Fundamental Cases in Criminal Justice

Adam J. McKee

University of Arkansas at Monticello

Table of Contents

Preface

Most criminal justice textbooks divide the criminal justice system into three components: Police, Courts, and Corrections. The Juvenile Justice system is usually discussed as a separate but parallel system. What brings these disparate systems together into a "system?" The answer is law. All of these systems are designed to promote the objectives of the criminal law, and the procedural law circumscribes them. One of the most important themes in the law of criminal procedure is the protection of civil liberties. Most of the liberties that Americans take for granted are enshrined in the Bill of Rights, which consists of the first ten Amendments to the Constitution of the United States. As written in the constitution, these rights are vague. This is no accident. They must be vague in order to be generally applied and withstand the test of time.

Because the constitution is so vague, the people depend on the Supreme Court of the United States (as well as other appellate courts) to both interpret and enforce their civil liberties. The Court performs this critical function by hearing cases, and their opinions are preserved in written opinions. This case law is the most prevalent type of procedural law. The following cases have been selected to demonstrate a cross-section of issues spanning the entire criminal justice system, and to show similarities and differences between the adult criminal justice system and the juvenile justice system. All of these cases deal with very specific questions that arose from criminal justice practice. For the student, they are of much broader use than merely answering a particular questions. These cases serve as a window into the chambers of the Supreme Court. From reading these cases, one can gain an in-depth understanding of what the specific clauses of the Bill of Rights mean in criminal justice practice.

Many academic programs require students to learn the names of cases and the rule of law, mostly drawn from a secondary source such as a synopsis in a textbook. While no doubt a time saving device, this method does a disservice to the student. Learning single sentence rules is of limited use. Professors often teach that the law is dynamic, but teach the law as if it were static. The law changes, and as new cases are handed down by the high courts, students need the ability to translate these new materials into practice. The best way to learn the fine art of reading court cases is to read court cases. Court cases have a similar anatomy, vocabulary, and way of unfolding that become comfortable with repeated exposure. As this text is designed to accompany an introductory course, students may well not feel that comfort in the beginning. Sadly, the ample jargon and stilted diction of high court cases can be intimidating for the novice. Near the end of a first course, however, the Court's method of revealing the law will seem comfortable and familiar.

The cases that follow have been heavily edited and abridged. With only a few exceptions, only the decision of the majority is retained, and all footnotes and parenthetical reference material has been stripped away. The logic is to make material that is very complicated for the novice less intimidating and more approachable. Simply put, I have endeavored to make these cases *readable*. Those wanting access to these omitted details can find the full text of these cases in myriad online collections, including those of the Administrative Offices of the United States Courts.

Please feel free to contact me with any commends, criticisms, and suggestions for future editions. I am quick to acknowledge that this is an imperfect work and that future editions have much room for improvement.

Adam J. McKee, Ph.D.
Associate Professor of Criminal Justice

www.DocMcKee.com

Part I: Safeguards

Freedom is an American birthright. The freedoms we enjoy as American citizens are vital to our national identity and way of life. These freedoms were so important, in fact, that many of the founding fathers would not sign the Constitution until these rights, mostly protections from government intrusion on the liberty of the new republic's citizens, were made part of the Constitution itself. The first ten Amendments date from the time of the Constitution's signing, and are known as the Bill of Rights. *The body entrusted with guarding these important rights is the Supreme Court of the United States. In their cases, the court establishes just what the various Amendments mean in legal practice, and updates them to keep up with changes in society and technology.*

Barron v. Baltimore (1833)
32 U.S. 243

This case provides an excellent overview of how the constitution of the United States affects the states. In general, the court concludes, the constitution only limits the power of the states when such an application is expressly stated in the text of some constitutional passage. This would change with the passage of the Fourteenth Amendment, which includes the Due Process Clause. The phrase due process *means can be considered synonymous with* fundamental fairness. *This case is also an interesting example of how the courts view of the constitution changes over time.*

....

The plaintiff in error contends that it comes within that clause in the Fifth Amendment to the constitution, which inhibits the taking of private property for public use, without just compensation. He insists that this amendment, being in favor of the liberty of the citizen, ought to be so construed as to restrain the legislative power of a state, as well as that of the United States. If this proposition be untrue, the court can take no jurisdiction of the cause.

The question thus presented is, we think, of great importance, but not of much difficulty.

The constitution was ordained and established by the people of the United States for themselves, for their own government, and not for the government of the individual states. Each state established a constitution for itself, and, in that constitution, provided such limitations and restrictions on the powers of its particular government as its judgment dictated. The people of the United States framed such a government for the United States as they supposed best adapted to their situation, and best calculated to promote their interests. The powers they conferred on this government were to be exercised by itself; and the limitations on power, if expressed in general terms, are naturally, and, we think, necessarily applicable to the government created by the instrument. They are limitations of power granted in the instrument itself; not of distinct governments, framed by different persons and for different purposes.

If these propositions be correct, the fifth amendment must be understood as restraining the power of the general government, not as applicable to the states. In their several constitutions they have imposed such restrictions on their respective governments as their own wisdom suggested; such as they deemed most proper for themselves. It is a subject on which they judge exclusively, and with which others interfere no farther than they are supposed to have a common interest.

The counsel for the plaintiff in error insists that the constitution was intended to secure the people of the several states against the undue exercise of power by their respective state governments; as well as against that which might be attempted by their general government. In support of this argument he relies on the inhibitions contained in the tenth section of the first article.

We think that section affords a strong if not a conclusive argument in support of the opinion already indicated by the court.

The preceding section contains restrictions which are obviously intended for the exclusive purpose of restraining the exercise of power by the departments of the general government. Some of them use language applicable only to congress: others are expressed in general terms. The third clause, for example, declares that "no bill of attainder or ex post facto law shall be passed." No language can be more general; yet the demonstration is complete that it applies solely to the government of the United States. In addition to the general arguments furnished by the instrument itself, some of which have been already suggested, the succeeding section, the avowed purpose of which is to restrain state legislation, contains in terms the very prohibition. It declares that "no state shall pass any bill of attainder or ex post facto law." This provision, then, of the ninth section, however comprehensive its language, contains no restriction on state legislation.

The ninth section having enumerated, in the nature of a bill of rights, the limitations intended to be imposed on the powers of the general government, the tenth proceeds to enumerate those which were to operate on the state legislatures. These restrictions are brought together in the same section, and are by express words applied to the states. "No state shall enter into any treaty," &c. Perceiving that in a constitution framed by the people of the United States for the government of all, no limitation of the action of government on the people would apply to the state government, unless expressed in terms; the restrictions contained in the tenth section are in direct words so applied to the states.

It is worthy of remark, too, that these inhibitions generally restrain state legislation on subjects entrusted to the general government, or in which the people of all the states feel an interest.

A state is forbidden to enter into any treaty, alliance or confederation. If these compacts are with foreign nations, they interfere with the treaty making power which is conferred entirely on the general government; if with each other, for political purposes, they can scarcely fail to interfere with the general purpose and intent of the constitution. To grant letters of marque and reprisal, would lead directly to war; the power of declaring which is expressly given to congress. To coin money is also the exercise of a power conferred on congress. It would be tedious to recapitulate the several limitations on the powers of the states which are contained in this section. They will be found, generally, to restrain state legislation on subjects entrusted to the government of the union, in which the citizens of all the states are interested. In these alone were the whole people concerned. The question of their application to states is not left to construction. It is averred in positive words.

If the original constitution, in the ninth and tenth sections of the first article, draws this plain and marked line of discrimination between the limitations it imposes on the powers of the general government, and on those of the states; if in every inhibition intended to act on state power, words are employed which directly express that intent; some strong reason must be assigned for departing from this safe and judicious course in framing the amendments, before that departure can be assumed.

We search in vain for that reason.

Had the people of the several states, or any of them, required changes in their constitutions; had they required additional safeguards to liberty from the apprehended encroachments of their particular governments: the remedy was in their own hands, and would have been applied by themselves. A convention would have been assembled by the discontented state, and the required improvements would have been made by itself. The unwieldy and cumbrous machinery of procuring a recommendation from two-thirds of congress, and the assent of three-fourths of their sister states, could never have occurred to any human being as a mode of doing that which might be effected by the state itself. Had the framers of these amendments intended them to be limitations on the powers of the state governments, they would have imitated the framers of the original constitution, and have expressed that intention. Had congress engaged in the extraordinary occupation of improving the constitutions of the several states by affording the people additional protection from the exercise of power by their own governments in matters which concerned themselves alone, they would have declared this purpose in plain and intelligible language.

But it is universally understood, it is a part of the history of the day, that the great revolution which established the constitution of the United States, was not effected without immense opposition. Serious fears were extensively entertained that those powers which the patriot statesmen, who then watched over the interests of our country, deemed essential to union, and to the attainment of those invaluable objects for which union was sought, might be exercised in a manner dangerous to liberty. In almost every convention by which the constitution was adopted, amendments to guard against the abuse of power were recommended. These amendments demanded security against the apprehended encroachments of the general government–not against those of the local governments.

In compliance with a sentiment thus generally expressed, to quiet fears thus extensively entertained, amendments were proposed by the required majority in congress, and adopted by the states. These amendments contain no expression indicating an intention to apply them to the state governments. This court cannot so apply them.

We are of opinion that the provision in the fifth amendment to the constitution, declaring that private property shall not be taken for public use without just compensation, is intended solely as a limitation on the exercise of power by the government of the United States, and is not applicable to the legislation of the states. We are therefore of opinion that there is no repugnancy between the several acts of the general assembly of Maryland, given in evidence by the defendants at the trial of this cause, in the court of that state, and the constitution of the United States. This court, therefore, has no jurisdiction of the cause; and it is dismissed.

This cause came on to be heard on the transcript of the record from the court of appeals for the western shore of the state of Maryland, and was argued by counsel: on consideration whereof, it is the opinion of this court that there is no repugnancy between the several acts of the general assembly of Maryland, given in evidence by the defendants at the trial of this cause in the court of that state, and the constitution of the United States; whereupon, it is ordered and adjudged by this court that this writ of error be, and the same is hereby dismissed for the want of jurisdiction.

Gideon v. Wainwright (1963)
372 U.S. 335

In addition to the important question of appointed counsel for indigent offenders, this case is an excellent example of how the Fourteenth Amendment's Due Process Clause can apply federal constitutional protections to the states. This type of inclusion was used frequently by the Warren court in what has been called the "civil rights revolution" that took place during the 1960s.

Petitioner was charged in a Florida state court with having broken and entered a poolroom with intent to commit a misdemeanor. This offense is a felony under Florida law. Appearing in court without funds and without a lawyer, petitioner asked the court to appoint counsel for him, whereupon the following colloquy took place:

The COURT: Mr. Gideon, I am sorry, but I cannot appoint Counsel to represent you in this case. Under the laws of the State of Florida, the only time the Court can appoint Counsel to represent a Defendant is when that person is charged with a capital offense. I am sorry, but I will have to deny your request to appoint Counsel to defend you in this case.

The DEFENDANT: The United States Supreme Court says I am entitled to be represented by Counsel.

Put to trial before a jury, Gideon conducted his defense about as well as could be expected from a layman. He made an opening statement to the jury, cross—examined the State's witnesses, presented witnesses in his own defense, declined to testify himself, and made a short argument "emphasizing his innocence to the charge contained in the Information filed in this case." The jury returned a verdict of guilty, and petitioner was sentenced to serve five years in the state prison. Later, petitioner filed in the Florida Supreme Court this habeas corpus petition attacking his conviction and sentence on the ground that the trial court's refusal to appoint counsel for him denied him rights "guaranteed by the Constitution and the Bill of Rights by the United States Government."

Treating the petition for habeas corpus as properly before it, the State Supreme Court, "upon consideration thereof" but without an opinion, denied all relief. Since 1942, when *Betts v. Brady* was decided by a divided Court, the problem of a defendant's federal constitutional right to counsel in a state court has been a continuing source of controversy and litigation in both state and federal courts. To give this problem another review here, we granted certiorari. Since Gideon was proceeding *in forma pauperis*, we appointed counsel to represent him and requested both sides to discuss in their briefs and oral arguments the following: "Should this Court's holding in *Betts v. Brady* be reconsidered?"

....

The facts upon which Betts claimed that he had been unconstitutionally denied the right to have counsel appointed to assist him are strikingly like the facts upon which Gideon here bases his federal constitutional claim. Betts was indicted for robbery in a Maryland state court. On arraignment, he told the trial judge of his lack of funds to hire a lawyer and asked the court to appoint one for him. Betts was advised that it was not the practice in that county to appoint counsel for indigent defendants except in murder and rape cases. He then pleaded not guilty, had witnesses summoned, cross-examined the State's witnesses, examined his own, and chose not to testify himself. He was found guilty by the judge, sitting without a jury, and sentenced to eight years in prison. Like Gideon, Betts sought release by habeas corpus, alleging that he had been denied the right to assistance of counsel in violation of the Fourteenth Amendment. Betts was denied any relief, and on review this Court affirmed. It was held that a refusal to appoint counsel for an indigent defendant charged with a felony did not necessarily violate the Due Process Clause of the Fourteenth Amendment, which for reasons given the Court deemed to be the only applicable federal constitutional provision. The Court said:

"Asserted denial of due process is to be tested by an appraisal of the totality of facts in a given case. That which may, in one setting, constitute a denial of fundamental fairness, shocking to the universal sense of justice, may, in other circumstances, and in the light of other considerations, fall short of such denial."

Treating due process as "a concept less rigid and more fluid than those envisaged in other specific and particular provisions of the Bill of Rights," the Court held that refusal to appoint counsel under the particular facts and circumstances in the Betts case was not so "offensive to the common and fundamental ideas of fairness" as to amount to a denial of due process. Since the facts and circumstances of the two cases are so nearly indistinguishable, we think the *Betts v. Brady* holding if left standing would require us to reject Gideon's claim that the Constitution guarantees him the assistance of counsel. Upon full reconsideration we conclude that *Betts v. Brady* should be overruled.

The Sixth Amendment provides, "In all criminal prosecutions, the accused shall enjoy the right . . . to have the Assistance of Counsel for his defense." We have construed this to mean that in federal courts counsel must be provided for defendants unable to employ counsel unless the right is competently and intelligently waived. Betts argued that this right is extended to indigent defendants in state courts by the Fourteenth Amendment. In response the Court stated that, while the Sixth Amendment laid down "no rule for the conduct of the States, the question recurs whether the constraint laid by the Amendment upon the national courts expresses a rule so fundamental and essential to a fair trial, and so, to due process of law, that it is made obligatory upon the States by the Fourteenth Amendment." In order to decide whether the Sixth Amendment's guarantee of counsel is of this fundamental nature, the Court in Betts set out and considered "relevant data on the subject . . . afforded by constitutional and statutory provisions subsisting in the colonies and the States prior to the inclusion of the Bill of Rights in the national Constitution, and in the constitutional, legislative, and judicial history of the States to the present date." On the basis of this historical data the Court concluded that "appointment of counsel is not a fundamental right, essential to a fair trial." It was for this reason the Betts Court refused to accept the contention that the Sixth Amendment's guarantee of counsel for indigent federal defendants was extended to or, in the words of that Court, "made obligatory upon the States by the Fourteenth Amendment." Plainly, had the Court concluded that appointment of counsel for an indigent criminal defendant was "a fundamental right, essential to a fair trial," it would have held that the Fourteenth Amendment requires appointment of counsel in a state court, just as the Sixth Amendment requires in a federal court.

We think the Court in *Betts* had ample precedent for acknowledging that those guarantees of the Bill of Rights which are fundamental safeguards of liberty immune from federal abridgment are equally protected against state invasion by the Due Process Clause of the Fourteenth Amendment. This same principle was recognized, explained, and applied in *Powell v. Alabama*, a case upholding the right of counsel, where the Court held that despite sweeping language to the contrary in *Hurtado v. California*, the Fourteenth Amendment "embraced" those "'fundamental principles of liberty and justice which lie at the base of all our civil and political institutions,'" even though they had been "specifically dealt with in another part of the federal Constitution." In many cases other than *Powell* and *Betts*, this Court has looked to the fundamental nature of original Bill of Rights guarantees to decide whether the Fourteenth Amendment makes them obligatory on the States. Explicitly recognized to be of this "fundamental nature" and therefore made immune from state invasion by the Fourteenth, or some part of it, are the First Amendment's freedoms of speech, press, religion, assembly, association, and petition for redress of grievances. For the same reason, though not always in precisely the same terminology, the Court has made obligatory on the States the Fifth Amendment's command that private property shall not be taken for public use without just compensation, the Fourth Amendment's prohibition of unreasonable searches and seizures, and the Eighth's ban on cruel and unusual punishment. On the other hand, this Court in *Palko v. Connecticut*, refused to hold that the Fourteenth Amendment made the double jeopardy provision of the Fifth Amendment obligatory on the States. In so refusing, however, the Court, speaking through Mr. Justice Cardozo, was careful to emphasize that "immunities that are valid as against the federal government by force of the specific pledges of particular amendments have been found to be implicit in the concept of ordered liberty, and thus, through the Fourteenth Amendment, become valid as against the states" and that guarantees "in their origin . . . effective against the federal government alone" had by prior cases "been taken over from the earlier articles of the federal bill of rights and brought within the Fourteenth Amendment by a process of absorption."

We accept *Betts v. Brady*'s assumption, based as it was on our prior cases, that a provision of the Bill of Rights which is "fundamental and essential to a fair trial" is made obligatory upon the States by the Fourteenth Amendment. We think the Court in *Betts* was wrong, however, in concluding that the Sixth Amendment's guarantee of counsel is not one of these fundamental rights. Ten years before *Betts v. Brady*, this Court, after full consideration of all the historical data examined in *Betts*, had unequivocally declared that "the right to the aid of counsel is of this fundamental character." While the Court at the close of its *Powell* opinion did by its language, as this Court frequently does, limit its holding to the particular facts and circumstances of that case, its conclusions about the fundamental nature of the right to counsel are unmistakable. Several years later, in 1936, the Court reemphasized what it had said about the fundamental nature of the right to counsel in this language:

"We concluded that certain fundamental rights, safeguarded by the first eight amendments against federal action, were also safeguarded against state action by the due process of law clause of the Fourteenth Amendment, and among them the fundamental right of the accused to the aid of counsel in a criminal prosecution."

And again in 1938 this Court said:

"The assistance of counsel is one of the safeguards of the Sixth Amendment deemed necessary to insure fundamental human rights of life and liberty. . . . The Sixth Amendment stands as a constant admonition that if the constitutional safeguards it provides be lost, justice will not still be done."

In light of these and many other prior decisions of this Court, it is not surprising that the *Betts* Court, when faced with the contention that "one charged with crime, who is unable to obtain counsel, must be furnished counsel by the State," conceded that "expressions in the opinions of this court lend color to the argument . . . ." The fact is that in deciding as it did—that "appointment of counsel is not a fundamental right, essential to a fair trial"—the Court in *Betts v. Brady* made an abrupt break with its own well-considered precedents. In returning to these old precedents, sounder we believe than the new, we but restore constitutional principles established to achieve a fair system of justice. Not only these precedents but also reason and reflection require us to recognize that in our adversary system of criminal justice, any person hauled into court, who is too poor to hire a lawyer, cannot be assured a fair trial unless counsel is provided for him. This seems to us to be an obvious truth. Governments, both state and federal, quite properly spend vast sums of money to establish machinery to try defendants accused of crime. Lawyers to prosecute are everywhere deemed essential to protect the public's interest in an orderly society. Similarly, there are few defendants charged with crime, few indeed, who fail to hire the best lawyers they can get to prepare and present their defenses. That government hires lawyers to prosecute and defendants who have the money hire lawyers to defend are the strongest indications of the widespread belief that lawyers in criminal courts are necessities, not luxuries. The right of one charged with crime to counsel may not be deemed fundamental and essential to fair trials in some countries, but it is in ours. From the very beginning, our state and national constitutions and laws have laid great emphasis on procedural and substantive safeguards designed to assure fair trials before impartial tribunals in which every defendant stands equal before the law. This noble ideal cannot be realized if the poor man charged with crime has to face his accusers without a lawyer to assist him. A defendant's need for a lawyer is nowhere better stated than in the moving words of Mr. Justice Sutherland in *Powell v. Alabama*:

"The right to be heard would be, in many cases, of little avail if it did not comprehend the right to be heard by counsel. Even the intelligent and educated layman has small and sometimes no skill in the science of law. If charged with crime, he is incapable, generally, of determining for himself whether the indictment is good or bad. He is unfamiliar with the rules of evidence. Left without the aid of counsel he may be put on trial without a proper charge, and convicted upon incompetent evidence, or evidence irrelevant to the issue or otherwise inadmissible. He lacks both the skill and knowledge adequately to prepare his defense, even though he have a perfect one. He requires the guiding hand of counsel at every step in the proceedings against him. Without it, though he be not guilty, he faces the danger of conviction because he does not know how to establish his innocence."

The Court in *Betts v. Brady* departed from the sound wisdom upon which the Court's holding in *Powell v. Alabama* rested. Florida, supported by two other States, has asked that *Betts v. Brady* be left intact. Twenty-two States, as friends of the Court, argue that Betts was "an anachronism when handed down" and that it should now be overruled. We agree.

. . . .

Reversed.

Powell v. Alabama (1932)
287 U.S. 45

This case is remarkable in that it was among the first instances where the Supreme Court held that a criminal defendant had the right to appointed counsel. The Court would broaden the scope of the rights enumerated in this case, but the constitutional logic of applying the right to an attorney to the states via the Fourteenth Amendment has not changed.

The petitioners, hereinafter referred to as defendants, are negroes charged with the crime of rape, committed upon the persons of two white girls. The crime is said to have been committed on March 25, 1931. The indictment was returned in a state court of first instance on March 31, and the record recites that on the same day the defendants were arraigned and entered pleas of not guilty. There is a further recital to the effect that upon the arraignment they were represented by counsel. But no counsel had been employed, and aside from a statement made by the trial judge several days later during a colloquy immediately preceding the trial, the record does not disclose when, or under what circumstances, an appointment of counsel was made, or who was appointed. During the colloquy referred to, the trial judge, in response to a question, said that he had appointed all the members of the bar for the purpose of arraigning the defendants and then of course anticipated that the members of the bar would continue to help the defendants if no counsel appeared. Upon the argument here both sides accepted that as a correct statement of the facts concerning the matter.

There was a severance upon the request of the state, and the defendants were tried in three several groups, as indicated above. As each of the three cases was called for trial, each defendant was arraigned, and, having the indictment read to him, entered a plea of not guilty. Whether the original arraignment and pleas were regarded as ineffective is not shown. Each of the three trials was completed within a single day. Under the Alabama statute the punishment for rape is to be fixed by the jury, and in its discretion may be from ten years imprisonment to death. The juries found defendants guilty and imposed the death penalty upon all. The trial court overruled motions for new trials and sentenced the defendants in accordance with the verdicts. The judgments were affirmed by the state supreme court. Chief Justice Anderson thought the defendants had not been accorded a fair trial and strongly dissented.

In this court the judgments are assailed upon the grounds that the defendants, and each of them, were denied due process of law and the equal protection of the laws, in contravention of the Fourteenth Amendment, specifically as follows: (1) they were not given a fair, impartial and deliberate trial; (2) they were denied the right of counsel, with the accustomed incidents of consultation and opportunity of preparation for trial; and (3) they were tried before juries from which qualified members of their own race were systematically excluded. These questions were properly raised and saved in the courts below.

The only one of the assignments which we shall consider is the second, in respect of the denial of counsel; and it becomes unnecessary to discuss the facts of the case or the circumstances surrounding the prosecution except in so far as they reflect light upon that question.

The record shows that on the day when the offense is said to have been committed, these defendants, together with a number of other negroes, were upon a freight train on its way through Alabama. On the same train were seven white boys and the two white girls. A fight took place between the negroes and the white boys, in the course of which the white boys, with the exception of one named Gilley, were thrown off the train. A message was sent ahead, reporting the fight and asking that every negro be gotten off the train. The participants in the fight, and the two girls, were in an open gondola car. The two girls testified that each of them was assaulted by six different negroes in turn, and they identified the seven defendants as having been among the number. None of the white boys was called to testify, with the exception of Gilley, who was called in rebuttal.

Before the train reached Scottsboro, Alabama, a sheriff's posse seized the defendants and two other negroes. Both girls and the negroes then were taken to Scottsboro, the county seat. Word of their coming and of the alleged assault had preceded them, and they were met at Scottsboro by a large crowd. It does not sufficiently appear that the defendants were seriously threatened with, or that they were actually in danger of, mob violence; but it does appear that the attitude of the community was one of great hostility. The sheriff thought it necessary to call for the militia to assist in safeguarding the prisoners. Chief Justice Anderson pointed out in his opinion that every step taken from the arrest and arraignment to the sentence was accompanied by the military. Soldiers took the defendants to Gadsden for safekeeping, brought them back to Scottsboro for arraignment, returned them to Gadsden for safekeeping while awaiting trial, escorted them to Scottsboro for trial a few days later, and guarded the court house and grounds at every stage of the proceedings. It is perfectly apparent that the proceedings, from beginning to end, took place in an atmosphere of tense, hostile and excited public sentiment. During the entire time, the defendants were closely confined or were under military guard. The record does not disclose their ages, except that one of them was nineteen; but the record

8

clearly indicates that most, if not all, of them were youthful, and they are constantly referred to as "the boys." They were ignorant and illiterate. All of them were residents of other states, where alone members of their families or friends resided.

However guilty defendants, upon due inquiry, might prove to have been, they were, until convicted, presumed to be innocent. It was the duty of the court having their cases in charge to see that they were denied no necessary incident of a fair trial. With any error of the state court involving alleged contravention of the state statutes or constitution we, of course, have nothing to do. The sole inquiry which we are permitted to make is whether the federal Constitution was contravened; and as to that, we confine ourselves, as already suggested, to the inquiry whether the defendants were in substance denied the right of counsel, and if so, whether such denial infringes the due process clause of the Fourteenth Amendment.

First. The record shows that immediately upon the return of the indictment defendants were arraigned and pleaded not guilty. Apparently they were not asked whether they had, or were able to employ, counsel, or wished to have counsel appointed; or whether they had friends or relatives who might assist in that regard if communicated with. That it would not have been an idle ceremony to have given the defendants reasonable opportunity to communicate with their families and endeavor to obtain counsel is demonstrated by the fact that, very soon after conviction, able counsel appeared in their behalf. This was pointed out by Chief Justice Anderson in the course of his dissenting opinion. "They were nonresidents," he said, "and had little time or opportunity to get in touch with their families and friends who were scattered throughout two other states, and time has demonstrated that they could or would have been represented by able counsel had a better opportunity been given by a reasonable delay in the trial of the cases, judging from the number and activity of counsel that appeared immediately or shortly after their conviction."

It is hardly necessary to say that, the right to counsel being conceded, a defendant should be afforded a fair opportunity to secure counsel of his own choice. Not only was that not done here, but such designation of counsel as was attempted was either so indefinite or so close upon the trial as to amount to a denial of effective and substantial aid in that regard. This will be amply demonstrated by a brief review of the record.

April 6, six days after indictment, the trials began. When the first case was called, the court inquired whether the parties were ready for trial. The state's attorney replied that he was ready to proceed. No one answered for the defendants or appeared to represent or defend them. Mr. Roddy, a Tennessee lawyer not a member of the local bar, addressed the court, saying that he had not been employed, but that people who were interested had spoken to him about the case. He was asked by the court whether he intended to appear for the defendants, and answered that he would like to appear along with counsel that the court might appoint. The record then proceeds:

The Court: If you appear for these defendants, then I will not appoint counsel; if local counsel are willing to appear and assist you under the circumstances all right, but I will not appoint them.

Mr. Roddy: Your Honor has appointed counsel, is that correct?

The Court: I appointed all the members of the bar for the purpose of arraigning the defendants and then of course I anticipated them to continue to help them if no counsel appears.

Mr. Roddy: Then I don't appear then as counsel but I do want to stay in and not be ruled out in this case.

The Court: Of course I would not do that—

Mr. Roddy: I just appear here through the courtesy of Your Honor.

The Court: Of course I give you that right; . . ."

And then, apparently addressing all the lawyers present, the court inquired: ". . . well are you all willing to assist?"

Mr. Moody: Your Honor appointed us all and we have been proceeding along every line we know about it under Your Honor's appointment.

The Court: The only thing I am trying to do is, if counsel appears for these defendants I don't want to impose on you all, but if you feel like counsel from Chattanooga –

Mr. Moody: I see his situation of course and I have not run out of anything yet. Of course, if Your Honor purposes to appoint us, Mr. Parks, I am willing to go on with it. Most of the bar have been down and conferred with these defendants in this case; they did not know what else to do.

The Court: The thing, I did not want to impose on the members of the bar if counsel unqualifiedly appears; if you all feel like Mr. Roddy is only interested in a limited way to assist, then I don't care to appoint.

Mr. Parks: Your Honor, I don't feel like you ought to impose on any member of the local bar if the defendants are represented by counsel.

The Court: That is what I was trying to ascertain, Mr. Parks.

Mr. Parks: Of course if they have counsel, I don't see the necessity of the Court appointing anybody; if they haven't counsel, of course I think it is up to the Court to appoint counsel to represent them.

The Court: I think you are right about it Mr. Parks and that is the reason I was trying to get an expression from Mr. Roddy.

Mr. Roddy: I think Mr. Parks is entirely right about it, if I was paid down here and employed, it would be a different thing, but I have not prepared this case for trial and have only been called into it by people who are interested in these boys from Chattanooga. Now, they have not given me an opportunity to prepare the case and I am not familiar with the procedure in Alabama, but I merely came down here as a friend of the people who are interested and not as paid counsel, and certainly I haven't any money to pay them and nobody I am interested in had me to come down here has put up any fund of money to come down here and pay counsel. If they should do it I would be glad to turn it over—a counsel but I am merely here at the solicitation of people who have become interested in this case without any payment of fee and without any preparation for trial and I think the boys would be better off if I step entirely out of the case according to my way of looking at it and according to my lack of preparation of it and not being familiar with the procedure in Alabama, . . ."

Mr. Roddy later observed: If there is anything I can do to be of help to them, I will be glad to do it; I am interested to that extent.

The Court: Well gentlemen, if Mr. Roddy only appears as assistant that way, I think it is proper that I appoint members of this bar to represent them, I expect that is right. If Mr. Roddy will appear, I wouldn't of course, I would not appoint anybody. I don't see, Mr. Roddy, how I can make a qualified appointment or a limited appointment. Of course, I don't mean to cut off your assistance in any way—Well gentlemen, I think you understand it.

Mr. Moody: I am willing to go ahead and help Mr. Roddy in anything I can do about it, under the circumstances.

The Court: All right, all the lawyers that will; of course I would not require a lawyer to appear if –

Mr. Moody: I am willing to do that for him as a member of the bar; I will go ahead and help do anything I can do.

The Court: All right.

And in this casual fashion the matter of counsel in a capital case was disposed of.

It thus will be seen that until the very morning of the trial no lawyer had been named or definitely designated to represent the defendants. Prior to that time, the trial judge had "appointed all the members of the bar" for the limited "purpose of arraigning the defendants." Whether they would represent the defendants thereafter if no counsel appeared in their behalf, was a matter of speculation only, or, as the judge indicated, of mere anticipation on the part of the court. Such a designation, even if made for all purposes, would, in our opinion, have fallen far short of meeting, in any proper sense, a requirement for the appointment of counsel. How many lawyers were members of the bar does not appear; but, in the very nature of things, whether many or few, they would not, thus collectively named, have been given that clear appreciation of responsibility or impressed with that individual sense of duty which should and naturally would accompany the appointment of a selected member of the bar, specifically named and assigned.

That this action of the trial judge in respect of appointment of counsel was little more than an expansive gesture, imposing no substantial or definite obligation upon any one, is borne out by the fact that prior to the calling of the case for trial on April 6, a leading member of the local bar accepted employment on the side of the prosecution and actively participated in the trial. It is true that he said that before doing so he had understood Mr. Roddy would be employed as counsel for the defendants. This the lawyer in question, of his own accord, frankly stated to the court; and no doubt he acted with the utmost good faith. Probably other members of the bar had a like understanding. In any event, the circumstance lends emphasis to the conclusion that during perhaps the most critical period of the proceedings against these defendants, that is to say, from the time of their arraignment until the beginning of their trial, when consultation, thoroughgoing investigation and preparation were vitally important, the defendants did not have the aid of counsel in any real sense, although they were as much entitled to such aid during that period as at the trial itself.

Nor do we think the situation was helped by what occurred on the morning of the trial. At that time, as appears from the colloquy printed above, Mr. Roddy stated to the court that he did not appear as counsel, but that he would like to appear along with counsel that the court might appoint; that he had not been given an opportunity to prepare the case; that he was not familiar with the procedure in Alabama, but merely came down as a friend of the people who were interested; that he thought the boys would be better off if he should step entirely out of the case. Mr. Moody, a member of the local bar, expressed a willingness to help Mr. Roddy in anything he could do under the circumstances. To this the court responded, "All right, all the lawyers that will; of course I would not require a lawyer to appear if—" And Mr. Moody continued, "I am willing to do that for him as a member of the bar; I will go ahead and help do anything I can do." With this dubious understanding, the trials immediately proceeded. The defendants, young, ignorant, illiterate, surrounded by hostile sentiment, hauled back and forth under guard of soldiers, charged with an atrocious crime regarded with especial horror in the community where they were to be tried, were thus put in peril of their lives within a few moments after counsel for the first time charged with any degree of responsibility began to represent them.

It is not enough to assume that counsel thus precipitated into the case thought there was no defense, and exercised their best judgment in proceeding to trial without preparation. Neither they nor the court could say what a prompt and thoroughgoing investigation might disclose as to the facts. No attempt was made to investigate. No opportunity to do so was given. Defendants were immediately hurried to trial. Chief Justice Anderson, after disclaiming any intention to criticize harshly counsel who attempted to represent defendants at the trials, said: ". . . the record indicates that the appearance was rather *pro forma* than zealous and active . . ." Under the circumstances disclosed, we hold that defendants were not accorded the right of counsel in any substantial sense. To decide otherwise, would simply be to ignore actualities. This conclusion finds ample support in the reasoning of an overwhelming array of state decisions....

It is true that great and inexcusable delay in the enforcement of our criminal law is one of the grave evils of our time. Continuances are frequently granted for unnecessarily long periods of time, and delays incident to the disposition of motions for new trial and hearings upon appeal have come in many cases to be a distinct reproach to the administration of justice. The prompt disposition of criminal cases is to be commended and encouraged. But in reaching that result a defendant, charged with a serious crime, must not be stripped of his right to have sufficient time to advise with counsel and prepare his defense. To do that is not to proceed promptly in the calm spirit of regulated justice but to go forward with the haste of the mob.

As the court said in *Commonwealth* v. *O'Keefe*:

"It is vain to give the accused a day in court, with no opportunity to prepare for it, or to guarantee him counsel without giving the latter any opportunity to acquaint himself with the facts or law of the case.

....

"A prompt and vigorous administration of the criminal law is commendable and we have no desire to clog the wheels of justice. What we here decide is that to force a defendant, charged with a serious misdemeanor, to trial within five hours of his arrest, is not due process of law, regardless of the merits of the case."

The Constitution of Alabama provides that in all criminal prosecutions the accused shall enjoy the right to have the assistance of counsel; and a state statute requires the court in a capital case, where the defendant is unable to employ counsel, to appoint counsel for him. The state supreme court held that these provisions had not been infringed, and with that holding we are powerless to interfere. The question, however, which it is our duty, and within our power, to decide, is whether the denial of the assistance of counsel contravenes the due process clause of the Fourteenth Amendment to the federal Constitution.

If recognition of the right of a defendant charged with a felony to have the aid of counsel depended upon the existence of a similar right at common law as it existed in England when our Constitution was adopted, there would be great difficulty in maintaining it as necessary to due process. Originally, in England, a person charged with treason or felony was denied the aid of counsel, except in respect of legal questions which the accused himself might suggest. At the same time parties in civil cases and persons accused of misdemeanors were entitled to the full assistance of counsel. After the revolution of 1688, the rule was abolished as to treason, but was otherwise steadily adhered to until 1836, when by act of Parliament the full right was granted in respect of felonies generally.

....

We do not overlook the case of *Hurtado* v. *California*, where this court determined that due process of law does not require an indictment by a grand jury as a prerequisite to prosecution by a state for murder. In support of that conclusion the court referred to the fact that the Fifth Amendment, in addition to containing the due process of law clause, provides in explicit terms that "No person shall be held to answer for a capital, or otherwise infamous crime, unless on a presentment or indictment of a grand jury, . . .", and said that since no part of this important amendment could be regarded as superfluous, the obvious inference is that in the sense of the Constitution due process of law was not intended to include, *ex vi termini*, the institution and procedure of a grand jury in any case; and that the same phrase, employed in the Fourteenth Amendment to restrain the action of the states, was to be interpreted as having been used in the same sense and with no greater extent; and that if it had been the purpose of that Amendment to perpetuate the institution of the grand jury in the states, it would have embodied, as did the Fifth Amendment, an express declaration to that effect.

The Sixth Amendment, in terms, provides that in all criminal prosecutions the accused shall enjoy the right "to have the assistance of counsel for his defense." In the face of the reasoning of the *Hurtado* case, if it stood alone, it would be difficult to justify the conclusion that the right to counsel, being thus specifically granted by the Sixth Amendment, was also within the intendment of the due process of law clause. But the *Hurtado* case does not stand alone. In the later case of *Chicago, Burlington & Quincy R. Co.* v. *Chicago*, this court held that a judgment of a state court, even though authorized by statute, by which private property was taken for public use without just compensation, was in violation of the due process of law required by the Fourteenth Amendment, notwithstanding that the Fifth Amendment explicitly declares that private property shall not be taken for public use without just compensation....

These later cases establish that notwithstanding the sweeping character of the language in the *Hurtado* case, the rule laid down is not without exceptions. The rule is an aid to construction, and in some instances may be conclusive; but it must yield to more compelling considerations whenever such considerations exist. The fact that the right involved is of such a character that it cannot be denied without violating those "fundamental principles of liberty and justice which lie at the base of all our civil and political institutions" is obviously one of those compelling considerations which must prevail in determining whether it is embraced within the due process clause of the Fourteenth Amendment, although it be specifically dealt with in another part of the federal Constitution. Evidently this court, in the later cases enumerated, regarded the rights there under consideration as of this fundamental character. That some such distinction must be observed is foreshadowed in *Twining* v. *New Jersey*, where Mr. Justice Moody, speaking for the court, said that ". . . it is possible that some of the personal rights safeguarded by the first eight Amendments against National action may also be safeguarded against state action, because a denial of them would be a denial of due process of law.

If this is so, it is not because those rights are enumerated in the first eight Amendments, but because they are of such a nature that they are included in the conception of due process of law." While the question has never been categorically determined by this court, a consideration of the nature of the right and a review of the expressions of this and other courts, makes it clear that the right to the aid of counsel is of this fundamental character.

It never has been doubted by this court, or any other so far as we know, that notice and hearing are preliminary steps essential to the passing of an enforceable judgment, and that they, together with a legally competent tribunal having jurisdiction of the case, constitute basic elements of the constitutional requirement of due process of law. The words of Webster, so often quoted, that by "the law of the land" is intended "a law which hears before it condemns," have been repeated in varying forms of expression in a multitude of decisions....

What, then, does a hearing include? Historically and in practice, in our own country at least, it has always included the right to the aid of counsel when desired and provided by the party asserting the right. The right to be heard would be, in many cases, of little avail if it did not comprehend the right to be heard by counsel. Even the intelligent and educated layman has small and sometimes no skill in the science of law. If charged with crime, he is incapable, generally, of determining for himself whether the indictment is good or bad. He is unfamiliar with the rules of evidence. Left without the aid of counsel he may be put on trial without a proper charge, and convicted upon incompetent evidence, or evidence irrelevant to the issue or otherwise inadmissible. He lacks both the skill and knowledge adequately to prepare his defense, even though he had a perfect one. He requires the guiding hand of counsel at every step in the proceedings against him. Without it, though he be not guilty, he faces the danger of conviction because he does not know how to establish his innocence. If that be true of men of intelligence, how much more true is it of the ignorant and illiterate, or those of feeble intellect. If in any case, civil or criminal, a state or federal court were arbitrarily to refuse to hear a party by counsel, employed by and appearing for him, it reasonably may not be doubted that such a refusal would be a denial of a hearing, and, therefore, of due process in the constitutional sense.

The decisions all point to that conclusion. In *Cooke* v. *United States*, it was held that where a contempt was not in open court, due process of law required charges and a reasonable opportunity to defend or explain. The court added, "We think this includes the assistance of counsel, if requested, . . ." In numerous other cases the court, in determining that due process was accorded, has frequently stressed the fact that the defendant had the aid of counsel.

....

In the light of the facts outlined in the forepart of this opinion—the ignorance and illiteracy of the defendants, their youth, the circumstances of public hostility, the imprisonment and the close surveillance of the defendants by the military forces, the fact that their friends and families were all in other states and communication with them necessarily difficult, and above all that they stood in deadly peril of their lives—we think the failure of the trial court to give them reasonable time and opportunity to secure counsel was a clear denial of due process.

But passing that, and assuming their inability, even if opportunity had been given, to employ counsel, as the trial court evidently did assume, we are of opinion that, under the circumstances just stated, the necessity of counsel was so vital and imperative that the failure of the trial court to make an effective appointment of counsel was likewise a denial of due process within the meaning of the Fourteenth Amendment. Whether this would be so in other criminal prosecutions, or under other circumstances, we need not determine. All that it is necessary now to decide, as we do decide, is that in a capital case, where the defendant is unable to employ counsel, and is incapable adequately of making his own defense because of ignorance, feeble mindedness, illiteracy, or the like, it is the duty of the court, whether requested or not, to assign counsel for him as a necessary requisite of due process of law; and that duty is not discharged by an assignment at such a time or under such circumstances as to preclude the giving of effective aid in the preparation and trial of the case. To hold otherwise would be to ignore the fundamental postulate, already adverted to, "that there are certain immutable principles of justice which inhere in the very idea of free government which no member of the Union may disregard." In a case such as this, whatever may be the rule in other cases, the right to have counsel appointed, when necessary, is a logical corollary from the constitutional right to be heard by counsel....

Let us suppose the extreme case of a prisoner charged with a capital offence, who is deaf and dumb, illiterate and feeble minded, unable to employ counsel, with the whole power of the state arrayed against him, prosecuted by counsel for the state without assignment of counsel for his defense, tried, convicted and sentenced to death. Such a result, which, if carried into execution, would be little short of judicial murder, it cannot be doubted would be a gross violation of the guarantee of due process of law; and we venture to think that no appellate court, state or federal, would hesitate so to decide.... The duty of the trial court to appoint counsel under such circumstances is clear, as it is clear under circumstances such as are disclosed by the record here; and its power to do so, even in the absence of a statute, cannot be questioned. Attorneys are officers of the court, and are bound to render service when required by such an appointment.

The United States by statute and every state in the Union by express provision of law, or by the determination of its courts, make it the duty of the trial judge, where the accused is unable to employ counsel, to appoint counsel for him. In most states the rule applies broadly to all criminal prosecutions, in others it is limited to the more serious crimes, and in a very limited number, to capital cases. A rule adopted with such unanimous accord reflects, if it does not establish, the inherent right to have counsel appointed, at least in cases like the present, and lends convincing support to the conclusion we have reached as to the fundamental nature of that right.

The judgments must be reversed and the causes remanded for further proceedings not inconsistent with this opinion.

Judgments reversed

Part II: Police

Almost no one will argue that the police are not necessary for a well-ordered society to exist. Most people value a public order and safety. In a democratic society, freedom is also highly valued. Often the values of public order and individual liberty are at odds. Public safety can be increased in an instant, but Americans are not willing to make the sacrifices to individual liberties that such a rapid increase would require. Liberties can be increased and better protected, but often people are not willing to accept the costs it would require in terms of public safety. Balancing these two issues is a primary goal of the Supreme Court. The cases in this section show how the Supreme Court has attempted to strike a balance between letting the police do what is necessary to bring criminals to justice, and preventing the abuse of civil liberties by the police.

Terry v. Ohio (1968)
392 U.S. 1

This case is remarkable in that it established an evidentiary standard between a mere hunch, which allows the police to do nothing without consent, and probable cause that is the Fourth Amendment standard for an arrest. This reasonable suspicion standard would later be applied by the courts in many different circumstances where the goal of a search is officer safety, and not the search for evidence of a crime.

This case presents serious questions concerning the role of the Fourth Amendment in the confrontation on the street between the citizen and the policeman investigating suspicious circumstances.

Petitioner Terry was convicted of carrying a concealed weapon and sentenced to the statutorily prescribed term of one to three years in the penitentiary. Following the denial of a pretrial motion to suppress, the prosecution introduced in evidence two revolvers and a number of bullets seized from Terry and a codefendant, Richard Chilton, by Cleveland Police Detective Martin McFadden. At the hearing on the motion to suppress this evidence, Officer McFadden testified that while he was patrolling in plain clothes in downtown Cleveland at approximately 2:30 in the afternoon of October 31, 1963, his attention was attracted by two men, Chilton and Terry, standing on the corner of Huron Road and Euclid Avenue. He had never seen the two men before, and he was unable to say precisely what first drew his eye to them. However, he testified that he had been a policeman for 39 years and a detective for 35 and that he had been assigned to patrol this vicinity of downtown Cleveland for shoplifters and pickpockets for 30 years. He explained that he had developed routine habits of observation over the years and that he would "stand and watch people or walk and watch people at many intervals of the day." He added: "Now, in this case when I looked over they didn't look right to me at the time."

His interest aroused, Officer McFadden took up a post of observation in the entrance to a store 300 to 400 feet away from the two men. "I get more purpose to watch them when I seen their movements," he testified. He saw one of the men leave the other one and walk southwest on Huron Road, past some stores. The man paused for a moment and looked in a store window, then walked on a short distance, turned around and walked back toward the corner, pausing once again to look in the same store window. He rejoined his companion at the corner, and the two conferred briefly. Then the second man went through the same series of motions, strolling down Huron Road, looking in the same window, walking on a short distance, turning back, peering in the store window again, and returning to confer with the first man at the corner. The two men repeated this ritual alternately between five and six times apiece—in all, roughly a dozen trips. At one point, while the two were standing together on the corner, a third man approached them and engaged them briefly in conversation. This man then left the two others and walked west on Euclid Avenue. Chilton and Terry resumed their measured pacing, peering, and conferring. After this had gone on for 10 to 12 minutes, the two men walked off together, heading west on Euclid Avenue, following the path taken earlier by the third man.

By this time Officer McFadden had become thoroughly suspicious. He testified that after observing their elaborately casual and oft-repeated reconnaissance of the store window on Huron Road, he suspected the two men of "casing a job, a stick-up," and that he considered it his duty as a police officer to investigate further. He added that he feared "they may have a gun." Thus, Officer McFadden followed Chilton and Terry and saw them stop in front of Zucker's store to talk to the same man who had conferred with them earlier on the street corner. Deciding that the situation was ripe for direct action, Officer McFadden approached the three men, identified himself as a police officer and asked for their names. At this point his knowledge was confined to what he had observed. He was not acquainted with any of the three men by name or by sight, and he had received no information concerning them from any other source. When the men "mumbled something" in response to his inquiries, Officer McFadden grabbed petitioner Terry, spun him around so that they were facing the other two, with Terry between McFadden and the others, and patted down the outside of his clothing. In the left breast pocket of Terry's overcoat Officer McFadden felt a pistol. He reached inside the overcoat pocket, but was unable to remove the gun. At this point, keeping Terry between himself and the others, the officer ordered all three men to enter Zucker's store.

As they went in, he removed Terry's overcoat completely, removed a .38-caliber revolver from the pocket and ordered all three men to face the wall with their hands raised. Officer McFadden proceeded to pat down the outer clothing of Chilton and the third man, Katz. He discovered another revolver in the outer pocket of Chilton's overcoat, but no weapons were found on Katz. The officer testified that he only patted the men down to see whether they had weapons, and that he did not put his hands beneath the outer garments of either Terry or Chilton until he felt their guns. So far as appears from the record, he never placed his hands beneath Katz' outer garments. Officer McFadden seized Chilton's gun, asked the proprietor of the store to call a police wagon, and took all three men to the station, where Chilton and Terry were formally charged with carrying concealed weapons.

On the motion to suppress the guns the prosecution took the position that they had been seized following a search incident to a lawful arrest. The trial court rejected this theory, stating that it "would be stretching the facts beyond reasonable comprehension" to find that Officer McFadden had had probable cause to arrest the men before he patted them down for weapons. However, the court denied the defendants' motion on the ground that Officer McFadden, on the basis of his experience, "had reasonable cause to believe . . . that the defendants were conducting themselves suspiciously, and some interrogation should be made of their action." Purely for his own protection, the court held, the officer had the right to pat down the outer clothing of these men, who he had reasonable cause to believe might be armed. The court distinguished between an investigatory "stop" and an arrest, and between a "frisk" of the outer clothing for weapons and a full-blown search for evidence of crime. The frisk, it held, was essential to the proper performance of the officer's investigatory duties, for without it "the answer to the police officer may be a bullet, and a loaded pistol discovered during the frisk is admissible."

After the court denied their motion to suppress, Chilton and Terry waived jury trial and pleaded not guilty. The court adjudged them guilty, and the Court of Appeals for the Eighth Judicial District, Cuyahoga County, affirmed. The Supreme Court of Ohio dismissed their appeal on the ground that no "substantial constitutional question" was involved. We granted certiorari to determine whether the admission of the revolvers in evidence violated petitioner's rights under the Fourth Amendment, made applicable to the States by the Fourteenth.

I.

The Fourth Amendment provides that "the right of the people to be secure in their persons, houses, papers, and effects, against unreasonable searches and seizures, shall not be violated . . . ." This inestimable right of personal security belongs as much to the citizen on the streets of our cities as to the homeowner closeted in his study to dispose of his secret affairs. For, as this Court has always recognized,

"No right is held more sacred, or is more carefully guarded, by the common law, than the right of every individual to the possession and control of his own person, free from all restraint or interference of others, unless by clear and unquestionable authority of law."

We have recently held that "the Fourth Amendment protects people, not places," and wherever an individual may harbor a reasonable "expectation of privacy," he is entitled to be free from unreasonable governmental intrusion. Of course, the specific content and incidents of this right must be shaped by the context in which it is asserted. For "what the Constitution forbids is not all searches and seizures, but unreasonable searches and seizures." Unquestionably petitioner was entitled to the protection of the Fourth Amendment as he walked down the street in Cleveland. The question is whether in all the circumstances of this on-the-street encounter, his right to personal security was violated by an unreasonable search and seizure.

We would be less than candid if we did not acknowledge that this question thrusts to the fore difficult and troublesome issues regarding a sensitive area of police activity—issues which have never before been squarely presented to this Court. Reflective of the tensions involved are the practical and constitutional arguments pressed with great vigor on both sides of the public debate over the power of the police to "stop and frisk"—as it is sometimes euphemistically termed—suspicious persons.

On the one hand, it is frequently argued that in dealing with the rapidly unfolding and often dangerous situations on city streets the police are in need of an escalating set of flexible responses, graduated in relation to the amount of information they possess. For this purpose it is urged that distinctions should be made between a "stop" and an "arrest" (or a "seizure" of a person), and between a "frisk" and a "search." Thus, it is argued, the police should be allowed to "stop" a person and detain him briefly for questioning upon suspicion that he may be connected with criminal activity. Upon suspicion that the person may be armed, the police should have the power to "frisk" him for weapons. If the "stop" and the "frisk" give rise to probable cause to believe that the suspect has committed a crime, then the police should be empowered to make a formal "arrest," and a full incident "search" of the person. This scheme is justified in part upon the notion that a "stop" and a "frisk" amount to a mere "minor inconvenience and petty indignity," which can properly be imposed upon the citizen in the interest of effective law enforcement on the basis of a police officer's suspicion.

On the other side the argument is made that the authority of the police must be strictly circumscribed by the law of arrest and search as it has developed to date in the traditional jurisprudence of the Fourth Amendment. It is contended with some force that there is not—and cannot be—a variety of police activity which does not depend solely upon the voluntary cooperation of the citizen and yet which stops short of an arrest based upon probable cause to make such an arrest. The heart of the Fourth Amendment, the argument runs, is a severe requirement of specific justification for any intrusion upon protected personal security, coupled with a highly developed system of judicial controls to enforce upon the agents of the State the commands of the Constitution. Acquiescence by the courts in the compulsion inherent in the field interrogation practices at issue here, it is urged, would constitute an abdication of judicial control over, and indeed an encouragement of, substantial interference with liberty and personal security by police officers whose judgment is necessarily colored by their primary involvement in "the often competitive enterprise of ferreting out crime." This, it is argued, can only serve to exacerbate police-community tensions in the crowded centers of our Nation's cities.

In this context we approach the issues in this case mindful of the limitations of the judicial function in controlling the myriad daily situations in which policemen and citizens confront each other on the street. The State has characterized the issue here as "the right of a police officer . . . to make an on-the-street stop, interrogate and pat down for weapons (known in street vernacular as 'stop and frisk')." But this is only partly accurate. For the issue is not the abstract propriety of the police conduct, but the admissibility against petitioner of the evidence uncovered by the search and seizure. Ever since its inception, the rule excluding evidence seized in violation of the Fourth Amendment has been recognized as a principal mode of discouraging lawless police conduct. Thus its major thrust is a deterrent one and experience has taught that it is the only effective deterrent to police misconduct in the criminal context, and that without it the constitutional guarantee against unreasonable searches and seizures would be a mere "form of words." The rule also serves another vital function—"the imperative of judicial integrity." Courts which sit under our Constitution cannot and will not be made party to lawless invasions of the constitutional rights of citizens by permitting unhindered governmental use of the fruits of such invasions. Thus in our system evidentiary rulings provide the context in which the judicial process of inclusion and exclusion approves some conduct as comporting with constitutional guarantees and disapproves other actions by state agents. A ruling admitting evidence in a criminal trial, we recognize, has the necessary effect of legitimizing the conduct which produced the evidence, while an application of the exclusionary rule withholds the constitutional imprimatur.

The exclusionary rule has its limitations, however, as a tool of judicial control. It cannot properly be invoked to exclude the products of legitimate police investigative techniques on the ground that much conduct which is closely similar involves unwarranted intrusions upon constitutional protections. Moreover, in some contexts the rule is ineffective as a deterrent. Street encounters between citizens and police officers are incredibly rich in diversity. They range from wholly friendly exchanges of pleasantries or mutually useful information to hostile confrontations of armed men involving arrests, or injuries, or loss of life. Moreover, hostile confrontations are not all of a piece. Some of them begin in a friendly enough manner, only to take a different turn upon the injection of some unexpected element into the conversation. Encounters are initiated by the police for a wide variety of purposes, some of which are wholly unrelated to a desire to prosecute for crime. Doubtless some police "field interrogation" conduct violates the Fourth Amendment. But a stern refusal by this Court to condone such activity does not necessarily render it responsive to the exclusionary rule. Regardless of how effective the rule may be where obtaining convictions is an important objective of the police, it is powerless to deter invasions of constitutionally guaranteed rights where the police either have no interest in prosecuting or are willing to forgo successful prosecution in the interest of serving some other goal.

Proper adjudication of cases in which the exclusionary rule is invoked demands a constant awareness of these limitations. The wholesale harassment by certain elements of the police community, of which minority groups, particularly Negroes, frequently complain, will not be stopped by the exclusion of any evidence from any criminal trial. Yet a rigid and unthinking application of the exclusionary rule, in futile protest against practices which it can never be used effectively to control, may exact a high toll in human injury and frustration of efforts to prevent crime. No judicial opinion can comprehend the protean variety of the street encounter, and we can only judge the facts of the case before us. Nothing we say today is to be taken as indicating approval of police conduct outside the legitimate investigative sphere. Under our decision, courts still retain their traditional responsibility to guard against police conduct which is overbearing or harassing, or which trenches upon personal security without the objective evidentiary justification which the Constitution requires. When such conduct is identified, it must be condemned by the judiciary and its fruits must be excluded from evidence in criminal trials. And, of course, our approval of legitimate and restrained investigative conduct undertaken on the basis of ample factual justification should in no way discourage the employment of other remedies than the exclusionary rule to curtail abuses for which that sanction may prove inappropriate.

Having thus roughly sketched the perimeters of the constitutional debate over the limits on police investigative conduct in general and the background against which this case presents itself, we turn our attention to the quite narrow question posed by the facts before us: whether it is always unreasonable for a policeman to seize a person and subject him to a limited search for weapons unless there is probable cause for an arrest. Given the narrowness of this question, we have no occasion to canvass in detail the constitutional limitations upon the scope of a policeman's power when he confronts a citizen without probable cause to arrest him.

Our first task is to establish at what point in this encounter the Fourth Amendment becomes relevant. That is, we must decide whether and when Officer McFadden "seized" Terry and whether and when he conducted a "search." There is some suggestion in the use of such terms as "stop" and "frisk" that such police conduct is outside the purview of the Fourth Amendment because neither action rises to the level of a "search" or "seizure" within the meaning of the Constitution. We emphatically reject this notion. It is quite plain that the Fourth Amendment governs "seizures" of the person which do not eventuate in a trip to the station house and prosecution for crime— "arrests" in traditional terminology. It must be recognized that whenever a police officer accosts an individual and restrains his freedom to walk away, he has "seized" that person. And it is nothing less than sheer torture of the English language to suggest that a careful exploration of the outer surfaces of a person's clothing all over his or her body in an attempt to find weapons is not a "search." Moreover, it is simply fantastic to urge that such a procedure performed in public by a policeman while the citizen stands helpless, perhaps facing a wall with his hands raised, is a "petty indignity." It is a serious intrusion upon the sanctity of the person, which may inflict great indignity and arouse strong resentment, and it is not to be undertaken lightly.

The danger in the logic which proceeds upon distinctions between a "stop" and an "arrest," or "seizure" of the person, and between a "frisk" and a "search" is twofold. It seeks to isolate from constitutional scrutiny the initial stages of the contact between the policeman and the citizen. And by suggesting a rigid all-or-nothing model of justification and regulation under the Amendment, it obscures the utility of limitations upon the scope, as well as the initiation, of police action as a means of constitutional regulation. This Court has held in the past that a search which is reasonable at its inception may violate the Fourth Amendment by virtue of its intolerable intensity and scope. The scope of the search must be "strictly tied to and justified by" the circumstances which rendered its initiation permissible.

The distinctions of classical "stop-and-frisk" theory thus serve to divert attention from the central inquiry under the Fourth Amendment—the reasonableness in all the circumstances of the particular governmental invasion of a citizen's personal security. "Search" and "seizure" are not talismans. We therefore reject the notions that the Fourth Amendment does not come into play at all as a limitation upon police conduct if the officers stop short of something called a "technical arrest" or a "full-blown search."

In this case there can be no question, then, that Officer McFadden "seized" petitioner and subjected him to a "search" when he took hold of him and patted down the outer surfaces of his clothing. We must decide whether at that point it was reasonable for Officer McFadden to have interfered with petitioner's personal security as he did. And in determining whether the seizure and search were "unreasonable" our inquiry is a dual one—whether the officer's action was justified at its inception, and whether it was reasonably related in scope to the circumstances which justified the interference in the first place.

If this case involved police conduct subject to the Warrant Clause of the Fourth Amendment, we would have to ascertain whether "probable cause" existed to justify the search and seizure which took place. However, that is not the case. We do not retreat from our holdings that the police must, whenever practicable, obtain advance judicial approval of searches and seizures through the warrant procedure or that in most instances failure to comply with the warrant requirement can only be excused by exigent circumstances. But we deal here with an entire rubric of police conduct—necessarily swift action predicated upon the on-the-spot observations of the officer on the beat—which historically has not been, and as a practical matter could not be, subjected to the warrant procedure. Instead, the conduct involved in this case must be tested by the Fourth Amendment's general proscription against unreasonable searches and seizures.

Nonetheless, the notions which underlie both the warrant procedure and the requirement of probable cause remain fully relevant in this context. In order to assess the reasonableness of Officer McFadden's conduct as a general proposition, it is necessary "first to focus upon the governmental interest which allegedly justifies official intrusion upon the constitutionally protected interests of the private citizen," for there is "no ready test for determining reasonableness other than by balancing the need to search [or seize] against the invasion which the search [or seizure] entails." And in justifying the particular intrusion the police officer must be able to point to specific and articulable facts which, taken together with rational inferences from those facts, reasonably warrant that intrusion.

The scheme of the Fourth Amendment becomes meaningful only when it is assured that at some point the conduct of those charged with enforcing the laws can be subjected to the more detached, neutral scrutiny of a judge who must evaluate the reasonableness of a particular search or seizure in light of the particular circumstances. And in making that assessment it is imperative that the facts be judged against an objective standard: would the facts available to the officer at the moment of the seizure or the search "warrant a man of reasonable caution in the belief" that the action taken was appropriate? Anything less would invite intrusions upon constitutionally guaranteed rights based on nothing more substantial than inarticulate hunches, a result this Court has consistently refused to sanction. And simple "'good faith on the part of the arresting officer is not enough.' . .

. If subjective good faith alone were the test, the protections of the Fourth Amendment would evaporate, and the people would be 'secure in their persons, houses, papers, and effects,' only in the discretion of the police."

Applying these principles to this case, we consider first the nature and extent of the governmental interests involved. One general interest is of course that of effective crime prevention and detection; it is this interest which underlies the recognition that a police officer may in appropriate circumstances and in an appropriate manner approach a person for purposes of investigating possibly criminal behavior even though there is no probable cause to make an arrest. It was this legitimate investigative function Officer McFadden was discharging when he decided to approach petitioner and his companions. He had observed Terry, Chilton, and Katz go through a series of acts, each of them perhaps innocent in itself, but which taken together warranted further investigation. There is nothing unusual in two men standing together on a street corner, perhaps waiting for someone. Nor is there anything suspicious about people in such circumstances strolling up and down the street, singly or in pairs. Store windows, moreover, are made to be looked in. But the story is quite different where, as here, two men hover about a street corner for an extended period of time, at the end of which it becomes apparent that they are not waiting for anyone or anything; where these men pace alternately along an identical route, pausing to stare in the same store window roughly 24 times; where each completion of this route is followed immediately by a conference between the two men on the corner; where they are joined in one of these conferences by a third man who leaves swiftly; and where the two men finally follow the third and rejoin him a couple of blocks away. It would have been poor police work indeed for an officer of 30 years' experience in the detection of thievery from stores in this same neighborhood to have failed to investigate this behavior further.

The crux of this case, however, is not the propriety of Officer McFadden's taking steps to investigate petitioner's suspicious behavior, but rather, whether there was justification for McFadden's invasion of Terry's personal security by searching him for weapons in the course of that investigation. We are now concerned with more than the governmental interest in investigating crime; in addition, there is the more immediate interest of the police officer in taking steps to assure himself that the person with whom he is dealing is not armed with a weapon that could unexpectedly and fatally be used against him. Certainly it would be unreasonable to require that police officers take unnecessary risks in the performance of their duties. American criminals have a long tradition of armed violence, and every year in this country many law enforcement officers are killed in the line of duty, and thousands more are wounded. Virtually all of these deaths and a substantial portion of the injuries are inflicted with guns and knives.

In view of these facts, we cannot blind ourselves to the need for law enforcement officers to protect themselves and other prospective victims of violence in situations where they may lack probable cause for an arrest. When an officer is justified in believing that the individual whose suspicious behavior he is investigating at close range is armed and presently dangerous to the officer or to others, it would appear to be clearly unreasonable to deny the officer the power to take necessary measures to determine whether the person is in fact carrying a weapon and to neutralize the threat of physical harm.

We must still consider, however, the nature and quality of the intrusion on individual rights which must be accepted if police officers are to be conceded the right to search for weapons in situations where probable cause to arrest for crime is lacking. Even a limited search of the outer clothing for weapons constitutes a severe, though brief, intrusion upon cherished personal security, and it must surely be an annoying, frightening, and perhaps humiliating experience. Petitioner contends that such an intrusion is permissible only incident to a lawful arrest, either for a crime involving the possession of weapons or for a crime the commission of which led the officer to investigate in the first place. However, this argument must be closely examined.

Petitioner does not argue that a police officer should refrain from making any investigation of suspicious circumstances until such time as he has probable cause to make an arrest; nor does he deny that police officers in properly discharging their investigative function may find themselves confronting persons who might well be armed and dangerous. Moreover, he does not say that an officer is always unjustified in searching a suspect to discover weapons. Rather, he says it is unreasonable for the policeman to take that step until such time as the situation evolves to a point where there is probable cause to make an arrest. When that point has been reached, petitioner would concede the officer's right to conduct a search of the suspect for weapons, fruits or instrumentalities of the crime, or "mere" evidence, incident to the arrest. There are two weaknesses in this line of reasoning, however.

First, it fails to take account of traditional limitations upon the scope of searches, and thus recognizes no distinction in purpose, character, and extent between a search incident to an arrest and a limited search for weapons. The former, although justified in part by the acknowledged necessity to protect the arresting officer from assault with a concealed weapon is also justified on other grounds, and can therefore involve a relatively extensive exploration of the person. A search for weapons in the absence of probable cause to arrest, however, must, like any other search, be strictly circumscribed by the exigencies which justify its initiation. Thus it must be limited to that which is necessary for the discovery of weapons which might be used to harm the officer or others nearby, and may realistically be characterized as something less than a "full" search, even though it remains a serious intrusion.

A second, and related, objection to petitioner's argument is that it assumes that the law of arrest has already worked out the balance between the particular interests involved here—the neutralization of danger to the policeman in the investigative circumstance and the sanctity of the individual. But this is not so. An arrest is a wholly different kind of intrusion upon individual freedom from a limited search for weapons, and the interests each is designed to serve are likewise quite different. An arrest is the initial stage of a criminal prosecution. It is intended to vindicate society's interest in having its laws obeyed, and it is inevitably accompanied by future interference with the individual's freedom of movement, whether or not trial or conviction ultimately follows.

The protective search for weapons, on the other hand, constitutes a brief, though far from inconsiderable, intrusion upon the sanctity of the person. It does not follow that because an officer may lawfully arrest a person only when he is apprised of facts sufficient to warrant a belief that the person has committed or is committing a crime, the officer is equally unjustified, absent that kind of evidence, in making any intrusions short of an arrest. Moreover, a perfectly reasonable apprehension of danger may arise long before the officer is possessed of adequate information to justify taking a person into custody for the purpose of prosecuting him for a crime. Petitioner's reliance on cases which have worked out standards of reasonableness with regard to "seizures" constituting arrests and searches incident thereto is thus misplaced. It assumes that the interests sought to be vindicated and the invasions of personal security may be equated in the two cases, and thereby ignores a vital aspect of the analysis of the reasonableness of particular types of conduct under the Fourth Amendment.

 Our evaluation of the proper balance that has to be struck in this type of case leads us to conclude that there must be a narrowly drawn authority to permit a reasonable search for weapons for the protection of the police officer, where he has reason to believe that he is dealing with an armed and dangerous individual, regardless of whether he has probable cause to arrest the individual for a crime. The officer need not be absolutely certain that the individual is armed; the issue is whether a reasonably prudent man in the circumstances would be warranted in the belief that his safety or that of others was in danger. And in determining whether the officer acted reasonably in such circumstances, due weight must be given, not to his inchoate and unparticularized suspicion or "hunch," but to the specific reasonable inferences which he is entitled to draw from the facts in light of his experience.

....

We must now examine the conduct of Officer McFadden in this case to determine whether his search and seizure of petitioner were reasonable, both at their inception and as conducted. He had observed Terry, together with Chilton and another man, acting in a manner he took to be preface to a "stick-up." We think on the facts and circumstances Officer McFadden detailed before the trial judge a reasonably prudent man would have been warranted in believing petitioner was armed and thus presented a threat to the officer's safety while he was investigating his suspicious behavior. The actions of Terry and Chilton were consistent with McFadden's hypothesis that these men were contemplating a daylight robbery—which, it is reasonable to assume, would be likely to involve the use of weapons—and nothing in their conduct from the time he first noticed them until the time he confronted them and identified himself as a police officer gave him sufficient reason to negate that hypothesis.

Although the trio had departed the original scene, there was nothing to indicate abandonment of an intent to commit a robbery at some point. Thus, when Officer McFadden approached the three men gathered before the display window at Zucker's store he had observed enough to make it quite reasonable to fear that they were armed; and nothing in their response to his hailing them, identifying himself as a police officer, and asking their names served to dispel that reasonable belief. We cannot say his decision at that point to seize Terry and pat his clothing for weapons was the product of a volatile or inventive imagination, or was undertaken simply as an act of harassment; the record evidences the tempered act of a policeman who in the course of an investigation had to make a quick decision as to how to protect himself and others from possible danger, and took limited steps to do so.

The manner in which the seizure and search were conducted is, of course, as vital a part of the inquiry as whether they were warranted at all. The Fourth Amendment proceeds as much by limitations upon the scope of governmental action as by imposing preconditions upon its initiation. The entire deterrent purpose of the rule excluding evidence seized in violation of the Fourth Amendment rests on the assumption that "limitations upon the fruit to be gathered tend to limit the quest itself." Thus, evidence may not be introduced if it was discovered by means of a seizure and search which were not reasonably related in scope to the justification for their initiation. We need not develop at length in this case, however, the limitations which the Fourth

Amendment places upon a protective seizure and search for weapons. These limitations will have to be developed in the concrete factual circumstances of individual cases. Suffice it to note that such a search, unlike a search without a warrant incident to a lawful arrest, is not justified by any need to prevent the disappearance or destruction of evidence of crime. The sole justification of the search in the present situation is the protection of the police officer and others nearby, and it must therefore be confined in scope to an intrusion reasonably designed to discover guns, knives, clubs, or other hidden instruments for the assault of the police officer.

The scope of the search in this case presents no serious problem in light of these standards. Officer McFadden patted down the outer clothing of petitioner and his two companions. He did not place his hands in their pockets or under the outer surface of their garments until he had felt weapons, and then he merely reached for and removed the guns. He never did invade Katz' person beyond the outer surfaces of his clothes, since he discovered nothing in his pat-down which might have been a weapon. Officer McFadden confined his search strictly to what was minimally necessary to learn whether the men were armed and to disarm them once he discovered the weapons. He did not conduct a general exploratory search for whatever evidence of criminal activity he might find.

....

We conclude that the revolver seized from Terry was properly admitted in evidence against him. At the time he seized petitioner and searched him for weapons, Officer McFadden had reasonable grounds to believe that petitioner was armed and dangerous, and it was necessary for the protection of himself and others to take swift measures to discover the true facts and neutralize the threat of harm if it materialized. The policeman carefully restricted his search to what was appropriate to the discovery of the particular items which he sought. Each case of this sort will, of course, have to be decided on its own facts. We merely hold today that where a police officer observes unusual conduct which leads him reasonably to conclude in light of his experience that criminal activity may be afoot and that the persons with whom he is dealing may be armed and presently dangerous, where in the course of investigating this behavior he identifies himself as a policeman and makes reasonable inquiries, and where nothing in the initial stages of the encounter serves to dispel his reasonable fear for his own or others' safety, he is entitled for the protection of himself and others in the area to conduct a carefully limited search of the outer clothing of such persons in an attempt to discover weapons which might be used to assault him. Such a search is a reasonable search under the Fourth Amendment, and any weapons seized may properly be introduced in evidence against the person from whom they were taken.

Affirmed.

Chimel v. California (1969)
395 U.S. 752

When a person is arrested, it makes sense that police officers can search the person. Otherwise, the arrestee may have a weapon, a means of escape such as a handcuff key, or contraband. This kind of search—known as a search "incident to arrest"—has long been upheld by the courts as constitutional. The situation becomes more complicated when police search the area around the arrestee. The court considers the proper scope of such a search in this case. In addition, the court makes a compelling argument as to why search warrants and the probable cause requirement are important to the liberties of all Americans.

This case raises basic questions concerning the permissible scope under the Fourth Amendment of a search incident to a lawful arrest.

The relevant facts are essentially undisputed. Late in the afternoon of September 13, 1965, three police officers arrived at the Santa Ana, California, home of the petitioner with a warrant authorizing his arrest for the burglary of a coin shop. The officers knocked on the door, identified themselves to the petitioner's wife, and asked if they might come inside. She ushered them into the house, where they waited 10 or 15 minutes until the petitioner returned home from work. When the petitioner entered the house, one of the officers handed him the arrest warrant and asked for permission to "look around." The petitioner objected, but was advised that "on the basis of the lawful arrest," the officers would nonetheless conduct a search. No search warrant had been issued.

Accompanied by the petitioner's wife, the officers then looked through the entire three-bedroom house, including the attic, the garage, and a small workshop. In some rooms the search was relatively cursory. In the master bedroom and sewing room, however, the officers directed the petitioner's wife to open drawers and "to physically move contents of the drawers from side to side so that they might view any items that would have come from the burglary." After completing the search, they seized numerous items—primarily coins, but also several medals, tokens, and a few other objects. The entire search took between 45 minutes and an hour.

At the petitioner's subsequent state trial on two charges of burglary, the items taken from his house were admitted into evidence against him, over his objection that they had been unconstitutionally seized. He was convicted, and the judgments of conviction were affirmed by both the California Court of Appeal and the California Supreme Court. Both courts accepted the petitioner's contention that the arrest warrant was invalid because the supporting affidavit was set out in conclusory terms, but held that since the arresting officers had procured the warrant "in good faith," and since in any event they had had sufficient information to constitute probable cause for the petitioner's arrest, that arrest had been lawful. From this conclusion the appellate courts went on to hold that the search of the petitioner's home had been justified, despite the absence of a search warrant, on the ground that it had been incident to a valid arrest. We granted certiorari in order to consider the petitioner's substantial constitutional claims.

Without deciding the question, we proceed on the hypothesis that the California courts were correct in holding that the arrest of the petitioner was valid under the Constitution. This brings us directly to the question whether the warrantless search of the petitioner's entire house can be constitutionally justified as incident to that arrest. The decisions of this Court bearing upon that question have been far from consistent, as even the most cursory review makes evident.

Approval of a warrantless search incident to a lawful arrest seems first to have been articulated by the Court in 1914 as dictum in *Weeks v. United States*, in which the Court stated:

"What then is the present case? Before answering that inquiry specifically, it may be well by a process of exclusion to state what it is not. It is not an assertion of the right on the part of the Government, always recognized under English and American law, to search the person of the accused when legally arrested to discover and seize the fruits or evidences of crime."

That statement made no reference to any right to search the place where an arrest occurs, but was limited to a right to search the "person." Eleven years later the case of *Carroll v. United States*, brought the following embellishment of the *Weeks* statement:

"When a man is legally arrested for an offense, whatever is found upon his person or in his control which it is unlawful for him to have and which may be used to prove the offense may be seized and held as evidence in the prosecution."

Still, that assertion too was far from a claim that the "place" where one is arrested may be searched so long as the arrest is valid. Without explanation, however, the principle emerged in expanded form a few months later in *Agnello v. United States*—although still by way of dictum:

"The right without a search warrant contemporaneously to search persons lawfully arrested while committing crime and to search the place where the arrest is made in order to find and seize things connected with the crime as its fruits or as the means by which it was committed, as well as weapons and other things to effect an escape from custody, is not to be doubted."

And in *Marron v. United States*, two years later, the dictum of *Agnello* appeared to be the foundation of the Court's decision. In that case federal agents had secured a search warrant authorizing the seizure of liquor and certain articles used in its manufacture. When they arrived at the premises to be searched, they saw "that the place was used for retailing and drinking intoxicating liquors." They proceeded to arrest the person in charge and to execute the warrant. In searching a closet for the items listed in the warrant they came across an incriminating ledger, concededly not covered by the warrant, which they also seized. The Court upheld the seizure of the ledger by holding that since the agents had made a lawful arrest, "they had a right without a warrant contemporaneously to search the place in order to find and seize the things used to carry on the criminal enterprise."

....

In that case, officers had obtained a warrant for Harris' arrest on the basis of his alleged involvement with the cashing and interstate transportation of a forged check. He was arrested in the living room of his four-room apartment, and in an attempt to recover two canceled checks thought to have been used in effecting the forgery, the officers undertook a thorough search of the entire apartment. Inside a desk drawer they found a sealed envelope marked "George Harris, personal papers." The envelope, which was then torn open, was found to contain altered Selective Service documents, and those documents were used to secure Harris' conviction for violating the *Selective Training and Service Act of 1940*. The Court rejected Harris' Fourth Amendment claim, sustaining the search as "incident to arrest."

Only a year after *Harris*, however, the pendulum swung again. In *Trupiano v. United States*, agents raided the site of an illicit distillery, saw one of several conspirators operating the still, and arrested him, contemporaneously "seizing the illicit distillery." The Court held that the arrest and others made subsequently had been valid, but that the unexplained failure of the agents to procure a search warrant—in spite of the fact that they had had more than enough time before the raid to do so—rendered the search unlawful. The opinion stated:

"It is a cardinal rule that, in seizing goods and articles, law enforcement agents must secure and use search warrants wherever reasonably practicable. . . . This rule rests upon the desirability of having magistrates rather than police officers determine when searches and seizures are permissible and what limitations should be placed upon such activities. . . . To provide the necessary security against unreasonable intrusions upon the private lives of individuals, the framers of the Fourth Amendment required adherence to judicial processes wherever possible. And subsequent history has confirmed the wisdom of that requirement . . . A search or seizure without a warrant as an incident to a lawful arrest has always been considered to be a strictly limited right. It grows out of the inherent necessities of the situation at the time of the arrest. But there must be something more in the way of necessity than merely a lawful arrest."

In 1950, two years after *Trupiano*, came *United States v. Rabinowitz*, the decision upon which California primarily relies in the case now before us. In *Rabinowitz*, federal authorities had been informed that the defendant was dealing in stamps bearing forged overprints. On the basis of that information they secured a warrant for his arrest, which they executed at his one-room business office. At the time of the arrest, the officers "searched the desk, safe, and file cabinets in the office for about an hour and a half," and seized 573 stamps with forged overprints. The stamps were admitted into evidence at the defendant's trial, and this Court affirmed his conviction, rejecting the contention that the warrantless search had been unlawful. The Court held that the search in its entirety fell within the principle giving law enforcement authorities "the right 'to search the place where the arrest is made in order to find and seize things connected with the crime . . . .'" *Harris* was regarded as "ample authority" for that conclusion. The opinion rejected the rule of *Trupiano* that "in seizing goods and articles, law enforcement agents must secure and use search warrants wherever reasonably practicable." The test, said the Court, "is not whether it is reasonable to procure a search warrant, but whether the search was reasonable."

Rabinowitz has come to stand for the proposition...that a warrantless search "incident to a lawful arrest" may generally extend to the area that is considered to be in the "possession" or under the "control" of the person arrested. And it was on the basis of that proposition that the California courts upheld the search of the petitioner's entire house in this case. That doctrine, however, at least in the broad sense in which it was applied by the California courts in this case, can withstand neither historical nor rational analysis.

Even limited to its own facts, the *Rabinowitz* decision was, as we have seen, hardly founded on an unimpeachable line of authority. As Mr. Justice Frankfurter commented in dissent in that case, the "hint" contained in *Weeks* was, without persuasive justification, "loosely turned into dictum and finally elevated to a decision." And the approach taken in cases such as *Go-Bart*, *Lefkowitz*, and *Trupiano* was essentially disregarded by the *Rabinowitz* Court.

Nor is the rationale by which the State seeks here to sustain the search of the petitioner's house supported by a reasoned view of the background and purpose of the Fourth Amendment. Mr. Justice Frankfurter wisely pointed out in his *Rabinowitz* dissent that the Amendment's proscription of "unreasonable searches and seizures" must be read in light of "the history that gave rise to the words"—a history of "abuses so deeply felt by the Colonies as to be one of the potent causes of the Revolution . . . ." The Amendment was in large part a reaction to the general warrants and warrantless searches that had so alienated the colonists and had helped speed the movement for independence. In the scheme of the Amendment, therefore, the requirement that "no Warrants shall issue, but upon probable cause," plays a crucial part. As the Court put it in *McDonald v. United States*:

"We are not dealing with formalities. The presence of a search warrant serves a high function. Absent some grave emergency, the Fourth Amendment has interposed a magistrate between the citizen and the police. This was done not to shield criminals nor to make the home a safe haven for illegal activities. It was done so that an objective mind might weigh the need to invade that privacy in order to enforce the law. The right of privacy was deemed too precious to entrust to the discretion of those whose job is the detection of crime and the arrest of criminals. . . . And so the Constitution requires a magistrate to pass on the desires of the police before they violate the privacy of the home. We cannot be true to that constitutional requirement and excuse the absence of a search warrant without a showing by those who seek exemption from the constitutional mandate that the exigencies of the situation made that course imperative."

Even in the *Agnello* case the Court relied upon the rule that "belief, however well founded, that an article sought is concealed in a dwelling house furnishes no justification for a search of that place without a warrant. And such searches are held unlawful notwithstanding facts unquestionably showing probable cause." Clearly, the general requirement that a search warrant be obtained is not lightly to be dispensed with, and "the burden is on those seeking an exemption from the requirement to show the need for it . . . ."

 Only last Term in *Terry v. Ohio*, we emphasized that "the police must, whenever practicable, obtain advance judicial approval of searches and seizures through the warrant procedure," and that "the scope of a search must be 'strictly tied to and justified by' the circumstances which rendered its initiation permissible. The search undertaken by the officer in that "stop and frisk" case was sustained under that test, because it was no more than a "protective . . . search for weapons." But in a companion case, *Sibron v. New York*, we applied the same standard to another set of facts and reached a contrary result, holding that a policeman's action in thrusting his hand into a suspect's pocket had been neither motivated by nor limited to the objective of protection. Rather, the search had been made in order to find narcotics, which were in fact found.

A similar analysis underlies the "search incident to arrest" principle, and marks its proper extent. When an arrest is made, it is reasonable for the arresting officer to search the person arrested in order to remove any weapons that the latter might seek to use in order to resist arrest or effect his escape. Otherwise, the officer's safety might well be endangered, and the arrest itself frustrated. In addition, it is entirely reasonable for the arresting officer to search for and seize any evidence on the arrestee's person in order to prevent its concealment or destruction. And the area into which an arrestee might reach in order to grab a weapon or evidentiary items must, of course, be governed by a like rule. A gun on a table or in a drawer in front of one who is arrested can be as dangerous to the arresting officer as one concealed in the clothing of the person arrested. There is ample justification, therefore, for a search of the arrestee's person and the area "within his immediate control"—construing that phrase to mean the area from within which he might gain possession of a weapon or destructible evidence.

There is no comparable justification, however, for routinely searching any room other than that in which an arrest occurs—or, for that matter, for searching through all the desk drawers or other closed or concealed areas in that room itself. Such searches, in the absence of well-recognized exceptions, may be made only under the authority of a search warrant. The "adherence to judicial processes" mandated by the Fourth Amendment requires no less.

This is the principle that underlay our decision in *Preston v. United States*. In that case three men had been arrested in a parked car, which had later been towed to a garage and searched by police. We held the search to have been unlawful under the Fourth Amendment, despite the contention that it had been incidental to a valid arrest. Our reasoning was straightforward:

"The rule allowing contemporaneous searches is justified, for example, by the need to seize weapons and other things which might be used to assault an officer or effect an escape, as well as by the need to prevent the destruction of evidence of the crime—things which might easily happen where the weapon or evidence is on the accused's person or under his immediate control. But these justifications are absent where a search is remote in time or place from the arrest."

The same basic principle was reflected in our opinion last Term in *Sibron*. That opinion dealt with *Peters v. New York*, as well as with Sibron's case, and *Peters* involved a search that we upheld as incident to a proper arrest. We sustained the search, however, only because its scope had been "reasonably limited" by the "need to seize weapons" and "to prevent the destruction of evidence," to which *Preston* had referred. We emphasized that the arresting officer "did not engage in an unrestrained and thoroughgoing examination of Peters and his personal effects. He seized him to cut short his flight, and he searched him primarily for weapons."

It is argued in the present case that it is "reasonable" to search a man's house when he is arrested in it. But that argument is founded on little more than a subjective view regarding the acceptability of certain sorts of police conduct, and not on considerations relevant to Fourth Amendment interests. Under such an unconfined analysis, Fourth Amendment protection in this area would approach the evaporation point. It is not easy to explain why, for instance, it is less subjectively "reasonable" to search a man's house when he is arrested on his front lawn—or just down the street—than it is when he happens to be in the house at the time of arrest. As Mr. Justice Frankfurter put it:

"To say that the search must be reasonable is to require some criterion of reason. It is no guide at all either for a jury or for district judges or the police to say that an 'unreasonable search' is forbidden—that the search must be reasonable. What is the test of reason which makes a search reasonable? The test is the reason underlying and expressed by the Fourth Amendment: the history and the experience which it embodies and the safeguards afforded by it against the evils to which it was a response."

Thus, although "the recurring questions of the reasonableness of searches" depend upon "the facts and circumstances—the total atmosphere of the case," those facts and circumstances must be viewed in the light of established Fourth Amendment principles.

It would be possible, of course, to draw a line between *Rabinowitz* and *Harris* on the one hand, and this case on the other. For *Rabinowitz* involved a single room, and *Harris* a four-room apartment, while in the case before us an entire house was searched. But such a distinction would be highly artificial. The rationale that allowed the searches and seizures in *Rabinowitz* and *Harris* would allow the searches and seizures in this case. No consideration relevant to the Fourth Amendment suggests any point of rational limitation, once the search is allowed to go beyond the area from which the person arrested might obtain weapons or evidentiary items. The only reasoned distinction is one between a search of the person arrested and the area within his reach on the one hand, and more extensive searches on the other.

The petitioner correctly points out that one result of decisions such as *Rabinowitz* and *Harris* is to give law enforcement officials the opportunity to engage in searches not justified by probable cause, by the simple expedient of arranging to arrest suspects at home rather than elsewhere. We do not suggest that the petitioner is necessarily correct in his assertion that such a strategy was utilized here, but the fact remains that had he been arrested earlier in the day, at his place of employment rather than at home, no search of his house could have been made without a search warrant. In any event, even apart from the possibility of such police tactics, the general point so forcefully made by Judge Learned Hand in *United States v. Kirschenblatt* remains:

"After arresting a man in his house, to rummage at will among his papers in search of whatever will convict him, appears to us to be indistinguishable from what might be done under a general warrant; indeed, the warrant would give more protection, for presumably it must be issued by a magistrate. True, by hypothesis the power would not exist, if the supposed offender were not found on the premises; but it is small consolation to know that one's papers are safe only so long as one is not at home."

Rabinowitz and *Harris* have been the subject of critical commentary for many years, and have been relied upon less and less in our own decisions. It is time, for the reasons we have stated, to hold that on their own facts, and insofar as the principles they stand for are inconsistent with those that we have endorsed today, they are no longer to be followed.

Application of sound Fourth Amendment principles to the facts of this case produces a clear result. The search here went far beyond the petitioner's person and the area from within which he might have obtained either a weapon or something that could have been used as evidence against him. There was no constitutional justification, in the absence of a search warrant, for extending the search beyond that area. The scope of the search was, therefore, "unreasonable" under the Fourth and Fourteenth Amendments, and the petitioner's conviction cannot stand.

Reversed.

United States v. Drayton (2002)
536 U.S. 194

On its face, this case deals with the warrantless search of bus passengers. At its heart is the issue of the waiver of the right to be free from unreasonable searches and seizures. The court concludes that voluntary consent and participation in the search constituted a valid waiver of the right, regardless of failure to articulate the right to refuse consent by police.

The Fourth Amendment permits police officers to approach bus passengers at random to ask questions and to request their consent to searches, provided a reasonable person would understand that he or she is free to refuse. This case requires us to determine whether officers must advise bus passengers during these encounters of their right not to cooperate.

....

On February 4, 1999, respondents Christopher Drayton and Clifton Brown, Jr., were traveling on a Greyhound bus en route from Ft. Lauderdale, Florida, to Detroit, Michigan. The bus made a scheduled stop in Tallahassee, Florida. The passengers were required to disembark so the bus could be refueled and cleaned. As the passengers reboarded, the driver checked their tickets and then left to complete paperwork inside the terminal. As he left, the driver allowed three members of the Tallahassee Police Department to board the bus as part of a routine drug and weapons interdiction effort. The officers were dressed in plain clothes and carried concealed weapons and visible badges.

Once onboard Officer Hoover knelt on the driver's seat and faced the rear of the bus. He could observe the passengers and ensure the safety of the two other officers without blocking the aisle or otherwise obstructing the bus exit. Officers Lang and Blackburn went to the rear of the bus. Blackburn remained stationed there, facing forward. Lang worked his way toward the front of the bus, speaking with individual passengers as he went. He asked the passengers about their travel plans and sought to match passengers with luggage in the overhead racks. To avoid blocking the aisle, Lang stood next to or just behind each passenger with whom he spoke.

According to Lang's testimony, passengers who declined to cooperate with him or who chose to exit the bus at any time would have been allowed to do so without argument. In Lang's experience, however, most people are willing to cooperate. Some passengers go so far as to commend the police for their efforts to ensure the safety of their travel. Lang could recall five to six instances in the previous year in which passengers had declined to have their luggage searched. It also was common for passengers to leave the bus for a cigarette or a snack while the officers were on board. Lang sometimes informed passengers of their right to refuse to cooperate. On the day in question, however, he did not.

Respondents were seated next to each other on the bus. Drayton was in the aisle seat, Brown in the seat next to the window. Lang approached respondents from the rear and leaned over Drayton's shoulder. He held up his badge long enough for respondents to identify him as a police officer. With his face 12-to-18 inches away from Drayton's, Lang spoke in a voice just loud enough for respondents to hear:

"I'm Investigator Lang with the Tallahassee Police Department. We're conducting bus interdiction [sic], attempting to deter drugs and illegal weapons being transported on the bus. Do you have any bags on the bus?"

Both respondents pointed to a single green bag in the overhead luggage rack. Lang asked, "Do you mind if I check it?" and Brown responded, "Go ahead." Lang handed the bag to Officer Blackburn to check. The bag contained no contraband.

Officer Lang noticed that both respondents were wearing heavy jackets and baggy pants despite the warm weather. In Lang's experience drug traffickers often use baggy clothing to conceal weapons or narcotics. The officer thus asked Brown if he had any weapons or drugs in his possession. And he asked Brown: "Do you mind if I check your person?" Brown answered, "Sure," and cooperated by leaning up in his seat, pulling a cell phone out of his pocket, and opening up his jacket. Lang reached across Drayton and patted down Brown's jacket and pockets, including his waist area, sides, and upper thighs. In both thigh areas, Lang detected hard objects similar to drug packages detected on other occasions. Lang arrested and handcuffed Brown. Officer Hoover escorted Brown from the bus.

Lang then asked Drayton, "Mind if I check you?" Drayton responded by lifting his hands about eight inches from his legs. Lang conducted a pat-down of Drayton's thighs and detected hard objects similar to those found on Brown. He arrested Drayton and escorted him from the bus. A further search revealed that respondents had duct-taped plastic bundles of powder cocaine between several pairs of their boxer shorts. Brown possessed three bundles containing 483 grams of cocaine. Drayton possessed two bundles containing 295 grams of cocaine.

Respondents were charged with conspiring to distribute cocaine, in and with possessing cocaine with intent to distribute it. They moved to suppress the cocaine, arguing that the consent to the pat-down search was invalid. Following a hearing at which only Officer Lang testified, the United States District Court for the Northern District of Florida denied their motions to suppress. The District Court determined that the police conduct was not coercive and respondents' consent to the search was voluntary. The District Court pointed to the fact that the officers were dressed in plain clothes, did not brandish their badges in an authoritative manner, did not make a general announcement to the entire bus, and did not address anyone in a menacing tone of voice. It noted that the officers did not block the aisle or the exit, and stated that it was "obvious that respondents can get up and leave, as can the people ahead of them." The District Court concluded: "Everything that took place between Officer Lang and Mr. Drayton and Mr. Brown suggests that it was cooperative. There was nothing coercive, there was nothing confrontational about it."

The Court of Appeals for the Eleventh Circuit reversed and remanded with instructions to grant respondents' motions to suppress. The court held that this disposition was compelled by its previous decisions in *United States v. Washington*, and *United States v. Guapi*. Those cases had held that bus passengers do not feel free to disregard police officers' requests to search absent "some positive indication that consent could have been refused."

We granted certiorari. The respondents, we conclude, were not seized and their consent to the search was voluntary; and we reverse.

....

Law enforcement officers do not violate the Fourth Amendment's prohibition of unreasonable seizures merely by approaching individuals on the street or in other public places and putting questions to them if they are willing to listen. Even when law enforcement officers have no basis for suspecting a particular individual, they may pose questions, ask for identification, and request consent to search luggage—provided they do not induce cooperation by coercive means. If a reasonable person would feel free to terminate the encounter, then he or she has not been seized.

The Court has addressed on a previous occasion the specific question of drug interdiction efforts on buses. In *Bostick*, two police officers requested a bus passenger's consent to a search of his luggage. The passenger agreed, and the resulting search revealed cocaine in his suitcase. The Florida Supreme Court suppressed the cocaine. In doing so it adopted a per se rule that due to the cramped confines onboard a bus the act of questioning would deprive a person of his or her freedom of movement and so constitute a seizure under the Fourth Amendment.

This Court reversed. *Bostick* first made it clear that for the most part per se rules are inappropriate in the Fourth Amendment context. The proper inquiry necessitates a consideration of "all the circumstances surrounding the encounter." The Court noted next that the traditional rule, which states that a seizure does not occur so long as a reasonable person would feel free "to disregard the police and go about his business," is not an accurate measure of the coercive effect of a bus encounter. A passenger may not want to get off a bus if there is a risk it will depart before the opportunity to reboard. A bus rider's movements are confined in this sense, but this is the natural result of choosing to take the bus; it says nothing about whether the police conduct is coercive. The proper inquiry "is whether a reasonable person would feel free to decline the officers' requests or otherwise terminate the encounter." Finally, the Court rejected Bostick's argument that he must have been seized because no reasonable person would consent to a search of luggage containing drugs. The reasonable person test, the Court explained, is objective and "presupposes an innocent person."

In light of the limited record, *Bostick* refrained from deciding whether a seizure occurred. The Court, however, identified two factors "particularly worth noting" on remand. First, although it was obvious that an officer was armed, he did not remove the gun from its pouch or use it in a threatening way. Second, the officer advised the passenger that he could refuse consent to the search.

Relying upon this latter factor, the Eleventh Circuit has adopted what is in effect a per se rule that evidence obtained during suspicionless drug interdiction efforts aboard buses must be suppressed unless the officers have advised passengers of their right not to cooperate and to refuse consent to a search. In *United States v. Guapi* the Court of Appeals described "the most glaring difference" between the encounters in *Guapi* and in *Bostick* as "the complete lack of any notification to the passengers that they were in fact free to decline the search request . . . . Providing this simple notification . . . is perhaps the most efficient and effective method to ensure compliance with the Constitution."

The Court of Appeals then listed other factors that contributed to the coerciveness of the encounter: (1) the officer conducted the interdiction before the passengers disembarked from the bus at a scheduled stop; (2) the officer explained his presence in the form of a general announcement to the entire bus; (3) the officer wore a police uniform; and (4) the officer questioned passengers as he moved from the front to the rear of the bus, thus obstructing the path to the exit.

After its decision in *Guapi* the Court of Appeals decided *United States v. Washington* and the instant case. The court suppressed evidence obtained during similar drug interdiction efforts despite the following facts: (1) the officers in both cases conducted the interdiction after the passengers had re-boarded the bus; (2) the officer in the present case did not make a general announcement to the entire bus but instead spoke with individual passengers; (3) the officers in both cases were not in uniform; and (4) the officers in both cases questioned passengers as they moved from the rear to the front of the bus and were careful not to obstruct passengers' means of egress from the bus.

Although the Court of Appeals has disavowed a per se requirement, the lack of an explicit warning to passengers is the only element common to all its cases.... Under these cases, it appears that the Court of Appeals would suppress any evidence obtained during suspicionless drug interdiction efforts aboard buses in the absence of a warning that passengers may refuse to cooperate. The Court of Appeals erred in adopting this approach.

Applying the *Bostick* framework to the facts of this particular case, we conclude that the police did not seize respondents when they boarded the bus and began questioning passengers. The officers gave the passengers no reason to believe that they were required to answer the officers' questions. When Officer Lang approached respondents, he did not brandish a weapon or make any intimidating movements. He left the aisle free so that respondents could exit. He spoke to passengers one by one and in a polite, quiet voice. Nothing he said would suggest to a reasonable person that he or she was barred from leaving the bus or otherwise terminating the encounter.

There were ample grounds for the District Court to conclude that "everything that took place between Officer Lang and respondents suggests that it was cooperative" and that there "was nothing coercive or confrontational" about the encounter. There was no application of force, no intimidating movement, no overwhelming show of force, no brandishing of weapons, no blocking of exits, no threat, no command, not even an authoritative tone of voice. It is beyond question that had this encounter occurred on the street, it would be constitutional. The fact that an encounter takes place on a bus does not on its own transform standard police questioning of citizens into an illegal seizure. Indeed, because many fellow passengers are present to witness officers' conduct, a reasonable person may feel even more secure in his or her decision not to cooperate with police on a bus than in other circumstances.

Respondents make much of the fact that Officer Lang displayed his badge.... Drayton contends that even if Brown's cooperation with the officers was consensual, Drayton was seized because no reasonable person would feel free to terminate the encounter with the officers after Brown had been arrested. The Court of Appeals did not address this claim; and in any event the argument fails. The arrest of one person does not mean that everyone around him has been seized by police. If anything, Brown's arrest should have put Drayton on notice of the consequences of continuing the encounter by answering the officers' questions. Even after arresting Brown, Lang addressed Drayton in a polite manner and provided him with no indication that he was required to answer Lang's questions.

We turn now from the question whether respondents were seized to whether they were subjected to an unreasonable search, i.e., whether their consent to the suspicionless search was involuntary. Circumstances such as these, where the question of voluntariness pervades both the search and seizure inquiries, the respective analyses turn on very similar facts. And, as the facts above suggest, respondents' consent to the search of their luggage and their persons was voluntary. Nothing Officer Lang said indicated a command to consent to the search. Rather, when respondents informed Lang that they had a bag on the bus, he asked for their permission to check it. And when Lang requested to search Brown and Drayton's persons, he asked first if they objected, thus indicating to a reasonable person that he or she was free to refuse. Even after arresting Brown, Lang provided Drayton with no indication that he was required to consent to a search. To the contrary, Lang asked for Drayton's permission to search him ("Mind if I check you?"), and Drayton agreed.

The Court has rejected in specific terms the suggestion that police officers must always inform citizens of their right to refuse when seeking permission to conduct a warrantless consent search. "While knowledge of the right to refuse consent is one factor to be taken into account, the government need not establish such knowledge as the *sine qua non* of an effective consent." Nor do this Court's decisions suggest that even though there are no per se rules, a presumption of invalidity attaches if a citizen consented without explicit notification that he or she was free to refuse to cooperate. Instead, the Court has repeated that the totality of the circumstances must control, without giving extra weight to the absence of this type of warning.... Although Officer Lang did not inform respondents of their right to refuse the search, he did request permission to search, and the totality of the circumstances indicates that their consent was voluntary, so the searches were reasonable.

In a society based on law, the concept of agreement and consent should be given a weight and dignity of its own. Police officers act in full accord with the law when they ask citizens for consent. It reinforces the rule of law for the citizen to advise the police of his or her wishes and for the police to act in reliance on that understanding. When this exchange takes place, it dispels inferences of coercion.

We need not ask the alternative question whether, after the arrest of Brown, there were grounds for a *Terry* stop and frisk of Drayton, though this may have been the case. It was evident that Drayton and Brown were traveling together—Officer Lang observed the pair reboarding the bus together; they were each dressed in heavy, baggy clothes that were ill-suited for the day's warm temperatures; they were seated together on the bus; and they each claimed responsibility for the single piece of green carry-on luggage. Once Lang had identified Brown as carrying what he believed to be narcotics, he may have had reasonable suspicion to conduct a *Terry* stop and frisk on Drayton as well. That question, however, has not been presented to us. The fact the officers may have had reasonable suspicion does not prevent them from relying on a citizen's consent to the search. It would be a paradox, and one most puzzling to law enforcement officials and courts alike, were we to say, after holding that Brown's consent was voluntary, that Drayton's consent was ineffectual simply because the police at that point had more compelling grounds to detain him. After taking Brown into custody, the officers were entitled to continue to proceed on the basis of consent and to ask for Drayton's cooperation.

The judgment of the Court of Appeals is reversed, and the case is remanded for further proceedings consistent with this opinion.

It is so ordered.

Caroll v. United States (1925)
267 U.S. 132

This case carved out the now well-known automobile exception to the search warrant requirement. In addition, it provides insight into the courts analysis of the circumstances under which a warrant may not be required. The court reiterates that when it is practicable to do so, a warrant should be obtained. Where there is a bona fide reason that a warrant cannot reasonably be obtained, the court is likely to make an exception to the warrant requirement.

The constitutional and statutory provisions involved in this case include the Fourth Amendment and the National Prohibition Act.

The Fourth Amendment is in part as follows:

"The right of the people to be secure in their persons, houses, papers, and effects, against unreasonable searches and seizures, shall not be violated, and no Warrants shall issue, but upon probable cause, supported by Oath or affirmation, and particularly describing the place to be searched, and the person, or things to be seized."

Section 25, Title II, of the National Prohibition Act, passed to enforce the Eighteenth Amendment, makes it unlawful to have or possess any liquor intended for use in violating the Act, or which has been so used, and provides that no property rights shall exist in such liquor. A search warrant may issue and such liquor, with the containers thereof, may be seized under the warrant and be ultimately destroyed. The section further provides:

"No search warrant shall issue to search any private dwelling occupied as such unless it is being used for the unlawful sale of intoxicating liquor, or unless it is in part used for some business purpose such as a store, shop, saloon, restaurant, hotel, or boarding house. The term 'private dwelling' shall be construed to include the room or rooms used and occupied not transiently but solely as a residence in an apartment house, hotel, or boarding house."

Section 26, Title II, under which the seizure herein was made, provides in part as follows:

"When the commissioner, his assistants, inspectors, or any officer of the law shall discover any person in the act of transporting in violation of the law, intoxicating liquors in any wagon, buggy, automobile, water or air craft, or other vehicle, it shall be his duty to seize any and all intoxicating liquors found therein being transported contrary to law. Whenever intoxicating liquors transported or possessed illegally shall be seized by an officer he shall take possession of the vehicle and team or automobile, boat, air or water craft, or any other conveyance, and shall arrest any person in charge thereof."

The section then provides that the court upon conviction of the person so arrested shall order the liquor destroyed, and except for good cause shown shall order a sale by public auction of the other property seized, and that the proceeds shall be paid into the Treasury of the United States.

By Section 6 of an Act supplemental to the National Prohibition Act, it is provided that if any officer or agent or employee of the United States engaged in the enforcement of the Prohibition Act or this Amendment, "shall search any private dwelling," as defined in that Act, "without a warrant directing such search," or "shall without a search warrant maliciously and without reasonable cause search any other building or property," he shall be guilty of a misdemeanor and subject to fine or imprisonment or both.

In the passage of the supplemental Act through the Senate, known as the Stanley Amendment, was adopted, the relevant part of which was as follows:

"Section 6. That any officer, agent or employee of the United States engaged in the enforcement of this Act or the National Prohibition Act, or any other law of the United States, who shall search or attempt to search the property or premises of any person without previously securing a search warrant, as provided by law, shall be guilty of a misdemeanor and upon conviction thereof shall be fined not to exceed $ 1000, or imprisoned not to exceed one year, or both so fined and imprisoned in the discretion of the Court."

....

The intent of Congress to make a distinction between the necessity for a search warrant in the searching of private dwellings and in that of automobiles and other road vehicles is the enforcement of the Prohibition Act is thus clearly established by the legislative history of the Stanley Amendment. Is such a distinction consistent with the Fourth Amendment? We think that it is. The Fourth Amendment does not denounce all searches or seizures, but only such as are unreasonable.

The leading case on the subject of search and seizure is *Boyd v. United States*. An Act of Congress of June 22, 1874, authorized a court of the United States, in revenue cases, on motion of the government attorney, to require the defendant to produce in court his private books, invoices and papers on pain in case of refusal of having the allegations of the attorney in his motion taken as confessed. This was held to be unconstitutional and void as applied to suits for penalties or to establish a forfeiture of goods, on the ground that under the Fourth Amendment the compulsory production of invoices to furnish evidence for forfeiture of goods constituted an unreasonable search even where made upon a search warrant, and that it was also a violation of the Fifth Amendment, in that it compelled the defendant in a criminal case to produce evidence against himself or be in the attitude of confessing his guilt.

In *Weeks v. United States* it was held that a court in a criminal prosecution could not retain letters of the accused seized in his house, in his absence and without his authority, by a United States marshal holding no warrant for his arrest and none for the search of his premises, to be used as evidence against him, the accused having made timely application to the court for an order for the return of the letters.

In *Silverthorne Lumber Company v. United States* a writ of error was brought to reverse a judgment of contempt of the District Court, fining the company and imprisoning one Silverthorne, its president, until he should purge himself of contempt in not producing books and documents of the company before the grand jury to prove violation of the statutes of the United States by the company and Silverthorne. Silverthorne had been arrested and while under arrest the marshal had gone to the office of the company without a warrant and made a clean sweep of all books, papers and documents found there and had taken copies and photographs of the papers. The District Court ordered the return of the originals, but impounded the photographs and copies. This was held to be an unreasonable search of the property and possessions of the corporation and a violation of the Fourth Amendment and the judgment for contempt was reversed.

In *Gouled v. United States* the obtaining through stealth by a representative of the Government, from the office of one suspected of defrauding the Government, of a paper which had no pecuniary value in itself but was only to be used as evidence against its owner, was held to be a violation of the Fourth Amendment. It was further held that when the paper was offered in evidence and duly objected to it must be ruled inadmissible because obtained through an unreasonable search and seizure, and also in violation of the Fifth Amendment because working compulsory incrimination.

In *Amos v. United States,* it was held that where concealed liquor was found by government officers without a search warrant in the home of the defendant, in his absence, and after a demand made upon his wife, it was inadmissible as evidence against the defendant, because acquired by an unreasonable seizure.

In none of the cases cited is there any ruling as to the validity under the Fourth Amendment of a seizure without a warrant of contraband goods in the course of transportation and subject to forfeiture or destruction.

On reason and authority the true rule is that if the search and seizure without a warrant are made upon probable cause, that is, upon a belief, reasonably arising out of circumstances known to the seizing officer, that an automobile or other vehicle contains that which by law is subject to seizure and destruction, the search and seizure are valid. The Fourth Amendment is to be construed in the light of what was deemed an unreasonable search and seizure when it was adopted, and in a manner which will conserve public interests as well as the interests and rights of individual citizens.

In *Boyd v. United States*, as already said, the decision did not turn on whether a reasonable search might be made without a warrant; but for the purpose of showing the principle on which the Fourth Amendment proceeds, and to avoid any misapprehension of what was decided, the Court, speaking through Mr. Justice Bradley, used language which is of particular significance and applicability here. It was there said:

"The search for and seizure of stolen or forfeited goods, or goods liable to duties and concealed to avoid the payment thereof, are totally different things from a search for and seizure of a man's private books and papers for the purpose of obtaining information therein contained, or of using them as evidence against him. The two things differ *toto coelo*. In the one case, the government is entitled to the possession of the property; in the other it is not. The seizure of stolen goods is authorized by the common law; and the seizure of goods forfeited for a breach of the revenue laws, or concealed to avoid the duties payable on them, has been authorized by English statutes for at least two centuries past; and the like seizures have been authorized by our own revenue acts from the commencement of the government..."

....

We have made a somewhat extended reference to these statutes to show that the guaranty of freedom from unreasonable searches and seizures by the Fourth Amendment has been construed, practically since the beginning of the Government, as recognizing a necessary difference between a search of a store, dwelling house or other structure in respect of which a proper official warrant readily may be obtained, and a search of a ship, motor boat, wagon or automobile, for contraband goods, where it is not practicable to secure a warrant because the vehicle can be quickly moved out of the locality or jurisdiction in which the warrant must be sought.

Having thus established that contraband goods concealed and illegally transported in an automobile or other vehicle may be searched for without a warrant, we come now to consider under what circumstances such search may be made. It would be intolerable and unreasonable if a prohibition agent were authorized to stop every automobile on the chance of finding liquor and thus subject all persons lawfully using the highways to the inconvenience and indignity of such a search. Travelers may be so stopped in crossing an international boundary because of national self protection reasonably requiring one entering the country to identify himself as entitled to come in, and his belongings as effects which may be lawfully brought in. But those lawfully within the country, entitled to use the public highways, have a right to free passage without interruption or search unless there is known to a competent official authorized to search, probable cause for believing that their vehicles are carrying contraband or illegal merchandise.

....

The measure of legality of such a seizure is, therefore, that the seizing officer shall have reasonable or probable cause for believing that the automobile which he stops and seizes has contraband liquor therein which is being illegally transported.

We here find the line of distinction between legal and illegal seizures of liquor in transport in vehicles. It is certainly a reasonable distinction. It gives the owner of an automobile or other vehicle seized under Section 26, in absence of probable cause, a right to have restored to him the automobile, it protects him under the *Weeks* and *Amos* cases from use of the liquor as evidence against him, and it subjects the officer making the seizures to damages. On the other hand, in a case showing probable cause, the Government and its officials are given the opportunity which they should have, to make the investigation necessary to trace reasonably suspected contraband goods and to seize them.

Such a rule fulfills the guaranty of the Fourth Amendment. In cases where the securing of a warrant is reasonably practicable, it must be used, and when properly supported by affidavit and issued after judicial approval protects the seizing officer against a suit for damages. In cases where seizure is impossible except without warrant, the seizing officer acts unlawfully and at his peril unless he can show the court probable cause.

But we are pressed with the argument that if the search of the automobile discloses the presence of liquor and leads under the statute to the arrest of the person in charge of the automobile, the right of seizure should be limited by the common law rule as to the circumstances justifying an arrest without warrant for a misdemeanor. The usual rule is that a police officer may arrest without warrant one believed by the officer upon reasonable cause to have been guilty of a felony, and that he may only arrest without a warrant one guilty of a misdemeanor if committed in his presence. The rule is sometimes expressed as follows:

"In cases of misdemeanor, a peace officer like a private person has at common law no power of arresting without a warrant except when a breach of the peace has been committed in his presence or there is reasonable ground for supposing that a breach of peace is about to be committed or renewed in his presence."

The reason for arrest for misdemeanors without warrant at common law was promptly to suppress breaches of the peace, while the reason for arrest without warrant on a reliable report of a felony was because the public safety and the due apprehension of criminals charged with heinous offenses required that such arrests should be made at once without warrant. The argument for defendants is that as the misdemeanor to justify arrest without warrant must be committed in the presence of the police officer, the offense is not committed in his presence unless he can by his senses detect that the liquor is being transported, no matter how reliable his previous information by which he can identify the automobile as loaded with it.

....

When a man is legally arrested for an offense, whatever is found upon his person or in his control which it is unlawful for him to have and which may be used to prove the offense may be seized and held as evidence in the prosecution. The argument of defendants is based on the theory that the seizure in this case can only be thus justified. If their theory were sound, their conclusion would be. The validity of the seizure then would turn wholly on the validity of the arrest without a seizure. But the theory is unsound. The right to search and the validity of the seizure are not dependent on the right to arrest. They are dependent on the reasonable cause the seizing officer has for belief that the contents of the automobile offend against the law....

....

In the light of these authorities, and what is shown by this record, it is clear the officers here had justification for the search and seizure. This is to say that the facts and circumstances within their knowledge and of which they had reasonably trustworthy information were sufficient in themselves to warrant a man of reasonable caution in the belief that intoxicating liquor was being transported in the automobile which they stopped and searched.

....

The judgment is affirmed.

Maryland v. Wilson (1997)
519 U.S. 408

In this case, the court held that ordering passengers out of a vehicle stopped for a traffic violation is constitutional. In addition, the court articulates the important concept of a compelling state interest and how that concept relates to officer safety.

In this case we consider whether the rule of *Pennsylvania v. Mimms* that a police officer may as a matter of course order the driver of a lawfully stopped car to exit his vehicle, extends to passengers as well. We hold that it does.

At about 7:30 p.m. on a June evening, Maryland state trooper David Hughes observed a passenger car driving southbound on I-95 in Baltimore County at a speed of 64 miles per hour. The posted speed limit was 55 miles per hour, and the car had no regular license tag; there was a torn piece of paper reading "Enterprise Rent-A-Car" dangling from its rear. Hughes activated his lights and sirens, signaling the car to pull over, but it continued driving for another mile and a half until it finally did so.

During the pursuit, Hughes noticed that there were three occupants in the car and that the two passengers turned to look at him several times, repeatedly ducking below sight level and then reappearing. As Hughes approached the car on foot, the driver alighted and met him halfway. The driver was trembling and appeared extremely nervous, but nonetheless produced a valid Connecticut driver's license. Hughes instructed him to return to the car and retrieve the rental documents, and he complied. During this encounter, Hughes noticed that the front-seat passenger, respondent Jerry Lee Wilson, was sweating and also appeared extremely nervous. While the driver was sitting in the driver's seat looking for the rental papers, Hughes ordered Wilson out of the car.

When Wilson exited the car, a quantity of crack cocaine fell to the ground. Wilson was then arrested and charged with possession of cocaine with intent to distribute. Before trial, Wilson moved to suppress the evidence, arguing that Hughes' ordering him out of the car constituted an unreasonable seizure under the Fourth Amendment. The Circuit Court for Baltimore County agreed, and granted respondent's motion to suppress. On appeal….we granted certiorari, and now reverse.

In *Mimms*, we considered a traffic stop much like the one before us today. There, Mimms had been stopped for driving with an expired license plate, and the officer asked him to step out of his car. When Mimms did so, the officer noticed a bulge in his jacket that proved to be a .38-caliber revolver, whereupon Mimms was arrested for carrying a concealed deadly weapon. Mimms, like Wilson, urged the suppression of the evidence on the ground that the officer's ordering him out of the car was an unreasonable seizure, and the Pennsylvania Supreme Court, like the Court of Special Appeals of Maryland, agreed.

We reversed, explaining that "the touchstone of our analysis under the Fourth Amendment is always 'the reasonableness in all the circumstances of the particular governmental invasion of a citizen's personal security,'" and that reasonableness "depends 'on a balance between the public interest and the individual's right to personal security free from arbitrary interference by law officers,'"

On the public interest side of the balance, we noted that the State "freely conceded" that there had been nothing unusual or suspicious to justify ordering Mimms out of the car, but that it was the officer's "practice to order all drivers stopped in traffic stops out of their vehicles as a matter of course" as a "precautionary measure" to protect the officer's safety. We thought it "too plain for argument" that this justification—officer safety—was "both legitimate and weighty." In addition, we observed that the danger to the officer of standing by the driver's door and in the path of oncoming traffic might also be "appreciable."

On the other side of the balance, we considered the intrusion into the driver's liberty occasioned by the officer's ordering him out of the car. Noting that the driver's car was already validly stopped for a traffic infraction, we deemed the additional intrusion of asking him to step outside his car "*de minimis.*" Accordingly, we concluded that "once a motor vehicle has been lawfully detained for a traffic violation, the police officers may order the driver to get out of the vehicle without violating the Fourth Amendment's proscription of unreasonable seizures."

Respondent urges, and the lower courts agreed, that this per se rule does not apply to Wilson because he was a passenger, not the driver. Maryland, in turn, argues that we have already implicitly decided this question by our statement in *Michigan v. Long* that "in *Mimms*, we held that police may order persons out of an automobile during a stop for a traffic violation," and by Justice Powell's statement in *Rakas v. Illinois*, that "this Court determined in *Mimms* that passengers in automobiles have no Fourth Amendment right not to be ordered from their vehicle, once a proper stop is made." We agree with respondent that the former statement was dictum, and the latter was contained in a concurrence, so that neither constitutes binding precedent.

We must therefore now decide whether the rule of *Mimms* applies to passengers as well as to drivers. On the public interest side of the balance, the same weighty interest in officer safety is present regardless of whether the occupant of the stopped car is a driver or passenger. Regrettably, traffic stops may be dangerous encounters. In 1994 alone, there were 5,762 officer assaults and 11 officers killed during traffic pursuits and stops. In the case of passengers, the danger of the officer's standing in the path of oncoming traffic would not be present except in the case of a passenger in the left rear seat, but the fact that there is more than one occupant of the vehicle increases the possible sources of harm to the officer.

On the personal liberty side of the balance, the case for the passengers is in one sense stronger than that for the driver. There is probable cause to believe that the driver has committed a minor vehicular offense, but there is no such reason to stop or detain the passengers. But as a practical matter, the passengers are already stopped by virtue of the stop of the vehicle. The only change in their circumstances which will result from ordering them out of the car is that they will be outside of, rather than inside of, the stopped car. Outside the car, the passengers will be denied access to any possible weapon that might be concealed in the interior of the passenger compartment. It would seem that the possibility of a violent encounter stems not from the ordinary reaction of a motorist stopped for a speeding violation, but from the fact that evidence of a more serious crime might be uncovered during the stop. And the motivation of a passenger to employ violence to prevent apprehension of such a crime is every bit as great as that of the driver.

We think that our opinion in *Michigan v. Summers* offers guidance by analogy here. There the police had obtained a search warrant for contraband thought to be located in a residence, but when they arrived to execute the warrant they found Summers coming down the front steps. The question in the case depended "upon a determination whether the officers had the authority to require him to re-enter the house and to remain there while they conducted their search." In holding as it did, the Court said:

"Although no special danger to the police is suggested by the evidence in this record, the execution of a warrant to search for narcotics is the kind of transaction that may give rise to sudden violence or frantic efforts to conceal or destroy evidence. The risk of harm to both the police and the occupants is minimized if the officers routinely exercise unquestioned command of the situation."

In summary, danger to an officer from a traffic stop is likely to be greater when there are passengers in addition to the driver in the stopped car. While there is not the same basis for ordering the passengers out of the car as there is for ordering the driver out, the additional intrusion on the passenger is minimal. We therefore hold that an officer making a traffic stop may order passengers to get out of the car pending completion of the stop.

The judgment of the Court of Special Appeals of Maryland is reversed, and the case is remanded for proceedings not inconsistent with this opinion.

It is so ordered.

Warden v. Hayden (1967)
387 U.S. 294

In this case, the court carves out a hot pursuit exception to the search warrant requirement. In addition, the court articulates the sort of circumstances under which a warrant may not be necessary. The court also addresses an old legal doctrine of differentiating between types of things that may be seized, and finds the doctrine wanting.

We review in this case the validity of the proposition that there is under the Fourth Amendment a "distinction between merely evidentiary materials, on the one hand, which may not be seized either under the authority of a search warrant or during the course of a search incident to arrest, and on the other hand, those objects which may validly be seized including the instrumentalities and means by which a crime is committed, the fruits of crime such as stolen property, weapons by which escape of the person arrested might be effected, and property the possession of which is a crime."

A Maryland court sitting without a jury convicted respondent of armed robbery. Items of his clothing, a cap, jacket, and trousers, among other things, were seized during a search of his home, and were admitted in evidence without objection. After unsuccessful state court proceedings, he sought and was denied federal habeas corpus relief in the District Court for Maryland. A divided panel of the Court of Appeals for the Fourth Circuit reversed. The Court of Appeals believed that *Harris v. United States* sustained the validity of the search, but held that respondent was correct in his contention that the clothing seized was improperly admitted in evidence because the items had "evidential value only" and therefore were not lawfully subject to seizure. We granted certiorari. We reverse.

....

About 8 a. m. on March 17, 1962, an armed robber entered the business premises of the Diamond Cab Company in Baltimore, Maryland. He took some $ 363 and ran. Two cab drivers in the vicinity, attracted by shouts of "Holdup," followed the man to 2111 Cocoa Lane. One driver notified the company dispatcher by radio that the man was a Negro about 5'8' tall, wearing a light cap and dark jacket, and that he had entered the house on Cocoa Lane. The dispatcher relayed the information to police who were proceeding to the scene of the robbery. Within minutes, police arrived at the house in a number of patrol cars. An officer knocked and announced their presence. Mrs. Hayden answered, and the officers told her they believed that a robber had entered the house, and asked to search the house. She offered no objection.

The officers spread out through the first and second floors and the cellar in search of the robber. Hayden was found in an upstairs bedroom feigning sleep. He was arrested when the officers on the first floor and in the cellar reported that no other man was in the house. Meanwhile an officer was attracted to an adjoining bathroom by the noise of running water, and discovered a shotgun and a pistol in a flush tank; another officer who, according to the District Court, "was searching the cellar for a man or the money" found in a washing machine a jacket and trousers of the type the fleeing man was said to have worn. A clip of ammunition for the pistol and a cap were found under the mattress of Hayden's bed, and ammunition for the shotgun was found in a bureau drawer in Hayden's room. All these items of evidence were introduced against respondent at his trial.

....

We agree with the Court of Appeals that neither the entry without warrant to search for the robber, nor the search for him without warrant was invalid. Under the circumstances of this case, "the exigencies of the situation made that course imperative." The police were informed that an armed robbery had taken place, and that the suspect had entered 2111 Cocoa Lane less than five minutes before they reached it. They acted reasonably when they entered the house and began to search for a man of the description they had been given and for weapons which he had used in the robbery or might use against them. The Fourth Amendment does not require police officers to delay in the course of an investigation if to do so would gravely endanger their lives or the lives of others. Speed here was essential, and only a thorough search of the house for persons and weapons could have insured that Hayden was the only man present and that the police had control of all weapons which could be used against them or to effect an escape.

We do not rely upon *Harris v. United States* in sustaining the validity of the search. The principal issue in *Harris* was whether the search there could properly be regarded as incident to the lawful arrest, since Harris was in custody before the search was made and the evidence seized. Here, the seizures occurred prior to or immediately contemporaneous with Hayden's arrest, as part of an effort to find a suspected felon, armed, within the house into which he had run only minutes before the police arrived. The permissible scope of search must, therefore, at the least, be as broad as may reasonably be necessary to prevent the dangers that the suspect at large in the house may resist or escape.

It is argued that, while the weapons, ammunition, and cap may have been seized in the course of a search for weapons, the officer who seized the clothing was searching neither for the suspect nor for weapons when he looked into the washing machine in which he found the clothing. But even if we assume, although we do not decide, that the exigent circumstances in this case made lawful a search without warrant only for the suspect or his weapons, it cannot be said on this record that the officer who found the clothes in the washing machine was not searching for weapons. He testified that he was searching for the man or the money, but his failure to state explicitly that he was searching for weapons, in the absence of a specific question to that effect, can hardly be accorded controlling weight. He knew that the robber was armed and he did not know that some weapons had been found at the time he opened the machine. In these circumstances the inference that he was in fact also looking for weapons is fully justified.

....

We come, then, to the question whether, even though the search was lawful, the Court of Appeals was correct in holding that the seizure and introduction of the items of clothing violated the Fourth Amendment because they are "mere evidence." The distinction made by some of our cases between seizure of items of evidential value only and seizure of instrumentalities, fruits, or contraband has been criticized by courts and commentators. The Court of Appeals, however, felt "obligated to adhere to it." We today reject the distinction as based on premises no longer accepted as rules governing the application of the Fourth Amendment.

We have examined on many occasions the history and purposes of the Amendment. It was a reaction to the evils of the use of the general warrant in England and the writs of assistance in the Colonies, and was intended to protect against invasions of "the sanctity of a man's home and the privacies of life," from searches under indiscriminate, general authority. Protection of these interests was assured by prohibiting all "unreasonable" searches and seizures, and by requiring the use of warrants, which particularly describe "the place to be searched, and the persons or things to be seized," thereby interposing "a magistrate between the citizen and the police."

Nothing in the language of the Fourth Amendment supports the distinction between "mere evidence" and instrumentalities, fruits of crime, or contraband. On its face, the provision assures the "right of the people to be secure in their persons, houses, papers, and effects . . . ," without regard to the use to which any of these things are applied. This "right of the people" is certainly unrelated to the "mere evidence" limitation. Privacy is disturbed no more by a search directed to a purely evidentiary object than it is by a search directed to an instrumentality, fruit, or contraband. A magistrate can intervene in both situations, and the requirements of probable cause and specificity can be preserved intact. Moreover, nothing in the nature of property seized as evidence renders it more private than property seized, for example, as an instrumentality; quite the opposite may be true. Indeed, the distinction is wholly irrational, since, depending on the circumstances, the same "papers and effects" may be "mere evidence" in one case and "instrumentality" in another.

In *Gouled v. United States* the Court said that search warrants "may not be used as a means of gaining access to a man's house or office and papers solely for the purpose of making search to secure evidence to be used against him in a criminal or penal proceeding . . . ." The Court derived from *Boyd v. United States* the proposition that warrants "may be resorted to only when a primary right to such search and seizure may be found in the interest which the public or the complainant may have in the property to be seized, or in the right to the possession of it, or when a valid exercise of the police power renders possession of the property by the accused unlawful and provides that it may be taken"; that is, when the property is an instrumentality or fruit of crime, or contraband.

Since it was "impossible to say, on the record . . . that the Government had any interest" in the papers involved "other than as evidence against the accused . . . ," "to permit them to be used in evidence would be, in effect, as ruled in the *Boyd* Case, to compel the defendant to become a witness against himself."

The items of clothing involved in this case are not "testimonial" or "communicative" in nature, and their introduction therefore did not compel respondent to become a witness against himself in violation of the Fifth Amendment. This case thus does not require that we consider whether there are items of evidential value whose very nature precludes them from being the object of a reasonable search and seizure.

The Fourth Amendment ruling in *Gouled* was based upon the dual, related premises that historically the right to search for and seize property depended upon the assertion by the Government of a valid claim of superior interest, and that it was not enough that the purpose of the search and seizure was to obtain evidence to use in apprehending and convicting criminals..... Thus stolen property—the fruits of crime—was always subject to seizure. And the power to search for stolen property was gradually extended to cover "any property which the private citizen was not permitted to possess," which included instrumentalities of crime (because of the early notion that items used in crime were forfeited to the State) and contraband.

No separate governmental interest in seizing evidence to apprehend and convict criminals was recognized; it was required that some property interest be asserted. The remedial structure also reflected these dual premises. Trespass, replevin, and the other means of redress for persons aggrieved by searches and seizures, depended upon proof of a superior property interest. And since a lawful seizure presupposed a superior claim, it was inconceivable that a person could recover property lawfully seized....

The premise that property interests control the right of the Government to search and seize has been discredited. Searches and seizures may be "unreasonable" within the Fourth Amendment even though the Government asserts a superior property interest at common law. We have recognized that the principal object of the Fourth Amendment is the protection of privacy rather than property, and have increasingly discarded fictional and procedural barriers rested on property concepts. This shift in emphasis from property to privacy has come about through a subtle interplay of substantive and procedural reform. The remedial structure at the time even of *Weeks v. United States* was arguably explainable in property terms. The Court held in *Weeks* that a defendant could petition before trial for the return of his illegally seized property, a proposition not necessarily inconsistent with *Adams v. New York*, which held in effect that the property issues involved in search and seizure are collateral to a criminal proceeding. The remedial structure finally escaped the bounds of common law property limitations in *Silverthorne Lumber Co. v. United States* and *Gouled v. United States*, when it became established that suppression might be sought during a criminal trial, and under circumstances which would not sustain an action in trespass or replevin. Recognition that the role of the Fourth Amendment was to protect against invasions of privacy demanded a remedy to condemn the seizure in *Silverthorne*, although no possible common law claim existed for the return of the copies made by the Government of the papers it had seized. The remedy of suppression, necessarily involving only the limited, functional consequence of excluding the evidence from trial, satisfied that demand.

The development of search and seizure law since *Silverthorne* and *Gouled* is replete with examples of the transformation in substantive law brought about through the interaction of the felt need to protect privacy from unreasonable invasions and the flexibility in rulemaking made possible by the remedy of exclusion. We have held, for example, that intangible as well as tangible evidence may be suppressed, and that an actual trespass under local property law is unnecessary to support a remediable violation of the Fourth Amendment. In determining whether someone is a "person aggrieved by an unlawful search and seizure" we have refused "to import into the law . . . subtle distinctions, developed and refined by the common law in evolving the body of private property law which, more than almost any other branch of law, has been shaped by distinctions whose validity is largely historical." And with particular relevance here, we have given recognition to the interest in privacy despite the complete absence of a property claim by suppressing the very items which at common law could be seized with impunity....

The premise in *Gouled* that government may not seize evidence simply for the purpose of proving crime has likewise been discredited. The requirement that the Government assert in addition some property interest in material it seizes has long been a fiction, obscuring the reality that government has an interest in solving crime. *Schmerber* settled the proposition that it is reasonable, within the terms of the Fourth Amendment, to conduct otherwise permissible searches for the purpose of obtaining evidence which would aid in apprehending and convicting criminals. The requirements of the Fourth Amendment can secure the same protection of privacy whether the search is for "mere evidence" or for fruits, instrumentalities or contraband. There must, of course, be a nexus—automatically provided in the case of fruits, instrumentalities or contraband—between the item to be seized and criminal behavior. Thus in the case of "mere evidence," probable cause must be examined in terms of cause to believe that the evidence sought will aid in a particular apprehension or conviction. In so doing, consideration of police purposes will be required. But no such problem is presented in this case. The clothes found in the washing machine matched the description of those worn by the robber and the police therefore could reasonably believe that the items would aid in the identification of the culprit.

The remedy of suppression, moreover, which made possible protection of privacy from unreasonable searches without regard to proof of a superior property interest, likewise provides the procedural device necessary for allowing otherwise permissible searches and seizures conducted solely to obtain evidence of crime. For just as the suppression of evidence does not entail a declaration of superior property interest in the person aggrieved, thereby enabling him to suppress evidence unlawfully seized despite his inability to demonstrate such an interest (as with fruits, instrumentalities, contraband), the refusal to suppress evidence carries no declaration of superior property interest in the State, and should thereby enable the State to introduce evidence lawfully seized despite its inability to demonstrate such an interest. And, unlike the situation at common law, the owner of property would not be rendered remediless if "mere evidence" could lawfully be seized to prove crime. For just as the suppression of evidence does not in itself necessarily entitle the aggrieved person to its return (as, for example, contraband), the introduction of "mere evidence" does not in itself entitle the State to its retention. Where public officials "unlawfully seize or hold a citizen's realty or chattels, recoverable by appropriate action at law or in equity . . . ," the true owner may "bring his possessory action to reclaim that which is wrongfully withheld."

The survival of the *Gouled* distinction is attributable more to chance than considered judgment. Legislation has helped perpetuate it. Thus, Congress has never authorized the issuance of search warrants for the seizure of mere evidence of crime.

The rationale most frequently suggested for the rule preventing the seizure of evidence is that "limitations upon the fruit to be gathered tend to limit the quest itself." But privacy "would be just as well served by a restriction on search to the even-numbered days of the month. . . . And it would have the extra advantage of avoiding hair-splitting questions . . . ." The "mere evidence" limitation has spawned exceptions so numerous and confusion so great, in fact, that it is questionable whether it affords meaningful protection. But if its rejection does enlarge the area of permissible searches, the intrusions are nevertheless made after fulfilling the probable cause and particularity requirements of the Fourth Amendment and after the intervention of "a neutral and detached magistrate . . . ." The Fourth Amendment allows intrusions upon privacy under these circumstances, and there is no viable reason to distinguish intrusions to secure "mere evidence" from intrusions to secure fruits, instrumentalities, or contraband.

The judgment of the Court of Appeals is Reversed.

Miranda v. Arizona (1966)
384 U.S. 436

This case famously sets forth the warnings that police must issue before a custodial interrogation can legally begin. In addition, this case sheds much light on the important notion of due process in American jurisprudence.

The cases before us raise questions which go to the roots of our concepts of American criminal jurisprudence: the restraints society must observe consistent with the Federal Constitution in prosecuting individuals for crime. More specifically, we deal with the admissibility of statements obtained from an individual who is subjected to custodial police interrogation and the necessity for procedures which assure that the individual is accorded his privilege under the Fifth Amendment to the Constitution not to be compelled to incriminate himself.

We dealt with certain phases of this problem recently in *Escobedo v. Illinois*. There, as in the four cases before us, law enforcement officials took the defendant into custody and interrogated him in a police station for the purpose of obtaining a confession. The police did not effectively advise him of his right to remain silent or of his right to consult with his attorney. Rather, they confronted him with an alleged accomplice who accused him of having perpetrated a murder. When the defendant denied the accusation and said "I didn't shoot Manuel, you did it," they handcuffed him and took him to an interrogation room. There, while handcuffed and standing, he was questioned for four hours until he confessed. During this interrogation, the police denied his request to speak to his attorney, and they prevented his retained attorney, who had come to the police station, from consulting with him. At his trial, the State, over his objection, introduced the confession against him. We held that the statements thus made were constitutionally inadmissible.

This case has been the subject of judicial interpretation and spirited legal debate since it was decided two years ago. Both state and federal courts, in assessing its implications, have arrived at varying conclusions. A wealth of scholarly material has been written tracing its ramifications and underpinnings. Police and prosecutor have speculated on its range and desirability. We granted certiorari in these cases in order further to explore some facets of the problems, thus exposed, of applying the privilege against self-incrimination to in-custody interrogation, and to give concrete constitutional guidelines for law enforcement agencies and courts to follow.

We start here, as we did in *Escobedo*, with the premise that our holding is not an innovation in our jurisprudence, but is an application of principles long recognized and applied in other settings. We have undertaken a thorough re-examination of the *Escobedo* decision and the principles it announced, and we reaffirm it. That case was but an explication of basic rights that are enshrined in our Constitution–that "No person . . . shall be compelled in any criminal case to be a witness against himself," and that "the accused shall . . . have the Assistance of Counsel"– rights which were put in jeopardy in that case through official overbearing. These precious rights were fixed in our Constitution only after centuries of persecution and struggle. And in the words of Chief Justice Marshall, they were secured "for ages to come, and . . . designed to approach immortality as nearly as human institutions can approach it."

....

In stating the obligation of the judiciary to apply these constitutional rights, this Court declared in *Weems v. United States*:

". . . our contemplation cannot be only of what has been but of what may be. Under any other rule a constitution would indeed be as easy of application as it would be deficient in efficacy and power. Its general principles would have little value and be converted by precedent into impotent and lifeless formulas. Rights declared in words might be lost in reality. And this has been recognized. The meaning and vitality of the Constitution have developed against narrow and restrictive construction."

This was the spirit in which we delineated, in meaningful language, the manner in which the constitutional rights of the individual could be enforced against overzealous police practices. It was necessary in *Escobedo*, as here, to insure that what was proclaimed in the Constitution had not become but a "form of words" in the hands of government officials. And it is in this spirit, consistent with our role as judges, that we adhere to the principles of *Escobedo* today.

Our holding will be spelled out with some specificity in the pages which follow but briefly stated it is this: the prosecution may not use statements, whether exculpatory or inculpatory, stemming from custodial interrogation of the defendant unless it demonstrates the use of procedural safeguards effective to secure the privilege against self-incrimination. By custodial interrogation, we mean questioning initiated by law enforcement officers after a person has been taken into custody or otherwise deprived of his freedom of action in any significant way. As for the procedural safeguards to be employed, unless other fully effective means are devised to inform accused persons of their right of silence and to assure a continuous opportunity to exercise it, the following measures are required. Prior to any questioning, the person must be warned that he has a right to remain silent, that any statement he does make may be used as evidence against him, and that he has a right to the presence of an attorney, either retained or appointed. The defendant may waive effectuation of these rights, provided the waiver is made voluntarily, knowingly and intelligently. If, however, he indicates in any manner and at any stage of the process that he wishes to consult with an attorney before speaking there can be no questioning. Likewise, if the individual is alone and indicates in any manner that he does not wish to be interrogated, the police may not question him. The mere fact that he may have answered some questions or volunteered some statements on his own does not deprive him of the right to refrain from answering any further inquiries until he has consulted with an attorney and thereafter consents to be questioned.

....

The constitutional issue we decide in each of these cases is the admissibility of statements obtained from a defendant questioned while in custody or otherwise deprived of his freedom of action in any significant way. In each, the defendant was questioned by police officers, detectives, or a prosecuting attorney in a room in which he was cut off from the outside world. In none of these cases was the defendant given a full and effective warning of his rights at the outset of the interrogation process. In all the cases, the questioning elicited oral admissions, and in three of them, signed statements as well which were admitted at their trials. They all thus share salient features—incommunicado interrogation of individuals in a police-dominated atmosphere, resulting in self-incriminating statements without full warnings of constitutional rights.

An understanding of the nature and setting of this in-custody interrogation is essential to our decisions today. The difficulty in depicting what transpires at such interrogations stems from the fact that in this country they have largely taken place incommunicado. From extensive factual studies undertaken in the early 1930's, including the famous *Wickersham Report* to Congress by a Presidential Commission, it is clear that police violence and the "third degree" flourished at that time. In a series of cases decided by this Court long after these studies, the police resorted to physical brutality—beating, hanging, whipping— and to sustained and protracted questioning incommunicado in order to extort confessions. The Commission on Civil Rights in 1961 found much evidence to indicate that "some policemen still resort to physical force to obtain confessions." The use of physical brutality and violence is not, unfortunately, relegated to the past or to any part of the country. Only recently in Kings County, New York, the police brutally beat, kicked and placed lighted cigarette butts on the back of a potential witness under interrogation for the purpose of securing a statement incriminating a third party.

The examples given above are undoubtedly the exception now, but they are sufficiently widespread to be the object of concern. Unless a proper limitation upon custodial interrogation is achieved—such as these decisions will advance—there can be no assurance that practices of this nature will be eradicated in the foreseeable future. The conclusion of the *Wickersham Commission Report*, made over 30 years ago, is still pertinent:

"To the contention that the third degree is necessary to get the facts, the reporters aptly reply in the language of the present Lord Chancellor of England (Lord Sankey): 'It is not admissible to do a great right by doing a little wrong. . . . It is not sufficient to do justice by obtaining a proper result by irregular or improper means.' Not only does the use of the third degree involve a flagrant violation of law by the officers of the law, but it involves also the dangers of false confessions, and it tends to make police and prosecutors less zealous in the search for objective evidence. As the New York prosecutor quoted in the report said, 'It is a short cut and makes the police lazy and unenterprising.' Or, as another official quoted remarked: 'If you use your fists, you are not so likely to use your wits.' We agree with the conclusion expressed in the report, that 'The third degree brutalizes the police, hardens the prisoner against society, and lowers the esteem in which the administration of justice is held by the public.'"

Again we stress that the modern practice of in-custody interrogation is psychologically rather than physically oriented. As we have stated before, "Since *Chambers v. Florida* this Court has recognized that coercion can be mental as well as physical, and that the blood of the accused is not the only hallmark of an unconstitutional inquisition." Interrogation still takes place in privacy. Privacy results in secrecy and this in turn results in a gap in our knowledge as to what in fact goes on in the interrogation rooms. A valuable source of information about present police practices, however, may be found in various police manuals and texts which document procedures employed with success in the past, and which recommend various other effective tactics. These texts are used by law enforcement agencies themselves as guides. It should be noted that these texts professedly present the most enlightened and effective means presently used to obtain statements through custodial interrogation. By considering these texts and other data, it is possible to describe procedures observed and noted around the country.

The officers are told by the manuals that the "principal psychological factor contributing to a successful interrogation is privacy—being alone with the person under interrogation." The efficacy of this tactic has been explained as follows:

"If at all practicable, the interrogation should take place in the investigator's office or at least in a room of his own choice. The subject should be deprived of every psychological advantage. In his own home he may be confident, indignant, or recalcitrant. He is more keenly aware of his rights and more reluctant to tell of his indiscretions or criminal behavior within the walls of his home. Moreover his family and other friends are nearby, their presence lending moral support. In his own office, the investigator possesses all the advantages. The atmosphere suggests the invincibility of the forces of the law."

To highlight the isolation and unfamiliar surroundings, the manuals instruct the police to display an air of confidence in the suspect's guilt and from outward appearance to maintain only an interest in confirming certain details. The guilt of the subject is to be posited as a fact. The interrogator should direct his comments toward the reasons why the subject committed the act, rather than court failure by asking the subject whether he did it. Like other men, perhaps the subject has had a bad family life, had an unhappy childhood, had too much to drink, had an unrequited desire for women. The officers are instructed to minimize the moral seriousness of the offense, to cast blame on the victim or on society. These tactics are designed to put the subject in a psychological state where his story is but an elaboration of what the police purport to know already—that he is guilty. Explanations to the contrary are dismissed and discouraged.

The texts thus stress that the major qualities an interrogator should possess are patience and perseverance. One writer describes the efficacy of these characteristics in this manner:

"In the preceding paragraphs emphasis has been placed on kindness and stratagems. The investigator will, however, encounter many situations where the sheer weight of his personality will be the deciding factor. Where emotional appeals and tricks are employed to no avail, he must rely on an oppressive atmosphere of dogged persistence. He must interrogate steadily and without relent, leaving the subject no prospect of surcease. He must dominate his subject and overwhelm him with his inexorable will to obtain the truth. He should interrogate for a spell of several hours pausing only for the subject's necessities in acknowledgment of the need to avoid a charge of duress that can be technically substantiated. In a serious case, the interrogation may continue for days, with the required intervals for food and sleep, but with no respite from the atmosphere of domination. It is possible in this way to induce the subject to talk without resorting to duress or coercion. The method should be used only when the guilt of the subject appears highly probable."

The manuals suggest that the suspect be offered legal excuses for his actions in order to obtain an initial admission of guilt. Where there is a suspected revenge-killing, for example, the interrogator may say:

"Joe, you probably didn't go out looking for this fellow with the purpose of shooting him. My guess is, however, that you expected something from him and that's why you carried a gun—for your own protection. You knew him for what he was, no good. Then when you met him he probably started using foul, abusive language and he gave some indication that he was about to pull a gun on you, and that's when you had to act to save your own life. That's about it, isn't it, Joe?"

Having then obtained the admission of shooting, the interrogator is advised to refer to circumstantial evidence which negates the self-defense explanation. This should enable him to secure the entire story. One text notes that "Even if he fails to do so, the inconsistency between the subject's original denial of the shooting and his present admission of at least doing the shooting will serve to deprive him of a self-defense 'out' at the time of trial."

When the techniques described above prove unavailing, the texts recommend they be alternated with a show of some hostility. One ploy often used has been termed the "friendly-unfriendly" or the "Mutt and Jeff" act:

". . . In this technique, two agents are employed. Mutt, the relentless investigator, who knows the subject is guilty and is not going to waste any time. He's sent a dozen men away for this crime and he's going to send the subject away for the full term. Jeff, on the other hand, is obviously a kindhearted man. He has a family himself. He has a brother who was involved in a little scrape like this. He disapproves of Mutt and his tactics and will arrange to get him off the case if the subject will cooperate. He can't hold Mutt off for very long. The subject would be wise to make a quick decision. The technique is applied by having both investigators present while Mutt acts out his role. Jeff may stand by quietly and demur at some of Mutt's tactics. When Jeff makes his plea for cooperation, Mutt is not present in the room."

The interrogators sometimes are instructed to induce a confession out of trickery. The technique here is quite effective in crimes which require identification or which run in series. In the identification situation, the interrogator may take a break in his questioning to place the subject among a group of men in a line-up. "The witness or complainant (previously coached, if necessary) studies the line-up and confidently points out the subject as the guilty party." Then the questioning resumes "as though there were now no doubt about the guilt of the subject." A variation on this technique is called the "reverse line-up":

"The accused is placed in a line-up, but this time he is identified by several fictitious witnesses or victims who associated him with different offenses. It is expected that the subject will become desperate and confess to the offense under investigation in order to escape from the false accusations."

The manuals also contain instructions for police on how to handle the individual who refuses to discuss the matter entirely, or who asks for an attorney or relatives. The examiner is to concede him the right to remain silent. "This usually has a very undermining effect. First of all, he is disappointed in his expectation of an unfavorable reaction on the part of the interrogator. Secondly, a concession of this right to remain silent impresses the subject with the apparent fairness of his interrogator." After this psychological conditioning, however, the officer is told to point out the incriminating significance of the suspect's refusal to talk:

"Joe, you have a right to remain silent. That's your privilege and I'm the last person in the world who'll try to take it away from you. If that's the way you want to leave this, O. K. But let me ask you this. Suppose you were in my shoes and I were in yours and you called me in to ask me about this and I told you, 'I don't want to answer any of your questions.' You'd think I had something to hide, and you'd probably be right in thinking that. That's exactly what I'll have to think about you, and so will everybody else. So let's sit here and talk this whole thing over."

Few will persist in their initial refusal to talk, it is said, if this monologue is employed correctly.

In the event that the subject wishes to speak to a relative or an attorney, the following advice is tendered:

"The interrogator should respond by suggesting that the subject first tell the truth to the interrogator himself rather than get anyone else involved in the matter. If the request is for an attorney, the interrogator may suggest that the subject save himself or his family the expense of any such professional service, particularly if he is innocent of the offense under investigation. The interrogator may also add, 'Joe, I'm only looking for the truth, and if you're telling the truth, that's it. You can handle this by yourself.'"

From these representative samples of interrogation techniques, the setting prescribed by the manuals and observed in practice becomes clear. In essence, it is this: To be alone with the subject is essential to prevent distraction and to deprive him of any outside support. The aura of confidence in his guilt undermines his will to resist. He merely confirms the preconceived story the police seek to have him describe. Patience and persistence, at times relentless questioning, are employed. To obtain a confession, the interrogator must "patiently maneuver himself or his quarry into a position from which the desired objective may be attained." When normal procedures fail to produce the needed result, the police may resort to deceptive stratagems such as giving false legal advice. It is important to keep the subject off balance, for example, by trading on his insecurity about himself or his surroundings. The police then persuade, trick, or cajole him out of exercising his constitutional rights.

Even without employing brutality, the "third degree" or the specific stratagems described above, the very fact of custodial interrogation exacts a heavy toll on individual liberty and trades on the weakness of individuals....In other settings, these individuals might have exercised their constitutional rights. In the incommunicado police-dominated atmosphere, they succumbed.

In the cases before us today, given this background, we concern ourselves primarily with this interrogation atmosphere and the evils it can bring. In *Miranda v. Arizona*, the police arrested the defendant and took him to a special interrogation room where they secured a confession.

....

In these cases, we might not find the defendants' statements to have been involuntary in traditional terms. Our concern for adequate safeguards to protect precious Fifth Amendment rights is, of course, not lessened in the slightest. In each of the cases, the defendant was thrust into an unfamiliar atmosphere and run through menacing police interrogation procedures. The potentiality for compulsion is forcefully apparent, for example, in *Miranda*, where the indigent Mexican defendant was a seriously disturbed individual with pronounced sexual fantasies, and in *Stewart*, in which the defendant was an indigent Los Angeles Negro who had dropped out of school in the sixth grade. To be sure, the records do not evince overt physical coercion or patent psychological ploys. The fact remains that in none of these cases did the officers undertake to afford appropriate safeguards at the outset of the interrogation to insure that the statements were truly the product of free choice.

It is obvious that such an interrogation environment is created for no purpose other than to subjugate the individual to the will of his examiner. This atmosphere carries its own badge of intimidation. To be sure, this is not physical intimidation, but it is equally destructive of human dignity. The current practice of incommunicado interrogation is at odds with one of our Nation's most cherished principles—that the individual may not be compelled to incriminate himself. Unless adequate protective devices are employed to dispel the compulsion inherent in custodial surroundings, no statement obtained from the defendant can truly be the product of his free choice.

From the foregoing, we can readily perceive an intimate connection between the privilege against self-incrimination and police custodial questioning. It is fitting to turn to history and precedent underlying the Self-Incrimination Clause to determine its applicability in this situation.

....

We sometimes forget how long it has taken to establish the privilege against self-incrimination, the sources from which it came and the fervor with which it was defended. Its roots go back into ancient times....

On account of the *Lilburn* Trial, Parliament abolished the inquisitorial Court of Star Chamber and went further in giving him generous reparation. The lofty principles to which Lilburn had appealed during his trial gained popular acceptance in England. These sentiments worked their way over to the Colonies and were implanted after great struggle into the Bill of Rights. Those who framed our Constitution and the Bill of Rights were ever aware of subtle encroachments on individual liberty. They knew that "illegitimate and unconstitutional practices get their first footing . . . by silent approaches and slight deviations from legal modes of procedure." The privilege was elevated to constitutional status and has always been "as broad as the mischief against which it seeks to guard." We cannot depart from this noble heritage.

Thus we may view the historical development of the privilege as one which groped for the proper scope of governmental power over the citizen. As a "noble principle often transcends its origins," the privilege has come rightfully to be recognized in part as an individual's substantive right, a "right to a private enclave where he may lead a private life. That right is the hallmark of our democracy." We have recently noted that the privilege against self-incrimination—the essential mainstay of our adversary system—is founded on a complex of values. All these policies point to one overriding thought: the constitutional foundation underlying the privilege is the respect a government—state or federal—must accord to the dignity and integrity of its citizens. To maintain a "fair state-individual balance," to require the government "to shoulder the entire load" to respect the inviolability of the human personality, our accusatory system of criminal justice demands that the government seeking to punish an individual produce the evidence against him by its own independent labors, rather than by the cruel, simple expedient of compelling it from his own mouth. In sum, the privilege is fulfilled only when the person is guaranteed the right "to remain silent unless he chooses to speak in the unfettered exercise of his own will."

The question in these cases is whether the privilege is fully applicable during a period of custodial interrogation. In this Court, the privilege has consistently been accorded a liberal construction. We are satisfied that all the principles embodied in the privilege apply to informal compulsion exerted by law-enforcement officers during in-custody questioning. An individual swept from familiar surroundings into police custody, surrounded by antagonistic forces, and subjected to the techniques of persuasion described above cannot be otherwise than under compulsion to speak. As a practical matter, the compulsion to speak in the isolated setting of the police station may well be greater than in courts or other official investigations, where there are often impartial observers to guard against intimidation or trickery.

....

Our decision in *Malloy v. Hogan* necessitates an examination of the scope of the privilege in state cases as well. In *Malloy*, we squarely held the privilege applicable to the States, and held that the substantive standards underlying the privilege applied with full force to state court proceedings. There, as in *Murphy v. Waterfront Comm'n*, we applied the existing Fifth Amendment standards to the case before us. Aside from the holding itself, the reasoning in *Malloy* made clear what had already become apparent–that the substantive and procedural safeguards surrounding admissibility of confessions in state cases had become exceedingly exacting, reflecting all the policies embedded in the privilege, voluntariness doctrine in the state cases, as *Malloy* indicates, encompasses all interrogation practices which are likely to exert such pressure upon an individual as to disable him from making a free and rational choice. ...

The decisions of this Court have guaranteed the same procedural protection for the defendant whether his confession was used in a federal or state court. It is now axiomatic that the defendant's constitutional rights have been violated if his conviction is based, in whole or in part, on an involuntary confession, regardless of its truth or falsity. This is so even if there is ample evidence aside from the confession to support the conviction... Both state and federal courts now adhere to trial procedures which seek to assure a reliable and clear-cut determination of the voluntariness of the confession offered at trial. Appellate review is exacting. Whether his conviction was in a federal or state court, the defendant may secure a post-conviction hearing based on the alleged involuntary character of his confession, provided he meets the procedural requirements.

....

Our holding there stressed the fact that the police had not advised the defendant of his constitutional privilege to remain silent at the outset of the interrogation, and we drew attention to that fact at several points in the decision. This was no isolated factor, but an essential ingredient in our decision. The entire thrust of police interrogation there, as in all the cases today, was to put the defendant in such an emotional state as to impair his capacity for rational judgment. The abdication of the constitutional privilege—the choice on his part to speak to the police—was not made knowingly or competently because of the failure to apprise him of his rights; the compelling atmosphere of the in-custody interrogation, and not an independent decision on his part, caused the defendant to speak.

A different phase of the *Escobedo* decision was significant in its attention to the absence of counsel during the questioning. There, as in the cases today, we sought a protective device to dispel the compelling atmosphere of the interrogation. In *Escobedo*, however, the police did not relieve the defendant of the anxieties which they had created in the interrogation rooms. Rather, they denied his request for the assistance of counsel. This heightened his dilemma, and made his later statements the product of this compulsion. The denial of the defendant's request for his attorney thus undermined his ability to exercise the privilege—to remain silent if he chose or to speak without any intimidation, blatant or subtle. The presence of counsel, in all the cases before us today, would be the adequate protective device necessary to make the process of police interrogation conform to the dictates of the privilege. His presence would insure that statements made in the government-established atmosphere are not the product of compulsion.

It was in this manner that *Escobedo* explicated another facet of the pre-trial privilege, noted in many of the Court's prior decisions: the protection of rights at trial. That counsel is present when statements are taken from an individual during interrogation obviously enhances the integrity of the fact-finding processes in court. The presence of an attorney, and the warnings delivered to the individual, enable the defendant under otherwise compelling circumstances to tell his story without fear, effectively, and in a way that eliminates the evils in the interrogation process. Without the protections flowing from adequate warnings and the rights of counsel, "all the careful safeguards erected around the giving of testimony, whether by an accused or any other witness, would become empty formalities in a procedure where the most compelling possible evidence of guilt, a confession, would have already been obtained at the unsupervised pleasure of the police."

....

Today, then, there can be no doubt that the Fifth Amendment privilege is available outside of criminal court proceedings and serves to protect persons in all settings in which their freedom of action is curtailed in any significant way from being compelled to incriminate themselves. We have concluded that without proper safeguards the process of in-custody interrogation of persons suspected or accused of crime contains inherently compelling pressures which work to undermine the individual's will to resist and to compel him to speak where he would not otherwise do so freely. In order to combat these pressures and to permit a full opportunity to exercise the privilege against self-incrimination, the accused must be adequately and effectively apprised of his rights and the exercise of those rights must be fully honored.

It is impossible for us to foresee the potential alternatives for protecting the privilege which might be devised by Congress or the States in the exercise of their creative rule-making capacities. Therefore we cannot say that the Constitution necessarily requires adherence to any particular solution for the inherent compulsions of the interrogation process as it is presently conducted. Our decision in no way creates a constitutional straitjacket which will handicap sound efforts at reform, nor is it intended to have this effect. We encourage Congress and the States to continue their laudable search for increasingly effective ways of protecting the rights of the individual while promoting efficient enforcement of our criminal laws. However, unless we are shown other procedures which are at least as effective in apprising accused persons of their right of silence and in assuring a continuous opportunity to exercise it, the following safeguards must be observed.

At the outset, if a person in custody is to be subjected to interrogation, he must first be informed in clear and unequivocal terms that he has the right to remain silent. For those unaware of the privilege, the warning is needed simply to make them aware of it—the threshold requirement for an intelligent decision as to its exercise. More important, such a warning is an absolute prerequisite in overcoming the inherent pressures of the interrogation atmosphere. It is not just the subnormal or woefully ignorant who succumb to an interrogator's imprecations, whether implied or expressly stated, that the interrogation will continue until a confession is obtained or that silence in the face of accusation is itself damning and will bode ill when presented to a jury. Further, the warning will show the individual that his interrogators are prepared to recognize his privilege should he choose to exercise it.

The Fifth Amendment privilege is so fundamental to our system of constitutional rule and the expedient of giving an adequate warning as to the availability of the privilege so simple, we will not pause to inquire in individual cases whether the defendant was aware of his rights without a warning being given. Assessments of the knowledge the defendant possessed, based on information as to his age, education, intelligence, or prior contact with authorities, can never be more than speculation; a warning is a clear-cut fact. More important, whatever the background of the person interrogated, a warning at the time of the interrogation is indispensable to overcome its pressures and to insure that the individual knows he is free to exercise the privilege at that point in time.

The warning of the right to remain silent must be accompanied by the explanation that anything said can and will be used against the individual in court. This warning is needed in order to make him aware not only of the privilege, but also of the consequences of forgoing it. It is only through an awareness of these consequences that there can be any assurance of real understanding and intelligent exercise of the privilege. Moreover, this warning may serve to make the individual more acutely aware that he is faced with a phase of the adversary system—that he is not in the presence of persons acting solely in his interest.

The circumstances surrounding in-custody interrogation can operate very quickly to overbear the will of one merely made aware of his privilege by his interrogators. Therefore, the right to have counsel present at the interrogation is indispensable to the protection of the Fifth Amendment privilege under the system we delineate today. Our aim is to assure that the individual's right to choose between silence and speech remains unfettered throughout the interrogation process. A once-stated warning, delivered by those who will conduct the interrogation, cannot itself suffice to that end among those who most require knowledge of their rights. A mere warning given by the interrogators is not alone sufficient to accomplish that end. Prosecutors themselves claim that the admonishment of the right to remain silent without more "will benefit only the recidivist and the professional." Thus, the need for counsel to protect the Fifth Amendment privilege comprehends not merely a right to consult with counsel prior to questioning, but also to have counsel present during any questioning if the defendant so desires.

The presence of counsel at the interrogation may serve several significant subsidiary functions as well. If the accused decides to talk to his interrogators, the assistance of counsel can mitigate the dangers of untrustworthiness. With a lawyer present the likelihood that the police will practice coercion is reduced, and if coercion is nevertheless exercised the lawyer can testify to it in court. The presence of a lawyer can also help to guarantee that the accused gives a fully accurate statement to the police and that the statement is rightly reported by the prosecution at trial.

An individual need not make a pre-interrogation request for a lawyer. While such request affirmatively secures his right to have one, his failure to ask for a lawyer does not constitute a waiver. No effective waiver of the right to counsel during interrogation can be recognized unless specifically made after the warnings we here delineate have been given. The accused who does not know his rights and therefore does not make a request may be the person who most needs counsel. As the California Supreme Court has aptly put it:

"Finally, we must recognize that the imposition of the requirement for the request would discriminate against the defendant who does not know his rights. The defendant who does not ask for counsel is the very defendant who most needs counsel. We cannot penalize a defendant who, not understanding his constitutional rights, does not make the formal request and by such failure demonstrates his helplessness. To require the request would be to favor the defendant whose sophistication or status had fortuitously prompted him to make it."

In *Carnley v. Cochran*, we stated: "It is settled that where the assistance of counsel is a constitutional requisite, the right to be furnished counsel does not depend on a request." This proposition applies with equal force in the context of providing counsel to protect an accused's Fifth Amendment privilege in the face of interrogation. Although the role of counsel at trial differs from the role during interrogation, the differences are not relevant to the question whether a request is a prerequisite.

Accordingly we hold that an individual held for interrogation must be clearly informed that he has the right to consult with a lawyer and to have the lawyer with him during interrogation under the system for protecting the privilege we delineate today. As with the warnings of the right to remain silent and that anything stated can be used in evidence against him, this warning is an absolute prerequisite to interrogation. No amount of circumstantial evidence that the person may have been aware of this right will suffice to stand in its stead. Only through such a warning is there ascertainable assurance that the accused was aware of this right.

If an individual indicates that he wishes the assistance of counsel before any interrogation occurs, the authorities cannot rationally ignore or deny his request on the basis that the individual does not have or cannot afford a retained attorney. The financial ability of the individual has no relationship to the scope of the rights involved here. The privilege against self-incrimination secured by the Constitution applies to all individuals. The need for counsel in order to protect the privilege exists for the indigent as well as the affluent. In fact, were we to limit these constitutional rights to those who can retain an attorney, our decisions today would be of little significance. The cases before us as well as the vast majority of confession cases with which we have dealt in the past involve those unable to retain counsel. While authorities are not required to relieve the accused of his poverty, they have the obligation not to take advantage of indigence in the administration of justice. Denial of counsel to the indigent at the time of interrogation while allowing an attorney to those who can afford one would be no more supportable by reason or logic than the similar situation at trial and on appeal struck down in *Gideon v. Wainwright*.

In order fully to apprise a person interrogated of the extent of his rights under this system then, it is necessary to warn him not only that he has the right to consult with an attorney, but also that if he is indigent a lawyer will be appointed to represent him. Without this additional warning, the admonition of the right to consult with counsel would often be understood as meaning only that he can consult with a lawyer if he has one or has the funds to obtain one. The warning of a right to counsel would be hollow if not couched in terms that would convey to the indigent—the person most often subjected to interrogation—the knowledge that he too has a right to have counsel present. As with the warnings of the right to remain silent and of the general right to counsel, only by effective and express explanation to the indigent of this right can there be assurance that he was truly in a position to exercise it.

Once warnings have been given, the subsequent procedure is clear. If the individual indicates in any manner, at any time prior to or during questioning, that he wishes to remain silent, the interrogation must cease. At this point he has shown that he intends to exercise his Fifth Amendment privilege; any statement taken after the person invokes his privilege cannot be other than the product of compulsion, subtle or otherwise. Without the right to cut off questioning, the setting of in-custody interrogation operates on the individual to overcome free choice in producing a statement after the privilege has been once invoked. If the individual states that he wants an attorney, the interrogation must cease until an attorney is present. At that time, the individual must have an opportunity to confer with the attorney and to have him present during any subsequent questioning. If the individual cannot obtain an attorney and he indicates that he wants one before speaking to police, they must respect his decision to remain silent.

This does not mean, as some have suggested, that each police station must have a "station house lawyer" present at all times to advise prisoners. It does mean, however, that if police propose to interrogate a person they must make known to him that he is entitled to a lawyer and that if he cannot afford one, a lawyer will be provided for him prior to any interrogation. If authorities conclude that they will not provide counsel during a reasonable period of time in which investigation in the field is carried out, they may refrain from doing so without violating the person's Fifth Amendment privilege so long as they do not question him during that time.

If the interrogation continues without the presence of an attorney and a statement is taken, a heavy burden rests on the government to demonstrate that the defendant knowingly and intelligently waived his privilege against self-incrimination and his right to retained or appointed counsel. This Court has always set high standards of proof for the waiver of constitutional rights, and we re-assert these standards as applied to in-custody interrogation. Since the State is responsible for establishing the isolated circumstances under which the interrogation takes place and has the only means of making available corroborated evidence of warnings given during incommunicado interrogation, the burden is rightly on its shoulders.

An express statement that the individual is willing to make a statement and does not want an attorney followed closely by a statement could constitute a waiver. But a valid waiver will not be presumed simply from the silence of the accused after warnings are given or simply from the fact that a confession was in fact eventually obtained.... Moreover, where in-custody interrogation is involved, there is no room for the contention that the privilege is waived if the individual answers some questions or gives some information on his own prior to invoking his right to remain silent when interrogated.

Whatever the testimony of the authorities as to waiver of rights by an accused, the fact of lengthy interrogation or incommunicado incarceration before a statement is made is strong evidence that the accused did not validly waive his rights. In these circumstances the fact that the individual eventually made a statement is consistent with the conclusion that the compelling influence of the interrogation finally forced him to do so. It is inconsistent with any notion of a voluntary relinquishment of the privilege. Moreover, any evidence that the accused was threatened, tricked, or cajoled into a waiver will, of course, show that the defendant did not voluntarily waive his privilege. The requirement of warnings and waiver of rights is a fundamental with respect to the Fifth Amendment privilege and not simply a preliminary ritual to existing methods of interrogation.

The warnings required and the waiver necessary in accordance with our opinion today are, in the absence of a fully effective equivalent, prerequisites to the admissibility of any statement made by a defendant. No distinction can be drawn between statements which are direct confessions and statements which amount to "admissions" of part or all of an offense. The privilege against self-incrimination protects the individual from being compelled to incriminate himself in any manner; it does not distinguish degrees of incrimination. Similarly, for precisely the same reason, no distinction may be drawn between inculpatory statements and statements alleged to be merely "exculpatory." If a statement made were in fact truly exculpatory it would, of course, never be used by the prosecution. In fact, statements merely intended to be exculpatory by the defendant are often used to impeach his testimony at trial or to demonstrate untruths in the statement given under interrogation and thus to prove guilt by implication. These statements are incriminating in any meaningful sense of the word and may not be used without the full warnings and effective waiver required for any other statement. In *Escobedo* itself, the defendant fully intended his accusation of another as the slayer to be exculpatory as to himself.

The principles announced today deal with the protection which must be given to the privilege against self-incrimination when the individual is first subjected to police interrogation while in custody at the station or otherwise deprived of his freedom of action in any significant way. It is at this point that our adversary system of criminal proceedings commences, distinguishing itself at the outset from the inquisitorial system recognized in some countries. Under the system of warnings we delineate today or under any other system which may be devised and found effective, the safeguards to be erected about the privilege must come into play at this point.

Our decision is not intended to hamper the traditional function of police officers in investigating crime. When an individual is in custody on probable cause, the police may, of course, seek out evidence in the field to be used at trial against him. Such investigation may include inquiry of persons not under restraint. General on-the-scene questioning as to facts surrounding a crime or other general questioning of citizens in the fact-finding process is not affected by our holding. It is an act of responsible citizenship for individuals to give whatever information they may have to aid in law enforcement. In such situations the compelling atmosphere inherent in the process of in-custody interrogation is not necessarily present.

In dealing with statements obtained through interrogation, we do not purport to find all confessions inadmissible. Confessions remain a proper element in law enforcement. Any statement given freely and voluntarily without any compelling influences is, of course, admissible in evidence. The fundamental import of the privilege while an individual is in custody is not whether he is allowed to talk to the police without the benefit of warnings and counsel, but whether he can be interrogated. There is no requirement that police stop a person who enters a police station and states that he wishes to confess to a crime, or a person who calls the police to offer a confession or any other statement he desires to make. Volunteered statements of any kind are not barred by the Fifth Amendment and their admissibility is not affected by our holding today.

To summarize, we hold that when an individual is taken into custody or otherwise deprived of his freedom by the authorities in any significant way and is subjected to questioning, the privilege against self-incrimination is jeopardized. Procedural safeguards must be employed to protect the privilege, and unless other fully effective means are adopted to notify the person of his right of silence and to assure that the exercise of the right will be scrupulously honored, the following measures are required. He must be warned prior to any questioning that he has the right to remain silent, that anything he says can be used against him in a court of law, that he has the right to the presence of an attorney, and that if he cannot afford an attorney one will be appointed for him prior to any questioning if he so desires. Opportunity to exercise these rights must be afforded to him throughout the interrogation. After such warnings have been given, and such opportunity afforded him, the individual may knowingly and intelligently waive these rights and agree to answer questions or make a statement. But unless and until such warnings and waiver are demonstrated by the prosecution at trial, no evidence obtained as a result of interrogation can be used against him.

....

A recurrent argument made in these cases is that society's need for interrogation outweighs the privilege. This argument is not unfamiliar to this Court. The whole thrust of our foregoing discussion demonstrates that the Constitution has prescribed the rights of the individual when confronted with the power of government when it provided in the Fifth Amendment that an individual cannot be compelled to be a witness against himself. That right cannot be abridged. As Mr. Justice Brandeis once observed:

"Decency, security and liberty alike demand that government officials shall be subjected to the same rules of conduct that are commands to the citizen. In a government of laws, existence of the government will be imperiled if it fails to observe the law scrupulously. Our Government is the potent, the omnipresent teacher. For good or for ill, it teaches the whole people by its example. Crime is contagious. If the Government becomes a lawbreaker, it breeds contempt for law; it invites every man to become a law unto himself; it invites anarchy. To declare that in the administration of the criminal law the end justifies the means . . . would bring terrible retribution. Against that pernicious doctrine this Court should resolutely set its face."

In this connection, one of our country's distinguished jurists has pointed out: "The quality of a nation's civilization can be largely measured by the methods it uses in the enforcement of its criminal law."

If the individual desires to exercise his privilege, he has the right to do so. This is not for the authorities to decide. An attorney may advise his client not to talk to police until he has had an opportunity to investigate the case, or he may wish to be present with his client during any police questioning. In doing so an attorney is merely exercising the good professional judgment he has been taught. This is not cause for considering the attorney a menace to law enforcement. He is merely carrying out what he is sworn to do under his oath—to protect to the extent of his ability the rights of his client. In fulfilling this responsibility the attorney plays a vital role in the administration of criminal justice under our Constitution.

In announcing these principles, we are not unmindful of the burdens which law enforcement officials must bear, often under trying circumstances. We also fully recognize the obligation of all citizens to aid in enforcing the criminal laws. This Court, while protecting individual rights, has always given ample latitude to law enforcement agencies in the legitimate exercise of their duties. The limits we have placed on the interrogation process should not constitute an undue interference with a proper system of law enforcement. As we have noted, our decision does not in any way preclude police from carrying out their traditional investigatory functions. Although confessions may play an important role in some convictions, the cases before us present graphic examples of the overstatement of the "need" for confessions. In each case authorities conducted interrogations ranging up to five days in duration despite the presence, through standard investigating practices, of considerable evidence against each defendant. Further examples are chronicled in our prior cases.

It is also urged that an unfettered right to detention for interrogation should be allowed because it will often redound to the benefit of the person questioned. When police inquiry determines that there is no reason to believe that the person has committed any crime, it is said, he will be released without need for further formal procedures. The person who has committed no offense, however, will be better able to clear himself after warnings with counsel present than without. It can be assumed that in such circumstances a lawyer would advise his client to talk freely to police in order to clear himself.

Custodial interrogation, by contrast, does not necessarily afford the innocent an opportunity to clear themselves. A serious consequence of the present practice of the interrogation alleged to be beneficial for the innocent is that many arrests "for investigation" subject large numbers of innocent persons to detention and interrogation. In one of the cases before us, *California v. Stewart*, police held four persons, who were in the defendant's house at the time of the arrest, in jail for five days until defendant confessed. At that time they were finally released. Police stated that there was "no evidence to connect them with any crime." Available statistics on the extent of this practice where it is condoned indicate that these four are far from alone in being subjected to arrest, prolonged detention, and interrogation without the requisite probable cause.

Over the years the Federal Bureau of Investigation has compiled an exemplary record of effective law enforcement while advising any suspect or arrested person, at the outset of an interview, that he is not required to make a statement, that any statement may be used against him in court, that the individual may obtain the services of an attorney of his own choice and, more recently, that he has a right to free counsel if he is unable to pay.

....

The experience in some other countries also suggests that the danger to law enforcement in curbs on interrogation is overplayed. The English procedure since 1912 under the Judges' Rules is significant. As recently strengthened, the Rules require that a cautionary warning be given an accused by a police officer as soon as he has evidence that affords reasonable grounds for suspicion; they also require that any statement made be given by the accused without questioning by police. The right of the individual to consult with an attorney during this period is expressly recognized.

The safeguards present under Scottish law may be even greater than in England. Scottish judicial decisions bar use in evidence of most confessions obtained through police interrogation. In India, confessions made to police not in the presence of a magistrate have been excluded by rule of evidence since 1872, at a time when it operated under British law. Identical provisions appear in the Evidence Ordinance of Ceylon, enacted in 1895. Similarly, in our country the Uniform Code of Military Justice has long provided that no suspect may be interrogated without first being warned of his right not to make a statement and that any statement he makes may be used against him. Denial of the right to consult counsel during interrogation has also been proscribed by military tribunals. There appears to have been no marked detrimental effect on criminal law enforcement in these jurisdictions as a result of these rules. Conditions of law enforcement in our country are sufficiently similar to permit reference to this experience as assurance that lawlessness will not result from warning an individual of his rights or allowing him to exercise them. Moreover, it is consistent with our legal system that we give at least as much protection to these rights as is given in the jurisdictions described. We deal in our country with rights grounded in a specific requirement of the Fifth Amendment of the Constitution, whereas other jurisdictions arrived at their conclusions on the basis of principles of justice not so specifically defined.

It is also urged upon us that we withhold decision on this issue until state legislative bodies and advisory groups have had an opportunity to deal with these problems by rule making. We have already pointed out that the Constitution does not require any specific code of procedures for protecting the privilege against self-incrimination during custodial interrogation. Congress and the States are free to develop their own safeguards for the privilege, so long as they are fully as effective as those described above in informing accused persons of their right of silence and in affording a continuous opportunity to exercise it. In any event, however, the issues presented are of constitutional dimensions and must be determined by the courts. The admissibility of a statement in the face of a claim that it was obtained in violation of the defendant's constitutional rights is an issue the resolution of which has long since been undertaken by this Court. Judicial solutions to problems of constitutional dimension have evolved decade by decade. As courts have been presented with the need to enforce constitutional rights, they have found means of doing so. That was our responsibility when *Escobedo* was before us and it is our responsibility today. Where rights secured by the Constitution are involved, there can be no rule making or legislation which would abrogate them.

....

Because of the nature of the problem and because of its recurrent significance in numerous cases, we have to this point discussed the relationship of the Fifth Amendment privilege to police interrogation without specific concentration on the facts of the cases before us. We turn now to these facts to consider the application to these cases of the constitutional principles discussed above. In each instance, we have concluded that statements were obtained from the defendant under circumstances that did not meet constitutional standards for protection of the privilege....

On March 13, 1963, petitioner, Ernesto Miranda, was arrested at his home and taken in custody to a Phoenix police station. He was there identified by the complaining witness. The police then took him to "Interrogation Room No. 2" of the detective bureau. There he was questioned by two police officers. The officers admitted at trial that Miranda was not advised that he had a right to have an attorney present. Two hours later, the officers emerged from the interrogation room with a written confession signed by Miranda. At the top of the statement was a typed paragraph stating that the confession was made voluntarily, without threats or promises of immunity and "with full knowledge of my legal rights, understanding any statement I make may be used against me."

At his trial before a jury, the written confession was admitted into evidence over the objection of defense counsel, and the officers testified to the prior oral confession made by Miranda during the interrogation. Miranda was found guilty of kidnapping and rape. He was sentenced to 20 to 30 years' imprisonment on each count, the sentences to run concurrently. On appeal, the Supreme Court of Arizona held that Miranda's constitutional rights were not violated in obtaining the confession and affirmed the conviction. In reaching its decision, the court emphasized heavily the fact that Miranda did not specifically request counsel.

We reverse. From the testimony of the officers and by the admission of respondent, it is clear that Miranda was not in any way apprised of his right to consult with an attorney and to have one present during the interrogation, nor was his right not to be compelled to incriminate himself effectively protected in any other manner. Without these warnings the statements were inadmissible. The mere fact that he signed a statement which contained a typed-in clause stating that he had "full knowledge" of his "legal rights" does not approach the knowing and intelligent waiver required to relinquish constitutional rights.

…In dealing with custodial interrogation, we will not presume that a defendant has been effectively apprised of his rights and that his privilege against self-incrimination has been adequately safeguarded on a record that does not show that any warnings have been given or that any effective alternative has been employed. Nor can a knowing and intelligent waiver of these rights be assumed on a silent record.

It is so ordered.

New York v. Quarles (1984)
467 U.S. 649

In this case, the Supreme Court created an "exigent circumstances exception" to the general warning requirements established by the Court in Miranda v. Arizona. *The court describes* Miranda *not as a constitutional requirement, but as a "prophylactic rule."*

Respondent Benjamin Quarles was charged in the New York trial court with criminal possession of a weapon. The trial court suppressed the gun in question, and a statement made by respondent, because the statement was obtained by police before they read respondent his "*Miranda* rights." That ruling was affirmed on appeal through the New York Court of Appeals. We granted certiorari, and we now reverse. We conclude that under the circumstances involved in this case, overriding considerations of public safety justify the officer's failure to provide *Miranda* warnings before he asked questions devoted to locating the abandoned weapon.

On September 11, 1980, at approximately 12:30 a. m., Officer Frank Kraft and Officer Sal Scarring were on road patrol in Queens, N. Y., when a young woman approached their car. She told them that she had just been raped by a black male, approximately six feet tall, who was wearing a black jacket with the name "Big Ben" printed in yellow letters on the back. She told the officers that the man had just entered an A & P supermarket located nearby and that the man was carrying a gun.

The officers drove the woman to the supermarket, and Officer Kraft entered the store while Officer Scarring radioed for assistance. Officer Kraft quickly spotted respondent, who matched the description given by the woman, approaching a checkout counter. Apparently upon seeing the officer, respondent turned and ran toward the rear of the store, and Officer Kraft pursued him with a drawn gun. When respondent turned the corner at the end of an aisle, Officer Kraft lost sight of him for several seconds, and upon regaining sight of respondent, ordered him to stop and put his hands over his head.

Although more than three other officers had arrived on the scene by that time, Officer Kraft was the first to reach respondent. He frisked him and discovered that he was wearing a shoulder holster which was then empty. After handcuffing him, Officer Kraft asked him where the gun was. Respondent nodded in the direction of some empty cartons and responded, "the gun is over there." Officer Kraft thereafter retrieved a loaded .38-caliber revolver from one of the cartons, formally placed respondent under arrest, and read him his *Miranda* rights from a printed card. Respondent indicated that he would be willing to answer questions without an attorney present. Officer Kraft then asked respondent if he owned the gun and where he had purchased it. Respondent answered that he did own it and that he had purchased it in Miami, Fla.

In the subsequent prosecution of respondent for criminal possession of a weapon, the judge excluded the statement, "the gun is over there," and the gun because the officer had not given respondent the warnings required by our decision in *Miranda v. Arizona* before asking him where the gun was located. The judge excluded the other statements about respondent's ownership of the gun and the place of purchase, as evidence tainted by the prior *Miranda* violation. The Appellate Division of the Supreme Court of New York affirmed without opinion.

The Court of Appeals … concluded that respondent was in "custody" within the meaning of *Miranda* during all questioning and rejected the State's argument that the exigencies of the situation justified Officer Kraft's failure to read respondent his *Miranda* rights until after he had located the gun. The court declined to recognize an exigency exception to the usual requirements of *Miranda* because it found no indication from Officer Kraft's testimony at the suppression hearing that his subjective motivation in asking the question was to protect his own safety or the safety of the public. For the reasons which follow, we believe that this case presents a situation where concern for public safety must be paramount to adherence to the literal language of the prophylactic rules enunciated in *Miranda*.

The Fifth Amendment guarantees that "[no] person . . . shall be compelled in any criminal case to be a witness against himself." In *Miranda* this Court for the first time extended the Fifth Amendment privilege against compulsory self-incrimination to individuals subjected to custodial interrogation by the police. The Fifth Amendment itself does not prohibit all incriminating admissions; "[absent] some officially coerced self-accusation, the Fifth Amendment privilege is not violated by even the most damning admissions." The *Miranda* Court, however, presumed that interrogation in certain custodial circumstances is inherently coercive and held that statements made under those circumstances are inadmissible unless the suspect is specifically informed of his *Miranda* rights and freely decides to forgo those rights. The prophylactic *Miranda* warnings therefore are "not themselves rights protected by the Constitution but are instead measures to insure that the right against compulsory self-incrimination is protected." In this case we have before us no claim that respondent's statements were actually compelled by police conduct which overcame his will to resist. Thus the only issue before us is whether Officer Kraft was justified in failing to make available to respondent the procedural safeguards associated with the privilege against compulsory self-incrimination since *Miranda*.

The New York Court of Appeals was undoubtedly correct in deciding that the facts of this case come within the ambit of the *Miranda* decision as we have subsequently interpreted it. We agree that respondent was in police custody because we have noted that "the ultimate inquiry is simply whether there is a 'formal arrest or restraint on freedom of movement' of the degree associated with a formal arrest," Here Quarles was surrounded by at least four police officers and was handcuffed when the questioning at issue took place. As the New York Court of Appeals observed, there was nothing to suggest that any of the officers were any longer concerned for their own physical safety. The New York Court of Appeals' majority declined to express an opinion as to whether there might be an exception to the *Miranda* rule if the police had been acting to protect the public, because the lower courts in New York had made no factual determination that the police had acted with that motive.

We hold that on these facts there is a "public safety" exception to the requirement that *Miranda* warnings be given before a suspect's answers may be admitted into evidence, and that the availability of that exception does not depend upon the motivation of the individual officers involved. In a kaleidoscopic situation such as the one confronting these officers, where spontaneity rather than adherence to a police manual is necessarily the order of the day, the application of the exception which we recognize today should not be made to depend on post hoc findings at a suppression hearing concerning the subjective motivation of the arresting officer. Undoubtedly most police officers, if placed in Officer Kraft's position, would act out of a host of different, instinctive, and largely unverifiable motives—their own safety, the safety of others, and perhaps as well the desire to obtain incriminating evidence from the suspect.

Whatever the motivation of individual officers in such a situation, we do not believe that the doctrinal underpinnings of *Miranda* require that it be applied in all its rigor to a situation in which police officers ask questions reasonably prompted by a concern for the public safety. The *Miranda* decision was based in large part on this Court's view that the warnings which it required police to give to suspects in custody would reduce the likelihood that the suspects would fall victim to constitutionally impermissible practices of police interrogation in the presumptively coercive environment of the station house. The dissenters warned that the requirement of *Miranda* warnings would have the effect of decreasing the number of suspects who respond to police questioning. The *Miranda* majority, however, apparently felt that whatever the cost to society in terms of fewer convictions of guilty suspects, that cost would simply have to be borne in the interest of enlarged protection for the Fifth Amendment privilege.

The police in this case, in the very act of apprehending a suspect, were confronted with the immediate necessity of ascertaining the whereabouts of a gun which they had every reason to believe the suspect had just removed from his empty holster and discarded in the supermarket. So long as the gun was concealed somewhere in the supermarket, with its actual whereabouts unknown, it obviously posed more than one danger to the public safety: an accomplice might make use of it, a customer or employee might later come upon it.

In such a situation, if the police are required to recite the familiar *Miranda* warnings before asking the whereabouts of the gun, suspects in Quarles' position might well be deterred from responding. Procedural safeguards which deter a suspect from responding were deemed acceptable in *Miranda* in order to protect the Fifth Amendment privilege; when the primary social cost of those added protections is the possibility of fewer convictions, the *Miranda* majority was willing to bear that cost. Here, had *Miranda* warnings deterred Quarles from responding to Officer Kraft's question about the whereabouts of the gun, the cost would have been something more than merely the failure to obtain evidence useful in convicting Quarles. Officer Kraft needed an answer to his question not simply to make his case against Quarles but to insure that further danger to the public did not result from the concealment of the gun in a public area.

We conclude that the need for answers to questions in a situation posing a threat to the public safety outweighs the need for the prophylactic rule protecting the Fifth Amendment's privilege against self-incrimination. We decline to place officers such as Officer Kraft in the untenable position of having to consider, often in a matter of seconds, whether it best serves society for them to ask the necessary questions without the *Miranda* warnings and render whatever probative evidence they uncover inadmissible, or for them to give the warnings in order to preserve the admissibility of evidence they might uncover but possibly damage or destroy their ability to obtain that evidence and neutralize the volatile situation confronting them.

In recognizing a narrow exception to the *Miranda* rule in this case, we acknowledge that to some degree we lessen the desirable clarity of that rule. At least in part in order to preserve its clarity, we have over the years refused to sanction attempts to expand our *Miranda* holding. As we have in other contexts, we recognize here the importance of a workable rule "to guide police officers, who have only limited time and expertise to reflect on and balance the social and individual interests involved in the specific circumstances they confront." But as we have pointed out, we believe that the exception which we recognize today lessens the necessity of that on-the-scene balancing process. The exception will not be difficult for police officers to apply because in each case it will be circumscribed by the exigency which justifies it. We think police officers can and will distinguish almost instinctively between questions necessary to secure their own safety or the safety of the public and questions designed solely to elicit testimonial evidence from a suspect.

The facts of this case clearly demonstrate that distinction and an officer's ability to recognize it. Officer Kraft asked only the question necessary to locate the missing gun before advising respondent of his rights. It was only after securing the loaded revolver and giving the warnings that he continued with investigatory questions about the ownership and place of purchase of the gun. The exception which we recognize today, far from complicating the thought processes and the on-the-scene judgments of police officers, will simply free them to follow their legitimate instincts when confronting situations presenting a danger to the public safety.

We hold that the Court of Appeals in this case erred in excluding the statement, "the gun is over there," and the gun because of the officer's failure to read respondent his *Miranda* rights before attempting to locate the weapon. Accordingly, we hold that it also erred in excluding the subsequent statements as illegal fruits of a *Miranda* violation.

We therefore reverse and remand for further proceedings not inconsistent with this opinion.

It is so ordered.

Weeks v. United States (1914)
232 U.S. 383

This landmark case was the Supreme Court's first articulation of the exclusionary rule. This rule is now considered by most as a fundamental principle of criminal justice; it states that evidence obtained by the police in violation of a person's Fourth Amendment rights cannot be used against them in a criminal court.

....

The defendant was arrested by a police officer, so far as the record shows, without warrant, at the Union Station in Kansas City, Missouri, where he was employed by an express company. Other police officers had gone to the house of the defendant and being told by a neighbor where the key was kept, found it and entered the house. They searched the defendant's room and took possession of various papers and articles found there, which were afterwards turned over to the United States Marshal. Later in the same day police officers returned with the Marshal, who thought he might find additional evidence, and, being admitted by someone in the house, probably a boarder, in response to a rap, the Marshal searched the defendant's room and carried away certain letters and envelopes found in the drawer of a chiffonier. Neither the marshal nor the police officers had a search warrant.

The defendant filed in the cause before the time for trial the following petition:

"Petition to Return Private Papers, Books and Other Property.

"Now comes defendant and states that he is a citizen and resident of Kansas City, Missouri, and that he resides, owns and occupies a home at 1834 Penn Street in said City;

"That on the 21st day of December, 1911, while plaintiff was absent at his daily vocation certain officers of the government whose names are to plaintiff unknown, unlawfully and without warrant or authority so to do, broke open the door to plaintiff's said home and seized all of his books, letters, money, papers, notes, evidences of indebtedness, stock, certificates, insurance policies, deeds, abstracts, and other muniments of title, bonds, candies, clothes and other property in said home, and this in violation of Sections 11 and 23 of the Constitution of Missouri and of the 4th and 5th Amendments to the Constitution of the United States:

"That the District Attorney, Marshal and Clerk of the United States Court for the Western District of Missouri took the above described property so seized into their possession and have failed and refused to return to defendant portion of same, to-wit:

"One (1) leather grip, value about $ 7.00; one (1) tin box valued at $ 3.00; one (1) Pettis County, Missouri, bond, value $ 500.00; three (3) Mining stock certificates which defendant is unable to more particularly describe valued at $ 12,000.00, and certain stock certificates in addition thereto issued by the San Domingo Mining Loan and Investment Company, about $ 75.00 in currency; one (1) newspaper published about 1790, an heirloom; and certain other property which plaintiff is now unable to describe:

"That said property is being unlawfully and improperly held by said District Attorney, Marshal and Clerk in violation of defendant's rights under the Constitution of the United States and the State of Missouri:

"That said District Attorney purposes to use said books, letters, papers, certificates of stock, etc., at the trial of the above entitled cause and that by reason thereof and of the facts above set forth defendant's rights under the amendments aforesaid to the Constitution of Missouri, and the United States have been and will be violated unless the Court order the return prayed for:

"Wherefore, defendant prays that said District Attorney, Marshal and Clerk be notified, and that the Court direct and order said District Attorney, Marshal and Clerk to return said property to said defendant."

Upon consideration of the petition, the court entered in the cause an order directing the return of such property as was not pertinent to the charge against the defendant, but denied the petition as to pertinent matter, reserving the right to pass upon the pertinency at a later time. In obedience to the order the District Attorney returned part of the property taken and retained the remainder, concluding a list of the latter with the statement that, "all of which last above described property is to be used in evidence in the trial of the above entitled cause, and pertains to the alleged sale of lottery tickets of the company above named."

After the jury had been sworn and before any evidence had been given, the defendant again urged his petition for the return of his property, which was denied by the court. Upon the introduction of such papers during the trial, the defendant objected on the ground that the papers had been obtained without a search warrant and by breaking open his home, in violation of the Fourth and Fifth Amendments to the Constitution of the United States, which objection was overruled by the court. Among the papers retained and put in evidence were a number of lottery tickets and statements with reference to the lottery, taken at the first visit of the police to the defendant's room, and a number of letters written to the defendant in respect to the lottery, taken by the Marshal upon his search of defendant's room.

The defendant assigns error, among other things, in the court's refusal to grant his petition for the return of his property and in permitting the papers to be used at the trial.

It is thus apparent that the question presented involves the determination of the duty of the court with reference to the motion made by the defendant for the return of certain letters, as well as other papers, taken from his room by the United States Marshal, who, without authority of process, if any such could have been legally issued, visited the room of the defendant for the declared purpose of obtaining additional testimony to support the charge against the accused, and having gained admission to the house took from the drawer of a chiffonier there found certain letters written to the defendant, tending to show his guilt. These letters were placed in the control of the District Attorney and were subsequently produced by him and offered in evidence against the accused at the trial. The defendant contends that such appropriation of his private correspondence was in violation of rights secured to him by the Fourth and Fifth Amendments to the Constitution of the United States. We shall deal with the Fourth Amendment, which provides:

"The right of the people to be secure in their persons, houses, papers, and effects, against unreasonable searches and seizures, shall not be violated, and no warrants shall issue, but upon probable cause, supported by oath or affirmation and particularly describing the place to be searched, and the persons or things to be seized."

The history of this Amendment is given with particularity in the opinion of Mr. Justice Bradley, speaking for the court in *Boyd v. United States*. As was there shown, it took its origin in the determination of the framers of the Amendments to the Federal Constitution to provide for that instrument a Bill of Rights, securing to the American people, among other things, those safeguards which had grown up in England to protect the people from unreasonable searches and seizures, such as were permitted under the general warrants issued under authority of the Government by which there had been invasions of the home and privacy of the citizens and the seizure of their private papers in support of charges, real or imaginary, made against them. Such practices had also received sanction under warrants and seizures under the so-called writs of assistance, issued in the American colonies.... Resistance to these practices had established the principle which was enacted into the fundamental law in the Fourth Amendment, that a man's house was his castle and not to be invaded by any general authority to search and seize his goods and papers. Judge Cooley, in his *Constitutional Limitations*, in treating of this feature of our Constitution, said: "The maxim that 'every man's house is his castle,' is made a part of our constitutional law in the clauses prohibiting unreasonable searches and seizures, and has always been looked upon as of high value to the citizen."

"Accordingly," ... "no man's house can be forcibly opened, or he or his goods be carried away after it has thus been forced, except in cases of felony, and then the sheriff must be furnished with a warrant, and take great care lest he commit a trespass. This principle is jealously insisted upon." In *Ex parte Jackson*, this court recognized the principle of protection as applicable to letters and sealed packages in the mail, and held that consistently with this guaranty of the right of the people to be secure in their papers against unreasonable searches and seizures such matter could only be opened and examined upon warrants issued on oath or affirmation particularly describing the thing to be seized, "as is required when papers are subjected to search in one's own household."

....

In *Bram v. United States*, this court in speaking by the present Chief Justice of Boyd's Case, dealing with the Fourth and Fifth Amendments, said:

"It was in that case demonstrated that both of these Amendments contemplated perpetuating, in their full efficacy, by means of a constitutional provision, principles of humanity and civil liberty, which had been secured in the mother country only after years of struggle, so as to implant them in our institutions in the fullness of their integrity, free from the possibilities of future legislative change."

The effect of the Fourth Amendment is to put the courts of the United States and Federal officials, in the exercise of their power and authority, under limitations and restraints as to the exercise of such power and authority, and to forever secure the people, their persons, houses, papers and effects against all unreasonable searches and seizures under the guise of law. This protection reaches all alike, whether accused of crime or not, and the duty of giving to it force and effect is obligatory upon all entrusted under our Federal system with the enforcement of the laws. The tendency of those who execute the criminal laws of the country to obtain conviction by means of unlawful seizures and enforced confessions, the latter often obtained after subjecting accused persons to unwarranted practices destructive of rights secured by the Federal Constitution, should find no sanction in the judgments of the courts which are charged at all times with the support of the Constitution and to which people of all conditions have a right to appeal for the maintenance of such fundamental rights.

What then is the present case? Before answering that inquiry specifically, it may be well by a process of exclusion to state what it is not. It is not an assertion of the right on the part of the Government, always recognized under English and American law, to search the person of the accused when legally arrested to discover and seize the fruits or evidences of crime. This right has been uniformly maintained in many cases. Nor is it the case of testimony offered at a trial where the court is asked to stop and consider the illegal means by which proofs, otherwise competent, were obtained—of which we shall have occasion to treat later in this opinion. Nor is it the case of burglar's tools or other proofs of guilt found upon his arrest within the control of the accused.

The case in the aspect in which we are dealing with it involves the right of the court in a criminal prosecution to retain for the purposes of evidence the letters and correspondence of the accused, seized in his house in his absence and without his authority, by a United States Marshal holding no warrant for his arrest and none for the search of his premises. The accused, without awaiting his trial, made timely application to the court for an order for the return of these letters, as well as other property. This application was denied, the letters retained and put in evidence, after a further application at the beginning of the trial, both applications asserting the rights of the accused under the Fourth and Fifth Amendments to the Constitution. If letters and private documents can thus be seized and held and used in evidence against a citizen accused of an offense, the protection of the Fourth Amendment declaring his right to be secure against such searches and seizures is of no value, and, so far as those thus placed are concerned, might as well be stricken from the Constitution.

The efforts of the courts and their officials to bring the guilty to punishment, praiseworthy as they are, are not to be aided by the sacrifice of those great principles established by years of endeavor and suffering which have resulted in their embodiment in the fundamental law of the land. The United States Marshal could only have invaded the house of the accused when armed with a warrant issued as required by the Constitution, upon sworn information and describing with reasonable particularity the thing for which the search was to be made. Instead, he acted without sanction of law, doubtless prompted by the desire to bring further proof to the aid of the Government, and under color of his office undertook to make a seizure of private papers in direct violation of the constitutional prohibition against such action. Under such circumstances, without sworn information and particular description, not even an order of court would have justified such procedure, much less was it within the authority of the United States Marshal to thus invade the house and privacy of the accused.

In *Adams v. New York*, this court said that the Fourth Amendment was intended to secure the citizen in person and property against unlawful invasion of the sanctity of his home by officers of the law acting under legislative or judicial sanction. This protection is equally extended to the action of the Government and officers of the law acting under it. To sanction such proceedings would be to affirm by judicial decision a manifest neglect if not an open defiance of the prohibitions of the Constitution, intended for the protection of the people against such unauthorized action.

The court before which the application was made in this case recognized the illegal character of the seizure and ordered the return of property not in its judgment competent to be offered at the trial, but refused the application of the accused to turn over the letters, which were afterwards put in evidence on behalf of the Government. While there is no opinion in the case, the court in this proceeding doubtless relied upon what is now contended by the Government to be the correct rule of law under such circumstances, that the letters having come into the control of the court, it would not inquire into the manner in which they were obtained, but if competent would keep them and permit their use in evidence. Such proposition, the Government asserts, is conclusively established by certain decisions of this court, the first of which is *Adams v. New York*. In that case the plaintiff in error had been convicted in the Supreme Court of the State of New York for having in his possession certain gambling paraphernalia used in the game known as policy, in violation of the Penal Code of New York.

At the trial certain papers, which had been seized by police officers executing a search warrant for the discovery and seizure of policy slips and which had been found in addition to the policy slips, were offered in evidence over his objection. The conviction was affirmed by the Court of Appeals of New York, and the case was brought here for alleged violation of the Fourth and Fifth

Amendments to the Constitution of the United States. Pretermitting the question whether these amendments applied to the action of the States, this court proceeded to examine the alleged violations of the Fourth and Fifth Amendments, and put its decision upon the ground that the papers found in the execution of the search warrant, which warrant had a legal purpose in the attempt to find gambling paraphernalia, were competent evidence against the accused, and their offer in testimony did not violate his constitutional privilege against unlawful search or seizure, for it was held that such incriminatory documents thus discovered were not the subject of an unreasonable search and seizure, and in effect that the same were incidentally seized in the lawful execution of a warrant and not in the wrongful invasion of the home of the citizen and the unwarranted seizure of his papers and property.

....

We therefore reach the conclusion that the letters in question were taken from the house of the accused by an official of the United States acting under color of his office in direct violation of the constitutional rights of the defendant; that having made a seasonable application for their return, which was heard and passed upon by the court, there was involved in the order refusing the application a denial of the constitutional rights of the accused, and that the court should have restored these letters to the accused. In holding them and permitting their use upon the trial, we think prejudicial error was committed. As to the papers and property seized by the policemen, it does not appear that they acted under any claim of Federal authority such as would make the Amendment applicable to such unauthorized seizures. The record shows that what they did by way of arrest and search and seizure was done before the finding of the indictment in the Federal court, under what supposed right or authority does not appear. What remedies the defendant may have against them we need not inquire, as the Fourth Amendment is not directed to individual misconduct of such officials. Its limitations reach the Federal Government and its agencies.

It results that the judgment of the court below must be reversed, and the case remanded for further proceedings in accordance with this opinion.

Reversed.

Mapp v. Ohio (1961)
367 U.S. 643

Weeks established the exclusionary rule as it applied to federal officers and federal courts. It did not, however, reach local officers and state courts. In this landmark decision, the Court extended the reach of the exclusionary rule to the states via the Fourteenth Amendment.

Appellant stands convicted of knowingly having had in her possession and under her control certain lewd and lascivious books, pictures, and photographs in violation of 2905.34 of Ohio's Revised Code. As officially stated in the syllabus to its opinion, the Supreme Court of Ohio found that her conviction was valid though "based primarily upon the introduction in evidence of lewd and lascivious books and pictures unlawfully seized during an unlawful search of defendant's home . . . ."

On May 23, 1957, three Cleveland police officers arrived at appellant's residence in that city pursuant to information that "a person [was] hiding out in the home, who was wanted for questioning in connection with a recent bombing, and that there was a large amount of policy paraphernalia being hidden in the home." Miss Mapp and her daughter by a former marriage lived on the top floor of the two-family dwelling. Upon their arrival at that house, the officers knocked on the door and demanded entrance but appellant, after telephoning her attorney, refused to admit them without a search warrant. They advised their headquarters of the situation and undertook a surveillance of the house.

The officers again sought entrance some three hours later when four or more additional officers arrived on the scene. When Miss Mapp did not come to the door immediately, at least one of the several doors to the house was forcibly opened and the policemen gained admittance. Meanwhile Miss Mapp's attorney arrived, but the officers, having secured their own entry, and continuing in their defiance of the law, would permit him neither to see Miss Mapp nor to enter the house. It appears that Miss Mapp was halfway down the stairs from the upper floor to the front door when the officers, in this highhanded manner, broke into the hall. She demanded to see the search warrant. A paper, claimed to be a warrant, was held up by one of the officers. She grabbed the "warrant" and placed it in her bosom. A struggle ensued in which the officers recovered the piece of paper and as a result of which they handcuffed appellant because she had been "belligerent" in resisting their official rescue of the "warrant" from her person. Running roughshod over appellant, a policeman "grabbed" her, "twisted [her] hand," and she "yelled [and] pleaded with him" because "it was hurting."

Appellant, in handcuffs, was then forcibly taken upstairs to her bedroom where the officers searched a dresser, a chest of drawers, a closet and some suitcases. They also looked into a photo album and through personal papers belonging to the appellant. The search spread to the rest of the second floor including the child's bedroom, the living room, the kitchen and a dinette. The basement of the building and a trunk found therein were also searched. The obscene materials for possession of which she was ultimately convicted were discovered in the course of that widespread search.

At the trial no search warrant was produced by the prosecution, nor was the failure to produce one explained or accounted for. At best, "There is, in the record, considerable doubt as to whether there ever was any warrant for the search of defendant's home." The Ohio Supreme Court believed a "reasonable argument" could be made that the conviction should be reversed "because the 'methods' employed to obtain the [evidence] . . . were such as to 'offend "a sense of justice," ' but the court found determinative the fact that the evidence had not been taken "from defendant's person by the use of brutal or offensive physical force against defendant."

The State says that even if the search were made without authority, or otherwise unreasonably, it is not prevented from using the unconstitutionally seized evidence at trial, citing *Wolf v. Colorado*, in which this Court did indeed hold "that in a prosecution in a State court for a State crime the Fourteenth Amendment does not forbid the admission of evidence obtained by an unreasonable search and seizure." On this appeal, of which we have noted probable jurisdiction, it is urged once again that we review that holding.

I.

Seventy-five years ago, in *Boyd v. United States*, considering the Fourth and Fifth Amendments as running "almost into each other" on the facts before it, this Court held that the doctrines of those Amendments

"apply to all invasions on the part of the government and its employs of the sanctity of a man's home and the privacies of life. It is not the breaking of his doors, and the rummaging of his drawers, that constitutes the essence of the offence; but it is the invasion of his indefeasible right of personal security, personal liberty and private property. . . . Breaking into a house and opening boxes and drawers are circumstances of aggravation; but any forcible and compulsory extortion of a man's own testimony or of his private papers to be used as evidence to convict him of crime or to forfeit his goods, is within the condemnation . . . [of those Amendments]."

The Court noted that

"constitutional provisions for the security of person and property should be liberally construed. . . . It is the duty of courts to be watchful for the constitutional rights of the citizen, and against any stealthy encroachments thereon."

In this jealous regard for maintaining the integrity of individual rights, the Court gave life to Madison's prediction that "independent tribunals of justice . . . will be naturally led to resist every encroachment upon rights expressly stipulated for in the Constitution by the declaration of rights." Concluding, the Court specifically referred to the use of the evidence there seized as "unconstitutional."

....

There are in the cases of this Court some passing references to the *Weeks* rule as being one of evidence. But the plain and unequivocal language of *Weeks*— and its later paraphrase in *Wolf*— to the effect that the *Weeks* rule is of constitutional origin, remains entirely undisturbed. In *Byars v. United States*, a unanimous Court declared that "the doctrine [cannot] . . . be tolerated under our constitutional system, that evidences of crime discovered by a federal officer in making a search without lawful warrant may be used against the victim of the unlawful search where a timely challenge has been interposed." The Court, in *Olmstead v. United States*, in unmistakable language restated the *Weeks* rule:

"The striking outcome of the *Weeks* case and those which followed it was the sweeping declaration that the Fourth Amendment, although not referring to or limiting the use of evidence in courts, really forbade its introduction if obtained by government officers through a violation of the Amendment."

In *McNabb v. United States*, we note this statement:

"A conviction in the federal courts, the foundation of which is evidence obtained in disregard of liberties deemed fundamental by the Constitution, cannot stand. *Boyd v. United States* . . . *Weeks v. United States* . . . And this Court has, on Constitutional grounds, set aside convictions, both in the federal and state courts, which were based upon confessions 'secured by protracted and repeated questioning of ignorant and untutored persons, in whose minds the power of officers was greatly magnified'. . . or 'who have been unlawfully held incommunicado without advice of friends or counsel' . . . ."

Significantly in *McNabb*, the Court did then pass on to formulate a rule of evidence, saying, "in the view we take of the case, however, it becomes unnecessary to reach the Constitutional issue for . . . the principles governing the admissibility of evidence in federal criminal trials have not been restricted . . . to those derived solely from the Constitution."

II.

In 1949, 35 years after *Weeks* was announced, this Court, in *Wolf v. Colorado*, again for the first time, discussed the effect of the Fourth Amendment upon the States through the operation of the Due Process Clause of the Fourteenth Amendment. It said:

"We have no hesitation in saying that were a State affirmatively to sanction such police incursion into privacy it would run counter to the guaranty of the Fourteenth Amendment."

Nevertheless, after declaring that the "security of one's privacy against arbitrary intrusion by the police" is "implicit in the concept of ordered liberty' and as such enforceable against the States through the Due Process Clause," and announcing that it "stoutly adhered" to the *Weeks* decision, the Court decided that the *Weeks* exclusionary rule would not then be imposed upon the States as "an essential ingredient of the right." The Court's reasons for not considering essential to the right to privacy, as a curb imposed upon the States by the Due Process Clause, that which decades before had been posited as part and parcel of the Fourth Amendment's limitation upon federal encroachment of individual privacy, were bottomed on factual considerations.

While they are not basically relevant to a decision that the exclusionary rule is an essential ingredient of the Fourth Amendment as the right it embodies is vouchsafed against the States by the Due Process Clause, we will consider the current validity of the factual grounds upon which *Wolf* was based.

The Court in *Wolf* first stated that "the contrariety of views of the States" on the adoption of the exclusionary rule of *Weeks* was "particularly impressive"; and, in this connection, that it could not "brush aside the experience of States which deem the incidence of such conduct by the police too slight to call for a deterrent remedy . . . by overriding the States' relevant rules of evidence."

While in 1949, prior to the *Wolf* case, almost two-thirds of the States were opposed to the use of the exclusionary rule, now, despite the *Wolf* case, more than half of those since passing upon it, by their own legislative or judicial decision, have wholly or partly adopted or adhered to the *Weeks* rule. Significantly, among those now following the rule is California, which, according to its highest court, was "compelled to reach that conclusion because other remedies have completely failed to secure compliance with the constitutional provisions . . . ." In connection with this California case, we note that the second basis elaborated in *Wolf* in support of its failure to enforce the exclusionary doctrine against the States was that "other means of protection" have been afforded "the right to privacy." The experience of California that such other remedies have been worthless and futile is buttressed by the experience of other States. The obvious futility of relegating the Fourth Amendment to the protection of other remedies has, moreover, been recognized by this Court since *Wolf*.

Likewise, time has set its face against what *Wolf* called the "weighty testimony" of There Justice (then Judge) Cardozo, rejecting adoption of the *Weeks* exclusionary rule in New York, had said that "the Federal rule as it stands is either too strict or too lax." However, the force of that reasoning has been largely vitiated by later decisions of this Court. These include the recent discarding of the "silver platter" doctrine which allowed federal judicial use of evidence seized in violation of the Constitution by state agents, the relaxation of the formerly strict requirements as to standing to challenge the use of evidence thus seized, so that now the procedure of exclusion, "ultimately referable to constitutional safeguards," is available to anyone even "legitimately on the premises" unlawfully searched; and, finally, the formulation of a method to prevent state use of evidence unconstitutionally seized by federal agents. Because there can be no fixed formula, we are admittedly met with "recurring questions of the reasonableness of searches," but less is not to be expected when dealing with a Constitution, and, at any rate, "reasonableness is in the first instance for the trial court . . . to determine."

It, therefore, plainly appears that the factual considerations supporting the failure of the *Wolf* Court to include the *Weeks* exclusionary rule when it recognized the enforceability of the right to privacy against the States in 1949, while not basically relevant to the constitutional consideration, could not, in any analysis, now be deemed controlling.

III.

Some five years after *Wolf*, in answer to a plea made here Term after Term that we overturn its doctrine on applicability of the *Weeks* exclusionary rule, this Court indicated that such should not be done until the States had "adequate opportunity to adopt or reject the *Weeks* rule." There again it was said:

"Never until June of 1949 did this Court hold the basic search-and-seizure prohibition in any way applicable to the states under the Fourteenth Amendment."

And only last Term, after again carefully re-examining the *Wolf* doctrine in *Elkins v. United States*, the Court pointed out that "the controlling principles" as to search and seizure and the problem of admissibility "seemed clear" until the announcement in *Wolf* "that the Due Process Clause of the Fourteenth Amendment does not itself require state courts to adopt the exclusionary rule" of the *Weeks* case. At the same time, the Court pointed out, "the underlying constitutional doctrine which Wolf established . . . that the Federal Constitution . . . prohibits unreasonable searches and seizures by state officers" had undermined the "foundation upon which the admissibility of state-seized evidence in a federal trial originally rested . . . ." The Court concluded that it was therefore obliged to hold, although it chose the narrower ground on which to do so, that all evidence obtained by an unconstitutional search and seizure was inadmissible in a federal court regardless of its source. Today we once again examine *Wolf's* constitutional documentation of the right to privacy free from unreasonable state intrusion, and, after its dozen years on our books, are led by it to close the only courtroom door remaining open to evidence secured by official lawlessness in flagrant abuse of that basic right, reserved to all persons as a specific guarantee against that very same unlawful conduct. We hold that all evidence obtained by searches and seizures in violation of the Constitution is, by that same authority, inadmissible in a state court.

IV.

Since the Fourth Amendment's right of privacy has been declared enforceable against the States through the Due Process Clause of the Fourteenth, it is enforceable against them by the same sanction of exclusion as is used against the Federal Government. Were it otherwise, then just as without the *Weeks* rule the assurance against unreasonable federal searches and seizures would be "a form of words," valueless and undeserving of mention in a perpetual charter of inestimable human liberties, so too, without that rule the freedom from state invasions of privacy would be so ephemeral and so neatly severed from its conceptual nexus with the freedom from all brutish means of coercing evidence as not to merit this Court's high regard as a freedom "implicit in the concept of ordered liberty."

At the time that the Court held in *Wolf* that the Amendment was applicable to the States through the Due Process Clause, the cases of this Court, as we have seen, had steadfastly held that as to federal officers the Fourth Amendment included the exclusion of the evidence seized in violation of its provisions. Even *Wolf* "stoutly adhered" to that proposition. The right to privacy, when conceded operatively enforceable against the States, was not susceptible of destruction by avulsion of the sanction upon which its protection and enjoyment had always been deemed dependent under the *Boyd*, *Weeks,* and *Silverthorne* cases.

Therefore, in extending the substantive protections of due process to all constitutionally unreasonable searches—state or federal—it was logically and constitutionally necessary that the exclusion doctrine—an essential part of the right to privacy—be also insisted upon as an essential ingredient of the right newly recognized by the *Wolf* case. In short, the admission of the new constitutional right by *Wolf* could not consistently tolerate denial of its most important constitutional privilege, namely, the exclusion of the evidence which an accused had been forced to give by reason of the unlawful seizure. To hold otherwise is to grant the right but in reality to withhold its privilege and enjoyment. Only last year the Court itself recognized that the purpose of the exclusionary rule "is to deter—to compel respect for the constitutional guaranty in the only effectively available way—by removing the incentive to disregard it."

Indeed, we are aware of no restraint, similar to that rejected today, conditioning the enforcement of any other basic constitutional right. The right to privacy, no less important than any other right carefully and particularly reserved to the people, would stand in marked contrast to all other rights declared as "basic to a free society." This Court has not hesitated to enforce as strictly against the States as it does against the Federal Government the rights of free speech and of a free press, the rights to notice and to a fair, public trial, including, as it does, the right not to be convicted by use of a coerced confession, however logically relevant it be, and without regard to its reliability.

And nothing could be more certain than that when a coerced confession is involved, "the relevant rules of evidence" are overridden without regard to "the incidence of such conduct by the police," slight or frequent. Why should not the same rule apply to what is tantamount to coerced testimony by way of unconstitutional seizure of goods, papers, effects, documents, etc.? We find that as to the Federal Government, the Fourth and Fifth Amendments and, as to the States, the freedom from unconscionable invasions of privacy and the freedom from convictions based upon coerced confessions do enjoy an "intimate relation" in their perpetuation of "principles of humanity and civil liberty secured . . . only after years of struggle." They express "supplementing phases of the same constitutional purpose—to maintain inviolate large areas of personal privacy." The philosophy of each Amendment and of each freedom is complementary to, although not dependent upon, that of the other in its sphere of influence—the very least that together they assure in either sphere is that no man is to be convicted on unconstitutional evidence.

V.

Moreover, our holding that the exclusionary rule is an essential part of both the Fourth and Fourteenth Amendments is not only the logical dictate of prior cases, but it also makes very good sense. There is no war between the Constitution and common sense. Presently, a federal prosecutor may make no use of evidence illegally seized, but a State's attorney across the street may, although he supposedly is operating under the enforceable prohibitions of the same Amendment. Thus the State, by admitting evidence unlawfully seized, serves to encourage disobedience to the Federal Constitution which it is bound to uphold.

Moreover, as was said in *Elkins*, "the very essence of a healthy federalism depends upon the avoidance of needless conflict between state and federal courts." Such a conflict, hereafter needless, arose this very Term, in *Wilson v. Schnettler*, in which, and in spite of the promise made by *Rea*, we gave full recognition to our practice in this regard by refusing to restrain a federal officer from testifying in a state court as to evidence unconstitutionally seized by him in the performance of his duties. Yet the double standard recognized until today hardly put such a thesis into practice. In non-exclusionary States, federal officers, being human, were by it invited to and did, as our cases indicate, step across the street to the State's attorney with their unconstitutionally seized evidence. Prosecution on the basis of that evidence was then had in a state court in utter disregard of the enforceable Fourth Amendment. If the fruits of an unconstitutional search had been inadmissible in both state and federal courts, this inducement to evasion would have been sooner eliminated. There would be no need to reconcile such cases as *Rea* and *Schnettler*, each pointing up the hazardous uncertainties of our heretofore ambivalent approach.

Federal-state cooperation in the solution of crime under constitutional standards will be promoted, if only by recognition of their now mutual obligation to respect the same fundamental criteria in their approaches. "However much in a particular case insistence upon such rules may appear as a technicality that inures to the benefit of a guilty person, the history of the criminal law proves that tolerance of shortcut methods in law enforcement impairs its enduring effectiveness." Denying shortcuts to only one of two cooperating law enforcement agencies tends naturally to breed legitimate suspicion of "working arrangements" whose results are equally tainted.

There are those who say, as did Justice (then Judge) Cardozo, that under our constitutional exclusionary doctrine "the criminal is to go free because the constable has blundered." In some cases this will undoubtedly be the result. But, as was said in *Elkins*, "there is another consideration—the imperative of judicial integrity." The criminal goes free, if he must, but it is the law that sets him free. Nothing can destroy a government more quickly than its failure to observe its own laws, or worse, its disregard of the charter of its own existence. As Mr. Justice Brandeis, dissenting, said in *Olmstead v. United States*: "Our Government is the potent, the omnipresent teacher. For good or for ill, it teaches the whole people by its example. . . . If the Government becomes a lawbreaker, it breeds contempt for law; it invites every man to become a law unto himself; it invites anarchy." Nor can it lightly be assumed that, as a practical matter, adoption of the exclusionary rule fetters law enforcement.

Only last year this Court expressly considered that contention and found that "pragmatic evidence of a sort" to the contrary was not wanting. The Court noted that

"The federal courts themselves have operated under the exclusionary rule of *Weeks* for almost half a century; yet it has not been suggested either that the Federal Bureau of Investigation has thereby been rendered ineffective, or that the administration of criminal justice in the federal courts has thereby been disrupted. Moreover, the experience of the states is impressive. . . . The movement towards the rule of exclusion has been halting but seemingly inexorable."

The ignoble shortcut to conviction left open to the State tends to destroy the entire system of constitutional restraints on which the liberties of the people rest. Having once recognized that the right to privacy embodied in the Fourth Amendment is enforceable against the States, and that the right to be secure against rude invasions of privacy by state officers is, therefore, constitutional in origin, we can no longer permit that right to remain an empty promise. Because it is enforceable in the same manner and to like effect as other basic rights secured by the Due Process Clause, we can no longer permit it to be revocable at the whim of any police officer who, in the name of law enforcement itself, chooses to suspend its enjoyment. Our decision, founded on reason and truth, gives to the individual no more than that which the Constitution guarantees him, to the police officer no less than that to which honest law enforcement is entitled, and, to the courts, that judicial integrity so necessary in the true administration of justice.

The judgment of the Supreme Court of Ohio is reversed and the cause remanded for further proceedings not inconsistent with this opinion.

Reversed and remanded.

United States v. Leon (1984)
468 U.S. 897

This case presents the question whether the Fourth Amendment exclusionary rule should be modified so as not to bar the use in the prosecution's case in chief of evidence obtained by officers acting in reasonable reliance on a search warrant issued by a detached and neutral magistrate but ultimately found to be unsupported by probable cause. To resolve this question, we must consider once again the tension between the sometimes competing goals of, on the one hand, deterring official misconduct and removing inducements to unreasonable invasions of privacy and, on the other, establishing procedures under which criminal defendants are "acquitted or convicted on the basis of all the evidence which exposes the truth."

I.

In August 1981, a confidential informant of unproven reliability informed an officer of the Burbank Police Department that two persons known to him as "Armando" and "Patsy" were selling large quantities of cocaine and methaqualone from their residence at 620 Price Drive in Burbank, Cal. The informant also indicated that he had witnessed a sale of methaqualone by "Patsy" at the residence approximately five months earlier and had observed at that time a shoebox containing a large amount of cash that belonged to "Patsy." He further declared that "Armando" and "Patsy" generally kept only small quantities of drugs at their residence and stored the remainder at another location in Burbank.

On the basis of this information, the Burbank police initiated an extensive investigation focusing first on the Price Drive residence and later on two other residences as well. Cars parked at the Price Drive residence were determined to belong to respondents Armando Sanchez, who had previously been arrested for possession of marihuana, and Patsy Stewart, who had no criminal record. During the course of the investigation, officers observed an automobile belonging to respondent Ricardo Del Castillo, who had previously been arrested for possession of 50 pounds of marihuana, arrive at the Price Drive residence. The driver of that car entered the house, exited shortly thereafter carrying a small paper sack, and drove away. A check of Del Castillo's probation records led the officers to respondent Alberto Leon, whose telephone number Del Castillo had listed as his employer's. Leon had been arrested in 1980 on drug charges, and a companion had informed the police at that time that Leon was heavily involved in the importation of drugs into this country. Before the current investigation began, the Burbank officers had learned that an informant had told a Glendale police officer that Leon stored a large quantity of methaqualone at his residence in Glendale. During the course of this investigation, the Burbank officers learned that Leon was living at 716 South Sunset Canyon in Burbank.

Subsequently, the officers observed several persons, at least one of whom had prior drug involvement, arriving at the Price Drive residence and leaving with small packages; observed a variety of other material activity at the two residences as well as at a condominium at 7902 Via Magdalena; and witnessed a variety of relevant activity involving respondents' automobiles. The officers also observed respondents Sanchez and Stewart board separate flights for Miami. The pair later returned to Los Angeles together, consented to a search of their luggage that revealed only a small amount of marihuana, and left the airport. Based on these and other observations summarized in the affidavit, Officer Cyril Rombach of the Burbank Police Department, an experienced and well-trained narcotics investigator, prepared an application for a warrant to search 620 Price Drive, 716 South Sunset Canyon, 7902 Via Magdalena, and automobiles registered to each of the respondents for an extensive list of items believed to be related to respondents' drug-trafficking activities. Officer Rombach's extensive application was reviewed by several Deputy District Attorneys.

A facially valid search warrant was issued in September 1981 by a State Superior Court Judge. The ensuing searches produced large quantities of drugs at the Via Magdalena and Sunset Canyon addresses and a small quantity at the Price Drive residence. Other evidence was discovered at each of the residences and in Stewart's and Del Castillo's automobiles. Respondents were indicted by a grand jury in the District Court for the Central District of California and charged with conspiracy to possess and distribute cocaine and a variety of substantive counts.

The respondents then filed motions to suppress the evidence seized pursuant to the warrant. The District Court held an evidentiary hearing and, while recognizing that the case was a close one, granted the motions to suppress in part. It concluded that the affidavit was insufficient to establish probable cause, but did not suppress all of the evidence as to all of the respondents because none of the respondents had standing to challenge all of the searches. In response to a request from the Government, the court made clear that Officer Rombach had acted in good faith, but it rejected the Government's suggestion that the Fourth Amendment exclusionary rule should not apply where evidence is seized in reasonable, good-faith reliance on a search warrant.

The District Court denied the Government's motion for reconsideration, and a divided panel of the Court of Appeals for the Ninth Circuit affirmed. The Court of Appeals first concluded that Officer Rombach's affidavit could not establish probable cause to search the Price Drive residence. To the extent that the affidavit set forth facts demonstrating the basis of the informant's knowledge of criminal activity, the information included was fatally stale. The affidavit, moreover, failed to establish the informant's credibility. Accordingly, the Court of Appeals concluded that the information provided by the informant was inadequate under both prongs of the two-part test established in *Aguilar v. Texas* and *Spinelli v. United States*. The officers' independent investigation neither cured the staleness nor corroborated the details of the informant's declarations. The Court of Appeals then considered whether the affidavit formed a proper basis for the search of the Sunset Canyon residence. In its view, the affidavit included no facts indicating the basis for the informants' statements concerning respondent Leon's criminal activities and was devoid of information establishing the informants' reliability. Because these deficiencies had not been cured by the police investigation, the District Court properly suppressed the fruits of the search. The Court of Appeals refused the Government's invitation to recognize a good-faith exception to the Fourth Amendment exclusionary rule.

The Government's petition for certiorari expressly declined to seek review of the lower courts' determinations that the search warrant was unsupported by probable cause and presented only the question "whether the Fourth Amendment exclusionary rule should be modified so as not to bar the admission of evidence seized in reasonable, good-faith reliance on a search warrant that is subsequently held to be defective." We granted certiorari to consider the propriety of such a modification. Although it undoubtedly is within our power to consider the question whether probable cause existed under the "totality of the circumstances" test announced last Term in *Illinois v. Gates*, that question has not been briefed or argued; and it is also within our authority, which we choose to exercise, to take the case as it comes to us, accepting the Court of Appeals' conclusion that probable cause was lacking under the prevailing legal standards.

We have concluded that, in the Fourth Amendment context, the exclusionary rule can be modified somewhat without jeopardizing its ability to perform its intended functions. Accordingly, we reverse the judgment of the Court of Appeals.

II.

Language in opinions of this Court and of individual Justices has sometimes implied that the exclusionary rule is a necessary corollary of the Fourth Amendment, or that the rule is required by the conjunction of the Fourth and Fifth Amendments. These implications need not detain us long. The Fifth Amendment theory has not withstood critical analysis or the test of time, and the Fourth Amendment "has never been interpreted to proscribe the introduction of illegally seized evidence in all proceedings or against all persons."

A.

The Fourth Amendment contains no provision expressly precluding the use of evidence obtained in violation of its commands, and an examination of its origin and purposes makes clear that the use of fruits of a past unlawful search or seizure "works no new Fourth Amendment wrong." The wrong condemned by the Amendment is "fully accomplished" by the unlawful search or seizure itself, and the exclusionary rule is neither intended nor able to "cure the invasion of the defendant's rights which he has already suffered." The rule thus operates as "a judicially created remedy designed to safeguard Fourth Amendment rights generally through its deterrent effect, rather than a personal constitutional right of the party aggrieved."

Whether the exclusionary sanction is appropriately imposed in a particular case, our decisions make clear, is "an issue separate from the question whether the Fourth Amendment rights of the party seeking to invoke the rule were violated by police conduct." Only the former question is currently before us, and it must be resolved by weighing the costs and benefits of preventing the use in the prosecution's case in chief of inherently trustworthy tangible evidence obtained in reliance on a search warrant issued by a detached and neutral magistrate that ultimately is found to be defective.

The substantial social costs exacted by the exclusionary rule for the vindication of Fourth Amendment rights have long been a source of concern. "Our cases have consistently recognized that unbending application of the exclusionary sanction to enforce ideals of governmental rectitude would impede unacceptably the truth-finding functions of judge and jury." An objectionable collateral consequence of this interference with the criminal justice system's truth-finding function is that some guilty defendants may go free or receive reduced sentences as a result of favorable plea bargains. Particularly when law enforcement officers have acted in objective good faith or their transgressions have been minor, the magnitude of the benefit conferred on such guilty defendants offends basic concepts of the criminal justice system. Indiscriminate application of the exclusionary rule, therefore, may well "generate disrespect for the law and administration of justice." Accordingly, "as with any remedial device, the application of the rule has been restricted to those areas where its remedial objectives are thought most efficaciously served."

B.

Close attention to those remedial objectives has characterized our recent decisions concerning the scope of the Fourth Amendment exclusionary rule. The Court has, to be sure, not seriously questioned, "in the absence of a more efficacious sanction, the continued application of the rule to suppress evidence from the prosecution's case where a Fourth Amendment violation has been substantial and deliberate. . . ." Nevertheless, the balancing approach that has evolved in various contexts—including criminal trials—"forcefully suggests that the exclusionary rule be more generally modified to permit the introduction of evidence obtained in the reasonable good-faith belief that a search or seizure was in accord with the Fourth Amendment."

In *Stone v. Powell*, the Court emphasized the costs of the exclusionary rule, expressed its view that limiting the circumstances under which Fourth Amendment claims could be raised in federal habeas corpus proceedings would not reduce the rule's deterrent effect, and held that a state prisoner who has been afforded a full and fair opportunity to litigate a Fourth Amendment claim may not obtain federal habeas relief on the ground that unlawfully obtained evidence had been introduced at his trial. Proposed extensions of the exclusionary rule to proceedings other than the criminal trial itself have been evaluated and rejected under the same analytic approach. In *United States v. Calandra*, for example, we declined to allow grand jury witnesses to refuse to answer questions based on evidence obtained from an unlawful search or seizure since "any incremental deterrent effect which might be achieved by extending the rule to grand jury proceedings is uncertain at best." Similarly, in *United States v. Janis*, we permitted the use in federal civil proceedings of evidence illegally seized by state officials since the likelihood of deterring police misconduct through such an extension of the exclusionary rule was insufficient to outweigh its substantial social costs. In so doing, we declared that, "if . . . the exclusionary rule does not result in appreciable deterrence, then, clearly, its use in the instant situation is unwarranted."

As cases considering the use of unlawfully obtained evidence in criminal trials themselves make clear, it does not follow from the emphasis on the exclusionary rule's deterrent value that "anything which deters illegal searches is thereby commanded by the Fourth Amendment." In determining whether persons aggrieved solely by the introduction of damaging evidence unlawfully obtained from their co-conspirators or codefendants could seek suppression, for example, we found that the additional benefits of such an extension of the exclusionary rule would not outweigh its costs. Standing to invoke the rule has thus been limited to cases in which the prosecution seeks to use the fruits of an illegal search or seizure against the victim of police misconduct.

Even defendants with standing to challenge the introduction in their criminal trials of unlawfully obtained evidence cannot prevent every conceivable use of such evidence. Evidence obtained in violation of the Fourth Amendment and inadmissible in the prosecution's case in chief may be used to impeach a defendant's direct testimony. A similar assessment of the "incremental furthering" of the ends of the exclusionary rule led us to conclude in *United States v. Havens* that evidence inadmissible in the prosecution's case in chief or otherwise as substantive evidence of guilt may be used to impeach statements made by a defendant in response to "proper cross-examination reasonably suggested by the defendant's direct examination."

When considering the use of evidence obtained in violation of the Fourth Amendment in the prosecution's case in chief, moreover, we have declined to adopt a per se or "but for" rule that would render inadmissible any evidence that came to light through a chain of causation that began with an illegal arrest. We also have held that a witness' testimony may be admitted even when his identity was discovered in an unconstitutional search. The perception underlying these decisions—that the connection between police misconduct and evidence of crime may be sufficiently attenuated to permit the use of that evidence at trial—is a product of considerations relating to the exclusionary rule and the constitutional principles it is designed to protect. In short, the "dissipation of the taint" concept that the Court has applied in deciding whether exclusion is appropriate in a particular case "attempts to mark the point at which the detrimental consequences of illegal police action become so attenuated that the deterrent effect of the exclusionary rule no longer justifies its cost." Not surprisingly in view of this purpose, an assessment of the flagrancy of the police misconduct constitutes an important step in the calculus.

The same attention to the purposes underlying the exclusionary rule also has characterized decisions not involving the scope of the rule itself. We have not required suppression of the fruits of a search incident to an arrest made in good-faith reliance on a substantive criminal statute that subsequently is declared unconstitutional. Similarly, although the Court has been unwilling to conclude that new Fourth Amendment principles are always to have only prospective effect, no Fourth Amendment decision marking a "clear break with the past" has been applied retroactively. The propriety of retroactive application of a newly announced Fourth Amendment principle, moreover, has been assessed largely in terms of the contribution retroactivity might make to the deterrence of police misconduct.

As yet, we have not recognized any form of good-faith exception to the Fourth Amendment exclusionary rule. But the balancing approach that has evolved during the years of experience with the rule provides strong support for the modification currently urged upon us. As we discuss below, our evaluation of the costs and benefits of suppressing reliable physical evidence seized by officers reasonably relying on a warrant issued by a detached and neutral magistrate leads to the conclusion that such evidence should be admissible in the prosecution's case in chief.

III. A.

Because a search warrant "provides the detached scrutiny of a neutral magistrate, which is a more reliable safeguard against improper searches than the hurried judgment of a law enforcement officer 'engaged in the often competitive enterprise of ferreting out crime,'" we have expressed a strong preference for warrants and declared that "in a doubtful or marginal case a search under a warrant may be sustainable where without one it would fall." Reasonable minds frequently may differ on the question whether a particular affidavit establishes probable cause, and we have thus concluded that the preference for warrants is most appropriately effectuated by according "great deference" to a magistrate's determination.

Deference to the magistrate, however, is not boundless. It is clear, first, that the deference accorded to a magistrate's finding of probable cause does not preclude inquiry into the knowing or reckless falsity of the affidavit on which that determination was based. Second, the courts must also insist that the magistrate purport to "perform his 'neutral and detached' function and not serve merely as a rubber stamp for the police." A magistrate failing to "manifest that neutrality and detachment demanded of a judicial officer when presented with a warrant application" and who acts instead as "an adjunct law enforcement officer" cannot provide valid authorization for an otherwise unconstitutional search.

Third, reviewing courts will not defer to a warrant based on an affidavit that does not "provide the magistrate with a substantial basis for determining the existence of probable cause." "Sufficient information must be presented to the magistrate to allow that official to determine probable cause; his action cannot be a mere ratification of the bare conclusions of others." Even if the warrant application was supported by more than a "bare bones" affidavit, a reviewing court may properly conclude that, notwithstanding the deference that magistrates deserve, the warrant was invalid because the magistrate's probable-cause determination reflected an improper analysis of the totality of the circumstances, or because the form of the warrant was improper in some respect.

Only in the first of these three situations, however, has the Court set forth a rationale for suppressing evidence obtained pursuant to a search warrant; in the other areas, it has simply excluded such evidence without considering whether Fourth Amendment interests will be advanced. To the extent that proponents of exclusion rely on its behavioral effects on judges and magistrates in these areas, their reliance is misplaced. First, the exclusionary rule is designed to deter police misconduct rather than to punish the errors of judges and magistrates. Second, there exists no evidence suggesting that judges and magistrates are inclined to ignore or subvert the Fourth Amendment or that lawlessness among these actors requires application of the extreme sanction of exclusion.

Third, and most important, we discern no basis, and are offered none, for believing that exclusion of evidence seized pursuant to a warrant will have a significant deterrent effect on the issuing judge or magistrate. Many of the factors that indicate that the exclusionary rule cannot provide an effective "special" or "general" deterrent for individual offending law enforcement officers apply as well to judges or magistrates. And, to the extent that the rule is thought to operate as a "systemic" deterrent on a wider audience, it clearly can have no such effect on individuals empowered to issue search warrants. Judges and magistrates are not adjuncts to the law enforcement team; as neutral judicial officers, they have no stake in the outcome of particular criminal prosecutions. The threat of exclusion thus cannot be expected significantly to deter them. Imposition of the exclusionary sanction is not necessary meaningfully to inform judicial officers of their errors, and we cannot conclude that admitting evidence obtained pursuant to a warrant while at the same time declaring that the warrant was somehow defective will in any way reduce judicial officers' professional incentives to comply with the Fourth Amendment, encourage them to repeat their mistakes, or lead to the granting of all colorable warrant requests.

If exclusion of evidence obtained pursuant to a subsequently invalidated warrant is to have any deterrent effect, therefore, it must alter the behavior of individual law enforcement officers or the policies of their departments. One could argue that applying the exclusionary rule in cases where the police failed to demonstrate probable cause in the warrant application deters future inadequate presentations or "magistrate shopping" and thus promotes the ends of the Fourth Amendment. Suppressing evidence obtained pursuant to a technically defective warrant supported by probable cause also might encourage officers to scrutinize more closely the form of the warrant and to point out suspected judicial errors. We find such arguments speculative and conclude that suppression of evidence obtained pursuant to a warrant should be ordered only on a case-by-case basis and only in those unusual cases in which exclusion will further the purposes of the exclusionary rule.

We have frequently questioned whether the exclusionary rule can have any deterrent effect when the offending officers acted in the objectively reasonable belief that their conduct did not violate the Fourth Amendment. "No empirical researcher, proponent or opponent of the rule, has yet been able to establish with any assurance whether the rule has a deterrent effect. . . ." But even assuming that the rule effectively deters some police misconduct and provides incentives for the law enforcement profession as a whole to conduct itself in accord with the Fourth Amendment, it cannot be expected, and should not be applied, to deter objectively reasonable law enforcement activity.

As we observed in *Michigan v. Tucker*, and reiterated in *United States v. Peltier*:

"The deterrent purpose of the exclusionary rule necessarily assumes that the police have engaged in willful, or at the very least negligent, conduct which has deprived the defendant of some right. By refusing to admit evidence gained as a result of such conduct, the courts hope to instill in those particular investigating officers, or in their future counterparts, a greater degree of care toward the rights of an accused. Where the official action was pursued in complete good faith, however, the deterrence rationale loses much of its force."

....

In short, where the officer's conduct is objectively reasonable,

"excluding the evidence will not further the ends of the exclusionary rule in any appreciable way; for it is painfully apparent that . . . the officer is acting as a reasonable officer would and should act in similar circumstances. Excluding the evidence can in no way affect his future conduct unless it is to make him less willing to do his duty."

This is particularly true, we believe, when an officer acting with objective good faith has obtained a search warrant from a judge or magistrate and acted within its scope. In most such cases, there is no police illegality and thus nothing to deter. It is the magistrate's responsibility to determine whether the officer's allegations establish probable cause and, if so, to issue a warrant comporting in form with the requirements of the Fourth Amendment. In the ordinary case, an officer cannot be expected to question the magistrate's probable-cause determination or his judgment that the form of the warrant is technically sufficient. "Once the warrant issues, there is literally nothing more the policeman can do in seeking to comply with the law." Penalizing the officer for the magistrate's error, rather than his own, cannot logically contribute to the deterrence of Fourth Amendment violations.

We conclude that the marginal or nonexistent benefits produced by suppressing evidence obtained in objectively reasonable reliance on a subsequently invalidated search warrant cannot justify the substantial costs of exclusion. We do not suggest, however, that exclusion is always inappropriate in cases where an officer has obtained a warrant and abided by its terms. "Searches pursuant to a warrant will rarely require any deep inquiry into reasonableness," for "a warrant issued by a magistrate normally suffices to establish" that a law enforcement officer has "acted in good faith in conducting the search." Nevertheless, the officer's reliance on the magistrate's probable-cause determination and on the technical sufficiency of the warrant he issues must be objectively reasonable, and it is clear that in some circumstances the officer will have no reasonable grounds for believing that the warrant was properly issued.

Suppression therefore remains an appropriate remedy if the magistrate or judge in issuing a warrant was misled by information in an affidavit that the affiant knew was false or would have known was false except for his reckless disregard of the truth. The exception we recognize today will also not apply in cases where the issuing magistrate wholly abandoned his judicial role in the manner condemned in *Lo-Ji Sales, Inc. v. New York*; in such circumstances, no reasonably well trained officer should rely on the warrant. Nor would an officer manifest objective good faith in relying on a warrant based on an affidavit "so lacking in indicia of probable cause as to render official belief in its existence entirely unreasonable." Finally, depending on the circumstances of the particular case, a warrant may be so facially deficient—i.e., in failing to particularize the place to be searched or the things to be seized–that the executing officers cannot reasonably presume it to be valid.

In so limiting the suppression remedy, we leave untouched the probable-cause standard and the various requirements for a valid warrant. Other objections to the modification of the Fourth Amendment exclusionary rule we consider to be insubstantial. The good-faith exception for searches conducted pursuant to warrants is not intended to signal our unwillingness strictly to enforce the requirements of the Fourth Amendment, and we do not believe that it will have this effect. As we have already suggested, the good-faith exception, turning as it does on objective reasonableness, should not be difficult to apply in practice. When officers have acted pursuant to a warrant, the prosecution should ordinarily be able to establish objective good faith without a substantial expenditure of judicial time.

Nor are we persuaded that application of a good-faith exception to searches conducted pursuant to warrants will preclude review of the constitutionality of the search or seizure, deny needed guidance from the courts, or freeze Fourth Amendment law in its present state. There is no need for courts to adopt the inflexible practice of always deciding whether the officers' conduct manifested objective good faith before turning to the question whether the Fourth Amendment has been violated. Defendants seeking suppression of the fruits of allegedly unconstitutional searches or seizures undoubtedly raise live controversies which Art. III empowers federal courts to adjudicate....

If the resolution of a particular Fourth Amendment question is necessary to guide future action by law enforcement officers and magistrates, nothing will prevent reviewing courts from deciding that question before turning to the good-faith issue. Indeed, it frequently will be difficult to determine whether the officers acted reasonably without resolving the Fourth Amendment issue. Even if the Fourth Amendment question is not one of broad import, reviewing courts could decide in particular cases that magistrates under their supervision need to be informed of their errors and so evaluate the officers' good faith only after finding a violation. In other circumstances, those courts could reject suppression motions posing no important Fourth Amendment questions by turning immediately to a consideration of the officers' good faith. We have no reason to believe that our Fourth Amendment jurisprudence would suffer by allowing reviewing courts to exercise an informed discretion in making this choice.

IV.

When the principles we have enunciated today are applied to the facts of this case, it is apparent that the judgment of the Court of Appeals cannot stand. The Court of Appeals applied the prevailing legal standards to Officer Rombach's warrant application and concluded that the application could not support the magistrate's probable-cause determination. In so doing, the court clearly informed the magistrate that he had erred in issuing the challenged warrant. This aspect of the court's judgment is not under attack in this proceeding.

Having determined that the warrant should not have issued, the Court of Appeals understandably declined to adopt a modification of the Fourth Amendment exclusionary rule that this Court had not previously sanctioned. Although the modification finds strong support in our previous cases, the Court of Appeals' commendable self-restraint is not to be criticized. We have now reexamined the purposes of the exclusionary rule and the propriety of its application in cases where officers have relied on a subsequently invalidated search warrant. Our conclusion is that the rule's purposes will only rarely be served by applying it in such circumstances.

In the absence of an allegation that the magistrate abandoned his detached and neutral role, suppression is appropriate only if the officers were dishonest or reckless in preparing their affidavit or could not have harbored an objectively reasonable belief in the existence of probable cause. Only respondent Leon has contended that no reasonably well trained police officer could have believed that there existed probable cause to search his house; significantly, the other respondents advance no comparable argument. Officer Rombach's application for a warrant clearly was supported by much more than a "bare bones" affidavit. The affidavit related the results of an extensive investigation and, as the opinions of the divided panel of the Court of Appeals make clear, provided evidence sufficient to create disagreement among thoughtful and competent judges as to the existence of probable cause. Under these circumstances, the officers' reliance on the magistrate's determination of probable cause was objectively reasonable, and application of the extreme sanction of exclusion is inappropriate.

Accordingly, the judgment of the Court of Appeals is Reversed.

Nix v. Williams (1984)
467 U.S. 431

This case established the "inevitable discovery" exception to the exclusionary rule. That is, if police would have found the evidence by legal means anyway, then invoking the exclusionary rule serves no purpose.

We granted certiorari to consider whether, at respondent Williams' second murder trial in state court, evidence pertaining to the discovery and condition of the victim's body was properly admitted on the ground that it would ultimately or inevitably have been discovered even if no violation of any constitutional or statutory provision had taken place.

I. A.

On December 24, 1968, 10-year-old Pamela Powers disappeared from a YMCA building in Des Moines, Iowa, where she had accompanied her parents to watch an athletic contest. Shortly after she disappeared, Williams was seen leaving the YMCA carrying a large bundle wrapped in a blanket; a 14-year-old boy who had helped Williams open his car door reported that he had seen "two legs in it and they were skinny and white."

Williams' car was found the next day 160 miles east of Des Moines in Davenport, Iowa. Later several items of clothing belonging to the child, some of Williams' clothing, and an army blanket like the one used to wrap the bundle that Williams carried out of the YMCA were found at a rest stop on Interstate 80 near Grinnell, between Des Moines and Davenport. A warrant was issued for Williams' arrest.

Police surmised that Williams had left Pamela Powers or her body somewhere between Des Moines and the Grinnell rest stop where some of the young girl's clothing had been found. On December 26, the Iowa Bureau of Criminal Investigation initiated a large-scale search. Two hundred volunteers divided into teams began the search 21 miles east of Grinnell, covering an area several miles to the north and south of Interstate 80. They moved westward from Poweshiek County, in which Grinnell was located, into Jasper County. Searchers were instructed to check all roads, abandoned farm buildings, ditches, culverts, and any other place in which the body of a small child could be hidden.

Meanwhile, Williams surrendered to local police in Davenport, where he was promptly arraigned. Williams contacted a Des Moines attorney who arranged for an attorney in Davenport to meet Williams at the Davenport police station. Des Moines police informed counsel they would pick Williams up in Davenport and return him to Des Moines without questioning him. Two Des Moines detectives then drove to Davenport, took Williams into custody, and proceeded to drive him back to Des Moines.

During the return trip, one of the policemen, Detective Leaming, began a conversation with Williams, saying:

"I want to give you something to think about while we're traveling down the road. . . . They are predicting several inches of snow for tonight, and I feel that you yourself are the only person that knows where this little girl's body is. . . and if you get a snow on top of it you yourself may be unable to find it. And since we will be going right past the area where the body is on the way into Des Moines, I feel that we could stop and locate the body, that the parents of this little girl should be entitled to a Christian burial for the little girl who was snatched away from them on Christmas Eve and murdered. . . . After a snow storm we may not be able to find it at all."

Leaming told Williams he knew the body was in the area of Mitchellville—a town they would be passing on the way to Des Moines. He concluded the conversation by saying: "I do not want you to answer me. . . . Just think about it. . . ."

Later, as the police car approached Grinnell, Williams asked Leaming whether the police had found the young girl's shoes. After Leaming replied that he was unsure, Williams directed the police to a point near a service station where he said he had left the shoes; they were not found. As they continued the drive to Des Moines, Williams asked whether the blanket had been found and then directed the officers to a rest area in Grinnell where he said he had disposed of the blanket; they did not find the blanket. At this point Leaming and his party were joined by the officers in charge of the search. As they approached Mitchellville, Williams, without any further conversation, agreed to direct the officers to the child's body.

The officers directing the search had called off the search at 3 p. m., when they left the Grinnell Police Department to join Leaming at the rest area. At that time, one search team near the Jasper County-Polk County line was only two and one-half miles from where Williams soon guided Leaming and his party to the body. The child's body was found next to a culvert in a ditch beside a gravel road in Polk County, about two miles south of Interstate 80, and essentially within the area to be searched.

B. First Trial

In February 1969 Williams was indicted for first-degree murder. Before trial in the Iowa court, his counsel moved to suppress evidence of the body and all related evidence including the condition of the body as shown by the autopsy. The ground for the motion was that such evidence was the "fruit" or product of Williams' statements made during the automobile ride from Davenport to Des Moines and prompted by Leaming's statements. The motion to suppress was denied.

The jury found Williams guilty of first-degree murder; the judgment of conviction was affirmed by the Iowa Supreme Court. Williams then sought release on habeas corpus in the United States District Court for the Southern District of Iowa. That court concluded that the evidence in question had been wrongly admitted at Williams' trial; a divided panel of the Court of Appeals for the Eighth Circuit agreed.

We granted certiorari, and a divided Court affirmed, holding that Detective Leaming had obtained incriminating statements from Williams by what was viewed as interrogation in violation of his right to counsel. This Court's opinion noted, however, that although Williams' incriminating statements could not be introduced into evidence at a second trial, evidence of the body's location and condition "might well be admissible on the theory that the body would have been discovered in any event, even had incriminating statements not been elicited from Williams."

C. Second Trial

At Williams' second trial in 1977 in the Iowa court, the prosecution did not offer Williams' statements into evidence, nor did it seek to show that Williams had directed the police to the child's body. However, evidence of the condition of her body as it was found, articles and photographs of her clothing, and the results of post mortem medical and chemical tests on the body were admitted. The trial court concluded that the State had proved by a preponderance of the evidence that, if the search had not been suspended and Williams had not led the police to the victim, her body would have been discovered "within a short time" in essentially the same condition as it was actually found. The trial court also ruled that if the police had not located the body, "the search would clearly have been taken up again where it left off, given the extreme circumstances of this case and the body would have been found in short order."

In finding that the body would have been discovered in essentially the same condition as it was actually found, the court noted that freezing temperatures had prevailed and tissue deterioration would have been suspended. The challenged evidence was admitted and the jury again found Williams guilty of first-degree murder; he was sentenced to life in prison.

On appeal, the Supreme Court of Iowa again affirmed. That court held that there was in fact a "hypothetical independent source" exception to the exclusionary rule:

"After the defendant has shown unlawful conduct on the part of the police, the State has the burden to show by a preponderance of the evidence that (1) the police did not act in bad faith for the purpose of hastening discovery of the evidence in question, and (2) that the evidence in question would have been discovered by lawful means."

As to the first element, the Iowa Supreme Court, having reviewed the relevant cases, stated:

"The issue of the propriety of the police conduct in this case, as noted earlier in this opinion, has caused the closest possible division of views in every appellate court which has considered the question. In light of the legitimate disagreement among individuals well versed in the law of criminal procedure who were given the opportunity for calm deliberation, it cannot be said that the actions of the police were taken in bad faith."

The Iowa court then reviewed the evidence *de novo* and concluded that the State had shown by a preponderance of the evidence that, even if Williams had not guided police to the child's body, it would inevitably have been found by lawful activity of the search party before its condition had materially changed.

In 1980 Williams renewed his attack on the state-court conviction by seeking a writ of habeas corpus in the United States District Court for the Southern District of Iowa. The District Court conducted its own independent review of the evidence and concluded, as had the state courts, that the body would inevitably have been found by the searchers in essentially the same condition it was in when Williams led police to its discovery. The District Court denied Williams' petition.

The Court of Appeals for the Eighth Circuit reversed; an equally divided court denied rehearing *en banc*. That court assumed, without deciding, that there is an inevitable discovery exception to the exclusionary rule and that the Iowa Supreme Court correctly stated that exception to require proof that the police did not act in bad faith and that the evidence would have been discovered absent any constitutional violation. In reversing the District Court's denial of habeas relief, the Court of Appeals stated:

"We hold that the State has not met the first requirement. It is therefore unnecessary to decide whether the state courts' finding that the body would have been discovered anyway is fairly supported by the record. It is also unnecessary to decide whether the State must prove the two elements of the exception by clear and convincing evidence, as defendant argues, or by a preponderance of the evidence, as the state courts held. The state trial court, in denying the motion to suppress, made no finding one way or the other on the question of bad faith. Its opinion does not even mention the issue and seems to proceed on the assumption—contrary to the rule of law later laid down by the Supreme Court of Iowa—that the State needed to show only that the body would have been discovered in any event. The Iowa Supreme Court did expressly address the issue . . . and a finding by an appellate court of a state is entitled to the same presumption of correctness that attaches to trial-court findings under 28 U. S. C. § 2254(d). . . . We conclude, however, that the state Supreme Court's finding that the police did not act in bad faith is not entitled to the shield of § 2254(d). . . ."

We granted the State's petition for certiorari, and we reverse.

I. A.

The Iowa Supreme Court correctly stated that the "vast majority" of all courts, both state and federal, recognize an inevitable discovery exception to the exclusionary rule. We are now urged to adopt and apply the so-called ultimate or inevitable discovery exception to the exclusionary rule.

Williams contends that evidence of the body's location and condition is "fruit of the poisonous tree," i. e., the "fruit" or product of Detective Leaming's plea to help the child's parents give her "a Christian burial," which this Court had already held equated to interrogation. He contends that admitting the challenged evidence violated the Sixth Amendment whether it would have been inevitably discovered or not. Williams also contends that, if the inevitable discovery doctrine is constitutionally permissible, it must include a threshold showing of police good faith.

B.

The doctrine requiring courts to suppress evidence as the tainted "fruit" of unlawful governmental conduct had its genesis in *Silverthorne Lumber Co. v. United States*; there, the Court held that the exclusionary rule applies not only to the illegally obtained evidence itself, but also to other incriminating evidence derived from the primary evidence. The holding of *Silverthorne* was carefully limited, however, for the Court emphasized that such information does not automatically become "sacred and inaccessible."

"If knowledge of such facts is gained from an independent source, they may be proved like any others. . . ."

Wong Sun v. United States extended the exclusionary rule to evidence that was the indirect product or "fruit" of unlawful police conduct, but there again the Court emphasized that evidence that has been illegally obtained need not always be suppressed, stating:

"We need not hold that all evidence is 'fruit of the poisonous tree' simply because it would not have come to light but for the illegal actions of the police. Rather, the more apt question in such a case is 'whether, granting establishment of the primary illegality, the evidence to which instant objection is made has been come at by exploitation of that illegality or instead by means sufficiently distinguishable to be purged of the primary taint.'"

The Court thus pointedly negated the kind of good-faith requirement advanced by the Court of Appeals in reversing the District Court.

Although *Silverthorne* and *Wong Sun* involved violations of the Fourth Amendment, the "fruit of the poisonous tree" doctrine has not been limited to cases in which there has been a Fourth Amendment violation. The Court has applied the doctrine where the violations were of the Sixth Amendment.

The core rationale consistently advanced by this Court for extending the exclusionary rule to evidence that is the fruit of unlawful police conduct has been that this admittedly drastic and socially costly course is needed to deter police from violations of constitutional and statutory protections. This Court has accepted the argument that the way to ensure such protections is to exclude evidence seized as a result of such violations notwithstanding the high social cost of letting persons obviously guilty go unpunished for their crimes. On this rationale, the prosecution is not to be put in a better position than it would have been in if no illegality had transpired.

By contrast, the derivative evidence analysis ensures that the prosecution is not put in a worse position simply because of some earlier police error or misconduct. The independent source doctrine allows admission of evidence that has been discovered by means wholly independent of any constitutional violation. That doctrine, although closely related to the inevitable discovery doctrine, does not apply here; Williams' statements to Leaming indeed led police to the child's body, but that is not the whole story. The independent source doctrine teaches us that the interest of society in deterring unlawful police conduct and the public interest in having juries receive all probative evidence of a crime are properly balanced by putting the police in the same, not a worse, position that they would have been in if no police error or misconduct had occurred.

When the challenged evidence has an independent source, exclusion of such evidence would put the police in a worse position than they would have been in absent any error or violation. There is a functional similarity between these two doctrines in that exclusion of evidence that would inevitably have been discovered would also put the government in a worse position, because the police would have obtained that evidence if no misconduct had taken place. Thus, while the independent source exception would not justify admission of evidence in this case, its rationale is wholly consistent with and justifies our adoption of the ultimate or inevitable discovery exception to the exclusionary rule.

It is clear that the cases implementing the exclusionary rule "begin with the premise that the challenged evidence is in some sense the product of illegal governmental activity." Of course, this does not end the inquiry. If the prosecution can establish by a preponderance of the evidence that the information ultimately or inevitably would have been discovered by lawful means—here the volunteers' search—then the deterrence rationale has so little basis that the evidence should be received. Anything less would reject logic, experience, and common sense.

The requirement that the prosecution must prove the absence of bad faith, imposed here by the Court of Appeals, would place courts in the position of withholding from juries relevant and undoubted truth that would have been available to police absent any unlawful police activity. Of course, that view would put the police in a worse position than they would have been in if no unlawful conduct had transpired. And, of equal importance, it wholly fails to take into account the enormous societal cost of excluding truth in the search for truth in the administration of justice. Nothing in this Court's prior holdings supports any such formalistic, pointless, and punitive approach.

The Court of Appeals concluded, without analysis, that if an absence-of-bad-faith requirement were not imposed, "the temptation to risk deliberate violations of the Sixth Amendment would be too great, and the deterrent effect of the Exclusionary Rule reduced too far." We reject that view. A police officer who is faced with the opportunity to obtain evidence illegally will rarely, if ever, be in a position to calculate whether the evidence sought would inevitably be discovered....

On the other hand, when an officer is aware that the evidence will inevitably be discovered, he will try to avoid engaging in any questionable practice. In that situation, there will be little to gain from taking any dubious "shortcuts" to obtain the evidence. Significant disincentives to obtaining evidence illegally—including the possibility of departmental discipline and civil liability—also lessen the likelihood that the ultimate or inevitable discovery exception will promote police misconduct. In these circumstances, the societal costs of the exclusionary rule far outweigh any possible benefits to deterrence that a good-faith requirement might produce.

Williams contends that because he did not waive his right to the assistance of counsel, the Court may not balance competing values in deciding whether the challenged evidence was properly admitted. He argues that, unlike the exclusionary rule in the Fourth Amendment context, the essential purpose of which is to deter police misconduct, the Sixth Amendment exclusionary rule is designed to protect the right to a fair trial and the integrity of the factfinding process. Williams contends that, when those interests are at stake, the societal costs of excluding evidence obtained from responses presumed involuntary are irrelevant in determining whether such evidence should be excluded. We disagree.

Exclusion of physical evidence that would inevitably have been discovered adds nothing to either the integrity or fairness of a criminal trial. The Sixth Amendment right to counsel protects against unfairness by preserving the adversary process in which the reliability of proffered evidence may be tested in cross-examination. Here, however, Detective Leaming's conduct did nothing to impugn the reliability of the evidence in question—the body of the child and its condition as it was found, articles of clothing found on the body, and the autopsy. No one would seriously contend that the presence of counsel in the police car when Leaming appealed to Williams' decent human instincts would have had any bearing on the reliability of the body as evidence. Suppression, in these circumstances, would do nothing whatever to promote the integrity of the trial process, but would inflict a wholly unacceptable burden on the administration of criminal justice.

Nor would suppression ensure fairness on the theory that it tends to safeguard the adversary system of justice. To assure the fairness of trial proceedings, this Court has held that assistance of counsel must be available at pretrial confrontations where "the subsequent trial cannot cure an otherwise one-sided confrontation between prosecuting authorities and the uncounseled defendant." Fairness can be assured by placing the State and the accused in the same positions they would have been in had the impermissible conduct not taken place. However, if the government can prove that the evidence would have been obtained inevitably and, therefore, would have been admitted regardless of any overreaching by the police, there is no rational basis to keep that evidence from the jury in order to ensure the fairness of the trial proceedings. In that situation, the State has gained no advantage at trial and the defendant has suffered no prejudice. Indeed, suppression of the evidence would operate to undermine the adversary system by putting the State in a worse position than it would have occupied without any police misconduct. Williams' argument that inevitable discovery constitutes impermissible balancing of values is without merit.

More than a half century ago, Judge, later Justice, Cardozo made his seminal observation that under the exclusionary rule "the criminal is to go free because the constable has blundered." Prophetically, he went on to consider "how far-reaching in its effect upon society" the exclusionary rule would be when

"the pettiest peace officer would have it in his power through overzeal or indiscretion to confer immunity upon an offender for crimes the most flagitious."

Someday, Cardozo speculated, some court might press the exclusionary rule to the outer limits of its logic—or beyond—and suppress evidence relating to the "body of a murdered" victim because of the means by which it was found. But when, as here, the evidence in question would inevitably have been discovered without reference to the police error or misconduct, there is no nexus sufficient to provide a taint and the evidence is admissible.

C.

The Court of Appeals did not find it necessary to consider whether the record fairly supported the finding that the volunteer search party would ultimately or inevitably have discovered the victim's body. However, three courts independently reviewing the evidence have found that the body of the child inevitably would have been found by the searchers. Williams challenges these findings, asserting that the record contains only the "post hoc rationalization" that the search efforts would have proceeded two and one-half miles into Polk County where Williams had led police to the body.

When that challenge was made at the suppression hearing preceding Williams' second trial, the prosecution offered the testimony of Agent Ruxlow of the Iowa Bureau of Criminal Investigation. Ruxlow had organized and directed some 200 volunteers who were searching for the child's body. The searchers were instructed "to check all the roads, the ditches, any culverts. . . . If they came upon any abandoned farm buildings, they were instructed to go onto the property and search those abandoned farm buildings or any other places where a small child could be secreted." Ruxlow testified that he marked off highway maps of Poweshiek and Jasper Counties in grid fashion, divided the volunteers into teams of four to six persons, and assigned each team to search specific grid areas. Ruxlow also testified that, if the search had not been suspended because of Williams' promised cooperation, it would have continued into Polk County, using the same grid system. Although he had previously marked off into grids only the highway maps of Poweshiek and Jasper Counties, Ruxlow had obtained a map of Polk County, which he said he would have marked off in the same manner had it been necessary for the search to continue.

The search had commenced at approximately 10 a. m. and moved westward through Poweshiek County into Jasper County. At approximately 3 p. m., after Williams had volunteered to cooperate with the police, Detective Leaming, who was in the police car with Williams, sent word to Ruxlow and the other Special Agent directing the search to meet him at the Grinnell truck stop and the search was suspended at that time. Ruxlow also stated that he was "under the impression that there was a possibility" that Williams would lead them to the child's body at that time. The search was not resumed once it was learned that Williams had led the police to the body, which was found two and one-half miles from where the search had stopped in what would have been the easternmost grid to be searched in Polk County. There was testimony that it would have taken an additional three to five hours to discover the body if the search had continued; the body was found near a culvert, one of the kinds of places the teams had been specifically directed to search.

On this record it is clear that the search parties were approaching the actual location of the body, and we are satisfied, along with three courts earlier, that the volunteer search teams would have resumed the search had Williams not earlier led the police to the body and the body inevitably would have been found. The evidence asserted by Williams as newly discovered, i.e., certain photographs of the body and deposition testimony of Agent Ruxlow made in connection with the federal habeas proceeding, does not demonstrate that the material facts were inadequately developed in the suppression hearing in state court or that Williams was denied a full, fair, and adequate opportunity to present all relevant facts at the suppression hearing.

The judgment of the Court of Appeals is reversed, and the case is remanded for further proceedings consistent with this opinion.

It is so ordered.

Tennessee v. Garner (1985)
471 U.S. 1

In this case, the court examined the ancient "fleeing felon" rule. Under this common law doctrine, a felon trying to escape law enforcement could be captured via the use of deadly force. The Supreme Court determined that such a brutal arrest is a seizure under the Fourth Amendment. The court further determined that such a seizure was inherently a violation of the Constitution of the fleeing felon did not pose a deadly danger to the officer or the community.

This case requires us to determine the constitutionality of the use of deadly force to prevent the escape of an apparently unarmed suspected felon. We conclude that such force may not be used unless it is necessary to prevent the escape and the officer has probable cause to believe that the suspect poses a significant threat of death or serious physical injury to the officer or others.

I.

At about 10:45 p. m. on October 3, 1974, Memphis Police Officers Elton Hymon and Leslie Wright were dispatched to answer a "prowler inside call." Upon arriving at the scene they saw a woman standing on her porch and gesturing toward the adjacent house. She told them she had heard glass breaking and that "they" or "someone" was breaking in next door. While Wright radioed the dispatcher to say that they were on the scene, Hymon went behind the house. He heard a door slam and saw someone run across the backyard. The fleeing suspect, who was appellee-respondent's decedent, Edward Garner, stopped at a 6-feet-high chain link fence at the edge of the yard. With the aid of a flashlight, Hymon was able to see Garner's face and hands. He saw no sign of a weapon, and, though not certain, was "reasonably sure" and "figured" that Garner was unarmed. He thought Garner was 17 or 18 years old and about 5'5" or 5'7" tall. While Garner was crouched at the base of the fence, Hymon called out "police, halt" and took a few steps toward him. Garner then began to climb over the fence. Convinced that if Garner made it over the fence he would elude capture, Hymon shot him. The bullet hit Garner in the back of the head. Garner was taken by ambulance to a hospital, where he died on the operating table. Ten dollars and a purse taken from the house were found on his body.

In using deadly force to prevent the escape, Hymon was acting under the authority of a Tennessee statute and pursuant to Police Department policy. The statute provides that "if, after notice of the intention to arrest the defendant, he either flee or forcibly resist, the officer may use all the necessary means to effect the arrest." The Department policy was slightly more restrictive than the statute, but still allowed the use of deadly force in cases of burglary. The incident was reviewed by the Memphis Police Firearm's Review Board and presented to a grand jury. Neither took any action.

Garner's father then brought this action in the Federal District Court for the Western District of Tennessee, seeking damages under 42 U. S. C. § 1983 for asserted violations of Garner's constitutional rights. The complaint alleged that the shooting violated the Fourth, Fifth, Sixth, Eighth, and Fourteenth Amendments of the United States Constitution. It named as defendants Officer Hymon, the Police Department, its Director, and the Mayor and city of Memphis. After a 3-day bench trial, the District Court entered judgment for all defendants. It dismissed the claims against the Mayor and the Director for lack of evidence. It then concluded that Hymon's actions were authorized by the Tennessee statute, which in turn was constitutional. Hymon had employed the only reasonable and practicable means of preventing Garner's escape. Garner had "recklessly and heedlessly attempted to vault over the fence to escape, thereby assuming the risk of being fired upon."

The Court of Appeals for the Sixth Circuit affirmed with regard to Hymon, finding that he had acted in good-faith reliance on the Tennessee statute and was therefore within the scope of his qualified immunity. It remanded for reconsideration of the possible liability of the city, however, in light of *Monell v. New York City Dept. of Social Services*, which had come down after the District Court's decision. The District Court was directed to consider whether a city enjoyed a qualified immunity, whether the use of deadly force and hollow point bullets in these circumstances was constitutional, and whether any unconstitutional municipal conduct flowed from a "policy or custom" as required for liability under *Monell*.

The District Court concluded that Monell did not affect its decision. While acknowledging some doubt as to the possible immunity of the city, it found that the statute, and Hymon's actions, were constitutional. Given this conclusion, it declined to consider the "policy or custom" question.

The Court of Appeals reversed and remanded. It reasoned that the killing of a fleeing suspect is a "seizure" under the Fourth Amendment, and is therefore constitutional only if "reasonable." The Tennessee statute failed as applied to this case because it did not adequately limit the use of deadly force by distinguishing between felonies of different magnitudes—"the facts, as found, did not justify the use of deadly force under the Fourth Amendment." Officers cannot resort to deadly force unless they "have probable cause . . . to believe that the suspect has committed a felony and poses a threat to the safety of the officers or a danger to the community if left at large."

The State of Tennessee, which had intervened to defend the statute, appealed to this Court. The city filed a petition for certiorari. We noted probable jurisdiction in the appeal and granted the petition.

II.

Whenever an officer restrains the freedom of a person to walk away, he has seized that person. While it is not always clear just when minimal police interference becomes a seizure, there can be no question that apprehension by the use of deadly force is a seizure subject to the reasonableness requirement of the Fourth Amendment.

A.

A police officer may arrest a person if he has probable cause to believe that person committed a crime. Petitioners and appellant argue that if this requirement is satisfied the Fourth Amendment has nothing to say about how that seizure is made. This submission ignores the many cases in which this Court, by balancing the extent of the intrusion against the need for it, has examined the reasonableness of the manner in which a search or seizure is conducted. To determine the constitutionality of a seizure "we must balance the nature and quality of the intrusion on the individual's Fourth Amendment interests against the importance of the governmental interests alleged to justify the intrusion." We have described "the balancing of competing interests" as "the key principle of the Fourth Amendment." Because one of the factors is the extent of the intrusion, it is plain that reasonableness depends on not only when a seizure is made, but also how it is carried out.

Applying these principles to particular facts, the Court has held that governmental interests did not support a lengthy detention of luggage, *United States v. Place* an airport seizure not "carefully tailored to its underlying justification," surgery under general anesthesia to obtain evidence, or detention for fingerprinting without probable cause. On the other hand, under the same approach it has upheld the taking of fingernail scrapings from a suspect an unannounced entry into a home to prevent the destruction of evidence, administrative housing inspections without probable cause to believe that a code violation will be found, and a blood test of a drunken-driving suspect. In each of these cases, the question was whether the totality of the circumstances justified a particular sort of search or seizure.

B.

The same balancing process applied in the cases cited above demonstrates that, notwithstanding probable cause to seize a suspect, an officer may not always do so by killing him. The intrusiveness of a seizure by means of deadly force is unmatched. The suspect's fundamental interest in his own life need not be elaborated upon. The use of deadly force also frustrates the interest of the individual, and of society, in judicial determination of guilt and punishment. Against these interests are ranged governmental interests in effective law enforcement. It is argued that overall violence will be reduced by encouraging the peaceful submission of suspects who know that they may be shot if they flee. Effectiveness in making arrests requires the resort to deadly force, or at least the meaningful threat thereof. "Being able to arrest such individuals is a condition precedent to the state's entire system of law enforcement."

Without in any way disparaging the importance of these goals, we are not convinced that the use of deadly force is a sufficiently productive means of accomplishing them to justify the killing of nonviolent suspects. The use of deadly force is a self-defeating way of apprehending a suspect and so setting the criminal justice mechanism in motion. If successful, it guarantees that that mechanism will not be set in motion. And while the meaningful threat of deadly force might be thought to lead to the arrest of more live suspects by discouraging escape attempts, the presently available evidence does not support this thesis. The fact is that a majority of police departments in this country have forbidden the use of deadly force against nonviolent suspects. If those charged with the enforcement of the criminal law have abjured the use of deadly force in arresting nondangerous felons, there is a substantial basis for doubting that the use of such force is an essential attribute of the arrest power in all felony cases. Petitioners and appellant have not persuaded us that shooting nondangerous fleeing suspects is so vital as to outweigh the suspect's interest in his own life.

The use of deadly force to prevent the escape of all felony suspects, whatever the circumstances, is constitutionally unreasonable. It is not better that all felony suspects die than that they escape. Where the suspect poses no immediate threat to the officer and no threat to others, the harm resulting from failing to apprehend him does not justify the use of deadly force to do so. It is no doubt unfortunate when a suspect who is in sight escapes, but the fact that the police arrive a little late or are a little slower afoot does not always justify killing the suspect. A police officer may not seize an unarmed, nondangerous suspect by shooting him dead. The Tennessee statute is unconstitutional insofar as it authorizes the use of deadly force against such fleeing suspects.

It is not, however, unconstitutional on its face. Where the officer has probable cause to believe that the suspect poses a threat of serious physical harm, either to the officer or to others, it is not constitutionally unreasonable to prevent escape by using deadly force. Thus, if the suspect threatens the officer with a weapon or there is probable cause to believe that he has committed a crime involving the infliction or threatened infliction of serious physical harm, deadly force may be used if necessary to prevent escape, and if, where feasible, some warning has been given. As applied in such circumstances, the Tennessee statute would pass constitutional muster.

I. A.

It is insisted that the Fourth Amendment must be construed in light of the common-law rule, which allowed the use of whatever force was necessary to effect the arrest of a fleeing felon, though not a misdemeanant. As stated in Hale's posthumously published *Pleas of the Crown*:

"If persons that are pursued by these officers for felony or the just suspicion thereof . . . shall not yield themselves to these officers, but shall either resist or fly before they are apprehended or being apprehended shall rescue themselves and resist or fly, so that they cannot be otherwise apprehended, and are upon necessity slain therein, because they cannot be otherwise taken, it is no felony."

....

The State and city argue that because this was the prevailing rule at the time of the adoption of the Fourth Amendment and for some time thereafter, and is still in force in some States, use of deadly force against a fleeing felon must be "reasonable." It is true that this Court has often looked to the common law in evaluating the reasonableness, for Fourth Amendment purposes, of police activity. On the other hand, it "has not simply frozen into constitutional law those law enforcement practices that existed at the time of the Fourth Amendment's passage." Because of sweeping change in the legal and technological context, reliance on the common-law rule in this case would be a mistaken literalism that ignores the purposes of a historical inquiry.

B.

It has been pointed out many times that the common-law rule is best understood in light of the fact that it arose at a time when virtually all felonies were punishable by death. "Though effected without the protections and formalities of an orderly trial and conviction, the killing of a resisting or fleeing felon resulted in no greater consequences than those authorized for punishment of the felony of which the individual was charged or suspected." Courts have also justified the common-law rule by emphasizing the relative dangerousness of felons.

Neither of these justifications makes sense today. Almost all crimes formerly punishable by death no longer are or can be. And while in earlier times "the gulf between the felonies and the minor offences was broad and deep," today the distinction is minor and often arbitrary. Many crimes classified as misdemeanors, or nonexistent, at common law are now felonies. These changes have undermined the concept, which was questionable to begin with, that use of deadly force against a fleeing felon is merely a speedier execution of someone who has already forfeited his life. They have also made the assumption that a "felon" is more dangerous than a misdemeanant untenable. Indeed, numerous misdemeanors involve conduct more dangerous than many felonies.

There is an additional reason why the common-law rule cannot be directly translated to the present day. The common-law rule developed at a time when weapons were rudimentary. Deadly force could be inflicted almost solely in a hand-to-hand struggle during which, necessarily, the safety of the arresting officer was at risk. Handguns were not carried by police officers until the latter half of the last century. Only then did it become possible to use deadly force from a distance as a means of apprehension. As a practical matter, the use of deadly force under the standard articulation of the common-law rule has an altogether different meaning—and harsher consequences—now than in past centuries.

One other aspect of the common-law rule bears emphasis. It forbids the use of deadly force to apprehend a misdemeanant, condemning such action as disproportionately severe. In short, though the common-law pedigree of Tennessee's rule is pure on its face, changes in the legal and technological context mean the rule is distorted almost beyond recognition when literally applied.

C.

In evaluating the reasonableness of police procedures under the Fourth Amendment, we have also looked to prevailing rules in individual jurisdictions. The rules in the States are varied. Some States have codified the common-law rule, though in two of these the courts have significantly limited the statute. Four States, though without a relevant statute, apparently retain the common-law rule. Two States have adopted the *Model Penal Code's* provision verbatim. Eighteen others allow, in slightly varying language, the use of deadly force only if the suspect has committed a felony involving the use or threat of physical or deadly force, or is escaping with a deadly weapon, or is likely to endanger life or inflict serious physical injury if not arrested. Louisiana and Vermont, though without statutes or case law on point, do forbid the use of deadly force to prevent any but violent felonies. The remaining States either have no relevant statute or case law, or have positions that are unclear.

It cannot be said that there is a constant or overwhelming trend away from the common-law rule. In recent years, some States have reviewed their laws and expressly rejected abandonment of the common-law rule. Nonetheless, the long-term movement has been away from the rule that deadly force may be used against any fleeing felon, and that remains the rule in less than half the States.

This trend is more evident and impressive when viewed in light of the policies adopted by the police departments themselves. Overwhelmingly, these are more restrictive than the common-law rule. The Federal Bureau of Investigation and the New York City Police Department, for example, both forbid the use of firearms except when necessary to prevent death or grievous bodily harm. For accreditation by the Commission on Accreditation for Law Enforcement Agencies, a department must restrict the use of deadly force to situations where "the officer reasonably believes that the action is in defense of human life . . . or in defense of any person in immediate danger of serious physical injury." A 1974 study reported that the police department regulations in a majority of the large cities of the United States allowed the firing of a weapon only when a felon presented a threat of death or serious bodily harm.

Overall, only 7.5% of departmental and municipal policies explicitly permit the use of deadly force against any felon; 86.8% explicitly do not. In light of the rules adopted by those who must actually administer them, the older and fading common-law view is a dubious indicium of the constitutionality of the Tennessee statute now before us.

D.

Actual departmental policies are important for an additional reason. We would hesitate to declare a police practice of long standing "unreasonable" if doing so would severely hamper effective law enforcement. But the indications are to the contrary. There has been no suggestion that crime has worsened in any way in jurisdictions that have adopted, by legislation or departmental policy, rules similar to that announced today....

Nor do we agree with petitioners and appellant that the rule we have adopted requires the police to make impossible, split-second evaluations of unknowable facts. We do not deny the practical difficulties of attempting to assess the suspect's dangerousness. However, similarly difficult judgments must be made by the police in equally uncertain circumstances. Nor is there any indication that in States that allow the use of deadly force only against dangerous suspects the standard has been difficult to apply or has led to a rash of litigation involving inappropriate second-guessing of police officers' split-second decisions. Moreover, the highly technical felony/misdemeanor distinction is equally, if not more, difficult to apply in the field. An officer is in no position to know, for example, the precise value of property stolen, or whether the crime was a first or second offense. Finally, as noted above, this claim must be viewed with suspicion in light of the similar self-imposed limitations of so many police departments.

IV.

The District Court concluded that Hymon was justified in shooting Garner because state law allows, and the Federal Constitution does not forbid, the use of deadly force to prevent the escape of a fleeing felony suspect if no alternative means of apprehension is available. This conclusion made a determination of Garner's apparent dangerousness unnecessary. The court did find, however, that Garner appeared to be unarmed, though Hymon could not be certain that was the case. Restated in Fourth Amendment terms, this means Hymon had no articulable basis to think Garner was armed.

In reversing, the Court of Appeals accepted the District Court's factual conclusions and held that "the facts, as found, did not justify the use of deadly force." We agree. Officer Hymon could not reasonably have believed that Garner—young, slight, and unarmed—posed any threat. Indeed, Hymon never attempted to justify his actions on any basis other than the need to prevent an escape. The District Court stated in passing that "facts of this case did not indicate to Officer Hymon that Garner was 'non-dangerous.'" This conclusion is not explained, and seems to be based solely on the fact that Garner had broken into a house at night. However, the fact that Garner was a suspected burglar could not, without regard to the other circumstances, automatically justify the use of deadly force. Hymon did not have probable cause to believe that Garner, whom he correctly believed to be unarmed, posed any physical danger to himself or others.

The dissent argues that the shooting was justified by the fact that Officer Hymon had probable cause to believe that Garner had committed a nighttime burglary. While we agree that burglary is a serious crime, we cannot agree that it is so dangerous as automatically to justify the use of deadly force. The FBI classifies burglary as a "property" rather than a "violent" crime. Although the armed burglar would present a different situation, the fact that an unarmed suspect has broken into a dwelling at night does not automatically mean he is physically dangerous. This case demonstrates as much. In fact, the available statistics demonstrate that burglaries only rarely involve physical violence. During the 10-year period from 1973-1982, only 3.8% of all burglaries involved violent crime.

V.

We wish to make clear what our holding means in the context of this case. The complaint has been dismissed as to all the individual defendants. The State is a party only by virtue of 28 U. S. C. § 2403(b) and is not subject to liability. The possible liability of the remaining defendants—the Police Department and the city of Memphis—hinges on *Monell v. New York City Dept. of Social Services*. We hold that the statute is invalid insofar as it purported to give Hymon the authority to act as he did. As for the policy of the Police Department, the absence of any discussion of this issue by the courts below, and the uncertain state of the record, preclude any consideration of its validity.

The judgment of the Court of Appeals is affirmed, and the case is remanded for further proceedings consistent with this opinion.

So ordered.

Monell v. Department of Social Services (1978)
436 U.S. 658

In this case, the court overruled the previous decision in Monroe v. Pape. *The effect of this was to add local governments to the list of "people" that can be sued for damages under Section 1983. This decision radically changed the contours of police civil liability.*

Petitioners, a class of female employees of the Department of Social Services and of the Board of Education of the city of New York, commenced this action under 42 U. S. C. § 1983 in July 1971. The gravamen of the complaint was that the Board and the Department had as a matter of official policy compelled pregnant employees to take unpaid leaves of absence before such leaves were required for medical reasons. The suit sought injunctive relief and backpay for periods of unlawful forced leave. Named as defendants in the action were the Department and its Commissioner, the Board and its Chancellor, and the city of New York and its Mayor. In each case, the individual defendants were sued solely in their official capacities.

On cross-motions for summary judgment, the District Court for the Southern District of New York held moot petitioners' claims for injunctive and declaratory relief since the city of New York and the Board, after the filing of the complaint, had changed their policies relating to maternity leaves so that no pregnant employee would have to take leave unless she was medically unable to continue to perform her job. No one now challenges this conclusion. The court did conclude, however, that the acts complained of were unconstitutional under *LaFleur*. Nonetheless plaintiffs' prayers for backpay were denied because any such damages would come ultimately from the city of New York and, therefore, to hold otherwise would be to "circumvent" the immunity conferred on municipalities by *Monroe v. Pape*.

On appeal, petitioners renewed their arguments that the Board of Education was not a "municipality" within the meaning of *Monroe v. Pape*, and that, in any event, the District Court had erred in barring a damages award against the individual defendants. The Court of Appeals for the Second Circuit rejected both contentions. The court first held that the Board of Education was not a "person" under § 1983 because "it performs a vital governmental function . . . , and, significantly, while it has the right to determine how the funds appropriated to it shall be spent . . . , it has no final say in deciding what its appropriations shall be." The individual defendants, however, were "persons" under § 1983, even when sued solely in their official capacities. Yet, because a damages award would "have to be paid by a city that was held not to be amenable to such an action in *Monroe v. Pape*," a damages action against officials sued in their official capacities could not proceed.

We granted certiorari in this case, to consider

"Whether local governmental officials and/or local independent school boards are 'persons' within the meaning of 42 U. S. C. § 1983 when equitable relief in the nature of back pay is sought against them in their official capacities?"

Although, after plenary consideration, we have decided the merits of over a score of cases brought under § 1983 in which the principal defendant was a school board and, indeed, in some of which § 1983 and its jurisdictional counterpart, 28 U. S. C. § 1343, provided the only basis for jurisdiction—we indicated in *Mt. Healthy City Board of Education v. Doyle*, last Term that the question presented here was open and would be decided "another day." That other day has come and we now overrule *Monroe v. Pape*, insofar as it holds that local governments are wholly immune from suit under § 1983.

I.

In *Monroe v. Pape*, we held that "Congress did not undertake to bring municipal corporations within the ambit of § 1983." The sole basis for this conclusion was an inference drawn from Congress' rejection of the "Sherman amendment" to the bill which became the Civil Rights Act of 1871, 17 Stat. 13, the precursor of § 1983. The amendment would have held a municipal corporation liable for damage done to the person or property of its inhabitants by private persons "riotously and tumultuously assembled."

....

A. An Overview

There are three distinct stages in the legislative consideration of the bill which became the Civil Rights Act of 1871. On March 28, 1871, Representative Shellabarger, acting for a House select committee, reported H. R. 320, a bill "to enforce the provisions of the fourteenth amendment to the Constitution of the United States, and for other purposes." H. R. 320 contained four sections. Section 1, now codified as 42 U. S. C. § 1983, was the subject of only limited debate and was passed without amendment. Sections 2 through 4 dealt primarily with the "other purpose" of suppressing Ku Klux Klan violence in the Southern States. The wisdom and constitutionality of these sections—not § 1, now § 1983—were the subject of almost all congressional debate and each of these sections was amended. The House finished its initial debates on H. R. 320 on April 7, 1871, and one week later the Senate also voted out a bill. Again, debate on § 1 of the bill was limited and that section was passed as introduced.

Immediately prior to the vote on H. R. 320 in the Senate, Senator Sherman introduced his amendment. This was not an amendment to § 1 of the bill, but was to be added as § 7 at the end of the bill. Under the Senate rules, no discussion of the amendment was allowed and, although attempts were made to amend the amendment, it was passed as introduced. In this form, the amendment did not place liability on municipal corporations, but made any inhabitant of a municipality liable for damage inflicted by persons "riotously and tumultuously assembled."

The House refused to acquiesce in a number of amendments made by the Senate, including the Sherman amendment, and the respective versions of H. R. 320 were therefore sent to a conference committee. Section 1 of the bill, however, was not a subject of this conference since, as noted, it was passed verbatim as introduced in both Houses of Congress.

On April 18, 1871, the first conference committee completed its work on H. R. 320. The main features of the conference committee draft of the Sherman amendment were these:

"First, a cause of action was given to persons injured by any persons riotously and tumultuously assembled together . . . with intent to deprive any person of any right conferred upon him by the Constitution and laws of the United States, or to deter him or punish him for exercising such right, or by reason of his race, color, or previous condition of servitude . . . ."

Second, the bill provided that the action would be against the county, city, or parish in which the riot had occurred and that it could be maintained by either the person injured or his legal representative.

Third, unlike the amendment as proposed, the conference substitute made the government defendant liable on the judgment if it was not satisfied against individual defendants who had committed the violence. If a municipality were liable, the judgment against it could be collected

"by execution, attachment, mandamus, garnishment, or any other proceeding in aid of execution or applicable to the enforcement of judgments against municipal corporations; and such judgment would become a lien as well upon all moneys in the treasury of such county, city, or parish, as upon the other property thereof."

In the ensuing debate on the first conference report, which was the first debate of any kind on the Sherman amendment, Senator Sherman explained that the purpose of his amendment was to enlist the aid of persons of property in the enforcement of the civil rights laws by making their property "responsible" for Ku Klux Klan damage. Statutes drafted on a similar theory, he stated, had long been in force in England and were in force in 1871 in a number of States.

                                       ....

Because the House rejected the first conference report a second conference was called and it duly issued its report. The second conference substitute for the Sherman amendment abandoned municipal liability and, instead, made "any person or persons having knowledge that a conspiracy to violate civil rights was afoot, and having power to prevent or aid in preventing the same," who did not attempt to stop the same, liable to any person injured by the conspiracy. The amendment in this form was adopted by both Houses of Congress and is now codified as 42 U. S. C. § 1986.

The meaning of the legislative history sketched above can most readily be developed by first considering the debate on the report of the first conference committee. This debate shows conclusively that the constitutional objections raised against the Sherman amendment—on which our holding in *Monroe* was based—would not have prohibited congressional creation of a civil remedy against state municipal corporations that infringed federal rights. Because § 1 of the Civil Rights Act does not state expressly that municipal corporations come within its ambit, it is finally necessary to interpret § 1 to confirm that such corporations were indeed intended to be included within the "persons" to whom that section applies.

B. Debate on the First Conference Report

The style of argument adopted by both proponents and opponents of the Sherman amendment in both Houses of Congress was largely legal, with frequent references to cases decided by this Court and the Supreme Courts of the several States. Proponents of the Sherman amendment did not, however, discuss in detail the argument in favor of its constitutionality....

Finally, the very votes of those Members of Congress, who opposed the Sherman amendment but who had voted for § 1, confirm that the liability imposed by § 1 was something very different from that imposed by the amendment. Section 1 without question could be used to obtain a damages judgment against state or municipal officials who violated federal constitutional rights while acting under color of law. However, for Prigg-Dennison-Day purposes, as Blair and others recognized, there was no distinction of constitutional magnitude between officers and agents—including corporate agents—of the State: Both were state instrumentalities and the State could be impeded no matter over which sort of instrumentality the Federal Government sought to assert its power. Dennison and Day, after all, were not suits against municipalities but against officers, and Blair was quite conscious that he was extending these cases by applying them to municipal corporations....

C. Debate on § 1 of the Civil Rights Bill

From the foregoing discussion, it is readily apparent that nothing said in debate on the Sherman amendment would have prevented holding a municipality liable under § 1 of the Civil Rights Act for its own violations of the Fourteenth Amendment. The question remains, however, whether the general language describing those to be liable under § 1—"any person"—covers more than natural persons. An examination of the debate on § 1 and application of appropriate rules of construction show unequivocally that § 1 was intended to cover legal as well as natural persons.

....

That the "usual" meaning of the word "person" would extend to municipal corporations is also evidenced by an Act of Congress which had been passed only months before the Civil Rights Act was passed. This Act provided that
"in all acts hereafter passed . . . the word 'person' may extend and be applied to bodies politic and corporate . . . unless the context shows that such words were intended to be used in a more limited sense."

Municipal corporations in 1871 were included within the phrase "bodies politic and corporate" and, accordingly, the "plain meaning" of § 1 is that local government bodies were to be included within the ambit of the persons who could be sued under § 1 of the Civil Rights Act. Indeed, a Circuit Judge, writing in 1873 in what is apparently the first reported case under § 1, read the Dictionary Act in precisely this way in a case involving a corporate plaintiff and a municipal defendant.

II.

Our analysis of the legislative history of the Civil Rights Act of 1871 compels the conclusion that Congress did intend municipalities and other local government units to be included among those persons to whom § 1983 applies. Local governing bodies, therefore, can be sued directly under § 1983 for monetary, declaratory, or injunctive relief where, as here, the action that is alleged to be unconstitutional implements or executes a policy statement, ordinance, regulation, or decision officially adopted and promulgated by that body's officers. Moreover, although the touchstone of the § 1983 action against a government body is an allegation that official policy is responsible for a deprivation of rights protected by the Constitution, local governments, like every other § 1983 "person," by the very terms of the statute, may be sued for constitutional deprivations visited pursuant to governmental "custom" even though such a custom has not received formal approval through the body's official decisionmaking channels. As Mr. Justice Harlan, writing for the Court, said in *Adickes v. S. H. Kress & Co.*: "Congress included customs and usages in § 1983 because of the persistent and widespread discriminatory practices of state officials . . . . Although not authorized by written law, such practices of state officials could well be so permanent and well settled as to institute a 'custom or usage' with the force of law."

On the other hand, the language of § 1983, read against the background of the same legislative history, compels the conclusion that Congress did not intend municipalities to be held liable unless action pursuant to official municipal policy of some nature caused a constitutional tort. In particular, we conclude that municipality cannot be held liable solely because it employs a tortfeasor—or, in other words, a municipality cannot be held liable under § 1983 on a *respondeat superior* theory.

We begin with the language of § 1983 as originally passed:

"Any person who, under color of any law, statute, ordinance, regulation, custom, or usage of any State, shall subject, or cause to be subjected, any person . . . to the deprivation of any rights, privileges, or immunities secured by the Constitution of the United States, shall, any such law, statute, ordinance, regulation, custom, or usage of the State to the contrary notwithstanding, be liable to the party injured in any action at law, suit in equity, or other proper proceeding for redress . . . ."

The ... language plainly imposes liability on a government that, under color of some official policy, "causes" an employee to violate another's constitutional rights. At the same time, that language cannot be easily read to impose liability vicariously on governing bodies solely on the basis of the existence of an employer-employee relationship with a tortfeasor. Indeed, the fact that Congress did specifically provide that A's tort became B's liability if B "caused" A to subject another to a tort suggests that Congress did not intend § 1983 liability to attach where such causation was absent.

Equally important, creation of a federal law of respondeat superior would have raised all the constitutional problems associated with the obligation to keep the peace, an obligation Congress chose not to impose because it thought imposition of such an obligation unconstitutional. To this day, there is disagreement about the basis for imposing liability on an employer for the torts of an employee when the sole nexus between the employer and the tort is the fact of the employer-employee relationship. Nonetheless, two justifications tend to stand out. First is the common-sense notion that no matter how blameless an employer appears to be in an individual case, accidents might nonetheless be reduced if employers had to bear the cost of accidents. Second is the argument that the cost of accidents should be spread to the community as a whole on an insurance theory.

The first justification is of the same sort that was offered for statutes like the Sherman amendment: "The obligation to make compensation for injury resulting from riot is, by arbitrary enactment of statutes, affirmatory law, and the reason of passing the statute is to secure a more perfect police regulation." This justification was obviously insufficient to sustain the amendment against perceived constitutional difficulties and there is no reason to suppose that a more general liability imposed for a similar reason would have been thought less constitutionally objectionable. The second justification was similarly put forward as a justification for the Sherman amendment: "we do not look upon the Sherman amendment as a punishment . . . . It is a mutual insurance." Again, this justification was insufficient to sustain the amendment.

We conclude, therefore, that a local government may not be sued under § 1983 for an injury inflicted solely by its employees or agents. Instead, it is when execution of a government's policy or custom, whether made by its lawmakers or by those whose edicts or acts may fairly be said to represent official policy, inflicts the injury that the government as an entity is responsible under § 1983. Since this case unquestionably involves official policy as the moving force of the constitutional violation found by the District Court, and we must reverse the judgment below. In so doing, we have no occasion to address, and do not address, what the full contours of municipal liability under § 1983 may be. We have attempted only to sketch so much of the § 1983 cause of action against a local government as is apparent from the history of the 1871 Act and our prior cases, and we expressly leave further development of this action to another day.

III.

Although we have stated that *stare decisis* has more force in statutory analysis than in constitutional adjudication because, in the former situation, Congress can correct our mistakes through legislation, we have never applied *stare decisis* mechanically to prohibit overruling our earlier decisions determining the meaning of statutes. Nor is this a case where we should "place on the shoulders of Congress the burden of the Court's own error."

First, *Monroe v. Pape*, insofar as it completely immunizes municipalities from suit under § 1983, was a departure from prior practice...in each of which municipalities were defendants in § 1983 suits. Moreover, the constitutional defect that led to the rejection of the Sherman amendment would not have distinguished between municipalities and school boards, each of which is an instrumentality of state administration. For this reason, our cases—decided both before and after *Monroe*—holding school boards liable in § 1983 actions are inconsistent with *Monroe*, especially as *Monroe's* immunizing principle was extended to suits for injunctive relief in *City of Kenosha v. Bruno*. And although in many of these cases jurisdiction was not questioned, we ought not "disregard the implications of an exercise of judicial authority assumed to be proper for 100 years." Thus, while we have reaffirmed *Monroe* without further examination on three occasions, it can scarcely be said that *Monroe* is so consistent with the warp and woof of civil rights law as to be beyond question.

Second, the principle of blanket immunity established in *Monroe* cannot be cabined short of school boards. Yet such an extension would itself be inconsistent with recent expressions of congressional intent. In the wake of our decisions, Congress not only has shown no hostility to federal-court decisions against school boards, but it has indeed rejected efforts to strip the federal courts of jurisdiction over school boards.

....

Third, municipalities can assert no reliance claim which can support an absolute immunity. As Mr. Justice Frankfurter said in *Monroe*, "this is not an area of commercial law in which, presumably, individuals may have arranged their affairs in reliance on the expected stability of decision."

Indeed, municipalities simply cannot "arrange their affairs" on an assumption that they can violate constitutional rights indefinitely since injunctive suits against local officials under § 1983 would prohibit any such arrangement. And it scarcely need be mentioned that nothing in *Monroe* encourages municipalities to violate constitutional rights or even suggests that such violations are anything other than completely wrong.

Finally, even under the most stringent test for the propriety of overruling a statutory decision proposed by Mr. Justice Harlan in *Monroe*—"that it appear beyond doubt from the legislative history of the 1871 statute that Monroe misapprehended the meaning of the section"—the overruling of *Monroe* insofar as it holds that local governments are not "persons" who may be defendants in § 1983 suits is clearly proper. It is simply beyond doubt that, under the 1871 Congress' view of the law, were § 1983 liability unconstitutional as to local governments, it would have been equally unconstitutional as to state officers. Yet everyone—proponents and opponents alike—knew § 1983 would be applied to state officers and nonetheless stated that § 1983 was constitutional. And, moreover, there can be no doubt that § 1 of the Civil Rights Act was intended to provide a remedy, to be broadly construed, against all forms of official violation of federally protected rights. Therefore, absent a clear statement in the legislative history supporting the conclusion that § 1 was not to apply to the official acts of a municipal corporation—which simply is not present—there is no justification for excluding municipalities from the "persons" covered by § 1.

For the reasons stated above, therefore, we hold that *stare decisis* does not bar our overruling of *Monroe* insofar as it is inconsistent with Parts I and II of this opinion.

IV.

Since the question whether local government bodies should be afforded some form of official immunity was not presented as a question to be decided on this petition and was not briefed by the parties or addressed by the courts below, we express no views on the scope of any municipal immunity beyond holding that municipal bodies sued under § 1983 cannot be entitled to an absolute immunity, lest our decision that such bodies are subject to suit under § 1983 "be drained of meaning."

V.

For the reasons stated above, the judgment of the Court of Appeals is Reversed.

Part III: Courts and Sentencing

United States v. Salerno (1987)
481 U.S. 739

In this case, the court held that the Bail Reform Act of 1984 was constitutional in allowing for the denial of bail when the accused was deemed a danger to the community. In addition, the court outlines the right to bail and the limitations that may be constitutionally placed on those rights.

The Bail Reform Act of 1984 (Act) allows a federal court to detain an arrestee pending trial if the Government demonstrates by clear and convincing evidence after an adversary hearing that no release conditions "will reasonably assure . . . the safety of any other person and the community." The United States Court of Appeals for the Second Circuit struck down this provision of the Act as facially unconstitutional, because, in that court's words, this type of pretrial detention violates "substantive due process." We granted certiorari because of a conflict among the Courts of Appeals regarding the validity of the Act. We hold that, as against the facial attack mounted by these respondents, the Act fully comports with constitutional requirements. We therefore reverse.

I.

Responding to "the alarming problem of crimes committed by persons on release," Congress formulated the Bail Reform Act of 1984 as the solution to a bail crisis in the federal courts. The Act represents the National Legislature's considered response to numerous perceived deficiencies in the federal bail process. By providing for sweeping changes in both the way federal courts consider bail applications and the circumstances under which bail is granted, Congress hoped to "give the courts adequate authority to make release decisions that give appropriate recognition to the danger a person may pose to others if released."

To this end, § 3141(a) of the Act requires a judicial officer to determine whether an arrestee shall be detained. Section 3142(e) provides that "if, after a hearing pursuant to the provisions of subsection (f), the judicial officer finds that no condition or combination of conditions will reasonably assure the appearance of the person as required and the safety of any other person and the community, he shall order the detention of the person prior to trial."

Section 3142(f) provides the arrestee with a number of procedural safeguards. He may request the presence of counsel at the detention hearing, he may testify and present witnesses in his behalf, as well as proffer evidence, and he may cross-examine other witnesses appearing at the hearing. If the judicial officer finds that no conditions of pretrial release can reasonably assure the safety of other persons and the community, he must state his findings of fact in writing, and support his conclusion with "clear and convincing evidence."

The judicial officer is not given unbridled discretion in making the detention determination. Congress has specified the considerations relevant to that decision. These factors include the nature and seriousness of the charges, the substantiality of the Government's evidence against the arrestee, the arrestee's background and characteristics, and the nature and seriousness of the danger posed by the suspect's release. Should a judicial officer order detention, the detainee is entitled to expedited appellate review of the detention order.

Respondents Anthony Salerno and Vincent Cafaro were arrested on March 21, 1986, after being charged in a 29-count indictment alleging various Racketeer Influenced and Corrupt Organizations Act (RICO) violations, mail and wire fraud offenses, extortion, and various criminal gambling violations. The RICO counts alleged 35 acts of racketeering activity, including fraud, extortion, gambling, and conspiracy to commit murder. At respondents' arraignment, the Government moved to have Salerno and Cafaro detained pursuant to § 3142(e), on the ground that no condition of release would assure the safety of the community or any person. The District Court held a hearing at which the Government made a detailed proffer of evidence. The Government's case showed that Salerno was the "boss" of the Genovese crime family of La Cosa Nostra and that Cafaro was a "captain" in the Genovese family.

According to the Government's proffer, based in large part on conversations intercepted by a court-ordered wiretap, the two respondents had participated in wide-ranging conspiracies to aid their illegitimate enterprises through violent means. The Government also offered the testimony of two of its trial witnesses, who would assert that Salerno personally participated in two murder conspiracies. Salerno opposed the motion for detention, challenging the credibility of the Government's witnesses. He offered the testimony of several character witnesses as well as a letter from his doctor stating that he was suffering from a serious medical condition. Cafaro presented no evidence at the hearing, but instead characterized the wiretap conversations as merely "tough talk."

The District Court granted the Government's detention motion, concluding that the Government had established by clear and convincing evidence that no condition or combination of conditions of release would ensure the safety of the community or any person:

"The activities of a criminal organization such as the Genovese Family do not cease with the arrest of its principals and their release on even the most stringent of bail conditions. The illegal businesses, in place for many years, require constant attention and protection, or they will fail. Under these circumstances, this court recognizes a strong incentive on the part of its leadership to continue business as usual. When business as usual involves threats, beatings, and murder, the present danger such people pose in the community is self-evident."

Respondents appealed, contending that to the extent that the Bail Reform Act permits pretrial detention on the ground that the arrestee is likely to commit future crimes, it is unconstitutional on its face. Over a dissent, the United States Court of Appeals for the Second Circuit agreed. Although the court agreed that pretrial detention could be imposed if the defendants were likely to intimidate witnesses or otherwise jeopardize the trial process, it found "§ 3142(e)'s authorization of pretrial detention on the ground of future dangerousness repugnant to the concept of substantive due process, which we believe prohibits the total deprivation of liberty simply as a means of preventing future crimes."

The court concluded that the Government could not, consistent with due process, detain persons who had not been accused of any crime merely because they were thought to present a danger to the community. It reasoned that our criminal law system holds persons accountable for past actions, not anticipated future actions. Although a court could detain an arrestee who threatened to flee before trial, such detention would be permissible because it would serve the basic objective of a criminal system—bringing the accused to trial. The court distinguished our decision in *Gerstein v. Pugh* in which we upheld police detention pursuant to arrest. The court construed *Gerstein* as limiting such detention to the "'administrative steps incident to arrest.'" The Court of Appeals also found our decision in *Schall v. Martin*, upholding postarrest, pretrial detention of juveniles, inapposite because juveniles have a lesser interest in liberty than do adults. The dissenting judge concluded that on its face, the Bail Reform Act adequately balanced the Federal Government's compelling interests in public safety against the detainee's liberty interests.

II.

A facial challenge to a legislative Act is, of course, the most difficult challenge to mount successfully, since the challenger must establish that no set of circumstances exists under which the Act would be valid. The fact that the Bail Reform Act might operate unconstitutionally under some conceivable set of circumstances is insufficient to render it wholly invalid, since we have not recognized an "overbreadth" doctrine outside the limited context of the First Amendment. We think respondents have failed to shoulder their heavy burden to demonstrate that the Act is "facially" unconstitutional.

Respondents present two grounds for invalidating the Bail Reform Act's provisions permitting pretrial detention on the basis of future dangerousness. First, they rely upon the Court of Appeals' conclusion that the Act exceeds the limitations placed upon the Federal Government by the Due Process Clause of the Fifth Amendment. Second, they contend that the Act contravenes the Eighth Amendment's proscription against excessive bail. We treat these contentions in turn.

A.

The Due Process Clause of the Fifth Amendment provides that "No person shall . . . be deprived of life, liberty, or property, without due process of law . . . ." This Court has held that the Due Process Clause protects individuals against two types of government action. So-called "substantive due process" prevents the government from engaging in conduct that "shocks the conscience," or interferes with rights "implicit in the concept of ordered liberty." When government action depriving a person of life, liberty, or property survives substantive due process scrutiny, it must still be implemented in a fair manner. This requirement has traditionally been referred to as "procedural" due process.

Respondents first argue that the Act violates substantive due process because the pretrial detention it authorizes constitutes impermissible punishment before trial. The Government, however, has never argued that pretrial detention could be upheld if it were "punishment." The Court of Appeals assumed that pretrial detention under the Bail Reform Act is regulatory, not penal, and we agree that it is.

As an initial matter, the mere fact that a person is detained does not inexorably lead to the conclusion that the government has imposed punishment. To determine whether a restriction on liberty constitutes impermissible punishment or permissible regulation, we first look to legislative intent. Unless Congress expressly intended to impose punitive restrictions, the punitive/regulatory distinction turns on "whether an alternative purpose to which the restriction may rationally be connected is assignable for it, and whether it appears excessive in relation to the alternative purpose assigned to it."

We conclude that the detention imposed by the Act falls on the regulatory side of the dichotomy. The legislative history of the Bail Reform Act clearly indicates that Congress did not formulate the pretrial detention provisions as punishment for dangerous individuals. Congress instead perceived pretrial detention as a potential solution to a pressing societal problem. There is no doubt that preventing danger to the community is a legitimate regulatory goal.

Nor are the incidents of pretrial detention excessive in relation to the regulatory goal Congress sought to achieve. The Bail Reform Act carefully limits the circumstances under which detention may be sought to the most serious of crimes. The arrestee is entitled to a prompt detention hearing, and the maximum length of pretrial detention is limited by the stringent time limitations of the Speedy Trial Act. Moreover, as in *Schall v. Martin*, the conditions of confinement envisioned by the Act "appear to reflect the regulatory purposes relied upon by the" Government. As in *Schall*, the statute at issue here requires that detainees be housed in a "facility separate, to the extent practicable, from persons awaiting or serving sentences or being held in custody pending appeal." We conclude, therefore, that the pretrial detention contemplated by the Bail Reform Act is regulatory in nature, and does not constitute punishment before trial in violation of the Due Process Clause.

The Court of Appeals nevertheless concluded that "the Due Process Clause prohibits pretrial detention on the ground of danger to the community as a regulatory measure, without regard to the duration of the detention." Respondents characterize the Due Process Clause as erecting an impenetrable "wall" in this area that "no governmental interest—rational, important, compelling or otherwise—may surmount."

We do not think the Clause lays down any such categorical imperative. We have repeatedly held that the Government's regulatory interest in community safety can, in appropriate circumstances, outweigh an individual's liberty interest. For example, in times of war or insurrection, when society's interest is at its peak, the Government may detain individuals whom the Government believes to be dangerous. Even outside the exigencies of war, we have found that sufficiently compelling governmental interests can justify detention of dangerous persons. Thus, we have found no absolute constitutional barrier to detention of potentially dangerous resident aliens pending deportation proceedings. We have also held that the government may detain mentally unstable individuals who present a danger to the public, and dangerous defendants who become incompetent to stand trial. We have approved of postarrest regulatory detention of juveniles when they present a continuing danger to the community. Even competent adults may face substantial liberty restrictions as a result of the operation of our criminal justice system. If the police suspect an individual of a crime, they may arrest and hold him until a neutral magistrate determines whether probable cause exists. Finally, respondents concede and the Court of Appeals noted that an arrestee may be incarcerated until trial if he presents a risk of flight, or a danger to witnesses.

Respondents characterize all of these cases as exceptions to the "general rule" of substantive due process that the government may not detain a person prior to a judgment of guilt in a criminal trial. Such a "general rule" may freely be conceded, but we think that these cases show a sufficient number of exceptions to the rule that the congressional action challenged here can hardly be characterized as totally novel. Given the well-established authority of the government, in special circumstances, to restrain individuals' liberty prior to or even without criminal trial and conviction, we think that the present statute providing for pretrial detention on the basis of dangerousness must be evaluated in precisely the same manner that we evaluated the laws in the cases discussed above.

The government's interest in preventing crime by arrestees is both legitimate and compelling. In *Schall*, we recognized the strength of the State's interest in preventing juvenile crime. This general concern with crime prevention is no less compelling when the suspects are adults. Indeed, "the harm suffered by the victim of a crime is not dependent upon the age of the perpetrator." The Bail Reform Act of 1984 responds to an even more particularized governmental interest than the interest we sustained in *Schall*. The statute we upheld in Schall permitted pretrial detention of any juvenile arrested on any charge after a showing that the individual might commit some undefined further crimes. The Bail Reform Act, in contrast, narrowly focuses on a particularly acute problem in which the Government interests are overwhelming. The Act operates only on individuals who have been arrested for a specific category of extremely serious offenses. Congress specifically found that these individuals are far more likely to be responsible for dangerous acts in the community after arrest. Nor is the Act by any means a scattershot attempt to incapacitate those who are merely suspected of these serious crimes. The Government must first of all demonstrate probable cause to believe that the charged crime has been committed by the arrestee, but that is not enough. In a full-blown adversary hearing, the Government must convince a neutral decisionmaker by clear and convincing evidence that no conditions of release can reasonably assure the safety of the community or any person. While the Government's general interest in preventing crime is compelling, even this interest is heightened when the Government musters convincing proof that the arrestee, already indicted or held to answer for a serious crime, presents a demonstrable danger to the community. Under these narrow circumstances, society's interest in crime prevention is at its greatest.

On the other side of the scale, of course, is the individual's strong interest in liberty. We do not minimize the importance and fundamental nature of this right. But, as our cases hold, this right may, in circumstances where the government's interest is sufficiently weighty, be subordinated to the greater needs of society. We think that Congress' careful delineation of the circumstances under which detention will be permitted satisfies this standard. When the Government proves by clear and convincing evidence that an arrestee presents an identified and articulable threat to an individual or the community, we believe that, consistent with the Due Process Clause, a court may disable the arrestee from executing that threat. Under these circumstances, we cannot categorically state that pretrial detention "offends some principle of justice so rooted in the traditions and conscience of our people as to be ranked as fundamental."

Finally, we may dispose briefly of respondents' facial challenge to the procedures of the Bail Reform Act. To sustain them against such a challenge, we need only find them "adequate to authorize the pretrial detention of at least some persons charged with crimes," whether or not they might be insufficient in some particular circumstances. We think they pass that test. As we stated in Schall, "there is nothing inherently unattainable about a prediction of future criminal conduct."

Under the Bail Reform Act, the procedures by which a judicial officer evaluates the likelihood of future dangerousness are specifically designed to further the accuracy of that determination. Detainees have a right to counsel at the detention hearing. They may testify in their own behalf, present information by proffer or otherwise, and cross-examine witnesses who appear at the hearing. The judicial officer charged with the responsibility of determining the appropriateness of detention is guided by statutorily enumerated factors, which include the nature and the circumstances of the charges, the weight of the evidence, the history and characteristics of the putative offender, and the danger to the community. The Government must prove its case by clear and convincing evidence. Finally, the judicial officer must include written findings of fact and a written statement of reasons for a decision to detain. The Act's review provisions, provide for immediate appellate review of the detention decision.

We think these extensive safeguards suffice to repel a facial challenge. The protections are more exacting than those we found sufficient in the juvenile context, and they far exceed what we found necessary to effect limited postarrest detention in *Gerstein v. Pugh*. Given the legitimate and compelling regulatory purpose of the Act and the procedural protections it offers, we conclude that the Act is not facially invalid under the Due Process Clause of the Fifth Amendment.

B.

Respondents also contend that the Bail Reform Act violates the Excessive Bail Clause of the Eighth Amendment. The Court of Appeals did not address this issue because it found that the Act violates the Due Process Clause. We think that the Act survives a challenge founded upon the Eighth Amendment.

The Eighth Amendment addresses pretrial release by providing merely that "excessive bail shall not be required." This Clause, of course, says nothing about whether bail shall be available at all. Respondents nevertheless contend that this Clause grants them a right to bail calculated solely upon considerations of flight. They rely on *Stack v. Boyle*, in which the Court stated that "bail set at a figure higher than an amount reasonably calculated to ensure the defendant's presence at trial is 'excessive' under the Eighth Amendment." In respondents' view, since the Bail Reform Act allows a court essentially to set bail at an infinite amount for reasons not related to the risk of flight, it violates the Excessive Bail Clause. Respondents concede that the right to bail they have discovered in the Eighth Amendment is not absolute. A court may, for example, refuse bail in capital cases. And, as the Court of Appeals noted and respondents admit, a court may refuse bail when the defendant presents a threat to the judicial process by intimidating witnesses. Respondents characterize these exceptions as consistent with what they claim to be the sole purpose of bail—to ensure the integrity of the judicial process.

While we agree that a primary function of bail is to safeguard the courts' role in adjudicating the guilt or innocence of defendants, we reject the proposition that the Eighth Amendment categorically prohibits the government from pursuing other admittedly compelling interests through regulation of pretrial release. The above-quoted dictum in *Stack v. Boyle* is far too slender a reed on which to rest this argument. The Court in *Stack* had no occasion to consider whether the Excessive Bail Clause requires courts to admit all defendants to bail, because the statute before the Court in that case in fact allowed the defendants to be bailed. Thus, the Court had to determine only whether bail, admittedly available in that case, was excessive if set at a sum greater than that necessary to ensure the arrestees' presence at trial.

The holding of *Stack* is illuminated by the Court's holding just four months later in *Carlson v. Landon*. In that case, remarkably similar to the present action, the detainees had been arrested and held without bail pending a determination of deportability. The Attorney General refused to release the individuals, "on the ground that there was reasonable cause to believe that their release would be prejudicial to the public interest and would endanger the welfare and safety of the United States." The detainees brought the same challenge that respondents bring to us today: the Eighth Amendment required them to be admitted to bail. The Court squarely rejected this proposition:

"The bail clause was lifted with slight changes from the English Bill of Rights Act. In England that clause has never been thought to accord a right to bail in all cases, but merely to provide that bail shall not be excessive in those cases where it is proper to grant bail. When this clause was carried over into our Bill of Rights, nothing was said that indicated any different concept. The Eighth Amendment has not prevented Congress from defining the classes of cases in which bail shall be allowed in this country. Thus, in criminal cases bail is not compulsory where the punishment may be death. Indeed, the very language of the Amendment fails to say all arrests must be bailable."

Carlson v. Landon was a civil case, and we need not decide today whether the Excessive Bail Clause speaks at all to Congress' power to define the classes of criminal arrestees who shall be admitted to bail. For even if we were to conclude that the Eighth Amendment imposes some substantive limitations on the National Legislature's powers in this area, we would still hold that the Bail Reform Act is valid. Nothing in the text of the Bail Clause limits permissible Government considerations solely to questions of flight. The only arguable substantive limitation of the Bail Clause is that the Government's proposed conditions of release or detention not be "excessive" in light of the perceived evil. Of course, to determine whether the Government's response is excessive, we must compare that response against the interest the Government seeks to protect by means of that response. Thus, when the Government has admitted that its only interest is in preventing flight, bail must be set by a court at a sum designed to ensure that goal, and no more. We believe that when Congress has mandated detention on the basis of a compelling interest other than prevention of flight, as it has here, the Eighth Amendment does not require release on bail.

III.

In our society liberty is the norm, and detention prior to trial or without trial is the carefully limited exception. We hold that the provisions for pretrial detention in the Bail Reform Act of 1984 fall within that carefully limited exception. The Act authorizes the detention prior to trial of arrestees charged with serious felonies who are found after an adversary hearing to pose a threat to the safety of individuals or to the community which no condition of release can dispel. The numerous procedural safeguards detailed above must attend this adversary hearing. We are unwilling to say that this congressional determination, based as it is upon that primary concern of every government—a concern for the safety and indeed the lives of its citizens—on its face violates either the Due Process Clause of the Fifth Amendment or the Excessive Bail Clause of the Eighth Amendment.

The judgment of the Court of Appeals is therefore Reversed.

Blackledge v. Allison (1977)
431 U.S. 63

In this case, the court examines the question of whether the government must keep promises made in plea bargain agreements. In addition, the court sheds light on the development, justification, and correct process of plea bargaining.

The respondent, Gary Darrell Allison, an inmate of a North Carolina penitentiary, petitioned a Federal District Court for a writ of habeas corpus. The court dismissed his petition without a hearing, and the Court of Appeals reversed, ruling that in the circumstances of this case summary dismissal was improper. We granted certiorari to review the judgment of the Court of Appeals.

I.

Allison was indicted by a North Carolina grand jury for breaking and entering, attempted safe robbery, and possession of burglary tools. At his arraignment, where he was represented by court-appointed counsel, he initially pleaded not guilty. But after learning that his codefendant planned to plead guilty, he entered a guilty plea to a single count of attempted safe robbery, for which the minimum prison sentence was 10 years and the maximum was life.

In accord with the procedure for taking guilty pleas then in effect in North Carolina, the judge in open court read from a printed form 13 questions, generally concerning the defendant's understanding of the charge, its consequences, and the voluntariness of his plea. Allison answered "yes" or "no" to each question, and the court clerk transcribed those responses on a copy of the form, which Allison signed. So far as the record shows, there was no questioning beyond this routine; no inquiry was made of either defense counsel or prosecutor. Two questions from the form are of particular relevance to the issues before us: Question No. 8 - "Do you understand that upon your plea of guilty you could be imprisoned for as much as minimum [sic] of 10 years to life?" to which Allison answered "Yes"; and Question No. 11 - "Has the Solicitor, or your lawyer, or any policeman, law officer or anyone else made any promises or threat to you to influence you to plead guilty in this case?" to which Allison answered "No."

The trial judge then accepted the plea by signing his name at the bottom of the form under a text entitled "Adjudication," which recited the three charges for which Allison had been indicted, that he had been fully advised of his rights, was in fact guilty, and pleaded guilty to attempted safe robbery "freely, understandingly and voluntarily," with full awareness of the consequences, and "without undue… compulsion… duress, or promise of leniency." Three days later, at a sentencing hearing, of which there is no record whatsoever, Allison was sentenced to 17-21 years in prison.

After unsuccessfully exhausting a state collateral remedy, Allison filed a *pro se* petition in a Federal District Court seeking a writ of habeas corpus. The petition alleged:

"his guilty plea was induced by an unkept promise, and therefore was not the free and willing choice of the petitioner, and should be set aside by this Court. An unkept bargain which has induced a guilty plea is grounds for relief."

The petition went on to explain and support this allegation as follows:

"The petitioner was led to believe and did believe, by Mr. Pickard [Allison's attorney], that he Mr. N. Glenn Pickard had talked the case over with the Solicitor and the Judge, and that if the petitioner would plead guilty, that he would only get a 10 year sentence of penal servitude. This conversation, where the petitioner was assured that if he pleaded guilty, he would only get ten years was witnessed by another party other than the petitioner and counsel. . . . The petitioner believing that he was only going to get a ten year active sentence, allowed himself to be pled guilty to the charge of attempted safe robbery, and was shocked by the Court with a 17-21 year sentence.... "The petitioner was promised by his Attorney, who had consulted presumably with the Judge and Solicitor, that he was only going to get a ten year sentence, and therefore because of this unkept bargain, he is entitled to relief in this Court. . . . The petitioner is aware of the fact that he was questioned by the trial Judge prior to sentencing, but as he thought he was only going to get ten years, and had been instructed to answer the questions, so that the Court would accept the guilty plea, this fact does not preclude him from raising this matter especially since he was not given the promised sentence by the Court. . . ." The fact that the Judge, said that he could get more, did not affect, the belief of the petitioner, that he was only going to get a ten year sentence."

The petitioner here, Warden Blackledge, filed a motion to dismiss and attached to it the "transcript" of the plea hearing, consisting of nothing more than the printed form filled in by the clerk and signed by Allison and the state-court judge. The motion contended that the form conclusively showed that Allison had chosen to plead guilty knowingly, voluntarily, and with full awareness of the consequences. The Federal District Court agreed that the printed form "conclusively shows that Allison was carefully examined by the Court before the plea was accepted. Therefore, it must stand." Construing Allison's petition as alleging merely that his lawyer's prediction of the severity of the sentence turned out to be inaccurate, the District Court found no basis for relief and, accordingly, dismissed the petition.

One week later Allison filed a petition for rehearing. He contended that his statements during the guilty-plea proceeding in the state court were "evidentiary, but NOT conclusory"; that if true the allegations in his petition entitled him to relief; and that he deserved a chance to establish their truth. Apparently impressed by these arguments and recognizing that Allison was alleging more than a mere "prediction" by his lawyer, the District Court referred the rehearing petition to a United States Magistrate, who directed Allison to submit evidence in support of his allegations. After an inconclusive exchange of correspondence, the Magistrate concluded that despite "ample opportunity" Allison had failed to comply with the directive, and recommended that the petition for rehearing be denied. The District Court accepted the Magistrate's recommendation and denied the petition. A motion for reconsideration was also denied.

The Court of Appeals for the Fourth Circuit reversed. It held that Allison's allegation of a broken promise, as amplified by the explanation that his lawyer instructed him to deny the existence of any promises, was not foreclosed by his responses to the form questions at the state guilty-plea proceeding. The appellate court reasoned that when a pro se, indigent prisoner makes allegations that, if proved, would entitle him to habeas corpus relief, he should not be required to prove his allegations in advance of an evidentiary hearing, at least in the absence of counter affidavits conclusively proving their falsity. The case was therefore remanded for an evidentiary hearing.

The petitioner warden sought review in this Court, and we granted certiorari to consider the significant federal question presented.

II.

Whatever might be the situation in an ideal world, the fact is that the guilty plea and the often concomitant plea bargain are important components of this country's criminal justice system. Properly administered, they can benefit all concerned. The defendant avoids extended pretrial incarceration and the anxieties and uncertainties of a trial; he gains a speedy disposition of his case, the chance to acknowledge his guilt, and a prompt start in realizing whatever potential there may be for rehabilitation. Judges and prosecutors conserve vital and scarce resources. The public is protected from the risks posed by those charged with criminal offenses who are at large on bail while awaiting completion of criminal proceedings.

These advantages can be secured, however, only if dispositions by guilty plea are accorded a great measure of finality. To allow indiscriminate hearings in federal postconviction proceedings, whether for federal prisoners under 28 U.S.C. § 2255 or state prisoners under 28 U.S.C. §§ 2241-2254, would eliminate the chief virtues of the plea system—speed, economy, and finality. And there is reason for concern about that prospect. More often than not a prisoner has everything to gain and nothing to lose from filing a collateral attack upon his guilty plea. If he succeeds in vacating the judgment of conviction, retrial may be difficult. If he convinces a court that his plea was induced by an advantageous plea agreement that was violated, he may obtain the benefit of its terms. A collateral attack may also be inspired by "a mere desire to be freed temporarily from the confines of the prison."

Yet arrayed against the interest in finality is the very purpose of the writ of habeas corpus - to safeguard a person's freedom from detention in violation of constitutional guarantees... "The writ of habeas corpus has played a great role in the history of human freedom. It has been the judicial method of lifting undue restraints upon personal liberty." And a prisoner in custody after pleading guilty, no less than one tried and convicted by a jury, is entitled to avail himself of the writ in challenging the constitutionality of his custody.

In *Machibroda v. United States*, the defendant had pleaded guilty in federal court to bank robbery charges and been sentenced to 40 years in prison. He later filed a § 2255 motion alleging that his plea had been induced by an Assistant United States Attorney's promises that his sentence would not exceed 20 years, that the prosecutor had admonished him not to tell his lawyer about the agreement, and that the trial judge had wholly failed to inquire whether the guilty plea was made voluntarily before accepting it. This Court noted that the allegations, if proved, would entitle the defendant to relief, and that they raised an issue of fact that could not be resolved simply on the basis of an affidavit from the prosecutor denying the allegations. Because those allegations "related primarily to purported occurrences outside the courtroom and upon which the record could, therefore, cast no real light," and were not so "vague or conclusory" as to permit summary disposition, the Court ruled that the defendant was entitled to the opportunity to substantiate them at an evidentiary hearing.

The later case of *Fontaine v. United States* followed the same approach. The defendant there, having waived counsel, had also pleaded guilty to federal bank robbery charges. Before accepting the plea, the District Judge addressed the defendant personally, and the defendant stated in substance "that his plea was given voluntarily and knowingly, that he understood the nature of the charge and the consequences of the plea, and that he was in fact guilty." The defendant later filed a § 2255 motion to vacate his sentence on the ground that his plea had been coerced "by a combination of fear, coercive police tactics, and illness, including mental illness." The motion included supporting factual allegations, as well as hospital records documenting some of the contentions.

Although noting that in collaterally attacking a plea of guilty a prisoner "may not ordinarily repudiate" statements made to the sentencing judge when the plea was entered, the Court observed that no procedural device for the taking of guilty pleas is so perfect in design and exercise as to warrant a per se rule rendering it "uniformly invulnerable to subsequent challenge." Because the record of the plea hearing did not, in view of the allegations made, "'conclusively show that the prisoner was entitled to no relief,'" the Court ruled that the prisoner should be given an evidentiary hearing.

These cases do not in the least reduce the force of the original plea hearing. For the representations of the defendant, his lawyer, and the prosecutor at such a hearing, as well as any findings made by the judge accepting the plea, constitute a formidable barrier in any subsequent collateral proceedings. Solemn declarations in open court carry a strong presumption of verity. The subsequent presentation of conclusory allegations unsupported by specifics is subject to summary dismissal, as are contentions that in the face of the record are wholly incredible.

What *Machibroda* and *Fontaine* indisputably teach, however, is that the barrier of the plea or sentencing proceeding record, although imposing, is not invariably insurmountable. In administering the writ of habeas corpus and its § 2255 counterpart, the federal courts cannot fairly adopt a per se rule excluding all possibility that a defendant's representations at the time his guilty plea was accepted were so much the product of such factors as misunderstanding, duress, or misrepresentation by others as to make the guilty plea a constitutionally inadequate basis for imprisonment.

III.

The allegations in this case were not in themselves so "vague or conclusory," as to warrant dismissal for that reason alone. Allison alleged as a ground for relief that his plea was induced by an unkept promise. But he did not stop there. He proceeded to elaborate upon this claim with specific factual allegations. The petition indicated exactly what the terms of the promise were; when, where, and by whom the promise had been made; and the identity of one witness to its communication. The critical question is whether these allegations, when viewed against the record of the plea hearing, were so "palpably incredible," so "patently frivolous or false," to warrant summary dismissal. In the light of the nature of the record of the proceeding at which the guilty plea was accepted, and of the ambiguous status of the process of plea bargaining at the time the guilty plea was made, we conclude that Allison's petition should not have been summarily dismissed.

Only recently has plea bargaining become a visible practice accepted as a legitimate component in the administration of criminal justice. For decades it was a *sub rosa* process shrouded in secrecy and deliberately concealed by participating defendants, defense lawyers, prosecutors, and even judges. Indeed, it was not until our decision in *Santobello v. New York*, that lingering doubts about the legitimacy of the practice were finally dispelled.

Allison was arraigned a mere 37 days after the *Santobello* decision was announced, under a North Carolina procedure that had not been modified in light of *Santobello* or earlier decisions of this Court recognizing the process of plea bargaining. That procedure itself reflected the atmosphere of secrecy which then characterized plea bargaining generally. No transcript of the proceeding was made. The only record was a standard printed form. There is no way of knowing whether the trial judge in any way deviated from or supplemented the text of the form. The record is silent as to what statements Allison, his lawyer, or the prosecutor might have made regarding promised sentencing concessions. And there is no record at all of the sentencing hearing three days later, at which one of the participants might well have made a statement shedding light upon the veracity of the allegations Allison later advanced.

The litany of form questions followed by the trial judge at arraignment nowhere indicated to Allison (or indeed to the lawyers involved) that plea bargaining was a legitimate practice that could be freely disclosed in open court. Neither lawyer was asked to disclose any agreement that had been reached, or sentencing recommendation that had been promised. The process thus did nothing to dispel a defendant's belief that any bargain struck must remain concealed—a belief here allegedly reinforced by the admonition of Allison's lawyer himself that disclosure could jeopardize the agreement. Rather than challenging respondent's counsel's contention at oral argument in this Court that "at that time in North Carolina plea bargains were never disclosed in response to such a question on such a form," counsel for the petitioners conceded at oral argument that "that form was a minimum inquiry."

Although "logically the general inquiry should elicit information about plea bargaining... it seldom has in the past." Particularly if, as Allison alleged, he was advised by counsel to conceal any plea bargain, his denial that any promises had been made might have been a courtroom ritual more sham than real. We thus cannot conclude that the allegations in Allison's habeas corpus petition, when measured against the "record" of the arraignment, were so "patently false or frivolous" as to warrant summary dismissal.

North Carolina has recently undertaken major revisions of its plea-bargaining procedures, in part to prevent the very kind of problem now before us. Plea bargaining is expressly legitimated. The judge is directed to advise the defendant that courts have approved plea bargaining and he may thus admit to any promises without fear of jeopardizing an advantageous agreement or prejudicing himself in the judge's eyes. Specific inquiry about whether a plea bargain has been struck is then made not only of the defendant, but also of his counsel and the prosecutor. Finally, the entire proceeding is to be transcribed verbatim.

Had these commendable procedures been followed in the present case, Allison's petition would have been cast in a very different light. The careful explication of the legitimacy of plea bargaining, the questioning of both lawyers, and the verbatim record of their answers at the guilty-plea proceedings would almost surely have shown whether any bargain did exist and, if so, insured that it was not ignored. But the salutary reforms recently implemented by North Carolina highlight even more sharply the deficiencies in the record before the District Court in the present case.

A principal purpose of the North Carolina statutory reforms was to permit quick disposition of baseless collateral attacks. Indeed, a petitioner challenging a plea given pursuant to procedures like those now mandated in North Carolina will necessarily be asserting that not only his own transcribed responses, but those given by two lawyers, were untruthful. Especially as it becomes routine for prosecutors and defense lawyers to acknowledge that plea bargains have been made, such a contention will entitle a petitioner to an evidentiary hearing only in the most extraordinary circumstances.

This is not to suggest that a plea of guilty entered pursuant to procedures like those in effect at Allison's arraignment is necessarily vulnerable to collateral attack. It is simply to say that procedures like those now in effect in North Carolina serve (1) to prevent the occurrence of constitutional errors in the arraignment process, and (2) to discourage the filing of baseless petitions for habeas corpus and facilitate speedy but fair disposition of those that are filed.

....

This is not to say that every set of allegations not on its face without merit entitles a habeas corpus petitioner to an evidentiary hearing. As in civil cases generally, there exists a procedure whose purpose is to test whether facially adequate allegations have sufficient basis in fact to warrant plenary presentation of evidence. That procedure is, of course, the motion for summary judgment. Upon remand the warden will be free to make such a motion, supporting it with whatever proof he wishes to attach. If he chooses to do so, Allison will then be required either to produce some contrary proof indicating that there is a genuine issue of fact to be resolved by the District Court or to explain his inability to provide such proof.

Moreover, as is now expressly provided in the Rules Governing Habeas Corpus Cases, the district judge (or a magistrate to whom the case may be referred) may employ a variety of measures in an effort to avoid the need for an evidentiary hearing. Under Rule 6, a party may request and the judge may direct that discovery take place, and "there may be instances in which discovery would be appropriate [before an evidentiary hearing, and would show such a hearing to be unnecessary...." Under Rule 7, the judge can direct expansion of the record to include any appropriate materials that "enable the judge to dispose of some habeas petitions not dismissed on the pleadings, without the time and expense required for an evidentiary hearing."

In short, it may turn out upon remand that a full evidentiary hearing is not required. But Allison is "entitled to careful consideration and plenary processing of his claim, including full opportunity for presentation of the relevant facts." Upon that understanding, the judgment of the Court of Appeals is affirmed.

It is so ordered.

Santobello v. New York (1971)
404 U.S. 257

In this case, the Supreme Court considers whether or not a state's failure to keep a commitment regarding a plea agreement requires a new trial for the defendant. The court explains that once a promise is made by prosecutors as an inducement for an accused person to plead guilty, then the promise must subsequently be honored.

We granted certiorari in this case to determine whether the State's failure to keep a commitment concerning the sentence recommendation on a guilty plea required a new trial.

The facts are not in dispute. The State of New York indicted petitioner in 1969 on two felony counts, Promoting Gambling in the First Degree, and Possession of Gambling Records in the First Degree, N. Y. Penal Law §§ 225.10, 225.20. Petitioner first entered a plea of not guilty to both counts. After negotiations, the Assistant District Attorney in charge of the case agreed to permit petitioner to plead guilty to a lesser-included offense, Possession of Gambling Records in the Second Degree, conviction of which would carry a maximum prison sentence of one year. The prosecutor agreed to make no recommendation as to the sentence.

On June 16, 1969, petitioner accordingly withdrew his plea of not guilty and entered a plea of guilty to the lesser charge. Petitioner represented to the sentencing judge that the plea was voluntary and that the facts of the case, as described by the Assistant District Attorney, were true. The court accepted the plea and set a date for sentencing. A series of delays followed, owing primarily to the absence of a pre-sentence report, so that by September 23, 1969, petitioner had still not been sentenced. By that date petitioner acquired new defense counsel.

Petitioner's new counsel moved immediately to withdraw the guilty plea. In an accompanying affidavit, petitioner alleged that he did not know at the time of his plea that crucial evidence against him had been obtained as a result of an illegal search. The accuracy of this affidavit is subject to challenge since petitioner had filed and withdrawn a motion to suppress, before pleading guilty. In addition to his motion to withdraw his guilty plea, petitioner renewed the motion to suppress and filed a motion to inspect the grand jury minutes.

These three motions in turn caused further delay until November 26, 1969, when the court denied all three and set January 9, 1970, as the date for sentencing. On January 9 petitioner appeared before a different judge, the judge who had presided over the case to this juncture having retired. Petitioner renewed his motions, and the court again rejected them. The court then turned to consideration of the sentence.

At this appearance, another prosecutor had replaced the prosecutor who had negotiated the plea. The new prosecutor recommended the maximum one-year sentence. In making this recommendation, he cited petitioner's criminal record and alleged links with organized crime. Defense counsel immediately objected on the ground that the State had promised petitioner before the plea was entered that there would be no sentence recommendation by the prosecution. He sought to adjourn the sentence hearing in order to have time to prepare proof of the first prosecutor's promise. The second prosecutor, apparently ignorant of his colleague's commitment, argued that there was nothing in the record to support petitioner's claim of a promise, but the State, in subsequent proceedings, has not contested that such a promise was made.

The sentencing judge ended discussion, with the following statement, quoting extensively from the presentence report:

"Mr. Aronstein [Defense Counsel], I am not at all influenced by what the District Attorney says, so that there is no need to adjourn the sentence, and there is no need to have any testimony. It doesn't make a particle of difference what the District Attorney says he will do, or what he doesn't do.

"I have here, Mr. Aronstein, a probation report. I have here a history of a long, long serious criminal record. I have here a picture of the life history of this man. . . .

"'He is unamenable to supervision in the community. He is a professional criminal.' This is in quotes. 'And a recidivist. Institutionalization—'; that means, in plain language, just putting him away, 'is the only means of halting his anti-social activities,' and protecting you, your family, me, my family, protecting society. 'Institutionalization.' Plain language, put him behind bars.

"Under the plea, I can only send him to the New York City Correctional Institution for men for one year, which I am hereby doing."

The judge then imposed the maximum sentence of one year.

Petitioner sought and obtained a certificate of reasonable doubt and was admitted to bail pending an appeal. The Supreme Court of the State of New York, Appellate Division, First Department, unanimously affirmed petitioner's conviction, and petitioner was denied leave to appeal to the New York Court of Appeals. Petitioner then sought certiorari in this Court. Mr. Justice Harlan granted bail pending our disposition of the case.

This record represents another example of an unfortunate lapse in orderly prosecutorial procedures, in part, no doubt, because of the enormous increase in the workload of the often understaffed prosecutor's offices. The heavy workload may well explain these episodes, but it does not excuse them. The disposition of criminal charges by agreement between the prosecutor and the accused, sometimes loosely called "plea bargaining," is an essential component of the administration of justice. Properly administered, it is to be encouraged. If every criminal charge were subjected to a full-scale trial, the States and the Federal Government would need to multiply by many times the number of judges and court facilities.

Disposition of charges after plea discussions is not only an essential part of the process but a highly desirable part for many reasons. It leads to prompt and largely final disposition of most criminal cases; it avoids much of the corrosive impact of enforced idleness during pretrial confinement for those who are denied release pending trial; it protects the public from those accused persons who are prone to continue criminal conduct even while on pretrial release; and, by shortening the time between charge and disposition, it enhances whatever may be the rehabilitative prospects of the guilty when they are ultimately imprisoned.

However, all of these considerations presuppose fairness in securing agreement between an accused and a prosecutor. It is now clear, for example, that the accused pleading guilty must be counseled, absent a waiver. Fed. Rule Crim. Proc. 11, governing pleas in federal courts, now makes clear that the sentencing judge must develop, on the record, the factual basis for the plea, as, for example, by having the accused describe the conduct that gave rise to the charge. The plea must, of course, be voluntary and knowing and if it was induced by promises, the essence of those promises must in some way be made known. There is, of course, no absolute right to have a guilty plea accepted. A court may reject a plea in exercise of sound judicial discretion.

This phase of the process of criminal justice, and the adjudicative element inherent in accepting a plea of guilty, must be attended by safeguards to insure the defendant what is reasonably due in the circumstances. Those circumstances will vary, but a constant factor is that when a plea rests in any significant degree on a promise or agreement of the prosecutor, so that it can be said to be part of the inducement or consideration, such promise must be fulfilled.

On this record, petitioner "bargained" and negotiated for a particular plea in order to secure dismissal of more serious charges, but also on condition that no sentence recommendation would be made by the prosecutor. It is now conceded that the promise to abstain from a recommendation was made, and at this stage the prosecution is not in a good position to argue that its inadvertent breach of agreement is immaterial. The staff lawyers in a prosecutor's office have the burden of "letting the left hand know what the right hand is doing" or has done. That the breach of agreement was inadvertent does not lessen its impact.

We need not reach the question whether the sentencing judge would or would not have been influenced had he known all the details of the negotiations for the plea. He stated that the prosecutor's recommendation did not influence him and we have no reason to doubt that. Nevertheless, we conclude that the interests of justice and appropriate recognition of the duties of the prosecution in relation to promises made in the negotiation of pleas of guilty will be best served by remanding the case to the state courts for further consideration. The ultimate relief to which petitioner is entitled we leave to the discretion of the state court, which is in a better position to decide whether the circumstances of this case require only that there be specific performance of the agreement on the plea, in which case petitioner should be resentenced by a different judge, or whether, in the view of the state court, the circumstances require granting the relief sought by petitioner, i.e., the opportunity to withdraw his plea of guilty. We emphasize that this is in no sense to question the fairness of the sentencing judge; the fault here rests on the prosecutor, not on the sentencing judge.

The judgment is vacated and the case is remanded for reconsideration not inconsistent with this opinion.

Boykin v. Alabama (1969)
395 U.S. 238

As a rule, accused persons have the right to plead guilty to crimes. People do so for a variety of reasons, the most common being a plea bargain. In this case, the court considers what, exactly, circumstances must be found in the record before a guilty plea will be lawfully accepted by the courts.

In the spring of 1966, within the period of a fortnight, a series of armed robberies occurred in Mobile, Alabama. The victims, in each case, were local shopkeepers open at night who were forced by a gunman to hand over money. While robbing one grocery store, the assailant fired his gun once, sending a bullet through a door into the ceiling. A few days earlier in a drugstore, the robber had allowed his gun to discharge in such a way that the bullet, on ricochet from the floor, struck a customer in the leg. Shortly thereafter, a local grand jury returned five indictments against petitioner, a 27-year-old Negro, for common-law robbery—an offense punishable in Alabama by death.

Before the matter came to trial, the court determined that petitioner was indigent and appointed counsel to represent him. Three days later, at his arraignment, petitioner pleaded guilty to all five indictments. So far as the record shows, the judge asked no questions of petitioner concerning his plea, and petitioner did not address the court.

Trial strategy may of course make a plea of guilty seem the desirable course. But the record is wholly silent on that point and throws no light on it.

Alabama provides that when a defendant pleads guilty, "the court must cause the punishment to be determined by a jury" (except where it is required to be fixed by the court) and may "cause witnesses to be examined, to ascertain the character of the offense." In the present case a trial of that dimension was held, the prosecution presenting its case largely through eyewitness testimony. Although counsel for petitioner engaged in cursory cross-examination, petitioner neither testified himself nor presented testimony concerning his character and background. There was nothing to indicate that he had a prior criminal record.

In instructing the jury, the judge stressed that petitioner had pleaded guilty in five cases of robbery, defined as "the felonious taking of money . . . from another against his will . . . by violence or by putting him in fear . . . carrying from ten years minimum in the penitentiary to the supreme penalty of death by electrocution." The jury, upon deliberation, found petitioner guilty and sentenced him severally to die on each of the five indictments.

Taking an automatic appeal to the Alabama Supreme Court, petitioner argued that a sentence of death for common-law robbery was cruel and unusual punishment within the meaning of the Federal Constitution, a suggestion which that court unanimously rejected. On their own motion, however, four of the seven justices discussed the constitutionality of the process by which the trial judge had accepted petitioner's guilty plea. From the order affirming the trial court, three justices dissented on the ground that the record was inadequate to show that petitioner had intelligently and knowingly pleaded guilty. The fourth member concurred separately, conceding that "a trial judge should not accept a guilty plea unless he has determined that such a plea was voluntarily and knowingly entered by the defendant," but refusing "for aught appearing" "to presume that the trial judge failed to do his duty." We granted certiorari.

Respondent does not suggest that we lack jurisdiction to review the voluntary character of petitioner's guilty plea because he failed to raise that federal question below and the state court failed to pass upon it. But the question was raised on oral argument and we conclude that it is properly presented. The very Alabama statute that provides automatic appeal in capital cases also requires the reviewing court to comb the record for "any error prejudicial to the appellant, even though not called to our attention in brief of counsel." The automatic appeal statute "is the only provision under the Plain Error doctrine of which we are aware in Alabama criminal appellate review." In the words of the Alabama Supreme Court:

"Perhaps it is well to note that in reviewing a death case under the automatic appeal statute, . . . we may consider any testimony that was seriously prejudicial to the rights of the appellant and may reverse thereon, even though no lawful objection or exception was made thereto. Our review is not limited to the matters brought to our attention in brief of counsel."

It was error, plain on the face of the record, for the trial judge to accept petitioner's guilty plea without an affirmative showing that it was intelligent and voluntary. That error, under Alabama procedure, was properly before the court below and considered explicitly by a majority of the justices and is properly before us on review.

A plea of guilty is more than a confession which admits that the accused did various acts; it is itself a conviction; nothing remains but to give judgment and determine punishment. Admissibility of a confession must be based on a "reliable determination on the voluntariness issue which satisfies the constitutional rights of the defendant." The requirement that the prosecution spread on the record the prerequisites of a valid waiver is no constitutional innovation. In *Carnley v. Cochran*, we dealt with a problem of waiver of the right to counsel, a Sixth Amendment right. We held: "Presuming waiver from a silent record is impermissible. The record must show, or there must be an allegation and evidence which show, that an accused was offered counsel but intelligently and understandingly rejected the offer. Anything less is not waiver."

We think that the same standard must be applied to determining whether a guilty plea is voluntarily made. For, as we have said, a plea of guilty is more than an admission of conduct; it is a conviction. Ignorance, incomprehension, coercion, terror, inducements, subtle or blatant threats might be a perfect cover-up of unconstitutionality. The question of an effective waiver of a federal constitutional right in a proceeding is of course governed by federal standards.

Several federal constitutional rights are involved in a waiver that takes place when a plea of guilty is entered in a state criminal trial. First, is the privilege against compulsory self-incrimination guaranteed by the Fifth Amendment and applicable to the States by reason of the Fourteenth. Second, is the right to trial by jury. Third, is the right to confront one's accusers. We cannot presume a waiver of these three important federal rights from a silent record.

What is at stake for an accused facing death or imprisonment demands the utmost solicitude of which courts are capable in canvassing the matter with the accused to make sure he has a full understanding of what the plea connotes and of its consequence. When the judge discharges that function, he leaves a record adequate for any review that may be later sought and forestalls the spin-off of collateral proceedings that seek to probe murky memories.

The three dissenting justices in the Alabama Supreme Court stated the law accurately when they concluded that there was reversible error "because the record does not disclose that the defendant voluntarily and understandingly entered his pleas of guilty."

Reversed.

North Carolina v. Alford (1970)
400 U.S. 25

In this case, the court considers the issues of whether a defendant can maintain innocence and at the same time enter a guilty plea. After this case was decided, such contradictory pleas have been referred to as Alford pleas.

On December 2, 1963, Alford was indicted for first-degree murder, a capital offense under North Carolina law. The court appointed an attorney to represent him, and this attorney questioned all but one of the various witnesses who appellee said would substantiate his claim of innocence. The witnesses, however, did not support Alford's story but gave statements that strongly indicated his guilt. Faced with strong evidence of guilt and no substantial evidentiary support for the claim of innocence, Alford's attorney recommended that he plead guilty, but left the ultimate decision to Alford himself. The prosecutor agreed to accept a plea of guilty to a charge of second-degree murder, and on December 10, 1963, Alford pleaded guilty to the reduced charge.

Before the plea was finally accepted by the trial court, the court heard the sworn testimony of a police officer who summarized the State's case. Two other witnesses besides Alford were also heard. Although there was no eyewitness to the crime, the testimony indicated that shortly before the killing Alford took his gun from his house, stated his intention to kill the victim, and returned home with the declaration that he had carried out the killing. After the summary presentation of the State's case, Alford took the stand and testified that he had not committed the murder but that he was pleading guilty because he faced the threat of the death penalty if he did not do so. In response to the questions of his counsel, he acknowledged that his counsel had informed him of the difference between second- and first-degree murder and of his rights in case he chose to go to trial. The trial court then asked appellee if, in light of his denial of guilt, he still desired to plead guilty to second-degree murder and appellee answered, "Yes, sir. I plead guilty on—from the circumstances that he [Alford's attorney] told me." After eliciting information about Alford's prior criminal record, which was a long one, the trial court sentenced him to 30 years' imprisonment, the maximum penalty for second-degree murder.

Alford sought post-conviction relief in the state court. Among the claims raised was the claim that his plea of guilty was invalid because it was the product of fear and coercion. After a hearing, the state court in 1965 found that the plea was "willingly, knowingly, and understandingly" made on the advice of competent counsel and in the face of a strong prosecution case. Subsequently, Alford petitioned for a writ of habeas corpus, first in the United States District Court for the Middle District of North Carolina, and then in the Court of Appeals for the Fourth Circuit. Both courts denied the writ on the basis of the state court's findings that Alford voluntarily and knowingly agreed to plead guilty. In 1967, Alford again petitioned for a writ of habeas corpus in the District Court for the Middle District of North Carolina. That court, without an evidentiary hearing, again denied relief on the grounds that the guilty plea was voluntary and waived all defenses and nonjurisdictional defects in any prior stage of the proceedings, and that the findings of the state court in 1965 clearly required rejection of Alford's claim that he was denied effective assistance of counsel prior to pleading guilty. On appeal, a divided panel of the Court of Appeals for the Fourth Circuit reversed on the ground that Alford's guilty plea was made involuntarily.

In reaching its conclusion, the Court of Appeals relied heavily on *United States v. Jackson*, which the court read to require invalidation of the North Carolina statutory framework for the imposition of the death penalty because North Carolina statutes encouraged defendants to waive constitutional rights by the promise of no more than life imprisonment if a guilty plea was offered and accepted. Conceding that Jackson did not require the automatic invalidation of pleas of guilty entered under the North Carolina statutes, the Court of Appeals ruled that Alford's guilty plea was involuntary because its principal motivation was fear of the death penalty. By this standard, even if both the judge and the jury had possessed the power to impose the death penalty for first-degree murder or if guilty pleas to capital charges had not been permitted, Alford's plea of guilty to second-degree murder should still have been rejected because impermissibly induced by his desire to eliminate the possibility of a death sentence. We noted probable jurisdiction. We vacate the judgment of the Court of Appeals and remand the case for further proceedings.

We held in *Brady v. United States*, that a plea of guilty which would not have been entered except for the defendant's desire to avoid a possible death penalty and to limit the maximum penalty to life imprisonment or a term of years was not for that reason compelled within the meaning of the Fifth Amendment. Jackson established no new test for determining the validity of guilty pleas. The standard was and remains whether the plea represents a voluntary and intelligent choice among the alternative courses of action open to the defendant. That he would not have pleaded except for the opportunity to limit the possible penalty does not necessarily demonstrate that the plea of guilty was not the product of a free and rational choice, especially where the defendant was represented by competent counsel whose advice was that the plea would be to the defendant's advantage. The standard fashioned and applied by the Court of Appeals was therefore erroneous and we would, without more, vacate and remand the case for further proceedings with respect to any other claims of Alford which are properly before that court, if it were not for other circumstances appearing in the record which might seem to warrant an affirmance of the Court of Appeals.

As previously recounted, after Alford's plea of guilty was offered and the State's case was placed before the judge, Alford denied that he had committed the murder but reaffirmed his desire to plead guilty to avoid a possible death sentence and to limit the penalty to the 30-year maximum provided for second-degree murder. Ordinarily, a judgment of conviction resting on a plea of guilty is justified by the defendant's admission that he committed the crime charged against him and his consent that judgment be entered without a trial of any kind. The plea usually subsumes both elements, and justifiably so, even though there is no separate, express admission by the defendant that he committed the particular acts claimed to constitute the crime charged in the indictment. Here Alford entered his plea but accompanied it with the statement that he had not shot the victim.

If Alford's statements were to be credited as sincere assertions of his innocence, there obviously existed a factual and legal dispute between him and the State. Without more, it might be argued that the conviction entered on his guilty plea was invalid, since his assertion of innocence negatived any admission of guilt, which, as we observed last Term in *Brady*, is normally "central to the plea and the foundation for entering judgment against the defendant . . . ."

In addition to Alford's statement, however, the court had heard an account of the events on the night of the murder, including information from Alford's acquaintances that he had departed from his home with his gun stating his intention to kill and that he had later declared that he had carried out his intention. Nor had Alford wavered in his desire to have the trial court determine his guilt without a jury trial. Although denying the charge against him, he nevertheless preferred the dispute between him and the State to be settled by the judge in the context of a guilty plea proceeding rather than by a formal trial. Thereupon, with the State's telling evidence and Alford's denial before it, the trial court proceeded to convict and sentence Alford for second-degree murder.

State and lower federal courts are divided upon whether a guilty plea can be accepted when it is accompanied by protestations of innocence and hence contains only a waiver of trial but no admission of guilt. Some courts, giving expression to the principle that "our law only authorizes a conviction where guilt is shown," require that trial judges reject such pleas. But others have concluded that they should not "force any defense on a defendant in a criminal case," particularly when advancement of the defense might "end in disaster . . . ." They have argued that, since "guilt, or the degree of guilt, is at times uncertain and elusive," "an accused, though believing in or entertaining doubts respecting his innocence, might reasonably conclude a jury would be convinced of his guilt and that he would fare better in the sentence by pleading guilty . . . ." As one state court observed nearly a century ago, "reasons other than the fact that he is guilty may induce a defendant to so plead . . . and he must be permitted to judge for himself in this respect."

This Court has not confronted this precise issue, but prior decisions do yield relevant principles. In *Lynch v. Overholser*, Lynch, who had been charged in the Municipal Court of the District of Columbia with drawing and negotiating bad checks, a misdemeanor punishable by a maximum of one year in jail, sought to enter a plea of guilty, but the trial judge refused to accept the plea since a psychiatric report in the judge's possession indicated that Lynch had been suffering from "a manic depressive psychosis, at the time of the crime charged," and hence might have been not guilty by reason of insanity. Although at the subsequent trial Lynch did not rely on the insanity defense, he was found not guilty by reason of insanity and committed for an indeterminate period to a mental institution. On habeas corpus, the Court ordered his release, construing the congressional legislation seemingly authorizing the commitment as not reaching a case where the accused preferred a guilty plea to a plea of insanity. The Court expressly refused to rule that Lynch had an absolute right to have his guilty plea accepted, but implied that there would have been no constitutional error had his plea been accepted even though evidence before the judge indicated that there was a valid defense.

The issue in *Hudson v. United States*, was whether a federal court has power to impose a prison sentence after accepting a plea of nolo contendere, a plea by which a defendant does not expressly admit his guilt, but nonetheless waives his right to a trial and authorizes the court for purposes of the case to treat him as if he were guilty. The Court held that a trial court does have such power, and, except for the cases which were rejected in *Hudson*, the federal courts have uniformly followed this rule, even in cases involving moral turpitude. Implicit in the nolo contendere cases is a recognition that the Constitution does not bar imposition of a prison sentence upon an accused who is unwilling expressly to admit his guilt but who, faced with grim alternatives, is willing to waive his trial and accept the sentence.

These cases would be directly in point if Alford had simply insisted on his plea but refused to admit the crime. The fact that his plea was denominated a plea of guilty rather than a plea of nolo contendere is of no constitutional significance with respect to the issue now before us, for the Constitution is concerned with the practical consequences, not the formal categorizations, of state law. Thus, while most pleas of guilty consist of both a waiver of trial and an express admission of guilt, the latter element is not a constitutional requisite to the imposition of criminal penalty. An individual accused of crime may voluntarily, knowingly, and understandingly consent to the imposition of a prison sentence even if he is unwilling or unable to admit his participation in the acts constituting the crime.

Nor can we perceive any material difference between a plea that refuses to admit commission of the criminal act and a plea containing a protestation of innocence when, as in the instant case, a defendant intelligently concludes that his interests require entry of a guilty plea and the record before the judge contains strong evidence of actual guilt. Here the State had a strong case of first-degree murder against Alford. Whether he realized or disbelieved his guilt, he insisted on his plea because in his view he had absolutely nothing to gain by a trial and much to gain by pleading. Because of the overwhelming evidence against him, a trial was precisely what neither Alford nor his attorney desired. Confronted with the choice between a trial for first-degree murder, on the one hand, and a plea of guilty to second-degree murder, on the other, Alford quite reasonably chose the latter and thereby limited the maximum penalty to a 30-year term. When his plea is viewed in light of the evidence against him, which substantially negated his claim of innocence and which further provided a means by which the judge could test whether the plea was being intelligently entered its validity cannot be seriously questioned. In view of the strong factual basis for the plea demonstrated by the State and Alford's clearly expressed desire to enter it despite his professed belief in his innocence, we hold that the trial judge did not commit constitutional error in accepting it.

Relying on *United States v. Jackson*, Alford now argues in effect that the State should not have allowed him this choice but should have insisted on proving him guilty of murder in the first degree. The States in their wisdom may take this course by statute or otherwise and may prohibit the practice of accepting pleas to lesser included offenses under any circumstances. But this is not the mandate of the Fourteenth Amendment and the Bill of Rights. The prohibitions against involuntary or unintelligent pleas should not be relaxed, but neither should an exercise in arid logic render those constitutional guarantees counterproductive and put in jeopardy the very human values they were meant to preserve.

The Court of Appeals for the Fourth Circuit was in error to find Alford's plea of guilty invalid because it was made to avoid the possibility of the death penalty. That court's judgment directing the issuance of the writ of habeas corpus is vacated and the case is remanded to the Court of Appeals for further proceedings consistent with this opinion.

It is so ordered.

Ricketts v. Adamson (1987)
483 U.S. 1

In this case, the court considered the constitutional implications of an accused persons refusal to meet the conditions stated in a plea agreement. The court ruled that it is no double jeopardy to return an accused person to the legal status he or she held prior to the plea agreement being made.

The question for decision is whether the Double Jeopardy Clause bars the prosecution of respondent for first-degree murder following his breach of a plea agreement under which he had pleaded guilty to a lesser offense, had been sentenced, and had begun serving a term of imprisonment. The Court of Appeals for the Ninth Circuit held that the prosecution of respondent violated double jeopardy principles and directed the issuance of a writ of habeas corpus. We reverse.

In 1976, Donald Bolles, a reporter for the Arizona Republic, was fatally injured when a dynamite bomb exploded underneath his car. Respondent was arrested and charged with first-degree murder in connection with Bolles' death. Shortly after his trial had commenced, while jury selection was underway, respondent and the state prosecutor reached an agreement whereby respondent agreed to plead guilty to a charge of second-degree murder and to testify against two other individuals—Max Dunlap and James Robison—who were allegedly involved in Bolles' murder. Specifically, respondent agreed to "testify fully and completely in any Court, State or Federal, when requested by proper authorities against any and all parties involved in the murder of Don Bolles. . . ." The agreement provided that "should the defendant refuse to testify or should he at any time testify untruthfully . . . then this entire agreement is null and void and the original charge will be automatically reinstated." The parties agreed that respondent would receive a prison sentence of 48-49 years, with a total incarceration time of 20 years and 2 months. In January 1977, the state trial court accepted the plea agreement and the proposed sentence, but withheld imposition of the sentence. Thereafter, respondent testified as obligated under the agreement, and both Dunlap and Robison were convicted of the first-degree murder of Bolles. While their convictions and sentences were on appeal, the trial court, upon motion of the State, sentenced respondent. In February 1980, the Arizona Supreme Court reversed the convictions of Dunlap and Robison and remanded their cases for retrial. This event sparked the dispute now before us.

The State sought respondent's cooperation and testimony in preparation for the retrial of Dunlap and Robison. On April 3, 1980, however, respondent's counsel informed the prosecutor that respondent believed his obligation to provide testimony under the agreement had terminated when he was sentenced. Respondent would again testify against Dunlap and Robison only if certain conditions were met, including, among others, that the State release him from custody following the retrial. The State then informed respondent's attorney on April 9, 1980, that it deemed respondent to be in breach of the plea agreement. On April 18, 1980, the State called respondent to testify in pretrial proceedings. In response to questions, and upon advice of counsel, respondent invoked his Fifth Amendment privilege against self-incrimination. The trial judge, after respondent's counsel apprised him of the State's letter of April 9 indicating that the State considered respondent to be in breach of the plea agreement, refused to compel respondent to answer questions. The Arizona Supreme Court declined to accept jurisdiction of the State's petition for special action to review the trial judge's decision.

On May 8, 1980, the State filed a new information charging respondent with first-degree murder. Respondent's motion to quash the information on double jeopardy grounds was denied. Respondent challenged this decision by a special action in the Arizona Supreme Court. That court, after reviewing the plea agreement, the transcripts of the plea hearing and the sentencing hearing, respondent's April 3 letter to the state prosecutor, and the prosecutor's April response to that letter, held with "no hesitation" that "the plea agreement contemplates availability of respondent's testimony whether at trial or retrial after reversal," and that respondent "violated the terms of the plea agreement." The court also rejected respondent's double jeopardy claim, holding that the plea agreement "by its very terms waives the defense of double jeopardy if the agreement is violated." Finally, the court held that under state law and the terms of the plea agreement, the State should not have filed a new information, but should have merely reinstated the initial charge. Accordingly, the court vacated respondent's second-degree murder conviction, reinstated the original charge, and dismissed the new information.

After these rulings, respondent offered to testify at the retrials, but the State declined his offer. Respondent sought federal habeas relief, arguing that the Arizona Supreme Court had misconstrued the terms of the plea agreement. The District Court dismissed his petition, the Court of Appeals for the Ninth Circuit affirmed, and we denied respondent's petition for a writ of certiorari.

Respondent was then convicted of first-degree murder and sentenced to death. The judgment was affirmed on direct appeal, and we denied certiorari. Respondent sought federal habeas corpus for the second time, asserting a number of claims relating to his trial and sentence. The District Court dismissed the petition; a Court of Appeals panel affirmed. The Court of Appeals went en banc, held that the State had violated respondent's rights under the Double Jeopardy Clause, and directed the issuance of a writ of habeas corpus. The en banc opinion reasoned that respondent had not waived his double jeopardy rights by entering into the plea agreement, asserting that "it may well be argued that the only manner in which respondent could have made an intentional relinquishment of a known double jeopardy right would be by waiver 'spread on the record' of the court after an adequate explanation." Even if double jeopardy rights could be waived by implication, no such waiver occurred here since "agreeing that charges may be reinstituted under certain circumstances is not equivalent to agreeing that if they are reinstituted a double jeopardy defense is waived."

Finally, the court stated that even were the agreement read to waive double jeopardy rights impliedly, no waiver was effected here because a "defendant's action constituting the breach must be taken with the knowledge that in so doing he waives his double jeopardy rights." Because there was a "reasonable dispute as to respondent's obligation to testify," the court continued, "there could be no knowing or intentional waiver until his obligation to testify was announced by the court." The dissenting judges emphasized that respondent's refusal to testify triggered the second prosecution and the Double Jeopardy Clause "'does not relieve a defendant from the consequences of his voluntary choice.'" We granted the State's petition for a writ of certiorari to review the Court of Appeals' decision that the Double Jeopardy Clause barred prosecution of respondent for first-degree murder.

We may assume that jeopardy attached at least when respondent was sentenced in December 1978, on his plea of guilty to second-degree murder. Assuming also that under Arizona law second-degree murder is a lesser included offense of first-degree murder, the Double Jeopardy Clause, absent special circumstances, would have precluded prosecution of respondent for the greater charge on which he now stands convicted.

The State submits, however, that respondent's breach of the plea arrangement to which the parties had agreed removed the double jeopardy bar to prosecution of respondent on the first-degree murder charge. We agree with the State.

Under the terms of the plea agreement, both parties bargained for and received substantial benefits. The State obtained respondent's guilty plea and his promise to testify against "any and all parties involved in the murder of Don Bolles" and in certain specified other crimes. Respondent, a direct participant in a premeditated and brutal murder, received a specified prison sentence accompanied with a guarantee that he would serve actual incarceration time of 20 years and 2 months. He further obtained the State's promise that he would not be prosecuted for his involvement in certain other crimes.

The agreement specifies in two separate paragraphs the consequences that would flow from respondent's breach of his promises. Paragraph 5 provides that if respondent refused to testify, "this entire agreement is null and void and the original charge will be automatically reinstated." Similarly, Paragraph 15 of the agreement states that "in the event this agreement becomes null and void, then the parties shall be returned to the positions they were in before this agreement." Respondent unquestionably understood the meaning of these provisions. At the plea hearing, the trial judge read the plea agreement to respondent, line by line, and pointedly asked respondent whether he understood the provisions in Paragraphs 5 and 15. Respondent replied "Yes, sir," to each question. On this score, we do not find it significant, as did the Court of Appeals, that "double jeopardy" was not specifically waived by name in the plea agreement. Nor are we persuaded by the court's assertion that "agreeing that charges may be reinstituted . . . is not equivalent to agreeing that if they are reinstituted a double jeopardy defense is waived."

The terms of the agreement could not be clearer: in the event of respondent's breach occasioned by a refusal to testify, the parties would be returned to the status quo ante, in which case respondent would have no double jeopardy defense to waive. And, an agreement specifying that charges may be reinstated given certain circumstances is, at least under the provisions of this plea agreement, precisely equivalent to an agreement waiving a double jeopardy defense. The approach taken by the Court of Appeals would render the agreement meaningless: first-degree murder charges could not be reinstated against respondent if he categorically refused to testify after sentencing even if the agreement specifically provided that he would so testify, because, under the Court of Appeals' view, he never waived his double jeopardy protection. Even respondent, however, conceded at oral argument that "a waiver could be found under those circumstances . . . ."

We are also unimpressed by the Court of Appeals' holding that there was a good-faith dispute about whether respondent was bound to testify a second time and that until the extent of his obligation was decided, there could be no knowing and intelligent waiver of his double jeopardy defense. But respondent knew that if he breached the agreement he could be retried, and it is incredible to believe that he did not anticipate that the extent of his obligation would be decided by a court. Here he sought a construction of the agreement in the Arizona Supreme Court, and that court found that he had failed to live up to his promise. The result was that respondent was returned to the position he occupied prior to execution of the plea bargain: he stood charged with first-degree murder. Trial on that charge did not violate the Double Jeopardy Clause. *United States v. Scott* supports this conclusion.

At the close of all the evidence in *Scott*, the trial judge granted defendant's motion to dismiss two counts of the indictment against him on the basis of preindictment delay. This Court held that the Double Jeopardy Clause did not bar the Government from appealing the trial judge's decision, because "in a case such as this the defendant, by deliberately choosing to seek termination of the proceedings against him on a basis unrelated to factual guilt or innocence of the offense of which he was accused, suffers no injury cognizable under the Double Jeopardy Clause. . . ." The Court reasoned further that "the Double Jeopardy Clause . . . does not relieve a defendant from the consequences of his voluntary choice." The "voluntary choice" to which the *Scott* Court referred was the defendant's decision to move for dismissal of two counts of the indictment, seeking termination of that portion of the proceedings before the empaneled jury, rather than facing the risk that he might be convicted if his case were submitted to the jury. The respondent in this case had a similar choice. He could submit to the State's request that he testify at the retrial, and in so doing risk that he would be providing testimony that pursuant to the agreement he had no obligation to provide, or he could stand on his interpretation of the agreement, knowing that if he were wrong, his breach of the agreement would restore the parties to their original positions and he could be prosecuted for first-degree murder. Respondent chose the latter course, and the Double Jeopardy Clause does not relieve him from the consequences of that choice.

Respondent cannot escape the Arizona Supreme Court's interpretation of his obligations under the agreement. The State did not force the breach; respondent chose, perhaps for strategic reasons or as a gamble, to advance an interpretation of the agreement that proved erroneous. And, there is no indication that respondent did not fully understand the potential seriousness of the position he adopted. In the April 3 letter, respondent's counsel advised the prosecutor that respondent "is fully aware of the fact that your office may feel that he has not completed his obligations under the plea agreement . . . and, further, that your office may attempt to withdraw the plea agreement from him, and that he may be prosecuted for the killing of Donald Bolles on a first degree murder charge." This statement of respondent's awareness of the operative terms of the plea agreement only underscores that which respondent's plea hearing made evident: respondent clearly appreciated and understood the consequences were he found to be in breach of the agreement.

Finally, it is of no moment that following the Arizona Supreme Court's decision respondent offered to comply with the terms of the agreement. At this point, respondent's second-degree murder conviction had already been ordered vacated and the original charge reinstated. The parties did not agree that respondent would be relieved from the consequences of his refusal to testify if he were able to advance a colorable argument that a testimonial obligation was not owing. The parties could have struck a different bargain, but permitting the State to enforce the agreement the parties actually made does not violate the Double Jeopardy Clause.

The judgment of the Court of Appeals is reversed.

It is so ordered.

Bordenkircher v. Hayes (1978)
434 U.S. 357

In this case, the Supreme Court considers whether the Fourteenth Amendment's Due Process Clause prohibits prosecutors from carrying out threats made during plea negotiations to re-indict accused persons on more serious charges if they do not plead guilty to the offense with which they were originally charged. In addition, the court considers the importance of the plea bargaining process in the modern criminal justice system.

The question in this case is whether the Due Process Clause of the Fourteenth Amendment is violated when a state prosecutor carries out a threat made during plea negotiations to reindict the accused on more serious charges if he does not plead guilty to the offense with which he was originally charged.

I.

The respondent, Paul Lewis Hayes, was indicted by a Fayette County, Ky., grand jury on a charge of uttering a forged instrument in the amount of $ 88.30, an offense then punishable by a term of 2 to 10 years in prison. After arraignment, Hayes, his retained counsel, and the Commonwealth's Attorney met in the presence of the Clerk of the Court to discuss a possible plea agreement. During these conferences the prosecutor offered to recommend a sentence of five years in prison if Hayes would plead guilty to the indictment. He also said that if Hayes did not plead guilty and "saved the court the inconvenience and necessity of a trial," he would return to the grand jury to seek an indictment under the Kentucky Habitual Criminal Act, which would subject Hayes to a mandatory sentence of life imprisonment by reason of his two prior felony convictions. Hayes chose not to plead guilty, and the prosecutor did obtain an indictment charging him under the Habitual Criminal Act. It is not disputed that the recidivist charge was fully justified by the evidence, that the prosecutor was in possession of this evidence at the time of the original indictment, and that Hayes' refusal to plead guilty to the original charge was what led to his indictment under the habitual criminal statute.

A jury found Hayes guilty on the principal charge of uttering a forged instrument and, in a separate proceeding, further found that he had twice before been convicted of felonies. As required by the habitual offender statute, he was sentenced to a life term in the penitentiary. The Kentucky Court of Appeals rejected Hayes' constitutional objections to the enhanced sentence, holding in an unpublished opinion that imprisonment for life with the possibility of parole was constitutionally permissible in light of the previous felonies of which Hayes had been convicted, and that the prosecutor's decision to indict him as a habitual offender was a legitimate use of available leverage in the plea bargaining process.

On Hayes' petition for a federal writ of habeas corpus, the United States District Court for the Eastern District of Kentucky agreed that there had been no constitutional violation in the sentence or the indictment procedure, and denied the writ. The Court of Appeals for the Sixth Circuit reversed the District Court's judgment. While recognizing "that plea bargaining now plays an important role in our criminal justice system," the appellate court thought that the prosecutor's conduct during the bargaining negotiations had violated the principles of *Blackledge v. Perry*, which "protected defendants from the vindictive exercise of a prosecutor's discretion." Accordingly, the court ordered that Hayes be discharged "except for his confinement under a lawful sentence imposed solely for the crime of uttering a forged instrument." We granted certiorari to consider a constitutional question of importance in the administration of criminal justice.

II.

It may be helpful to clarify at the outset the nature of the issue in this case. While the prosecutor did not actually obtain the recidivist indictment until after the plea conferences had ended, his intention to do so was clearly expressed at the outset of the plea negotiations. Hayes was thus fully informed of the true terms of the offer when he made his decision to plead not guilty. This is not a situation, therefore, where the prosecutor without notice brought an additional and more serious charge after plea negotiations relating only to the original indictment had ended with the defendant's insistence on pleading not guilty. As a practical matter, in short, this case would be no different if the grand jury had indicted Hayes as a recidivist from the outset, and the prosecutor had offered to drop that charge as part of the plea bargain.

The Court of Appeals nonetheless drew a distinction between "concessions relating to prosecution under an existing indictment," and threats to bring more severe charges not contained in the original indictment—a line it thought necessary in order to establish a prophylactic rule to guard against the evil of prosecutorial vindictiveness. Quite apart from this chronological distinction, however, the Court of Appeals found that the prosecutor had acted vindictively in the present case since he had conceded that the indictment was influenced by his desire to induce a guilty plea. The ultimate conclusion of the Court of Appeals thus seems to have been that a prosecutor acts vindictively and in violation of due process of law whenever his charging decision is influenced by what he hopes to gain in the course of plea bargaining negotiations.

III.

We have recently had occasion to observe that: Whatever might be the situation in an ideal world, the fact is that the guilty plea and the often concomitant plea bargain are important components of this country's criminal justice system. Properly administered, they can benefit all concerned." The open acknowledgment of this previously clandestine practice has led this Court to recognize the importance of counsel during plea negotiations, the need for a public record indicating that a plea was knowingly and voluntarily made, and the requirement that a prosecutor's plea bargaining promise must be kept. The decision of the Court of Appeals in the present case, however, did not deal with considerations such as these, but held that the substance of the plea offer itself violated the limitations imposed by the Due Process Clause of the Fourteenth Amendment. For the reasons that follow, we have concluded that the Court of Appeals was mistaken in so ruling.

IV.

This Court held in *North Carolina v. Pearce* that the Due Process Clause of the Fourteenth Amendment "requires that vindictiveness against a defendant for having successfully attacked his first conviction must play no part in the sentence he receives after a new trial." The same principle was later applied to prohibit a prosecutor from reindicting a convicted misdemeanant on a felony charge after the defendant had invoked an appellate remedy, since in this situation there was also a "realistic likelihood of vindictiveness."

In those cases the Court was dealing with the State's unilateral imposition of a penalty upon a defendant who had chosen to exercise a legal right to attack his original conviction—a situation "very different from the give-and-take negotiation common in plea bargaining between the prosecution and defense, which arguably possess relatively equal bargaining power." The Court has emphasized that the due process violation in cases such as *Pearce* and *Perry* lay not in the possibility that a defendant might be deterred from the exercise of a legal right, but rather in the danger that the State might be retaliating against the accused for lawfully attacking his conviction.

To punish a person because he has done what the law plainly allows him to do is a due process violation of the most basic sort, and for an agent of the State to pursue a course of action whose objective is to penalize a person's reliance on his legal rights is "patently unconstitutional." But in the "give-and-take" of plea bargaining, there is no such element of punishment or retaliation so long as the accused is free to accept or reject the prosecution's offer.

Plea bargaining flows from "the mutuality of advantage" to defendants and prosecutors, each with his own reasons for wanting to avoid trial. Defendants advised by competent counsel and protected by other procedural safeguards are presumptively capable of intelligent choice in response to prosecutorial persuasion, and unlikely to be driven to false self-condemnation. Indeed, acceptance of the basic legitimacy of plea bargaining necessarily implies rejection of any notion that a guilty plea is involuntary in a constitutional sense simply because it is the end result of the bargaining process. By hypothesis, the plea may have been induced by promises of a recommendation of a lenient sentence or a reduction of charges, and thus by fear of the possibility of a greater penalty upon conviction after a trial.

While confronting a defendant with the risk of more severe punishment clearly may have a "discouraging effect on the defendant's assertion of his trial rights, the imposition of these difficult choices is an inevitable"—and permissible—"attribute of any legitimate system which tolerates and encourages the negotiation of pleas." It follows that, by tolerating and encouraging the negotiation of pleas, this Court has necessarily accepted as constitutionally legitimate the simple reality that the prosecutor's interest at the bargaining table is to persuade the defendant to forgo his right to plead not guilty.

It is not disputed here that Hayes was properly chargeable under the recidivist statute, since he had in fact been convicted of two previous felonies. In our system, so long as the prosecutor has probable cause to believe that the accused committed an offense defined by statute, the decision whether or not to prosecute, and what charge to file or bring before a grand jury, generally rests entirely in his discretion. Within the limits set by the legislature's constitutionally valid definition of chargeable offenses, "the conscious exercise of some selectivity in enforcement is not in itself a federal constitutional violation" so long as "the selection was not deliberately based upon an unjustifiable standard such as race, religion, or other arbitrary classification." To hold that the prosecutor's desire to induce a guilty plea is an "unjustifiable standard," which, like race or religion, may play no part in his charging decision, would contradict the very premises that underlie the concept of plea bargaining itself. Moreover, a rigid constitutional rule that would prohibit a prosecutor from acting forthrightly in his dealings with the defense could only invite unhealthy subterfuge that would drive the practice of plea bargaining back into the shadows from which it has so recently emerged.

There is no doubt that the breadth of discretion that our country's legal system vests in prosecuting attorneys carries with it the potential for both individual and institutional abuse. And broad though that discretion may be, there are undoubtedly constitutional limits upon its exercise. We hold only that the course of conduct engaged in by the prosecutor in this case, which no more than openly presented the defendant with the unpleasant alternatives of forgoing trial or facing charges on which he was plainly subject to prosecution, did not violate the Due Process Clause of the Fourteenth Amendment.

Accordingly, the judgment of the Court of Appeals is Reversed.

Williams v. Florida (1970)
399 U.S. 78

This case is an example of a case that raises more than one constitutional issue. The first issue the Court deals with in this case is whether a requirement that alibi witnesses be identified to the prosecution violates the defendant's fifth Amendment Right to not incriminate himself. The second is a Sixth Amendment claim regarding the number of jurors that are constitutionally required to hear a criminal case.

Prior to his trial for robbery in the State of Florida, petitioner filed a "Motion for a Protective Order," seeking to be excused from the requirements of Rule 1.200 of the Florida Rules of Criminal Procedure. That rule requires a defendant, on written demand of the prosecuting attorney, to give notice in advance of trial if the defendant intends to claim an alibi, and to furnish the prosecuting attorney with information as to the place where he claims to have been and with the names and addresses of the alibi witnesses he intends to use. In his motion petitioner openly declared his intent to claim an alibi, but objected to the further disclosure requirements on the ground that the rule "compels the Defendant in a criminal case to be a witness against himself" in violation of his Fifth and Fourteenth Amendment rights. The motion was denied. Petitioner also filed a pretrial motion to impanel a 12-man jury instead of the six-man jury provided by Florida law in all but capital cases. That motion too was denied. Petitioner was convicted as charged and was sentenced to life imprisonment. The District Court of Appeal affirmed, rejecting petitioner's claims that his Fifth and Sixth Amendment rights had been violated. We granted certiorari.

I.

Florida's notice-of-alibi rule is in essence a requirement that a defendant submit to a limited form of pretrial discovery by the State whenever he intends to rely at trial on the defense of alibi. In exchange for the defendant's disclosure of the witnesses he proposes to use to establish that defense, the State in turn is required to notify the defendant of any witnesses it proposes to offer in rebuttal to that defense. Both sides are under a continuing duty promptly to disclose the names and addresses of additional witnesses bearing on the alibi as they become available. The threatened sanction for failure to comply is the exclusion at trial of the defendant's alibi evidence—except for his own testimony—or, in the case of the State, the exclusion of the State's evidence offered in rebuttal of the alibi.

In this case, following the denial of his Motion for a Protective Order, petitioner complied with the alibi rule and gave the State the name and address of one Mary Scotty. Mrs. Scotty was summoned to the office of the State Attorney on the morning of the trial, where she gave pretrial testimony. At the trial itself, Mrs. Scotty, petitioner, and petitioner's wife all testified that the three of them had been in Mrs. Scotty's apartment during the time of the robbery. On two occasions during cross-examination of Mrs. Scotty, the prosecuting attorney confronted her with her earlier deposition in which she had given dates and times that in some respects did not correspond with the dates and times given at trial. Mrs. Scotty adhered to her trial story, insisting that she had been mistaken in her earlier testimony. The State also offered in rebuttal the testimony of one of the officers investigating the robbery who claimed that Mrs. Scotty had asked him for directions on the afternoon in question during the time when she claimed to have been in her apartment with petitioner and his wife.

We need not linger over the suggestion that the discovery permitted the State against petitioner in this case deprived him of "due process" or a "fair trial." Florida law provides for liberal discovery by the defendant against the State, and the notice-of-alibi rule is itself carefully hedged with reciprocal duties requiring state disclosure to the defendant. Given the ease with which an alibi can be fabricated, the State's interest in protecting itself against an eleventh-hour defense is both obvious and legitimate. Reflecting this interest, notice-of-alibi provisions, dating at least from 1927, are now in existence in a substantial number of States. The adversary system of trial is hardly an end in itself; it is not yet a poker game in which players enjoy an absolute right always to conceal their cards until played. We find ample room in that system, at least as far as "due process" is concerned, for the instant Florida rule, which is designed to enhance the search for truth in the criminal trial by insuring both the defendant and the State ample opportunity to investigate certain facts crucial to the determination of guilt or innocence.

Petitioner's major contention is that he was "compelled . . . to be a witness against himself" contrary to the commands of the Fifth and Fourteenth Amendments because the notice-of-alibi rule required him to give the State the name and address of Mrs. Scotty in advance of trial and thus to furnish the State with information useful in convicting him. No pretrial statement of petitioner was introduced at trial; but armed with Mrs. Scotty's name and address and the knowledge that she was to be petitioner's alibi witness, the State was able to take her deposition in advance of trial and to find rebuttal testimony. Also, requiring him to reveal the elements of his defense is claimed to have interfered with his right to wait until after the State had presented its case to decide how to defend against it.

We conclude, however, as has apparently every other court that has considered the issue, that the privilege against self-incrimination is not violated by a requirement that the defendant give notice of an alibi defense and disclose his alibi witnesses.

The defendant in a criminal trial is frequently forced to testify himself and to call other witnesses in an effort to reduce the risk of conviction. When he presents his witnesses, he must reveal their identity and submit them to cross-examination which in itself may prove incriminating or which may furnish the State with leads to incriminating rebuttal evidence. That the defendant faces such a dilemma demanding a choice between complete silence and presenting a defense has never been thought an invasion of the privilege against compelled self-incrimination. The pressures generated by the State's evidence may be severe but they do not vitiate the defendant's choice to present an alibi defense and witnesses to prove it, even though the attempted defense ends in catastrophe for the defendant. However "testimonial" or "incriminating" the alibi defense proves to be, it cannot be considered "compelled" within the meaning of the Fifth and Fourteenth Amendments.

Very similar constraints operate on the defendant when the State requires pretrial notice of alibi and the naming of alibi witnesses. Nothing in such a rule requires the defendant to rely on an alibi or prevents him from abandoning the defense; these matters are left to his unfettered choice. That choice must be made, but the pressures that bear on his pretrial decision are of the same nature as those that would induce him to call alibi witnesses at the trial: the force of historical fact beyond both his and the State's control and the strength of the State's case built on these facts. Response to that kind of pressure by offering evidence or testimony is not compelled self-incrimination transgressing the Fifth and Fourteenth Amendments.

In the case before us, the notice-of-alibi rule by itself in no way affected petitioner's crucial decision to call alibi witnesses or added to the legitimate pressures leading to that course of action. At most, the rule only compelled petitioner to accelerate the timing of his disclosure, forcing him to divulge at an earlier date information that the petitioner from the beginning planned to divulge at trial. Nothing in the Fifth Amendment privilege entitles a defendant as a matter of constitutional right to await the end of the State's case before announcing the nature of his defense, any more than it entitles him to await the jury's verdict on the State's case-in-chief before deciding whether or not to take the stand himself.

Petitioner concedes that absent the notice-of-alibi rule the Constitution would raise no bar to the court's granting the State a continuance at trial on the ground of surprise as soon as the alibi witness is called. Nor would there be self-incrimination problems if, during that continuance, the State was permitted to do precisely what it did here prior to trial: take the deposition of the witness and find rebuttal evidence. But if so utilizing a continuance is permissible under the Fifth and Fourteenth Amendments, then surely the same result may be accomplished through pretrial discovery, as it was here, avoiding the necessity of a disrupted trial. We decline to hold that the privilege against compulsory self-incrimination guarantees the defendant the right to surprise the State with an alibi defense.

II.

In *Duncan v. Louisiana*, we held that the Fourteenth Amendment guarantees a right to trial by jury in all criminal cases that—were they to be tried in a federal court—would come within the Sixth Amendment's guarantee. Petitioner's trial for robbery on July 3, 1968, clearly falls within the scope of that holding. The question in this case then is whether the constitutional guarantee of a trial by "jury" necessarily requires trial by exactly 12 persons, rather than some lesser number—in this case six. We hold that the 12-man panel is not a necessary ingredient of "trial by jury," and that respondent's refusal to impanel more than the six members provided for by Florida law did not violate petitioner's Sixth Amendment rights as applied to the States through the Fourteenth.

We had occasion in *Duncan v. Louisiana*, to review briefly the oft-told history of the development of trial by jury in criminal cases. That history revealed a long tradition attaching great importance to the concept of relying on a body of one's peers to determine guilt or innocence as a safeguard against arbitrary law enforcement. That same history, however, affords little insight into the considerations that gradually led the size of that body to be generally fixed at 12. Some have suggested that the number 12 was fixed upon simply because that was the number of the presentment jury from the hundred, from which the petit jury developed. Other, less circular but more fanciful reasons for the number 12 have been given, "but they were all brought forward after the number was fixed," and rest on little more than mystical or superstitious insights into the significance of "12." Lord Coke's explanation that the "number of twelve is much respected in holy writ, as 12 apostles, 12 stones, 12 tribes, etc.," is typical. In short, while sometime in the 14th century the size of the jury at common law came to be fixed generally at 12, that particular feature of the jury system appears to have been a historical accident, unrelated to the great purposes which gave rise to the jury in the first place. The question before us is whether this accidental feature of the jury has been immutably codified into our Constitution.

This Court's earlier decisions have assumed an affirmative answer to this question. The leading case so construing the Sixth Amendment is *Thompson v. Utah*. There the defendant had been tried and convicted by a 12-man jury for a crime committed in the Territory of Utah. A new trial was granted, but by that time Utah had been admitted as a State. The defendant's new trial proceeded under Utah's Constitution, providing for a jury of only eight members. This Court reversed the resulting conviction, holding that Utah's constitutional provision was an *ex post facto* law as applied to the defendant. In reaching its conclusion, the Court announced that the Sixth Amendment was applicable to the defendant's trial when Utah was a Territory, and that the jury referred to in the Amendment was a jury "constituted, as it was at common law, of twelve persons, neither more nor less." Arguably unnecessary for the result, this announcement was supported simply by referring to the *Magna Carta*, and by quoting passages from treatises which noted—what has already been seen—that at common law the jury did indeed consist of 12. Noticeably absent was any discussion of the essential step in the argument: namely, that every feature of the jury as it existed at common law—whether incidental or essential to that institution—was necessarily included in the Constitution wherever that document referred to a "jury." Subsequent decisions have reaffirmed the announcement in *Thompson*, often in dictum and usually by relying—where there was any discussion of the issue at all—solely on the fact that the common-law jury consisted of 12.

While "the intent of the Framers" is often an elusive quarry, the relevant constitutional history casts considerable doubt on the easy assumption in our past decisions that if a given feature existed in a jury at common law in 1789, then it was necessarily preserved in the Constitution. Provisions for jury trial were first placed in the Constitution in Article III's provision that "the Trial of all Crimes . . . shall be by Jury; and such Trial shall be held in the State where the said Crimes shall have been committed." The "very scanty history of this provision in the records of the Constitutional Convention" sheds little light either way on the intended correlation between Article III's "jury" and the features of the jury at common law. Indeed, pending and after the adoption of the Constitution, fears were expressed that Article III's provision failed to preserve the common-law right to be tried by a "jury of the vicinage."

That concern, as well as the concern to preserve the right to jury in civil as well as criminal cases, furnished part of the impetus for introducing amendments to the Constitution that ultimately resulted in the jury trial provisions of the Sixth and Seventh Amendments. As introduced by James Madison in the House, the Amendment relating to jury trial in criminal cases would have provided that:

"The trial of all crimes . . . shall be by an impartial jury of freeholders of the vicinage, with the requisite of unanimity for conviction, of the right of challenge, and other accustomed requisites. . . ."

. . . .

Three significant features may be observed in this sketch of the background of the Constitution's jury trial provisions. First, even though the vicinage requirement was as much a feature of the common-law jury as was the 12-man requirement, the mere reference to "trial by jury" in Article III was not interpreted to include that feature. Indeed, as the subsequent debates over the Amendments indicate, disagreement arose over whether the feature should be included at all in its common-law sense, resulting in the compromise described above. Second, provisions that would have explicitly tied the "jury" concept to the "accustomed requisites" of the time were eliminated. Such action is concededly open to the explanation that the "accustomed requisites" were thought to be already included in the concept of a "jury." But that explanation is no more plausible than the contrary one: that the deletion had some substantive effect. Indeed, given the clear expectation that a substantive change would be effected by the inclusion or deletion of an explicit "vicinage" requirement, the latter explanation is, if anything, the more plausible. Finally, contemporary legislative and constitutional provisions indicate that where Congress wanted to leave no doubt that it was incorporating existing common-law features of the jury system, it knew how to use express language to that effect.... And the Seventh Amendment, providing for jury trial in civil cases, explicitly added that "no fact tried by a jury, shall be otherwise re-examined in any Court of the United States, than according to the rules of the common law."

We do not pretend to be able to divine precisely what the word "jury" imported to the Framers, the First Congress, or the States in 1789. It may well be that the usual expectation was that the jury would consist of 12, and that hence, the most likely conclusion to be drawn is simply that little thought was actually given to the specific question we face today. But there is absolutely no indication in "the intent of the Framers" of an explicit decision to equate the constitutional and common-law characteristics of the jury. Nothing in this history suggests, then, that we do violence to the letter of the Constitution by turning to other than purely historical considerations to determine which features of the jury system, as it existed at common law, were preserved in the Constitution. The relevant inquiry, as we see it, must be the function that the particular feature performs and its relation to the purposes of the jury trial. Measured by this standard, the 12-man requirement cannot be regarded as an indispensable component of the Sixth Amendment.

The purpose of the jury trial, as we noted in *Duncan*, is to prevent oppression by the Government. "Providing an accused with the right to be tried by a jury of his peers gave him an inestimable safeguard against the corrupt or overzealous prosecutor and against the compliant, biased, or eccentric judge." Given this purpose, the essential feature of a jury obviously lies in the interposition between the accused and his accuser of the commonsense judgment of a group of laymen, and in the community participation and shared responsibility that results from that group's determination of guilt or innocence. The performance of this role is not a function of the particular number of the body that makes up the jury. To be sure, the number should probably be large enough to promote group deliberation, free from outside attempts at intimidation, and to provide a fair possibility for obtaining a representative cross-section of the community. But we find little reason to think that these goals are in any meaningful sense less likely to be achieved when the jury numbers six, than when it numbers 12—particularly if the requirement of unanimity is retained. And, certainly the reliability of the jury as a factfinder hardly seems likely to be a function of its size.

It might be suggested that the 12-man jury gives a defendant a greater advantage since he has more "chances" of finding a juror who will insist on acquittal and thus prevent conviction. But the advantage might just as easily belong to the State, which also needs only one juror out of twelve insisting on guilt to prevent acquittal. What few experiments have occurred—usually in the civil area—indicate that there is no discernible difference between the results reached by the two different-sized juries. In short, neither currently available evidence nor theory suggests that the 12-man jury is necessarily more advantageous to the defendant than a jury composed of fewer members.

Similarly, while in theory the number of viewpoints represented on a randomly selected jury ought to increase as the size of the jury increases, in practice the difference between the 12-man and the six-man jury in terms of the cross-section of the community represented seems likely to be negligible. Even the 12-man jury cannot insure representation of every distinct voice in the community, particularly given the use of the peremptory challenge. As long as arbitrary exclusions of a particular class from the jury rolls are forbidden, the concern that the cross-section will be significantly diminished if the jury is decreased in size from 12 to six seems an unrealistic one.

We conclude, in short, as we began: the fact that the jury at common law was composed of precisely 12 is a historical accident, unnecessary to effect the purposes of the jury system and wholly without significance "except to mystics." To read the Sixth Amendment as forever codifying a feature so incidental to the real purpose of the Amendment is to ascribe a blind formalism to the Framers which would require considerably more evidence than we have been able to discover in the history and language of the Constitution or in the reasoning of our past decisions. We do not mean to intimate that legislatures can never have good reasons for concluding that the 12-man jury is preferable to the smaller jury, or that such conclusions—reflected in the provisions of most States and in our federal system—are in any sense unwise. Legislatures may well have their own views about the relative value of the larger and smaller juries, and may conclude that, wholly apart from the jury's primary function, it is desirable to spread the collective responsibility for the determination of guilt among the larger group. In capital cases, for example, it appears that no State provides for less than 12 jurors—a fact that suggests implicit recognition of the value of the larger body as a means of legitimating society's decision to impose the death penalty. Our holding does no more than leave these considerations to Congress and the States, unrestrained by an interpretation of the Sixth Amendment that would forever dictate the precise number that can constitute a jury. Consistent with this holding, we conclude that petitioner's Sixth Amendment rights, as applied to the States through the Fourteenth Amendment, were not violated by Florida's decision to provide a six-man rather than a 12-man jury.

The judgment of the Florida District Court of Appeal is Affirmed.

Batson v. Kentucky (1986)
476 U.S. 79

In the jury selection process, both the prosecution and the defense have the right to dismiss potential jurors for cause, such as when a prosecutor dismisses a juror that as adamantly opposed to the death penalty in a death penalty case. When there is a stated, logical reason for dismissing a juror, the juror is said to have been dismissed for cause. Both sides also get a limited number of preemptory challenges whereby the reason for the challenge need not be revealed. In this case, the Supreme Court examines the issue of using such preemptory challenges with racist motives is unconstitutional. The court ultimately finds that the racist use of preemptory challenges is unconstitutional. When a defense attorney objects to the removal of a juror because the challenge was believed to have a racist motive, it is referred to as a Batson challenge. Since Batson, the Courts have extended the protection to civil cases, as well as cases where preemptory challenges are used with sexist motives.

This case requires us to reexamine that portion of *Swain v. Alabama*, concerning the evidentiary burden placed on a criminal defendant who claims that he has been denied equal protection through the State's use of peremptory challenges to exclude members of his race from the petit jury.

I.

Petitioner, a black man, was indicted in Kentucky on charges of second-degree burglary and receipt of stolen goods. On the first day of trial in Jefferson Circuit Court, the judge conducted voir dire examination of the venire, excused certain jurors for cause, and permitted the parties to exercise peremptory challenges. The prosecutor used his peremptory challenges to strike all four black persons on the venire, and a jury composed only of white persons was selected. Defense counsel moved to discharge the jury before it was sworn on the ground that the prosecutor's removal of the black veniremen violated petitioner's rights under the Sixth and Fourteenth Amendments to a jury drawn from a cross section of the community, and under the Fourteenth Amendment to equal protection of the laws. Counsel requested a hearing on his motion. Without expressly ruling on the request for a hearing, the trial judge observed that the parties were entitled to use their peremptory challenges to "strike anybody they want to." The judge then denied petitioner's motion, reasoning that the cross-section requirement applies only to selection of the venire and not to selection of the petit jury itself.

The jury convicted petitioner on both counts. On appeal to the Supreme Court of Kentucky, petitioner pressed, among other claims, the argument concerning the prosecutor's use of peremptory challenges. Conceding that *Swain v. Alabama* apparently foreclosed an equal protection claim based solely on the prosecutor's conduct in this case, petitioner urged the court to follow decisions of other and to hold that such conduct violated his rights under the Sixth Amendment and § 11 of the Kentucky Constitution to a jury drawn from a cross section of the community.

Petitioner also contended that the facts showed that the prosecutor had engaged in a "pattern" of discriminatory challenges in this case and established an equal protection violation under *Swain*. The Supreme Court of Kentucky affirmed. In a single paragraph, the court declined petitioner's invitation to adopt the reasoning of *People v. Wheeler* and *Commonwealth v. Soares*. The court observed that it recently had reaffirmed its reliance on *Swain*, and had held that a defendant alleging lack of a fair cross section must demonstrate systematic exclusion of a group of jurors from the venire. We granted certiorari, and now reverse.

II.

In *Swain v. Alabama*, this Court recognized that a "State's purposeful or deliberate denial to Negroes on account of race of participation as jurors in the administration of justice violates the Equal Protection Clause." This principle has been "consistently and repeatedly" reaffirmed in numerous decisions of this Court both preceding and following *Swain*.

A.

More than a century ago, the Court decided that the State denies a black defendant equal protection of the laws when it puts him on trial before a jury from which members of his race have been purposefully excluded. That decision laid the foundation for the Court's unceasing efforts to eradicate racial discrimination in the procedures used to select the venire from which individual jurors are drawn. In *Strauder*, the Court explained that the central concern of the recently ratified Fourteenth Amendment was to put an end to governmental discrimination on account of race. Exclusion of black citizens from service as jurors constitutes a primary example of the evil the Fourteenth Amendment was designed to cure.

In holding that racial discrimination in jury selection offends the Equal Protection Clause, the Court in *Strauder* recognized, however, that a defendant has no right to a "petit jury composed in whole or in part of persons of his own race." "The number of our races and nationalities stands in the way of evolution of such a conception" of the demand of equal protection. But the defendant does have the right to be tried by a jury whose members are selected pursuant to non-discriminatory criteria. The Equal Protection Clause guarantees the defendant that the State will not exclude members of his race from the jury venire on account of race, or on the false assumption that members of his race as a group are not qualified to serve as jurors.

Purposeful racial discrimination in selection of the venire violates a defendant's right to equal protection because it denies him the protection that a trial by jury is intended to secure. "The very idea of a jury is a body . . . composed of the peers or equals of the person whose rights it is selected or summoned to determine; that is, of his neighbors, fellows, associates, persons having the same legal status in society as that which he holds." The petit jury has occupied a central position in our system of justice by safeguarding a person accused of crime against the arbitrary exercise of power by prosecutor or judge. Those on the venire must be "indifferently chosen," to secure the defendant's right under the Fourteenth Amendment to "protection of life and liberty against race or color prejudice."

Racial discrimination in selection of jurors harms not only the accused whose life or liberty they are summoned to try. Competence to serve as a juror ultimately depends on an assessment of individual qualifications and ability impartially to consider evidence presented at a trial. A person's race simply "is unrelated to his fitness as a juror." As long ago as *Strauder*, therefore, the Court recognized that by denying a person participation in jury service on account of his race, the State unconstitutionally discriminated against the excluded juror.

The harm from discriminatory jury selection extends beyond that inflicted on the defendant and the excluded juror to touch the entire community. Selection procedures that purposefully exclude black persons from juries undermine public confidence in the fairness of our system of justice. Discrimination within the judicial system is most pernicious because it is "a stimulant to that race prejudice which is an impediment to securing to black citizens that equal justice which the law aims to secure to all others."

B.

 In *Strauder*, the Court invalidated a state statute that provided that only white men could serve as jurors. We can be confident that no State now has such a law. The Constitution requires, however, that we look beyond the face of the statute defining juror qualifications and also consider challenged selection practices to afford "protection against action of the State through its administrative officers in effecting the prohibited discrimination." Thus, the Court has found a denial of equal protection where the procedures implementing a neutral statute operated to exclude persons from the venire on racial grounds, and has made clear that the Constitution prohibits all forms of purposeful racial discrimination in selection of jurors. While decisions of this Court have been concerned largely with discrimination during selection of the venire, the principles announced there also forbid discrimination on account of race in selection of the petit jury. Since the Fourteenth Amendment protects an accused throughout the proceedings bringing him to justice, the State may not draw up its jury lists pursuant to neutral procedures but then resort to discrimination at "other stages in the selection process."

Accordingly, the component of the jury selection process at issue here, the State's privilege to strike individual jurors through peremptory challenges, is subject to the commands of the Equal Protection Clause. Although a prosecutor ordinarily is entitled to exercise permitted peremptory challenges "for any reason at all, as long as that reason is related to his view concerning the outcome" of the case to be tried, the Equal Protection Clause forbids the prosecutor to challenge potential jurors solely on account of their race or on the assumption that black jurors as a group will be unable impartially to consider the State's case against a black defendant.

III.

The principles announced in *Strauder* never have been questioned in any subsequent decision of this Court. Rather, the Court has been called upon repeatedly to review the application of those principles to particular facts. A recurring question in these cases, as in any case alleging a violation of the Equal Protection Clause, was whether the defendant had met his burden of proving purposeful discrimination on the part of the State. That question also was at the heart of the portion of *Swain v. Alabama* we reexamine today.

A.

Swain required the Court to decide, among other issues, whether a black defendant was denied equal protection by the State's exercise of peremptory challenges to exclude members of his race from the petit jury. The record in *Swain* showed that the prosecutor had used the State's peremptory challenges to strike the six black persons included on the petit jury venire. While rejecting the defendant's claim for failure to prove purposeful discrimination, the Court nonetheless indicated that the Equal Protection Clause placed some limits on the State's exercise of peremptory challenges.

The Court sought to accommodate the prosecutor's historical privilege of peremptory challenge free of judicial control and the constitutional prohibition on exclusion of persons from jury service on account of race. While the Constitution does not confer a right to peremptory challenges, those challenges traditionally have been viewed as one means of assuring the selection of a qualified and unbiased jury. To preserve the peremptory nature of the prosecutor's challenge, the Court in *Swain* declined to scrutinize his actions in a particular case by relying on a presumption that he properly exercised the State's challenges.

The Court went on to observe, however, that a State may not exercise its challenges in contravention of the Equal Protection Clause. It was impermissible for a prosecutor to use his challenges to exclude blacks from the jury "for reasons wholly unrelated to the outcome of the particular case on trial" or to deny to blacks "the same right and opportunity to participate in the administration of justice enjoyed by the white population." Accordingly, a black defendant could make out a *prima facie* case of purposeful discrimination on proof that the peremptory challenge system was "being perverted" in that manner. For example, an inference of purposeful discrimination would be raised on evidence that a prosecutor, "in case after case, whatever the circumstances, whatever the crime and whoever the defendant or the victim may be, is responsible for the removal of Negroes who have been selected as qualified jurors by the jury commissioners and who have survived challenges for cause, with the result that no Negroes ever serve on petit juries." Evidence offered by the defendant in *Swain* did not meet that standard. While the defendant showed that prosecutors in the jurisdiction had exercised their strikes to exclude blacks from the jury, he offered no proof of the circumstances under which prosecutors were responsible for striking black jurors beyond the facts of his own case.

A number of lower courts following the teaching of *Swain* reasoned that proof of repeated striking of blacks over a number of cases was necessary to establish a violation of the Equal Protection Clause. Since this interpretation of *Swain* has placed on defendants a crippling burden of proof, prosecutors' peremptory challenges are now largely immune from constitutional scrutiny. For reasons that follow, we reject this evidentiary formulation as inconsistent with standards that have been developed since *Swain* for assessing a prima facie case under the Equal Protection Clause.

B.

Since the decision in *Swain*, we have explained that our cases concerning selection of the venire reflect the general equal protection principle that the "invidious quality" of governmental action claimed to be racially discriminatory "must ultimately be traced to a racially discriminatory purpose." As in any equal protection case, the "burden is, of course," on the defendant who alleges discriminatory selection of the venire "to prove the existence of purposeful discrimination." In deciding if the defendant has carried his burden of persuasion, a court must undertake "a sensitive inquiry into such circumstantial and direct evidence of intent as may be available." Circumstantial evidence of invidious intent may include proof of disproportionate impact. We have observed that under some circumstances proof of discriminatory impact "may for all practical purposes demonstrate unconstitutionality because in various circumstances the discrimination is very difficult to explain on nonracial grounds." For example, "total or seriously disproportionate exclusion of Negroes from jury venires,"…"is itself such an unequal application of the law . . . as to show intentional discrimination."

Moreover, since *Swain*, we have recognized that a black defendant alleging that members of his race have been impermissibly excluded from the venire may make out a *prima facie* case of purposeful discrimination by showing that the totality of the relevant facts gives rise to an inference of discriminatory purpose. Once the defendant makes the requisite showing, the burden shifts to the State to explain adequately the racial exclusion. The State cannot meet this burden on mere general assertions that its officials did not discriminate or that they properly performed their official duties. Rather, the State must demonstrate that "permissible racially neutral selection criteria and procedures have produced the monochromatic result."

The showing necessary to establish a *prima facie* case of purposeful discrimination in selection of the venire may be discerned in this Court's decisions. The defendant initially must show that he is a member of a racial group capable of being singled out for differential treatment. In combination with that evidence, a defendant may then make a *prima facie* case by proving that in the particular jurisdiction members of his race have not been summoned for jury service over an extended period of time. Proof of systematic exclusion from the venire raises an inference of purposeful discrimination because the "result bespeaks discrimination."

Since the ultimate issue is whether the State has discriminated in selecting the defendant's venire, however, the defendant may establish a *prima facie* case "in other ways than by evidence of long-continued unexplained absence" of members of his race "from many panels." In cases involving the venire, this Court has found a *prima facie* case on proof that members of the defendant's race were substantially underrepresented on the venire from which his jury was drawn, and that the venire was selected under a practice providing "the opportunity for discrimination." This combination of factors raises the necessary inference of purposeful discrimination because the Court has declined to attribute to chance the absence of black citizens on a particular jury array where the selection mechanism is subject to abuse. When circumstances suggest the need, the trial court must undertake a "factual inquiry" that "takes into account all possible explanatory factors" in the particular case.

Thus, since the decision in *Swain*, this Court has recognized that a defendant may make a *prima facie* showing of purposeful racial discrimination in selection of the venire by relying solely on the facts concerning its selection in his case. These decisions are in accordance with the proposition, articulated in *Arlington Heights v. Metropolitan Housing Development Corp.*, that "a consistent pattern of official racial discrimination" is not "a necessary predicate to a violation of the Equal Protection Clause. A single invidiously discriminatory governmental act" is not "immunized by the absence of such discrimination in the making of other comparable decisions." For evidentiary requirements to dictate that "several must suffer discrimination" before one could object would be inconsistent with the promise of equal protection to all.

C.

The standards for assessing a *prima facie* case in the context of discriminatory selection of the venire have been fully articulated since *Swain*. These principles support our conclusion that a defendant may establish a *prima facie* case of purposeful discrimination in selection of the petit jury solely on evidence concerning the prosecutor's exercise of peremptory challenges at the defendant's trial. To establish such a case, the defendant first must show that he is a member of a cognizable racial group, and that the prosecutor has exercised peremptory challenges to remove from the venire members of the defendant's race. Second, the defendant is entitled to rely on the fact, as to which there can be no dispute, that peremptory challenges constitute a jury selection practice that permits "those to discriminate who are of a mind to discriminate." Finally, the defendant must show that these facts and any other relevant circumstances raise an inference that the prosecutor used that practice to exclude the veniremen from the petit jury on account of their race. This combination of factors in the empaneling of the petit jury, as in the selection of the venire, raises the necessary inference of purposeful discrimination.

In deciding whether the defendant has made the requisite showing, the trial court should consider all relevant circumstances. For example, a "pattern" of strikes against black jurors included in the particular venire might give rise to an inference of discrimination. Similarly, the prosecutor's questions and statements during *voir dire* examination and in exercising his challenges may support or refute an inference of discriminatory purpose. These examples are merely illustrative. We have confidence that trial judges, experienced in supervising *voir dire*, will be able to decide if the circumstances concerning the prosecutor's use of peremptory challenges creates a *prima facie* case of discrimination against black jurors.

Once the defendant makes a *prima facie* showing, the burden shifts to the State to come forward with a neutral explanation for challenging black jurors. Though this requirement imposes a limitation in some cases on the full peremptory character of the historic challenge, we emphasize that the prosecutor's explanation need not rise to the level justifying exercise of a challenge for cause. But the prosecutor may not rebut the defendant's *prima facie* case of discrimination by stating merely that he challenged jurors of the defendant's race on the assumption—or his intuitive judgment—that they would be partial to the defendant because of their shared race. Just as the Equal Protection Clause forbids the States to exclude black persons from the venire on the assumption that blacks as a group are unqualified to serve as jurors, so it forbids the States to strike black veniremen on the assumption that they will be biased in a particular case simply because the defendant is black.

The core guarantee of equal protection, ensuring citizens that their State will not discriminate on account of race, would be meaningless were we to approve the exclusion of jurors on the basis of such assumptions, which arise solely from the jurors' race. Nor may the prosecutor rebut the defendant's case merely by denying that he had a discriminatory motive or "affirming his good faith in making individual selections." If these general assertions were accepted as rebutting a defendant's *prima facie* case, the Equal Protection Clause "would be but a vain and illusory requirement." The prosecutor therefore must articulate a neutral explanation related to the particular case to be tried. The trial court then will have the duty to determine if the defendant has established purposeful discrimination.

IV.

The State contends that our holding will eviscerate the fair trial values served by the peremptory challenge. Conceding that the Constitution does not guarantee a right to peremptory challenges and that *Swain* did state that their use ultimately is subject to the strictures of equal protection, the State argues that the privilege of unfettered exercise of the challenge is of vital importance to the criminal justice system.

While we recognize, of course, that the peremptory challenge occupies an important position in our trial procedures, we do not agree that our decision today will undermine the contribution the challenge generally makes to the administration of justice. The reality of practice, amply reflected in many state- and federal-court opinions, shows that the challenge may be, and unfortunately at times has been, used to discriminate against black jurors. By requiring trial courts to be sensitive to the racially discriminatory use of peremptory challenges, our decision enforces the mandate of equal protection and furthers the ends of justice. In view of the heterogeneous population of our Nation, public respect for our criminal justice system and the rule of law will be strengthened if we ensure that no citizen is disqualified from jury service because of his race.

Nor are we persuaded by the State's suggestion that our holding will create serious administrative difficulties. In those States applying a version of the evidentiary standard we recognize today, courts have not experienced serious administrative burdens, and the peremptory challenge system has survived. We decline, however, to formulate particular procedures to be followed upon a defendant's timely objection to a prosecutor's challenges.

V.

In this case, petitioner made a timely objection to the prosecutor's removal of all black persons on the venire. Because the trial court flatly rejected the objection without requiring the prosecutor to give an explanation for his action, we remand this case for further proceedings. If the trial court decides that the facts establish, *prima facie*, purposeful discrimination and the prosecutor does not come forward with a neutral explanation for his action, our precedents require that petitioner's conviction be reversed.

It is so ordered.

Furman v. Georgia (1972)
408 U.S. 238

This landmark decision marks a departure from the usual formatting of this book. That is, the full case is provided, not merely the majority decision. This is because the issue is very controversial, and students will benefit from the various ways of looking at the death penalty presented. Note that this case effectively held the death penalty unconstitutional; this is not how the law stands today. Many of the limits placed on the death penalty today, however, are first articulated here. This case is unusual as Supreme Court cases go because every justice wrote an opinion. While very long because of this, the case provides unparalleled insight into the different legal arguments for and against the death penalty.

Petitioner in No. 69-5003 was convicted of murder in Georgia and was sentenced to death pursuant to Ga. Code Ann. § 26-1005 (Supp. 1971) (effective prior to July 1, 1969). Petitioner was convicted of rape in Georgia and was sentenced to death pursuant to Ga. Code Ann. § 26-1302 (Supp. 1971) (effective prior to July 1, 1969). Petitioner in No. 69-5031 was convicted of rape in Texas and was sentenced to death pursuant to Tex. Penal Code, Art. 1189 (1961). Certiorari was granted limited to the following question: "Does the imposition and carrying out of the death penalty in these cases constitute cruel and unusual punishment in violation of the Eighth and Fourteenth Amendments?" The Court holds that the imposition and carrying out of the death penalty in these cases constitute cruel and unusual punishment in violation of the Eighth and Fourteenth Amendments. The judgment in each case is therefore reversed insofar as it leaves undisturbed the death sentence imposed, and the cases are remanded for further proceedings.

So ordered.

MR. JUSTICE DOUGLAS, concurring.

In these three cases the death penalty was imposed, one of them for murder, and two for rape. In each the determination of whether the penalty should be death or a lighter punishment was left by the State to the discretion of the judge or of the jury. In each of the three cases the trial was to a jury. They are here on petitions for certiorari which we granted limited to the question whether the imposition and execution of the death penalty constitute "cruel and unusual punishment" within the meaning of the Eighth Amendment as applied to the States by the Fourteenth. I vote to vacate each judgment, believing that the exaction of the death penalty does violate the Eighth and Fourteenth Amendments.

That the requirements of due process ban cruel and unusual punishment is now settled. It is also settled that the proscription of cruel and unusual punishments forbids the judicial imposition of them as well as their imposition by the legislature.

Congressman Bingham, in proposing the Fourteenth Amendment, maintained that "the privileges or immunities of citizens of the United States" as protected by the Fourteenth Amendment included protection against "cruel and unusual punishments:"

"Many instances of State injustice and oppression have already occurred in the State legislation of this Union, of flagrant violations of the guaranteed privileges of citizens of the United States, for which the national Government furnished and could furnish by law no remedy whatever. Contrary to the express letter of your Constitution, 'cruel and unusual punishments' have been inflicted under State laws within this Union upon citizens, not only for crimes committed, but for sacred duty done, for which and against which the Government of the United States had provided no remedy and could provide none."

Whether the privileges and immunities route is followed, or the due process route, the result is the same.

It has been assumed in our decisions that punishment by death is not cruel, unless the manner of execution can be said to be inhuman and barbarous. It is also said in our opinions that the proscription of cruel and unusual punishments "is not fastened to the obsolete but may acquire meaning as public opinion becomes enlightened by a humane justice." A like statement was made in *Trop v. Dulles* that the Eighth Amendment "must draw its meaning from the evolving standards of decency that mark the progress of a maturing society."

The generality of a law inflicting capital punishment is one thing. What may be said of the validity of a law on the books and what may be done with the law in its application do, or may, lead to quite different conclusions.

It would seem to be incontestable that the death penalty inflicted on one defendant is "unusual" if it discriminates against him by reason of his race, religion, wealth, social position, or class, or if it is imposed under a procedure that gives room for the play of such prejudices.

There is evidence that the provision of the English Bill of Rights of 1689, from which the language of the Eighth Amendment was taken, was concerned primarily with selective or irregular application of harsh penalties and that its aim was to forbid arbitrary and discriminatory penalties of a severe nature:

"Following the Norman conquest of England in 1066, the old system of penalties, which ensured equality between crime and punishment, suddenly disappeared. By the time systematic judicial records were kept, its demise was almost complete. With the exception of certain grave crimes for which the punishment was death or outlawry, the arbitrary fine was replaced by a discretionary amercement. Although amercement's discretionary character allowed the circumstances of each case to be taken into account and the level of cash penalties to be decreased or increased accordingly, the amercement presented an opportunity for excessive or oppressive fines.

"The problem of excessive amercements became so prevalent that three chapters of the *Magna Carta* were devoted to their regulation. Maitland said of Chapter 14 that 'very likely there was no clause in the *Magna Carta* more grateful to the mass of the people.' Chapter 14 clearly stipulated as fundamental law a prohibition of excessiveness in punishments:

"A free man shall not be amerced for a trivial offence, except in accordance with the degree of the offence; and for a serious offence he shall be amerced according to its gravity, saving his livelihood; and a merchant likewise, saving his merchandise; in the same way a villein shall be amerced saving his wainage; if they fall into our mercy. And none of the aforesaid amercements shall be imposed except by the testimony of reputable men of the neighborhood."

The English Bill of Rights, enacted December 16, 1689, stated that "excessive bail ought not to be required, nor excessive fines imposed, nor cruel and unusual punishments inflicted." These were the words chosen for our Eighth Amendment. A like provision had been in Virginia's Constitution of 1776 and in the constitutions of seven other States. The Northwest Ordinance, enacted under the Articles of Confederation, included a prohibition of cruel and unusual punishments. But the debates of the First Congress on the Bill of Rights throw little light on its intended meaning. All that appears is the following:

"Mr. SMITH, of South Carolina, objected to the words 'nor cruel and unusual punishments;' the import of them being too indefinite.

"Mr. LIVERMORE: The clause seems to express a great deal of humanity, on which account I have no objection to it; but as it seems to have no meaning in it, I do not think it necessary. What is meant by the terms excessive bail? Who are to be the judges? What is understood by excessive fines? It lies with the court to determine. No cruel and unusual punishment is to be inflicted; it is sometimes necessary to hang a man, villains often deserve whipping, and perhaps having their ears cut off; but are we in future to be prevented from inflicting these punishments because they are cruel? If a more lenient mode of correcting vice and deterring others from the commission of it could be invented, it would be very prudent in the Legislature to adopt it; but until we have some security that this will be done, we ought not to be restrained from making necessary laws by any declaration of this kind."

The words "cruel and unusual" certainly include penalties that are barbaric. But the words, at least when read in light of the English proscription against selective and irregular use of penalties, suggest that it is "cruel and unusual" to apply the death penalty—or any other penalty—selectively to minorities whose numbers are few, who are outcasts of society, and who are unpopular, but whom society is willing to see suffer though it would not countenance general application of the same penalty across the board. Judge Tuttle, indeed, made abundantly clear in *Novak v. Beto* that solitary confinement may at times be "cruel and unusual" punishment.

The Court in *McGautha v. California* noted that in this country there was almost from the beginning a "rebellion against the common-law rule imposing a mandatory death sentence on all convicted murderers." The first attempted remedy was to restrict the death penalty to defined offenses such as "premeditated" murder. But juries "took the law into their own hands" and refused to convict on the capital offense.

"In order to meet the problem of jury nullification, legislatures did not try, as before, to refine further the definition of capital homicides. Instead they adopted the method of forthrightly granting juries the discretion which they had been exercising in fact."

The Court concluded: "In light of history, experience, and the present limitations of human knowledge, we find it quite impossible to say that committing to the untrammeled discretion of the jury the power to pronounce life or death in capital cases is offensive to anything in the Constitution."

The Court refused to find constitutional dimensions in the argument that those who exercise their discretion to send a person to death should be given standards by which that discretion should be exercised.

....

The high service rendered by the "cruel and unusual" punishment clause of the Eighth Amendment is to require legislatures to write penal laws that are evenhanded, nonselective, and nonarbitrary, and to require judges to see to it that general laws are not applied sparsely, selectively, and spottily to unpopular groups.

A law that stated that anyone making more than $ 50,000 would be exempt from the death penalty would plainly fall, as would a law that in terms said that blacks, those who never went beyond the fifth grade in school, those who made less than $ 3,000 a year, or those who were unpopular or unstable should be the only people executed. A law which in the overall view reaches that result in practice has no more sanctity than a law which in terms provides the same.

Thus, these discretionary statutes are unconstitutional in their operation. They are pregnant with discrimination and discrimination is an ingredient not compatible with the idea of equal protection of the laws that is implicit in the ban on "cruel and unusual" punishments.

Any law which is nondiscriminatory on its face may be applied in such a way as to violate the Equal Protection Clause of the Fourteenth Amendment. Such conceivably might be the fate of a mandatory death penalty, where equal or lesser sentences were imposed on the elite, a harsher one on the minorities or members of the lower castes.

Whether a mandatory death penalty would otherwise be constitutional is a question I do not reach.

I concur in the judgments of the Court.

MR. JUSTICE BRENNAN, concurring.

The question presented in these cases is whether death is today a punishment for crime that is "cruel and unusual" and consequently, by virtue of the Eighth and Fourteenth Amendments, beyond the power of the State to inflict.

Almost a century ago, this Court observed that "difficulty would attend the effort to define with exactness the extent of the constitutional provision which provides that cruel and unusual punishments shall not be inflicted." Less than 15 years ago, it was again noted that "the exact scope of the constitutional phrase 'cruel and unusual' has not been detailed by this Court." Those statements remain true today. The Cruel and Unusual Punishments Clause, like the other great clauses of the Constitution, is not susceptible of precise definition. Yet we know that the values and ideals it embodies are basic to our scheme of government. And we know also that the Clause imposes upon this Court the duty, when the issue is properly presented, to determine the constitutional validity of a challenged punishment, whatever that punishment may be. In these cases, "that issue confronts us, and the task of resolving it is inescapably ours."

I.

We have very little evidence of the Framers' intent in including the Cruel and Unusual Punishments Clause among those restraints upon the new Government enumerated in the Bill of Rights. The absence of such a restraint from the body of the Constitution was alluded to, so far as we now know, in the debates of only two of the state ratifying conventions. In the Massachusetts convention, Mr. Holmes protested:

"What gives an additional glare of horror to these gloomy circumstances is the consideration, that Congress have to ascertain, point out, and determine, what kind of punishments shall be inflicted on persons convicted of crimes. They are nowhere restrained from inventing the most cruel and unheard-of punishments, and annexing them to crimes; and there is no constitutional check on them, but that racks and gibbets may be amongst the most mild instruments of their discipline."

Holmes' fear that Congress would have unlimited power to prescribe punishments for crimes was echoed by Patrick Henry at the Virginia convention:

". . . Congress, from their general powers, may fully go into business of human legislation. They may legislate, in criminal cases, from treason to the lowest offence—petty larceny. They may define crimes and prescribe punishments. In the definition of crimes, I trust they will be directed by what wise representatives ought to be governed by. But when we come to punishments, no latitude ought to be left, nor dependence put on the virtue of representatives. What says our Virginia bill of rights?—'that excessive bail ought not to be required, nor excessive fines imposed, nor cruel and unusual punishments inflicted.' Are you not, therefore, now calling on those gentlemen who are to compose Congress, to . . . define punishments without this control? Will they find sentiments there similar to this bill of rights? You let them loose; you do more—you depart from the genius of your country. . . .

"In this business of legislation, your members of Congress will loose the restriction of not imposing excessive fines, demanding excessive bail, and inflicting cruel and unusual punishments. These are prohibited by your Virginia declaration of rights. What has distinguished our ancestors?—That they would not admit of tortures, or cruel and barbarous punishment."

These two statements shed some light on what the Framers meant by "cruel and unusual punishments." Holmes referred to "the most cruel and unheard-of punishments," Henry to "tortures, or cruel and barbarous punishment." It does not follow, however, that the Framers were exclusively concerned with prohibiting torturous punishments. Holmes and Henry were objecting to the absence of a Bill of Rights, and they cited to support their objections the unrestrained legislative power to prescribe punishments for crimes. Certainly we may suppose that they invoked the specter of the most drastic punishments a legislature might devise.

In addition, it is quite clear that Holmes and Henry focused wholly upon the necessity to restrain the legislative power. Because they recognized "that Congress have to ascertain, point out, and determine, what kinds of punishments shall be inflicted on persons convicted of crimes," they insisted that Congress must be limited in its power to punish. Accordingly, they called for a "constitutional check" that would ensure that "when we come to punishments, no latitude ought to be left, nor dependence put on the virtue of representatives."

....

Several conclusions thus emerge from the history of the adoption of the Clause. We know that the Framers' concern was directed specifically at the exercise of legislative power. They included in the Bill of Rights a prohibition upon "cruel and unusual punishments" precisely because the legislature would otherwise have had the unfettered power to prescribe punishments for crimes. Yet we cannot now know exactly what the Framers thought "cruel and unusual punishments" were. Certainly they intended to ban torturous punishments, but the available evidence does not support the further conclusion that only torturous punishments were to be outlawed. As Livermore's comments demonstrate, the Framers were well aware that the reach of the Clause was not limited to the proscription of unspeakable atrocities. Nor did they intend simply to forbid punishments considered "cruel and unusual" at the time. The "import" of the Clause is, indeed, "indefinite," and for good reason. A constitutional provision "is enacted, it is true, from an experience of evils, but its general language should not, therefore, be necessarily confined to the form that evil had theretofore taken. Time works changes, brings into existence new conditions and purposes. Therefore a principle to be vital must be capable of wider application than the mischief which gave it birth."

It was almost 80 years before this Court had occasion to refer to the Clause. These early cases, as the Court pointed out in *Weems v. United States* did not undertake to provide "an exhaustive definition" of "cruel and unusual punishments." Most of them proceeded primarily by "looking backwards for examples by which to fix the meaning of the clause," concluding simply that a punishment would be "cruel and unusual" if it were similar to punishments considered "cruel and unusual" at the time the Bill of Rights was adopted. In *Wilkerson v. Utah*, for instance, the Court found it "safe to affirm that punishments of torture . . . and all others in the same line of unnecessary cruelty, are forbidden." The "punishments of torture," which the Court labeled "atrocities," were cases where the criminal "was embowelled alive, beheaded, and quartered," and cases "of public dissection . . . and burning alive." Similarly, in *In re Kemmler*, the Court declared that "if the punishment prescribed for an offence against the laws of the State were manifestly cruel and unusual, as burning at the stake, crucifixion, breaking on the wheel, or the like, it would be the duty of the courts to adjudge such penalties to be within the constitutional prohibition." The Court then observed, commenting upon the passage just quoted from *Wilkerson v. Utah*, and applying the "manifestly cruel and unusual" test, that "punishments are cruel when they involve torture or a lingering death; but the punishment of death is not cruel, within the meaning of that word as used in the Constitution. It implies there something inhuman and barbarous, something more than the mere extinguishment of life."

Had this "historical" interpretation of the Cruel and Unusual Punishments Clause prevailed, the Clause would have been effectively read out of the Bill of Rights. As the Court noted in *Weems v. United States*, this interpretation led Story to conclude "that the provision 'would seem to be wholly unnecessary in a free government, since it is scarcely possible that any department of such a government should authorize or justify such atrocious conduct.'" And Cooley in his book, *Constitutional Limitations*, said the Court, "apparently in a struggle between the effect to be given to ancient examples and the inconsequence of a dread of them in these enlightened times, . . . hesitated to advance definite views." The result of a judicial application of this interpretation was not surprising. A state court, for example, upheld the constitutionality of the whipping post: "In comparison with the 'barbarities of quartering, hanging in chains, castration, etc.,' it was easily reduced to insignificance."

But this Court in *Weems* decisively repudiated the "historical" interpretation of the Clause. The Court, returning to the intention of the Framers, "relied on the conditions which existed when the Constitution was adopted." And the Framers knew "that government by the people instituted by the Constitution would not imitate the conduct of arbitrary monarchs. The abuse of power might, indeed, be apprehended, but not that it would be manifested in provisions or practices which would shock the sensibilities of men." The Clause, then, guards against "the abuse of power"; contrary to the implications in *Wilkerson v. Utah* and *In re Kemmler*, the prohibition of the Clause is not "confined . . . to such penalties and punishment as were inflicted by the Stuarts." Although opponents of the Bill of Rights "felt sure that the spirit of liberty could be trusted, and that its ideals would be represented, not debased, by legislation," the Framers disagreed:

"Patrick Henry and those who believed as he did would take no chances. Their predominant political impulse was distrust of power, and they insisted on constitutional limitations against its abuse. But surely they intended more than to register a fear of the forms of abuse that went out of practice with the Stuarts. Surely, their jealousy of power had a saner justification than that. They were men of action, practical and sagacious, not beset with vain imagining, and it must have come to them that there could be exercises of cruelty by laws other than those which inflicted bodily pain or mutilation. With power in a legislature great, if not unlimited, to give criminal character to the actions of men, with power unlimited to fix terms of imprisonment with what accompaniments they might, what more potent instrument of cruelty could be put into the hands of power? And it was believed that power might be tempted to cruelty. This was the motive of the clause, and if we are to attribute an intelligent providence to its advocates we cannot think that it was intended to prohibit only practices like the Stuarts', or to prevent only an exact repetition of history. We cannot think that the possibility of a coercive cruelty being exercised through other forms of punishment was overlooked."

The Court in *Weems* thus recognized that this "restraint upon legislatures" possesses an "expansive and vital character" that is "'essential . . . to the rule of law and the maintenance of individual freedom.'" Accordingly, the responsibility lies with the courts to make certain that the prohibition of the Clause is enforced. Referring to cases in which "prominence was given to the power of the legislature to define crimes and their punishment," the Court said:

"We concede the power in most of its exercises. We disclaim the right to assert a judgment against that of the legislature of the expediency of the laws or the right to oppose the judicial power to the legislative power to define crimes and fix their punishment, unless that power encounters in its exercise a constitutional prohibition. In such case not our discretion but our legal duty, strictly defined and imperative in its direction, is invoked."

In short, this Court finally adopted the Framers' view of the Clause as a "constitutional check" to ensure that "when we come to punishments, no latitude ought to be left, nor dependence put on the virtue of representatives." That, indeed, is the only view consonant with our constitutional form of government. If the judicial conclusion that a punishment is "cruel and unusual" "depended upon virtually unanimous condemnation of the penalty at issue," then, "like no other constitutional provision, the Clause's only function would be to legitimize advances already made by the other departments and opinions already the conventional wisdom." We know that the Framers did not envision "so narrow a role for this basic guaranty of human rights." The right to be free of cruel and unusual punishments, like the other guarantees of the Bill of Rights, "may not be submitted to vote; it depends on the outcome of no elections." "The very purpose of a Bill of Rights was to withdraw certain subjects from the vicissitudes of political controversy, to place them beyond the reach of majorities and officials and to establish them as legal principles to be applied by the courts."

Judicial enforcement of the Clause, then, cannot be evaded by invoking the obvious truth that legislatures have the power to prescribe punishments for crimes. That is precisely the reason the Clause appears in the Bill of Rights. The difficulty arises, rather, in formulating the "legal principles to be applied by the courts" when a legislatively prescribed punishment is challenged as "cruel and unusual." In formulating those constitutional principles, we must avoid the insertion of "judicial conceptions of . . . wisdom or propriety," yet we must not, in the guise of "judicial restraint," abdicate our fundamental responsibility to enforce the

Bill of Rights. Were we to do so, the "constitution would indeed be as easy of application as it would be deficient in efficacy and power. Its general principles would have little value and be converted by precedent into impotent and lifeless formulas. Rights declared in words might be lost in reality." The Cruel and Unusual Punishments Clause would become, in short, "little more than good advice."

II.

Ours would indeed be a simple task were we required merely to measure a challenged punishment against those that history has long condemned. That narrow and unwarranted view of the Clause, however, was left behind with the 19th century. Our task today is more complex. We know "that the words of the Clause are not precise, and that their scope is not static." We know, therefore, that the Clause "must draw its meaning from the evolving standards of decency that mark the progress of a maturing society." That knowledge, of course, is but the beginning of the inquiry.

In *Trop v. Dulles*, it was said that "the question is whether a penalty subjects the individual to a fate forbidden by the principle of civilized treatment guaranteed by the Clause." It was also said that a challenged punishment must be examined "in light of the basic prohibition against inhuman treatment" embodied in the Clause. It was said, finally, that:

"The basic concept underlying the Clause is nothing less than the dignity of man. While the State has the power to punish, the Clause stands to assure that this power be exercised within the limits of civilized standards."

At bottom, then, the Cruel and Unusual Punishments Clause prohibits the infliction of uncivilized and inhuman punishments. The State, even as it punishes, must treat its members with respect for their intrinsic worth as human beings. A punishment is "cruel and unusual," therefore, if it does not comport with human dignity.

This formulation, of course, does not of itself yield principles for assessing the constitutional validity of particular punishments. Nevertheless, even though "this Court has had little occasion to give precise content to the Clause," there are principles recognized in our cases and inherent in the Clause sufficient to permit a judicial determination whether a challenged punishment comports with human dignity.

The primary principle is that a punishment must not be so severe as to be degrading to the dignity of human beings. Pain, certainly, may be a factor in the judgment. The infliction of an extremely severe punishment will often entail physical suffering. Yet the Framers also knew "that there could be exercises of cruelty by laws other than those which inflicted bodily pain or mutilation." Even though "there may be involved no physical mistreatment, no primitive torture," severe mental pain may be inherent in the infliction of a particular punishment. That, indeed, was one of the conclusions underlying the holding of the plurality in *Trop v. Dulles* that the punishment of expatriation violates the Clause. And the physical and mental suffering inherent in the punishment of *cadena temporal*, was an obvious basis for the Court's decision in *Weems v. United States* that the punishment was "cruel and unusual."

More than the presence of pain, however, is comprehended in the judgment that the extreme severity of a punishment makes it degrading to the dignity of human beings. The barbaric punishments condemned by history, "punishments which inflict torture, such as the rack, the thumbscrew, the iron boot, the stretching of limbs and the like," are, of course, "attended with acute pain and suffering." When we consider why they have been condemned, however, we realize that the pain involved is not the only reason. The true significance of these punishments is that they treat members of the human race as nonhumans, as objects to be toyed with and discarded. They are thus inconsistent with the fundamental premise of the Clause that even the vilest criminal remains a human being possessed of common human dignity.

The infliction of an extremely severe punishment, then, like the one before the Court in *Weems v. United States*, from which "no circumstance of degradation was omitted," may reflect the attitude that the person punished is not entitled to recognition as a fellow human being. That attitude may be apparent apart from the severity of the punishment itself. In *Louisiana ex rel. Francis v. Resweber*, for example, the unsuccessful electrocution, although it caused "mental anguish and physical pain," was the result of "an unforeseeable accident." Had the failure been intentional, however, the punishment would have been, like torture, so degrading and indecent as to amount to a refusal to accord the criminal human status. Indeed, a punishment may be degrading to human dignity solely because it is a punishment. A State may not punish a person for being "mentally ill, or a leper, or . . . afflicted with a venereal disease," or for being addicted to narcotics. To inflict punishment for having a disease is to treat the individual as a diseased thing rather than as a sick human being. That the punishment is not severe, "in the abstract," is irrelevant; "even one day in prison would be a cruel and unusual punishment for the 'crime' of having a common cold." Finally, of course, a punishment may be degrading simply by reason of its enormity. A prime example is expatriation, a "punishment more primitive than torture," for it necessarily involves a denial by society of the individual's existence as a member of the human community.

In determining whether a punishment comports with human dignity, we are aided also by a second principle inherent in the Clause—that the State must not arbitrarily inflict a severe punishment. This principle derives from the notion that the State does not respect human dignity when, without reason, it inflicts upon some people a severe punishment that it does not inflict upon others. Indeed, the very words "cruel and unusual punishments" imply condemnation of the arbitrary infliction of severe punishments. And, as we now know, the English history of the Clause reveals a particular concern with the establishment of a safeguard against arbitrary punishments.

This principle has been recognized in our cases. In *Wilkerson v. Utah*, the Court reviewed various treatises on military law in order to demonstrate that under "the custom of war" shooting was a common method of inflicting the punishment of death. On that basis, the Court concluded:

"Cruel and unusual punishments are forbidden by the Constitution, but the authorities referred to treatises on military law are quite sufficient to show that the punishment of shooting as a mode of executing the death penalty for the crime of murder in the first degree is not included in that category, within the meaning of the Clause. Soldiers convicted of desertion or other capital military offenses are in the great majority of cases sentenced to be shot, and the ceremony for such occasions is given in great fullness by the writers upon the subject of courts-martial."

The Court thus upheld death by shooting, so far as appears, solely on the ground that it was a common method of execution.

As *Wilkerson v. Utah* suggests, when a severe punishment is inflicted "in the great majority of cases" in which it is legally available, there is little likelihood that the State is inflicting it arbitrarily. If, however, the infliction of a severe punishment is "something different from that which is generally done" in such cases, *Trop v. Dulles*, there is a substantial likelihood that the State, contrary to the requirements of regularity and fairness embodied in the Clause, is inflicting the punishment arbitrarily. This principle is especially important today. There is scant danger, given the political processes "in an enlightened democracy such as ours," that extremely severe punishments will be widely applied. The more significant function of the Clause, therefore, is to protect against the danger of their arbitrary infliction.

A third principle inherent in the Clause is that a severe punishment must not be unacceptable to contemporary society. Rejection by society, of course, is a strong indication that a severe punishment does not comport with human dignity. In applying this principle, however, we must make certain that the judicial determination is as objective as possible. Thus, for example, *Weems v. United States* and *Trop v. Dulles*, suggest that one factor that may be considered is the existence of the punishment in jurisdictions other than those before the Court. *Wilkerson v. Utah* suggests that another factor to be considered is the historic usage of the punishment. *Trop v. Dulles* combined present acceptance with past usage by observing that "the death penalty has been employed throughout our history, and, in a day when it is still widely accepted, it cannot be said to violate the constitutional concept of cruelty." In *Robinson v. California*, which involved the infliction of punishment for narcotics addiction, the Court went a step further, concluding simply that "in the light of contemporary human knowledge, a law which made a criminal offense of such a disease would doubtless be universally thought to be an infliction of cruel and unusual punishment."

The question under this principle, then, is whether there are objective indicators from which a court can conclude that contemporary society considers a severe punishment unacceptable. Accordingly, the judicial task is to review the history of a challenged punishment and to examine society's present practices with respect to its use. Legislative authorization, of course, does not establish acceptance. The acceptability of a severe punishment is measured, not by its availability, for it might become so offensive to society as never to be inflicted, but by its use.

The final principle inherent in the Clause is that a severe punishment must not be excessive. A punishment is excessive under this principle if it is unnecessary: The infliction of a severe punishment by the State cannot comport with human dignity when it is nothing more than the pointless infliction of suffering. If there is a significantly less severe punishment adequate to achieve the purposes for which the punishment is inflicted, the punishment inflicted is unnecessary and therefore excessive.
This principle first appeared in our cases in Mr. Justice Field's dissent in *O'Neil v. Vermont*. He there took the position that:

"The Clause is directed, not only against punishments of the character mentioned torturous punishments, but against all punishments which by their excessive length or severity are greatly disproportioned to the offences charged. The whole inhibition is against that which is excessive either in the bail required, or fine imposed, or punishment inflicted."

Although the determination that a severe punishment is excessive may be grounded in a judgment that it is disproportionate to the crime, the more significant basis is that the punishment serves no penal purpose more effectively than a less severe punishment. This view of the principle was explicitly recognized by the Court in *Weems v. United States*. There the Court, reviewing a severe punishment inflicted for the falsification of an official record, found that "the highest punishment possible for a crime which may cause the loss of many thousands of dollars, and to prevent which the duty of the State should be as eager as to prevent the perversion of truth in a public document, is not greater than that which may be imposed for falsifying a single item of a public account." Stating that "this contrast shows more than different exercises of legislative judgment," the Court concluded that the punishment was unnecessarily severe in view of the purposes for which it was imposed.

There are, then, four principles by which we may determine whether a particular punishment is "cruel and unusual." The primary principle, which I believe supplies the essential predicate for the application of the others, is that a punishment must not by its severity be degrading to human dignity. The paradigm violation of this principle would be the infliction of a torturous punishment of the type that the Clause has always prohibited. Yet "it is unlikely that any State at this moment in history," would pass a law providing for the infliction of such a punishment. Indeed, no such punishment has ever been before this Court. The same may be said of the other principles. It is unlikely that this Court will confront a severe punishment that is obviously inflicted in wholly arbitrary fashion; no State would engage in a reign of blind terror. Nor is it likely that this Court will be called upon to review a severe punishment that is clearly and totally rejected throughout society; no legislature would be able even to authorize the infliction of such a punishment. Nor, finally, is it likely that this Court will have to consider a severe punishment that is patently unnecessary; no State today would inflict a severe punishment knowing that there was no reason whatever for doing so. In short, we are unlikely to have occasion to determine that a punishment is fatally offensive under any one principle.

Since the Bill of Rights was adopted, this Court has adjudged only three punishments to be within the prohibition of the Clause. Each punishment, of course, was degrading to human dignity, but of none could it be said conclusively that it was fatally offensive under one or the other of the principles. Rather, these "cruel and unusual punishments" seriously implicated several of the principles, and it was the application of the principles in combination that supported the judgment. That, indeed, is not surprising. The function of these principles, after all, is simply to provide means by which a court can determine whether a challenged punishment comports with human dignity. They are, therefore, interrelated, and in most cases it will be their convergence that will justify the conclusion that a punishment is "cruel and unusual." The test, then, will ordinarily be a cumulative one: If a punishment is unusually severe, if there is a strong probability that it is inflicted arbitrarily, if it is substantially rejected by contemporary society, and if there is no reason to believe that it serves any penal purpose more effectively than some less severe punishment, then the continued infliction of that punishment violates the command of the Clause that the State may not inflict inhuman and uncivilized punishments upon those convicted of crimes.

III.

The punishment challenged in these cases is death. Death, of course, is a "traditional" punishment, one that "has been employed throughout our history," and its constitutional background is accordingly an appropriate subject of inquiry.

There is, first, a textual consideration raised by the Bill of Rights itself. The Fifth Amendment declares that if a particular crime is punishable by death, a person charged with that crime is entitled to certain procedural protections. We can thus infer that the Framers recognized the existence of what was then a common punishment. We cannot, however, make the further inference that they intended to exempt this particular punishment from the express prohibition of the Cruel and Unusual Punishments Clause. Nor is there any indication in the debates on the Clause that a special exception was to be made for death. If anything, the indication is to the contrary, for Livermore specifically mentioned death as a candidate for future proscription under the Clause. Finally, it does not advance analysis to insist that the Framers did not believe that adoption of the Bill of Rights would immediately prevent the infliction of the punishment of death; neither did they believe that it would immediately prevent the infliction of other corporal punishments that, although common at the time, are now acknowledged to be impermissible.

There is also the consideration that this Court has decided three cases involving constitutional challenges to particular methods of inflicting this punishment. In *Wilkerson v. Utah*, and *In re Kemmler*, the Court, expressing in both cases the since-rejected "historical" view of the Clause, approved death by shooting and death by electrocution. In *Wilkerson*, the Court concluded that shooting was a common method of execution, in *Kemmler*, the Court held that the Clause did not apply to the States. In *Louisiana ex rel. Francis v. Resweber*, the Court approved a second attempt at electrocution after the first had failed. It was said that "the Fourteenth Amendment would prohibit by its due process clause execution by a state in a cruel manner," but that the abortive attempt did not make the "subsequent execution any more cruel in the constitutional sense than any other execution." These three decisions thus reveal that the Court, while ruling upon various methods of inflicting death, has assumed in the past that death was a constitutionally permissible punishment. Past assumptions, however, are not sufficient to limit the scope of our examination of this punishment today. The constitutionality of death itself under the Cruel and Unusual Punishments Clause is before this Court for the first time; we cannot avoid the question by recalling past cases that never directly considered it.

The question, then, is whether the deliberate infliction of death is today consistent with the command of the Clause that the State may not inflict punishments that do not comport with human dignity. I will analyze the punishment of death in terms of the principles set out above and the cumulative test to which they lead: It is a denial of human dignity for the State arbitrarily to subject a person to an unusually severe punishment that society has indicated it does not regard as acceptable, and that cannot be shown to serve any penal purpose more effectively than a significantly less drastic punishment. Under these principles and this test, death is today a "cruel and unusual" punishment.

Death is a unique punishment in the United States. In a society that so strongly affirms the sanctity of life, not surprisingly the common view is that death is the ultimate sanction. This natural human feeling appears all about us. There has been no national debate about punishment, in general or by imprisonment, comparable to the debate about the punishment of death. No other punishment has been so continuously restricted, nor has any State yet abolished prisons, as some have abolished this punishment. And those States that still inflict death reserve it for the most heinous crimes. Juries, of course, have always treated death cases differently, as have governors exercising their commutation powers. Criminal defendants are of the same view. "As all practicing lawyers know, who have defended persons charged with capital offenses, often the only goal possible is to avoid the death penalty." Some legislatures have required particular procedures, such as two-stage trials and automatic appeals, applicable only in death cases. "It is the universal experience in the administration of criminal justice that those charged with capital offenses are granted special considerations." This Court, too, almost always treats death cases as a class apart. And the unfortunate effect of this punishment upon the functioning of the judicial process is well known; no other punishment has a similar effect.

The only explanation for the uniqueness of death is its extreme severity. Death is today an unusually severe punishment, unusual in its pain, in its finality, and in its enormity. No other existing punishment is comparable to death in terms of physical and mental suffering. Although our information is not conclusive, it appears that there is no method available that guarantees an immediate and painless death. Since the discontinuance of flogging as a constitutionally permissible punishment, death remains as the only punishment that may involve the conscious infliction of physical pain. In addition, we know that mental pain is an inseparable part of our practice of punishing criminals by death, for the prospect of pending execution exacts a frightful toll during the inevitable long wait between the imposition of sentence and the actual infliction of death.

....

Death is truly an awesome punishment. The calculated killing of a human being by the State involves, by its very nature, a denial of the executed person's humanity. The contrast with the plight of a person punished by imprisonment is evident. An individual in prison does not lose "the right to have rights." A prisoner retains, for example, the constitutional rights to the free exercise of religion, to be free of cruel and unusual punishments, and to treatment as a "person" for purposes of due process of law and the equal protection of the laws. A prisoner remains a member of the human family. Moreover, he retains the right of access to the courts. His punishment is not irrevocable. Apart from the common charge, grounded upon the recognition of human fallibility, that the punishment of death must inevitably be inflicted upon innocent men, we know that death has been the lot of men whose convictions were unconstitutionally secured in view of later, retroactively applied, holdings of this Court. The punishment itself may have been unconstitutionally inflicted, yet the finality of death precludes relief. An executed person has indeed "lost the right to have rights." As one 19th century proponent of punishing criminals by death declared, "When a man is hung, there is an end of our relations with him. His execution is a way of saying, 'You are not fit for this world, take your chance elsewhere.'"

In comparison to all other punishments today, then, the deliberate extinguishment of human life by the State is uniquely degrading to human dignity. I would not hesitate to hold, on that ground alone, that death is today a "cruel and unusual" punishment, were it not that death is a punishment of longstanding usage and acceptance in this country. I therefore turn to the second principle—that the State may not arbitrarily inflict an unusually severe punishment.

The outstanding characteristic of our present practice of punishing criminals by death is the infrequency with which we resort to it. The evidence is conclusive that death is not the ordinary punishment for any crime.

....

131

When a country of over 200 million people inflicts an unusually severe punishment no more than 50 times a year, the inference is strong that the punishment is not being regularly and fairly applied. To dispel it would indeed require a clear showing of nonarbitrary infliction.

Although there are no exact figures available, we know that thousands of murders and rapes are committed annually in States where death is an authorized punishment for those crimes. However the rate of infliction is characterized—as "freakishly" or "spectacularly" rare, or simply as rare—it would take the purest sophistry to deny that death is inflicted in only a minute fraction of these cases. How much rarer, after all, could the infliction of death be?

When the punishment of death is inflicted in a trivial number of the cases in which it is legally available, the conclusion is virtually inescapable that it is being inflicted arbitrarily. Indeed, it smacks of little more than a lottery system. The States claim, however, that this rarity is evidence not of arbitrariness, but of informed selectivity: Death is inflicted, they say, only in "extreme" cases.

Informed selectivity, of course, is a value not to be denigrated. Yet presumably the States could make precisely the same claim if there were 10 executions per year, or five, or even if there were but one. That there may be as many as 50 per year does not strengthen the claim. When the rate of infliction is at this low level, it is highly implausible that only the worst criminals or the criminals who commit the worst crimes are selected for this punishment. No one has yet suggested a rational basis that could differentiate in those terms the few who die from the many who go to prison. Crimes and criminals simply do not admit of a distinction that can be drawn so finely as to explain, on that ground, the execution of such a tiny sample of those eligible. Certainly the laws that provide for this punishment do not attempt to draw that distinction; all cases to which the laws apply are necessarily "extreme." Nor is the distinction credible in fact. If, for example, petitioner Furman or his crime illustrates the "extreme," then nearly all murderers and their murders are also "extreme." Furthermore, our procedures in death cases, rather than resulting in the selection of "extreme" cases for this punishment, actually sanction an arbitrary selection. For this Court has held that juries may, as they do, make the decision whether to impose a death sentence wholly unguided by standards governing that decision. In other words, our procedures are not constructed to guard against the totally capricious selection of criminals for the punishment of death.

Although it is difficult to imagine what further facts would be necessary in order to prove that death is, as my Brother STEWART puts it, "wantonly and . . . freakishly" inflicted, I need not conclude that arbitrary infliction is patently obvious. I am not considering this punishment by the isolated light of one principle. The probability of arbitrariness is sufficiently substantial that it can be relied upon, in combination with the other principles, in reaching a judgment on the constitutionality of this punishment.

When there is a strong probability that an unusually severe and degrading punishment is being inflicted arbitrarily, we may well expect that society will disapprove of its infliction. I turn, therefore, to the third principle. An examination of the history and present operation of the American practice of punishing criminals by death reveals that this punishment has been almost totally rejected by contemporary society.

....

Our practice of punishing criminals by death has changed greatly over the years. One significant change has been in our methods of inflicting death. Although this country never embraced the more violent and repulsive methods employed in England, we did for a long time rely almost exclusively upon the gallows and the firing squad. Since the development of the supposedly more humane methods of electrocution late in the 19th century and lethal gas in the 20th, however, hanging and shooting have virtually ceased. Our concern for decency and human dignity, moreover, has compelled changes in the circumstances surrounding the execution itself. No longer does our society countenance the spectacle of public executions, once thought desirable as a deterrent to criminal behavior by others. Today we reject public executions as debasing and brutalizing to us all.

Also significant is the drastic decrease in the crimes for which the punishment of death is actually inflicted. While esoteric capital crimes remain on the books, since 1930 murder and rape have accounted for nearly 99% of the total executions, and murder alone for about 87%. In addition, the crime of capital murder has itself been limited. As the Court noted in *McGautha v. California*, there was in this country a "rebellion against the common-law rule imposing a mandatory death sentence on all convicted murderers." Initially, that rebellion resulted in legislative definitions that distinguished between degrees of murder, retaining the mandatory death sentence only for murder in the first degree. Yet "this new legislative criterion for isolating crimes appropriately punishable by death soon proved as unsuccessful as the concept of 'malice aforethought,'" the common-law means of separating murder from manslaughter. Not only was the distinction between degrees of murder confusing and uncertain in practice, but even in clear cases of first-degree murder juries continued to take the law into their own hands: if they felt that death was an inappropriate punishment, "they simply refused to convict of the capital offense." The phenomenon of jury nullification thus remained to counteract the rigors of mandatory death sentences. Bowing to reality, "legislatures did not try, as before, to refine further the definition of capital homicides. Instead they adopted the method of forthrightly granting juries the discretion which they had been exercising in fact." In consequence, virtually all death sentences today are discretionarily imposed. Finally, it is significant that nine States no longer inflict the punishment of death under any circumstances, and five others have restricted it to extremely rare crimes.

Thus, although "the death penalty has been employed throughout our history," in fact the history of this punishment is one of successive restriction. What was once a common punishment has become, in the context of a continuing moral debate, increasingly rare. The evolution of this punishment evidences, not that it is an inevitable part of the American scene, but that it has proved progressively more troublesome to the national conscience. The result of this movement is our current system of administering the punishment, under which death sentences are rarely imposed and death is even more rarely inflicted. It is, of course, "We, the People" who are responsible for the rarity both of the imposition and the carrying out of this punishment. Juries, "expressing the conscience of the community on the ultimate question of life or death," have been able to bring themselves to vote for death in a mere 100 or so cases among the thousands tried each year where the punishment is available. Governors, elected by and acting for us, have regularly commuted a substantial number of those sentences. And it is our society that insists upon due process of law to the end that no person will be unjustly put to death, thus ensuring that many more of those sentences will not be carried out. In sum, we have made death a rare punishment today.

....

The final principle to be considered is that an unusually severe and degrading punishment may not be excessive in view of the purposes for which it is inflicted. This principle, too, is related to the others. When there is a strong probability that the State is arbitrarily inflicting an unusually severe punishment that is subject to grave societal doubts, it is likely also that the punishment cannot be shown to be serving any penal purpose that could not be served equally well by some less severe punishment.

The States' primary claim is that death is a necessary punishment because it prevents the commission of capital crimes more effectively than any less severe punishment. The first part of this claim is that the infliction of death is necessary to stop the individuals executed from committing further crimes. The sufficient answer to this is that if a criminal convicted of a capital crime poses a danger to society, effective administration of the State's pardon and parole laws can delay or deny his release from prison, and techniques of isolation can eliminate or minimize the danger while he remains confined.

The more significant argument is that the threat of death prevents the commission of capital crimes because it deters potential criminals who would not be deterred by the threat of imprisonment. The argument is not based upon evidence that the threat of death is a superior deterrent. Indeed, as my Brother MARSHALL establishes, the available evidence uniformly indicates, although it does not conclusively prove, that the threat of death has no greater deterrent effect than the threat of imprisonment. The States argue, however, that they are entitled to rely upon common human experience, and that experience, they say, supports the conclusion that death must be a more effective deterrent than any less severe punishment. Because people fear death the most, the argument runs, the threat of death must be the greatest deterrent.

It is important to focus upon the precise import of this argument. It is not denied that many, and probably most, capital crimes cannot be deterred by the threat of punishment. Thus the argument can apply only to those who think rationally about the commission of capital crimes. Particularly is that true when the potential criminal, under this argument, must not only consider the risk of punishment, but also distinguish between two possible punishments. The concern, then, is with a particular type of potential criminal, the rational person who will commit a capital crime knowing that the punishment is long-term imprisonment, which may well be for the rest of his life, but will not commit the crime knowing that the punishment is death. On the face of it, the assumption that such persons exist is implausible.

In any event, this argument cannot be appraised in the abstract. We are not presented with the theoretical question whether under any imaginable circumstances the threat of death might be a greater deterrent to the commission of capital crimes than the threat of imprisonment. We are concerned with the practice of punishing criminals by death as it exists in the United States today. Proponents of this argument necessarily admit that its validity depends upon the existence of a system in which the punishment of death is invariably and swiftly imposed. Our system, of course, satisfies neither condition. A rational person contemplating a murder or rape is confronted, not with the certainty of a speedy death, but with the slightest possibility that he will be executed in the distant future. The risk of death is remote and improbable; in contrast, the risk of long-term imprisonment is near and great. In short, whatever the speculative validity of the assumption that the threat of death is a superior deterrent, there is no reason to believe that as currently administered the punishment of death is necessary to deter the commission of capital crimes. Whatever might be the case were all or substantially all eligible criminals quickly put to death, unverifiable possibilities are an insufficient basis upon which to conclude that the threat of death today has any greater deterrent efficacy than the threat of imprisonment.

There is, however, another aspect to the argument that the punishment of death is necessary for the protection of society. The infliction of death, the States urge, serves to manifest the community's outrage at the commission of the crime. It is, they say, a concrete public expression of moral indignation that inculcates respect for the law and helps assure a more peaceful community. Moreover, we are told, not only does the punishment of death exert this widespread moralizing influence upon community values, it also satisfies the popular demand for grievous condemnation of abhorrent crimes and thus prevents disorder, lynching, and attempts by private citizens to take the law into their own hands.

The question, however, is not whether death serves these supposed purposes of punishment, but whether death serves them more effectively than imprisonment. There is no evidence whatever that utilization of imprisonment rather than death encourages private blood feuds and other disorders. Surely if there were such a danger, the execution of a handful of criminals each year would not prevent it. The assertion that death alone is a sufficiently emphatic denunciation for capital crimes suffers from the same defect. If capital crimes require the punishment of death in order to provide moral reinforcement for the basic values of the community, those values can only be undermined when death is so rarely inflicted upon the criminals who commit the crimes. Furthermore, it is certainly doubtful that the infliction of death by the State does in fact strengthen the community's moral code; if the deliberate extinguishment of human life has any effect at all, it more likely tends to lower our respect for life and brutalize our values. That, after all, is why we no longer carry out public executions. In any event, this claim simply means that one purpose of punishment is to indicate social disapproval of crime. To serve that purpose our laws distribute punishments according to the gravity of crimes and punish more severely the crimes society regards as more serious. That purpose cannot justify any particular punishment as the upper limit of severity.

There is, then, no substantial reason to believe that the punishment of death, as currently administered, is necessary for the protection of society. The only other purpose suggested, one that is independent of protection for society, is retribution. Shortly stated, retribution in this context means that criminals are put to death because they deserve it.

Although it is difficult to believe that any State today wishes to proclaim adherence to "naked vengeance," the States claim, in reliance upon its statutory authorization, that death is the only fit punishment for capital crimes and that this retributive purpose justifies its infliction. In the past, judged by its statutory authorization, death was considered the only fit punishment for the crime of forgery, for the first federal criminal statute provided a mandatory death penalty for that crime. Obviously, concepts of justice change; no immutable moral order requires death for murderers and rapists. The claim that death is a just punishment necessarily refers to the existence of certain public beliefs. The claim must be that for capital crimes death alone comports with society's notion of proper punishment. As administered today, however, the punishment of death cannot be justified as a necessary means of exacting retribution from criminals. When the overwhelming number of criminals who commit capital crimes go to prison, it cannot be concluded that death serves the purpose of retribution more effectively than imprisonment. The asserted public belief that murderers and rapists deserve to die is flatly inconsistent with the execution of a random few. As the history of the punishment of death in this country shows, our society wishes to prevent crime; we have no desire to kill criminals simply to get even with them.

In sum, the punishment of death is inconsistent with all four principles: Death is an unusually severe and degrading punishment; there is a strong probability that it is inflicted arbitrarily; its rejection by contemporary society is virtually total; and there is no reason to believe that it serves any penal purpose more effectively than the less severe punishment of imprisonment. The function of these principles is to enable a court to determine whether a punishment comports with human dignity. Death, quite simply, does not.

IV.

When this country was founded, memories of the Stuart horrors were fresh and severe corporal punishments were common. Death was not then a unique punishment. The practice of punishing criminals by death, moreover, was widespread and by and large acceptable to society. Indeed, without developed prison systems, there was frequently no workable alternative. Since that time, successive restrictions, imposed against the background of a continuing moral controversy, have drastically curtailed the use of this punishment. Today death is a uniquely and unusually severe punishment. When examined by the principles applicable under the Cruel and Unusual Punishments Clause, death stands condemned as fatally offensive to human dignity. The punishment of death is therefore "cruel and unusual," and the States may no longer inflict it as a punishment for crimes. Rather than kill an arbitrary handful of criminals each year, the States will confine them in prison. "The State thereby suffers nothing and loses no power. The purpose of punishment is fulfilled, crime is repressed by penalties of just, not tormenting, severity, its repetition is prevented, and hope is given for the reformation of the criminal."

I concur in the judgments of the Court.

MR. JUSTICE STEWART, concurring.

The penalty of death differs from all other forms of criminal punishment, not in degree but in kind. It is unique in its total irrevocability. It is unique in its rejection of rehabilitation of the convict as a basic purpose of criminal justice. And it is unique, finally, in its absolute renunciation of all that is embodied in our concept of humanity.

For these and other reasons, at least two of my Brothers have concluded that the infliction of the death penalty is constitutionally impermissible in all circumstances under the Eighth and Fourteenth Amendments. Their case is a strong one. But I find it unnecessary to reach the ultimate question they would decide.

The opinions of other Justices today have set out in admirable and thorough detail the origins and judicial history of the Eighth Amendment's guarantee against the infliction of cruel and unusual punishments, and the origin and judicial history of capital punishment. There is thus no need for me to review the historical materials here, and what I have to say can, therefore, be briefly stated.

Legislatures—state and federal—have sometimes specified that the penalty of death shall be the mandatory punishment for every person convicted of engaging in certain designated criminal conduct. Congress, for example, has provided that anyone convicted of acting as a spy for the enemy in time of war shall be put to death. The Rhode Island Legislature has ordained the death penalty for a life term prisoner who commits murder. Massachusetts has passed a law imposing the death penalty upon anyone convicted of murder in the commission of a forcible rape. An Ohio law imposes the mandatory penalty of death upon the assassin of the President of the United States or the Governor of a State.

If we were reviewing death sentences imposed under these or similar laws, we would be faced with the need to decide whether capital punishment is unconstitutional for all crimes and under all circumstances. We would need to decide whether a legislature—state or federal—could constitutionally determine that certain criminal conduct is so atrocious that society's interest in deterrence and retribution wholly outweighs any considerations of reform or rehabilitation of the perpetrator, and that, despite the inconclusive empirical evidence, only the automatic penalty of death will provide maximum deterrence.

On that score I would say only that I cannot agree that retribution is a constitutionally impermissible ingredient in the imposition of punishment. The instinct for retribution is part of the nature of man, and channeling that instinct in the administration of criminal justice serves an important purpose in promoting the stability of a society governed by law. When people begin to believe that organized society is unwilling or unable to impose upon criminal offenders the punishment they "deserve," then there are sown the seeds of anarchy—of self-help, vigilante justice, and lynch law.

The constitutionality of capital punishment in the abstract is not, however, before us in these cases. For the Georgia and Texas Legislatures have not provided that the death penalty shall be imposed upon all those who are found guilty of forcible rape. And the Georgia Legislature has not ordained that death shall be the automatic punishment for murder. In a word, neither State has made a legislative determination that forcible rape and murder can be deterred only by imposing the penalty of death upon all who perpetrate those offenses. As MR. JUSTICE WHITE so tellingly puts it, the "legislative will is not frustrated if the penalty is never imposed."

Instead, the death sentences now before us are the product of a legal system that brings them, I believe, within the very core of the Eighth Amendment's guarantee against cruel and unusual punishments, a guarantee applicable against the States through the Fourteenth Amendment. In the first place, it is clear that these sentences are "cruel" in the sense that they excessively go beyond, not in degree but in kind, the punishments that the state legislatures have determined to be necessary. In the second place, it is equally clear that these sentences are "unusual" in the sense that the penalty of death is infrequently imposed for murder, and that its imposition for rape is extraordinarily rare. But I do not rest my conclusion upon these two propositions alone.

These death sentences are cruel and unusual in the same way that being struck by lightning is cruel and unusual. For, of all the people convicted of rapes and murders in 1967 and 1968, many just as reprehensible as these, the petitioners are among a capriciously selected random handful upon whom the sentence of death has in fact been imposed. My concurring Brothers have demonstrated that, if any basis can be discerned for the selection of these few to be sentenced to die, it is the constitutionally impermissible basis of race. But racial discrimination has not been proved, and I put it to one side. I simply conclude that the Eighth and Fourteenth Amendments cannot tolerate the infliction of a sentence of death under legal systems that permit this unique penalty to be so wantonly and so freakishly imposed.

For these reasons I concur in the judgments of the Court.

MR. JUSTICE WHITE, concurring.

The facial constitutionality of statutes requiring the imposition of the death penalty for first-degree murder, for more narrowly defined categories of murder, or for rape would present quite different issues under the Eighth Amendment than are posed by the cases before us. In joining the Court's judgments, therefore, I do not at all intimate that the death penalty is unconstitutional per se or that there is no system of capital punishment that would comport with the Eighth Amendment. That question, ably argued by several of my Brethren, is not presented by these cases and need not be decided.

The narrower question to which I address myself concerns the constitutionality of capital punishment statutes under which (1) the legislature authorizes the imposition of the death penalty for murder or rape; (2) the legislature does not itself mandate the penalty in any particular class or kind of case (that is, legislative will is not frustrated if the penalty is never imposed), but delegates to judges or juries the decisions as to those cases, if any, in which the penalty will be utilized; and (3) judges and juries have ordered the death penalty with such infrequency that the odds are now very much against imposition and execution of the penalty with respect to any convicted murderer or rapist. It is in this context that we must consider whether the execution of these petitioners would violate the Eighth Amendment.

I begin with what I consider a near truism: that the death penalty could so seldom be imposed that it would cease to be a credible deterrent or measurably to contribute to any other end of punishment in the criminal justice system. It is perhaps true that no matter how infrequently those convicted of rape or murder are executed, the penalty so imposed is not disproportionate to the crime and those executed may deserve exactly what they received. It would also be clear that executed defendants are finally and completely incapacitated from again committing rape or murder or any other crime. But when imposition of the penalty reaches a certain degree of infrequency, it would be very doubtful that any existing general need for retribution would be measurably satisfied. Nor could it be said with confidence that society's need for specific deterrence justifies death for so few when for so many in like circumstances life imprisonment or shorter prison terms are judged sufficient, or that community values are measurably reinforced by authorizing a penalty so rarely invoked.

Most important, a major goal of the criminal law—to deter others by punishing the convicted criminal—would not be substantially served where the penalty is so seldom invoked that it ceases to be the credible threat essential to influence the conduct of others. For present purposes I accept the morality and utility of punishing one person to influence another. I accept also the effectiveness of punishment generally and need not reject the death penalty as a more effective deterrent than a lesser punishment. But common sense and experience tell us that seldom-enforced laws become ineffective measures for controlling human conduct and that the death penalty, unless imposed with sufficient frequency, will make little contribution to deterring those crimes for which it may be exacted.

The imposition and execution of the death penalty are obviously cruel in the dictionary sense. But the penalty has not been considered cruel and unusual punishment in the constitutional sense because it was thought justified by the social ends it was deemed to serve. At the moment that it ceases realistically to further these purposes, however, the emerging question is whether its imposition in such circumstances would violate the Eighth Amendment. It is my view that it would, for its imposition would then be the pointless and needless extinction of life with only marginal contributions to any discernible social or public purposes. A penalty with such negligible returns to the State would be patently excessive and cruel and unusual punishment violative of the Eighth Amendment.

It is also my judgment that this point has been reached with respect to capital punishment as it is presently administered under the statutes involved in these cases. Concededly, it is difficult to prove as a general proposition that capital punishment, however administered, more effectively serves the ends of the criminal law than does imprisonment. But however that may be, I cannot avoid the conclusion that as the statutes before us are now administered, the penalty is so infrequently imposed that the threat of execution is too attenuated to be of substantial service to criminal justice.

I need not restate the facts and figures that appear in the opinions of my Brethren. Nor can I "prove" my conclusion from these data. But, like my Brethren, I must arrive at judgment; and I can do no more than state a conclusion based on 10 years of almost daily exposure to the facts and circumstances of hundreds and hundreds of federal and state criminal cases involving crimes for which death is the authorized penalty. That conclusion, as I have said, is that the death penalty is exacted with great infrequency even for the most atrocious crimes and that there is no meaningful basis for distinguishing the few cases in which it is imposed from the many cases in which it is not. The short of it is that the policy of vesting sentencing authority primarily in juries—a decision largely motivated by the desire to mitigate the harshness of the law and to bring community judgment to bear on the sentence as well as guilt or innocence—has so effectively achieved its aims that capital punishment within the confines of the statutes now before us has for all practical purposes run its course.

Judicial review, by definition, often involves a conflict between judicial and legislative judgment as to what the Constitution means or requires. In this respect, Eighth Amendment cases come to us in no different posture. It seems conceded by all that the Amendment imposes some obligations on the judiciary to judge the constitutionality of punishment and that there are punishments that the Amendment would bar whether legislatively approved or not. Inevitably, then, there will be occasions when we will differ with Congress or state legislatures with respect to the validity of punishment. There will also be cases in which we shall strongly disagree among ourselves. Unfortunately, this is one of them. But as I see it, this case is no different in kind from many others, although it may have wider impact and provoke sharper disagreement.

In this respect, I add only that past and present legislative judgment with respect to the death penalty loses much of its force when viewed in light of the recurring practice of delegating sentencing authority to the jury and the fact that a jury, in its own discretion and without violating its trust or any statutory policy, may refuse to impose the death penalty no matter what the circumstances of the crime. Legislative "policy" is thus necessarily defined not by what is legislatively authorized but by what juries and judges do in exercising the discretion so regularly conferred upon them. In my judgment what was done in these cases violated the Eighth Amendment.

I concur in the judgments of the Court.

MR. JUSTICE MARSHALL, concurring.

These three cases present the question whether the death penalty is a cruel and unusual punishment prohibited by the Eighth Amendment to the United States Constitution.

....

Furman was convicted of murder for shooting the father of five children when he discovered that Furman had broken into his home early one morning.... Jackson was found guilty of rape during the course of a robbery in the victim's home. The rape was accomplished as he held the pointed ends of scissors at the victim's throat. Branch also was convicted of a rape committed in the victim's home. No weapon was utilized, but physical force and threats of physical force were employed.

The criminal acts with which we are confronted are ugly, vicious, reprehensible acts. Their sheer brutality cannot and should not be minimized. But, we are not called upon to condone the penalized conduct; we are asked only to examine the penalty imposed on each of the petitioners and to determine whether or not it violates the Eighth Amendment. The question then is not whether we condone rape or murder, for surely we do not; it is whether capital punishment is "a punishment no longer consistent with our own self-respect" and, therefore, violative of the Eighth Amendment.

The elasticity of the constitutional provision under consideration presents dangers of too little or too much self-restraint. Hence, we must proceed with caution to answer the question presented. By first examining the historical derivation of the Eighth Amendment and the construction given it in the past by this Court, and then exploring the history and attributes of capital punishment in this country, we can answer the question presented with objectivity and a proper measure of self-restraint.

Candor is critical to such an inquiry. All relevant material must be marshaled and sorted and forthrightly examined. We must not only be precise as to the standards of judgment that we are utilizing, but exacting in examining the relevant material in light of those standards.

Candor compels me to confess that I am not oblivious to the fact that this is truly a matter of life and death. Not only does it involve the lives of these three petitioners, but those of the almost 600 other condemned men and women in this country currently awaiting execution. While this fact cannot affect our ultimate decision, it necessitates that the decision be free from any possibility of error.

I.

The Eighth Amendment's ban against cruel and unusual punishments derives from English law. In 1583, John Whitgift, Archbishop of Canterbury, turned the High Commission into a permanent ecclesiastical court, and the Commission began to use torture to extract confessions from persons suspected of various offenses. Sir Robert Beale protested that cruel and barbarous torture violated *Magna Carta*, but his protests were made in vain.

....

Cruel punishments were not confined to those accused of crimes, but were notoriously applied with even greater relish to those who were convicted. Blackstone described in ghastly detail the myriad of inhumane forms of punishment imposed on persons found guilty of any of a large number of offenses. Death, of course, was the usual result.

....

Thus, the history of the clause clearly establishes that it was intended to prohibit cruel punishments. We must now turn to the case law to discover the manner in which courts have given meaning to the term "cruel."

II.

This Court did not squarely face the task of interpreting the cruel and unusual punishments language for the first time until *Wilkerson v. Utah,* although the language received a cursory examination in several prior cases. In *Wilkerson*, the Court unanimously upheld a sentence of public execution by shooting imposed pursuant to a conviction for premeditated murder. In his opinion for the Court, Mr. Justice Clifford wrote:

"Difficulty would attend the effort to define with exactness the extent of the constitutional provision which provides that cruel and unusual punishments shall not be inflicted; but it is safe to affirm that punishments of torture . . . and all others in the same line of unnecessary cruelty, are forbidden by that amendment to the Constitution."

Thus, the Court found that unnecessary cruelty was no more permissible than torture. To determine whether the punishment under attack was unnecessarily cruel, the Court examined the history of the Utah Territory and the then-current writings on capital punishment, and compared this Nation's practices with those of other countries. It is apparent that the Court felt it could not dispose of the question simply by referring to traditional practices; instead, it felt bound to examine developing thought.

Eleven years passed before the Court again faced a challenge to a specific punishment under the Eighth Amendment. In the case of *In re Kemmler*, Chief Justice Fuller wrote an opinion for a unanimous Court upholding electrocution as a permissible mode of punishment. While the Court ostensibly held that the Eighth Amendment did not apply to the States, it is very apparent that the nature of the punishment involved was examined under the Due Process Clause of the Fourteenth Amendment. The Court held that the punishment was not objectionable. Today, *Kemmler* stands primarily for the proposition that a punishment is not necessarily unconstitutional simply because it is unusual, so long as the legislature has a humane purpose in selecting it.

Two years later in *O'Neil v. Vermont*, the Court reaffirmed that the Eighth Amendment was not applicable to the States. O'Neil was found guilty on 307 counts of selling liquor in violation of Vermont law. A fine of $ 6,140 ($ 20 for each offense) and the costs of prosecution ($ 497.96) were imposed. O'Neil was committed to prison until the fine and the costs were paid; and the court provided that if they were not paid before a specified date, O'Neil was to be confined in the house of corrections for 19,914 days (approximately 54 years) at hard labor. Three Justices—Field, Harlan, and Brewer—dissented. They maintained not only that the Cruel and Unusual Punishments Clause was applicable to the States, but that in O'Neil's case it had been violated. Mr. Justice Field wrote:
"That designation [cruel and unusual], it is true, is usually applied to punishments which inflict torture, such as the rack, the thumbscrew, the iron boot, the stretching of limbs and the like, which are attended with acute pain and suffering. . . . The inhibition is directed, not only against punishments of the character mentioned, but against all punishments which by their

excessive length or severity are greatly disproportioned to the offences charged. The whole inhibition is against that which is excessive . . . ."

In *Howard v. Fleming* the Court, in essence, followed the approach advocated by the dissenters in *O'Neil*. In rejecting the claim that 10-year sentences for conspiracy to defraud were cruel and unusual, the Court (per Mr. Justice Brewer) considered the nature of the crime, the purpose of the law, and the length of the sentence imposed.

The Court used the same approach seven years later in the landmark case of *Weems v. United States*. Weems, an officer of the Bureau of Coast Guard and Transportation of the United States Government of the Philippine Islands, was convicted of falsifying a "public and official document." He was sentenced to 15 years' incarceration at hard labor with chains on his ankles, to an unusual loss of his civil rights, and to perpetual surveillance. Called upon to determine whether this was a cruel and unusual punishment, the Court found that it was. The Court emphasized that the Constitution was not an "ephemeral" enactment, or one "designed to meet passing occasions." Recognizing that "time works changes, and brings into existence new conditions and purposes," the Court commented that "in the application of a constitution . . . our contemplation cannot be only of what has been but of what may be."

In striking down the penalty imposed on Weems, the Court examined the punishment in relation to the offense, compared the punishment to those inflicted for other crimes and to those imposed in other jurisdictions, and concluded that the punishment was excessive. Justices White and Holmes dissented and argued that the cruel and unusual prohibition was meant to prohibit only those things that were objectionable at the time the Constitution was adopted.

Weems is a landmark case because it represents the first time that the Court invalidated a penalty prescribed by a legislature for a particular offense. The Court made it plain beyond any reasonable doubt that excessive punishments were as objectionable as those that were inherently cruel. Thus, it is apparent that the dissenters' position in *O'Neil* had become the opinion of the Court in *Weems*.

Weems was followed by two cases that added little to our knowledge of the scope of the cruel and unusual language, *Badders v. United States* and *United States ex rel. Milwaukee Social Democratic Publishing Co. v. Burleson*. Then came another landmark case, *Louisiana ex rel. Francis v. Resweber*.

Francis had been convicted of murder and sentenced to be electrocuted. The first time the current passed through him, there was a mechanical failure and he did not die. Thereafter, Francis sought to prevent a second electrocution on the ground that it would be a cruel and unusual punishment. Eight members of the Court assumed the applicability of the Eighth Amendment to the States. The Court was virtually unanimous in agreeing that "the traditional humanity of modern Anglo-American law forbids the infliction of unnecessary pain," but split 5-4 on whether Francis would, under the circumstances, be forced to undergo any excessive pain. Five members of the Court treated the case like *In re Kemmler* and held that the legislature adopted electrocution for a humane purpose, and that its will should not be thwarted because, in its desire to reduce pain and suffering in most cases, it may have inadvertently increased suffering in one particular case. The four dissenters felt that the case should be remanded for further facts.

As in *Weems*, the Court was concerned with excessive punishments. *Resweber* is perhaps most significant because the analysis of cruel and unusual punishment questions first advocated by the dissenters in *O'Neil* was at last firmly entrenched in the minds of an entire Court.

Trop v. Dulles marked the next major cruel and unusual punishment case in this Court. Trop, a native-born American, was declared to have lost his citizenship by reason of a conviction by court-martial for wartime desertion. Writing for himself and Justices Black, DOUGLAS, and Whittaker, Chief Justice Warren concluded that loss of citizenship amounted to a cruel and unusual punishment that violated the Eighth Amendment.

Emphasizing the flexibility inherent in the words "cruel and unusual," the Chief Justice wrote that "the Amendment must draw its meaning from the evolving standards of decency that mark the progress of a maturing society." His approach to the problem was that utilized by the Court in *Weems*: he scrutinized the severity of the penalty in relation to the offense, examined the practices of other civilized nations of the world, and concluded that involuntary statelessness was an excessive and, therefore, an unconstitutional punishment. Justice Frankfurter, dissenting, urged that expatriation was not punishment, and that even if it were, it was not excessive. While he criticized the conclusion arrived at by the Chief Justice, his approach to the Eighth Amendment question was identical.

Whereas in *Trop* a majority of the Court failed to agree on whether loss of citizenship was a cruel and unusual punishment, four years later a majority did agree in *Robinson v. California* that a sentence of 90 days' imprisonment for violation of a California statute making it a crime to "be addicted to the use of narcotics" was cruel and unusual. MR. JUSTICE STEWART, writing the opinion of the Court, reiterated what the Court had said in *Weems* and what Chief Justice Warren wrote in *Trop*—that the cruel and unusual punishment clause was not a static concept, but one that must be continually re-examined "in the light of contemporary human knowledge." The fact that the penalty under attack was only 90 days evidences the Court's willingness to carefully examine the possible excessiveness of punishment in a given case even where what is involved is a penalty that is familiar and widely accepted.

We distinguished *Robinson* in *Powell v. Texas*, where we sustained a conviction for drunkenness in a public place and a fine of $20. Four Justices dissented on the ground that Robinson was controlling. The analysis in both cases was the same; only the conclusion as to whether or not the punishment was excessive differed. *Powell* marked the last time prior to today's decision that the Court has had occasion to construe the meaning of the term "cruel and unusual" punishment.

Several principles emerge from these prior cases and serve as a beacon to an enlightened decision in the instant cases.

III.

Perhaps the most important principle in analyzing "cruel and unusual" punishment questions is one that is reiterated again and again in the prior opinions of the Court: i.e., the cruel and unusual language "must draw its meaning from the evolving standards of decency that mark the progress of a maturing society." Thus, a penalty that was permissible at one time in our Nation's history is not necessarily permissible today.

The fact, therefore, that the Court, or individual Justices, may have in the past expressed an opinion that the death penalty is constitutional is not now binding on us. A fair reading of *Wilkerson v. Utah*, *In re Kemmler*, and *Louisiana ex rel. Francis v. Resweber*, would certainly indicate an acceptance *sub silentio* of capital punishment as constitutionally permissible. Several Justices have also expressed their individual opinions that the death penalty is constitutional. Yet, some of these same Justices and others have at times expressed concern over capital punishment. There is no holding directly in point, and the very nature of the Eighth Amendment would dictate that unless a very recent decision existed, stare decisis would bow to changing values, and the question of the constitutionality of capital punishment at a given moment in history would remain open.

Faced with an open question, we must establish our standards for decision. The decisions discussed in the previous section imply that a punishment may be deemed cruel and unusual for any one of four distinct reasons.

First, there are certain punishments that inherently involve so much physical pain and suffering that civilized people cannot tolerate them—e.g., use of the rack, the thumbscrew, or other modes of torture. Regardless of public sentiment with respect to imposition of one of these punishments in a particular case or at any one moment in history, the Constitution prohibits it. These are punishments that have been barred since the adoption of the Bill of Rights.

Second, there are punishments that are unusual, signifying that they were previously unknown as penalties for a given offense. If these punishments are intended to serve a humane purpose, they may be constitutionally permissible.... Prior decisions leave open the question of just how much the word "unusual" adds to the word "cruel." I have previously indicated that use of the word "unusual" in the English Bill of Rights of 1689 was inadvertent, and there is nothing in the history of the Eighth Amendment to give flesh to its intended meaning. In light of the meager history that does exist, one would suppose that an innovative punishment would probably be constitutional if no more cruel than that punishment which it superseded. We need not decide this question here, however, for capital punishment is certainly not a recent phenomenon.

Third, a penalty may be cruel and unusual because it is excessive and serves no valid legislative purpose. The decisions previously discussed are replete with assertions that one of the primary functions of the cruel and unusual punishments clause is to prevent excessive or unnecessary penalties; these punishments are unconstitutional even though popular sentiment may favor them. Both THE CHIEF JUSTICE and MR. JUSTICE POWELL seek to ignore or to minimize this aspect of the Court's prior decisions. But, since Mr. Justice Field first suggested that "the whole inhibition of the prohibition against cruel and unusual punishments is against that which is excessive," this Court has steadfastly maintained that a penalty is unconstitutional whenever it is unnecessarily harsh or cruel. This is what the Founders of this country intended; this is what their fellow citizens believed the Eighth Amendment provided; and this was the basis for our decision in *Robinson v. California*, for the plurality opinion by Mr. Chief Justice Warren in *Trop v. Dulles*, and for the Court's decision in *Weems v. United States*. It should also be noted that the "cruel and unusual" language of the Eighth Amendment immediately follows language that prohibits excessive bail and excessive fines. The entire thrust of the Eighth Amendment is, in short, against "that which is excessive."

Fourth, where a punishment is not excessive and serves a valid legislative purpose, it still may be invalid if popular sentiment abhors it. For example, if the evidence clearly demonstrated that capital punishment served valid legislative purposes, such punishment would, nevertheless, be unconstitutional if citizens found it to be morally unacceptable. A general abhorrence on the part of the public would, in effect, equate a modern punishment with those barred since the adoption of the Eighth Amendment. There are no prior cases in this Court striking down a penalty on this ground, but the very notion of changing values requires that we recognize its existence.

It is immediately obvious, then, that since capital punishment is not a recent phenomenon, if it violates the Constitution, it does so because it is excessive or unnecessary, or because it is abhorrent to currently existing moral values.

We must proceed to the history of capital punishment in the United States.

IV.

Capital punishment has been used to penalize various forms of conduct by members of society since the beginnings of civilization. Its precise origins are difficult to perceive, but there is some evidence that its roots lie in violent retaliation by members of a tribe or group, or by the tribe or group itself, against persons committing hostile acts toward group members. Thus, infliction of death as a penalty for objectionable conduct appears to have its beginnings in private vengeance.

As individuals gradually ceded their personal prerogatives to a sovereign power, the sovereign accepted the authority to punish wrongdoing as part of its "divine right" to rule. Individual vengeance gave way to the vengeance of the state, and capital punishment became a public function. Capital punishment worked its way into the laws of various countries, and was inflicted in a variety of macabre and horrific ways.

....

During the 1830's, there was a rising tide of sentiment against capital punishment. In 1834, Pennsylvania abolished public executions, and two years later, The Report on Capital Punishment Made to the Maine Legislature was published. It led to a law that prohibited the executive from issuing a warrant for execution within one year after a criminal was sentenced by the courts. The totally discretionary character of the law was at odds with almost all prior practices. The "Maine Law" resulted in little enforcement of the death penalty, which was not surprising since the legislature's idea in passing the law was that the affirmative burden placed on the governor to issue a warrant one full year or more after a trial would be an effective deterrent to exercise of his power. The law spread throughout New England and led to Michigan's being the first State to abolish capital punishment in 1846.

Anti-capital-punishment feeling grew in the 1840's as the literature of the period pointed out the agony of the condemned man and expressed the philosophy that repentance atoned for the worst crimes, and that true repentance derived, not from fear, but from harmony with nature.

By 1850, societies for abolition existed in Massachusetts, New York, Pennsylvania, Tennessee, Ohio, Alabama, Louisiana, Indiana, and Iowa. New York, Massachusetts, and Pennsylvania constantly had abolition bills before their legislatures. In 1852, Rhode Island followed in the footsteps of Michigan and partially abolished capital punishment. Wisconsin totally abolished the death penalty the following year. Those States that did not abolish the death penalty greatly reduced its scope, and "few states outside the South had more than one or two . . . capital offenses" in addition to treason and murder.

But the Civil War halted much of the abolition furor. One historian has said that "after the Civil War, men's finer sensibilities, which had once been revolted by the execution of a fellow being, seemed hardened and blunted." Some of the attention previously given to abolition was diverted to prison reform. An abolitionist movement still existed, however. Maine abolished the death penalty in 1876, restored it in 1883, and abolished it again in 1887; Iowa abolished capital punishment from 1872-1878; Colorado began an erratic period of *de facto* abolition and revival in 1872; and Kansas also abolished it *de facto* in 1872, and by law in 1907.

One great success of the abolitionist movement in the period from 1830-1900 was almost complete elimination of mandatory capital punishment. Before the legislatures formally gave juries discretion to refrain from imposing the death penalty, the phenomenon of "jury nullification," in which juries refused to convict in cases in which they believed that death was an inappropriate penalty, was experienced. Tennessee was the first State to give juries discretion, but other States quickly followed suit. Then, Rep. Curtis of New York introduced a federal bill that ultimately became law in 1897 which reduced the number of federal capital offenses from 60 to 3 (treason, murder, and rape) and gave the jury sentencing discretion in murder and rape cases.

By 1917, 12 States had become abolitionist jurisdictions. But, under the nervous tension of World War I, four of these States reinstituted capital punishment and promising movements in other States came grinding to a halt. During the period following the First World War, the abolitionist movement never regained its momentum.

It is not easy to ascertain why the movement lost its vigor. Certainly, much attention was diverted from penal reform during the economic crisis of the depression and the exhausting years of struggle during World War II. Also, executions, which had once been frequent public spectacles, became infrequent private affairs. The manner of inflicting death changed, and the horrors of the punishment were, therefore, somewhat diminished in the minds of the general public.

In recent years there has been renewed interest in modifying capital punishment. New York has moved toward abolition, as have several other States. In 1967, a bill was introduced in the Senate to abolish capital punishment for all federal crimes, but it died in committee.

At the present time, 41 States, the District of Columbia, and other federal jurisdictions authorize the death penalty for at least one crime. It would be fruitless to attempt here to categorize the approach to capital punishment taken by the various States. It is sufficient to note that murder is the crime most often punished by death, followed by kidnapping and treason. Rape is a capital offense in 16 States and the federal system.

The foregoing history demonstrates that capital punishment was carried from Europe to America but, once here, was tempered considerably. At times in our history, strong abolitionist movements have existed. But, they have never been completely successful, as no more than one-quarter of the States of the Union have, at any one time, abolished the death penalty. They have had partial success, however, especially in reducing the number of capital crimes, replacing mandatory death sentences with jury discretion, and developing more humane methods of conducting executions.

This is where our historical foray leads. The question now to be faced is whether American society has reached a point where abolition is not dependent on a successful grass roots movement in particular jurisdictions, but is demanded by the Eighth Amendment. To answer this question, we must first examine whether or not the death penalty is today tantamount to excessive punishment.

V.

In order to assess whether or not death is an excessive or unnecessary penalty, it is necessary to consider the reasons why a legislature might select it as punishment for one or more offenses, and examine whether less severe penalties would satisfy the legitimate legislative wants as well as capital punishment. If they would, then the death penalty is unnecessary cruelty, and, therefore, unconstitutional.

There are six purposes conceivably served by capital punishment: retribution, deterrence, prevention of repetitive criminal acts, encouragement of guilty pleas and confessions, eugenics, and economy. These are considered *seriatim* below.

A.

The concept of retribution is one of the most misunderstood in all of our criminal jurisprudence. The principal source of confusion derives from the fact that, in dealing with the concept, most people confuse the question "why do men in fact punish?" with the question "what justifies men in punishing?" Men may punish for any number of reasons, but the one reason that punishment is morally good or morally justifiable is that someone has broken the law. Thus, it can correctly be said that breaking the law is the *sine qua non* of punishment, or, in other words, that we only tolerate punishment as it is imposed on one who deviates from the norm established by the criminal law.

The fact that the State may seek retribution against those who have broken its laws does not mean that retribution may then become the State's sole end in punishing. Our jurisprudence has always accepted deterrence in general, deterrence of individual recidivism, isolation of dangerous persons, and rehabilitation as proper goals of punishment. Retaliation, vengeance, and retribution have been roundly condemned as intolerable aspirations for a government in a free society.

Punishment as retribution has been condemned by scholars for centuries, and the Eighth Amendment itself was adopted to prevent punishment from becoming synonymous with vengeance.

....

I would reach an opposite conclusion—that only in a free society would men recognize their inherent weaknesses and seek to compensate for them by means of a Constitution.

The history of the Eighth Amendment supports only the conclusion that retribution for its own sake is improper.

B.

The most hotly contested issue regarding capital punishment is whether it is better than life imprisonment as a deterrent to crime.

While the contrary position has been argued, it is my firm opinion that the death penalty is a more severe sanction than life imprisonment. Admittedly, there are some persons who would rather die than languish in prison for a lifetime. But, whether or not they should be able to choose death as an alternative is a far different question from that presented here—i.e., whether the State can impose death as a punishment. Death is irrevocable; life imprisonment is not. Death, of course, makes rehabilitation impossible; life imprisonment does not. In short, death has always been viewed as the ultimate sanction, and it seems perfectly reasonable to continue to view it as such.

It must be kept in mind, then, that the question to be considered is not simply whether capital punishment is a deterrent, but whether it is a better deterrent than life imprisonment.

There is no more complex problem than determining the deterrent efficacy of the death penalty. "Capital punishment has obviously failed as a deterrent when a murder is committed. We can number its failures. But we cannot number its successes. No one can ever know how many people have refrained from murder because of the fear of being hanged." This is the nub of the problem and it is exacerbated by the paucity of useful data. The United States is more fortunate than most countries, however, in that it has what are generally considered to be the world's most reliable statistics.

The two strongest arguments in favor of capital punishment as a deterrent are both logical hypotheses devoid of evidentiary support, but persuasive nonetheless. The first proposition was best stated by Sir James Stephen in 1864:

"No other punishment deters men so effectually from committing crimes as the punishment of death. This is one of those propositions which it is difficult to prove, simply because they are in themselves more obvious than any proof can make them. It is possible to display ingenuity in arguing against it, but that is all. The whole experience of mankind is in the other direction. The threat of instant death is the one to which resort has always been made when there was an absolute necessity for producing some result. . . . No one goes to certain inevitable death except by compulsion. Put the matter the other way. Was there ever yet a criminal who, when sentenced to death and brought out to die, would refuse the offer of a commutation of his sentence for the severest secondary punishment? Surely not. Why is this? It can only be because 'All that a man has will he give for his life.' In any secondary punishment, however terrible, there is hope; but death is death; its terrors cannot be described more forcibly."

This hypothesis relates to the use of capital punishment as a deterrent for any crime. The second proposition is that "if life imprisonment is the maximum penalty for a crime such as murder, an offender who is serving a life sentence cannot then be deterred from murdering a fellow inmate or a prison officer." This hypothesis advocates a limited deterrent effect under particular circumstances.

Abolitionists attempt to disprove these hypotheses by amassing statistical evidence to demonstrate that there is no correlation between criminal activity and the existence or nonexistence of a capital sanction. Almost all of the evidence involves the crime of murder, since murder is punishable by death in more jurisdictions than are other offenses, and almost 90% of all executions since 1930 have been pursuant to murder convictions.

....

Statistics also show that the deterrent effect of capital punishment is no greater in those communities where executions take place than in other communities. In fact, there is some evidence that imposition of capital punishment may actually encourage crime, rather than deter it. And, while police and law enforcement officers are the strongest advocates of capital punishment, the evidence is overwhelming that police are no safer in communities that retain the sanction than in those that have abolished it.

There is also a substantial body of data showing that the existence of the death penalty has virtually no effect on the homicide rate in prisons. Most of the persons sentenced to death are murderers, and murderers tend to be model prisoners.

In sum, the only support for the theory that capital punishment is an effective deterrent is found in the hypotheses with which we began and the occasional stories about a specific individual being deterred from doing a contemplated criminal act. These claims of specific deterrence are often spurious, however, and may be more than counterbalanced by the tendency of capital punishment to incite certain crimes.

The United Nations Committee that studied capital punishment found that "it is generally agreed between the retentionists and abolitionists, whatever their opinions about the validity of comparative studies of deterrence, that the data which now exist show no correlation between the existence of capital punishment and lower rates of capital crime."

Despite the fact that abolitionists have not proved non-deterrence beyond a reasonable doubt, they have succeeded in showing by clear and convincing evidence that capital punishment is not necessary as a deterrent to crime in our society. This is all that they must do. We would shirk our judicial responsibilities if we failed to accept the presently existing statistics and demanded more proof. It may be that we now possess all the proof that anyone could ever hope to assemble on the subject. But, even if further proof were to be forthcoming, I believe there is more than enough evidence presently available for a decision in this case.

....

In light of the massive amount of evidence before us, I see no alternative but to conclude that capital punishment cannot be justified on the basis of its deterrent effect.

C.

Much of what must be said about the death penalty as a device to prevent recidivism is obvious—if a murderer is executed, he cannot possibly commit another offense. The fact is, however, that murderers are extremely unlikely to commit other crimes either in prison or upon their release. For the most part, they are first offenders, and when released from prison they are known to become model citizens. Furthermore, most persons who commit capital crimes are not executed. With respect to those who are sentenced to die, it is critical to note that the jury is never asked to determine whether they are likely to be recidivists. In light of these facts, if capital punishment were justified purely on the basis of preventing recidivism, it would have to be considered to be excessive; no general need to obliterate all capital offenders could have been demonstrated, nor any specific need in individual cases.

D.

The three final purposes which may underlie utilization of a capital sanction—encouraging guilty pleas and confessions, eugenics, and reducing state expenditures—may be dealt with quickly. If the death penalty is used to encourage guilty pleas and thus to deter suspects from exercising their rights under the Sixth Amendment to jury trials, it is unconstitutional. Its elimination would do little to impair the State's bargaining position in criminal cases, since life imprisonment remains a severe sanction which can be used as leverage for bargaining for pleas or confessions in exchange either for charges of lesser offenses or recommendations of leniency.

Moreover, to the extent that capital punishment is used to encourage confessions and guilty pleas, it is not being used for punishment purposes. A State that justifies capital punishment on its utility as part of the conviction process could not profess to rely on capital punishment as a deterrent. Such a State's system would be structured with twin goals only: obtaining guilty pleas and confessions and imposing imprisonment as the maximum sanction. Since life imprisonment is sufficient for bargaining purposes, the death penalty is excessive if used for the same purposes.

In light of the previous discussion on deterrence, any suggestions concerning the eugenic benefits of capital punishment are obviously meritless. As I pointed out above, there is not even any attempt made to discover which capital offenders are likely to be recidivists, let alone which are positively incurable. No test or procedure presently exists by which incurables can be screened from those who would benefit from treatment. On the one hand, due process would seem to require that we have some procedure to demonstrate incurability before execution; and, on the other hand, equal protection would then seemingly require that all incurables be executed. In addition, the "cruel and unusual" language would require that life imprisonment, treatment, and sterilization be inadequate for eugenic purposes. More importantly, this Nation has never formally professed eugenic goals, and the history of the world does not look kindly on them. If eugenics is one of our purposes, then the legislatures should say so forthrightly and design procedures to serve this goal. Until such time, I can only conclude, as has virtually everyone else who has looked at the problem, that capital punishment cannot be defended on the basis of any eugenic purposes.

During the period between conviction and execution, there are an inordinate number of collateral attacks on the conviction and attempts to obtain executive clemency, all of which exhaust the time, money, and effort of the State. There are also continual assertions that the condemned prisoner has gone insane. Because there is a formally established policy of not executing insane persons, great sums of money may be spent on detecting and curing mental illness in order to perform the execution. Since no one wants the responsibility for the execution, the condemned man is likely to be passed back and forth from doctors to custodial officials to courts like a ping-pong ball. The entire process is very costly.

When all is said and done, there can be no doubt that it costs more to execute a man than to keep him in prison for life.

E.

There is but one conclusion that can be drawn from all of this—i.e., the death penalty is an excessive and unnecessary punishment that violates the Eighth Amendment. The statistical evidence is not convincing beyond all doubt, but it is persuasive. It is not improper at this point to take judicial notice of the fact that for more than 200 years men have labored to demonstrate that capital punishment serves no purpose that life imprisonment could not serve equally well. And they have done so with great success. Little, if any, evidence has been adduced to prove the contrary. The point has now been reached at which deference to the legislatures is tantamount to abdication of our judicial roles as factfinders, judges, and ultimate arbiters of the Constitution. We know that at some point the presumption of constitutionality accorded legislative acts gives way to a realistic assessment of those acts. This point comes when there is sufficient evidence available so that judges can determine, not whether the legislature acted wisely, but whether it had any rational basis whatsoever for acting. We have this evidence before us now. There is no rational basis for concluding that capital punishment is not excessive. It therefore violates the Eighth Amendment.

VI.

In addition, even if capital punishment is not excessive, it nonetheless violates the Eighth Amendment because it is morally unacceptable to the people of the United States at this time in their history.

In judging whether or not a given penalty is morally acceptable, most courts have said that the punishment is valid unless "it shocks the conscience and sense of justice of the people."

Judge Frank once noted the problems inherent in the use of such a measuring stick:

"The court, before it reduces a sentence as 'cruel and unusual,' must have reasonably good assurances that the sentence offends the 'common conscience.' And, in any context, such a standard—the community's attitude—is usually an unknowable. It resembles a slithery shadow, since one can seldom learn, at all accurately, what the community, or a majority, actually feels. Even a carefully-taken 'public opinion poll' would be inconclusive in a case like this."

While a public opinion poll obviously is of some assistance in indicating public acceptance or rejection of a specific penalty, its utility cannot be very great. This is because whether or not a punishment is cruel and unusual depends, not on whether its mere mention "shocks the conscience and sense of justice of the people," but on whether people who were fully informed as to the purposes of the penalty and its liabilities would find the penalty shocking, unjust, and unacceptable.

In other words, the question with which we must deal is not whether a substantial proportion of American citizens would today, if polled, opine that capital punishment is barbarously cruel, but whether they would find it to be so in the light of all information presently available.

This is not to suggest that with respect to this test of unconstitutionality people are required to act rationally; they are not. With respect to this judgment, a violation of the Eighth Amendment is totally dependent on the predictable subjective, emotional reactions of informed citizens.

It has often been noted that American citizens know almost nothing about capital punishment. Some of the conclusions arrived at in the preceding section and the supporting evidence would be critical to an informed judgment on the morality of the death penalty: e.g., that the death penalty is no more effective a deterrent than life imprisonment, that convicted murderers are rarely executed, but are usually sentenced to a term in prison; that convicted murderers usually are model prisoners, and that they almost always become lawabiding citizens upon their release from prison; that the costs of executing a capital offender exceed the costs of imprisoning him for life; that while in prison, a convict under sentence of death performs none of the useful functions that life prisoners perform; that no attempt is made in the sentencing process to ferret out likely recidivists for execution; and that the death penalty may actually stimulate criminal activity.

....

There is also overwhelming evidence that the death penalty is employed against men and not women. Only 32 women have been executed since 1930, while 3,827 men have met a similar fate. It is difficult to understand why women have received such favored treatment since the purposes allegedly served by capital punishment seemingly are equally applicable to both sexes.

It also is evident that the burden of capital punishment falls upon the poor, the ignorant, and the underprivileged members of society. It is the poor, and the members of minority groups who are least able to voice their complaints against capital punishment. Their impotence leaves them victims of a sanction that the wealthier, better-represented, just-as-guilty person can escape. So long as the capital sanction is used only against the forlorn, easily forgotten members of society, legislators are content to maintain the status quo, because change would draw attention to the problem and concern might develop. Ignorance is perpetuated and apathy soon becomes its mate, and we have today's situation.

Just as Americans know little about who is executed and why, they are unaware of the potential dangers of executing an innocent man. Our "beyond a reasonable doubt" burden of proof in criminal cases is intended to protect the innocent, but we know it is not foolproof. Various studies have shown that people whose innocence is later convincingly established are convicted and sentenced to death.

Proving one's innocence after a jury finding of guilt is almost impossible. While reviewing courts are willing to entertain all kinds of collateral attacks where a sentence of death is involved, they very rarely dispute the jury's interpretation of the evidence. This is, perhaps, as it should be. But, if an innocent man has been found guilty, he must then depend on the good faith of the prosecutor's office to help him establish his innocence. There is evidence, however, that prosecutors do not welcome the idea of having convictions, which they labored hard to secure, overturned, and that their cooperation is highly unlikely.

No matter how careful courts are, the possibility of perjured testimony, mistaken honest testimony, and human error remain all too real. We have no way of judging how many innocent persons have been executed but we can be certain that there were some. Whether there were many is an open question made difficult by the loss of those who were most knowledgeable about the crime for which they were convicted. Surely there will be more as long as capital punishment remains part of our penal law.

While it is difficult to ascertain with certainty the degree to which the death penalty is discriminatorily imposed or the number of innocent persons sentenced to die, there is one conclusion about the penalty that is universally accepted—i.e., it "tends to distort the course of the criminal law."

As Mr. Justice Frankfurter said:

"I am strongly against capital punishment . . . . When life is at hazard in a trial, it sensationalizes the whole thing almost unwittingly; the effect on juries, the Bar, the public, the Judiciary, I regard as very bad. I think scientifically the claim of deterrence is not worth much. Whatever proof there may be in my judgment does not outweigh the social loss due to the inherent sensationalism of a trial for life."

The deleterious effects of the death penalty are also felt otherwise than at trial. For example, its very existence "inevitably sabotages a social or institutional program of reformation." In short "the presence of the death penalty as the keystone of our penal system bedevils the administration of criminal justice all the way down the line and is the stumbling block in the path of general reform and of the treatment of crime and criminals."

Assuming knowledge of all the facts presently available regarding capital punishment, the average citizen would, in my opinion, find it shocking to his conscience and sense of justice. For this reason alone capital punishment cannot stand.

VII.

To arrive at the conclusion that the death penalty violates the Eighth Amendment, we have had to engage in a long and tedious journey. The amount of information that we have assembled and sorted is enormous. Yet, I firmly believe that we have not deviated in the slightest from the principles with which we began.

At a time in our history when the streets of the Nation's cities inspire fear and despair, rather than pride and hope, it is difficult to maintain objectivity and concern for our fellow citizens. But, the measure of a country's greatness is its ability to retain compassion in time of crisis. No nation in the recorded history of man has a greater tradition of revering justice and fair treatment for all its citizens in times of turmoil, confusion, and tension than ours. This is a country which stands tallest in troubled times, a country that clings to fundamental principles, cherishes its constitutional heritage, and rejects simple solutions that compromise the values that lie at the roots of our democratic system.

In striking down capital punishment, this Court does not malign our system of government. On the contrary, it pays homage to it. Only in a free society could right triumph in difficult times, and could civilization record its magnificent advancement. In recognizing the humanity of our fellow beings, we pay ourselves the highest tribute. We achieve "a major milestone in the long road up from barbarism" and join the approximately 70 other jurisdictions in the world which celebrate their regard for civilization and humanity by shunning capital punishment.

I concur in the judgments of the Court.

DISSENT

At the outset it is important to note that only two members of the Court, MR. JUSTICE BRENNAN and MR. JUSTICE MARSHALL, have concluded that the Eighth Amendment prohibits capital punishment for all crimes and under all circumstances. MR. JUSTICE DOUGLAS has also determined that the death penalty contravenes the Eighth Amendment, although I do not read his opinion as necessarily requiring final abolition of the penalty. For the reasons set forth in Parts I-IV of this opinion, I conclude that the constitutional prohibition against "cruel and unusual punishments" cannot be construed to bar the imposition of the punishment of death.

MR. JUSTICE STEWART and MR. JUSTICE WHITE have concluded that petitioners' death sentences must be set aside because prevailing sentencing practices do not comply with the Eighth Amendment. For the reasons set forth in Part V of this opinion, I believe this approach fundamentally misconceives the nature of the Eighth Amendment guarantee and flies directly in the face of controlling authority of extremely recent vintage.

I.

If we were possessed of legislative power, I would either join with MR. JUSTICE BRENNAN and MR. JUSTICE MARSHALL or, at the very least, restrict the use of capital punishment to a small category of the most heinous crimes. Our constitutional inquiry, however, must be divorced from personal feelings as to the morality and efficacy of the death penalty, and be confined to the meaning and applicability of the uncertain language of the Eighth Amendment. There is no novelty in being called upon to interpret a constitutional provision that is less than self-defining, but, of all our fundamental guarantees, the ban on "cruel and unusual punishments" is one of the most difficult to translate into judicially manageable terms. The widely divergent views of the Amendment expressed in today's opinions reveal the haze that surrounds this constitutional command. Yet it is essential to our role as a court that we not seize upon the enigmatic character of the guarantee as an invitation to enact our personal predilections into law.

Although the Eighth Amendment literally reads as prohibiting only those punishments that are both "cruel" and "unusual," history compels the conclusion that the Constitution prohibits all punishments of extreme and barbarous cruelty, regardless of how frequently or infrequently imposed.

The most persuasive analysis of Parliament's adoption of the English Bill of Rights of 1689—the unquestioned source of the Eighth Amendment wording—suggests that the prohibition against "cruel and unusual punishments" was included therein out of aversion to severe punishments not legally authorized and not within the jurisdiction of the courts to impose. To the extent that the term "unusual" had any importance in the English version, it was apparently intended as a reference to illegal punishments.

From every indication, the Framers of the Eighth Amendment intended to give the phrase a meaning far different from that of its English precursor. The records of the debates in several of the state conventions called to ratify the 1789 draft Constitution submitted prior to the addition of the Bill of Rights show that the Framers' exclusive concern was the absence of any ban on tortures. The later inclusion of the "cruel and unusual punishments" clause was in response to these objections. There was no discussion of the interrelationship of the terms "cruel" and "unusual," and there is nothing in the debates supporting the inference that the Founding Fathers would have been receptive to torturous or excessively cruel punishments even if usual in character or authorized by law.

The cases decided under the Eighth Amendment are consistent with the tone of the ratifying debates. In *Wilkerson v. Utah*, this Court held that execution by shooting was not a prohibited mode of carrying out a sentence of death. Speaking to the meaning of the Cruel and Unusual Punishments Clause, the Court stated,

"It is safe to affirm that punishments of torture . . . and all others in the same line of unnecessary cruelty, are forbidden by that amendment to the Constitution."

The Court made no reference to the role of the term "unusual" in the constitutional guarantee.

In the case of *In re Kemmler*, the Court held the Eighth Amendment inapplicable to the States and added the following dictum:

"So that, if the punishment prescribed for an offence against the laws of the State were manifestly cruel and unusual, as burning at the stake, crucifixion, breaking on the wheel, or the like, it would be the duty of the courts to adjudge such penalties to be within the . . . prohibition of the New York constitution. And we think this equally true of the Eighth Amendment, in its application to Congress. . . . Punishments are cruel when they involve torture or a lingering death; but the punishment of death is not cruel, within the meaning of that word as used in the Constitution. It implies there something inhuman and barbarous, something more than the mere extinguishment of life."

This language again reveals an exclusive concern with extreme cruelty. The Court made passing reference to the finding of the New York courts that electrocution was an "unusual" punishment, but it saw no need to discuss the significance of that term as used in the Eighth Amendment.

Opinions in subsequent cases also speak of extreme cruelty as though that were the sum and substance of the constitutional prohibition. As summarized by Mr. Chief Justice Warren in the plurality opinion in *Trop v. Dulles*:

"Whether the word 'unusual' has any qualitative meaning different from 'cruel' is not clear. On the few occasions this Court has had to consider the meaning of the phrase, precise distinctions between cruelty and unusualness do not seem to have been drawn. These cases indicate that the Court simply examines the particular punishment involved in light of the basic prohibition against inhuman treatment, without regard to any subtleties of meaning that might be latent in the word 'unusual.'"

I do not suggest that the presence of the word "unusual" in the Eighth Amendment is merely vestigial, having no relevance to the constitutionality of any punishment that might be devised. But where, as here, we consider a punishment well known to history, and clearly authorized by legislative enactment, it disregards the history of the Eighth Amendment and all the judicial comment that has followed to rely on the term "unusual" as affecting the outcome of these cases. Instead, I view these cases as turning on the single question whether capital punishment is "cruel" in the constitutional sense. The term "unusual" cannot be read as limiting the ban on "cruel" punishments or as somehow expanding the meaning of the term "cruel." For this reason I am unpersuaded by the facile argument that since capital punishment has always been cruel in the everyday sense of the word, and has become unusual due to decreased use, it is, therefore, now "cruel and unusual."

II.

Counsel for petitioners properly concede that capital punishment was not impermissibly cruel at the time of the adoption of the Eighth Amendment. Not only do the records of the debates indicate that the Founding Fathers were limited in their concern to the prevention of torture, but it is also clear from the language of the Constitution itself that there was no thought whatever of the elimination of capital punishment. The opening sentence of the Fifth Amendment is a guarantee that the death penalty not be imposed "unless on a presentment or indictment of a Grand Jury." The Double Jeopardy Clause of the Fifth Amendment is a prohibition against being "twice put in jeopardy of life" for the same offense. Similarly, the Due Process Clause commands "due process of law" before an accused can be "deprived of life, liberty, or property." Thus, the explicit language of the Constitution affirmatively acknowledges the legal power to impose capital punishment; it does not expressly or by implication acknowledge the legal power to impose any of the various punishments that have been banned as cruel since 1791. Since the Eighth Amendment was adopted on the same day in 1791 as the Fifth Amendment, it hardly needs more to establish that the death penalty was not "cruel" in the constitutional sense at that time.

In the 181 years since the enactment of the Eighth Amendment, not a single decision of this Court has cast the slightest shadow of a doubt on the constitutionality of capital punishment. In rejecting Eighth Amendment attacks on particular modes of execution, the Court has more than once implicitly denied that capital punishment is impermissibly "cruel" in the constitutional sense. It is only 14 years since Mr. Chief Justice Warren, speaking for four members of the Court, stated without equivocation:

"Whatever the arguments may be against capital punishment, both on moral grounds and in terms of accomplishing the purposes of punishment—and they are forceful—the death penalty has been employed throughout our history, and, in a day when it is still widely accepted, it cannot be said to violate the constitutional concept of cruelty."

It is only one year since Mr. Justice Black made his feelings clear on the constitutional issue:

"The Eighth Amendment forbids 'cruel and unusual punishments.' In my view, these words cannot be read to outlaw capital punishment because that penalty was in common use and authorized by law here and in the countries from which our ancestors came at the time the Amendment was adopted. It is inconceivable to me that the framers intended to end capital punishment by the Amendment."

By limiting its grants of certiorari, the Court has refused even to hear argument on the Eighth Amendment claim on two occasions in the last four years. In these cases the Court confined its attention to the procedural aspects of capital trials, it being implicit that the punishment itself could be constitutionally imposed. Nonetheless, the Court has now been asked to hold that a punishment clearly permissible under the Constitution at the time of its adoption and accepted as such by every member of the Court until today, is suddenly so cruel as to be incompatible with the Eighth Amendment.

Before recognizing such an instant evolution in the law, it seems fair to ask what factors have changed that capital punishment should now be "cruel" in the constitutional sense as it has not been in the past. It is apparent that there has been no change of constitutional significance in the nature of the punishment itself. Twentieth century modes of execution surely involve no greater physical suffering than the means employed at the time of the Eighth Amendment's adoption. And although a man awaiting execution must inevitably experience extraordinary mental anguish, no one suggests that this anguish is materially different from that experienced by condemned men in 1791, even though protracted appellate review processes have greatly increased the waiting time on "death row." To be sure, the ordeal of the condemned man may be thought cruel in the sense that all suffering is thought cruel. But if the Constitution proscribed every punishment producing severe emotional stress, then capital punishment would clearly have been impermissible in 1791.

However, the inquiry cannot end here. For reasons unrelated to any change in intrinsic cruelty, the Eighth Amendment prohibition cannot fairly be limited to those punishments thought excessively cruel and barbarous at the time of the adoption of the Eighth Amendment. A punishment is inordinately cruel, in the sense we must deal with it in these cases, chiefly as perceived by the society so characterizing it. The standard of extreme cruelty is not merely descriptive, but necessarily embodies a moral judgment. The standard itself remains the same, but its applicability must change as the basic mores of society change. This notion is not new to Eighth Amendment adjudication. In *Weems v. United States*, the Court referred with apparent approval to the opinion of the commentators that "the clause of the Constitution . . . may be therefore progressive, and is not fastened to the obsolete but may acquire meaning as public opinion becomes enlightened by a humane justice." Mr. Chief Justice Warren, writing the plurality opinion in *Trop v. Dulles* stated, "The Amendment must draw its meaning from the evolving standards of decency that mark the progress of a maturing society." Nevertheless, the Court up to now has never actually held that a punishment has become impermissibly cruel due to a shift in the weight of accepted social values; nor has the Court suggested judicially manageable criteria for measuring such a shift in moral consensus.

The Court's quiescence in this area can be attributed to the fact that in a democratic society legislatures, not courts, are constituted to respond to the will and consequently the moral values of the people. For this reason, early commentators suggested that the "cruel and unusual punishments" clause was an unnecessary constitutional provision. As acknowledged in the principal brief for petitioners, "both in constitutional contemplation and in fact, it is the legislature, not the Court, which responds to public opinion and immediately reflects the society's standards of decency." Accordingly, punishments such as branding and the cutting off of ears, which were commonplace at the time of the adoption of the Constitution, passed from the penal scene without judicial intervention because they became basically offensive to the people and the legislatures responded to this sentiment.

Beyond any doubt, if we were today called upon to review such punishments, we would find them excessively cruel because we could say with complete assurance that contemporary society universally rejects such bizarre penalties. However, this speculation on the Court's probable reaction to such punishments is not of itself significant. The critical fact is that this Court has never had to hold that a mode of punishment authorized by a domestic legislature was so cruel as to be fundamentally at odds with our basic notions of decency. Judicial findings of impermissible cruelty have been limited, for the most part, to offensive punishments devised without specific authority by prison officials, not by legislatures. The paucity of judicial decisions invalidating legislatively prescribed punishments is powerful evidence that in this country legislatures have in fact been responsive—albeit belatedly at times—to changes in social attitudes and moral values.

I do not suggest that the validity of legislatively authorized punishments presents no justiciable issue under the Eighth Amendment, but, rather, that the primacy of the legislative role narrowly confines the scope of judicial inquiry. Whether or not provable, and whether or not true at all times, in a democracy the legislative judgment is presumed to embody the basic standards of decency prevailing in the society. This presumption can only be negated by unambiguous and compelling evidence of legislative default.

III.

There are no obvious indications that capital punishment offends the conscience of society to such a degree that our traditional deference to the legislative judgment must be abandoned. It is not a punishment such as burning at the stake that everyone would ineffably find to be repugnant to all civilized standards. Nor is it a punishment so roundly condemned that only a few aberrant legislatures have retained it on the statute books. Capital punishment is authorized by statute in 40 States, the District of Columbia, and in the federal courts for the commission of certain crimes. On four occasions in the last 11 years Congress has added to the list of federal crimes punishable by death. In looking for reliable indicia of contemporary attitude, none more trustworthy has been advanced.

One conceivable source of evidence that legislatures have abdicated their essentially barometric role with respect to community values would be public opinion polls, of which there have been many in the past decade addressed to the question of capital punishment. Without assessing the reliability of such polls, or intimating that any judicial reliance could ever be placed on them, it need only be noted that the reported results have shown nothing approximating the universal condemnation of capital punishment that might lead us to suspect that the legislatures in general have lost touch with current social values.

Counsel for petitioners rely on a different body of empirical evidence. They argue, in effect, that the number of cases in which the death penalty is imposed, as compared with the number of cases in which it is statutorily available, reflects a general revulsion toward the penalty that would lead to its repeal if only it were more generally and widely enforced. It cannot be gainsaid that by the choice of juries—and sometimes judges—the death penalty is imposed in far fewer than half the cases in which it is available. To go further and characterize the rate of imposition as "freakishly rare," as petitioners insist, is unwarranted hyperbole. And regardless of its characterization, the rate of imposition does not impel the conclusion that capital punishment is now regarded as intolerably cruel or uncivilized.

It is argued that in those capital cases where juries have recommended mercy, they have given expression to civilized values and effectively renounced the legislative authorization for capital punishment. At the same time it is argued that where juries have made the awesome decision to send men to their deaths, they have acted arbitrarily and without sensitivity to prevailing standards of decency. This explanation for the infrequency of imposition of capital punishment is unsupported by known facts, and is inconsistent in principle with everything this Court has ever said about the functioning of juries in capital cases.

In *McGautha v. California*, decided only one year ago, the Court held that there was no mandate in the Due Process Clause of the Fourteenth Amendment that juries be given instructions as to when the death penalty should be imposed. After reviewing the autonomy that juries have traditionally exercised in capital cases and noting the practical difficulties of framing manageable instructions, this Court concluded that judicially articulated standards were not needed to insure a responsible decision as to penalty. Nothing in *McGautha* licenses capital juries to act arbitrarily or assumes that they have so acted in the past. On the contrary, the assumption underlying the *McGautha* ruling is that juries "will act with due regard for the consequences of their decision."

The responsibility of juries deciding capital cases in our system of justice was nowhere better described than in *Witherspoon v. Illinois*:

"A jury that must choose between life imprisonment and capital punishment can do little more—and must do nothing less—than express the conscience of the community on the ultimate question of life or death."

"And one of the most important functions any jury can perform in making such a selection is to maintain a link between contemporary community values and the penal system—a link without which the determination of punishment could hardly reflect 'the evolving standards of decency that mark the progress of a maturing society'"

The selectivity of juries in imposing the punishment of death is properly viewed as a refinement on, rather than a repudiation of, the statutory authorization for that penalty. Legislatures prescribe the categories of crimes for which the death penalty should be available, and, acting as "the conscience of the community," juries are entrusted to determine in individual cases that the ultimate punishment is warranted. Juries are undoubtedly influenced in this judgment by myriad factors. The motive or lack of motive of the perpetrator, the degree of injury or suffering of the victim or victims, and the degree of brutality in the commission of the crime would seem to be prominent among these factors. Given the general awareness that death is no longer a routine punishment for the crimes for which it is made available, it is hardly surprising that juries have been increasingly meticulous in their imposition of the penalty. But to assume from the mere fact of relative infrequency that only a random assortment of pariahs are sentenced to death, is to cast grave doubt on the basic integrity of our jury system.

It would, of course, be unrealistic to assume that juries have been perfectly consistent in choosing the cases where the death penalty is to be imposed, for no human institution performs with perfect consistency. There are doubtless prisoners on death row who would not be there had they been tried before a different jury or in a different State. In this sense their fate has been controlled by a fortuitous circumstance. However, this element of fortuity does not stand as an indictment either of the general functioning of juries in capital cases or of the integrity of jury decisions in individual cases. There is no empirical basis for concluding that juries have generally failed to discharge in good faith the responsibility described in *Witherspoon*—that of choosing between life and death in individual cases according to the dictates of community values.

The rate of imposition of death sentences falls far short of providing the requisite unambiguous evidence that the legislatures of 40 States and the Congress have turned their backs on current or evolving standards of decency in continuing to make the death penalty available. For, if selective imposition evidences a rejection of capital punishment in those cases where it is not imposed, it surely evidences a correlative affirmation of the penalty in those cases where it is imposed. Absent some clear indication that the continued imposition of the death penalty on a selective basis is violative of prevailing standards of civilized conduct, the Eighth Amendment cannot be said to interdict its use.

In two of these cases we have been asked to rule on the narrower question whether capital punishment offends the Eighth Amendment when imposed as the punishment for the crime of forcible rape. It is true that the death penalty is authorized for rape in fewer States than it is for murder, and that even in those States it is applied more sparingly for rape than for murder. But for the reasons aptly brought out in the opinion of MR. JUSTICE POWELL, I do not believe these differences can be elevated to the level of an Eighth Amendment distinction. This blunt constitutional command cannot be sharpened to carve neat distinctions corresponding to the categories of crimes defined by the legislatures.

IV.

Capital punishment has also been attacked as violative of the Eighth Amendment on the ground that it is not needed to achieve legitimate penal aims and is thus "unnecessarily cruel." As a pure policy matter, this approach has much to recommend it, but it seeks to give a dimension to the Eighth Amendment that it was never intended to have and promotes a line of inquiry that this Court has never before pursued.

The Eighth Amendment, as I have noted, was included in the Bill of Rights to guard against the use of torturous and inhuman punishments, not those of limited efficacy. One of the few to speak out against the adoption of the Eighth Amendment asserted that it is often necessary to use cruel punishments to deter crimes. But among those favoring the Amendment, no sentiment was expressed that a punishment of extreme cruelty could ever be justified by expediency. The dominant theme of the Eighth Amendment debates was that the ends of the criminal laws cannot justify the use of measures of extreme cruelty to achieve them.

The apparent seed of the "unnecessary cruelty" argument is the following language, quoted earlier, found in *Wilkerson v. Utah*:

"Difficulty would attend the effort to define with exactness the extent of the constitutional provision which provides that cruel and unusual punishments shall not be inflicted; but it is safe to affirm that punishments of torture . . . and all others in the same line of unnecessary cruelty, are forbidden by that amendment to the Constitution."

....

Apart from these isolated uses of the word "unnecessary," nothing in the cases suggests that it is for the courts to make a determination of the efficacy of punishments. The decision in *Weems v. United States* is not to the contrary. In *Weems* the Court held that for the crime of falsifying public documents, the punishment imposed under the Philippine Code of 15 years' imprisonment at hard labor under shackles, followed by perpetual surveillance, loss of voting rights, loss of the right to hold public office, and loss of right to change domicile freely, was violative of the Eighth Amendment. The case is generally regarded as holding that a punishment may be excessively cruel within the meaning of the Eighth Amendment because it is grossly out of proportion to the severity of the crime; some view the decision of the Court primarily as a reaction to the mode of the punishment itself.

Under any characterization of the holding, it is readily apparent that the decision grew out of the Court's overwhelming abhorrence of the imposition of the particular penalty for the particular crime; it was making an essentially moral judgment, not a dispassionate assessment of the need for the penalty. The Court specifically disclaimed "the right to assert a judgment against that of the legislature of the expediency of the laws. . . ." Thus, apart from the fact that the Court in *Weems* concerned itself with the crime committed as well as the punishment imposed, the case marks no departure from the largely unarticulable standard of extreme cruelty. However intractable that standard may be, that is what the Eighth Amendment is all about. The constitutional provision is not addressed to social utility and does not command that enlightened principles of penology always be followed.

By pursuing the necessity approach, it becomes even more apparent that it involves matters outside the purview of the Eighth Amendment. Two of the several aims of punishment are generally associated with capital punishment—retribution and deterrence. It is argued that retribution can be discounted because that, after all, is what the Eighth Amendment seeks to eliminate. There is no authority suggesting that the Eighth Amendment was intended to purge the law of its retributive elements, and the Court has consistently assumed that retribution is a legitimate dimension of the punishment of crimes. Furthermore, responsible legal thinkers of widely varying persuasions have debated the sociological and philosophical aspects of the retribution question for generations, neither side being able to convince the other. It would be reading a great deal into the Eighth Amendment to hold that the punishments authorized by legislatures cannot constitutionally reflect a retributive purpose.

The less esoteric but no less controversial question is whether the death penalty acts as a superior deterrent. Those favoring abolition find no evidence that it does. Those favoring retention start from the intuitive notion that capital punishment should act as the most effective deterrent and note that there is no convincing evidence that it does not. Escape from this empirical stalemate is sought by placing the burden of proof on the States and concluding that they have failed to demonstrate that capital punishment is a more effective deterrent than life imprisonment. Numerous justifications have been advanced for shifting the burden, and they are not without their rhetorical appeal.

However, these arguments are not descended from established constitutional principles, but are born of the urge to bypass an unresolved factual question. Comparative deterrence is not a matter that lends itself to precise measurement; to shift the burden to the States is to provide an illusory solution to an enormously complex problem. If it were proper to put the States to the test of demonstrating the deterrent value of capital punishment, we could just as well ask them to prove the need for life imprisonment or any other punishment. Yet I know of no convincing evidence that life imprisonment is a more effective deterrent than 20 years' imprisonment, or even that a $10 parking ticket is a more effective deterrent than a $5 parking ticket. In fact, there are some who go so far as to challenge the notion that any punishments deter crime. If the States are unable to adduce convincing proof rebutting such assertions, does it then follow that all punishments are suspect as being "cruel and unusual" within the meaning of the Constitution? On the contrary, I submit that the questions raised by the necessity approach are beyond the pale of judicial inquiry under the Eighth Amendment.

V.

Today the Court has not ruled that capital punishment is per se violative of the Eighth Amendment; nor has it ruled that the punishment is barred for any particular class or classes of crimes. The substantially similar concurring opinions of MR. JUSTICE STEWART and MR. JUSTICE WHITE, which are necessary to support the judgment setting aside petitioners' sentences, stop short of reaching the ultimate question. The actual scope of the Court's ruling, which I take to be embodied in these concurring opinions, is not entirely clear. This much, however, seems apparent: if the legislatures are to continue to authorize capital punishment for some crimes, juries and judges can no longer be permitted to make the sentencing determination in the same manner they have in the past. This approach—not urged in oral arguments or briefs—misconceives the nature of the constitutional command against "cruel and unusual punishments," disregards controlling case law, and demands a rigidity in capital cases which, if possible of achievement, cannot be regarded as a welcome change. Indeed the contrary seems to be the case.

As I have earlier stated, the Eighth Amendment forbids the imposition of punishments that are so cruel and inhumane as to violate society's standards of civilized conduct. The Amendment does not prohibit all punishments the States are unable to prove necessary to deter or control crime. The Amendment is not concerned with the process by which a State determines that a particular punishment is to be imposed in a particular case. And the Amendment most assuredly does not speak to the power of legislatures to confer sentencing discretion on juries, rather than to fix all sentences by statute.

The critical factor in the concurring opinions of both MR. JUSTICE STEWART and MR. JUSTICE WHITE is the infrequency with which the penalty is imposed. This factor is taken not as evidence of society's abhorrence of capital punishment—the inference that petitioners would have the Court draw—but as the earmark of a deteriorated system of sentencing. It is concluded that petitioners' sentences must be set aside, not because the punishment is impermissibly cruel, but because juries and judges have failed to exercise their sentencing discretion in acceptable fashion.

To be sure, there is a recitation cast in Eighth Amendment terms: petitioners' sentences are "cruel" because they exceed that which the legislatures have deemed necessary for all cases; petitioners' sentences are "unusual" because they exceed that which is imposed in most cases. This application of the words of the Eighth Amendment suggests that capital punishment can be made to satisfy Eighth Amendment values if its rate of imposition is somehow multiplied; it seemingly follows that the flexible sentencing system created by the legislatures, and carried out by juries and judges, has yielded more mercy than the Eighth Amendment can stand. The implications of this approach are mildly ironical. For example, by this measure of the Eighth Amendment, the elimination of death-qualified juries in *Witherspoon v. Illinois*, can only be seen in retrospect as a setback to "the evolving standards of decency that mark the progress of a maturing society."

This novel formulation of Eighth Amendment principles—albeit necessary to satisfy the terms of our limited grant of certiorari—does not lie at the heart of these concurring opinions. The decisive grievance of the opinions—not translated into Eighth Amendment terms—is that the present system of discretionary sentencing in capital cases has failed to produce evenhanded justice; the problem is not that too few have been sentenced to die, but that the selection process has followed no rational pattern. This claim of arbitrariness is not only lacking in empirical support, but also it manifestly fails to establish that the death penalty is a "cruel and unusual" punishment. The Eighth Amendment was included in the Bill of Rights to assure that certain types of punishments would never be imposed, not to channelize the sentencing process. The approach of these concurring opinions has no antecedent in the Eighth Amendment cases. It is essentially and exclusively a procedural due process argument.

This ground of decision is plainly foreclosed as well as misplaced. Only one year ago, in *McGautha v. California*, the Court upheld the prevailing system of sentencing in capital cases. The Court concluded:

"In light of history, experience, and the present limitations of human knowledge, we find it quite impossible to say that committing to the untrammeled discretion of the jury the power to pronounce life or death in capital cases is offensive to anything in the Constitution."

In reaching this decision, the Court had the benefit of extensive briefing, full oral argument, and six months of careful deliberations. The Court's labors are documented by 130 pages of opinions in the United States Reports. All of the arguments and factual contentions accepted in the concurring opinions today were considered and rejected by the Court one year ago. *McGautha* was an exceedingly difficult case, and reasonable men could fairly disagree as to the result. But the Court entered its judgment, and if *stare decisis* means anything, that decision should be regarded as a controlling pronouncement of law.

Although the Court's decision in *McGautha* was technically confined to the dictates of the Due Process Clause of the Fourteenth Amendment, rather than the Eighth Amendment as made applicable to the States through the Due Process Clause of the Fourteenth Amendment, it would be disingenuous to suggest that today's ruling has done anything less than overrule *McGautha* in the guise of an Eighth Amendment adjudication. It may be thought appropriate to subordinate principles of *stare decisis* where the subject is as sensitive as capital punishment and the stakes are so high, but these external considerations were no less weighty last year. This pattern of decisionmaking will do little to inspire confidence in the stability of the law.

While I would not undertake to make a definitive statement as to the parameters of the Court's ruling, it is clear that if state legislatures and the Congress wish to maintain the availability of capital punishment, significant statutory changes will have to be made. Since the two pivotal concurring opinions turn on the assumption that the punishment of death is now meted out in a random and unpredictable manner, legislative bodies may seek to bring their laws into compliance with the Court's ruling by providing standards for juries and judges to follow in determining the sentence in capital cases or by more narrowly defining the crimes for which the penalty is to be imposed. If such standards can be devised or the crimes more meticulously defined, the result cannot be detrimental. However, Mr. Justice Harlan's opinion for the Court in *McGautha* convincingly demonstrates that all past efforts "to identify before the fact" the cases in which the penalty is to be imposed have been "uniformly unsuccessful."

One problem is that "the factors which determine whether the sentence of death is the appropriate penalty in particular cases are too complex to be compressed within the limits of a simple formula . . . ." As the Court stated in *McGautha*, "the infinite variety of cases and facets to each case would make general standards either meaningless 'boilerplate' or a statement of the obvious that no jury would need." But even assuming that suitable guidelines can be established, there is no assurance that sentencing patterns will change so long as juries are possessed of the power to determine the sentence or to bring in a verdict of guilt on a charge carrying a lesser sentence; juries have not been inhibited in the exercise of these powers in the past. Thus, unless the Court in *McGautha* misjudged the experience of history, there is little reason to believe that sentencing standards in any form will substantially alter the discretionary character of the prevailing system of sentencing in capital cases. That system may fall short of perfection, but it is yet to be shown that a different system would produce more satisfactory results.

Real change could clearly be brought about if legislatures provided mandatory death sentences in such a way as to deny juries the opportunity to bring in a verdict on a lesser charge; under such a system, the death sentence could only be avoided by a verdict of acquittal. If this is the only alternative that the legislatures can safely pursue under today's ruling, I would have preferred that the Court opt for total abolition.

It seems remarkable to me that with our basic trust in lay jurors as the keystone in our system of criminal justice, it should now be suggested that we take the most sensitive and important of all decisions away from them. I could more easily be persuaded that mandatory sentences of death, without the intervening and ameliorating impact of lay jurors, are so arbitrary and doctrinaire that they violate the Constitution. The very infrequency of death penalties imposed by jurors attests their cautious and discriminating reservation of that penalty for the most extreme cases. I had thought that nothing was clearer in history, as we noted in *McGautha* one year ago, than the American abhorrence of "the common-law rule imposing a mandatory death sentence on all convicted murderers."

As the concurring opinion of MR. JUSTICE MARSHALL shows, the 19th century movement away from mandatory death sentences marked an enlightened introduction of flexibility into the sentencing process. It recognized that individual culpability is not always measured by the category of the crime committed. This change in sentencing practice was greeted by the Court as a humanizing development. I do not see how this history can be ignored and how it can be suggested that the Eighth Amendment demands the elimination of the most sensitive feature of the sentencing system.

As a general matter, the evolution of penal concepts in this country has not been marked by great progress, nor have the results up to now been crowned with significant success. If anywhere in the whole spectrum of criminal justice fresh ideas deserve sober analysis, the sentencing and correctional area ranks high on the list. But it has been widely accepted that mandatory sentences for crimes do not best serve the ends of the criminal justice system. Now, after the long process of drawing away from the blind imposition of uniform sentences for every person convicted of a particular offense, we are confronted with an argument perhaps implying that only the legislatures may determine that a sentence of death is appropriate, without the intervening evaluation of jurors or judges. This approach threatens to turn back the progress of penal reform, which has moved until recently at too slow a rate to absorb significant setbacks.

VI.

Since there is no majority of the Court on the ultimate issue presented in these cases, the future of capital punishment in this country has been left in an uncertain limbo. Rather than providing a final and unambiguous answer on the basic constitutional question, the collective impact of the majority's ruling is to demand an undetermined measure of change from the various state legislatures and the Congress. While I cannot endorse the process of decisionmaking that has yielded today's result and the restraints that that result imposes on legislative action, I am not altogether displeased that legislative bodies have been given the opportunity, and indeed unavoidable responsibility, to make a thorough re-evaluation of the entire subject of capital punishment. If today's opinions demonstrate nothing else, they starkly show that this is an area where legislatures can act far more effectively than courts.

The legislatures are free to eliminate capital punishment for specific crimes or to carve out limited exceptions to a general abolition of the penalty, without adherence to the conceptual strictures of the Eighth Amendment. The legislatures can and should make an assessment of the deterrent influence of capital punishment, both generally and as affecting the commission of specific types of crimes. If legislatures come to doubt the efficacy of capital punishment, they can abolish it, either completely or on a selective basis. If new evidence persuades them that they have acted unwisely, they can reverse their field and reinstate the penalty to the extent it is thought warranted. An Eighth Amendment ruling by judges cannot be made with such flexibility or discriminating precision.

The world-wide trend toward limiting the use of capital punishment, a phenomenon to which we have been urged to give great weight, hardly points the way to a judicial solution in this country under a written Constitution. Rather, the change has generally come about through legislative action, often on a trial basis and with the retention of the penalty for certain limited classes of crimes. Virtually nowhere has change been wrought by so crude a tool as the Eighth Amendment. The complete and unconditional abolition of capital punishment in this country by judicial fiat would have undermined the careful progress of the legislative trend and foreclosed further inquiry on many as yet unanswered questions in this area.

Quite apart from the limitations of the Eighth Amendment itself, the preference for legislative action is justified by the inability of the courts to participate in the debate at the level where the controversy is focused. The case against capital punishment is not the product of legal dialectic, but rests primarily on factual claims, the truth of which cannot be tested by conventional judicial processes. The five opinions in support of the judgments differ in many respects, but they share a willingness to make sweeping factual assertions, unsupported by empirical data, concerning the manner of imposition and effectiveness of capital punishment in this country. Legislatures will have the opportunity to make a more penetrating study of these claims with the familiar and effective tools available to them as they are not to us.

The highest judicial duty is to recognize the limits on judicial power and to permit the democratic processes to deal with matters falling outside of those limits. The "hydraulic pressures" that Holmes spoke of as being generated by cases of great import have propelled the Court to go beyond the limits of judicial power, while fortunately leaving some room for legislative judgment.

MR. JUSTICE BLACKMUN, dissenting.

I join the respective opinions of THE CHIEF JUSTICE, MR. JUSTICE POWELL, and MR. JUSTICE REHNQUIST, and add only the following, somewhat personal, comments.

1. Cases such as these provide for me an excruciating agony of the spirit. I yield to no one in the depth of my distaste, antipathy, and, indeed, abhorrence, for the death penalty, with all its aspects of physical distress and fear and of moral judgment exercised by finite minds. That distaste is buttressed by a belief that capital punishment serves no useful purpose that can be demonstrated. For me, it violates childhood's training and life's experiences, and is not compatible with the philosophical convictions I have been able to develop. It is antagonistic to any sense of "reverence for life." Were I a legislator, I would vote against the death penalty for the policy reasons argued by counsel for the respective petitioners and expressed and adopted in the several opinions filed by the Justices who vote to reverse these judgments.

2. Having lived for many years in a State that does not have the death penalty, that effectively abolished it in 1911, and that carried out its last execution on February 13, 1906, capital punishment had never been a part of life for me. In my State, it just did not exist. So far as I can determine, the State, purely from a statistical deterrence point of view, was neither the worse nor the better for its abolition, for, as the concurring opinions observe, the statistics prove little, if anything. But the State and its citizens accepted the fact that the death penalty was not to be in the arsenal of possible punishments for any crime.

3. I, perhaps alone among the present members of the Court, am on judicial record as to this. As a member of the United States Court of Appeals, I first struggled silently with the issue of capital punishment in *Feguer v. United States*. The defendant in that case may have been one of the last to be executed under federal auspices. I struggled again with the issue, and once more refrained from comment, in my writing for an en banc court in *Pope v. United States*. Finally, in *Maxwell v. Bishop,* I revealed, solitarily and not for the panel, my distress and concern. And in *Jackson v. Bishop*, I had no hesitancy in writing a panel opinion that held the use of the strap by trusties upon fellow Arkansas prisoners to be a violation of the Eighth Amendment. That, however, was in-prison punishment imposed by inmate-foremen.

4. The several concurring opinions acknowledge, as they must, that until today capital punishment was accepted and assumed as not unconstitutional per se under the Eighth Amendment or the Fourteenth Amendment. This is either the flat or the implicit holding of a unanimous Court in *Wilkerson v. Utah*; of a unanimous Court in *In re Kemmler*; of the Court in *Weems v. United States*; of all those members of the Court, a majority, who addressed the issue in *Louisiana ex rel. Francis v. Resweber*; of Mr. Chief Justice Warren, speaking for himself and three others (Justices Black, DOUGLAS, and Whittaker) in *Trop v. Dulles*; in the denial of certiorari in *Rudolph v. Alabama*; and of Mr. Justice Black in *McGautha v. California*.

Suddenly, however, the course of decision is now the opposite way, with the Court evidently persuaded that somehow the passage of time has taken us to a place of greater maturity and outlook. The argument, plausible and high-sounding as it may be, is not persuasive, for it is only one year since *McGautha*, only eight and one-half years since *Rudolph*, 14 years since *Trop*, and 25 years since *Francis*, and we have been presented with nothing that demonstrates a significant movement of any kind in these brief periods. The Court has just decided that it is time to strike down the death penalty. There would have been as much reason to do this when any of the cited cases were decided. But the Court refrained from that action on each of those occasions.

The Court has recognized, and I certainly subscribe to the proposition, that the Cruel and Unusual Punishments Clause "may acquire meaning as public opinion becomes enlightened by a humane justice." And Mr. Chief Justice Warren, for a plurality of the Court, referred to "the evolving standards of decency that mark the progress of a maturing society." Mr. Jefferson expressed the same thought well.

My problem, however, as I have indicated, is the suddenness of the Court's perception of progress in the human attitude since decisions of only a short while ago.

5. To reverse the judgments in these cases is, of course, the easy choice. It is easier to strike the balance in favor of life and against death. It is comforting to relax in the thoughts—perhaps the rationalizations—that this is the compassionate decision for a maturing society; that this is the moral and the "right" thing to do; that thereby we convince ourselves that we are moving down the road toward human decency; that we value life even though that life has taken another or others or has grievously scarred another or others and their families; and that we are less barbaric than we were in 1879, or in 1890, or in 1910, or in 1947, or in 1958, or in 1963, or a year ago, in 1971, when *Wilkerson, Kemmler, Weems, Francis, Trop, Rudolph*, and *McGautha* were respectively decided.

This, for me, is good argument, and it makes some sense. But it is good argument and it makes sense only in a legislative and executive way and not as a judicial expedient. As I have said above, were I a legislator, I would do all I could to sponsor and to vote for legislation abolishing the death penalty. And were I the chief executive of a sovereign State, I would be sorely tempted to exercise executive clemency as Governor Rockefeller of Arkansas did recently just before he departed from office. There—on the Legislative Branch of the State or Federal Government, and secondarily, on the Executive Branch—is where the authority and responsibility for this kind of action lies. The authority should not be taken over by the judiciary in the modern guise of an Eighth Amendment issue.

I do not sit on these cases, however, as a legislator, responsive, at least in part, to the will of constituents. Our task here, as must so frequently be emphasized and re-emphasized, is to pass upon the constitutionality of legislation that has been enacted and that is challenged. This is the sole task for judges. We should not allow our personal preferences as to the wisdom of legislative and congressional action, or our distaste for such action, to guide our judicial decision in cases such as these. The temptations to cross that policy line are very great. In fact, as today's decision reveals, they are almost irresistible.

6. The Court, in my view, is somewhat propelled toward its result by the interim decision of the California Supreme Court, with one justice dissenting, that the death penalty is violative of that State's constitution. So far as I am aware, that was the first time the death penalty in its entirety has been nullified by judicial decision. California's moral problem was a profound one, for more

prisoners were on death row there than in any other State. California, of course, has the right to construe its constitution as it will. Its construction, however, is hardly a precedent for federal adjudication.

7. I trust the Court fully appreciates what it is doing when it decides these cases the way it does today. Not only are the capital punishment laws of 39 States and the District of Columbia struck down, but also all those provisions of the federal statutory structure that permit the death penalty apparently are voided. No longer is capital punishment possible, I suspect, for, among other crimes.... All these seem now to be discarded without a passing reference to the reasons, or the circumstances, that prompted their enactment, some very recent, and their retention in the face of efforts to repeal them.

8. It is of passing interest to note a few voting facts with respect to recent federal death penalty legislation....

It is impossible for me to believe that the many lawyer-members of the House and Senate—including, I might add, outstanding leaders and prominent candidates for higher office—were callously unaware and insensitive of constitutional overtones in legislation of this type. The answer, of course, is that in 1961, in 1965, and in 1970 these elected representatives of the people—far more conscious of the temper of the times, of the maturing of society, and of the contemporary demands for man's dignity, than are we who sit cloistered on this Court—took it as settled that the death penalty then, as it always had been, was not in itself unconstitutional. Some of those Members of Congress, I suspect, will be surprised at this Court's giant stride today.

9. If the reservations expressed by my Brother STEWART (which, as I read his opinion, my Brother WHITE shares) were to command support, namely, that capital punishment may not be unconstitutional so long as it be mandatorily imposed, the result, I fear, will be that statutes struck down today will be re-enacted by state legislatures to prescribe the death penalty for specified crimes without any alternative for the imposition of a lesser punishment in the discretion of the judge or jury, as the case may be. This approach, it seems to me, encourages legislation that is regressive and of an antique mold, for it eliminates the element of mercy in the imposition of punishment. I thought we had passed beyond that point in our criminology long ago.

10. It is not without interest, also, to note that, although the several concurring opinions acknowledge the heinous and atrocious character of the offenses committed by the petitioners, none of those opinions makes reference to the misery the petitioners' crimes occasioned to the victims, to the families of the victims, and to the communities where the offenses took place. The arguments for the respective petitioners, particularly the oral arguments, were similarly and curiously devoid of reference to the victims. There is risk, of course, in a comment such as this, for it opens one to the charge of emphasizing the retributive. Nevertheless, these cases are here because offenses to innocent victims were perpetrated. This fact, and the terror that occasioned it, and the fear that stalks the streets of many of our cities today perhaps deserve not to be entirely overlooked. Let us hope that, with the Court's decision, the terror imposed will be forgotten by those upon whom it was visited, and that our society will reap the hoped-for benefits of magnanimity.

Although personally I may rejoice at the Court's result, I find it difficult to accept or to justify as a matter of history, of law, or of constitutional pronouncement. I fear the Court has overstepped. It has sought and has achieved an end.

MR. JUSTICE POWELL, with whom THE CHIEF JUSTICE, MR. JUSTICE BLACKMUN, and MR. JUSTICE REHNQUIST join, dissenting.

The Court granted certiorari in these cases to consider whether the death penalty is any longer a permissible form of punishment. It is the judgment of five Justices that the death penalty, as customarily prescribed and implemented in this country today, offends the constitutional prohibition against cruel and unusual punishments. The reasons for that judgment are stated in five separate opinions, expressing as many separate rationales. In my view, none of these opinions provides a constitutionally adequate foundation for the Court's decision.

MR. JUSTICE DOUGLAS concludes that capital punishment is incompatible with notions of "equal protection" that he finds to be "implicit" in the Eighth Amendment. MR. JUSTICE BRENNAN bases his judgment primarily on the thesis that the penalty "does not comport with human dignity." MR. JUSTICE STEWART concludes that the penalty is applied in a "wanton" and "freakish" manner. For MR. JUSTICE WHITE it is the "infrequency" with which the penalty is imposed that renders its use unconstitutional. MR. JUSTICE MARSHALL finds that capital punishment is an impermissible form of punishment because it is "morally unacceptable" and "excessive."

Although the central theme of petitioners' presentations in these cases is that the imposition of the death penalty is per se unconstitutional, only two of today's opinions explicitly conclude that so sweeping a determination is mandated by the

Constitution. Both MR. JUSTICE BRENNAN and MR. JUSTICE MARSHALL call for the abolition of all existing state and federal capital punishment statutes. They intimate as well that no capital statute could be devised in the future that might comport with the Eighth Amendment. While the practical consequences of the other three opinions are less certain, they at least do not purport to render impermissible every possible statutory scheme for the use of capital punishment that legislatures might hereafter devise. Insofar as these latter opinions fail, at least explicitly, to go as far as petitioners' contentions would carry them, their reservations are attributable to a willingness to accept only a portion of petitioners' thesis.

For the reasons cogently set out in the CHIEF JUSTICE's dissenting opinion, and for reasons stated elsewhere in this opinion, I find my Brothers' less-than-absolute-abolition judgments unpersuasive. Because those judgments are, for me, not dispositive, I shall focus primarily on the broader ground upon which the petitions in these cases are premised. The foundations of my disagreement with that broader thesis are equally applicable to each of the concurring opinions. I will, therefore, not endeavor to treat each one separately. Nor will I attempt to predict what forms of capital statutes, if any, may avoid condemnation in the future under the variety of views expressed by the collective majority today. That difficult task, not performed in any of the controlling opinions, must go unanswered until other cases presenting these more limited inquiries arise.

Whatever uncertainties may hereafter surface, several of the consequences of today's decision are unmistakably clear. The decision is plainly one of the greatest importance. The Court's judgment removes the death sentences previously imposed on some 600 persons awaiting punishment in state and federal prisons throughout the country. At least for the present, it also bars the States and the Federal Government from seeking sentences of death for defendants awaiting trial on charges for which capital punishment was heretofore a potential alternative. The happy event for these countable few constitutes, however, only the most visible consequence of this decision. Less measurable, but certainly of no less significance, is the shattering effect this collection of views has on the root principles of stare decisis, federalism, judicial restraint and—most importantly—separation of powers.

The Court rejects as not decisive the clearest evidence that the Framers of the Constitution and the authors of the Fourteenth Amendment believed that those documents posed no barrier to the death penalty. The Court also brushes aside an unbroken line of precedent reaffirming the heretofore virtually unquestioned constitutionality of capital punishment. Because of the pervasiveness of the constitutional ruling sought by petitioners, and accepted in varying degrees by five members of the Court, today's departure from established precedent invalidates a staggering number of state and federal laws. The capital punishment laws of no less than 39 States and the District of Columbia are nullified. In addition, numerous provisions of the Criminal Code of the United States and of the Uniform Code of Military Justice also are voided. The Court's judgment not only wipes out laws presently in existence, but denies to Congress and to the legislatures of the 50 States the power to adopt new policies contrary to the policy selected by the Court. Indeed, it is the view of two of my Brothers that the people of each State must be denied the prerogative to amend their constitutions to provide for capital punishment even selectively for the most heinous crime.

In terms of the constitutional role of this Court, the impact of the majority's ruling is all the greater because the decision encroaches upon an area squarely within the historic prerogative of the legislative branch—both state and federal—to protect the citizenry through the designation of penalties for prohibitable conduct. It is the very sort of judgment that the legislative branch is competent to make and for which the judiciary is ill-equipped. Throughout our history, Justices of this Court have emphasized the gravity of decisions invalidating legislative judgments, admonishing the nine men who sit on this bench of the duty of self-restraint, especially when called upon to apply the expansive due process and cruel and unusual punishment rubrics. I can recall no case in which, in the name of deciding constitutional questions, this Court has subordinated national and local democratic processes to such an extent. Before turning to address the thesis of petitioners' case against capital punishment—a thesis that has proved, at least in large measure, persuasive to a majority of this Court—I first will set out the principles that counsel against the Court's sweeping decision.

I.

The Constitution itself poses the first obstacle to petitioners' argument that capital punishment is per se unconstitutional. The relevant provisions are the Fifth, Eighth, and Fourteenth Amendments. The first of these provides in part:

"No person shall be held to answer for a capital, or otherwise infamous crime, unless on a presentment or indictment of a Grand Jury . . . ; nor shall any person be subject for the same offence to be twice put in jeopardy of life or limb; . . . nor be deprived of life, liberty, or property, without due process of law . . . ."

Thus, the Federal Government's power was restricted in order to guarantee those charged with crimes that the prosecution would have only a single opportunity to seek imposition of the death penalty and that the death penalty could not be exacted without due process and a grand jury indictment. The Fourteenth Amendment, adopted about 77 years after the Bill of Rights, imposed the due process limitation of the Fifth Amendment upon the States' power to authorize capital punishment.

The Eighth Amendment, adopted at the same time as the Fifth, proscribes "cruel and unusual" punishments. In an effort to discern its meaning, much has been written about its history in the opinions of this Court and elsewhere. That history need not be restated here since, whatever punishments the Framers of the Constitution may have intended to prohibit under the "cruel and unusual" language, there cannot be the slightest doubt that they intended no absolute bar on the Government's authority to impose the death penalty. As much is made clear by the three references to capital punishment in the Fifth Amendment. Indeed, the same body that proposed the Eighth Amendment also provided, in the first Crimes Act of 1790, for the death penalty for a number of offenses.

Of course, the specific prohibitions within the Bill of Rights are limitations on the exercise of power; they are not an affirmative grant of power to the Government. I, therefore, do not read the several references to capital punishment as foreclosing this Court from considering whether the death penalty in a particular case offends the Eighth and Fourteenth Amendments. Nor are "cruel and unusual punishments" and "due process of law" static concepts whose meaning and scope were sealed at the time of their writing. They were designed to be dynamic and to gain meaning through application to specific circumstances, many of which were not contemplated by their authors. While flexibility in the application of these broad concepts is one of the hallmarks of our system of government, the Court is not free to read into the Constitution a meaning that is plainly at variance with its language. Both the language of the Fifth and Fourteenth Amendments and the history of the Eighth Amendment confirm beyond doubt that the death penalty was considered to be a constitutionally permissible punishment. It is, however, within the historic process of constitutional adjudication to challenge the imposition of the death penalty in some barbaric manner or as a penalty wholly disproportionate to a particular criminal act. And in making such a judgment in a case before it, a court may consider contemporary standards to the extent they are relevant. While this weighing of a punishment against the Eighth Amendment standard on a case-by-case basis is consonant with history and precedent, it is not what petitioners demand in these cases. They seek nothing less than the total abolition of capital punishment by judicial fiat.

II.

Petitioners assert that the constitutional issue is an open one uncontrolled by prior decisions of this Court. They view the several cases decided under the Eighth Amendment as assuming the constitutionality of the death penalty without focusing squarely upon the issue. I do not believe that the case law can be so easily cast aside. The Court on numerous occasions has both assumed and asserted the constitutionality of capital punishment. In several cases that assumption provided a necessary foundation for the decision, as the issue was whether a particular means of carrying out a capital sentence would be allowed to stand. Each of those decisions necessarily was premised on the assumption that some method of exacting the penalty was permissible.

The issue in the first capital case in which the Eighth Amendment was invoked, was whether carrying out a death sentence by public shooting was cruel and unusual punishment. A unanimous Court upheld that form of execution, noting first that the punishment itself, as distinguished from the mode of its infliction, was "not pretended by the counsel of the prisoner" to be cruel and unusual. The Court went on to hold that:

"Cruel and unusual punishments are forbidden by the Constitution, but the authorities . . . are quite sufficient to show that the punishment of shooting as a mode of executing the death penalty for the crime of murder in the first degree is not included in that category . . . ."

Eleven years later, in *In re Kemmler* the Court again faced a question involving the method of carrying out a capital sentence. On review of a denial of habeas corpus relief by the Supreme Court of New York, this Court was called on to decide whether electrocution, which only very recently had been adopted by the New York Legislature as a means of execution, was impermissibly cruel and unusual in violation of the Fourteenth Amendment. Chief Justice Fuller, speaking for the entire Court, ruled in favor of the State. Electrocution had been selected by the legislature, after careful investigation, as "the most humane and practical method known to modern science of carrying into effect the sentence of death." The Court drew a clear line between the penalty itself and the mode of its execution:

"Punishments are cruel when they involve torture or a lingering death; but the punishment of death is not cruel, within the meaning of that word as used in the Constitution. It implies there something inhuman and barbarous, something more than the mere extinguishment of life."

More than 50 years later, in *Louisiana ex rel. Francis v. Resweber*, the Court considered a case in which, due to a mechanical malfunction, Louisiana's initial attempt to electrocute a convicted murderer had failed. Petitioner sought to block a second attempt to execute the sentence on the ground that to do so would constitute cruel and unusual punishment. In the plurality opinion written by Mr. Justice Reed, concurred in by Chief Justice Vinson and Justices Black and Jackson, relief was denied. Again the Court focused on the manner of execution, never questioning the propriety of the death sentence itself.

"The case before us does not call for an examination into any punishments except that of death. . . . The traditional humanity of modern Anglo-American law forbids the infliction of unnecessary pain in the execution of the death sentence. . . .

". . . The cruelty against which the Constitution protects a convicted man is cruelty inherent in the method of punishment, not the necessary suffering involved in any method employed to extinguish life humanely."

Mr. Justice Frankfurter, unwilling to dispose of the case under the Eighth Amendment's specific prohibition, approved the second execution attempt under the Due Process Clause. He concluded that "a State may be found to deny a person due process by treating even one guilty of crime in a manner that violates standards of decency more or less universally accepted though not when it treats him by a mode about which opinion is fairly divided."

The four dissenting Justices, although finding a second attempt at execution to be impermissibly cruel, expressly recognized the validity of capital punishment:

"In determining whether the proposed procedure is unconstitutional, we must measure it against a lawful electrocution. . . . Electrocution, when instantaneous, can be inflicted by a state in conformity with due process of law. . . .

"The all-important consideration is that the execution shall be so instantaneous and substantially painless that the punishment shall be reduced, as nearly as possible, to no more than that of death itself."

Each of these cases involved the affirmance of a death sentence where its validity was attacked as violating the Eighth Amendment. Five opinions were written in these three cases, expressing the views of 23 Justices. While in the narrowest sense it is correct to say that in none was there a frontal attack upon the constitutionality of the death penalty, each opinion went well beyond an unarticulated assumption of validity. The power of the States to impose capital punishment was repeatedly and expressly recognized.

In addition to these cases in which the constitutionality of the death penalty was a necessary foundation for the decision, those who today would have this Court undertake the absolute abolition of the death penalty also must reject the opinions of other cases stipulating or assuming the constitutionality of capital punishment.

The plurality opinion in *Trop v. Dulles*, is of special interest since it is this opinion, in large measure, that provides the foundation for the present attack on the death penalty. It is anomalous that the standard urged by petitioners—"evolving standards of decency that mark the progress of a maturing society"—should be derived from an opinion that so unqualifiedly rejects their arguments. Chief Justice Warren, joined by Justices Black, DOUGLAS, and Whittaker, stated flatly:

"At the outset, let us put to one side the death penalty as an index of the constitutional limit on punishment. Whatever the arguments may be against capital punishment, both on moral grounds and in terms of accomplishing the purposes of punishment—and they are forceful—the death penalty has been employed throughout our history, and, in a day when it is still widely accepted, it cannot be said to violate the constitutional concept of cruelty."

The issue in *Trop* was whether forfeiture of citizenship was a cruel and unusual punishment when imposed on a wartime deserter who had gone "over the hill" for less than a day and had willingly surrendered. In examining the consequences of the relatively novel punishment of denationalization, Chief Justice Warren drew a line between "traditional" and "unusual" penalties:

"While the State has the power to punish, the Eighth Amendment stands to assure that this power be exercised within the limits of civilized standards. Fines, imprisonment and even execution may be imposed depending upon the enormity of the crime, but any technique outside the bounds of these traditional penalties is constitutionally suspect."

The plurality's repeated disclaimers of any attack on capital punishment itself must be viewed as more than offhand dicta since those views were written in direct response to the strong language in Mr. Justice Frankfurter's dissent arguing that denationalization could not be a disproportionate penalty for a concededly capital offense.

The most recent precedents of this Court—*Witherspoon v. Illinois* and *McGautha v. California*—are also premised to a significant degree on the constitutionality of the death penalty. While the scope of review in both cases was limited to questions involving the procedures for selecting juries and regulating their deliberations in capital cases, those opinions were "singularly academic exercises" if the members of this Court were prepared at those times to find in the Constitution the complete prohibition of the death penalty. This is especially true of Mr. Justice Harlan's opinion for the Court in *McGautha*, in which, after a full review of the history of capital punishment, he concluded that "we find it quite impossible to say that committing to the untrammeled discretion of the jury the power to pronounce life or death in capital cases is offensive to anything in the Constitution."

Perhaps enough has been said to demonstrate the unswerving position that this Court has taken in opinions spanning the last hundred years. On virtually every occasion that any opinion has touched on the question of the constitutionality of the death penalty, it has been asserted affirmatively, or tacitly assumed, that the Constitution does not prohibit the penalty. No Justice of the Court, until today, has dissented from this consistent reading of the Constitution. The petitioners in these cases now before the Court cannot fairly avoid the weight of this substantial body of precedent merely by asserting that there is no prior decision precisely in point. *Stare decisis*, if it is a doctrine founded on principle, surely applies where there exists a long line of cases endorsing or necessarily assuming the validity of a particular matter of constitutional interpretation. While these oft-repeated expressions of unchallenged belief in the constitutionality of capital punishment may not justify a summary disposition of the constitutional question before us, they are views expressed and joined in over the years by no less than 29 Justices of this Court and therefore merit the greatest respect. Those who now resolve to set those views aside indeed have a heavy burden.

III.

Petitioners seek to avoid the authority of the foregoing cases, and the weight of express recognition in the Constitution itself, by reasoning which will not withstand analysis. The thesis of petitioners' case derives from several opinions in which members of this Court have recognized the dynamic nature of the prohibition against cruel and unusual punishments. The final meaning of those words was not set in 1791. Rather, to use the words of Chief Justice Warren speaking for a plurality of the Court in *Trop v. Dulles*:

"The words of the Amendment are not precise, and . . . their scope is not static. The Amendment must draw its meaning from the evolving standards of decency that mark the progress of a maturing society."

But this was not new doctrine. It was the approach to the Eighth Amendment taken by Mr. Justice McKenna in his opinion for the Court in *Weems v. United States*. Writing for four Justices sitting as the majority of the six-man Court deciding the case, he concluded that the clause must be "progressive"; it is not "fastened to the obsolete but may acquire meaning as public opinion becomes enlightened by a humane justice." The same test was offered by Mr. Justice Frankfurter in his separate concurrence in *Louisiana ex rel. Francis v. Resweber*. While he rejected the notion that the Fourteenth Amendment made the Eighth Amendment fully applicable to the States, he nonetheless found as a matter of due process that the States were prohibited from "treating even one guilty of crime in a manner that violates standards of decency more or less universally accepted."

Whether one views the question as one of due process or of cruel and unusual punishment, as I do for convenience in this case, the issue is essentially the same. The fundamental premise upon which either standard is based is that notions of what constitutes cruel and unusual punishment or due process do evolve. Neither the Congress nor any state legislature would today tolerate pillorying, branding, or cropping or nailing of the ears—punishments that were in existence during our colonial era. Should, however, any such punishment be prescribed, the courts would certainly enjoin its execution. Likewise, no court would approve any method of implementation of the death sentence found to involve unnecessary cruelty in light of presently available alternatives. Similarly, there may well be a process of evolving attitude with respect to the application of the death sentence for particular crimes.

But we are not asked to consider the permissibility of any of the several methods employed in carrying out the death sentence. Nor are we asked, at least as part of the core submission in these cases, to determine whether the penalty might be a grossly excessive punishment for some specific criminal conduct. Either inquiry would call for a discriminating evaluation of particular means, or of the relationship between particular conduct and its punishment. Petitioners' principal argument goes far beyond the traditional process of case-by-case inclusion and exclusion. Instead the argument insists on an unprecedented constitutional rule of absolute prohibition of capital punishment for any crime, regardless of its depravity and impact on society. In calling for a precipitate and final judicial end to this form of penalty as offensive to evolving standards of decency, petitioners would have this Court abandon the traditional and more refined approach consistently followed in its prior Eighth Amendment precedents. What they are saying, in effect, is that the evolutionary process has come suddenly to an end; that the ultimate wisdom as to the appropriateness of capital punishment under all circumstances, and for all future generations, has somehow been revealed.

The prior opinions of this Court point with great clarity to reasons why those of us who sit on this Court at a particular time should act with restraint before assuming, contrary to a century of precedent, that we now know the answer for all time to come. First, whereas here, the language of the applicable provision provides great leeway and where the underlying social policies are felt to be of vital importance, the temptation to read personal preference into the Constitution is understandably great. It is too easy to propound our subjective standards of wise policy under the rubric of more or less universally held standards of decency.

The second consideration dictating judicial self-restraint arises from a proper recognition of the respective roles of the legislative and judicial branches. The designation of punishments for crimes is a matter peculiarly within the sphere of the state and federal legislative bodies. When asked to encroach on the legislative prerogative we are well counseled to proceed with the utmost reticence. The review of legislative choices, in the performance of our duty to enforce the Constitution, has been characterized most appropriately by Mr. Justice Holmes as "the gravest and most delicate duty that this Court is called on to perform."

How much graver is that duty when we are not asked to pass on the constitutionality of a single penalty under the facts of a single case but instead are urged to overturn the legislative judgments of 40 state legislatures as well as those of Congress. In so doing is the majority able to claim, as did the Court in *Weems*, that it appreciates "to the fullest the wide range of power that the legislature possesses to adapt its penal laws to conditions as they may exist and punish the crimes of men according to their forms and frequency"? I think not. No more eloquent statement of the essential separation of powers limitation on our prerogative can be found than the admonition of Mr. Justice Frankfurter, dissenting in *Trop*. His articulation of the traditional view takes on added significance where the Court undertakes to nullify the legislative judgments of the Congress and four-fifths of the States.

"What is always basic when the power of Congress to enact legislation is challenged is the appropriate approach to judicial review of congressional legislation . . . . When the power of Congress to pass a statute is challenged, the function of this Court is to determine whether legislative action lies clearly outside the constitutional grant of power to which it has been, or may fairly be, referred. In making this determination, the Court sits in judgment on the action of a co-ordinate branch of the Government while keeping unto itself—as it must under our constitutional system—the final determination of its own power to act. . . .

"Rigorous observance of the difference between limits of power and wise exercise of power—between questions of authority and questions of prudence—requires the most alert appreciation of this decisive but subtle relationship of two concepts that too easily coalesce. No less does it require a disciplined will to adhere to the difference. It is not easy to stand aloof and allow want of wisdom to prevail, to disregard one's own strongly held view of what is wise in the conduct of affairs. But it is not the business of this Court to pronounce policy. It must observe a fastidious regard for limitations on its own power, and this precludes the Court's giving effect to its own notions of what is wise or politic. That self-restraint is of the essence in the observance of the judicial oath, for the Constitution has not authorized the judges to sit in judgment on the wisdom of what Congress and the Executive Branch do."

IV.

Although determining the range of available punishments for a particular crime is a legislative function, the very presence of the Cruel and Unusual Punishments Clause within the Bill of Rights requires, in the context of a specific case, that courts decide whether particular acts of the Congress offend that Amendment. The Due Process Clause of the Fourteenth Amendment imposes on the judiciary a similar obligation to scrutinize state legislation. But the proper exercise of that constitutional obligation in the cases before us today must be founded on a full recognition of the several considerations set forth above—the affirmative references to capital punishment in the Constitution, the prevailing precedents of this Court, the limitations on the exercise of our power imposed by tested principles of judicial self-restraint, and the duty to avoid encroachment on the powers conferred upon state and federal legislatures. In the face of these considerations, only the most conclusive of objective demonstrations could warrant this Court in holding capital punishment per se unconstitutional. The burden of seeking so sweeping a decision against such formidable obstacles is almost insuperable. Viewed from this perspective, as I believe it must be, the case against the death penalty falls far short.

Petitioners' contentions are premised, as indicated above, on the long-accepted view that concepts embodied in the Eighth and Fourteenth Amendments evolve. They present, with skill and persistence, a list of "objective indicators" which are said to demonstrate that prevailing standards of human decency have progressed to the final point of requiring the Court to hold, for all cases and for all time, that capital punishment is unconstitutional.

Briefly summarized, these proffered indicia of contemporary standards of decency include the following: (i) a worldwide trend toward the disuse of the death penalty; (ii) the reflection in the scholarly literature of a progressive rejection of capital punishment founded essentially on moral opposition to such treatment; (iii) the decreasing numbers of executions over the last 40 years and especially over the last decade; (iv) the small number of death sentences rendered in relation to the number of cases in which they might have been imposed; and (v) the indication of public abhorrence of the penalty reflected in the circumstance that executions are no longer public affairs. The foregoing is an incomplete summary but it touches the major bases of petitioners' presentation. Although they are not appropriate for consideration as objective evidence, petitioners strongly urge two additional propositions. They contend, first, that the penalty survives public condemnation only through the infrequency, arbitrariness, and discriminatory nature of its application, and, second, that there no longer exists any legitimate justification for the utilization of the ultimate penalty. These contentions, which have proved persuasive to several of the Justices constituting the majority, deserve separate consideration and will be considered in the ensuing sections. Before turning to those arguments, I first address the argument based on "objective" factors.

Any attempt to discern contemporary standards of decency through the review of objective factors must take into account several overriding considerations which petitioners choose to discount or ignore. In a democracy the first indicator of the public's attitude must always be found in the legislative judgments of the people's chosen representatives. MR. JUSTICE MARSHALL's opinion today catalogues the salient statistics. Forty States, the District of Columbia, and the Federal Government still authorize the death penalty for a wide variety of crimes. That number has remained relatively static since the end of World War I. That does not mean, however, that capital punishment has become a forgotten issue in the legislative arena. As recently as January, 1971, Congress approved the death penalty for congressional assassination. In 1965 Congress added the death penalty for presidential and vice presidential assassinations. Additionally, the aircraft piracy statute passed in 1961 also carries the death penalty. MR. JUSTICE BLACKMUN's dissenting opinion catalogues the impressive ease with which each of these statutes was approved. On the converse side, a bill proposing the abolition of capital punishment for all federal crimes was introduced in 1967 but failed to reach the Senate floor.

At the state level, New York, among other States, has recently undertaken reconsideration of its capital crimes. A law passed in 1965 restricted the use of capital punishment to the crimes of murder of a police officer and murder by a person serving a sentence of life imprisonment.

I pause here to state that I am at a loss to understand how those urging this Court to pursue a course of absolute abolition as a matter of constitutional judgment can draw any support from the New York experience. As is also the case with respect to recent legislative activity in Canada and Great Britain, New York's decision to restrict the availability of the death penalty is a product of refined and discriminating legislative judgment, reflecting, not the total rejection of capital punishment as inherently cruel, but a desire to limit it to those circumstances in which legislative judgment deems retention to be in the public interest. No such legislative flexibility is permitted by the contrary course petitioners urge this Court to follow.

In addition to the New York experience, a number of other States have undertaken reconsideration of capital punishment in recent years. In four States the penalty has been put to a vote of the people through public referenda—a means likely to supply objective evidence of community standards. In Oregon a referendum seeking abolition of capital punishment failed in 1958 but was subsequently approved in 1964. Two years later the penalty was approved in Colorado by a wide margin. In Massachusetts in 1968, in an advisory referendum, the voters there likewise recommended retention of the penalty. In 1970, approximately 64% of the voters in Illinois approved the penalty. In addition, the National Commission on Reform of Federal Criminal Laws reports that legislative committees in Massachusetts, Pennsylvania, and Maryland recommended abolition, while committees in New Jersey and Florida recommended retention. The legislative views of other States have been summarized by Professor Hugo Bedau in his compilation of sources on capital punishment entitled *The Death Penalty in America*:

"What our legislative representatives think in the two score states which still have the death penalty may be inferred from the fate of the bills to repeal or modify the death penalty filed during recent years in the legislatures of more than half of these states. In about a dozen instances, the bills emerged from committee for a vote. But in none except Delaware did they become law. In those states where these bills were brought to the floor of the legislatures, the vote in most instances wasn't even close."

This recent history of activity with respect to legislation concerning the death penalty abundantly refutes the abolitionist position.

The second and even more direct source of information reflecting the public's attitude toward capital punishment is the jury. *In Witherspoon v. Illinois*, MR. JUSTICE STEWART, joined by JUSTICES BRENNAN and MARSHALL, characterized the jury's historic function in the sentencing process in the following terms:

"The jury is given broad discretion to decide whether or not death is 'the proper penalty' in a given case, and a juror's general views about capital punishment play an inevitable role in any such decision.

"A man who opposes the death penalty, no less than one who favors it, can make the discretionary judgment entrusted to him by the State and can thus obey the oath he takes as a juror. . . . Guided by neither rule nor standard . . . a jury that must choose between life imprisonment and capital punishment can do little more—and must do nothing less—than express the conscience of the community on the ultimate question of life or death."

"One of the most important functions any jury can perform in making such a selection is to maintain a link between contemporary community values and the penal system—a link without which the determination of punishment could hardly reflect 'the evolving standards of decency that mark the progress of a maturing society.'. . ."

Any attempt to discern, therefore, where the prevailing standards of decency lie must take careful account of the jury's response to the question of capital punishment. During the 1960's juries returned in excess of a thousand death sentences, a rate of approximately two per week. Whether it is true that death sentences were returned in less than 10% of the cases as petitioners estimate or whether some higher percentage is more accurate, these totals simply do not support petitioners' assertion at oral argument that "the death penalty is virtually unanimously repudiated and condemned by the conscience of contemporary society." It is also worthy of note that the annual rate of death sentences has remained relatively constant over the last 10 years and that the figure for 1970—127 sentences— is the highest annual total since 1961. It is true that the sentencing rate might be expected to rise, rather than remain constant, when the number of violent crimes increases as it has in this country. And it may be conceded that the constancy in these statistics indicates the unwillingness of juries to demand the ultimate penalty in many cases where it might be imposed. But these considerations fall short of indicating that juries are imposing the death penalty with such rarity as to justify this Court in reading into this circumstance a public rejection of capital punishment.

One must conclude, contrary to petitioners' submission, that the indicators most likely to reflect the public's view— legislative bodies, state referenda and the juries which have the actual responsibility—do not support the contention that evolving standards of decency require total abolition of capital punishment. Indeed, the weight of the evidence indicates that the public generally has not accepted either the morality or the social merit of the views so passionately advocated by the articulate spokesmen for abolition. But however one may assess the amorphous ebb and flow of public opinion generally on this volatile issue, this type of inquiry lies at the periphery—not the core— of the judicial process in constitutional cases. The assessment of popular opinion is essentially a legislative, not a judicial, function.

V.

Petitioners seek to salvage their thesis by arguing that the infrequency and discriminatory nature of the actual resort to the ultimate penalty tend to diffuse public opposition. We are told that the penalty is imposed exclusively on uninfluential minorities—"the poor and powerless, personally ugly and socially unacceptable." It is urged that this pattern of application assures that large segments of the public will be either uninformed or unconcerned and will have no reason to measure the punishment against prevailing moral standards.

Implicitly, this argument concedes the unsoundness of petitioners' contention, examined above under Part IV, that objective evidence shows a present and widespread community rejection of the death penalty. It is now said, in effect, not that capital punishment presently offends our citizenry, but that the public would be offended if the penalty were enforced in a nondiscriminatory manner against a significant percentage of those charged with capital crimes, and if the public were thereby made aware of the moral issues surrounding capital punishment. Rather than merely registering the objective indicators on a judicial balance, we are asked ultimately to rest a far-reaching constitutional determination on a prediction regarding the subjective judgments of the mass of our people under hypothetical assumptions that may or may not be realistic.

Apart from the impermissibility of basing a constitutional judgment of this magnitude on such speculative assumptions, the argument suffers from other defects. If, as petitioners urge, we are to engage in speculation, it is not at all certain that the public would experience deep-felt revulsion if the States were to execute as many sentenced capital offenders this year as they executed in the mid-1930's. It seems more likely that public reaction, rather than being characterized by undifferentiated rejection, would depend upon the facts and circumstances surrounding each particular case.

Members of this Court know, from the petitions and appeals that come before us regularly, that brutish and revolting murders continue to occur with disquieting frequency. Indeed, murders are so commonplace in our society that only the most sensational receive significant and sustained publicity. It could hardly be suggested that in any of these highly publicized murder cases—the several senseless assassinations or the too numerous shocking multiple murders that have stained this country's recent history— the public has exhibited any signs of "revulsion" at the thought of executing the convicted murderers. The public outcry, as we all know, has been quite to the contrary. Furthermore, there is little reason to suspect that the public's reaction would differ significantly in response to other less publicized murders. It is certainly arguable that many such murders, because of their senselessness or barbarousness, would evoke a public demand for the death penalty rather than a public rejection of that alternative. Nor is there any rational basis for arguing that the public reaction to any of these crimes would be muted if the murderer were "rich and powerful." The demand for the ultimate sanction might well be greater, as a wealthy killer is hardly a sympathetic figure. While there might be specific cases in which capital punishment would be regarded as excessive and shocking to the conscience of the community, it can hardly be argued that the public's dissatisfaction with the penalty in particular cases would translate into a demand for absolute abolition.

In pursuing the foregoing speculation, I do not suggest that it is relevant to the appropriate disposition of these cases. The purpose of the digression is to indicate that judicial decisions cannot be founded on such speculations and assumptions, however appealing they may seem.

But the discrimination argument does not rest alone on a projection of the assumed effect on public opinion of more frequent executions. Much also is made of the undeniable fact that the death penalty has a greater impact on the lower economic strata of society, which include a relatively higher percentage of persons of minority racial and ethnic group backgrounds. The argument drawn from this fact is two-pronged. In part it is merely an extension of the speculative approach pursued by petitioners, i.e., that public revulsion is suppressed in callous apathy because the penalty does not affect persons from the white middle class which constitutes the majority in this country. This aspect, however, adds little to the infrequency rationalization for public apathy which I have found unpersuasive.

As MR. JUSTICE MARSHALL's opinion today demonstrates, the argument does have a more troubling aspect. It is his contention that if the average citizen were aware of the disproportionate burden of capital punishment borne by the "poor, the ignorant, and the underprivileged," he would find the penalty "shocking to his conscience and sense of justice" and would not stand for its further use. This argument, like the apathy rationale, calls for further speculation on the part of the Court. It also illuminates the quicksands upon which we are asked to base this decision. Indeed, the two contentions seem to require contradictory assumptions regarding the public's moral attitude toward capital punishment. The apathy argument is predicated on the assumption that the penalty is used against the less influential elements of society, that the public is fully aware of this, and that it tolerates use of capital punishment only because of a callous indifference to the offenders who are sentenced. MR. JUSTICE MARSHALL's argument, on the other hand, rests on the contrary assumption that the public does not know against whom the penalty is enforced and that if the public were educated to this fact it would find the punishment intolerable. Neither assumption can claim to be an entirely accurate portrayal of public attitude; for some acceptance of capital punishment might be a consequence of hardened apathy based on the knowledge of infrequent and uneven application, while for others acceptance may grow only out of ignorance. More significantly, however, neither supposition acknowledges what, for me, is a more basic flaw.

Certainly the claim is justified that this criminal sanction falls more heavily on the relatively impoverished and underprivileged elements of society. The "have-nots" in every society always have been subject to greater pressure to commit crimes and to fewer constraints than their more affluent fellow citizens. This is, indeed, a tragic byproduct of social and economic deprivation, but it is not an argument of constitutional proportions under the Eighth or Fourteenth Amendment. The same discriminatory impact argument could be made with equal force and logic with respect to those sentenced to prison terms. The Due Process Clause admits of no distinction between the deprivation of "life" and the deprivation of "liberty." If discriminatory impact renders capital punishment cruel and unusual, it likewise renders invalid most of the prescribed penalties for crimes of violence. The root causes of the higher incidence of criminal penalties on "minorities and the poor" will not be cured by abolishing the system of penalties. Nor, indeed, could any society have a viable system of criminal justice if sanctions were abolished or ameliorated because most of those who commit crimes happen to be underprivileged. The basic problem results not from the penalties imposed for criminal conduct but from social and economic factors that have plagued humanity since the beginning of recorded history, frustrating all efforts to create in any country at any time the perfect society in which there are no "poor," no "minorities" and no "underprivileged." The causes underlying this problem are unrelated to the constitutional issue before the Court.

Finally, yet another theory for abolishing the death penalty—reflected in varying degrees in each of the concurring opinions today—is predicated on the discriminatory impact argument. Quite apart from measuring the public's acceptance or rejection of the death penalty under the "standards of decency" rationale, MR. JUSTICE DOUGLAS finds the punishment cruel and unusual because it is "arbitrarily" invoked. He finds that "the basic theme of equal protection is implicit" in the Eighth Amendment, and that the Amendment is violated when jury sentencing may be characterized as arbitrary or discriminatory. While MR. JUSTICE STEWART does not purport to rely on notions of equal protection, he also rests primarily on what he views to be a history of arbitrariness. Whatever may be the facts with respect to jury sentencing, this argument calls for a reconsideration of the "standards" aspects of the Court's decision in *McGautha v. California*. Although that is the unmistakable thrust of these opinions today, I see no reason to reassess the standards question considered so carefully in Mr. Justice Harlan's opinion for the Court last Term. Having so recently reaffirmed our historic dedication to entrusting the sentencing function to the jury's "untrammeled discretion," it is difficult to see how the Court can now hold the entire process constitutionally defective under the Eighth Amendment. For all of these reasons I find little merit in the various discrimination arguments, at least in the several lights in which they have been cast in these cases.

. . . .

I agree that discriminatory application of the death penalty in the past, admittedly indefensible, is no justification for holding today that capital punishment is invalid in all cases in which sentences were handed out to members of the class discriminated against. But *Maxwell* does point the way to a means of raising the equal protection challenge that is more consonant with precedent and the Constitution's mandates than the several courses pursued by today's concurring opinions.

A final comment on the racial discrimination problem seems appropriate. The possibility of racial bias in the trial and sentencing process has diminished in recent years. The segregation of our society in decades past, which contributed substantially to the severity of punishment for interracial crimes, is now no longer prevalent in this country. Likewise, the day is past when juries do not represent the minority group elements of the community. The assurance of fair trials for all citizens is greater today than at any previous time in our history. Because standards of criminal justice have "evolved" in a manner favorable to the accused, discriminatory imposition of capital punishment is far less likely today than in the past.

VI.

Petitioner in …the other cases before us today, urge that capital punishment is cruel and unusual because it no longer serves any rational legislative interests. Before turning to consider whether any of the traditional aims of punishment justify the death penalty, I should make clear the context in which I approach this aspect of the cases.

First, I find no support—in the language of the Constitution, in its history, or in the cases arising under it—for the view that this Court may invalidate a category of penalties because we deem less severe penalties adequate to serve the ends of penology. While the cases affirm our authority to prohibit punishments that are cruelly inhumane (e.g., *Wilkerson v. Utah, In re Kemmler*), and punishments that are cruelly excessive in that they are disproportionate to particular crimes, the precedents of this Court afford no basis for striking down a particular form of punishment because we may be persuaded that means less stringent would be equally efficacious.

Secondly, if we were free to question the justifications for the use of capital punishment, a heavy burden would rest on those who attack the legislatures' judgments to prove the lack of rational justifications. This Court has long held that legislative decisions in this area, which lie within the special competency of that branch, are entitled to a presumption of validity. I come now to consider, subject to the reservations above expressed, the two justifications most often cited for the retention of capital punishment. The concept of retribution—though popular for centuries— is now criticized as unworthy of a civilized people. Yet this Court has acknowledged the existence of a retributive element in criminal sanctions and has never heretofore found it impermissible. In *Williams v. New York*, Mr. Justice Black stated that,

"Retribution is no longer the dominant objective of the criminal law. Reformation and rehabilitation of offenders have become important goals of criminal jurisprudence."

It is clear, however, that the Court did not reject retribution altogether. The record in that case indicated that one of the reasons why the trial judge imposed the death penalty was his sense of revulsion at the "shocking details of the crime." Although his motivation was clearly retributive, the Court upheld the trial judge's sentence. Similarly, MR. JUSTICE MARSHALL noted in his plurality opinion in *Powell v. Texas* that this Court "has never held that anything in the Constitution requires that penal sanctions be designed solely to achieve therapeutic or rehabilitative effects."

While retribution alone may seem an unworthy justification in a moral sense, its utility in a system of criminal justice requiring public support has long been recognized. Lord Justice Denning, now Master of the Rolls of the Court of Appeal in England, testified on this subject before the British Royal Commission on Capital Punishment:

"Many are inclined to test the efficacy of punishment solely by its value as a deterrent: but this is too narrow a view. Punishment is the way in which society expresses its denunciation of wrongdoing: and, in order to maintain respect for law, it is essential that the punishment inflicted for grave crimes should adequately reflect the revulsion felt by the great majority of citizens for them. It is a mistake to consider the objects of punishment as being deterrent or reformative or preventive and nothing else. If this were so, we should not send to prison a man who was guilty of motor manslaughter, but only disqualify him from driving; but would public opinion be content with this? The truth is that some crimes are so outrageous that society insists on adequate punishment, because the wrong-doer deserves it, irrespective of whether it is a deterrent or not."

The view expressed by Lord Denning was cited approvingly in the Royal Commission's Report, recognizing "a strong and widespread demand for retribution." MR. JUSTICE STEWART makes much the same point in his opinion today when he concludes that expression of man's retributive instincts in the sentencing process "serves an important purpose in promoting the stability of a society governed by law." The view, moreover, is not without respectable support in the jurisprudential literature in this country, despite a substantial body of opinion to the contrary. And it is conceded on all sides that, not infrequently, cases arise that are so shocking or offensive that the public demands the ultimate penalty for the transgressor.

Deterrence is a more appealing justification, although opinions again differ widely. Indeed, the deterrence issue lies at the heart of much of the debate between the abolitionists and retentionists. Statistical studies, based primarily on trends in States that have abolished the penalty, tend to support the view that the death penalty has not been proved to be a superior deterrent. Some dispute the validity of this conclusion, pointing out that the studies do not show that the death penalty has no deterrent effect on any categories of crimes. On the basis of the literature and studies currently available, I find myself in agreement with the conclusions drawn by the Royal Commission following its exhaustive study of this issue:

"The general conclusion which we reach, after careful review of all the evidence we have been able to obtain as to the deterrent effect of capital punishment, may be stated as follows. *Prima facie* the penalty of death is likely to have a stronger effect as a deterrent to normal human beings than any other form of punishment, and there is some evidence (though no convincing statistical evidence) that this is in fact so. But this effect does not operate universally or uniformly, and there are many offenders on whom it is limited and may often be negligible. It is accordingly important to view this question in a just perspective and not base a penal policy in relation to murder on exaggerated estimates of the uniquely deterrent force of the death penalty."

Only recently this Court was called on to consider the deterrence argument in relation to punishment by fines for public drunkenness. The Court was unwilling to strike down the Texas statute on grounds that it lacked a rational foundation. What MR. JUSTICE MARSHALL said there would seem to have equal applicability in this case:

"The long-standing and still raging debate over the validity of the deterrence justification for penal sanctions has not reached any sufficiently clear conclusions to permit it to be said that such sanctions are ineffective in any particular context or for any particular group of people who are able to appreciate the consequences of their acts. . . ."

As I noted at the outset of this section, legislative judgments as to the efficacy of particular punishments are presumptively rational and may not be struck down under the Eighth Amendment because this Court may think that some alternative sanction would be more appropriate. Even if such judgments were within the judicial prerogative, petitioners have failed to show that there exist no justifications for the legislative enactments challenged in these cases. While the evidence and arguments advanced by petitioners might have proved profoundly persuasive if addressed to a legislative body, they do not approach the showing traditionally required before a court declares that the legislature has acted irrationally.

VII.

In two of the cases before us today juries imposed sentences of death after convictions for rape. In these cases we are urged to hold that even if capital punishment is permissible for some crimes, it is a cruel and unusual punishment for this crime. Petitioners in these cases rely on the Court's opinions holding that the Eighth Amendment, in addition to prohibiting punishments deemed barbarous and inhumane, also condemns punishments that are greatly disproportionate to the crime charged. This reading of the Amendment was first expressed by Mr. Justice Field in his dissenting opinion in *O'Neil v. Vermont* a case in which a defendant charged with a large number of violations of Vermont's liquor laws received a fine in excess of $ 6,600, or a 54-year jail sentence if the fine was not paid. The majority refused to consider the question on the ground that the Eighth Amendment did not apply to the States. The dissent, after carefully examining the history of that Amendment and the Fourteenth, concluded that its prohibition was binding on Vermont and that it was directed against "all punishments which by their excessive length or severity are greatly disproportioned to the offences charged."

The Court, in *Weems v. United States*, adopted Mr. Justice Field's view. The defendant, in *Weems*, charged with falsifying Government documents, had been sentenced to serve 15 years in *cadena temporal*, a punishment which included carrying chains at the wrists and ankles and the perpetual loss of the right to vote and hold office. Finding the sentence grossly excessive in length and condition of imprisonment, the Court struck it down. This notion of disproportionality–that particular sentences may be cruelly excessive for particular crimes—has been cited with approval in more recent decisions of this Court.

These cases, while providing a rationale for gauging the constitutionality of capital sentences imposed for rape, also indicate the existence of necessary limitations on the judicial function. The use of limiting terms in the various expressions of this test found in the opinions—grossly excessive, greatly disproportionate—emphasizes that the Court's power to strike down punishments as excessive must be exercised with the greatest circumspection. As I have noted earlier, nothing in the history of the Cruel and Unusual Punishments Clause indicates that it may properly be utilized by the judiciary to strike down punishments—authorized by legislatures and imposed by juries—in any but the extraordinary case. This Court is not empowered to sit as a court of sentencing review, implementing the personal views of its members on the proper role of penology. To do so is to usurp a function committed to the Legislative Branch and beyond the power and competency of this Court.

Operating within these narrow limits, I find it quite impossible to declare the death sentence grossly excessive for all rapes. Rape is widely recognized as among the most serious of violent crimes, as witnessed by the very fact that it is punishable by death in 16 States and by life imprisonment in most other States. The several reasons why rape stands so high on the list of serious crimes are well known: It is widely viewed as the most atrocious of intrusions upon the privacy and dignity of the victim; never is the crime committed accidentally; rarely can it be said to be unpremeditated; often the victim suffers serious physical injury; the psychological impact can often be as great as the physical consequences; in a real sense, the threat of both types of injury is always present. For these reasons, and for the reasons arguing against abolition of the death penalty altogether, the excessiveness rationale provides no basis for rejection of the penalty for rape in all cases.

The argument that the death penalty for rape lacks rational justification because less severe punishments might be viewed as accomplishing the proper goals of penology is as inapposite here as it was in considering per se abolition. The state of knowledge with respect to the deterrent value of the sentence for this crime is inconclusive. Moreover, what has been said about the concept of retribution applies with equal force where the crime is rape. There are many cases in which the sordid, heinous nature of a particular crime, demeaning, humiliating, and often physically or psychologically traumatic, will call for public condemnation. In a period in our country's history when the frequency of this crime is increasing alarmingly, it is indeed a grave event for the Court to take from the States whatever deterrent and retributive weight the death penalty retains.

Other less sweeping applications of the disproportionality concept have been suggested. Recently the Fourth Circuit struck down a death sentence in *Ralph v. Warden*, holding that the death penalty was an appropriate punishment for rape only where life is "endangered." Chief Judge Haynsworth, who joined in the panel's opinion, wrote separately in denying the State of Maryland's petition for rehearing in order to make clear the basis for his joinder. He stated that, for him, the appropriate test was not whether life was endangered, but whether the victim in fact suffered "grievous physical or psychological harm."

It seems to me that both of these tests depart from established principles and also raise serious practical problems. How are those cases in which the victim's life is endangered to be distinguished from those in which no danger is found? The threat of serious injury is implicit in the definition of rape; the victim is either forced into submission by physical violence or by the threat of violence. Certainly that test would provide little comfort for either of the rape defendants in the cases presently before us. Both criminal acts were accomplished only after a violent struggle. Petitioner Jackson held a scissors blade against his victim's neck. Petitioner Branch had less difficulty subduing his 65-year-old victim. Both assailants threatened to kill their victims. The alternate test, limiting the penalty to cases in which the victim suffers physical or emotional harm, might present even greater problems of application. While most physical effects may be seen and objectively measured, the emotional impact may be impossible to gauge at any particular point in time. The extent and duration of psychological trauma may not be known or ascertainable prior to the date of trial.

While I reject each of these attempts to establish specific categories of cases in which the death penalty may be deemed excessive, I view them as groping toward what is for me the appropriate application of the Eighth Amendment. While in my view the disproportionality test may not be used either to strike down the death penalty for rape altogether or to install the Court as a tribunal for sentencing review, that test may find its application in the peculiar circumstances of specific cases. Its utilization should be limited to the rare case in which the death penalty is rendered for a crime technically falling within the legislatively defined class but factually falling outside the likely legislative intent in creating the category. Specific rape cases (and specific homicides as well) can be imagined in which the conduct of the accused would render the ultimate penalty a grossly excessive punishment. Although this case-by-case approach may seem painfully slow and inadequate to those who wish the Court to assume an activist legislative role in reforming criminal punishments, it is the approach dictated both by our prior opinions and by a due recognition of the limitations of judicial power. This approach, rather than the majority's more pervasive and less refined judgment, marks for me the appropriate course under the Eighth Amendment.

VIII.

I now return to the overriding question in these cases: whether this Court, acting in conformity with the Constitution, can justify its judgment to abolish capital punishment as heretofore known in this country. It is important to keep in focus the enormity of the step undertaken by the Court today. Not only does it invalidate hundreds of state and federal laws, it deprives those jurisdictions of the power to legislate with respect to capital punishment in the future, except in a manner consistent with the cloudily outlined views of those Justices who do not purport to undertake total abolition. Nothing short of an amendment to the United States Constitution can reverse the Court's judgments. Meanwhile, all flexibility is foreclosed. The normal democratic process, as well as the opportunities for the several States to respond to the will of their people expressed through ballot referenda (as in Massachusetts, Illinois, and Colorado), is now shut off.

The sobering disadvantage of constitutional adjudication of this magnitude is the universality and permanence of the judgment. The enduring merit of legislative action is its responsiveness to the democratic process, and to revision and change: mistaken judgments may be corrected and refinements perfected. In England and Canada critical choices were made after studies canvassing all competing views, and in those countries revisions may be made in light of experience.

As recently as 1967 a presidential commission did consider, as part of an overall study of crime in this country, whether the death penalty should be abolished. The commission's unanimous recommendation was as follows:

"The question whether capital punishment is an appropriate sanction is a policy decision to be made by each State. Where it is retained, the types of offenses for which it is available should be strictly limited, and the law should be enforced in an evenhanded and nondiscriminatory manner, with procedures for review of death sentences that are fair and expeditious. When a State finds that it cannot administer the penalty in such a manner, or that the death penalty is being imposed but not carried into effect, the penalty should be abandoned."

The thrust of the Commission's recommendation, as presently relevant, is that this question "is a policy decision to be made by each State." There is no hint that this decision could or should be made by the judicial branch.

The National Commission on Reform of Federal Criminal Laws also considered the capital punishment issue. The introductory commentary of its final report states that "a sharp division existed within the Commission on the subject of capital punishment," although a majority favored its abolition. Again, consideration of the question was directed to the propriety of retention or abolition as a legislative matter. There was no suggestion that the difference of opinion existing among commission members, and generally across the country, could or should be resolved in one stroke by a decision of this Court. Similar activity was, before today, evident at the state level with re-evaluation having been undertaken by special legislative committees in some States and by public ballot in others.

....

MR. JUSTICE REHNQUIST, with whom THE CHIEF JUSTICE, MR. JUSTICE BLACKMUN, and MR. JUSTICE POWELL join, dissenting.

The Court's judgments today strike down a penalty that our Nation's legislators have thought necessary since our country was founded. My Brothers DOUGLAS, BRENNAN, and MARSHALL would at one fell swoop invalidate laws enacted by Congress and 40 of the 50 state legislatures, and would consign to the limbo of unconstitutionality under a single rubric penalties for offenses as varied and unique as murder, piracy, mutiny, highjacking, and desertion in the face of the enemy. My Brothers STEWART and WHITE, asserting reliance on a more limited rationale—the reluctance of judges and juries actually to impose the death penalty in the majority of capital cases— join in the judgments in these cases. Whatever its precise rationale, today's holding necessarily brings into sharp relief the fundamental question of the role of judicial review in a democratic society. How can government by the elected representatives of the people co-exist with the power of the federal judiciary, whose members are constitutionally insulated from responsiveness to the popular will, to declare invalid laws duly enacted by the popular branches of government?

The answer, of course, is found in Hamilton's Federalist Paper No. 78 and in Chief Justice Marshall's classic opinion in *Marbury v. Madison.* An oft-told story since then, it bears summarization once more. Sovereignty resides ultimately in the people as a whole and, by adopting through their States a written Constitution for the Nation and subsequently adding amendments to that instrument, they have both granted certain powers to the National Government, and denied other powers to the National and the State Governments. Courts are exercising no more than the judicial function conferred upon them by Art. III of the Constitution when they assess, in a case before them, whether or not a particular legislative enactment is within the authority granted by the Constitution to the enacting body, and whether it runs afoul of some limitation placed by the Constitution on the authority of that body. For the theory is that the people themselves have spoken in the Constitution, and therefore its commands are superior to the commands of the legislature, which is merely an agent of the people.

The Founding Fathers thus wisely sought to have the best of both worlds, the undeniable benefits of both democratic self-government and individual rights protected against possible excesses of that form of government.

The courts in cases properly before them have been entrusted under the Constitution with the last word, short of constitutional amendment, as to whether a law passed by the legislature conforms to the Constitution. But just because courts in general, and this Court in particular, do have the last word, the admonition of Mr. Justice Stone dissenting in *United States v. Butler* must be constantly borne in mind:

"While unconstitutional exercise of power by the executive and legislative branches of the government is subject to judicial restraint, the only check upon our own exercise of power is our own sense of self-restraint."

Rigorous attention to the limits of this Court's authority is likewise enjoined because of the natural desire that beguiles judges along with other human beings into imposing their own views of goodness, truth, and justice upon others. Judges differ only in that they have the power, if not the authority, to enforce their desires. This is doubtless why nearly two centuries of judicial precedent from this Court counsel the sparing use of that power. The most expansive reading of the leading constitutional cases does not remotely suggest that this Court has been granted a roving commission, either by the Founding Fathers or by the framers of the Fourteenth Amendment, to strike down laws that are based upon notions of policy or morality suddenly found unacceptable by a majority of this Court. The Framers of the Constitution would doubtless have agreed with the great English political philosopher John Stuart Mill when he observed:

"The disposition of mankind, whether as rulers or as fellow-citizens, to impose their own opinions and inclinations as a rule of conduct on others, is so energetically supported by some of the best and by some of the worst feelings incident to human nature, that it is hardly ever kept under restraint by anything but want of power."

A separate reason for deference to the legislative judgment is the consequence of human error on the part of the judiciary with respect to the constitutional issue before it. Human error there is bound to be, judges being men and women, and men and women being what they are. But an error in mistakenly sustaining the constitutionality of a particular enactment, while wrongfully depriving the individual of a right secured to him by the Constitution, nonetheless does so by simply letting stand a duly enacted law of a democratically chosen legislative body. The error resulting from a mistaken upholding of an individual's constitutional claim against the validity of a legislative enactment is a good deal more serious. For the result in such a case is not to leave standing a law duly enacted by a representative assembly, but to impose upon the Nation the judicial fiat of a majority of a court of judges whose connection with the popular will is remote at best.

The task of judging constitutional cases imposed by Art. III cannot for this reason be avoided, but it must surely be approached with the deepest humility and genuine deference to legislative judgment. Today's decision to invalidate capital punishment is, I respectfully submit, significantly lacking in those attributes. For the reasons well stated in the opinions of THE CHIEF JUSTICE, MR. JUSTICE BLACKMUN, and MR. JUSTICE POWELL, I conclude that this decision holding unconstitutional capital punishment is not an act of judgment, but rather an act of will. It completely ignores the strictures of Mr. Justice Holmes, writing more than 40 years ago in *Baldwin v. Missouri*:

"I have not yet adequately expressed the more than anxiety that I feel at the ever increasing scope given to the Fourteenth Amendment in cutting down what I believe to be the constitutional rights of the States. As the decisions now stand, I see hardly any limit but the sky to the invalidating of those rights if they happen to strike a majority of this Court as for any reason undesirable. I cannot believe that the Amendment was intended to give us carte blanche to embody our economic or moral beliefs in its prohibitions. Yet I can think of no narrower reason that seems to me to justify the present and the earlier decisions to which I have referred. Of course the words 'due process of law,' if taken in their literal meaning, have no application to this case; and while it is too late to deny that they have been given a much more extended and artificial signification, still we ought to remember the great caution shown by the Constitution in limiting the power of the States, and should be slow to construe the clause in the Fourteenth Amendment as committing to the Court, with no guide but the Court's own discretion, the validity of whatever laws the States may pass."

More than 20 years ago, Justice Jackson made a similar observation with respect to this Court's restriction of the States in the enforcement of their own criminal laws:

"The use of the due process clause to disable the States in protection of society from crime is quite as dangerous and delicate a use of federal judicial power as to use it to disable them from social or economic experimentation."

If there can be said to be one dominant theme in the Constitution, perhaps more fully articulated in the *Federalist Papers* than in the instrument itself, it is the notion of checks and balances. The Framers were well aware of the natural desire of office holders as well as others to seek to expand the scope and authority of their particular office at the expense of others. They sought to provide against success in such efforts by erecting adequate checks and balances in the form of grants of authority to each branch of the government in order to counteract and prevent usurpation on the part of the others.

This philosophy of the Framers is best described by one of the ablest and greatest of their number, James Madison, in *Federalist No. 51*:

"In framing a government which is to be administered by men over men, the great difficulty lies in this: You must first enable the government to controul the governed; and in the next place, oblige it to controul itself."

Madison's observation applies to the Judicial Branch with at least as much force as to the Legislative and Executive Branches. While overreaching by the Legislative and Executive Branches may result in the sacrifice of individual protections that the Constitution was designed to secure against action of the State, judicial overreaching may result in sacrifice of the equally important right of the people to govern themselves. The Due Process and Equal Protection Clauses of the Fourteenth Amendment were "never intended to destroy the States' power to govern themselves."

The very nature of judicial review, as pointed out by Justice Stone in his dissent in the *Butler* case, makes the courts the least subject to Madisonian check in the event that they shall, for the best of motives, expand judicial authority beyond the limits contemplated by the Framers. It is for this reason that judicial self-restraint is surely an implied, if not an expressed, condition of the grant of authority of judicial review. The Court's holding in these cases has been reached, I believe, in complete disregard of that implied condition.

Gregg v. Georgia (1976)
428 U.S. 153

In essence, this case restored the death penalty after it was abolished in four years earlier in Furman v. Georgia. *The key elements in the restoration of the penalty were the procedural safeguards put in place by the Georgia legislature. The death penalty itself was determined not to violate the Eighth and Fourteenth Amendments.*

The issue in this case is whether the imposition of the sentence of death for the crime of murder under the law of Georgia violates the Eighth and Fourteenth Amendments.

I.

The petitioner, Troy Gregg, was charged with committing armed robbery and murder. In accordance with Georgia procedure in capital cases, the trial was in two stages, a guilt stage and a sentencing stage. The evidence at the guilt trial established that on November 21, 1973, the petitioner and a traveling companion, Floyd Allen, while hitchhiking north in Florida were picked up by Fred Simmons and Bob Moore. Their car broke down, but they continued north after Simmons purchased another vehicle with some of the cash he was carrying. While still in Florida, they picked up another hitchhiker, Dennis Weaver, who rode with them to Atlanta, where he was let out about 11 p.m. A short time later the four men interrupted their journey for a rest stop along the highway. The next morning the bodies of Simmons and Moore were discovered in a ditch nearby.

On November 23, after reading about the shootings in an Atlanta newspaper, Weaver communicated with the Gwinnett County police and related information concerning the journey with the victims, including a description of the car. The next afternoon, the petitioner and Allen, while in Simmons' car, were arrested in Asheville, N.C. In the search incident to the arrest a .25-caliber pistol, later shown to be that used to kill Simmons and Moore, was found in the petitioner's pocket. After receiving the warnings required by *Miranda v. Arizona* and signing a written waiver of his rights, the petitioner signed a statement in which he admitted shooting, then robbing Simmons and Moore. He justified the slayings on grounds of self-defense. The next day, while being transferred to Lawrenceville, Ga., the petitioner and Allen were taken to the scene of the shootings. Upon arriving there, Allen recounted the events leading to the slayings. His version of these events was as follows: After Simmons and Moore left the car, the petitioner stated that he intended to rob them. The petitioner then took his pistol in hand and positioned himself on the car to improve his aim. As Simmons and Moore came up an embankment toward the car, the petitioner fired three shots and the two men fell near a ditch. The petitioner, at close range, then fired a shot into the head of each. He robbed them of valuables and drove away with Allen.

A medical examiner testified that Simmons died from a bullet wound in the eye and that Moore died from bullet wounds in the cheek and in the back of the head. He further testified that both men had several bruises and abrasions about the face and head which probably were sustained either from the fall into the ditch or from being dragged or pushed along the embankment. Although Allen did not testify, a police detective recounted the substance of Allen's statements about the slayings and indicated that directly after Allen had made these statements the petitioner had admitted that Allen's account was accurate. The petitioner testified in his own defense. He confirmed that Allen had made the statements described by the detective, but denied their truth or ever having admitted to their accuracy. He indicated that he had shot Simmons and Moore because of fear and in self-defense, testifying they had attacked Allen and him, one wielding a pipe and the other a knife.

The trial judge submitted the murder charges to the jury on both felony-murder and nonfelony-murder theories. He also instructed on the issue of self-defense but declined to instruct on manslaughter. He submitted the robbery case to the jury on both an armed-robbery theory and on the lesser included offense of robbery by intimidation. The jury found the petitioner guilty of two counts of armed robbery and two counts of murder.

At the penalty stage, which took place before the same jury, neither the prosecutor nor the petitioner's lawyer offered any additional evidence. Both counsel, however, made lengthy arguments dealing generally with the propriety of capital punishment under the circumstances and with the weight of the evidence of guilt. The trial judge instructed the jury that it could recommend either a death sentence or a life prison sentence on each count. The judge further charged the jury that in determining what sentence was appropriate the jury was free to consider the facts and circumstances, if any, presented by the parties in mitigation or aggravation.

Finally, the judge instructed the jury that it "would not be authorized to consider imposing the penalty of death" unless it first found beyond a reasonable doubt one of these aggravating circumstances:

"One—That the offense of murder was committed while the offender was engaged in the commission of two other capital felonies, to-wit the armed robbery of Simmons and Moore.

"Two—That the offender committed the offense of murder for the purpose of receiving money and the automobile described in the indictment.

"Three—The offense of murder was outrageously and wantonly vile, horrible and inhuman, in that they [sic] involved the depravity of the mind of the defendant."

Finding the first and second of these circumstances, the jury returned verdicts of death on each count.

The Supreme Court of Georgia affirmed the convictions and the imposition of the death sentences for murder. After reviewing the trial transcript and the record, including the evidence, and comparing the evidence and sentence in similar cases in accordance with the requirements of Georgia law, the court concluded that, considering the nature of the crime and the defendant, the sentences of death had not resulted from prejudice or any other arbitrary factor and were not excessive or disproportionate to the penalty applied in similar cases. The death sentences imposed for armed robbery, however, were vacated on the grounds that the death penalty had rarely been imposed in Georgia for that offense and that the jury improperly considered the murders as aggravating circumstances for the robberies after having considered the armed robberies as aggravating circumstances for the murders.

We granted the petitioner's application for a writ of certiorari limited to his challenge to the imposition of the death sentences in this case as "cruel and unusual" punishment in violation of the Eighth and the Fourteenth Amendments.

II.

Before considering the issues presented it is necessary to understand the Georgia statutory scheme for the imposition of the death penalty. The Georgia statute, as amended after our decision in *Furman v. Georgia*, retains the death penalty for six categories of crime: murder, kidnapping for ransom or where the victim is harmed, armed robbery, rape, treason, and aircraft hijacking. The capital defendant's guilt or innocence is determined in the traditional manner, either by a trial judge or a jury, in the first stage of a bifurcated trial.

If trial is by jury, the trial judge is required to charge lesser included offenses when they are supported by any view of the evidence. After a verdict, finding, or plea of guilty to a capital crime, a presentence hearing is conducted before whoever made the determination of guilt. The sentencing procedures are essentially the same in both bench and jury trials. At the hearing:

"The judge or jury shall hear additional evidence in extenuation, mitigation, and aggravation of punishment, including the record of any prior criminal convictions and pleas of guilty or pleas of nolo contendere of the defendant, or the absence of any prior conviction and pleas: Provided, however, that only such evidence in aggravation as the State has made known to the defendant prior to his trial shall be admissible. The judge or jury shall also hear argument by the defendant or his counsel and the prosecuting attorney… regarding the punishment to be imposed."

The defendant is accorded substantial latitude as to the types of evidence that he may introduce. Evidence considered during the guilt stage may be considered during the sentencing stage without being resubmitted.

In the assessment of the appropriate sentence to be imposed the judge is also required to consider or to include in his instructions to the jury "any mitigating circumstances or aggravating circumstances otherwise authorized by law and any of 10 statutory aggravating circumstances which may be supported by the evidence…." The scope of the nonstatutory aggravating or mitigating circumstances is not delineated in the statute. Before a convicted defendant may be sentenced to death, however, except in cases of treason or aircraft hijacking, the jury, or the trial judge in cases tried without a jury, must find beyond a reasonable doubt one of the 10 aggravating circumstances specified in the statute. The sentence of death may be imposed only if the jury (or judge) finds one of the statutory aggravating circumstances and then elects to impose that sentence. If the verdict is death, the jury or judge must specify the aggravating circumstance(s) found. In jury cases, the trial judge is bound by the jury's recommended sentence.

In addition to the conventional appellate process available in all criminal cases, provision is made for special expedited direct review by the Supreme Court of Georgia of the appropriateness of imposing the sentence of death in the particular case. The court is directed to consider "the punishment as well as any errors enumerated by way of appeal," and to determine:

"(1) Whether the sentence of death was imposed under the influence of passion, prejudice, or any other arbitrary factor, and

"(2) Whether, in cases other than treason or aircraft hijacking, the evidence supports the jury's or judge's finding of a statutory aggravating circumstance as enumerated in section 27.2534.1 (b), and

"(3) Whether the sentence of death is excessive or disproportionate to the penalty imposed in similar cases, considering both the crime and the defendant."

If the court affirms a death sentence, it is required to include in its decision reference to similar cases that it has taken into consideration.

A transcript and complete record of the trial, as well as a separate report by the trial judge, are transmitted to the court for its use in reviewing the sentence. The report is in the form of a 6 1/2-page questionnaire, designed to elicit information about the defendant, the crime, and the circumstances of the trial. It requires the trial judge to characterize the trial in several ways designed to test for arbitrariness and disproportionality of sentence. Included in the report are responses to detailed questions concerning the quality of the defendant's representation, whether race played a role in the trial, and, whether, in the trial court's judgment, there was any doubt about the defendant's guilt or the appropriateness of the sentence. A copy of the report is served upon defense counsel. Under its special review authority, the court may either affirm the death sentence or remand the case for resentencing. In cases in which the death sentence is affirmed there remains the possibility of executive clemency.

III.

We address initially the basic contention that the punishment of death for the crime of murder is, under all circumstances, "cruel and unusual" in violation of the Eighth and Fourteenth Amendments of the Constitution. In Part IV of this opinion, we will consider the sentence of death imposed under the Georgia statutes at issue in this case.

The Court on a number of occasions has both assumed and asserted the constitutionality of capital punishment. In several cases that assumption provided a necessary foundation for the decision, as the Court was asked to decide whether a particular method of carrying out a capital sentence would be allowed to stand under the Eighth Amendment. But until *Furman v. Georgia*, the Court never confronted squarely the fundamental claim that the punishment of death always, regardless of the enormity of the offense or the procedure followed in imposing the sentence, is cruel and unusual punishment in violation of the Constitution. Although this issue was presented and addressed in *Furman*, it was not resolved by the Court. Four Justices would have held that capital punishment is not unconstitutional per se; two Justices would have reached the opposite conclusion; and three Justices, while agreeing that the statutes then before the Court were invalid as applied, left open the question whether such punishment may ever be imposed. We now hold that the punishment of death does not invariably violate the Constitution.

A.

The history of the prohibition of "cruel and unusual" punishment already has been reviewed at length. The phrase first appeared in the English Bill of Rights of 1689, which was drafted by Parliament at the accession of William and Mary. The English version appears to have been directed against punishments unauthorized by statute and beyond the jurisdiction of the sentencing court, as well as those disproportionate to the offense involved. The American draftsmen, who adopted the English phrasing in drafting the Eighth Amendment, were primarily concerned, however, with proscribing "tortures" and other "barbarous" methods of punishment."

In the earliest cases raising Eighth Amendment claims, the Court focused on particular methods of execution to determine whether they were too cruel to pass constitutional muster. The constitutionality of the sentence of death itself was not at issue, and the criterion used to evaluate the mode of execution was its similarity to "torture" and other "barbarous" methods....

But the Court has not confined the prohibition embodied in the Eighth Amendment to "barbarous" methods that were generally outlawed in the 18th century. Instead, the Amendment has been interpreted in a flexible and dynamic manner. The Court early recognized that "a principle to be vital must be capable of wider application than the mischief which gave it birth." Thus the

Clause forbidding "cruel and unusual" punishments "is not fastened to the obsolete but may acquire meaning as public opinion becomes enlightened by a humane justice."

In *Weems* the Court addressed the constitutionality of the Philippine punishment of *cadena temporal* for the crime of falsifying an official document. That punishment included imprisonment for at least 12 years and one day, in chains, at hard and painful labor; the loss of many basic civil rights; and subjection to lifetime surveillance. Although the Court acknowledged the possibility that "the cruelty of pain" may be present in the challenged punishment, it did not rely on that factor, for it rejected the proposition that the Eighth Amendment reaches only punishments that are "inhuman and barbarous, torture and the like." Rather, the Court focused on the lack of proportion between the crime and the offense:

"Such penalties for such offenses amaze those who have formed their conception of the relation of a state to even its offending citizens from the practice of the American commonwealths, and believe that it is a precept of justice that punishment for crime should be graduated and proportioned to offense."

Later, in *Trop v. Dulles*, the Court reviewed the constitutionality of the punishment of denationalization imposed upon a soldier who escaped from an Army stockade and became a deserter for one day. Although the concept of proportionality was not the basis of the holding, the plurality observed in dicta that "fines, imprisonment and even execution may be imposed depending upon the enormity of the crime."

The substantive limits imposed by the Eighth Amendment on what can be made criminal and punished were discussed in *Robinson v. California*. The Court found unconstitutional a state statute that made the status of being addicted to a narcotic drug a criminal offense. It held, in effect, that it is "cruel and unusual" to impose any punishment at all for the mere status of addiction. The cruelty in the abstract of the actual sentence imposed was irrelevant: "Even one day in prison would be a cruel and unusual punishment for the 'crime' of having a common cold." Most recently, in *Furman v. Georgia*, three Justices in separate concurring opinions found the Eighth Amendment applicable to procedures employed to select convicted defendants for the sentence of death.

It is clear from the foregoing precedents that Eighth Amendment has not been regarded as a static concept. As Mr. Chief Justice Warren said, in an often-quoted phrase, "the Amendment must draw its meaning from the evolving standards of decency that mark the progress of a maturing society." …Thus, an assessment of contemporary values concerning the infliction of a challenged sanction is relevant to the application of the Eighth Amendment. As we develop below more fully, this assessment does not call for a subjective judgment. It requires, rather, that we look to objective indicia that reflect the public attitude toward a given sanction.

But our cases also make clear that public perceptions of standards of decency with respect to criminal sanctions are not conclusive. A penalty also must accord with "the dignity of man," which is the "basic concept underlying the Eighth Amendment." This means, at least, that the punishment not be "excessive." When a form of punishment in the abstract (in this case, whether capital punishment may ever be imposed as a sanction for murder) rather than in the particular (the propriety of death as a penalty to be applied to a specific defendant for a specific crime) is under consideration, the inquiry into "excessiveness" has two aspects. First, the punishment must not involve the unnecessary and wanton infliction of pain. Second, the punishment must not be grossly out of proportion to the severity of the crime.

B.

Of course, the requirements of the Eighth Amendment must be applied with an awareness of the limited role to be played by the courts. This does not mean that judges have no role to play, for the Eighth Amendment is a restraint upon the exercise of legislative power.

"Judicial review, by definition, often involves a conflict between judicial and legislative judgment as to what the Constitution means or requires. In this respect, Eighth Amendment cases come to us in no different posture. It seems conceded by all that the Amendment imposes some obligations on the judiciary to judge the constitutionality of punishment and that there are punishments that the Amendment would bar whether legislatively approved or not."

But, while we have an obligation to insure that constitutional bounds are not overreached, we may not act as judges as we might as legislators.

"Courts are not representative bodies. They are not designed to be a good reflex of a democratic society. Their judgment is best informed, and therefore most dependable, within narrow limits. Their essential quality is detachment, founded on independence. History teaches that the independence of the judiciary is jeopardized when courts become embroiled in the passions of the day and assume primary responsibility in choosing between competing political, economic and social pressures."

Therefore, in assessing a punishment selected by a democratically elected legislature against the constitutional measure, we presume its validity. We may not require the legislature to select the least severe penalty possible so long as the penalty selected is not cruelly inhumane or disproportionate to the crime involved. And a heavy burden rests on those who would attack the judgment of the representatives of the people.

This is true in part because the constitutional test is intertwined with an assessment of contemporary standards and the legislative judgment weighs heavily in ascertaining such standards. "In a democratic society legislatures, not courts, are constituted to respond to the will and consequently the moral values of the people." The deference we owe to the decisions of the state legislatures under our federal system is enhanced where the specification of punishments is concerned, for "these are peculiarly questions of legislative policy." Caution is necessary lest this Court become, "under the aegis of the Cruel and Unusual Punishment Clause, the ultimate arbiter of the standards of criminal responsibility... throughout the country." A decision that a given punishment is impermissible under the Eighth Amendment cannot be reversed short of a constitutional amendment. The ability of the people to express their preference through the normal democratic processes, as well as through ballot referenda, is shut off. Revisions cannot be made in the light of further experience.

C.

In the discussion to this point we have sought to identify the principles and considerations that guide a court in addressing an Eighth Amendment claim. We now consider specifically whether the sentence of death for the crime of murder is a per se violation of the Eighth and Fourteenth Amendments to the Constitution. We note first that history and precedent strongly support a negative answer to this question.

The imposition of the death penalty for the crime of murder has a long history of acceptance both in the United States and in England. The common-law rule imposed a mandatory death sentence on all convicted murderers. And the penalty continued to be used into the 20th century by most American States, although the breadth of the common-law rule was diminished, initially by narrowing the class of murders to be punished by death and subsequently by widespread adoption of laws expressly granting juries the discretion to recommend mercy.

It is apparent from the text of the Constitution itself that the existence of capital punishment was accepted by the Framers. At the time the Eighth Amendment was ratified, capital punishment was a common sanction in every State. Indeed, the First Congress of the United States enacted legislation providing death as the penalty for specified crimes. The Fifth Amendment, adopted at the same time as the Eighth, contemplated the continued existence of the capital sanction by imposing certain limits on the prosecution of capital cases:
"No person shall be held to answer for a capital, or otherwise infamous crime, unless on a presentment or indictment of a Grand Jury...; nor shall any person be subject for the same offense to be twice put in jeopardy of life or limb... nor be deprived of life, liberty, or property, without due process of law...."

And the Fourteenth Amendment, adopted over three-quarters of a century later, similarly contemplates the existence of the capital sanction in providing that no State shall deprive any person of "life, liberty, or property" without due process of law.

For nearly two centuries, this Court, repeatedly and often expressly, has recognized that capital punishment is not invalid per se. In *Wilkerson v. Utah*, where the Court found no constitutional violation in inflicting death by public shooting, it said:

"Cruel and unusual punishments are forbidden by the Constitution, but the authorities referred to are quite sufficient to show that the punishment of shooting as a mode of executing the death penalty for the crime of murder in the first degree is not included in that category, within the meaning of the eighth amendment."

Rejecting the contention that death by electrocution was "cruel and unusual," the Court in *In re Kemmler* reiterated:

"The punishment of death is not cruel, within the meaning of that word as used in the Constitution. It implies there something inhuman and barbarous, something more than the mere extinguishment of life."

Again, in *Louisiana ex rel. Francis v. Resweber*, the Court remarked: "The cruelty against which the Constitution protects a convicted man is cruelty inherent in the method of punishment, not the necessary suffering involved in any method employed to extinguish life humanely." And in *Trop v. Dulles*, Mr. Chief Justice Warren, for himself and three other Justices, wrote:

"Whatever the arguments may be against capital punishment, both on moral grounds and in terms of accomplishing the purposes of punishment... the death penalty has been employed throughout our history, and, in a day when it is still widely accepted, it cannot be said to violate the constitutional concept of cruelty."

Four years ago, the petitioners in *Furman* and its companion cases predicated their argument primarily upon the asserted proposition that standards of decency had evolved to the point where capital punishment no longer could be tolerated. The petitioners in those cases said, in effect, that the evolutionary process had come to an end, and that standards of decency required that the Eighth Amendment be construed finally as prohibiting capital punishment for any crime regardless of its depravity and impact on society. This view was accepted by two Justices. Three other Justices were unwilling to go so far; focusing on the procedures by which convicted defendants were selected for the death penalty rather than on the actual punishment inflicted, they joined in the conclusion that the statutes before the Court were constitutionally invalid.

The petitioners in the capital cases before the Court today renew the "standards of decency" argument, but developments during the four years since *Furman* have undercut substantially the assumptions upon which their argument rested. Despite the continuing debate, dating back to the 19th century, over the morality and utility of capital punishment, it is now evident that a large proportion of American society continues to regard it as an appropriate and necessary criminal sanction.

The most marked indication of society's endorsement of the death penalty for murder is the legislative response to *Furman*. The legislatures of at least 35 States have enacted new statutes that provide for the death penalty for at least some crimes that result in the death of another person. And the Congress of the United States, in 1974, enacted a statute providing the death penalty for aircraft piracy that results in death. These recently adopted statutes have attempted to address the concerns expressed by the Court in *Furman* primarily (i) by specifying the factors to be weighed and the procedures to be followed in deciding when to impose a capital sentence, or (ii) by making the death penalty mandatory for specified crimes. But all of the post-*Furman* statutes make clear that capital punishment itself has not been rejected by the elected representatives of the people.

In the only statewide referendum occurring since *Furman* and brought to our attention, the people of California adopted a constitutional amendment that authorized capital punishment, in effect negating a prior ruling by the Supreme Court of California in *People v. Anderson*, that the death penalty violated the California Constitution.

The jury also is a significant and reliable objective index of contemporary values because it is so directly involved. The Court has said that "one of the most important functions any jury can perform in making... a selection between life imprisonment and death for a defendant convicted in a capital case is to maintain a link between contemporary community values and the penal system." It may be true that evolving standards have influenced juries in recent decades to be more discriminating in imposing the sentence of death. But the relative infrequency of jury verdicts imposing the death sentence does not indicate rejection of capital punishment per se. Rather, the reluctance of juries in many cases to impose the sentence may well reflect the humane feeling that this most irrevocable of sanctions should be reserved for a small number of extreme cases. Indeed, the actions of juries in many States since *Furman* are fully compatible with the legislative judgments, reflected in the new statutes, as to the continued utility and necessity of capital punishment in appropriate cases. At the close of 1974 at least 254 persons had been sentenced to death since *Furman*, and by the end of March 1976, more than 460 persons were subject to death sentences.

As we have seen, however, the Eighth Amendment demands more than that a challenged punishment be acceptable to contemporary society. The Court also must ask whether it comports with the basic concept of human dignity at the core of the Amendment. Although we cannot "invalidate a category of penalties because we deem less severe penalties adequate to serve the ends of penology," the sanction imposed cannot be so totally without penological justification that it results in the gratuitous infliction of suffering. The death penalty is said to serve two principal social purposes: retribution and deterrence of capital crimes by prospective offenders.

In part, capital punishment is an expression of society's moral outrage at particularly offensive conduct. This function may be unappealing to many, but it is essential in an ordered society that asks its citizens to rely on legal processes rather than self-help to vindicate their wrongs.

"The instinct for retribution is part of the nature of man, and channeling that instinct in the administration of criminal justice serves an important purpose in promoting the stability of a society governed by law. When people begin to believe that organized society is unwilling or unable to impose upon criminal offenders the punishment they 'deserve,' then there are sown the seeds of anarchy—of self-help, vigilante justice, and lynch law."

Retribution is no longer the dominant objective of the criminal law," but neither is it a forbidden objective nor one inconsistent with our respect for the dignity of men. Indeed, the decision that capital punishment may be the appropriate sanction in extreme cases is an expression of the community's belief that certain crimes are themselves so grievous an affront to humanity that the only adequate response may be the penalty of death.

Statistical attempts to evaluate the worth of the death penalty as a deterrent to crimes by potential offenders have occasioned a great deal of debate. The results simply have been inconclusive. As one opponent of capital punishment has said:

"After all possible inquiry, including the probing of all possible methods of inquiry, we do not know, and for systematic and easily visible reasons cannot know, what the truth about this 'deterrent' effect may be....

"The inescapable flaw is… that social conditions in any state are not constant through time, and that social conditions are not the same in any two states. If an effect were observed (and the observed effects, one way or another, are not large) then one could not at all tell whether any of this effect is attributable to the presence or absence of capital punishment. A 'scientific'—that is to say, a soundly based—conclusion is simply impossible, and no methodological path out of this tangle suggests itself."

Although some of the studies suggest that the death penalty may not function as a significantly greater deterrent than lesser penalties, there is no convincing empirical evidence either supporting or refuting this view. We may nevertheless assume safely that there are murderers, such as those who act in passion, for whom the threat of death has little or no deterrent effect. But for many others, the death penalty undoubtedly is a significant deterrent. There are carefully contemplated murders, such as murder for hire, where the possible penalty of death may well enter into the cold calculus that precedes the decision to act. And there are some categories of murder, such as murder by a life prisoner, where other sanctions may not be adequate.

The value of capital punishment as a deterrent of crime is a complex factual issue the resolution of which properly rests with the legislatures, which can evaluate the results of statistical studies in terms of their own local conditions and with a flexibility of approach that is not available to the courts. Indeed, many of the post-*Furman* statutes reflect just such a responsible effort to define those crimes and those criminals for which capital punishment is most probably an effective deterrent.

In sum, we cannot say that the judgment of the Georgia Legislature that capital punishment may be necessary in some cases is clearly wrong. Considerations of federalism, as well as respect for the ability of a legislature to evaluate, in terms of its particular State, the moral consensus concerning the death penalty and its social utility as a sanction, require us to conclude, in the absence of more convincing evidence, that the infliction of death as a punishment for murder is not without justification and thus is not unconstitutionally severe.

Finally, we must consider whether the punishment of death is disproportionate in relation to the crime for which it is imposed. There is no question that death as a punishment is unique in its severity and irrevocability. When a defendant's life is at stake, the Court has been particularly sensitive to insure that every safeguard is observed. But we are concerned here only with the imposition of capital punishment for the crime of murder, and when a life has been taken deliberately by the offender, we cannot say that the punishment is invariably disproportionate to the crime. It is an extreme sanction, suitable to the most extreme of crimes.

We hold that the death penalty is not a form of punishment that may never be imposed, regardless of the circumstances of the offense, regardless of the character of the offender, and regardless of the procedure followed in reaching the decision to impose it.

IV.

We now consider whether Georgia may impose the death penalty on the petitioner in this case.

A.

While *Furman* did not hold that the infliction of the death penalty per se violates the Constitution's ban on cruel and unusual punishments, it did recognize that the penalty of death is different in kind from any other punishment imposed under our system of criminal justice. Because of the uniqueness of the death penalty, *Furman* held that it could not be imposed under sentencing procedures that created a substantial risk that it would be inflicted in an arbitrary and capricious manner. MR. JUSTICE WHITE concluded that "the death penalty is exacted with great infrequency even for the most atrocious crimes and... there is no meaningful basis for distinguishing the few cases in which it is imposed from the many cases in which it is not." Indeed, the death sentences examined by the Court in *Furman* were "cruel and unusual in the same way that being struck by lightning is cruel and unusual. For, of all the people convicted of capital crimes, many just as reprehensible as these, the petitioners in *Furman* were among a capriciously selected random handful upon whom the sentence of death has in fact been imposed.... The Eighth and Fourteenth Amendments cannot tolerate the infliction of a sentence of death under legal systems that permit this unique penalty to be so wantonly and so freakishly imposed."

Furman mandates that where discretion is afforded a sentencing body on a matter so grave as the determination of whether a human life should be taken or spared, that discretion must be suitably directed and limited so as to minimize the risk of wholly arbitrary and capricious action.

It is certainly not a novel proposition that discretion in the area of sentencing be exercised in an informed manner. We have long recognized that "for the determination of sentences, justice generally requires... that there be taken into account the circumstances of the offense together with the character and propensities of the offender." Otherwise, "the system cannot function in a consistent and a rational manner."

The cited studies assumed that the trial judge would be the sentencing authority. If an experienced trial judge, who daily faces the difficult task of imposing sentences, has a vital need for accurate information about a defendant and the crime he committed in order to be able to impose a rational sentence in the typical criminal case, then accurate sentencing information is an indispensable prerequisite to a reasoned determination of whether a defendant shall live or die by a jury of people who may never before have made a sentencing decision.

Jury sentencing has been considered desirable in capital cases in order to maintain a link between contemporary community values and the penal system—a link without which the determination of punishment could hardly reflect 'the evolving standards of decency that mark the progress of a maturing society.' But it creates special problems. Much of the information that is relevant to the sentencing decision may have no relevance to the question of guilt, or may even be extremely prejudicial to a fair determination of that question. This problem, however, is scarcely insurmountable. Those who have studied the question suggest that a bifurcated procedure—one in which the question of sentence is not considered until the determination of guilt has been made—is the best answer. The drafters of the Model Penal Code concluded:

"If a unitary proceeding is used the determination of the punishment must be based on less than all the evidence that has a bearing on that issue, such for example as a previous criminal record of the accused, or evidence must be admitted on the ground that it is relevant to sentence, though it would be excluded as irrelevant or prejudicial with respect to guilt or innocence alone. Trial lawyers understandably have little confidence in a solution that admits the evidence and trusts to an instruction to the jury that it should be considered only in determining the penalty and disregarded in assessing guilt.

"... The obvious solution... is to bifurcate the proceeding, abiding strictly by the rules of evidence until and unless there is a conviction, but once guilt has been determined opening the record to the further information that is relevant to sentence. This is the analogue of the procedure in the ordinary case when capital punishment is not in issue; the court conducts a separate inquiry before imposing sentence."

When a human life is at stake and when the jury must have information prejudicial to the question of guilt but relevant to the question of penalty in order to impose a rational sentence, a system is more likely to ensure elimination of the constitutional deficiencies identified in *Furman*.

But the provision of relevant information under fair procedural rules is not alone sufficient to guarantee that the information will be properly used in the imposition of punishment, especially if sentencing is performed by a jury. Since the members of a jury will have had little, if any, previous experience in sentencing, they are unlikely to be skilled in dealing with the information they are given. To the extent that this problem is inherent in jury sentencing, it may not be totally correctable. It seems clear, however, that the problem will be alleviated if the jury is given guidance regarding the factors about the crime and the defendant that the State, representing organized society, deems particularly relevant to the sentencing decision.

The idea that a jury should be given guidance in its decisionmaking is also hardly a novel proposition. Juries are invariably given careful instructions on the law and how to apply it before they are authorized to decide the merits of a lawsuit. It would be virtually unthinkable to follow any other course in a legal system that has traditionally operated by following prior precedents and fixed rules of law. When erroneous instructions are given, retrial is often required. It is quite simply a hallmark of our legal system that juries be carefully and adequately guided in their deliberations.

While some have suggested that standards to guide a capital jury's sentencing deliberations are impossible to formulate, the fact is that such standards have been developed. When the drafters of the Model Penal Code faced this problem, they concluded "that it is within the realm of possibility to point to the main circumstances of aggravation and of mitigation that should be weighed and weighed against each other when they are presented in a concrete case." While such standards are by necessity somewhat general, they do provide guidance to the sentencing authority and thereby reduce the likelihood that it will impose a sentence that fairly can be called capricious or arbitrary. Where the sentencing authority is required to specify the factors it relied upon in reaching its decision, the further safeguard of meaningful appellate review is available to ensure that death sentences are not imposed capriciously or in a freakish manner.

In summary, the concerns expressed in *Furman* that the penalty of death not be imposed in an arbitrary or capricious manner can be met by a carefully drafted statute that ensures that the sentencing authority is given adequate information and guidance. As a general proposition these concerns are best met by a system that provides for a bifurcated proceeding at which the sentencing authority is apprised of the information relevant to the imposition of sentence and provided with standards to guide its use of the information.

We do not intend to suggest that only the above described procedures would be permissible under *Furman* or that any sentencing system constructed along these general lines would inevitably satisfy the concerns of *Furman*, for each distinct system must be examined on an individual basis. Rather, we have embarked upon this general exposition to make clear that it is possible to construct capital-sentencing systems capable of meeting *Furman's* constitutional concerns.

B.

We now turn to consideration of the constitutionality of Georgia's capital-sentencing procedures. In the wake of *Furman*, Georgia amended its capital punishment statute, but chose not to narrow the scope of its murder provisions. Thus, now as before *Furman*, in Georgia "a person commits murder when he unlawfully and with malice aforethought, either express or implied, causes the death of another human being." All persons convicted of murder "shall be punished by death or by imprisonment for life."

Georgia did act, however, to narrow the class of murderers subject to capital punishment by specifying 10 statutory aggravating circumstances, one of which must be found by the jury to exist beyond a reasonable doubt before a death sentence can ever be imposed. In addition, the jury is authorized to consider any other appropriate aggravating or mitigating circumstances. The jury is not required to find any mitigating circumstance in order to make a recommendation of mercy that is binding on the trial court, but it must find a statutory aggravating circumstance before recommending a sentence of death.

These procedures require the jury to consider the circumstances of the crime and the criminal before it recommends sentence. No longer can a Georgia jury do as Furman's jury did: reach a finding of the defendant's guilt and then, without guidance or direction, decide whether he should live or die. Instead, the jury's attention is directed to the specific circumstances of the crime: Was it committed in the course of another capital felony? Was it committed for money? Was it committed upon a peace officer or judicial officer? Was it committed in a particularly heinous way or in a manner that endangered the lives of many persons? In addition, the jury's attention is focused on the characteristics of the person who committed the crime: Does he have a record of prior convictions for capital offenses? Are there any special facts about this defendant that mitigate against imposing capital punishment (e.g., his youth, the extent of his cooperation with the police, his emotional state at the time of the crime). As a result, while some jury discretion still exists, "the discretion to be exercised is controlled by clear and objective standards so as to produce non-discriminatory application."

As an important additional safeguard against arbitrariness and caprice, the Georgia statutory scheme provides for automatic appeal of all death sentences to the State's Supreme Court. That court is required by statute to review each sentence of death and determine whether it was imposed under the influence of passion or prejudice, whether the evidence supports the jury's finding of a statutory aggravating circumstance, and whether the sentence is disproportionate compared to those sentences imposed in similar cases.

In short, Georgia's new sentencing procedures require as a prerequisite to the imposition of the death penalty, specific jury findings as to the circumstances of the crime or the character of the defendant. Moreover, to guard further against a situation comparable to that presented in *Furman*, the Supreme Court of Georgia compares each death sentence with the sentences imposed on similarly situated defendants to ensure that the sentence of death in a particular case is not disproportionate. On their face these procedures seem to satisfy the concerns of *Furman*. No longer should there be "no meaningful basis for distinguishing the few cases in which the death penalty is imposed from the many cases in which it is not."

The petitioner contends, however, that the changes in the Georgia sentencing procedures are only cosmetic, that the arbitrariness and capriciousness condemned by *Furman* continue to exist in Georgia—both in traditional practices that still remain and in the new sentencing procedures adopted in response to *Furman*.

First, the petitioner focuses on the opportunities for discretionary action that are inherent in the processing of any murder case under Georgia law. He notes that the state prosecutor has unfettered authority to select those persons whom he wishes to prosecute for a capital offense and to plea bargain with them. Further, at the trial the jury may choose to convict a defendant of a lesser included offense rather than find him guilty of a crime punishable by death, even if the evidence would support a capital verdict. And finally, a defendant who is convicted and sentenced to die may have his sentence commuted by the Governor of the State and the Georgia Board of Pardons and Paroles.

The existence of these discretionary stages is not determinative of the issues before us. At each of these stages an actor in the criminal justice system makes a decision which may remove a defendant from consideration as a candidate for the death penalty. *Furman*, in contrast, dealt with the decision to impose the death sentence on a specific individual who had been convicted of a capital offense. Nothing in any of our cases suggests that the decision to afford an individual defendant mercy violates the Constitution. *Furman* held only that, in order to minimize the risk that the death penalty would be imposed on a capriciously selected group of offenders, the decision to impose it had to be guided by standards so that the sentencing authority would focus on the particularized circumstances of the crime and the defendant.

The petitioner further contends that the capital sentencing procedures adopted by Georgia in response to *Furman* do not eliminate the dangers of arbitrariness and caprice in jury sentencing that were held in *Furman* to be violative of the Eighth and Fourteenth Amendments. He claims that the statute is so broad and vague as to leave juries free to act as arbitrarily and capriciously as they wish in deciding whether to impose the death penalty. While there is no claim that the jury in this case relied upon a vague or overbroad provision to establish the existence of a statutory aggravating circumstance, the petitioner looks to the sentencing system as a whole (as the Court did in *Furman* and we do today) and argues that it fails to reduce sufficiently the risk of arbitrary infliction of death sentences. Specifically, Gregg urges that the statutory aggravating circumstances are too broad and too vague, that the sentencing procedure allows for arbitrary grants of mercy, and that the scope of the evidence and argument that can be considered at the presentence hearing is too wide.

The petitioner attacks the seventh statutory aggravating circumstance, which authorizes imposition of the death penalty if the murder was "outrageously or wantonly vile, horrible or inhuman in that it involved torture, depravity of mind, or an aggravated battery to the victim," contending that it is so broad that capital punishment could be imposed in any murder case. It is, of course, arguable that any murder involves depravity of mind or an aggravated battery. But this language need not be construed in this way, and there is no reason to assume that the Supreme Court of Georgia will adopt such an open-ended construction. In only one case has it upheld a jury's decision to sentence a defendant to death when the only statutory aggravating circumstance found was that of the seventh, and that homicide was a horrifying torture-murder.

The petitioner also argues that two of the statutory aggravating circumstances are vague and therefore susceptible of widely differing interpretations, thus creating a substantial risk that the death penalty will be arbitrarily inflicted by Georgia juries. In light of the decisions of the Supreme Court of Georgia we must disagree. First, the petitioner attacks that part of § 27-2534.1 (b)(1) that authorizes a jury to consider whether a defendant has a "substantial history of serious assaultive criminal convictions." The Supreme Court of Georgia, however, has demonstrated a concern that the new sentencing procedures provide guidance to juries. It held this provision to be impermissibly vague in *Arnold v. State* because it did not provide the jury with "sufficiently 'clear and objective standards.'" Second, the petitioner points to § 27-2534.1 (b)(3) which speaks of creating a "great risk of death to more than one person." While such a phrase might be susceptible of an overly broad interpretation, the Supreme Court of

Georgia has not so construed it. The only case in which the court upheld a conviction in reliance on this aggravating circumstance involved a man who stood up in a church and fired a gun indiscriminately into the audience. On the other hand, the court expressly reversed a finding of great risk when the victim was simply kidnaped in a parking lot.

The petitioner next argues that the requirements of *Furman* are not met here because the jury has the power to decline to impose the death penalty even if it finds that one or more statutory aggravating circumstances are present in the case. This contention misinterprets *Furman*. Moreover, it ignores the role of the Supreme Court of Georgia which reviews each death sentence to determine whether it is proportional to other sentences imposed for similar crimes. Since the proportionality requirement on review is intended to prevent caprice in the decision to inflict the penalty, the isolated decision of a jury to afford mercy does not render unconstitutional death sentences imposed on defendants who were sentenced under a system that does not create a substantial risk of arbitrariness or caprice.

The petitioner objects, finally, to the wide scope of evidence and argument allowed at presentence hearings. We think that the Georgia court wisely has chosen not to impose unnecessary restrictions on the evidence that can be offered at such a hearing and to approve open and far-ranging argument. So long as the evidence introduced and the arguments made at the presentence hearing do not prejudice a defendant, it is preferable not to impose restrictions. We think it desirable for the jury to have as much information before it as possible when it makes the sentencing decision.

Finally, the Georgia statute has an additional provision designed to assure that the death penalty will not be imposed on a capriciously selected group of convicted defendants. The new sentencing procedures require that the State Supreme Court review every death sentence to determine whether it was imposed under the influence of passion, prejudice, or any other arbitrary factor, whether the evidence supports the findings of a statutory aggravating circumstance, and "whether the sentence of death is excessive or disproportionate to the penalty imposed in similar cases, considering both the crime and the defendant." In performing its sentence-review function, the Georgia court has held that "if the death penalty is only rarely imposed for an act or it is substantially out of line with sentences imposed for other acts it will be set aside as excessive." The court on another occasion stated that "we view it to be our duty under the similarity standard to assure that no death sentence is affirmed unless in similar cases throughout the state the death penalty has been imposed generally...."

It is apparent that the Supreme Court of Georgia has taken its review responsibilities seriously. In *Coley*, it held that "the prior cases indicate that the past practice among juries faced with similar factual situations and like aggravating circumstances has been to impose only the sentence of life imprisonment for the offense of rape, rather than death." It thereupon reduced Coley's sentence from death to life imprisonment. Similarly, although armed robbery is a capital offense under Georgia law, the Georgia court concluded that the death sentences imposed in this case for that crime were "unusual in that they are rarely imposed for armed robbery. Thus, under the test provided by statute... they must be considered to be excessive or disproportionate to the penalties imposed in similar cases." The court therefore vacated Gregg's death sentences for armed robbery and has followed a similar course in every other armed robbery death penalty case to come before it.

The provision for appellate review in the Georgia capital-sentencing system serves as a check against the random or arbitrary imposition of the death penalty. In particular, the proportionality review substantially eliminates the possibility that a person will be sentenced to die by the action of an aberrant jury. If a time comes when juries generally do not impose the death sentence in a certain kind of murder case, the appellate review procedures assure that no defendant convicted under such circumstances will suffer a sentence of death.

V.

The basic concern of *Furman* centered on those defendants who were being condemned to death capriciously and arbitrarily. Under the procedures before the Court in that case, sentencing authorities were not directed to give attention to the nature or circumstances of the crime committed or to the character or record of the defendant. Left unguided, juries imposed the death sentence in a way that could only be called freakish. The new Georgia sentencing procedures, by contrast, focus the jury's attention on the particularized nature of the crime and the particularized characteristics of the individual defendant. While the jury is permitted to consider any aggravating or mitigating circumstances, it must find and identify at least one statutory aggravating factor before it may impose a penalty of death. In this way the jury's discretion is channeled. No longer can a jury wantonly and freakishly impose the death sentence; it is always circumscribed by the legislative guidelines. In addition, the review function of the Supreme Court of Georgia affords additional assurance that the concerns that prompted our decision in *Furman* are not present to any significant degree in the Georgia procedure applied here.

For the reasons expressed in this opinion, we hold that the statutory system under which Gregg was sentenced to death does not violate the Constitution. Accordingly, the judgment of the Georgia Supreme Court is affirmed.

It is so ordered.

McCleskey v. Kemp (1987)
481 U.S. 279

This case presents the question whether a complex statistical study that indicates a risk that racial considerations enter into capital sentencing determinations proves that petitioner McCleskey's capital sentence is unconstitutional under the Eighth or Fourteenth Amendment.

I.

McCleskey, a black man, was convicted of two counts of armed robbery and one count of murder in the Superior Court of Fulton County, Georgia, on October 12, 1978. McCleskey's convictions arose out of the robbery of a furniture store and the killing of a white police officer during the course of the robbery. The evidence at trial indicated that McCleskey and three accomplices planned and carried out the robbery. All four were armed. McCleskey entered the front of the store while the other three entered the rear. McCleskey secured the front of the store by rounding up the customers and forcing them to lie face down on the floor. The other three rounded up the employees in the rear and tied them up with tape. The manager was forced at gunpoint to turn over the store receipts, his watch, and $ 6. During the course of the robbery, a police officer, answering a silent alarm, entered the store through the front door. As he was walking down the center aisle of the store, two shots were fired. Both struck the officer. One hit him in the face and killed him.

Several weeks later, McCleskey was arrested in connection with an unrelated offense. He confessed that he had participated in the furniture store robbery, but denied that he had shot the police officer. At trial, the State introduced evidence that at least one of the bullets that struck the officer was fired from a .38 caliber Rossi revolver. This description matched the description of the gun that McCleskey had carried during the robbery. The State also introduced the testimony of two witnesses who had heard McCleskey admit to the shooting.

The jury convicted McCleskey of murder. At the penalty hearing, the jury heard arguments as to the appropriate sentence. Under Georgia law, the jury could not consider imposing the death penalty unless it found beyond a reasonable doubt that the murder was accompanied by one of the statutory aggravating circumstances. The jury in this case found two aggravating circumstances to exist beyond a reasonable doubt: the murder was committed during the course of an armed robbery, and the murder was committed upon a peace officer engaged in the performance of his duties. In making its decision whether to impose the death sentence, the jury considered the mitigating and aggravating circumstances of McCleskey's conduct. McCleskey offered no mitigating evidence. The jury recommended that he be sentenced to death on the murder charge and to consecutive life sentences on the armed robbery charges. The court followed the jury's recommendation and sentenced McCleskey to death.

On appeal, the Supreme Court of Georgia affirmed the convictions and the sentences. This Court denied a petition for a writ of certiorari. The Superior Court of Fulton County denied McCleskey's extraordinary motion for a new trial. McCleskey then filed a petition for a writ of habeas corpus in the Superior Court of Butts County. After holding an evidentiary hearing, the Superior Court denied relief. The Supreme Court of Georgia denied McCleskey's application for a certificate of probable cause to appeal the Superior Court's denial of his petition and this Court again denied certiorari.

McCleskey next filed a petition for a writ of habeas corpus in the Federal District Court for the Northern District of Georgia. His petition raised 18 claims, one of which was that the Georgia capital sentencing process is administered in a racially discriminatory manner in violation of the Eighth and Fourteenth Amendments to the United States Constitution. In support of his claim, McCleskey proffered a statistical study performed by Professors David C. Baldus, Charles Pulaski, and George Woodworth (the Baldus study) that purports to show a disparity in the imposition of the death sentence in Georgia based on the race of the murder victim and, to a lesser extent, the race of the defendant. The Baldus study is actually two sophisticated statistical studies that examine over 2,000 murder cases that occurred in Georgia during the 1970's. The raw numbers collected by Professor Baldus indicate that defendants charged with killing white persons received the death penalty in 11% of the cases, but defendants charged with killing blacks received the death penalty in only 1% of the cases. The raw numbers also indicate a reverse racial disparity according to the race of the defendant: 4% of the black defendants received the death penalty, as opposed to 7% of the white defendants.

Baldus also divided the cases according to the combination of the race of the defendant and the race of the victim. He found that the death penalty was assessed in 22% of the cases involving black defendants and white victims; 8% of the cases involving white defendants and white victims; 1% of the cases involving black defendants and black victims; and 3% of the cases involving white defendants and black victims. Similarly, Baldus found that prosecutors sought the death penalty in 70% of the cases involving black defendants and white victims; 32% of the cases involving white defendants and white victims; 15% of the cases involving black defendants and black victims; and 19% of the cases involving white defendants and black victims.

Baldus subjected his data to an extensive analysis, taking account of 230 variables that could have explained the disparities on nonracial grounds. One of his models concludes that, even after taking account of 39 nonracial variables, defendants charged with killing white victims were 4.3 times as likely to receive a death sentence as defendants charged with killing blacks. According to this model, black defendants were 1.1 times as likely to receive a death sentence as other defendants. Thus, the Baldus study indicates that black defendants, such as McCleskey, who kill white victims have the greatest likelihood of receiving the death penalty.

The District Court held an extensive evidentiary hearing on McCleskey's petition. Although it believed that McCleskey's Eighth Amendment claim was foreclosed by the Fifth Circuit's decision in *Spinkellink v. Wainwright*, it nevertheless considered the Baldus study with care. It concluded that McCleskey's "statistics do not demonstrate a *prima facie* case in support of the contention that the death penalty was imposed upon him because of his race, because of the race of the victim, or because of any Eighth Amendment concern. As to McCleskey's Fourteenth Amendment claim, the court found that the methodology of the Baldus study was flawed in several respects. Because of these defects, the court held that the Baldus study "failed to contribute anything of value" to McCleskey's claim. Accordingly, the court denied the petition insofar as it was based upon the Baldus study.

The Court of Appeals for the Eleventh Circuit, sitting en banc, carefully reviewed the District Court's decision on McCleskey's claim. It assumed the validity of the study itself and addressed the merits of McCleskey's Eighth and Fourteenth Amendment claims. That is, the court assumed that the study "showed that systematic and substantial disparities existed in the penalties imposed upon homicide defendants in Georgia based on race of the homicide victim, that the disparities existed at a less substantial rate in death sentencing based on race of defendants, and that the factors of race of the victim and defendant were at work in Fulton County." Even assuming the study's validity, the Court of Appeals found the statistics "insufficient to demonstrate discriminatory intent or unconstitutional discrimination in the Fourteenth Amendment context, and insufficient to show irrationality, arbitrariness and capriciousness under any kind of Eighth Amendment analysis." The court noted:

"The very exercise of discretion means that persons exercising discretion may reach different results from exact duplicates. Assuming each result is within the range of discretion, all are correct in the eyes of the law. It would not make sense for the system to require the exercise of discretion in order to be facially constitutional, and at the same time hold a system unconstitutional in application where that discretion achieved different results for what appear to be exact duplicates, absent the state showing the reasons for the difference. . . . The Baldus approach . . . would take the cases with different results on what are contended to be duplicate facts, where the differences could not be otherwise explained, and conclude that the different result was based on race alone. . . . This approach ignores the realities. . . . There are, in fact, no exact duplicates in capital crimes and capital defendants. The type of research submitted here tends to show which of the directed factors were effective, but is of restricted use in showing what undirected factors control the exercise of constitutionally required discretion."

The court concluded:

"Viewed broadly, it would seem that the statistical evidence presented here, assuming its validity, confirms rather than condemns the system . . . . The marginal disparity based on the race of the victim tends to support the state's contention that the system is working far differently from the one which *Furman* condemned. In pre-*Furman* days, there was no rhyme or reason as to who got the death penalty and who did not. But now, in the vast majority of cases, the reasons for a difference are well documented. That they are not so clear in a small percentage of the cases is no reason to declare the entire system unconstitutional."

The Court of Appeals affirmed the denial by the District Court of McCleskey's petition for a writ of habeas corpus insofar as the petition was based upon the Baldus study, with three judges dissenting as to McCleskey's claims based on the Baldus study. We granted certiorari and now affirm.

II.

McCleskey's first claim is that the Georgia capital punishment statute violates the Equal Protection Clause of the Fourteenth Amendment. He argues that race has infected the administration of Georgia's statute in two ways: persons who murder whites are more likely to be sentenced to death than persons who murder blacks, and black murderers are more likely to be sentenced to death than white murderers. As a black defendant who killed a white victim, McCleskey claims that the Baldus study demonstrates that he was discriminated against because of his race and because of the race of his victim. In its broadest form, McCleskey's claim of discrimination extends to every actor in the Georgia capital sentencing process, from the prosecutor who sought the death penalty and the jury that imposed the sentence, to the State itself that enacted the capital punishment statute and allows it to remain in effect despite its allegedly discriminatory application. We agree with the Court of Appeals, and every other court that has considered such a challenge, that this claim must fail.

A.

Our analysis begins with the basic principle that defendant who alleges an equal protection violation has the burden of proving "the existence of purposeful discrimination." A corollary to this principle is that a criminal defendant must prove that the purposeful discrimination "had a discriminatory effect" on him. Thus, to prevail under the Equal Protection Clause, McCleskey must prove that the decisionmakers in his case acted with discriminatory purpose. He offers no evidence specific to his own case that would support an inference that racial considerations played a part in his sentence. Instead, he relies solely on the Baldus study. McCleskey argues that the Baldus study compels an inference that his sentence rests on purposeful discrimination. McCleskey's claim that these statistics are sufficient proof of discrimination, without regard to the facts of a particular case, would extend to all capital cases in Georgia, at least where the victim was white and the defendant is black.

The Court has accepted statistics as proof of intent to discriminate in certain limited contexts. First, this Court has accepted statistical disparities as proof of an equal protection violation in the selection of the jury venire in a particular district. Although statistical proof normally must present a "stark" pattern to be accepted as the sole proof of discriminatory intent under the Constitution "because of the nature of the jury-selection task . . . we have permitted a finding of constitutional violation even when the statistical pattern does not approach such extremes." Second, this Court has accepted statistics in the form of multiple-regression analysis to prove statutory violations under Title VII of the Civil Rights Act of 1964.

But the nature of the capital sentencing decision, and the relationship of the statistics to that decision, are fundamentally different from the corresponding elements in the venire-selection or Title VII cases. Most importantly, each particular decision to impose the death penalty is made by a petit jury selected from a properly constituted venire. Each jury is unique in its composition, and the Constitution requires that its decision rest on consideration of innumerable factors that vary according to the characteristics of the individual defendant and the facts of the particular capital offense. Thus, the application of an inference drawn from the general statistics to a specific decision in a trial and sentencing simply is not comparable to the application of an inference drawn from general statistics to a specific venire-selection or Title VII case. In those cases, the statistics relate to fewer entities, and fewer variables are relevant to the challenged decisions.

Another important difference between the cases in which we have accepted statistics as proof of discriminatory intent and this case is that, in the venire-selection and Title VII contexts, the decisionmaker has an opportunity to explain the statistical disparity. Here, the State has no practical opportunity to rebut the Baldus study. "Controlling considerations of . . . public policy" dictate that jurors "cannot be called . . . to testify to the motives and influences that led to their verdict." Similarly, the policy considerations behind a prosecutor's traditionally "wide discretion" suggest the impropriety of our requiring prosecutors to defend their decisions to seek death penalties, "often years after they were made." Moreover, absent far stronger proof, it is unnecessary to seek such a rebuttal, because a legitimate and unchallenged explanation for the decision is apparent from the record: McCleskey committed an act for which the United States Constitution and Georgia laws permit imposition of the death penalty.

Although *Imbler* was decided in the context of damages actions under 42 U. S. C. § 1983 brought against prosecutors, the considerations that led the Court to hold that a prosecutor should not be required to explain his decisions apply in this case as well: "If the prosecutor could be made to answer in court each time . . . a person charged him with wrongdoing, his energy and attention would be diverted from the pressing duty of enforcing the criminal law." Our refusal to require that the prosecutor provide an explanation for his decisions in this case is completely consistent with this Court's longstanding precedents that hold that a prosecutor need not explain his decisions unless the criminal defendant presents a *prima facie* case of unconstitutional conduct with respect to his case.

Finally, McCleskey's statistical proffer must be viewed in the context of his challenge. McCleskey challenges decisions at the heart of the State's criminal justice system. "One of society's most basic tasks is that of protecting the lives of its citizens and one of the most basic ways in which it achieves the task is through criminal laws against murder." Implementation of these laws necessarily requires discretionary judgments. Because discretion is essential to the criminal justice process, we would demand exceptionally clear proof before we would infer that the discretion has been abused. The unique nature of the decisions at issue in this case also counsels against adopting such an inference from the disparities indicated by the Baldus study. Accordingly, we hold that the Baldus study is clearly insufficient to support an inference that any of the decisionmakers in McCleskey's case acted with discriminatory purpose.

B.

McCleskey also suggests that the Baldus study proves that the State as a whole has acted with a discriminatory purpose. He appears to argue that the State has violated the Equal Protection Clause by adopting the capital punishment statute and allowing it to remain in force despite its allegedly discriminatory application. But "'discriminatory purpose' . . . implies more than intent as volition or intent as awareness of consequences. It implies that the decisionmaker, in this case a state legislature, selected or reaffirmed a particular course of action at least in part 'because of,' not merely 'in spite of,' its adverse effects upon an identifiable group." For this claim to prevail, McCleskey would have to prove that the Georgia Legislature enacted or maintained the death penalty statute because of an anticipated racially discriminatory effect. In *Gregg v. Georgia*, this Court found that the Georgia capital sentencing system could operate in a fair and neutral manner. There was no evidence then, and there is none now, that the Georgia Legislature enacted the capital punishment statute to further a racially discriminatory purpose.

Nor has McCleskey demonstrated that the legislature maintains the capital punishment statute because of the racially disproportionate impact suggested by the Baldus study. As legislatures necessarily have wide discretion in the choice of criminal laws and penalties, and as there were legitimate reasons for the Georgia Legislature to adopt and maintain capital punishment, we will not infer a discriminatory purpose on the part of the State of Georgia. Accordingly, we reject McCleskey's equal protection claims.

III.

McCleskey also argues that the Baldus study demonstrates that the Georgia capital sentencing system violates the Eighth Amendment. We begin our analysis of this claim by reviewing the restrictions on death sentences established by our prior decisions under that Amendment.

A.

The Eighth Amendment prohibits infliction of "cruel and unusual punishments." This Court's early Eighth Amendment cases examined only the "particular methods of execution to determine whether they were too cruel to pass constitutional muster." Subsequently, the Court recognized that the constitutional prohibition against cruel and unusual punishments "is not fastened to the obsolete but may acquire meaning as public opinion becomes enlightened by a humane justice." In *Weems*, the Court identified a second principle inherent in the Eighth Amendment, "that punishment for crime should be graduated and proportioned to offense." Chief Justice Warren, writing for the plurality in *Trop v. Dulles*, acknowledged the constitutionality of capital punishment. In his view, the "basic concept underlying the Eighth Amendment" in this area is that the penalty must accord with "the dignity of man." In applying this mandate, we have been guided by his statement that "the Amendment must draw its meaning from the evolving standards of decency that mark the progress of a maturing society." Thus, our constitutional decisions have been informed by "contemporary values concerning the infliction of a challenged sanction." In assessing contemporary values, we have eschewed subjective judgment, and instead have sought to ascertain "objective indicia that reflect the public attitude toward a given sanction." First among these indicia are the decisions of state legislatures, "because the . . . legislative judgment weighs heavily in ascertaining" contemporary standards. We also have been guided by the sentencing decisions of juries, because they are "a significant and reliable objective index of contemporary values," Most of our recent decisions as to the constitutionality of the death penalty for a particular crime have rested on such an examination of contemporary values.

B.

Two principal decisions guide our resolution of McCleskey's Eighth Amendment claim. In *Furman v. Georgia*, the Court concluded that the death penalty was so irrationally imposed that any particular death sentence could be presumed excessive. Under the statutes at issue in *Furman*, there was no basis for determining in any particular case whether the penalty was proportionate to the crime: "The death penalty was exacted with great infrequency even for the most atrocious crimes and . . . there was no meaningful basis for distinguishing the few cases in which it was imposed from the many cases in which it was not."

In *Gregg*, the Court specifically addressed the question left open in *Furman*—whether the punishment of death for murder is "under all circumstances, 'cruel and unusual' in violation of the Eighth and Fourteenth Amendments of the Constitution." We noted that the imposition of the death penalty for the crime of murder "has a long history of acceptance both in the United States and in England." "The most marked indication of society's endorsement of the death penalty for murder was the legislative response to *Furman*." During the 4-year period between *Furman* and *Gregg*, at least 35 States had reenacted the death penalty, and Congress had authorized the penalty for aircraft piracy. The "actions of juries" were "fully compatible with the legislative judgments." We noted that any punishment might be unconstitutionally severe if inflicted without penological justification, but concluded:

"Considerations of federalism, as well as respect for the ability of a legislature to evaluate, in terms of its particular State, the moral consensus concerning the death penalty and its social utility as a sanction, require us to conclude, in the absence of more convincing evidence, that the infliction of death as a punishment for murder is not without justification and thus is not unconstitutionally severe."

The second question before the Court in *Gregg* was the constitutionality of the particular procedures embodied in the Georgia capital punishment statute. We explained the fundamental principle of *Furman*, that "where discretion is afforded a sentencing body on a matter so grave as the determination of whether a human life should be taken or spared, that discretion must be suitably directed and limited so as to minimize the risk of wholly arbitrary and capricious action." Numerous features of the then new Georgia statute met the concerns articulated in *Furman*. The Georgia system bifurcates guilt and sentencing proceedings so that the jury can receive all relevant information for sentencing without the risk that evidence irrelevant to the defendant's guilt will influence the jury's consideration of that issue. The statute narrows the class of murders subject to the death penalty to cases in which the jury finds at least one statutory aggravating circumstance beyond a reasonable doubt. Conversely, it allows the defendant to introduce any relevant mitigating evidence that might influence the jury not to impose a death sentence. The procedures also require a particularized inquiry into "'the circumstances of the offense together with the character and propensities of the offender.'" Thus, "while some jury discretion still exists, 'the discretion to be exercised is controlled by clear and objective standards so as to produce non-discriminatory application.'"

Moreover, the Georgia system adds "an important additional safeguard against arbitrariness and caprice" in a provision for automatic appeal of a death sentence to the State Supreme Court. The statute requires that court to review each sentence to determine whether it was imposed under the influence of passion or prejudice, whether the evidence supports the jury's finding of a statutory aggravating circumstance, and whether the sentence is disproportionate to sentences imposed in generally similar murder cases. To aid the court's review, the trial judge answers a questionnaire about the trial, including detailed questions as to "the quality of the defendant's representation and whether race played a role in the trial."

C.

In the cases decided after *Gregg*, the Court has imposed a number of requirements on the capital sentencing process to ensure that capital sentencing decisions rest on the individualized inquiry contemplated in *Gregg*. In *Woodson v. North Carolina*, we invalidated a mandatory capital sentencing system, finding that the "respect for humanity underlying the Eighth Amendment requires consideration of the character and record of the individual offender and the circumstances of the particular offense as a constitutionally indispensable part of the process of inflicting the penalty of death." Similarly, State must "narrow the class of murderers subject to capital punishment" by providing "specific and detailed guidance" to the sentencer.

In contrast to the carefully defined standards that must narrow a sentencer's discretion to impose the death sentence, the Constitution limits a State's ability to narrow a sentencer's discretion to consider relevant evidence that might cause it to decline to impose the death sentence. "The sentencer . . . [cannot] be precluded from considering, as a mitigating factor, any aspect of a defendant's character or record and any of the circumstances of the offense that the defendant proffers as a basis for a sentence less than death." Any exclusion of the "compassionate or mitigating factors stemming from the diverse frailties of humankind" that are relevant to the sentencer's decision would fail to treat all persons as "uniquely individual human beings."

Although our constitutional inquiry has centered on the procedures by which a death sentence is imposed, we have not stopped at the face of a statute, but have probed the application of statutes to particular cases. For example, in *Godfrey v. Georgia*, the Court invalidated a Georgia Supreme Court interpretation of the statutory aggravating circumstance that the murder be "outrageously or wantonly vile, horrible or inhuman in that it involved torture, depravity of mind, or an aggravated battery to the victim." Although that court had articulated an adequate limiting definition of this phrase, we concluded that its interpretation in *Godfrey* was so broad that it may have vitiated the role of the aggravating circumstance in guiding the sentencing jury's discretion.

Finally, where the objective indicia of community values have demonstrated a consensus that the death penalty is disproportionate as applied to a certain class of cases, we have established substantive limitations on its application. In *Coker v. Georgia*, the Court held that a State may not constitutionally sentence an individual to death for the rape of an adult woman. *In Enmund v. Florida*, the Court prohibited imposition of the death penalty on a defendant convicted of felony murder absent a showing that the defendant possessed a sufficiently culpable mental state. Most recently, in *Ford v. Wainwright*, we prohibited execution of prisoners who are insane.

D.

In sum, our decisions since *Furman* have identified constitutionally permissible range of discretion in imposing the death penalty. First, there is a required threshold below which the death penalty cannot be imposed. In this context, the State must establish rational criteria that narrow the decisionmaker's judgment as to whether the circumstances of a particular defendant's case meet the threshold. Moreover, a societal consensus that the death penalty is disproportionate to a particular offense prevents a State from imposing the death penalty for that offense. Second, States cannot limit the sentencer's consideration of any relevant circumstance that could cause it to decline to impose the penalty. In this respect, the State cannot channel the sentencer's discretion, but must allow it to consider any relevant information offered by the defendant.

IV. A.

In light of our precedents under the Eighth Amendment, McCleskey cannot argue successfully that his sentence is "disproportionate to the crime in the traditional sense." He does not deny that he committed a murder in the course of a planned robbery, a crime for which this Court has determined that the death penalty constitutionally may be imposed. His disproportionality claim "is of a different sort." McCleskey argues that the sentence in his case is disproportionate to the sentences in other murder cases.

On the one hand, he cannot base a constitutional claim on an argument that his case differs from other cases in which defendants did receive the death penalty. On automatic appeal, the Georgia Supreme Court found that McCleskey's death sentence was not disproportionate to other death sentences imposed in the State. The court supported this conclusion with an appendix containing citations to 13 cases involving generally similar murders. Moreover, where the statutory procedures adequately channel the sentencer's discretion, such proportionality review is not constitutionally required.

On the other hand, absent a showing that the Georgia capital punishment system operates in an arbitrary and capricious manner, McCleskey cannot prove a constitutional violation by demonstrating that other defendants who may be similarly situated did not receive the death penalty. In *Gregg*, the Court confronted the argument that "the opportunities for discretionary action that are inherent in the processing of any murder case under Georgia law," specifically the opportunities for discretionary leniency, rendered the capital sentences imposed arbitrary and capricious. We rejected this contention:

"The existence of these discretionary stages is not determinative of the issues before us. At each of these stages an actor in the criminal justice system makes a decision which may remove a defendant from consideration as a candidate for the death penalty. *Furman*, in contrast, dealt with the decision to impose the death sentence on a specific individual who had been convicted of a capital offense. Nothing in any of our cases suggests that the decision to afford an individual defendant mercy violates the Constitution. *Furman* held only that, in order to minimize the risk that the death penalty would be imposed on a capriciously selected group of offenders, the decision to impose it had to be guided by standards so that the sentencing authority would focus on the particularized circumstances of the crime and the defendant."

Because McCleskey's sentence was imposed under Georgia sentencing procedures that focus discretion "on the particularized nature of the crime and the particularized characteristics of the individual defendant," we lawfully may presume that McCleskey's death sentence was not "wantonly and freakishly" imposed, and thus that the sentence is not disproportionate within any recognized meaning under the Eighth Amendment.

B.

Although our decision in *Gregg* as to the facial validity of the Georgia capital punishment statute appears to foreclose McCleskey's disproportionality argument, he further contends that the Georgia capital punishment system is arbitrary and capricious in application, and therefore his sentence is excessive, because racial considerations may influence capital sentencing decisions in Georgia. We now address this claim.

To evaluate McCleskey's challenge, we must examine exactly what the Baldus study may show. Even Professor Baldus does not contend that his statistics prove that race enters into any capital sentencing decisions or that race was a factor in McCleskey's particular case. Statistics at most may show only a likelihood that a particular factor entered into some decisions. There is, of course, some risk of racial prejudice influencing a jury's decision in a criminal case. There are similar risks that other kinds of prejudice will influence other criminal trials. The question "is at what point that risk becomes constitutionally unacceptable," McCleskey asks us to accept the likelihood allegedly shown by the Baldus study as the constitutional measure of an unacceptable risk of racial prejudice influencing capital sentencing decisions. This we decline to do.

Because of the risk that the factor of race may enter the criminal justice process, we have engaged in "unceasing efforts" to eradicate racial prejudice from our criminal justice system. Our efforts have been guided by our recognition that "the inestimable privilege of trial by jury . . . is a vital principle, underlying the whole administration of criminal justice," Thus, it is the jury that is a criminal defendant's fundamental "protection of life and liberty against race or color prejudice." Specifically, a capital sentencing jury representative of a criminal defendant's community assures a "'diffused impartiality'" in the jury's task of "expressing the conscience of the community on the ultimate question of life or death."

Individual jurors bring to their deliberations "qualities of human nature and varieties of human experience, the range of which is unknown and perhaps unknowable." The capital sentencing decision requires the individual jurors to focus their collective judgment on the unique characteristics of a particular criminal defendant. It is not surprising that such collective judgments often are difficult to explain. But the inherent lack of predictability of jury decisions does not justify their condemnation. On the contrary, it is the jury's function to make the difficult and uniquely human judgments that defy codification and that "build discretion, equity, and flexibility into a legal system."

McCleskey's argument that the Constitution condemns the discretion allowed decisionmakers in the Georgia capital sentencing system is antithetical to the fundamental role of discretion in our criminal justice system. Discretion in the criminal justice system offers substantial benefits to the criminal defendant. Not only can a jury decline to impose the death sentence, it can decline to convict or choose to convict of a lesser offense. Whereas decisions against a defendant's interest may be reversed by the trial judge or on appeal, these discretionary exercises of leniency are final and unreviewable. Similarly, the capacity of prosecutorial discretion to provide individualized justice is "firmly entrenched in American law." As we have noted, a prosecutor can decline to charge, offer a plea bargain, or decline to seek a death sentence in any particular case. Of course, "the power to be lenient also is the power to discriminate," but a capital punishment system that did not allow for discretionary acts of leniency "would be totally alien to our notions of criminal justice."

C.

At most, the Baldus study indicates a discrepancy that appears to correlate with race. Apparent disparities in sentencing are an inevitable part of our criminal justice system. The discrepancy indicated by the Baldus study is "a far cry from the major systemic defects identified in *Furman*," As this Court has recognized, any mode for determining guilt or punishment "has its weaknesses and the potential for misuse." Specifically, "there can be 'no perfect procedure for deciding in which cases governmental authority should be used to impose death.'" Despite these imperfections, our consistent rule has been that constitutional guarantees are met when "the mode for determining guilt or punishment itself has been surrounded with safeguards to make it as fair as possible." Where the discretion that is fundamental to our criminal process is involved, we decline to assume that what is unexplained is invidious. In light of the safeguards designed to minimize racial bias in the process, the fundamental value of jury trial in our criminal justice system, and the benefits that discretion provides to criminal defendants, we hold that the Baldus study does not demonstrate a constitutionally significant risk of racial bias affecting the Georgia capital sentencing process.

Two additional concerns inform our decision in this case. First, McCleskey's claim, taken to its logical conclusion, throws into serious question the principles that underlie our entire criminal justice system. The Eighth Amendment is not limited in application to capital punishment, but applies to all penalties. Thus, if we accepted McCleskey's claim that racial bias has impermissibly tainted the capital sentencing decision, we could soon be faced with similar claims as to other types of penalty. Moreover, the claim that his sentence rests on the irrelevant factor of race easily could be extended to apply to claims based on unexplained discrepancies that correlate to membership in other minority groups, and even to gender. Similarly, since McCleskey's claim relates to the race of his victim, other claims could apply with equally logical force to statistical disparities that correlate with the race or sex of other actors in the criminal justice system, such as defense attorneys or judges. Also, there is no logical reason that such a claim need be limited to racial or sexual bias. If arbitrary and capricious punishment is the touchstone under the Eighth Amendment, such a claim could—at least in theory—be based upon any arbitrary variable, such as the defendant's facial characteristics, or the physical attractiveness of the defendant or the victim, that some statistical study indicates may be influential in jury decisionmaking. As these examples illustrate, there is no limiting principle to the type of challenge brought by McCleskey. The Constitution does not require that a State eliminate any demonstrable disparity that correlates with a potentially irrelevant factor in order to operate a criminal justice system that includes capital punishment. As we have stated specifically in the context of capital punishment, the Constitution does not "place totally unrealistic conditions on its use."

Second, McCleskey's arguments are best presented to the legislative bodies. It is not the responsibility—or indeed even the right—of this Court to determine the appropriate punishment for particular crimes. It is the legislatures, the elected representatives of the people, that are "constituted to respond to the will and consequently the moral values of the people." Legislatures also are better qualified to weigh and "evaluate the results of statistical studies in terms of their own local conditions and with a flexibility of approach that is not available to the courts," Capital punishment is now the law in more than two-thirds of our States. It is the ultimate duty of courts to determine on a case-by-case basis whether these laws are applied consistently with the Constitution. Despite McCleskey's wide-ranging arguments that basically challenge the validity of capital punishment in our multiracial society, the only question before us is whether in his case, the law of Georgia was properly applied. We agree with the District Court and the Court of Appeals for the Eleventh Circuit that this was carefully and correctly done in this case.

VI.

Accordingly, we affirm the judgment of the Court of Appeals for the Eleventh Circuit.

It is so ordered.

Atkins v. Virginia (2002)
536 U.S. 304

In this case, the Supreme Court examined whether or not the death penalty applied to an intellectually challenged person violates the Eighth Amendment ban on Cruel and Unusual Punishment. The Court ruled that it did, but allowed states broad discretion in determining who would be considered intellectually challenged.

Those mentally retarded persons who meet the law's requirements for criminal responsibility should be tried and punished when they commit crimes. Because of their disabilities in areas of reasoning, judgment, and control of their impulses, however, they do not act with the level of moral culpability that characterizes the most serious adult criminal conduct. Moreover, their impairments can jeopardize the reliability and fairness of capital proceedings against mentally retarded defendants. Presumably for these reasons, in the 13 years since we decided *Penry v. Lynaugh* the American public, legislators, scholars, and judges have deliberated over the question whether the death penalty should ever be imposed on a mentally retarded criminal. The consensus reflected in those deliberations informs our answer to the question presented by this case: whether such executions are "cruel and unusual punishments" prohibited by the Eighth Amendment to the Federal Constitution.

I.

Petitioner, Daryl Renard Atkins, was convicted of abduction, armed robbery, and capital murder, and sentenced to death. At approximately midnight on August 16, 1996, Atkins and William Jones, armed with a semiautomatic handgun, abducted Eric Nesbitt, robbed him of the money on his person, drove him to an automated teller machine in his pickup truck where cameras recorded their withdrawal of additional cash, then took him to an isolated location where he was shot eight times and killed.

Jones and Atkins both testified in the guilt phase of Atkins' trial. Each confirmed most of the details in the other's account of the incident, with the important exception that each stated that the other had actually shot and killed Nesbitt. Jones' testimony, which was both more coherent and credible than Atkins', was obviously credited by the jury and was sufficient to establish Atkins' guilt. At the penalty phase of the trial, the State introduced victim impact evidence and proved two aggravating circumstances: future dangerousness and "vileness of the offense." To prove future dangerousness, the State relied on Atkins' prior felony convictions as well as the testimony of four victims of earlier robberies and assaults. To prove the second aggravator, the prosecution relied upon the trial record, including pictures of the deceased's body and the autopsy report.

In the penalty phase, the defense relied on one witness, Dr. Evan Nelson, a forensic psychologist who had evaluated Atkins before trial and concluded that he was "mildly mentally retarded." His conclusion was based on interviews with people who knew Atkins, a review of school and court records, and the administration of a standard intelligence test which indicated that Atkins had a full scale IQ of 59.5.

The jury sentenced Atkins to death, but the Virginia Supreme Court ordered a second sentencing hearing because the trial court had used a misleading verdict form. At the resentencing, Dr. Nelson again testified. The State presented an expert rebuttal witness, Dr. Stanton Samenow, who expressed the opinion that Atkins was not mentally retarded, but rather was of "average intelligence, at least," and diagnosable as having antisocial personality disorder. The jury again sentenced Atkins to death.

The Supreme Court of Virginia affirmed the imposition of the death penalty. Atkins did not argue before the Virginia Supreme Court that his sentence was disproportionate to penalties imposed for similar crimes in Virginia, but he did contend "that he is mentally retarded and thus cannot be sentenced to death." The majority of the state court rejected this contention, relying on our holding in *Penry*. The Court was "not willing to commute Atkins' sentence of death to life imprisonment merely because of his IQ score."

Justice Hassell and Justice Koontz dissented. They rejected Dr. Samenow's opinion that Atkins possesses average intelligence as "incredulous as a matter of law," and concluded that "the imposition of the sentence of death upon a criminal defendant who has the mental age of a child between the ages of 9 and 12 is excessive." In their opinion, "it is indefensible to conclude that individuals who are mentally retarded are not to some degree less culpable for their criminal acts. By definition, such individuals have substantial limitations not shared by the general population. A moral and civilized society diminishes itself if its system of justice does not afford recognition and consideration of those limitations in a meaningful way." Because of the gravity of the concerns expressed by the dissenters, and in light of the dramatic shift in the state legislative landscape that has occurred in the past 13 years, we granted certiorari to revisit the issue that we first addressed in the *Penry* case.

II.

The Eighth Amendment succinctly prohibits "excessive" sanctions. It provides: "Excessive bail shall not be required, nor excessive fines imposed, nor cruel and unusual punishments inflicted." In *Weems v. United States*, we held that a punishment of 12 years jailed in irons at hard and painful labor for the crime of falsifying records was excessive. We explained "that it is a precept of justice that punishment for crime should be graduated and proportioned to the offense." We have repeatedly applied this proportionality precept in later cases interpreting the Eighth Amendment. Thus, even though "imprisonment for ninety days is not, in the abstract, a punishment which is either cruel or unusual," it may not be imposed as a penalty for "the 'status' of narcotic addiction" because such a sanction would be excessive. As Justice Stewart explained in *Robinson*: "Even one day in prison would be a cruel and unusual punishment for the 'crime' of having a common cold."

A claim that punishment is excessive is judged not by the standards that prevailed in 1685 when Lord Jeffreys presided over the "Bloody Assizes" or when the Bill of Rights was adopted, but rather by those that currently prevail. As Chief Justice Warren explained in his opinion in *Trop v. Dulles*, "The basic concept underlying the Eighth Amendment is nothing less than the dignity of man. . . . The Amendment must draw its meaning from the evolving standards of decency that mark the progress of a maturing society."

Proportionality review under those evolving standards should be informed by "'objective factors to the maximum possible extent.'" We have pinpointed that the "clearest and most reliable objective evidence of contemporary values is the legislation enacted by the country's legislatures." Relying in part on such legislative evidence, we have held that death is an impermissibly excessive punishment for the rape of an adult woman, or for a defendant who neither took life, attempted to take life, nor intended to take life. In *Coker*, we focused primarily on the then-recent legislation that had been enacted in response to our decision 10 years earlier in *Furman v. Georgia* to support the conclusion that the "current judgment," though "not wholly unanimous," weighed very heavily on the side of rejecting capital punishment as a "suitable penalty for raping an adult woman." The "current legislative judgment" relevant to our decision in *Enmund* was less clear than in *Coker* but "nevertheless weighed on the side of rejecting capital punishment for the crime at issue."

We also acknowledged in *Coker* that the objective evidence, though of great importance, did not "wholly determine" the controversy, "for the Constitution contemplates that in the end our own judgment will be brought to bear on the question of the acceptability of the death penalty under the Eighth Amendment." For example, in *Enmund*, we concluded by expressing our own judgment about the issue:

"For purposes of imposing the death penalty, Enmund's criminal culpability must be limited to his participation in the robbery, and his punishment must be tailored to his personal responsibility and moral guilt. Putting Enmund to death to avenge two killings that he did not commit and had no intention of committing or causing does not measurably contribute to the retributive end of ensuring that the criminal gets his just deserts. This is the judgment of most of the legislatures that have recently addressed the matter, and we have no reason to disagree with that judgment for purposes of construing and applying the Eighth Amendment."

Thus, in cases involving a consensus, our own judgment is "brought to bear" by asking whether there is reason to disagree with the judgment reached by the citizenry and its legislators.

Guided by our approach in these cases, we shall first review the judgment of legislatures that have addressed the suitability of imposing the death penalty on the mentally retarded and then consider reasons for agreeing or disagreeing with their judgment.

III.

The parties have not called our attention to any state legislative consideration of the suitability of imposing the death penalty on mentally retarded offenders prior to 1986. In that year, the public reaction to the execution of a mentally retarded murderer in Georgia apparently led to the enactment of the first state statute prohibiting such executions. In 1988, when Congress enacted legislation reinstating the federal death penalty, it expressly provided that a "sentence of death shall not be carried out upon a person who is mentally retarded." In 1989, Maryland enacted a similar prohibition. It was in that year that we decided *Penry*, and concluded that those two state enactments, "even when added to the 14 States that have rejected capital punishment completely, do not provide sufficient evidence at present of a national consensus."

Much has changed since then. Responding to the national attention received by the Bowden execution and our decision in *Penry*, state legislatures across the country began to address the issue. In 1990 Kentucky and Tennessee enacted statutes similar to those in Georgia and Maryland, as did New Mexico in 1991, and Arkansas, Colorado, Washington, Indiana, and Kansas in 1993 and 1994. In 1995, when New York reinstated its death penalty, it emulated the Federal Government by expressly exempting the mentally retarded. Nebraska followed suit in 1998. There appear to have been no similar enactments during the next two years, but in 2000 and 2001 six more States— South Dakota, Arizona, Connecticut, Florida, Missouri, and North Carolina—joined the procession. The Texas Legislature unanimously adopted a similar bill, and bills have passed at least one house in other States, including Virginia and Nevada.

It is not so much the number of these States that is significant, but the consistency of the direction of change. Given the well-known fact that anticrime legislation is far more popular than legislation providing protections for persons guilty of violent crime, the large number of States prohibiting the execution of mentally retarded persons (and the complete absence of States passing legislation reinstating the power to conduct such executions) provides powerful evidence that today our society views mentally retarded offenders as categorically less culpable than the average criminal. The evidence carries even greater force when it is noted that the legislatures that have addressed the issue have voted overwhelmingly in favor of the prohibition. Moreover, even in those States that allow the execution of mentally retarded offenders, the practice is uncommon. Some States, for example New Hampshire and New Jersey, continue to authorize executions, but none have been carried out in decades. Thus there is little need to pursue legislation barring the execution of the mentally retarded in those States. And it appears that even among those States that regularly execute offenders and that have no prohibition with regard to the mentally retarded, only five have executed offenders possessing a known IQ less than 70 since we decided *Penry*. The practice, therefore, has become truly unusual, and it is fair to say that a national consensus has developed against it.

To the extent there is serious disagreement about the execution of mentally retarded offenders, it is in determining which offenders are in fact retarded. In this case, for instance, the Commonwealth of Virginia disputes that Atkins suffers from mental retardation. Not all people who claim to be mentally retarded will be so impaired as to fall within the range of mentally retarded offenders about whom there is a national consensus. As was our approach in *Ford v. Wainwright*, with regard to insanity, "we leave to the States the task of developing appropriate ways to enforce the constitutional restriction upon its execution of sentences."

IV.

This consensus unquestionably reflects widespread judgment about the relative culpability of mentally retarded offenders, and the relationship between mental retardation and the penological purposes served by the death penalty. Additionally, it suggests that some characteristics of mental retardation undermine the strength of the procedural protections that our capital jurisprudence steadfastly guards.

As discussed above, clinical definitions of mental retardation require not only subaverage intellectual functioning, but also significant limitations in adaptive skills such as communication, self-care, and self-direction that became manifest before age 18. Mentally retarded persons frequently know the difference between right and wrong and are competent to stand trial. Because of their impairments, however, by definition they have diminished capacities to understand and process information, to communicate, to abstract from mistakes and learn from experience, to engage in logical reasoning, to control impulses, and to understand the reactions of others. There is no evidence that they are more likely to engage in criminal conduct than others, but there is abundant evidence that they often act on impulse rather than pursuant to a premeditated plan, and that in group settings they are followers rather than leaders. Their deficiencies do not warrant an exemption from criminal sanctions, but they do diminish their personal culpability.

In light of these deficiencies, our death penalty jurisprudence provides two reasons consistent with the legislative consensus that the mentally retarded should be categorically excluded from execution. First, there is a serious question as to whether either justification that we have recognized as a basis for the death penalty applies to mentally retarded offenders. *Gregg v. Georgia* identified "retribution and deterrence of capital crimes by prospective offenders" as the social purposes served by the death penalty. Unless the imposition of the death penalty on a mentally retarded person "measurably contributes to one or both of these goals, it 'is nothing more than the purposeless and needless imposition of pain and suffering,' and hence an unconstitutional punishment."

With respect to retribution—the interest in seeing that the offender gets his "just deserts"—the severity of the appropriate punishment necessarily depends on the culpability of the offender. Since *Gregg*, our jurisprudence has consistently confined the imposition of the death penalty to a narrow category of the most serious crimes. For example, in *Godfrey v. Georgia*, we set aside a death sentence because the petitioner's crimes did not reflect "a consciousness materially more 'depraved' than that of any person guilty of murder." If the culpability of the average murderer is insufficient to justify the most extreme sanction available to the State, the lesser culpability of the mentally retarded offender surely does not merit that form of retribution. Thus, pursuant to our narrowing jurisprudence, which seeks to ensure that only the most deserving of execution are put to death, an exclusion for the mentally retarded is appropriate.

With respect to deterrence—the interest in preventing capital crimes by prospective offenders—"it seems likely that 'capital punishment can serve as a deterrent only when murder is the result of premeditation and deliberation,'" Exempting the mentally retarded from that punishment will not affect the "cold calculus that precedes the decision" of other potential murderers. Indeed, that sort of calculus is at the opposite end of the spectrum from behavior of mentally retarded offenders. The theory of deterrence in capital sentencing is predicated upon the notion that the increased severity of the punishment will inhibit criminal actors from carrying out murderous conduct. Yet it is the same cognitive and behavioral impairments that make these defendants less morally culpable—for example, the diminished ability to understand and process information, to learn from experience, to engage in logical reasoning, or to control impulses—that also make it less likely that they can process the information of the possibility of execution as a penalty and, as a result, control their conduct based upon that information. Nor will exempting the mentally retarded from execution lessen the deterrent effect of the death penalty with respect to offenders who are not mentally retarded. Such individuals are unprotected by the exemption and will continue to face the threat of execution. Thus, executing the mentally retarded will not measurably further the goal of deterrence.

The reduced capacity of mentally retarded offenders provides a second justification for a categorical rule making such offenders ineligible for the death penalty. The risk "that the death penalty will be imposed in spite of factors which may call for a less severe penalty" is enhanced, not only by the possibility of false confessions, but also by the lesser ability of mentally retarded defendants to make a persuasive showing of mitigation in the face of prosecutorial evidence of one or more aggravating factors..... As *Penry* demonstrated, moreover, reliance on mental retardation as a mitigating factor can be a two-edged sword that may enhance the likelihood that the aggravating factor of future dangerousness will be found by the jury. Mentally retarded defendants in the aggregate face a special risk of wrongful execution.

Our independent evaluation of the issue reveals no reason to disagree with the judgment of "the legislatures that have recently addressed the matter" and concluded that death is not a suitable punishment for a mentally retarded criminal. We are not persuaded that the execution of mentally retarded criminals will measurably advance the deterrent or the retributive purpose of the death penalty. Construing and applying the Eighth Amendment in the light of our "evolving standards of decency," we therefore conclude that such punishment is excessive and that the Constitution "places a substantive restriction on the State's power to take the life" of a mentally retarded offender.

The judgment of the Virginia Supreme Court is reversed and the case is remanded for further proceedings not inconsistent with this opinion.

It is so ordered.

Blakely v. Washington (2004)
542 U.S. 296

In this case, the court examined whether a sentencing scheme that allowed judges to enhance criminal penalties based on their own finding of facts (independent of a jury) was a violation of the defendant's Sixth Amendment right to a trial by jury.

Petitioner Ralph Howard Blakely, Jr., pleaded guilty to the kidnaping of his estranged wife. The facts admitted in his plea, standing alone, supported a maximum sentence of 53 months. Pursuant to state law, the court imposed an "exceptional" sentence of 90 months after making a judicial determination that he had acted with "deliberate cruelty." We consider whether this violated petitioner's Sixth Amendment right to trial by jury.

I.

Petitioner married his wife Yolanda in 1973. He was evidently a difficult man to live with, having been diagnosed at various times with psychological and personality disorders including paranoid schizophrenia. His wife ultimately filed for divorce. In 1998, he abducted her from their orchard home in Grant County, Washington, binding her with duct tape and forcing her at knifepoint into a wooden box in the bed of his pickup truck. In the process, he implored her to dismiss the divorce suit and related trust proceedings.

When the couple's 13-year-old son Ralphy returned home from school, petitioner ordered him to follow in another car, threatening to harm Yolanda with a shotgun if he did not do so. Ralphy escaped and sought help when they stopped at a gas station, but petitioner continued on with Yolanda to a friend's house in Montana. He was finally arrested after the friend called the police.

The State charged petitioner with first-degree kidnaping. Upon reaching a plea agreement, however, it reduced the charge to second-degree kidnaping involving domestic violence and use of a firearm. Petitioner entered a guilty plea admitting the elements of second-degree kidnaping and the domestic-violence and firearm allegations, but no other relevant facts.

The case then proceeded to sentencing. In Washington, second-degree kidnaping is a class B felony. State law provides that "no person convicted of a class B felony shall be punished by confinement . . . exceeding . . . a term of ten years." Other provisions of state law, however, further limit the range of sentences a judge may impose. Washington's Sentencing Reform Act specifies, for petitioner's offense of second-degree kidnaping with a firearm, a "standard range" of 49 to 53 months. A judge may impose a sentence above the standard range if he finds "substantial and compelling reasons justifying an exceptional sentence." The Act lists aggravating factors that justify such a departure, which it recites to be illustrative rather than exhaustive. Nevertheless, "a reason offered to justify an exceptional sentence can be considered only if it takes into account factors other than those which are used in computing the standard range sentence for the offense." When a judge imposes an exceptional sentence, he must set forth findings of fact and conclusions of law supporting it. A reviewing court will reverse the sentence if it finds that "under a clearly erroneous standard there is insufficient evidence in the record to support the reasons for imposing an exceptional sentence."

Pursuant to the plea agreement, the State recommended a sentence within the standard range of 49 to 53 months. After hearing Yolanda's description of the kidnaping, however, the judge rejected the State's recommendation and imposed an exceptional sentence of 90 months—37 months beyond the standard maximum. He justified the sentence on the ground that petitioner had acted with "deliberate cruelty," a statutorily enumerated ground for departure in domestic-violence cases.

Faced with an unexpected increase of more than three years in his sentence, petitioner objected. The judge accordingly conducted a 3-day bench hearing featuring testimony from petitioner, Yolanda, Ralphy, a police officer, and medical experts. After the hearing, he issued findings of fact, concluding:

"The defendant's motivation to commit kidnapping was complex, contributed to by his mental condition and personality disorders, the pressures of the divorce litigation, the impending trust litigation trial and anger over his troubled interpersonal relationships with his spouse and children. While he misguidedly intended to forcefully reunite his family, his attempt to do so was subservient to his desire to terminate lawsuits and modify title ownerships to his benefit.

"The defendant's methods were more homogeneous than his motive. He used stealth and surprise, and took advantage of the victim's isolation. He immediately employed physical violence, restrained the victim with tape, and threatened her with injury and death to herself and others. He immediately coerced the victim into providing information by the threatening application of a knife. He violated a subsisting restraining order."

The judge adhered to his initial determination of deliberate cruelty. Petitioner appealed, arguing that this sentencing procedure deprived him of his federal constitutional right to have a jury determine beyond a reasonable doubt all facts legally essential to his sentence. The State Court of Appeals affirmed, relying on the Washington Supreme Court's rejection of a similar challenge in *Gore*. The Washington Supreme Court denied discretionary review. We granted certiorari.

II.

This case requires us to apply the rule we expressed in *Apprendi v. New Jersey*: "Other than the fact of a prior conviction, any fact that increases the penalty for a crime beyond the prescribed statutory maximum must be submitted to a jury, and proved beyond a reasonable doubt." This rule reflects two longstanding tenets of common-law criminal jurisprudence: that the "truth of every accusation" against a defendant "should afterwards be confirmed by the unanimous suffrage of twelve of his equals and neighbours," and that "an accusation which lacks any particular fact which the law makes essential to the punishment is . . . no accusation within the requirements of the common law, and it is no accusation in reason," These principles have been acknowledged by courts and treatises since the earliest days of graduated sentencing; we compiled the relevant authorities in *Apprendi*, and need not repeat them here.

Apprendi involved a New Jersey hate-crime statute that authorized a 20-year sentence, despite the usual 10-year maximum, if the judge found the crime to have been committed "'with a purpose to intimidate . . . because of race, color, gender, handicap, religion, sexual orientation or ethnicity.'" In *Ring v. Arizona*, we applied *Apprendi* to an Arizona law that authorized the death penalty if the judge found 1 of 10 aggravating factors. In each case, we concluded that the defendant's constitutional rights had been violated because the judge had imposed a sentence greater than the maximum he could have imposed under state law without the challenged factual finding.

In this case, petitioner was sentenced to more than three years above the 53-month statutory maximum of the standard range because he had acted with "deliberate cruelty." The facts supporting that finding were neither admitted by petitioner nor found by a jury. The State nevertheless contends that there was no *Apprendi* violation because the relevant "statutory maximum" is not 53 months, but the 10-year maximum for class B felonies in § 9A.20.021(1)(b). It observes that no exceptional sentence may exceed that limit. Our precedents make clear, however, that the "statutory maximum" for *Apprendi* purposes is the maximum sentence a judge may impose solely on the basis of the facts reflected in the jury verdict or admitted by the defendant. In other words, the relevant "statutory maximum" is not the maximum sentence a judge may impose after finding additional facts, but the maximum he may impose without any additional findings. When a judge inflicts punishment that the jury's verdict alone does not allow, the jury has not found all the facts "which the law makes essential to the punishment," and the judge exceeds his proper authority.

The judge in this case could not have imposed the exceptional 90-month sentence solely on the basis of the facts admitted in the guilty plea. Those facts alone were insufficient because, as the Washington Supreme Court has explained, "a reason offered to justify an exceptional sentence can be considered only if it takes into account factors other than those which are used in computing the standard range sentence for the offense," which in this case included the elements of second-degree kidnaping and the use of a firearm. Had the judge imposed the 90-month sentence solely on the basis of the plea, he would have been reversed. The "maximum sentence" is no more 10 years here than it was 20 years in *Apprendi* (because that is what the judge could have imposed upon finding a hate crime) or death in *Ring* (because that is what the judge could have imposed upon finding an aggravator).

The State defends the sentence by drawing an analogy to those we upheld in *McMillan v. Pennsylvania* and *Williams v. New York*. Neither case is on point. *McMillan* involved a sentencing scheme that imposed a statutory minimum if a judge found a particular fact. We specifically noted that the statute "does not authorize a sentence in excess of that otherwise allowed for the underlying offense." *Williams* involved an indeterminate-sentencing regime that allowed a judge (but did not compel him) to rely on facts outside the trial record in determining whether to sentence a defendant to death. The judge could have "sentenced the defendant to death giving no reason at all." Thus, neither case involved a sentence greater than what state law authorized on the basis of the verdict alone.

Finally, the State tries to distinguish *Apprendi* and *Ring* by pointing out that the enumerated grounds for departure in its regime are illustrative rather than exhaustive. This distinction is immaterial. Whether the judge's authority to impose an enhanced sentence depends on finding a specified fact (as in *Apprendi*), one of several specified facts (as in *Ring*), or any aggravating fact (as here), it remains the case that the jury's verdict alone does not authorize the sentence. The judge acquires that authority only upon finding some additional fact.

Because the State's sentencing procedure did not comply with the Sixth Amendment, petitioner's sentence is invalid.

III.

Our commitment to *Apprendi* in this context reflects not just respect for longstanding precedent, but the need to give intelligible content to the right of jury trial. That right is no mere procedural formality, but a fundamental reservation of power in our constitutional structure. Just as suffrage ensures the people's ultimate control in the legislative and executive branches, jury trial is meant to ensure their control in the judiciary....

Those who would reject *Apprendi* are resigned to one of two alternatives. The first is that the jury need only find whatever facts the legislature chooses to label elements of the crime, and that those it labels sentencing factors—no matter how much they may increase the punishment—may be found by the judge. This would mean, for example, that a judge could sentence a man for committing murder even if the jury convicted him only of illegally possessing the firearm used to commit it—or of making an illegal lane change while fleeing the death scene. Not even *Apprendi's* critics would advocate this absurd result. The jury could not function as circuitbreaker in the State's machinery of justice if it were relegated to making a determination that the defendant at some point did something wrong, a mere preliminary to a judicial inquisition into the facts of the crime the State actually seeks to punish.

The second alternative is that legislatures may establish legally essential sentencing factors within limits—limits crossed when, perhaps, the sentencing factor is a "tail which wags the dog of the substantive offense." What this means in operation is that the law must not go too far—it must not exceed the judicial estimation of the proper role of the judge.

The subjectivity of this standard is obvious. Petitioner argued below that second-degree kidnaping with deliberate cruelty was essentially the same as first-degree kidnaping, the very charge he had avoided by pleading to a lesser offense. The court conceded this might be so but held it irrelevant. Petitioner's 90-month sentence exceeded the 53-month standard maximum by almost 70%; the Washington Supreme Court in other cases has upheld exceptional sentences 15 times the standard maximum. Did the court go too far in any of these cases? There is no answer that legal analysis can provide. With too far as the yardstick, it is always possible to disagree with such judgments and never to refute them.

Whether the Sixth Amendment incorporates this manipulable standard rather than *Apprendi's* bright-line rule depends on the plausibility of the claim that the Framers would have left definition of the scope of jury power up to judges' intuitive sense of how far is too far. We think that claim not plausible at all, because the very reason the Framers put a jury-trial guarantee in the Constitution is that they were unwilling to trust government to mark out the role of the jury.

IV.

By reversing the judgment below, we are not, as the State would have it, "finding determinate sentencing schemes unconstitutional." This case is not about whether determinate sentencing is constitutional, only about how it can be implemented in a way that respects the Sixth Amendment. Several policies prompted Washington's adoption of determinate sentencing, including proportionality to the gravity of the offense and parity among defendants. Nothing we have said impugns those salutary objectives.

Justice O'Connor argues that, because determinate sentencing schemes involving judicial factfinding entail less judicial discretion than indeterminate schemes, the constitutionality of the latter implies the constitutionality of the former. This argument is flawed on a number of levels. First, the Sixth Amendment by its terms is not a limitation on judicial power, but a reservation of jury power. It limits judicial power only to the extent that the claimed judicial power infringes on the province of the jury. Indeterminate sentencing does not do so. It increases judicial discretion, to be sure, but not at the expense of the jury's traditional function of finding the facts essential to lawful imposition of the penalty. Of course indeterminate schemes involve judicial factfinding, in that a judge (like a parole board) may implicitly rule on those facts he deems important to the exercise of his sentencing discretion. But the facts do not pertain to whether the defendant has a legal right to a lesser sentence—and that makes all the difference insofar as judicial impingement upon the traditional role of the jury is concerned. In a system that says the judge may punish burglary with 10 to 40 years, every burglar knows he is risking 40 years in jail. In a system that punishes burglary with a 10-year sentence, with another 30 added for use of a gun, the burglar who enters a home unarmed is entitled to no more than a 10-year sentence—and by reason of the Sixth Amendment the facts bearing upon that entitlement must be found by a jury.

But even assuming that restraint of judicial power unrelated to the jury's role is a Sixth Amendment objective, it is far from clear that *Apprendi* disserves that goal. Determinate judicial-factfinding schemes entail less judicial power than indeterminate schemes, but more judicial power than determinate jury-factfinding schemes. Whether *Apprendi* increases judicial power overall depends on what States with determinate judicial-factfinding schemes would do, given the choice between the two alternatives. Justice O'Connor simply assumes that the net effect will favor judges, but she has no empirical basis for that prediction. Indeed, what evidence we have points exactly the other way: When the Kansas Supreme Court found *Apprendi* infirmities in that State's determinate-sentencing regime in *State v. Gould*, the legislature responded not by reestablishing indeterminate sentencing but by applying *Apprendi's* requirements to its current regime. The result was less, not more, judicial power.

Justice Breyer argues that *Apprendi* works to the detriment of criminal defendants who plead guilty by depriving them of the opportunity to argue sentencing factors to a judge. But nothing prevents a defendant from waiving his *Apprendi* rights. When a defendant pleads guilty, the State is free to seek judicial sentence enhancements so long as the defendant either stipulates to the relevant facts or consents to judicial factfinding. If appropriate waivers are procured, States may continue to offer judicial factfinding as a matter of course to all defendants who plead guilty. Even a defendant who stands trial may consent to judicial factfinding as to sentence enhancements, which may well be in his interest if relevant evidence would prejudice him at trial. We do not understand how *Apprendi* can possibly work to the detriment of those who are free, if they think its costs outweigh its benefits, to render it inapplicable.

Nor do we see any merit to Justice Breyer's contention that *Apprendi* is unfair to criminal defendants because, if States respond by enacting "17-element robbery crimes," prosecutors will have more elements with which to bargain. Bargaining already exists with regard to sentencing factors because defendants can either stipulate or contest the facts that make them applicable. If there is any difference between bargaining over sentencing factors and bargaining over elements, the latter probably favors the defendant. Every new element that a prosecutor can threaten to charge is also an element that a defendant can threaten to contest at trial and make the prosecutor prove beyond a reasonable doubt. Moreover, given the sprawling scope of most criminal codes, and the power to affect sentences by making (even nonbinding) sentencing recommendations, there is already no shortage of *in terrorem* tools at prosecutors' disposal.

Any evaluation of *Apprendi's* "fairness" to criminal defendants must compare it with the regime it replaced, in which a defendant, with no warning in either his indictment or plea, would routinely see his maximum potential sentence balloon from as little as five years to as much as life imprisonment, based not on facts proved to his peers beyond a reasonable doubt, but on facts extracted after trial from a report compiled by a probation officer who the judge thinks more likely got it right than got it wrong. We can conceive of no measure of fairness that would find more fault in the utterly speculative bargaining effects Justice Breyer identifies than in the regime he champions. Suffice it to say that, if such a measure exists, it is not the one the Framers left us with.

The implausibility of Justice Breyer's contention that *Apprendi* is unfair to criminal defendants is exposed by the lineup of *amici* in this case. It is hard to believe that the National Association of Criminal Defense Lawyers was somehow duped into arguing for the wrong side. Justice Breyer's only authority asking that defendants be protected from *Apprendi* is an article written not by a criminal defense lawyer but by a law professor and former prosecutor. Justice Breyer also claims that *Apprendi* will attenuate the connection between "real criminal conduct and real punishment" by encouraging plea bargaining and by restricting alternatives to adversarial factfinding. The short answer to the former point is that the Sixth Amendment was not written for the benefit of those who choose to forgo its protection. It guarantees the right to jury trial. It does not guarantee that a particular number of jury trials will actually take place. That more defendants elect to waive that right (because, for example, government at the moment is not particularly oppressive) does not prove that a constitutional provision guaranteeing availability of that option is disserved.

Justice Breyer's more general argument—that *Apprendi* undermines alternatives to adversarial factfinding—is not so much a criticism of *Apprendi* as an assault on jury trial generally. His esteem for "non-adversarial" truth-seeking processes supports just as well an argument against either. Our Constitution and the common-law traditions it entrenches, however, do not admit the contention that facts are better discovered by judicial inquisition than by adversarial testing before a jury. Justice Breyer may be convinced of the equity of the regime he favors, but his views are not the ones we are bound to uphold.

Ultimately, our decision cannot turn on whether or to what degree trial by jury impairs the efficiency or fairness of criminal justice. One can certainly argue that both these values would be better served by leaving justice entirely in the hands of professionals; many nations of the world, particularly those following civil-law traditions, take just that course. There is not one shred of doubt, however, about the Framers' paradigm for criminal justice: not the civil-law ideal of administrative perfection, but the common-law ideal of limited state power accomplished by strict division of authority between judge and jury. As *Apprendi* held, every defendant has the right to insist that the prosecutor prove to a jury all facts legally essential to the punishment. Under the dissenters' alternative, he has no such right. That should be the end of the matter.

Petitioner was sentenced to prison for more than three years beyond what the law allowed for the crime to which he confessed, on the basis of a disputed finding that he had acted with "deliberate cruelty." The Framers would not have thought it too much to demand that, before depriving a man of three more years of his liberty, the State should suffer the modest inconvenience of submitting its accusation to "the unanimous suffrage of twelve of his equals and neighbours," rather than a lone employee of the State.

The judgment of the Washington Court of Appeals is reversed, and the case is remanded for further proceedings not inconsistent with this opinion.

It is so ordered.

District Attorney's Office v. Osborne (2009)
557 U.S. 52

In this case, the court considered the thorny legal issue of the retesting of DNA evidence used in a state criminal conviction. The appellant used the novel approach of a 1983 suit rather than the more traditional method of relief offered by habeas corpus. The Court acknowledged the usefulness of DNA evidence for both identifying the guilty and exonerating the innocent, but declined to create a general Constitutional right to access such evidence. The logic used by the court in reaching this decision was that there were adequate state remedies for the problem, and thus there was no need to "constitutionalize the issue" in federal courts.

DNA testing has an unparalleled ability both to exonerate the wrongly convicted and to identify the guilty. It has the potential to significantly improve both the criminal justice system and police investigative practices. The Federal Government and the States have recognized this, and have developed special approaches to ensure that this evidentiary tool can be effectively incorporated into established criminal procedure—usually but not always through legislation.

Against this prompt and considered response, the respondent, William Osborne, proposes a different approach: the recognition of a freestanding and far-reaching constitutional right of access to this new type of evidence. The nature of what he seeks is confirmed by his decision to file this lawsuit in federal court under 42 U.S.C. § 1983, not within the state criminal justice system. This approach would take the development of rules and procedures in this area out of the hands of legislatures and state courts shaping policy in a focused manner and turn it over to federal courts applying the broad parameters of the Due Process Clause. There is no reason to constitutionalize the issue in this way. Because the decision below would do just that, we reverse.

I. A.

This lawsuit arose out of a violent crime committed 16 years ago, which has resulted in a long string of litigation in the state and federal courts. On the evening of March 22, 1993, two men driving through Anchorage, Alaska, solicited sex from a female prostitute, K. G. She agreed to perform fellatio on both men for $100 and got in their car. The three spent some time looking for a place to stop and ended up in a deserted area near Earthquake Park. When K. G. demanded payment in advance, the two men pulled out a gun and forced her to perform fellatio on the driver while the passenger penetrated her vaginally, using a blue condom she had brought. The passenger then ordered K. G. out of the car and told her to lie face-down in the snow. Fearing for her life, she refused, and the two men choked her and beat her with the gun. When K. G. tried to flee, the passenger beat her with a wooden axe handle and shot her in the head while she lay on the ground. They kicked some snow on top of her and left her for dead.

K. G. did not die; the bullet had only grazed her head. Once the two men left, she found her way back to the road, and flagged down a passing car to take her home. Ultimately, she received medical care and spoke to the police. At the scene of the crime, the police recovered a spent shell casing, the axe handle, some of K. G.'s clothing stained with blood, and the blue condom.

Six days later, two military police officers at Fort Richardson pulled over Dexter Jackson for flashing his headlights at another vehicle. In his car they discovered a gun (which matched the shell casing), as well as several items K. G. had been carrying the night of the attack. The car also matched the description K. G. had given to the police. Jackson admitted that he had been the driver during the rape and assault, and told the police that William Osborne had been his passenger. Other evidence also implicated Osborne. K. G. picked out his photograph (with some uncertainty) and at trial she identified Osborne as her attacker. Other witnesses testified that shortly before the crime, Osborne had called Jackson from an arcade, and then driven off with him. An axe handle similar to the one at the scene of the crime was found in Osborne's room on the military base where he lived.

The State also performed DQ Alpha testing on sperm found in the blue condom. DQ Alpha testing is a relatively inexact form of DNA testing that can clear some wrongly accused individuals, but generally cannot narrow the perpetrator down to less than 5% of the population. The semen found on the condom had a genotype that matched a blood sample taken from Osborne, but not ones from Jackson, K. G., or a third suspect named James Hunter. Osborne is black, and approximately 16% of black individuals have such a genotype. In other words, the testing ruled out Jackson and Hunter as possible sources of the semen, and also ruled out over 80% of other black individuals. The State also examined some pubic hairs found at the scene of the crime, which were not susceptible to DQ Alpha testing, but which state witnesses attested to be similar to Osborne's.

B.

Osborne and Jackson were convicted by an Alaska jury of kidnaping, assault, and sexual assault. They were acquitted of an additional count of sexual assault and of attempted murder. Finding it "'nearly miraculous'" that K. G. had survived, the trial judge sentenced Osborne to 26 years in prison, with 5 suspended. His conviction and sentence were affirmed on appeal.

Osborne then sought postconviction relief in Alaska state court. He claimed that he had asked his attorney, Sidney Billingslea, to seek more discriminating restriction-fragment-length-polymorphism (RFLP) DNA testing during trial, and argued that she was constitutionally ineffective for not doing so. Billingslea testified that after investigation, she had concluded that further testing would do more harm than good. She planned to mount a defense of mistaken identity, and thought that the imprecision of the DQ Alpha test gave her "'very good numbers in a mistaken identity, cross-racial identification case, where the victim was in the dark and had bad eyesight.'" Because she believed Osborne was guilty, "'insisting on a more advanced . . . DNA test would have served to prove that Osborne committed the alleged crimes.'" The Alaska Court of Appeals concluded that Billingslea's decision had been strategic and rejected Osborne's claim.

In this proceeding, Osborne also sought the DNA testing that Billingslea had failed to perform, relying on an Alaska postconviction statute, Alaska Stat. § 12.72 (2008), and the State and Federal Constitutions. In two decisions, the Alaska Court of Appeals concluded that Osborne had no right to the RFLP test. According to the court, § 12.72 "apparently" did not apply to DNA testing that had been available at trial. The court found no basis in our precedents for recognizing a federal constitutional right to DNA evidence. After a remand for further findings, the Alaska Court of Appeals concluded that Osborne could not claim a state constitutional right either, because the other evidence of his guilt was too strong and RFLP testing was not likely to be conclusive. Two of the three judges wrote separately to say that "if Osborne could show that he were in fact innocent, it would be unconscionable to punish him," and that doing so might violate the Alaska Constitution.

The court relied heavily on the fact that Osborne had confessed to some of his crimes in a 2004 application for parole—in which it is a crime to lie. In this statement, Osborne acknowledged forcing K. G. to have sex at gunpoint, as well as beating her and covering her with snow. He repeated this confession before the parole board. Despite this acceptance of responsibility, the board did not grant him discretionary parole. In 2007, he was released on mandatory parole, but he has since been rearrested for another offense, and the State has petitioned to revoke this parole.

Meanwhile, Osborne had also been active in federal court, suing state officials under 42 U.S.C. § 1983. He claimed that the Due Process Clause and other constitutional provisions gave him a constitutional right to access the DNA evidence for what is known as short-tandem-repeat (STR) testing (at his own expense). This form of testing is more discriminating than the DQ Alpha or RFLP methods available at the time of Osborne's trial.

The District Court first dismissed the claim under *Heck v. Humphrey* (1994), holding it "inescapable" that Osborne sought to "set the stage" for an attack on his conviction, and therefore "must proceed through a writ of habeas corpus." The United States Court of Appeals for the Ninth Circuit reversed, concluding that § 1983 was the proper vehicle for Osborne's claims, while "expressing no opinion as to whether Osborne had been deprived of a federally protected right."

On cross-motions for summary judgment after remand, the District Court concluded that "there does exist, under the unique and specific facts presented, a very limited constitutional right to the testing sought." The court relied on several factors: that the testing Osborne sought had been unavailable at trial, that the testing could be accomplished at almost no cost to the State, and that the results were likely to be material. It therefore granted summary judgment in favor of Osborne.

The Court of Appeals affirmed, relying on the prosecutorial duty to disclose exculpatory evidence recognized in *Pennsylvania v. Ritchie* (1987) and *Brady v. Maryland* (1963). While acknowledging that our precedents "involved only the right to pre-trial disclosure," the court concluded that the Due Process Clause also "extends the government's duty to disclose (or the defendant's right of access) to post-conviction proceedings." Although Osborne's trial and appeals were over, the court noted that he had a "potentially viable" state constitutional claim of "actual innocence," and relied on the "well-established assumption" that a similar claim arose under the Federal Constitution. The court held that these potential claims extended some of the State's *Brady* obligations to the postconviction context.

The court declined to decide the details of what showing must be made to access the evidence because it found "Osborne's case for disclosure . . . so strong on the facts" that "wherever the bar is, he crosses it." While acknowledging that Osborne's prior confessions were "certainly relevant," the court concluded that they did not "necessarily trump . . . the right to obtain post-conviction access to evidence" in light of the "emerging reality of wrongful convictions based on false confessions."

We granted certiorari to decide whether Osborne's claims could be pursued using § 1983, and whether he has a right under the Due Process Clause to obtain postconviction access to the State's evidence for DNA testing. We now reverse on the latter ground.

II.

Modern DNA testing can provide powerful new evidence unlike anything known before. Since its first use in criminal investigations in the mid-1980s, there have been several major advances in DNA technology, culminating in STR technology. It is now often possible to determine whether a biological tissue matches a suspect with near certainty. While of course many criminal trials proceed without any forensic and scientific testing at all, there is no technology comparable to DNA testing for matching tissues when such evidence is at issue. DNA testing has exonerated wrongly convicted people, and has confirmed the convictions of many others.

At the same time, DNA testing alone does not always resolve a case. Where there is enough other incriminating evidence and an explanation for the DNA result, science alone cannot prove a prisoner innocent. The availability of technologies not available at trial cannot mean that every criminal conviction, or even every criminal conviction involving biological evidence, is suddenly in doubt. The dilemma is how to harness DNA's power to prove innocence without unnecessarily overthrowing the established system of criminal justice.

That task belongs primarily to the legislature. "The States are currently engaged in serious, thoughtful examinations," of how to ensure the fair and effective use of this testing within the existing criminal justice framework. Forty-six States have already enacted statutes dealing specifically with access to DNA evidence. The Federal Government has also passed the Innocence Protection Act of 2004, which allows federal prisoners to move for court-ordered DNA testing under certain specified conditions. That Act also grants money to States that enact comparable statutes, and as a consequence has served as a model for some state legislation. At oral argument, Osborne agreed that the federal statute is a model for how States ought to handle the issue.

These laws recognize the value of DNA evidence but also the need for certain conditions on access to the State's evidence. A requirement of demonstrating materiality is common.... The federal statute, for example, requires a sworn statement that the applicant is innocent. This requirement is replicated in several state statutes. States also impose a range of diligence requirements. Several require the requested testing to "have been technologically impossible at trial." Others deny testing to those who declined testing at trial for tactical reasons.

Alaska is one of a handful of States yet to enact legislation specifically addressing the issue of evidence requested for DNA testing. But that does not mean that such evidence is unavailable for those seeking to prove their innocence. Instead, Alaska courts are addressing how to apply existing laws for discovery and postconviction relief to this novel technology. The same is true with respect to other States that do not have DNA-specific statutes.

First, access to evidence is available under Alaska law for those who seek to subject it to newly available DNA testing that will prove them to be actually innocent. Under the State's general postconviction relief statute, a prisoner may challenge his conviction when "there exists evidence of material facts, not previously presented and heard by the court, that requires vacation of the conviction or sentence in the interest of justice." Such a claim is exempt from otherwise applicable time limits if "newly discovered evidence," pursued with due diligence, "establishes by clear and convincing evidence that the applicant is innocent."

Both parties agree that under these provisions of "a defendant is entitled to post-conviction relief if the defendant presents newly discovered evidence that establishes by clear and convincing evidence that the defendant is innocent." If such a claim is brought, state law permits general discovery. Alaska courts have explained that these procedures are available to request DNA evidence for newly available testing to establish actual innocence.

In addition to this statutory procedure, the Alaska Court of Appeals has invoked a widely accepted three-part test to govern additional rights to DNA access under the State Constitution. Drawing on the experience with DNA evidence of State Supreme Courts around the country, the Court of Appeals explained that it was "reluctant to hold that Alaska law offers no remedy to defendants who could prove their factual innocence." It was "prepared to hold, however, that a defendant who seeks postconviction DNA testing . . . must show (1) that the conviction rested primarily on eyewitness identification evidence, (2) that there was a demonstrable doubt concerning the defendant's identification as the perpetrator, and (3) that scientific testing would likely be conclusive on this issue." Thus, the Alaska courts have suggested that even those who do not get discovery under the State's criminal rules have available to them a safety valve under the State Constitution.

This is the background against which the Federal Court of Appeals ordered the State to turn over the DNA evidence in its possession, and it is our starting point in analyzing Osborne's constitutional claims.

III.

The parties dispute whether Osborne has invoked the proper federal statute in bringing his claim. He sued under the federal civil rights statute, 42 U.S.C. § 1983, which gives a cause of action to those who challenge a State's "deprivation of any rights . . . secured by the Constitution." The State insists that Osborne's claim must be brought under 28 U.S.C. § 2254, which allows a prisoner to seek "a writ of habeas corpus . . . on the ground that he is in custody in violation of the Constitution."

While Osborne's claim falls within the literal terms of § 1983, we have also recognized that § 1983 must be read in harmony with the habeas statute. "Stripped to its essence," the State says, "Osborne's § 1983 action is nothing more than a request for evidence to support a hypothetical claim that he is actually innocent. . . . This hypothetical claim sounds at the core of habeas corpus."

Osborne responds that his claim does not sound in habeas at all. Although invalidating his conviction is of course his ultimate goal, giving him the evidence he seeks "would not necessarily imply the invalidity of his confinement." If he prevails, he would receive only access to the DNA, and even if DNA testing exonerates him, his conviction is not automatically invalidated. He must bring an entirely separate suit or a petition for clemency to invalidate his conviction. If he were proved innocent, the State might also release him on its own initiative, avoiding any need to pursue habeas at all.

Osborne also invokes our recent decision in *Wilkinson v. Dotson* (2005). There, we held that prisoners who sought new hearings for parole eligibility and suitability need not proceed in habeas. We acknowledged that the two plaintiffs "hoped" their suits would "help bring about earlier release," but concluded that the § 1983 suit would not accomplish that without further proceedings. "Because neither prisoner's claim would necessarily spell speedier release, neither lay at the core of habeas corpus." Every Court of Appeals to consider the question since *Dotson* has decided that because access to DNA evidence similarly does not "necessarily spell speedier release," it can be sought under § 1983. On the other hand, the State argues that *Dotson* is distinguishable because the challenged procedures in that case did not affect the ultimate "exercise of discretion by the parole board." It also maintains that *Dotson* does not set forth "the exclusive test for whether a prisoner may proceed under § 1983."

While we granted certiorari on this question, our resolution of Osborne's claims does not require us to resolve this difficult issue. Accordingly, we will assume without deciding that the Court of Appeals was correct that *Heck* does not bar Osborne's § 1983 claim. Even under this assumption, it was wrong to find a due process violation.

IV. A.

"No State shall . . . deprive any person of life, liberty, or property, without due process of law." This Clause imposes procedural limitations on a State's power to take away protected entitlements. Osborne argues that access to the State's evidence is a "process" needed to vindicate his right to prove himself innocent and get out of jail. Process is not an end in itself, so a necessary premise of this argument is that he has an entitlement (what our precedents call a "liberty interest") to prove his innocence even after a fair trial has proved otherwise. We must first examine this asserted liberty interest to determine what process (if any) is due.

In identifying his potential liberty interest, Osborne first attempts to rely on the Governor's constitutional authority to "grant pardons, commutations, and reprieves." That claim can be readily disposed of. We have held that noncapital defendants do not have a liberty interest in traditional state executive clemency, to which no particular claimant is entitled as a matter of state law. Osborne therefore cannot challenge the constitutionality of any procedures available to vindicate an interest in state clemency.

Osborne does, however, have a liberty interest in demonstrating his innocence with new evidence under state law. As explained, Alaska law provides that those who use "newly discovered evidence" to "establish by clear and convincing evidence that they are innocent" may obtain "vacation of their conviction or sentence in the interest of justice." This "state-created right can, in some circumstances, beget yet other rights to procedures essential to the realization of the parent right."

The Court of Appeals went too far, however, in concluding that the Due Process Clause requires that certain familiar preconviction trial rights be extended to protect Osborne's postconviction liberty interest. After identifying Osborne's possible liberty interests, the court concluded that the State had an obligation to comply with the principles of *Brady v. Maryland*. In that case, we held that due process requires a prosecutor to disclose material exculpatory evidence to the defendant before trial. The Court of Appeals acknowledged that nothing in our precedents suggested that this disclosure obligation continued after the defendant was convicted and the case was closed, but it relied on prior Ninth Circuit precedent applying "Brady as a post-conviction right." Osborne does not claim that *Brady* controls this case, and with good reason.

A criminal defendant proved guilty after a fair trial does not have the same liberty interests as a free man. At trial, the defendant is presumed innocent and may demand that the government prove its case beyond reasonable doubt. But "once a defendant has been afforded a fair trial and convicted of the offense for which he was charged, the presumption of innocence disappears." "Given a valid conviction, the criminal defendant has been constitutionally deprived of his liberty."

The State accordingly has more flexibility in deciding what procedures are needed in the context of postconviction relief. "When a State chooses to offer help to those seeking relief from convictions," due process does not "dictate the exact form such assistance must assume." Osborne's right to due process is not parallel to a trial right, but rather must be analyzed in light of the fact that he has already been found guilty at a fair trial, and has only a limited interest in postconviction relief. *Brady* is the wrong framework.

Instead, the question is whether consideration of Osborne's claim within the framework of the State's procedures for postconviction relief "offends some principle of justice so rooted in the traditions and conscience of our people as to be ranked as fundamental," or "transgresses any recognized principle of fundamental fairness in operation." Federal courts may upset a State's postconviction relief procedures only if they are fundamentally inadequate to vindicate the substantive rights provided.

We see nothing inadequate about the procedures Alaska has provided to vindicate its state right to postconviction relief in general, and nothing inadequate about how those procedures apply to those who seek access to DNA evidence. Alaska provides a substantive right to be released on a sufficiently compelling showing of new evidence that establishes innocence. It exempts such claims from otherwise applicable time limits. The State provides for discovery in postconviction proceedings, and has—through judicial decision—specified that this discovery procedure is available to those seeking access to DNA evidence. These procedures are not without limits. The evidence must indeed be newly available to qualify under Alaska's statute, must have been diligently pursued, and must also be sufficiently material. These procedures are similar to those provided for DNA evidence by federal law and the law of other States, and they are not inconsistent with the "traditions and conscience of our people" or with "any recognized principle of fundamental fairness."

And there is more. While the Alaska courts have not had occasion to conclusively decide the question, the Alaska Court of Appeals has suggested that the State Constitution provides an additional right of access to DNA. In expressing its "reluctance to hold that Alaska law offers no remedy" to those who belatedly seek DNA testing, and in invoking the three-part test used by other state courts, the court indicated that in an appropriate case the State Constitution may provide a failsafe even for those who cannot satisfy the statutory requirements under general postconviction procedures.

To the degree there is some uncertainty in the details of Alaska's newly developing procedures for obtaining postconviction access to DNA, we can hardly fault the State for that. Osborne has brought this § 1983 action without ever using these procedures in filing a state or federal habeas claim relying on actual innocence. In other words, he has not tried to use the process provided to him by the State or attempted to vindicate the liberty interest that is now the centerpiece of his claim. When Osborne did request DNA testing in state court, he sought RFLP testing that had been available at trial, not the STR testing he now seeks, and the state court relied on that fact in denying him testing under Alaska law.

His attempt to sidestep state process through a new federal lawsuit puts Osborne in a very awkward position. If he simply seeks the DNA through the State's discovery procedures, he might well get it. If he does not, it may be for a perfectly adequate reason, just as the federal statute and all state statutes impose conditions and limits on access to DNA evidence. It is difficult to criticize the State's procedures when Osborne has not invoked them. This is not to say that Osborne must exhaust state-law remedies. But it is Osborne's burden to demonstrate the inadequacy of the state-law procedures available to him in state postconviction relief. These procedures are adequate on their face, and without trying them, Osborne can hardly complain that they do not work in practice.

As a fallback, Osborne also obliquely relies on an asserted federal constitutional right to be released upon proof of "actual innocence." Whether such a federal right exists is an open question. We have struggled with it over the years, in some cases assuming, *arguendo*, that it exists while also noting the difficult questions such a right would pose and the high standard any claimant would have to meet. In this case too we can assume without deciding that such a claim exists, because even if so there is no due process problem. Osborne does not dispute that a federal actual innocence claim (as opposed to a DNA access claim) would be brought in habeas. If such a habeas claim is viable, federal procedural rules permit discovery "for good cause." Just as with state law, Osborne cannot show that available discovery is facially inadequate, and cannot show that it would be arbitrarily denied to him.

B.

The Court of Appeals below relied only on procedural due process, but Osborne seeks to defend the judgment on the basis of substantive due process as well. He asks that we recognize a freestanding right to DNA evidence untethered from the liberty interests he hopes to vindicate with it. We reject the invitation and conclude, in the circumstances of this case, that there is no such substantive due process right. "As a general matter, the Court has always been reluctant to expand the concept of substantive due process because guideposts for responsible decisionmaking in this unchartered area are scarce and open-ended." Osborne seeks access to state evidence so that he can apply new DNA-testing technology that might prove him innocent. There is no long history of such a right, and "the mere novelty of such a claim is reason enough to doubt that 'substantive due process' sustains it."

And there are further reasons to doubt. The elected governments of the States are actively confronting the challenges DNA technology poses to our criminal justice systems and our traditional notions of finality, as well as the opportunities it affords. To suddenly constitutionalize this area would short-circuit what looks to be a prompt and considered legislative response. The first DNA testing statutes were passed in 1994 and 1997. In the past decade, 44 States and the Federal Government have followed suit, reflecting the increased availability of DNA testing. As noted, Alaska itself is considering such legislation. "By extending constitutional protection to an asserted right or liberty interest, we, to a great extent, place the matter outside the arena of public debate and legislative action. We must therefore exercise the utmost care whenever we are asked to break new ground in this field." "Judicial imposition of a categorical remedy . . . might pretermit other responsible solutions being considered in Congress and state legislatures." If we extended substantive due process to this area, we would cast these statutes into constitutional doubt and be forced to take over the issue of DNA access ourselves. We are reluctant to enlist the Federal Judiciary in creating a new constitutional code of rules….

Establishing a freestanding right to access DNA evidence for testing would force us to act as policymakers, and our substantive-due-process rulemaking authority would not only have to cover the right of access but a myriad of other issues. We would soon have to decide if there is a constitutional obligation to preserve forensic evidence that might later be tested. If so, for how long? Would it be different for different types of evidence? Would the State also have some obligation to gather such evidence in the first place? How much, and when? No doubt there would be a miscellany of other minor directives.

In this case, the evidence has already been gathered and preserved, but if we extend substantive due process to this area, these questions would be before us in short order, and it is hard to imagine what tools federal courts would use to answer them. At the end of the day, there is no reason to suppose that their answers to these questions would be any better than those of state courts and legislatures, and good reason to suspect the opposite.

DNA evidence will undoubtedly lead to changes in the criminal justice system. It has done so already. The question is whether further change will primarily be made by legislative revision and judicial interpretation of the existing system, or whether the Federal Judiciary must leap ahead—revising (or even discarding) the system by creating a new constitutional right and taking over responsibility for refining it.

Federal courts should not presume that state criminal procedures will be inadequate to deal with technological change. The criminal justice system has historically accommodated new types of evidence, and is a time-tested means of carrying out society's interest in convicting the guilty while respecting individual rights. That system, like any human endeavor, cannot be perfect. DNA evidence shows that it has not been. But there is no basis for Osborne's approach of assuming that because DNA has shown that these procedures are not flawless, DNA evidence must be treated as categorically outside the process, rather than within it. That is precisely what his § 1983 suit seeks to do, and that is the contention we reject.

The judgment of the Court of Appeals is reversed, and the case is remanded for further proceedings consistent with this opinion.

It is so ordered.

Part IV: Corrections

Hudson v. Palmer (1984)
468 U.S. 517

We granted certiorari in No. 82-1630 to decide whether a prison inmate has a reasonable expectation of privacy in his prison cell entitling him to the protection of the Fourth Amendment against unreasonable searches and seizures. We also granted certiorari in No. 82-6695, the cross-petition, to determine whether our decision in *Parratt v. Taylor* (1981), which held that a negligent deprivation of property by state officials does not violate the Fourteenth Amendment if an adequate postdeprivation state remedy exists, should extend to intentional deprivations of property.

I.

The facts underlying this dispute are relatively simple. Respondent Palmer is an inmate at the Bland Correctional Center in Bland, Va., serving sentences for forgery, uttering, grand larceny, and bank robbery convictions. On September 16, 1981, petitioner Hudson, an officer at the Correctional Center, with a fellow officer, conducted a "shakedown" search of respondent's prison locker and cell for contraband. During the "shakedown," the officers discovered a ripped pillowcase in a trash can near respondent's cell bunk. Charges against Palmer were instituted under the prison disciplinary procedures for destroying state property. After a hearing, Palmer was found guilty on the charge and was ordered to reimburse the State for the cost of the material destroyed; in addition, a reprimand was entered on his prison record.

Palmer subsequently brought this pro se action in United States District Court under 42 U. S. C. § 1983. Respondent claimed that Hudson had conducted the shakedown search of his cell and had brought a false charge against him solely to harass him, and that, in violation of his Fourteenth Amendment right not to be deprived of property without due process of law, Hudson had intentionally destroyed certain of his noncontraband personal property during the September 16 search. Hudson denied each allegation; he moved for and was granted summary judgment. The District Court accepted respondent's allegations as true but held nonetheless, relying on *Parratt v. Taylor,* that the alleged destruction of respondent's property, even if intentional, did not violate the Fourteenth Amendment because there were state tort remedies available to redress the deprivation, and that the alleged harassment did not "rise to the level of a constitutional deprivation."

The Court of Appeals affirmed in part, reversed in part, and remanded for further proceedings. The court affirmed the District Court's holding that respondent was not deprived of his property without due process. The court acknowledged that we considered only a claim of negligent property deprivation in *Parratt v. Taylor*. It agreed with the District Court, however, that the logic of *Parratt* applies equally to unauthorized intentional deprivations of property by state officials: "Once it is assumed that a postdeprivation remedy can cure an unintentional but negligent act causing injury, inflicted by a state agent which is unamendable to prior review, then that principle applies as well to random and unauthorized intentional acts." The Court of Appeals did not discuss the availability and adequacy of existing state-law remedies; it presumably accepted as correct the District Court's statement of the remedies available under Virginia law.

The Court of Appeals reversed the summary judgment on respondent's claim that the shakedown search was unreasonable. The court recognized that *Bell v. Wolfish* (1979) authorized irregular unannounced shakedown searches of prison cells. But the court held that an individual prisoner has a "limited privacy right" in his cell entitling him to protection against searches conducted solely to harass or to humiliate. The shakedown of a single prisoner's property, said the court, is permissible only if "done pursuant to an established program of conducting random searches of single cells or groups of cells reasonably designed to deter or discover the possession of contraband" or upon reasonable belief that the particular prisoner possessed contraband. Because the Court of Appeals concluded that the record reflected a factual dispute over whether the search of respondent's cell was routine or conducted to harass respondent, it held that summary judgment was inappropriate, and that a remand was necessary to determine the purpose of the cell search.

We granted certiorari. We affirm in part and reverse in part.

II. A.

The first question we address is whether respondent has a right of privacy in his prison cell entitling him to the protection of the Fourth Amendment against unreasonable searches. As we have noted, the Court of Appeals held that the District Court's summary judgment in petitioner's favor was premature because respondent had a "limited privacy right" in his cell that might have been breached. The court concluded that, to protect this privacy right, shakedown searches of an individual's cell should be performed only "pursuant to an established program of conducting random searches . . . reasonably designed to deter or discover

211

the possession of contraband" or upon reasonable belief that the prisoner possesses contraband. Petitioner contends that the Court of Appeals erred in holding that respondent had even a limited privacy right in his cell, and urges that we adopt the "bright line" rule that prisoners have no legitimate expectation of privacy in their individual cells that would entitle them to Fourth Amendment protection.

We have repeatedly held that prisons are not beyond the reach of the Constitution. No "iron curtain" separates one from the other. Indeed, we have insisted that prisoners be accorded those rights not fundamentally inconsistent with imprisonment itself or incompatible with the objectives of incarceration. For example, we have held that invidious racial discrimination is as intolerable within a prison as outside, except as may be essential to "prison security and discipline." Like others, prisoners have the constitutional right to petition the Government for redress of their grievances, which includes a reasonable right of access to the courts.

Prisoners must be provided "reasonable opportunities" to exercise their religious freedom guaranteed under the First Amendment. Similarly, they retain those First Amendment rights of speech "not inconsistent with their status as . . . prisoners or with the legitimate penological objectives of the corrections system." They enjoy the protection of due process. And the Eighth Amendment ensures that they will not be subject to "cruel and unusual punishments." The continuing guarantee of these substantial rights to prison inmates is testimony to a belief that the way a society treats those who have transgressed against it is evidence of the essential character of that society.

However, while persons imprisoned for crime enjoy many protections of the Constitution, it is also clear that imprisonment carries with it the circumscription or loss of many significant rights. These constraints on inmates, and in some cases the complete withdrawal of certain rights, are "justified by the considerations underlying our penal system." The curtailment of certain rights is necessary, as a practical matter, to accommodate a myriad of "institutional needs and objectives" of prison facilities, chief among which is internal security. Of course, these restrictions or retractions also serve, incidentally, as reminders that, under our system of justice, deterrence, and retribution are factors in addition to correction.

We have not before been called upon to decide the specific question whether the Fourth Amendment applies within a prison cell, but the nature of our inquiry is well defined. We must determine here, as in other Fourth Amendment contexts, if a "justifiable" expectation of privacy is at stake. The applicability of the Fourth Amendment turns on whether "the person invoking its protection can claim a 'justifiable,' a 'reasonable,' or a 'legitimate expectation of privacy' that has been invaded by government action." We must decide, in Justice Harlan's words, whether a prisoner's expectation of privacy in his prison cell is the kind of expectation that "society is prepared to recognize as 'reasonable.'"

Notwithstanding our caution in approaching claims that the Fourth Amendment is inapplicable in a given context, we hold that society is not prepared to recognize as legitimate any subjective expectation of privacy that a prisoner might have in his prison cell and that, accordingly, the Fourth Amendment proscription against unreasonable searches does not apply within the confines of the prison cell. The recognition of privacy rights for prisoners in their individual cells simply cannot be reconciled with the concept of incarceration and the needs and objectives of penal institutions.

Prisons, by definition, are places of involuntary confinement of persons who have a demonstrated proclivity for anti-social criminal, and often violent, conduct. Inmates have necessarily shown a lapse in ability to control and conform their behavior to the legitimate standards of society by the normal impulses of self-restraint; they have shown an inability to regulate their conduct in a way that reflects either a respect for law or an appreciation of the rights of others. Even a partial survey of the statistics on violent crime in our Nation's prisons illustrates the magnitude of the problem. During 1981 and the first half of 1982, there were over 120 prisoners murdered by fellow inmates in state and federal prisons. A number of prison personnel were murdered by prisoners during this period. Over 29 riots or similar disturbances were reported in these facilities for the same time frame. And there were over 125 suicides in these institutions. Additionally, informal statistics from the United States Bureau of Prisons show that in the federal system during 1983, there were 11 inmate homicides, 359 inmate assaults on other inmates, 227 inmate assaults on prison staff, and 10 suicides. There were in the same system in 1981 and 1982 over 750 inmate assaults on other inmates and over 570 inmate assaults on prison personnel.

Within this volatile "community," prison administrators are to take all necessary steps to ensure the safety of not only the prison staffs and administrative personnel, but also visitors. They are under an obligation to take reasonable measures to guarantee the safety of the inmates themselves. They must be ever alert to attempts to introduce drugs and other contraband into the premises which, we can judicially notice, is one of the most perplexing problems of prisons today; they must prevent, so far as possible, the flow of illicit weapons into the prison; they must be vigilant to detect escape plots, in which drugs or weapons may be involved, before the schemes materialize. In addition to these monumental tasks, it is incumbent upon these officials at the same time to maintain as sanitary an environment for the inmates as feasible, given the difficulties of the circumstances.

The administration of a prison, we have said, is "at best an extraordinarily difficult undertaking." But it would be literally impossible to accomplish the prison objectives identified above if inmates retained a right of privacy in their cells. Virtually the only place inmates can conceal weapons, drugs, and other contraband is in their cells. Unfettered access to these cells by prison officials, thus, is imperative if drugs and contraband are to be ferreted out and sanitary surroundings are to be maintained.

Determining whether an expectation of privacy is "legitimate" or "reasonable" necessarily entails a balancing of interests. The two interests here are the interest of society in the security of its penal institutions and the interest of the prisoner in privacy within his cell. The latter interest, of course, is already limited by the exigencies of the circumstances: A prison "shares none of the attributes of privacy of a home, an automobile, an office, or a hotel room." We strike the balance in favor of institutional security, which we have noted is "central to all other corrections goals." A right of privacy in traditional Fourth Amendment terms is fundamentally incompatible with the close and continual surveillance of inmates and their cells required to ensure institutional security and internal order. We are satisfied that society would insist that the prisoner's expectation of privacy always yield to what must be considered the paramount interest in institutional security. We believe that it is accepted by our society that "loss of freedom of choice and privacy are inherent incidents of confinement."

The Court of Appeals was troubled by the possibility of searches conducted solely to harass inmates; it reasoned that a requirement that searches be conducted only pursuant to an established policy or upon reasonable suspicion would prevent such searches to the maximum extent possible. Of course, there is a risk of maliciously motivated searches, and of course, intentional harassment of even the most hardened criminals cannot be tolerated by a civilized society. However, we disagree with the court's proposed solution. The uncertainty that attends random searches of cells renders these searches perhaps the most effective weapon of the prison administrator in the constant fight against the proliferation of knives and guns, illicit drugs, and other contraband. The Court of Appeals candidly acknowledged that "the device of random cell searches is of . . . obvious utility in achieving the goal of prison security."

A requirement that even random searches be conducted pursuant to an established plan would seriously undermine the effectiveness of this weapon. It is simply naive to believe that prisoners would not eventually decipher any plan officials might devise for "planned random searches," and thus be able routinely to anticipate searches. The Supreme Court of Virginia identified the shortcomings of an approach such as that adopted by the Court of Appeals and the necessity of allowing prison administrators flexibility:

"For one to advocate that prison searches must be conducted only pursuant to an enunciated general policy or when suspicion is directed at a particular inmate is to ignore the realities of prison operation. Random searches of inmates, individually or collectively, and their cells and lockers are valid and necessary to ensure the security of the institution and the safety of inmates and all others within its boundaries. This type of search allows prison officers flexibility and prevents inmates from anticipating, and thereby thwarting, a search for contraband."

We share the concerns so well expressed by the Supreme Court and its view that wholly random searches are essential to the effective security of penal institutions. We, therefore, cannot accept even the concededly limited holding of the Court of Appeals.

Respondent acknowledges that routine shakedowns of prison cells are essential to the effective administration of prisons. He contends, however, that he is constitutionally entitled not to be subjected to searches conducted only to harass. The crux of his claim is that "because searches and seizures to harass are unreasonable, a prisoner has a reasonable expectation of privacy not to have his cell, locker, personal effects, person invaded for such a purpose." This argument ,which assumes the answer to the predicate question whether a prisoner has a legitimate expectation of privacy in his prison cell at all, is merely a challenge to the reasonableness of the particular search of respondent's cell. Because we conclude that prisoners have no legitimate expectation of privacy and that the Fourth Amendment's prohibition on unreasonable searches does not apply in prison cells, we need not address this issue.

Our holding that respondent does not have a reasonable expectation of privacy enabling him to invoke the protections of the Fourth Amendment does not mean that he is without a remedy for calculated harassment unrelated to prison needs. Nor does it mean that prison attendants can ride roughshod over inmates' property rights with impunity. The Eighth Amendment always stands as a protection against "cruel and unusual punishments." By the same token, there are adequate state tort and common-law remedies available to respondent to redress the alleged destruction of his personal property.

B.

In his complaint in the District Court, in addition to his claim that the shakedown search of his cell violated his Fourth and Fourteenth Amendment privacy rights, respondent alleged under 42 U. S. C. § 1983 that petitioner intentionally destroyed certain of his personal property during the search. This destruction, respondent contended, deprived him of property without due process, in violation of the Due Process Clause of the Fourteenth Amendment. The District Court dismissed this portion of respondent's complaint for failure to state a claim. Reasoning under *Parratt v. Taylor* (1981), it held that even an intentional destruction of property by a state employee does not violate due process if the state provides a meaningful postdeprivation remedy. The Court of Appeals affirmed. The question presented for our review in Palmer's cross-petition is whether our decision in *Parratt v. Taylor* should extend, as the Court of Appeals held, to intentional deprivations of property by state employees acting under color of state law.

In *Parratt v. Taylor*, a state prisoner sued prison officials under 42 U. S. C. § 1983, alleging that their negligent loss of a hobby kit he ordered from a mail-order catalog deprived him of property without due process of law, in violation of the Fourteenth Amendment. The Court of Appeals for the Eighth Circuit had affirmed the District Court's summary judgment in the prisoner's favor. We reversed, holding that the Due Process Clause of the Fourteenth Amendment is not violated when a state employee negligently deprives an individual of property, provided that the state makes available a meaningful postdeprivation remedy.

We viewed our decision in *Parratt* as consistent with prior cases recognizing that

 "Either the necessity of quick action by the State or the impracticality of providing any meaningful predeprivation process, when coupled with the availability of some meaningful means by which to assess the propriety of the State's action at some time after the initial taking . . . satisfies the requirements of procedural due process."

We reasoned that where a loss of property is occasioned by a random, unauthorized act by a state employee, rather than by an established state procedure, the state cannot predict when the loss will occur. Under these circumstances, we observed:

"It is difficult to conceive of how the State could provide a meaningful hearing before the deprivation takes place. The loss of property, although attributable to the State as action under 'color of law,' is in almost all cases beyond the control of the State. Indeed, in most cases it is not only impracticable, but impossible, to provide a meaningful hearing before the deprivation."
Two Terms ago, we reaffirmed our holding in *Parratt* in *Logan v. Zimmerman Brush Co* (1982), in the course of holding that postdeprivation remedies do not satisfy due process where a deprivation of property is caused by conduct pursuant to established state procedure, rather than random and unauthorized action.

While *Parratt* is necessarily limited by its facts to negligent deprivations of property, it is evident, as the Court of Appeals recognized, that its reasoning applies as well to intentional deprivations of property. The underlying rationale of *Parratt* is that when deprivations of property are effected through random and unauthorized conduct of a state employee, predeprivation procedures are simply "impracticable" since the state cannot know when such deprivations will occur. We can discern no logical distinction between negligent and intentional deprivations of property insofar as the "practicability" of affording predeprivation process is concerned. The state can no more anticipate and control in advance the random and unauthorized intentional conduct of its employees than it can anticipate similar negligent conduct. Arguably, intentional acts are even more difficult to anticipate because one bent on intentionally depriving a person of his property might well take affirmative steps to avoid signaling his intent.

If negligent deprivations of property do not violate the Due Process Clause because predeprivation process is impracticable, it follows that intentional deprivations do not violate that Clause provided, of course, that adequate state postdeprivation remedies are available. Accordingly, we hold that an unauthorized intentional deprivation of property by a state employee does not constitute a violation of the procedural requirements of the Due Process Clause of the Fourteenth Amendment if a meaningful postdeprivation remedy for the loss is available. For intentional, as for negligent deprivations of property by state employees, the state's action is not complete until and unless it provides or refuses to provide a suitable postdeprivation remedy.

Respondent presses two arguments that require at least brief comment. First, he contends that, because an agent of the state who intends to deprive a person of his property "can provide predeprivation process, then as a matter of due process he must do so." This argument reflects a fundamental misunderstanding of *Parratt*. There we held that postdeprivation procedures satisfy due process because the state cannot possibly know in advance of a negligent deprivation of property. Whether an individual employee himself is able to foresee a deprivation is simply of no consequence. The controlling inquiry is solely whether the state is in a position to provide for predeprivation process.

Respondent also contends that the deliberate destruction of his property by petitioner constituted a due process violation despite the availability of postdeprivation remedies. In *Logan*, we decided a question about which our decision in *Parratt* left little doubt, that is, whether a postdeprivation state remedy satisfies due process where the property deprivation is effected pursuant to an established state procedure. We held that it does not. *Logan* plainly has no relevance here. Respondent does not even allege that the asserted destruction of his property occurred pursuant to a state procedure.

Having determined that *Parratt* extends to intentional deprivations of property, we need only decide whether the Commonwealth of Virginia provides respondent an adequate postdeprivation remedy for the alleged destruction of his property. Both the District Court and, at least implicitly, the Court of Appeals held that several common-law remedies available to respondent would provide adequate compensation for his property loss. We have no reason to question that determination, particularly given the speculative nature of respondent's arguments.

Palmer does not seriously dispute the adequacy of the existing state-law remedies themselves. He asserts in this respect only that, because certain of his legal papers allegedly taken "may have contained things irreplacable [sic], and incompensable" or "may also have involved sentimental items which are of equally intangible value." A suit in tort, for example, would not "necessarily" compensate him fully. If the loss is "incompensable," this is as much so under § 1983 as it would be under any other remedy. In any event, that Palmer might not be able to recover under these remedies the full amount which he might receive in a § 1983 action is not, as we have said, determinative of the adequacy of the state remedies.

Palmer contends also that relief under applicable state law "is far from certain and complete" because a state court might hold that petitioner, as a state employee, is entitled to sovereign immunity. This suggestion is unconvincing. The District Court and the Court of Appeals held that respondent's claim would not be barred by sovereign immunity. As the District Court noted, under Virginia law, "a State employee may be held liable for his intentional torts." Indeed, respondent candidly acknowledges that it is "probable that a Virginia trial court would rule that there should be no immunity bar in the present case."

Respondent attempts to cast doubt on the obvious breadth of *Elder* through the naked assertion that "the phrase 'may be held liable' could have meant . . . only the possibility of liability under certain circumstances rather than a blanket rule. . . ." We are equally unpersuaded by this speculation. The language of *Elder* is unambiguous that employees of the Commonwealth do not enjoy sovereign immunity for their intentional torts, and *Elder* has been so read by a number of federal courts, as respondent concedes. In sum, it is evident here, as in *Parratt*, that the State has provided an adequate postdeprivation remedy for the alleged destruction of property.

III.

We hold that the Fourth Amendment has no applicability to a prison cell. We hold also that, even if petitioner intentionally destroyed respondent's personal property during the challenged shakedown search, the destruction did not violate the Fourteenth Amendment since the Commonwealth of Virginia has provided respondent an adequate postdeprivation remedy.

Accordingly, the judgment of the Court of Appeals reversing and remanding the District Court's judgment on respondent's claim under the Fourth and Fourteenth Amendments is reversed. The judgment affirming the District Court's decision that respondent has not been denied due process under the Fourteenth Amendment is affirmed.

It is so ordered.

Wolf v. McDonnell (1974)
418 U.S. 539

In this case, the Supreme Court was called upon to consider if certain prison disciplinary proceedings violated the appellant's Due Process Rights. The court used this decision to articulate several due process rights that must be protected during prison disciplinary proceedings, as well as the accompanying procedures that must be used to protect them.

We granted the petition for writ of certiorari in this case, 414 U.S. 1156 (1974), because it raises important questions concerning the administration of a state prison.

Respondent, on behalf of himself and other inmates of the Nebraska Penal and Correctional Complex, Lincoln, Nebraska, filed a complaint under 42 U. S. C. § 1983 1 challenging several of the practices, rules, and regulations of the Complex. For present purposes, the pertinent allegations were that disciplinary proceedings did not comply with the Due Process Clause of the Fourteenth Amendment to the Federal Constitution; that the inmate legal assistance program did not meet constitutional standards, and that the regulations governing the inspection of mail to and from attorneys for inmates were unconstitutionally restrictive. Respondent requested damages and injunctive relief.

After an evidentiary hearing, the District Court granted partial relief. Considering itself bound by prior Circuit authority, it rejected the procedural due process claim; but it went on to hold that the prison's policy of inspecting all incoming and outgoing mail to and from attorneys violated prisoners' rights of access to the courts and that the restrictions placed on inmate legal assistance were not constitutionally defective.

The Court of Appeals reversed, with respect to the due process claim, holding that the procedural requirements outlined by this Court in *Morrissey v. Brewer* and *Gagnon v. Scarpelli* decided after the District Court's opinion in this case, should be generally followed in prison disciplinary hearings but left the specific requirements, including the circumstances in which counsel might be required, to be determined by the District Court on remand. With respect to a remedy, the court further held that *Preiser v. Rodriguez* forbade the actual restoration of good-time credits in this § 1983 suit but ordered expunged from prison records any determinations of misconduct arrived at in proceedings that failed to comport with due process as defined by the court. The court generally affirmed the judgment of the District Court with respect to correspondence with attorneys, but ordered further proceedings to determine whether the State was meeting its burden under *Johnson v. Avery* (1969) to provide legal assistance to prison inmates, the court holding that the State's duty extended to civil rights cases as well as to habeas corpus proceedings.

I.

We begin with the due process claim. An understanding of the issues involved requires a detailing of the prison disciplinary regime set down by Nebraska statutes and prison regulations.

Section 16 of the Nebraska Treatment and Corrections Act provides that chief executive officer of each penal facility is responsible for the discipline of inmates in a particular institution. The statute provides for a range of possible disciplinary action. "Except in flagrant or serious cases, punishment for misconduct shall consist of deprivation of privileges. In cases of flagrant or serious misconduct, the chief executive officer may order that a person's reduction of term as provided in section 83-1,107 [good-time credit] be forfeited or withheld and also that the person be confined in a disciplinary cell." Each breach of discipline is to be entered in the person's file together with the disposition or punishment therefor.

As the statute makes clear, there are basically two kinds of punishment for flagrant or serious misconduct. The first is the forfeiture or withholding of good-time credits, which affects the term of confinement, while the second, confinement in a disciplinary cell, involves alteration of the conditions of confinement. If the misconduct is less than flagrant or serious, only deprivation of privileges results.

The only statutory provision establishing procedures for the imposition of disciplinary sanctions which pertains to good time, § 38 of the Nebraska Treatment and Corrections Act, merely requires that an inmate be "consulted regarding the charges of misconduct" in connection with the forfeiture, withholding, or restoration of credit. But prison authorities have framed written regulations dealing with procedures and policies for controlling inmate misconduct. By regulation, misconduct is classified into two categories: major misconduct is a "serious violation" and must be formally reported to an Adjustment Committee, composed of the Associate Warden Custody, the Correctional Industries Superintendent, and the Reception Center Director. This Committee is directed to "review and evaluate all misconduct reports" and, among other things, to "conduct investigations, make findings, and impose disciplinary actions." If only minor misconduct, "a less serious violation," is involved, the problem may either be resolved informally by the inmate's supervisor or it can be formally reported for action to the Adjustment Committee. Repeated minor misconduct must be reported. The Adjustment Committee has available a wide range of sanctions. "Disciplinary action taken and recommended may include but not necessarily be limited to the following: reprimand, restrictions of various kinds, extra duty, confinement in the Adjustment Center [the disciplinary cell], withholding of statutory good time and/or extra earned good time, or a combination of the elements listed herein."

Additional procedures have been devised by the Complex governing the actions of the Adjustment Committee. Based on the testimony, the District Court found that the following procedures were in effect when an inmate is written up or charged with a prison violation:

"(a) The chief correction supervisor reviews the 'write-ups' on the inmates by the officers of the Complex daily;
"(b) the convict is called to a conference with the chief correction supervisor and the charging party;
"(c) following the conference, a conduct report is sent to the Adjustment Committee;
"(d) there follows a hearing before the Adjustment Committee and the report is read to the inmate and discussed;
"(e) if the inmate denies charge he may ask questions of the party writing him up;
"(f) the Adjustment Committee can conduct additional investigations if it desires;
"(g) punishment is imposed."

II.

This class action brought by respondent alleged that the rules, practices, and procedures at the Complex which might result in the taking of good time violated the Due Process Clause of the Fourteenth Amendment. Respondent sought three types of relief: (1) restoration of good time; (2) submission of a plan by the prison authorities for a hearing procedure in connection with withholding and forfeiture of good time which complied with the requirements of due process; and (3) damages for the deprivation of civil rights resulting from the use of the allegedly unconstitutional procedures.

At the threshold is the issue whether under *Preiser v. Rodriguez* (1973), the validity of the procedures for depriving prisoners of good-time credits may be considered in a civil rights suit brought under 42 U. S. C. § 1983. In *Preiser*, state prisoners brought a § 1983 suit seeking an injunction to compel restoration of good-time credits. The Court held that because the state prisoners were challenging the very fact or duration of their confinement and were seeking a speedier release, their sole federal remedy was by writ of habeas corpus, with the concomitant requirement of exhausting state remedies. But the Court was careful to point out that habeas corpus is not an appropriate or available remedy for damages claims, which, if not frivolous and of sufficient substance to invoke the jurisdiction of the federal court, could be pressed under § 1983 along with suits challenging the conditions of confinement rather than the fact or length of custody.

The complaint in this case sought restoration of good-time credits, and the Court of Appeals correctly held this relief foreclosed under *Preiser*. But the complaint also sought damages; and Preiser expressly contemplated that claims properly brought under § 1983 could go forward while actual restoration of good-time credits is sought in state proceedings. Respondent's damages claim was therefore properly before the District Court and required determination of the validity of the procedures employed for imposing sanctions, including loss of good time, for flagrant or serious misconduct. Such a declaratory judgment as a predicate to a damages award would not be barred by *Preiser*; and because under that case only an injunction restoring good time improperly taken is foreclosed, neither would it preclude a litigant with standing from obtaining by way of ancillary relief an otherwise proper injunction enjoining the prospective enforcement of invalid prison regulations.

We therefore conclude that it was proper for the Court of Appeals and the District Court to determine the validity of the procedures for revoking good-time credits and to fashion appropriate remedies for any constitutional violations ascertained, short of ordering the actual restoration of good time already canceled.

III.

Petitioners assert that the procedure for disciplining prison inmates for serious misconduct is a matter of policy raising no constitutional issue. If the position implies that prisoners in state institutions are wholly without the protections of the Constitution and the Due Process Clause, it is plainly untenable. Lawful imprisonment necessarily makes unavailable many rights and privileges of the ordinary citizen, a "retraction justified by the considerations underlying our penal system." But though his rights may be diminished by the needs and exigencies of the institutional environment, a prisoner is not wholly stripped of constitutional protections when he is imprisoned for crime. There is no iron curtain drawn between the Constitution and the prisons of this country. Prisoners have been held to enjoy substantial religious freedom under the First and Fourteenth Amendments. They retain right of access to the courts. Prisoners are protected under the Equal Protection Clause of the Fourteenth Amendment from invidious discrimination based on race. Prisoners may also claim the protections of the Due Process Clause. They may not be deprived of life, liberty, or property without due process of law.

Of course, as we have indicated, the fact that prisoners retain rights under the Due Process Clause in no way implies that these rights are not subject to restrictions imposed by the nature of the regime to which they have been lawfully committed. Prison disciplinary proceedings are not part of a criminal prosecution, and the full panoply of rights due a defendant in such proceedings does not apply. In sum, there must be mutual accommodation between institutional needs and objectives and the provisions of the Constitution that are of general application.

We also reject the assertion of the State that whatever may be true of the Due Process Clause in general or of other rights protected by that Clause against state infringement, the interest of prisoners in disciplinary procedures is not included in that "liberty" protected by the Fourteenth Amendment. It is true that the Constitution itself does not guarantee good-time credit for satisfactory behavior while in prison. But here the State itself has not only provided a statutory right to good time but also specifies that it is to be forfeited only for serious misbehavior. Nebraska may have the authority to create, or not, a right to a shortened prison sentence through the accumulation of credits for good behavior, and it is true that the Due Process Clause does not require a hearing "in every conceivable case of government impairment of private interest."

But the State having created the right to good time and itself recognizing that its deprivation is a sanction authorized for major misconduct, the prisoner's interest has real substance and is sufficiently embraced within Fourteenth Amendment "liberty" to entitle him to those minimum procedures appropriate under the circumstances and required by the Due Process Clause to insure that the state-created right is not arbitrarily abrogated. This is the thrust of recent cases in the prison disciplinary context. In *Haines v. Kerner*, the state prisoner asserted a "denial of due process in the steps leading to disciplinary confinement." We reversed the dismissal of the § 1983 complaint for failure to state a claim. In *Preiser v. Rodriguez*, the prisoner complained that he had been deprived of good-time credits without notice or hearing and without due process of law. We considered the claim a proper subject for a federal habeas corpus proceeding.

This analysis as to liberty parallels the accepted due process analysis as to property. The Court has consistently held that some kind of hearing is required at some time before a person is finally deprived of his property interests. The requirement for some kind of a hearing applies to the taking of private property, the revocation of licenses, the operation of state dispute-settlement mechanisms, when one person seeks to take property from another, or to government-created jobs held, absent "cause" for termination.

We think a person's liberty is equally protected, even when the liberty itself is a statutory creation of the State. The touchstone of due process is protection of the individual against arbitrary action of government. Since prisoners in Nebraska can only lose good-time credits if they are guilty of serious misconduct, the determination of whether such behavior has occurred becomes critical, and the minimum requirements of procedural due process appropriate for the circumstances must be observed.

IV.

As found by the District Court, the procedures employed are: (1) a preliminary conference with the Chief Corrections Supervisor and the charging party, where the prisoner is informed of the misconduct charge and engages in preliminary discussion on its merits; (2) the preparation of a conduct report and a hearing held before the Adjustment Committee, the disciplinary body of the prison, where the report is read to the inmate; and (3) the opportunity at the hearing to ask questions of the charging party. The State contends that the procedures already provided are adequate. The Court of Appeals held them insufficient and ordered that the due process requirements outlined in *Morrissey* and *Scarpelli* be satisfied in serious disciplinary cases at the prison.

Morrissey held that due process imposed certain minimum procedural requirements which must be satisfied before parole could finally be revoked. These procedures were:

"(a) written notice of the claimed violations of parole; (b) disclosure to the parolee of evidence against him; (c) opportunity to be heard in person and to present witnesses and documentary evidence; (d) the right to confront and cross-examine adverse witnesses (unless the hearing officer specifically finds good cause for not allowing confrontation); (e) a 'neutral and detached' hearing body such as a traditional parole board, members of which need not be judicial officers or lawyers; and (f) a written statement by the factfinders as to the evidence relied on and reasons for revoking parole."

The Court did not reach the question as to whether the parolee is entitled to the assistance of retained counsel or to appointed counsel, if he is indigent. Following the decision in *Morrissey*, in *Gagnon v. Scarpelli* (1973) the Court held the requirements of due process established for parole revocation were applicable to probation revocation proceedings. The Court added to the required minimum procedures of *Morrissey* the right to counsel, where a probationer makes a request, "based on a timely and colorable claim (i) that he has not committed the alleged violation of the conditions upon which he is at liberty; or (ii) that, even if the violation is a matter of public record or is uncontested, there are substantial reasons which justified or mitigated the violation and make revocation inappropriate, and that the reasons are complex or otherwise difficult to develop or present." In doubtful cases, the agency was to consider whether the probationer appeared to be capable of speaking effectively for himself, and a record was to be made of the grounds for refusing to appoint counsel.

We agree with neither petitioners nor the Court of Appeals: the Nebraska procedures are in some respects constitutionally deficient but the *Morrissey-Scarpelli* procedures need not in all respects be followed in disciplinary cases in state prisons.

We have often repeated that "the very nature of due process negates any concept of inflexible procedures universally applicable to every imaginable situation." "Consideration of what procedures due process may require under any given set of circumstances must begin with a determination of the precise nature of the government function involved as well as of the private interest that has been affected by governmental action." Viewed in this light it is immediately apparent that one cannot automatically apply procedural rules designed for free citizens in an open society, or for parolees or probationers under only limited restraints, to the very different situation presented by a disciplinary proceeding in a state prison.

Revocation of parole may deprive the parolee of only conditional liberty, but it nevertheless "inflicts a 'grievous loss' on the parolee and often on others." Simply put, revocation proceedings determine whether the parolee will be free or in prison, a matter of obvious great moment to him. For the prison inmate, the deprivation of good time is not the same immediate disaster that the revocation of parole is for the parolee. The deprivation, very likely, does not then and there work any change in the conditions of his liberty. It can postpone the date of eligibility for parole and extend the maximum term to be served, but it is not certain to do so, for good time may be restored. Even if not restored, it cannot be said with certainty that the actual date of parole will be affected; and if parole occurs, the extension of the maximum term resulting from loss of good time may affect only the termination of parole, and it may not even do that. The deprivation of good time is unquestionably a matter of considerable importance. The State reserves it as a sanction for serious misconduct, and we should not unrealistically discount its significance. But it is qualitatively and quantitatively different from the revocation of parole or probation.

In striking the balance that the Due Process Clause demands, however, we think the major consideration militating against adopting the full range of procedures suggested by *Morrissey* for alleged parole violators is the very different stake the State has in the structure and content of the prison disciplinary hearing. That the revocation of parole be justified and based on an accurate assessment of the facts is a critical matter to the State as well as the parolee; but the procedures by which it is determined whether the conditions of parole have been breached do not themselves threaten other important state interests, parole officers, the police, or witnesses–at least no more so than in the case of the ordinary criminal trial.

Prison disciplinary proceedings, on the other hand, take place in a closed, tightly controlled environment peopled by those who have chosen to violate the criminal law and who have been lawfully incarcerated for doing so. Some are first offenders, but many are recidivists who have repeatedly employed illegal and often very violent means to attain their ends. They may have little regard for the safety of others or their property or for the rules designed to provide an orderly and reasonably safe prison life. Although there are very many varieties of prisons with different degrees of security, we must realize that in many of them the inmates are closely supervised and their activities controlled around the clock. Guards and inmates co-exist in direct and intimate contact. Tension between them is unremitting. Frustration, resentment, and despair are commonplace. Relationships among the inmates are varied and complex and perhaps subject to the unwritten code that exhorts inmates not to inform on a fellow prisoner.

It is against this background that disciplinary proceedings must be structured by prison authorities; and it is against this background that we must make our constitutional judgments, realizing that we are dealing with the maximum security institution as well as those where security considerations are not paramount. The reality is that disciplinary hearings and the imposition of disagreeable sanctions necessarily involve confrontations between inmates and authority and between inmates who are being disciplined and those who would charge or furnish evidence against them. Retaliation is much more than a theoretical possibility;

and the basic and unavoidable task of providing reasonable personal safety for guards and inmates may be at stake, to say nothing of the impact of disciplinary confrontations and the resulting escalation of personal antagonisms on the important aims of the correctional process.

Indeed, it is pressed upon us that the proceedings to ascertain and sanction misconduct themselves play a major role in furthering the institutional goal of modifying the behavior and value systems of prison inmates sufficiently to permit them to live within the law when they are released. Inevitably there is a great range of personality and character among those who have transgressed the criminal law. Some are more amenable to suggestion and persuasion than others. Some may be incorrigible and would merely disrupt and exploit the disciplinary process for their own ends. With some, rehabilitation may be best achieved by simulating procedures of a free society to the maximum possible extent; but with others, it may be essential that discipline be swift and sure. In any event, it is argued, there would be great unwisdom in encasing the disciplinary procedures in an inflexible constitutional straitjacket that would necessarily call for adversary proceedings typical of the criminal trial, very likely raise the level of confrontation between staff and inmate, and make more difficult the utilization of the disciplinary process as a tool to advance the rehabilitative goals of the institution. This consideration, along with the necessity to maintain an acceptable level of personal security in the institution, must be taken into account as we now examine in more detail the Nebraska procedures that the Court of Appeals found wanting.

V.

Two of the procedures that the Court held should be extended to parolees facing revocation proceedings are not, but must be, provided to prisoners in the Nebraska Complex if the minimum requirements of procedural due process are to be satisfied. These are advance written notice of the claimed violation and a written statement of the factfinders as to the evidence relied upon and the reasons for the disciplinary action taken. As described by the Warden in his oral testimony, on the basis of which the District Court made its findings, the inmate is now given oral notice of the charges against him at least as soon as the conference with the Chief Corrections Supervisor and charging party. A written record is there compiled and the report read to the inmate at the hearing before the Adjustment Committee where the charges are discussed and pursued. There is no indication that the inmate is ever given a written statement by the Committee as to the evidence or informed in writing or otherwise as to the reasons for the disciplinary action taken.

Part of the function of notice is to give the charged party a chance to marshal the facts in his defense and to clarify what the charges are, in fact. Neither of these functions was performed by the notice described by the Warden. Although the charges are discussed orally with the inmate somewhat in advance of the hearing, the inmate is sometimes brought before the Adjustment Committee shortly after he is orally informed of the charges. Other times, after this initial discussion, further investigation takes place which may reshape the nature of the charges or the evidence relied upon. In those instances, under procedures in effect at the time of trial, it would appear that the inmate first receives notice of the actual charges at the time of the hearing before the Adjustment Committee. We hold that written notice of the charges must be given to the disciplinary-action defendant in order to inform him of the charges and to enable him to marshal the facts and prepare a defense. At least a brief period of time after the notice, no less than 24 hours, should be allowed to the inmate to prepare for the appearance before the Adjustment Committee.

We also hold that there must be a "written statement by the factfinders as to the evidence relied on and reasons" for the disciplinary action. Although Nebraska does not seem to provide administrative review of the action taken by the Adjustment Committee, the actions taken at such proceedings may involve review by other bodies. They might furnish the basis of a decision by the Director of Corrections to transfer an inmate to another institution because he is considered "to be incorrigible by reason of frequent intentional breaches of discipline," and are certainly likely to be considered by the state parole authorities in making parole decisions. Written records of proceedings will thus protect the inmate against collateral consequences based on a misunderstanding of the nature of the original proceeding. Further, as to the disciplinary action itself, the provision for a written record helps to insure that administrators, faced with possible scrutiny by state officials and the public, and perhaps even the courts, where fundamental constitutional rights may have been abridged, will act fairly. Without written records, the inmate will be at a severe disadvantage in propounding his own cause to or defending himself from others. It may be that there will be occasions when personal or institutional safety is so implicated that the statement may properly exclude certain items of evidence, but in that event the statement should indicate the fact of the omission. Otherwise, we perceive no conceivable rehabilitative objective or prospect of prison disruption that can flow from the requirement of these statements.

We are also of the opinion that the inmate facing disciplinary proceedings should be allowed to call witnesses and present documentary evidence in his defense when permitting him to do so will not be unduly hazardous to institutional safety or correctional goals. Ordinarily, the right to present evidence is basic to a fair hearing; but the unrestricted right to call witnesses from the prison population carries obvious potential for disruption and for interference with the swift punishment that in individual cases may be essential to carrying out the correctional program of the institution. We should not be too ready to exercise oversight and put aside the judgment of prison administrators. It may be that an individual threatened with serious sanctions would normally be entitled to present witnesses and relevant documentary evidence; but here we must balance the inmate's interest in avoiding loss of good time against the needs of the prison, and some amount of flexibility and accommodation is required.

Prison officials must have the necessary discretion to keep the hearing within reasonable limits and to refuse to call witnesses that may create a risk of reprisal or undermine authority, as well as to limit access to other inmates to collect statements or to compile other documentary evidence. Although we do not prescribe it, it would be useful for the Committee to state its reason for refusing to call a witness, whether it be for irrelevance, lack of necessity, or the hazards presented in individual cases. Any less flexible rule appears untenable as a constitutional matter, at least on the record made in this case. The operation of a correctional institution is at best an extraordinarily difficult undertaking. Many prison officials, on the spot and with the responsibility for the safety of inmates and staff, are reluctant to extend the unqualified right to call witnesses; and in our view, they must have the necessary discretion without being subject to unduly crippling constitutional impediments. There is this much play in the joints of the Due Process Clause, and we stop short of imposing a more demanding rule with respect to witnesses and documents.

Confrontation and cross-examination present greater hazards to institutional interests. If confrontation and cross-examination of those furnishing evidence against the inmate were to be allowed as a matter of course, as in criminal trials, there would be considerable potential for havoc inside the prison walls. Proceedings would inevitably be longer and tend to unmanageability. These procedures are essential in criminal trials where the accused, if found guilty, may be subjected to the most serious deprivations, or where a person may lose his job in society. But they are not rights universally applicable to all hearings. Rules of procedure may be shaped by consideration of the risks of error, and should also be shaped by the consequences which will follow their adoption. Although some States do seem to allow cross-examination in disciplinary hearings, we are not apprised of the conditions under which the procedure may be curtailed; and it does not appear that confrontation and cross-examination are generally required in this context. We think that the Constitution should not be read to impose the procedure at the present time and that adequate bases for decision in prison disciplinary cases can be arrived at without cross-examination.

Perhaps as the problems of penal institutions change and correctional goals are reshaped, the balance of interests involved will require otherwise. But in the current environment, where prison disruption remains a serious concern to administrators, we cannot ignore the desire and effort of many States, including Nebraska, and the Federal Government to avoid situations that may trigger deep emotions and that may scuttle the disciplinary process as a rehabilitation vehicle. To some extent, the American adversary trial presumes contestants who are able to cope with the pressures and aftermath of the battle, and such may not generally be the case of those in the prisons of this country. At least, the Constitution, as we interpret it today, does not require the contrary assumption. Within the limits set forth in this opinion we are content for now to leave the continuing development of measures to review adverse actions affecting inmates to the sound discretion of corrections officials administering the scope of such inquiries.

We recognize that the problems of potential disruption may differ depending on whom the inmate proposes to cross-examine. If he proposes to examine an unknown fellow inmate, the danger may be the greatest, since the disclosure of the identity of the accuser, and the cross-examination which will follow, may pose a high risk of reprisal within the institution. Conversely, the inmate accuser, who might freely tell his story privately to prison officials, may refuse to testify or admit any knowledge of the situation in question. Although the dangers posed by cross-examination of known inmate accusers, or guards, may be less, the resentment which may persist after confrontation may still be substantial. Also, even where the accuser or adverse witness is known, the disclosure of third parties may pose a problem.

There may be a class of cases where the facts are closely disputed, and the character of the parties minimizes the dangers involved. However, any constitutional rule tailored to meet these situations would undoubtedly produce great litigation and attendant costs in a much wider range of cases. Further, in the last analysis, even within the narrow range of cases where interest balancing may well dictate cross-examination, courts will be faced with the assessment of prison officials as to the dangers involved, and there would be a limited basis for upsetting such judgments. The better course at this time, in a period where prison practices are diverse and somewhat experimental, is to leave these matters to the sound discretion of the officials of state prisons.

As to the right to counsel, the problem as outlined in *Scarpelli* with respect to parole and probation revocation proceedings is even more pertinent here:

"The introduction of counsel into a revocation proceeding will alter significantly the nature of the proceeding. If counsel is provided for the probationer or parolee, the State in turn will normally provide its own counsel; lawyers, by training and disposition, are advocates and bound by professional duty to present all available evidence and arguments in support of their clients' positions and to contest with vigor all adverse evidence and views. The role of the hearing body itself, aptly described in *Morrissey* as being 'predictive and discretionary' as well as factfinding, may become more akin to that of a judge at a trial, and less attuned to the rehabilitative needs of the individual probationer or parolee. In the greater self-consciousness of its quasi-judicial role, the hearing body may be less tolerant of marginal deviant behavior and feel more pressure to reincarcerate than to continue nonpunitive rehabilitation. Certainly, the decisionmaking process will be prolonged, and the financial cost to the State– for appointed counsel, counsel for the State, a longer record, and the possibility of judicial review—will not be insubstantial."

The insertion of counsel into the disciplinary process would inevitably give the proceedings a more adversary cast and tend to reduce their utility as a means to further correctional goals. There would also be delay and very practical problems in providing counsel in sufficient numbers at the time and place where hearings are to be held. At this stage of the development of these procedures we are not prepared to hold that inmates have a right to either retained or appointed counsel in disciplinary proceedings.

Where an illiterate inmate is involved, however, or where the complexity of the issue makes it unlikely that the inmate will be able to collect and present the evidence necessary for an adequate comprehension of the case, he should be free to seek the aid of a fellow inmate, or if that is forbidden, to have adequate substitute aid in the form of help from the staff or from a sufficiently competent inmate designated by the staff. We need not pursue the matter further here, however, for there is no claim that respondent, McDonnell, is within the class of inmates entitled to advice or help from others in the course of a prison disciplinary hearing.

Finally, we decline to rule that the Adjustment Committee which conducts the required hearings at the Nebraska Prison Complex and determines whether to revoke good time is not sufficiently impartial to satisfy the Due Process Clause. The Committee is made up of the Associate Warden Custody as chairman, the Correctional Industries Superintendent, and the Reception Center Director. The Chief Corrections Supervisor refers cases to the Committee after investigation and an initial interview with the inmate involved. The Committee is not left at large with unlimited discretion. It is directed to meet daily and to operate within the principles stated in the controlling regulations, among which is the command that "full consideration must be given to the causes for the adverse behavior, the setting and circumstances in which it occurred, the man's accountability, and the correctional treatment goals," as well as the direction that "disciplinary measures will be taken only at such times and to such degrees as are necessary to regulate and control a man's behavior within acceptable limits and will never be rendered capriciously or in the nature of retaliation or revenge." We find no warrant in the record presented here for concluding that the Adjustment Committee presents such a hazard of arbitrary decisionmaking that it should be held violative of due process of law.

Our conclusion that some, but not all, of the procedures specified in *Morrissey* and *Scarpelli* must accompany the deprivation of good time by state prison authorities is not graven in stone. As the nature of the prison disciplinary process changes in future years, circumstances may then exist which will require further consideration and reflection of this Court. It is our view, however, that the procedures we have now required in prison disciplinary proceedings represent a reasonable accommodation between the interests of the inmates and the needs of the institution.

VI.

The Court of Appeals held that the due process requirements in prison disciplinary proceedings were to apply retroactively so as to require that prison records containing determinations of misconduct, not in accord with required procedures, be expunged. We disagree and reverse on this point.

The question of retroactivity of new procedural rules affecting inquiries into infractions of prison discipline is effectively foreclosed by this Court's ruling in *Morrissey* that the due process requirements there announced were to be "applicable to future revocations of parole." Despite the fact that procedures are related to the integrity of the factfinding process, in the context of disciplinary proceedings, where less is generally at stake for an individual than at a criminal trial, great weight should be given to the significant impact a retroactivity ruling would have on the administration of all prisons in the country, and the reliance prison officials placed, in good faith, on prior law not requiring such procedures. During 1973, the Federal Government alone conducted 19,000 misconduct hearings, as compared with 1,173 parole revocation hearings, and 2,023 probation revocation hearings. If *Morrissey-Scarpelli* rules are not retroactive out of consideration for the burden of federal and state officials, this case is *a fortiori*. We also note that a contrary holding would be very troublesome for the parole system since performance in prison is often a relevant criterion for parole. On the whole, we do not think that error was so pervasive in the system under the old procedures as to warrant this cost or result.

VII.

The issue of the extent to which prison authorities can open and inspect incoming mail from attorneys to inmates, has been considerably narrowed in the course of this litigation. The prison regulation under challenge provided that "all incoming and outgoing mail will be read and inspected," and no exception was made for attorney-prisoner mail. The District Court held that incoming mail from attorneys might be opened if normal contraband detection techniques failed to disclose contraband, and if there was a reasonable possibility that contraband would be included in the mail. It further held that if an incoming letter was marked "privileged," thus identifying it as from an attorney, the letter could not be opened except in the presence of the inmate. Prison authorities were not to read the mail from attorneys. The Court of Appeals affirmed the District Court order, but placed additional restrictions on prison authorities. If there was doubt that a letter was actually from an attorney, "a simple telephone call should be enough to settle the matter," the court thus implying that officials might have to go beyond the face of the envelope, and the "privileged" label, in ascertaining what kind of communication was involved. The court further stated that "the danger that a letter from an attorney, an officer of the court, will contain contraband is ordinarily too remote and too speculative to justify the petitioners' regulation permitting the opening and inspection of all legal mail." While methods to detect contraband could be employed, a letter was to be opened only "in the appropriate circumstances" in the presence of the inmate.

Petitioners now concede that they cannot open and read mail from attorneys to inmates, but contend that they may open all letters from attorneys as long as it is done in the presence of the prisoners. The narrow issue thus presented is whether letters determined or found to be from attorneys may be opened by prison authorities in the presence of the inmate or whether such mail must be delivered unopened if normal detection techniques fail to indicate contraband.

Respondent asserts that his First, Sixth, and Fourteenth Amendment rights are infringed, under a procedure whereby the State may open mail from his attorney, even though in his presence and even though it may not be read. To begin with, the constitutional status of the rights asserted, as applied in this situation, is far from clear. While First Amendment rights of correspondents with prisoners may protect against the censoring of inmate mail, when not necessary to protect legitimate governmental interests. This Court has not yet recognized First Amendment rights of prisoners in this context. Furthermore, freedom from censorship is not equivalent to freedom from inspection or perusal. As to the Sixth Amendment, its reach is only to protect the attorney-client relationship from intrusion in the criminal setting, while the claim here would insulate all mail from inspection, whether related to civil or criminal matters. Finally, the Fourteenth Amendment due process claim based on access to the courts, has not been extended by this Court to apply further than protecting the ability of an inmate to prepare a petition or complaint. Moreover, even if one were to accept the argument that inspection of incoming mail from an attorney placed an obstacle to access to the court, it is far from clear that this burden is a substantial one. We need not decide, however, which, if any, of the asserted rights are operative here, for the question is whether, assuming some constitutional right is implicated, it is infringed by the procedure now found acceptable by the State.

In our view, the approach of the Court of Appeals is unworkable and none of the above rights is infringed by the procedures petitioners now accept. If prison officials had to check in each case whether a communication was from an attorney before opening it for inspection, a near-impossible task of administration would be imposed. We think it entirely appropriate that the State require any such communications to be specially marked as originating from an attorney, with his name and address being given, if they are to receive special treatment. It would also certainly be permissible that prison authorities require that a lawyer desiring to correspond with a prisoner, first identify himself and his client to the prison officials, to assure that the letters marked privileged are actually from members of the bar. As to the ability to open the mail in the presence of inmates, this could in no way constitute censorship, since the mail would not be read. Neither could it chill such communications, since the inmate's presence insures that prison officials will not read the mail. The possibility that contraband will be enclosed in letters, even those from apparent attorneys, surely warrants prison officials' opening the letters. We disagree with the Court of Appeals that this should only be done in "appropriate circumstances." Since a flexible test, besides being unworkable, serves no arguable purpose in protecting any of the possible constitutional rights enumerated by respondent, we think that petitioners, by acceding to a rule whereby the inmate is present when mail from attorneys is inspected, have done all, and perhaps even more, than the Constitution requires.

VIII.

The last issue presented is whether the Complex must make available, and if so has made available, adequate legal assistance, under *Johnson v. Avery*, for the preparation of habeas corpus petitions and civil rights actions by inmates. The issue arises in the context of a challenge to a regulation providing, in pertinent part:

"Legal Work

"A legal advisor has been appointed by the Warden for the benefit of those offenders who are in need of legal assistance. This individual is an offender who has general knowledge of the law procedure. He is not an attorney and cannot represent you as such.

"No other offender than the legal advisor is permitted to assist you in the preparation of legal documents unless with the specific written permission of the Warden."

Respondent contended that this regulation was invalid because it failed to allow inmates to furnish assistance to one another. The District Court assumed that the Warden freely gave permission to inmates to give assistance to each other, and that *Johnson v. Avery* was thereby satisfied. The Court of Appeals found that the record did not support the assumption and that permission has been denied solely because of the existence of the inmate legal advisor, one of the inmates specially approved by the prison authorities. It decided, therefore, to remand the case to decide whether the one advisor satisfied the requirements of *Johnson v. Avery*. In so doing, the court stated that in determining the need for legal assistance, petitioners were to take into account the need for assistance in civil rights actions as well as habeas corpus suits.

In *Johnson v. Avery*, an inmate was disciplined for violating a prison regulation which prohibited inmates from assisting other prisoners in preparing habeas corpus petitions. The Court held that "unless and until the State provides some reasonable alternative to assist inmates in the preparation of petitions for post-conviction relief," inmates could not be barred from furnishing assistance to each other. The court emphasized that the writ of habeas corpus was of fundamental importance in our constitutional scheme, and since the basic purpose of the writ "is to enable those unlawfully incarcerated to obtain their freedom, it is fundamental that access of prisoners to the courts for the purpose of presenting their complaints may not be denied or obstructed." Following *Avery*, the Court, in *Younger v. Gilmore*, affirmed a three-judge court judgment which required state officials to provide indigent inmates with access to a reasonably adequate law library for preparation of legal actions.

Petitioners contend that *Avery* is limited to assistance in the preparation of habeas corpus petitions and disputes the direction of the Court of Appeals to the District Court that the capacity of the inmate adviser be assessed in light of the demand for assistance in civil rights actions as well as in the preparation of habeas petitions. Petitioners take too narrow a view of that decision.

First, the demarcation line between civil rights actions and habeas petitions is not always clear. The Court has already recognized instances where the same constitutional rights might be redressed under either form of relief. Second, while it is true that only in habeas actions may relief be granted which will shorten the term of confinement, *Preiser*, it is more pertinent that both actions serve to protect basic constitutional rights. The right of access to the courts, upon which *Avery* was premised, is founded in the Due Process Clause and assures that no person will be denied the opportunity to present to the judiciary allegations concerning violations of fundamental constitutional rights. It is futile to contend that the Civil Rights Act of 1871 has less importance in our constitutional scheme than does the Great Writ. The recognition by this Court that prisoners have certain constitutional rights which can be protected by civil rights actions would be diluted if inmates, often "totally or functionally illiterate," were unable to articulate their complaints to the courts. Although there may be additional burdens on the Complex, if inmates may seek help from other inmates, or from the inmate adviser if he proves adequate, in both habeas and civil rights actions, this should not prove overwhelming. At present only one inmate serves as legal adviser and it may be expected that other qualified inmates could be found for assistance if the Complex insists on naming the inmates from whom help may be sought.

Finding no reasonable distinction between the two forms of actions, we affirm the Court of Appeals on this point, and as the Court of Appeals suggested, the District Court will assess the adequacy of legal assistance under the reasonable-alternative standard of *Avery*.

Affirmed in part, reversed in part, and remanded.

Mempa v. Rhay (1967)
389 U.S. 128

In this case, the Supreme Court considered whether the appointment of counsel was a constitutional requirement in probation revocation hearings. The Court held that counsel was constitutionally required. The court cautioned that calling such a proceeding by any other name ("deferred sentencing" in this case) does not relieve the state of this burden.

These consolidated cases raise the question of the extent of the right to counsel at the time of sentencing where the sentencing has been deferred subject to probation.

Petitioner Jerry Douglas Mempa was convicted in the Spokane County Superior Court on June 17, 1959, of the offense of "joyriding." This conviction was based on his plea of guilty entered with the advice of court-appointed counsel. He was then placed on probation for two years on the condition, *inter alia*, that he first spend 30 days in the county jail, and the imposition of sentence was deferred....

About four months later the Spokane County prosecuting attorney moved to have petitioner's probation revoked on the ground that he had been involved in a burglary on September 15, 1959. A hearing was held in the Spokane County Superior Court on October 23, 1959. Petitioner Mempa, who was 17 years old at the time, was accompanied to the hearing by his stepfather. He was not represented by counsel and was not asked whether he wished to have counsel appointed for him. Nor was any inquiry made concerning the appointed counsel who had previously represented him.

At the hearing Mempa was asked if it was true that he had been involved in the alleged burglary and he answered in the affirmative. A probation officer testified without cross-examination that according to his information petitioner had been involved in the burglary and had previously denied participation in it. Without asking petitioner if he had anything to say or any evidence to supply, the court immediately entered an order revoking petitioner's probation and then sentenced him to 10 years in the penitentiary, but stated that it would recommend to the parole board that Mempa be required to serve only a year.

In 1965, Mempa filed a *pro se* petition for a writ of habeas corpus with the Washington Supreme Court, claiming that he had been deprived of his right to counsel at the proceeding at which his probation was revoked and sentence imposed. The Washington Supreme Court denied the petition on June 23, 1966, by a vote of six to three. We granted certiorari to consider the questions raised.

Petitioner William Earl Walkling was convicted in the Thurston County Superior Court on October 29, 1962, of burglary in the second degree on the basis of his plea of guilty entered with the advice of his retained counsel. He was placed on probation for three years and the imposition of sentence was deferred. As conditions of his probation he was required to serve 90 days in the county jail and make restitution. On May 2, 1963, a bench warrant for his arrest was issued based on a report that he had violated the terms of his probation and had left the State.

On February 24, 1964, Walkling was arrested and charged with forgery and grand larceny. After being transferred back to Thurston County he was brought before the court on May 12, 1964, for a hearing on the petition by the prosecuting attorney to revoke his probation. Petitioner then requested a continuance to enable him to retain counsel and was granted a week. On May 18, 1964, the hearing was called and Walkling appeared without a lawyer. He informed the court that he had retained an attorney who was supposed to be present. After waiting for 15 minutes the court went ahead with the hearing in the absence of petitioner's counsel. He was not offered appointed counsel and would not have had counsel appointed for him had he requested it. Whether he made such a request does not appear from the record.

At the hearing, a probation officer presented hearsay testimony to the effect that petitioner had committed the acts alleged in the 14 separate counts of forgery and 14 separate counts of grand larceny that had been charged against petitioner previously at the time of his arrest. The court thereupon revoked probation and imposed the maximum sentence of 15 years on Walkling on his prior second-degree burglary conviction. Because of the failure of the State to keep a record of the proceeding, nothing is known as to whether Walkling was advised of his right to appeal. He did not, however, take an appeal.

In May 1966 Walkling filed a habeas corpus petition with the Washington Supreme Court, claiming denial of his right to counsel at the combined probation revocation and sentencing proceeding. The petition was denied on the authority of the prior decision in *Mempa v. Rhay*. We granted certiorari, and the cases were consolidated for argument.

In 1948 this Court held in *Townsend v. Burke* that the absence of counsel during sentencing after a plea of guilty coupled with "assumptions concerning his criminal record which were materially untrue" deprived the defendant in that case of due process. Mr. Justice Jackson there stated in conclusion, "In this case, counsel might not have changed the sentence, but he could have taken steps to see that the conviction and sentence were not predicated on misinformation or misreading of court records, a requirement of fair play which absence of counsel withheld from this prisoner." Then, in *Moore v. Michigan* (1957), where a denial of due process was found when the defendant did not intelligently and understandingly waive counsel before entering a plea of guilty, this Court emphasized the prejudice stemming from the absence of counsel at the hearing on the degree of the crime following entry of the guilty plea and stated, "The right to counsel is not a right confined to representation during the trial on the merits."

In *Hamilton v. Alabama* (1961), it was held that failure to appoint counsel at arraignment deprived the petitioner of due process, notwithstanding the fact that he simply pleaded not guilty at that time, because under Alabama law certain defenses had to be raised then or be abandoned.

All the foregoing cases, with the exception of *White*, were decided during the reign of *Betts v. Brady* (1942), and accordingly relied on various "special circumstances" to make the right to counsel applicable. In *Gideon v. Wainwright* (1963), however, *Betts* was overruled and this Court held that the Sixth Amendment as applied through the Due Process Clause of the Fourteenth Amendment was applicable to the States and, accordingly, that there was an absolute right to appointment of counsel in felony cases.

There was no occasion in *Gideon* to enumerate the various stages in a criminal proceeding at which counsel was required, but *Townsend*, *Moore*, and *Hamilton*, when the *Betts* requirement of special circumstances is stripped away by *Gideon*, clearly stand for the proposition that appointment of counsel for an indigent is required at every stage of a criminal proceeding where substantial rights of a criminal accused may be affected. In particular, *Townsend v. Burke* illustrates the critical nature of sentencing in a criminal case and might well be considered to support by itself a holding that the right to counsel applies at sentencing. Many lower courts have concluded that the Sixth Amendment right to counsel extends to sentencing in federal cases.

The State, however, argues that the petitioners were sentenced at the time they were originally placed on probation and that the imposition of sentence following probation revocation is, in effect, a mere formality constituting part of the probation revocation proceeding. It is true that sentencing in Washington offers fewer opportunities for the exercise of judicial discretion than in many other jurisdictions. The applicable statute requires the trial judge in all cases to sentence the convicted person to the maximum term provided by law for the offense of which he was convicted. The actual determination of the length of time to be served is to be made by the Board of Prison Terms and Paroles within six months after the convicted person is admitted to prison.

On the other hand, the sentencing judge is required by statute, together with the prosecutor, to furnish the Board with a recommendation as to the length of time that the person should serve, in addition to supplying it with various information about the circumstances of the crime and the character of the individual. We were informed during oral argument that the Board places considerable weight on these recommendations, although it is in no way bound by them. Obviously to the extent such recommendations are influential in determining the resulting sentence, the necessity for the aid of counsel in marshaling the facts, introducing evidence of mitigating circumstances and in general aiding and assisting the defendant to present his case as to sentence is apparent.

 Even more important in a case such as this is the fact that certain legal rights may be lost if not exercised at this stage. For one, Washington law provides that an appeal in a case involving a plea of guilty followed by probation can only be taken after sentence is imposed following revocation of probation. Therefore, in a case where an accused agreed to plead guilty, although he had a valid defense, because he was offered probation, absence of counsel at the imposition of the deferred sentence might well result in loss of the right to appeal. While ordinarily appeals from a plea of guilty are less frequent than those following a trial on the merits, the incidence of improperly obtained guilty pleas is not so slight as to be capable of being characterized as *de minimis*.

Likewise, the Washington statutes provide that a plea of guilty can be withdrawn at any time prior to the imposition of sentence if the trial judge in his discretion finds that the ends of justice will be served. Without undertaking to catalog the various situations in which a lawyer could be of substantial assistance to a defendant in such a case, it can be reiterated that a plea of guilty might well be improperly obtained by the promise to have a defendant placed on the very probation the revocation of which furnishes the occasion for desiring to withdraw the plea. An uncounseled defendant might very likely be unaware of this opportunity.

The two foregoing factors assume increased significance when it is considered that, as happened in these two cases, the eventual imposition of sentence on the prior plea of guilty is based on the alleged commission of offenses for which the accused is never tried.

In sum, we do not question the authority of the State of Washington to provide for a deferred sentencing procedure coupled with its probation provisions. Indeed, it appears to be an enlightened step forward. All we decide here is that a lawyer must be afforded at this proceeding whether it be labeled a revocation of probation or a deferred sentencing. We assume that counsel appointed for the purpose of the trial or guilty plea would not be unduly burdened by being requested to follow through at the deferred sentencing stage of the proceeding.

The judgments below are reversed and the cases are remanded for further proceedings not inconsistent with this opinion.

Reversed and remanded.

Morrissey v. Brewer (1972)
408 U.S. 471

In this case, the Supreme Court was asked to decide whether a hearing was required before parole could be revoked. The court found that the Due Process Clause of the Fourteenth Amendment did indeed require such a hearing, but such a hearing did not require every procedural safeguard a criminal defendant enjoys in a trial.

We granted certiorari in this case to determine whether the Due Process Clause of the Fourteenth Amendment requires that a State afford an individual some opportunity to be heard prior to revoking his parole.

Petitioner Morrissey was convicted of false drawing or uttering of checks in 1967 pursuant to his guilty plea, and was sentenced to not more than seven years' confinement. He was paroled from the Iowa State Penitentiary in June 1968. Seven months later, at the direction of his parole officer, he was arrested in his home town as a parole violator and incarcerated in the county jail. One week later, after review of the parole officer's written report, the Iowa Board of Parole revoked Morrissey's parole, and he was returned to the penitentiary located about 100 miles from his home. Petitioner asserts he received no hearing prior to revocation of his parole.

The parole officer's report on which the Board of Parole acted shows that petitioner's parole was revoked on the basis of information that he had violated the conditions of parole by buying a car under an assumed name and operating it without permission, giving false statements to police concerning his address and insurance company after a minor accident, obtaining credit under an assumed name, and failing to report his place of residence to his parole officer. The report states that the officer interviewed Morrissey, and that he could not explain why he did not contact his parole officer despite his effort to excuse this on the ground that he had been sick. Further, the report asserts that Morrissey admitted buying the car and obtaining credit under an assumed name, and also admitted being involved in the accident. The parole officer recommended that his parole be revoked because of "his continual violating of his parole rules."

The situation as to petitioner Booher is much the same. Pursuant to his guilty plea, Booher was convicted of forgery in 1966 and sentenced to a maximum term of 10 years. He was paroled November 14, 1968. In August 1969, at his parole officer's direction, he was arrested in his home town for a violation of his parole and confined in the county jail several miles away. On September 13, 1969, on the basis of a written report by his parole officer, the Iowa Board of Parole revoked Booher's parole and Booher was recommitted to the state penitentiary, located about 250 miles from his home, to complete service of his sentence. Petitioner asserts he received no hearing prior to revocation of his parole.

The parole officer's report with respect to Booher recommended that his parole be revoked because he had violated the territorial restrictions of his parole without consent, had obtained a driver's license under an assumed name, operated a motor vehicle without permission, and had violated the employment condition of his parole by failing to keep himself in gainful employment. The report stated that the officer had interviewed Booher and that he had acknowledged to the parole officer that he had left the specified territorial limits and had operated the car and had obtained a license under an assumed name "knowing that it was wrong." The report further noted that Booher had stated that he had not found employment because he could not find work that would pay him what he wanted—he stated he would not work for $ 2.25 to $ 2.75 per hour—and that he had left the area to get work in another city.

After exhausting state remedies, both petitioners filed habeas corpus petitions in the United States District Court for the Southern District of Iowa alleging that they had been denied due process because their paroles had been revoked without a hearing. The State responded by arguing that no hearing was required. The District Court held on the basis of controlling authority that the State's failure to accord a hearing prior to parole revocation did not violate due process. On appeal, the two cases were consolidated.

The Court of Appeals, dividing 4 to 3, held that due process does not require a hearing. The majority recognized that the traditional view of parole as a privilege rather than a vested right is no longer dispositive as to whether due process is applicable; however, on a balancing of the competing interests involved, it concluded that no hearing is required. The court reasoned that parole is only "a correctional device authorizing service of sentence outside the penitentiary"; the parolee is still "in custody." Accordingly, the Court of Appeals was of the view that prison officials must have large discretion in making revocation determinations, and that courts should retain their traditional reluctance to interfere with disciplinary matters properly under the control of state prison authorities. The majority expressed the view that "non-legal, non-adversary considerations" were often the determinative factors in making a parole revocation decision. It expressed concern that if adversary hearings were required for

228

parole revocation, "with the full panoply of rights accorded in criminal proceedings," the function of the parole board as "an administrative body acting in the role of parens patriae would be aborted," and the board would be more reluctant to grant parole in the first instance—an apprehension that would not be without some basis if the choice were between a full-scale adversary proceeding or no hearing at all. Additionally, the majority reasoned that the parolee has no statutory right to remain on parole. Iowa law provides that a parolee may be returned to the institution at any time. Our holding in *Mempa v. Rhay* (1967), was distinguished on the ground that it involved deferred sentencing upon probation revocation, and thus involved a stage of the criminal proceeding, whereas parole revocation was not a stage in the criminal proceeding. The Court of Appeals' decision was consistent with many other decisions on parole revocations.

In their brief in this Court, respondents assert for the first time that petitioners were in fact granted hearings after they were returned to the penitentiary. More generally, respondents say that within two months after the Board revokes an individual's parole and orders him returned to the penitentiary, on the basis of the parole officer's written report it grants the individual a hearing before the Board. At that time, the Board goes over "each of the alleged parole violations with the returnee, and he is given an opportunity to orally present his side of the story to the Board." If the returnee denies the report, it is the practice of the Board to conduct a further investigation before making a final determination either affirming the initial revocation, modifying it, or reversing it. Respondents assert that Morrissey, whose parole was revoked on January 31, 1969, was granted a hearing before the Board on February 12, 1969. Booher's parole was revoked on September 13, 1969, and he was granted a hearing on October 14, 1969. At these hearings, respondents tell us—in the briefs—both Morrissey and Booher admitted the violations alleged in the parole violation reports.

Nothing in the record supplied to this Court indicates that respondent claimed, either in the District Court or the Court of Appeals, that petitioners had received hearings promptly after their paroles were revoked, or that in such hearing they admitted the violations; that information comes to us only in the respondents' brief here. Further, even the assertions that respondents make here are not based on any public record but on interviews with two of the members of the parole board. In the interview relied on to show that petitioners admitted their violations, the board member did not assert he could remember that both Morrissey and Booher admitted the parole violations with which they were charged. He stated only that, according to his memory, in the previous several years all but three returnees had admitted commission of the parole infractions alleged and that neither of the petitioners was among the three who denied them.

We must therefore treat this case in the posture and on the record respondents elected to rely on in the District Court and the Court of Appeals. If the facts are otherwise, respondents may make a showing in the District Court that petitioners in fact have admitted the violations charged before a neutral officer.

I.

Before reaching the issue of whether due process applies to the parole system, it is important to recall the function of parole in the correctional process.

During the past 60 years, the practice of releasing prisoners on parole before the end of their sentences has become an integral part of the penological system. Rather than being an ad hoc exercise of clemency, parole is an established variation on imprisonment of convicted criminals. Its purpose is to help individuals reintegrate into society as constructive individuals as soon as they are able, without being confined for the full term of the sentence imposed. It also serves to alleviate the costs to society of keeping an individual in prison. The essence of parole is release from prison, before the completion of sentence, on the condition that the prisoner abide by certain rules during the balance of the sentence. Under some systems, parole is granted automatically after the service of a certain portion of a prison term. Under others, parole is granted by the discretionary action of a board, which evaluates an array of information about a prisoner and makes a prediction whether he is ready to reintegrate into society.

To accomplish the purpose of parole, those who are allowed to leave prison early are subjected to specified conditions for the duration of their terms. These conditions restrict their activities substantially beyond the ordinary restrictions imposed by law on an individual citizen. Typically, parolees are forbidden to use liquor or to have associations or correspondence with certain categories of undesirable persons. Typically, also they must seek permission from their parole officers before engaging in specified activities, such as changing employment or living quarters, marrying, acquiring or operating a motor vehicle, traveling outside the community, and incurring substantial indebtedness. Additionally, parolees must regularly report to the parole officer to whom they are assigned and sometimes they must make periodic written reports of their activities.

The parole officers are part of the administrative system designed to assist parolees and to offer them guidance. The conditions of parole serve a dual purpose; they prohibit, either absolutely or conditionally, behavior that is deemed dangerous to the restoration of the individual into normal society. And through the requirement of reporting to the parole officer and seeking guidance and permission before doing many things, the officer is provided with information about the parolee and an opportunity to advise him. The combination puts the parole officer into the position in which he can try to guide the parolee into constructive development.

The enforcement leverage that supports the parole conditions derives from the authority to return the parolee to prison to serve out the balance of his sentence if he fails to abide by the rules. In practice, not every violation of parole conditions automatically leads to revocation. Typically, a parolee will be counseled to abide by the conditions of parole, and the parole officer ordinarily does not take steps to have parole revoked unless he thinks that the violations are serious and continuing so as to indicate that the parolee is not adjusting properly and cannot be counted on to avoid antisocial activity. The broad discretion accorded the parole officer is also inherent in some of the quite vague conditions, such as the typical requirement that the parolee avoid "undesirable" associations or correspondence. Yet revocation of parole is not an unusual phenomenon, affecting only a few parolees. It has been estimated that 35%-45% of all parolees are subjected to revocation and return to prison. Sometimes revocation occurs when the parolee is accused of another crime; it is often preferred to a new prosecution because of the procedural ease of recommitting the individual on the basis of a lesser showing by the State.

Implicit in the system's concern with parole violations is the notion that the parolee is entitled to retain his liberty as long as he substantially abides by the conditions of his parole. The first step in a revocation decision thus involves a wholly retrospective factual question: whether the parolee has in fact acted in violation of one or more conditions of his parole. Only if it is determined that the parolee did violate the conditions does the second question arise: should the parolee be recommitted to prison or should other steps be taken to protect society and improve chances of rehabilitation? The first step is relatively simple; the second is more complex. The second question involves the application of expertise by the parole authority in making a prediction as to the ability of the individual to live in society without committing antisocial acts. This part of the decision, too, depends on facts, and therefore it is important for the board to know not only that some violation was committed but also to know accurately how many and how serious the violations were. Yet this second step, deciding what to do about the violation once it is identified, is not purely factual but also predictive and discretionary.

If a parolee is returned to prison, he usually receives no credit for the time "served" on parole. Thus, the returnee may face a potential of substantial imprisonment.

II.

We begin with the proposition that the revocation of parole is not part of a criminal prosecution and thus the full panoply of rights due a defendant in such a proceeding does not apply to parole revocations. Parole arises after the end of the criminal prosecution, including imposition of sentence. Supervision is not directly by the court but by an administrative agency, which is sometimes an arm of the court and sometimes of the executive. Revocation deprives an individual, not of the absolute liberty to which every citizen is entitled, but only of the conditional liberty properly dependent on observance of special parole restrictions.

We turn, therefore, to the question whether the requirements of due process in general apply to parole revocations. As MR. JUSTICE BLACKMUN has written recently, "this Court now has rejected the concept that constitutional rights turn upon whether a governmental benefit is characterized as a 'right' or as a 'privilege.'" Whether any procedural protections are due depends on the extent to which an individual will be "condemned to suffer grievous loss." The question is not merely the "weight" of the individual's interest, but whether the nature of the interest is one within the contemplation of the "liberty or property" language of the Fourteenth Amendment. Once it is determined that due process applies, the question remains what process is due. It has been said so often by this Court and others as not to require citation of authority that due process is flexible and calls for such procedural protections as the particular situation demands. "Consideration of what procedures due process may require under any given set of circumstances must begin with a determination of the precise nature of the government function involved as well as of the private interest that has been affected by governmental action." To say that the concept of due process is flexible does not mean that judges are at large to apply it to any and all relationships. Its flexibility is in its scope once it has been determined that some process is due; it is a recognition that not all situations calling for procedural safeguards call for the same kind of procedure.

We turn to an examination of the nature of the interest of the parolee in his continued liberty. The liberty of a parolee enables him to do a wide range of things open to persons who have never been convicted of any crime. The parolee has been released from prison based on an evaluation that he shows reasonable promise of being able to return to society and function as a responsible, self-reliant person. Subject to the conditions of his parole, he can be gainfully employed and is free to be with family and friends and to form the other enduring attachments of normal life. Though the State properly subjects him to many restrictions not applicable to other citizens, his condition is very different from that of confinement in a prison. He may have been on parole for a number of years and may be living a relatively normal life at the time he is faced with revocation. The parolee has relied on at least an implicit promise that parole will be revoked only if he fails to live up to the parole conditions. In many cases, the parolee faces lengthy incarceration if his parole is revoked.

We see, therefore, that the liberty of a parolee, although indeterminate, includes many of the core values of unqualified liberty and its termination inflicts a "grievous loss" on the parolee and often on others. It is hardly useful any longer to try to deal with this problem in terms of whether the parolee's liberty is a "right" or a "privilege." By whatever name, the liberty is valuable and must be seen as within the protection of the Fourteenth Amendment. Its termination calls for some orderly process, however informal.

Turning to the question what process is due, we find that the State's interests are several. The State has found the parolee guilty of a crime against the people. That finding justifies imposing extensive restrictions on the individual's liberty. Release of the parolee before the end of his prison sentence is made with the recognition that with many prisoners there is a risk that they will not be able to live in society without committing additional antisocial acts. Given the previous conviction and the proper imposition of conditions, the State has an overwhelming interest in being able to return the individual to imprisonment without the burden of a new adversary criminal trial if in fact he has failed to abide by the conditions of his parole.

Yet, the State has no interest in revoking parole without some informal procedural guarantees. Although the parolee is often formally described as being "in custody," the argument cannot even be made here that summary treatment is necessary as it may be with respect to controlling a large group of potentially disruptive prisoners in actual custody. Nor are we persuaded by the argument that revocation is so totally a discretionary matter that some form of hearing would be administratively intolerable. A simple factual hearing will not interfere with the exercise of discretion. Serious studies have suggested that fair treatment on parole revocation will not result in fewer grants of parole.

This discretionary aspect of the revocation decision need not be reached unless there is first an appropriate determination that the individual has in fact breached the conditions of parole. The parolee is not the only one who has a stake in his conditional liberty. Society has a stake in whatever may be the chance of restoring him to normal and useful life within the law. Society thus has an interest in not having parole revoked because of erroneous information or because of an erroneous evaluation of the need to revoke parole, given the breach of parole conditions. And society has a further interest in treating the parolee with basic fairness: fair treatment in parole revocations will enhance the chance of rehabilitation by avoiding reactions to arbitrariness.

Given these factors, most States have recognized that there is no interest on the part of the State in revoking parole without any procedural guarantees at all. What is needed is an informal hearing structured to assure that the finding of a parole violation will be based on verified facts and that the exercise of discretion will be informed by an accurate knowledge of the parolee's behavior.

III.

We now turn to the nature of the process that is due, bearing in mind that the interest of both State and parolee will be furthered by an effective but informal hearing. In analyzing what is due, we see two important stages in the typical process of parole revocation.

(a) Arrest of Parolee and Preliminary Hearing. The first stage occurs when the parolee is arrested and detained, usually at the direction of his parole officer. The second occurs when parole is formally revoked. There is typically a substantial time lag between the arrest and the eventual determination by the parole board whether parole should be revoked. Additionally, it may be that the parolee is arrested at a place distant from the state institution, to which he may be returned before the final decision is made concerning revocation. Given these factors, due process would seem to require that some minimal inquiry be conducted at or reasonably near the place of the alleged parole violation or arrest and as promptly as convenient after arrest while information is fresh and sources are available. Such an inquiry should be seen as in the nature of a "preliminary hearing" to determine whether there is probable cause or reasonable ground to believe that the arrested parolee has committed acts that would constitute a violation of parole conditions.

In our view, due process requires that after the arrest, the determination that reasonable ground exists for revocation of parole should be made by someone not directly involved in the case. It would be unfair to assume that the supervising parole officer does not conduct an interview with the parolee to confront him with the reasons for revocation before he recommends an arrest.

231

It would also be unfair to assume that the parole officer bears hostility against the parolee that destroys his neutrality; realistically the failure of the parolee is in a sense a failure for his supervising officer. However, we need make no assumptions one way or the other to conclude that there should be an uninvolved person to make this preliminary evaluation of the basis for believing the conditions of parole have been violated. The officer directly involved in making recommendations cannot always have complete objectivity in evaluating them. *Goldberg v. Kelly* found it unnecessary to impugn the motives of the caseworker to find a need for an independent decisionmaker to examine the initial decision.

This independent officer need not be a judicial officer. The granting and revocation of parole are matters traditionally handled by administrative officers. In *Goldberg*, the Court pointedly did not require that the hearing on termination of benefits be conducted by a judicial officer or even before the traditional "neutral and detached" officer; it required only that the hearing be conducted by some person other than one initially dealing with the case. It will be sufficient, therefore, in the parole revocation context, if an evaluation of whether reasonable cause exists to believe that conditions of parole have been violated is made by someone such as a parole officer other than the one who has made the report of parole violations or has recommended revocation. A State could certainly choose some other independent decisionmaker to perform this preliminary function.

With respect to the preliminary hearing before this officer, the parolee should be given notice that the hearing will take place and that its purpose is to determine whether there is probable cause to believe he has committed a parole violation. The notice should state what parole violations have been alleged. At the hearing the parolee may appear and speak in his own behalf; he may bring letters, documents, or individuals who can give relevant information to the hearing officer. On request of the parolee, a person who has given adverse information on which parole revocation is to be based is to be made available for questioning in his presence. However, if the hearing officer determines that an informant would be subjected to risk of harm if his identity were disclosed, he need not be subjected to confrontation and cross-examination.

The hearing officer shall have the duty of making a summary, or digest, of what occurs at the hearing in terms of the responses of the parolee and the substance of the documents or evidence given in support of parole revocation and of the parolee's position. Based on the information before him, the officer should determine whether there is probable cause to hold the parolee for the final decision of the parole board on revocation. Such a determination would be sufficient to warrant the parolee's continued detention and return to the state correctional institution pending the final decision. As in *Goldberg*, "the decision maker should state the reasons for his determination and indicate the evidence he relied on . . ." but it should be remembered that this is not a final determination calling for "formal findings of fact and conclusions of law." No interest would be served by formalism in this process; informality will not lessen the utility of this inquiry in reducing the risk of error.

(b) The Revocation Hearing. There must also be an opportunity for a hearing, if it is desired by the parolee, prior to the final decision on revocation by the parole authority. This hearing must be the basis for more than determining probable cause; it must lead to a final evaluation of any contested relevant facts and consideration of whether the facts as determined warrant revocation. The parolee must have an opportunity to be heard and to show, if he can, that he did not violate the conditions, or, if he did, that circumstances in mitigation suggest that the violation does not warrant revocation. The revocation hearing must be tendered within a reasonable time after the parolee is taken into custody. A lapse of two months, as respondents suggests occurs in some cases, would not appear to be unreasonable.

We cannot write a code of procedure; that is the responsibility of each State. Most States have done so by legislation, others by judicial decision usually on due process grounds. Our task is limited to deciding the minimum requirements of due process. They include (a) written notice of the claimed violations of parole; (b) disclosure to the parolee of evidence against him; (c) opportunity to be heard in person and to present witnesses and documentary evidence; (d) the right to confront and cross-examine adverse witnesses (unless the hearing officer specifically finds good cause for not allowing confrontation); (e) a "neutral and detached" hearing body such as a traditional parole board, members of which need not be judicial officers or lawyers; and (f) a written statement by the factfinders as to the evidence relied on and reasons for revoking parole. We emphasize there is no thought to equate this second stage of parole revocation to a criminal prosecution in any sense. It is a narrow inquiry; the process should be flexible enough to consider evidence including letters, affidavits, and other material that would not be admissible in an adversary criminal trial.

We do not reach or decide the question whether the parolee is entitled to the assistance of retained counsel or to appointed counsel if he is indigent.

We have no thought to create an inflexible structure for parole revocation procedures. The few basic requirements set out above, which are applicable to future revocations of parole, should not impose a great burden on any State's parole system. Control over the required proceedings by the hearing officers can assure that delaying tactics and other abuses sometimes present in the traditional adversary trial situation do not occur. Obviously, a parolee cannot relitigate issues determined against him in other forums, as in the situation presented when the revocation is based on conviction of another crime.

In the peculiar posture of this case, given the absence of an adequate record, we conclude the ends of justice will be best served by remanding the case to the Court of Appeals for its return of the two consolidated cases to the District Court with directions to make findings on the procedures actually followed by the Parole Board in these two revocations. If it is determined that petitioners admitted parole violations to the Parole Board, as respondents contend, and if those violations are found to be reasonable grounds for revoking parole under state standards, that would end the matter. If the procedures followed by the Parole Board are found to meet the standards laid down in this opinion that, too, would dispose of the due process claims for these cases.

We reverse and remand to the Court of Appeals for further proceedings consistent with this opinion.

Reversed and remanded.

<h1 align="center">*Gagnon v. Scarpelli (1973)*</h1>
411 U.S. 778

This case presents the related questions whether a previously sentenced probationer is entitled to a hearing when his probation is revoked and, if so, whether he is entitled to be represented by appointed counsel at such a hearing.

I.

Respondent, Gerald Scarpelli, pleaded guilty in July 1965, to a charge of armed robbery in Wisconsin. The trial judge sentenced him to 15 years' imprisonment, but suspended the sentence and placed him on probation for seven years in the custody of the Wisconsin Department of Public Welfare (the Department). At that time, he signed an agreement specifying the terms of his probation and a "Travel Permit and Agreement to Return" allowing him to reside in Illinois, with supervision there under an interstate compact. On August 5, 1965, he was accepted for supervision by the Adult Probation Department of Cook County, Illinois.

On August 6, respondent was apprehended by Illinois police, who had surprised him and one Fred Kleckner, Jr., in the course of the burglary of a house. After being apprised of his constitutional rights, respondent admitted that he and Kleckner had broken into the house for the purpose of stealing merchandise or money, although he now asserts that his statement was made under duress and is false. Probation was revoked by the Wisconsin Department on September 1, without a hearing. The stated grounds for revocation were that:

"1. [Scarpelli] has associated with known criminals, in direct violation of his probation regulations and his supervising agent's instructions;

"2. [Scarpelli,] while associating with a known criminal, namely Fred Kleckner, Jr., was involved in, and arrested for, a burglary . . . in Deerfield, Illinois."

On September 4, 1965, he was incarcerated in the Wisconsin State Reformatory at Green Bay to begin serving the 15 years to which he had been sentenced by the trial judge. At no time was he afforded a hearing.

Some three years later, on December 16, 1968, respondent applied for a writ of habeas corpus. After the petition had been filed, but before it had been acted upon, the Department placed respondent on parole. The District Court found that his status as parolee was sufficient custody to confer jurisdiction on the court and that the petition was not moot because the revocation carried "collateral consequences," presumably including the restraints imposed by his parole. On the merits, the District Court held that revocation without a hearing and counsel was a denial of due process. The Court of Appeals affirmed *sub nom*, and we granted certiorari.

II.

Two prior decisions set the bounds of our present inquiry. In *Mempa v. Rhay* (1967), the Court held that a probationer is entitled to be represented by appointed counsel at a combined revocation and sentencing hearing. Reasoning that counsel is required "at every stage of a criminal proceeding where substantial rights of a criminal accused may be affected," and that sentencing is one such stage, the Court concluded that counsel must be provided an indigent at sentencing even when it is accomplished as part of a subsequent probation revocation proceeding. But this line of reasoning does not require a hearing or counsel at the time of probation revocation in a case such as the present one, where the probationer was sentenced at the time of trial.

Of greater relevance is our decision last Term in *Morrissey v. Brewer*. There we held that the revocation of parole is not a part of a criminal prosecution.

"Parole arises after the end of the criminal prosecution, including imposition of sentence. . . . Revocation deprives an individual, not of the absolute liberty to which every citizen is entitled, but only of the conditional liberty properly dependent on observance of special parole restrictions."

Even though the revocation of parole is not a part of the criminal prosecution, we held that the loss of liberty entailed is a serious deprivation requiring that the parolee be accorded due process. Specifically, we held that a parolee is entitled to two hearings, one a preliminary hearing at the time of his arrest and detention to determine whether there is probable cause to believe that he

234

has committed a violation of his parole, and the other a somewhat more comprehensive hearing prior to the making of the final revocation decision.

Petitioner does not contend that there is any difference relevant to the guarantee of due process between the revocation of parole and the revocation of probation, nor do we perceive one. Probation revocation, like parole revocation, is not a stage of a criminal prosecution, but does result in a loss of liberty. Accordingly, we hold that a probationer, like a parolee, is entitled to a preliminary and a final revocation hearing, under the conditions specified in *Morrissey v. Brewer*.

III.

The second, and more difficult, question posed by this case is whether an indigent probationer or parolee has a due process right to be represented by appointed counsel at these hearings. In answering that question, we draw heavily on the opinion in *Morrissey*. Our first point of reference is the character of probation or parole. As noted in *Morrissey* regarding parole, the "purpose is to help individuals reintegrate into society as constructive individuals as soon as they are able . . ." The duty and attitude of the probation or parole officer reflect this purpose:

"While the parole or probation officer recognizes his double duty to the welfare of his clients and to the safety of the general community, by and large concern for the client dominates his professional attitude. The parole agent ordinarily defines his role as representing his client's best interests as long as these do not constitute a threat to public safety."

Because the probation or parole officer's function is not so much to compel conformance to a strict code of behavior as to supervise a course of rehabilitation, he has been entrusted traditionally with broad discretion to judge the progress of rehabilitation in individual cases, and has been armed with the power to recommend or even to declare revocation.

In *Morrissey*, we recognized that the revocation decision has two analytically distinct components:

"The first step in a revocation decision thus involves a wholly retrospective factual question: whether the parolee has in fact acted in violation of one or more conditions of his parole. Only if it is determined that the parolee did violate the conditions does the second question arise: should the parolee be recommitted to prison or should other steps be taken to protect society and improve chances of rehabilitation?"

The parole officer's attitude toward these decisions reflects the rehabilitative rather than punitive focus of the probation/parole system:

"Revocation . . . is, if anything, commonly treated as a failure of supervision. While presumably it would be inappropriate for a field agent never to revoke, the whole thrust of the probation-parole movement is to keep men in the community, working with adjustment problems there, and using revocation only as a last resort when treatment has failed or is about to fail."

But an exclusive focus on the benevolent attitudes of those who administer the probation/parole system when it is working successfully obscures the modification in attitude which is likely to take place once the officer has decided to recommend revocation. Even though the officer is not by this recommendation converted into a prosecutor committed to convict, his role as counsellor to the probationer or parolee is then surely compromised.

When the officer's view of the probationer's or parolee's conduct differs in this fundamental way from the latter's own view, due process requires that the difference be resolved before revocation becomes final. Both the probationer or parolee and the State have interests in the accurate finding of fact and the informed use of discretion—the probationer or parolee to insure that his liberty is not unjustifiably taken away and the State to make certain that it is neither unnecessarily interrupting a successful effort at rehabilitation nor imprudently prejudicing the safety of the community.

It was to serve all of these interests that *Morrissey* mandated preliminary and final revocation hearings. At the preliminary hearing, a probationer or parolee is entitled to notice of the alleged violations of probation or parole, an opportunity to appear and to present evidence in his own behalf, a conditional right to confront adverse witnesses, an independent decisionmaker, and a written report of the hearing. The final hearing is a less summary one because the decision under consideration is the ultimate decision to revoke rather than a mere determination of probable cause, but the "minimum requirements of due process" include very similar elements:

"(a) written notice of the claimed violations of probation or parole; (b) disclosure to the probationer or parolee of evidence against him; (c) opportunity to be heard in person and to present witnesses and documentary evidence; (d) the right to confront and cross-examine adverse witnesses (unless the hearing officer specifically finds good cause for not allowing confrontation); (e) a 'neutral and detached' hearing body such as a traditional parole board, members of which need not be judicial officers or lawyers; and (f) a written statement by the factfinders as to the evidence relied on and reasons for revoking probation or parole."

These requirements in themselves serve as substantial protection against ill-considered revocation, and petitioner argues that counsel need never be supplied. What this argument overlooks is that the effectiveness of the rights guaranteed by *Morrissey* may in some circumstances depend on the use of skills which the probationer or parolee is unlikely to possess. Despite the informal nature of the proceedings and the absence of technical rules of procedure or evidence, the unskilled or uneducated probationer or parolee may well have difficulty in presenting his version of a disputed set of facts where the presentation requires the examining or cross-examining of witnesses or the offering or dissecting of complex documentary evidence.

By the same token, we think that the Court of Appeals erred in accepting respondent's contention that the State is under a constitutional duty to provide counsel for indigents in all probation or parole revocation cases. While such a rule has the appeal of simplicity, it would impose direct costs and serious collateral disadvantages without regard to the need or the likelihood in a particular case for a constructive contribution by counsel. In most cases, the probationer or parolee has been convicted of committing another crime or has admitted the charges against him. And while in some cases he may have a justifiable excuse for the violation or a convincing reason why revocation is not the appropriate disposition, mitigating evidence of this kind is often not susceptible of proof or is so simple as not to require either investigation or exposition by counsel.

The introduction of counsel into a revocation proceeding will alter significantly the nature of the proceeding. If counsel is provided for the probationer or parolee, the State in turn will normally provide its own counsel; lawyers, by training and disposition, are advocates and bound by professional duty to present all available evidence and arguments in support of their clients' positions and to contest with vigor all adverse evidence and views. The role of the hearing body itself, aptly described in *Morrissey* as being "predictive and discretionary" as well as factfinding, may become more akin to that of a judge at a trial, and less attuned to the rehabilitative needs of the individual probationer or parolee. In the greater self-consciousness of its quasi-judicial role, the hearing body may be less tolerant of marginal deviant behavior and feel more pressure to reincarcerate than to continue nonpunitive rehabilitation. Certainly, the decisionmaking process will be prolonged, and the financial cost to the State—for appointed counsel, counsel for the State, a longer record, and the possibility of judicial review—will not be insubstantial.

In some cases, these modifications in the nature of the revocation hearing must be endured and the costs borne because, as we have indicated above, the probationer's or parolee's version of a disputed issue can fairly be represented only by a trained advocate. But due process is not so rigid as to require that the significant interests in informality, flexibility, and economy must always be sacrificed.

In so concluding, we are of course aware that the case-by-case approach to the right to counsel in felony prosecutions adopted in *Betts v. Brady* (1942), was later rejected in favor of a *per se* rule in *Gideon v. Wainwright* (1963). We do not, however, draw from *Gideon* and *Argersinger* the conclusion that a case-by-case approach to furnishing counsel is necessarily inadequate to protect constitutional rights asserted in varying types of proceedings: there are critical differences between criminal trials and probation or parole revocation hearings, and both society and the probationer or parolee have stakes in preserving these differences.

In a criminal trial, the State is represented by a prosecutor; formal rules of evidence are in force; a defendant enjoys a number of procedural rights which may be lost if not timely raised; and, in a jury trial, a defendant must make a presentation understandable to untrained jurors. In short, a criminal trial under our system is an adversary proceeding with its own unique characteristics. In a revocation hearing, on the other hand, the State is represented, not by a prosecutor, but by a parole officer with the orientation described above; formal procedures and rules of evidence are not employed; and the members of the hearing body are familiar with the problems and practice of probation or parole. The need for counsel at revocation hearings derives, not from the invariable attributes of those hearings, but rather from the peculiarities of particular cases.

The differences between a criminal trial and a revocation hearing do not dispose altogether of the argument that under a case-by-case approach there may be cases in which a lawyer would be useful but in which none would be appointed because an arguable defense would be uncovered only by a lawyer. Without denying that there is some force in this argument, we think it a sufficient answer that we deal here, not with the right of an accused to counsel in a criminal prosecution, but with the more limited due process right of one who is a probationer or parolee only because he has been convicted of a crime.

We thus find no justification for a new inflexible constitutional rule with respect to the requirement of counsel. We think, rather, that the decision as to the need for counsel must be made on a case-by-case basis in the exercise of a sound discretion by the state authority charged with responsibility for administering the probation and parole system. Although the presence and participation of counsel will probably be both undesirable and constitutionally unnecessary in most revocation hearings, there will remain certain cases in which fundamental fairness—the touchstone of due process—will require that the State provide at its expense counsel for indigent probationers or parolees.

It is neither possible nor prudent to attempt to formulate a precise and detailed set of guidelines to be followed in determining when the providing of counsel is necessary to meet the applicable due process requirements. The facts and circumstances in preliminary and final hearings are susceptible of almost infinite variation, and a considerable discretion must be allowed the responsible agency in making the decision. Presumptively, it may be said that counsel should be provided in cases where, after being informed of his right to request counsel, the probationer or parolee makes such a request, based on a timely and colorable claim (i) that he has not committed the alleged violation of the conditions upon which he is at liberty; or (ii) that, even if the violation is a matter of public record or is uncontested, there are substantial reasons which justified or mitigated the violation and make revocation inappropriate, and that the reasons are complex or otherwise difficult to develop or present. In passing on a request for the appointment of counsel, the responsible agency also should consider, especially in doubtful cases, whether the probationer appears to be capable of speaking effectively for himself. In every case in which a request for counsel at a preliminary or final hearing is refused, the grounds for refusal should be stated succinctly in the record.

IV.

We return to the facts of the present case. Because respondent was not afforded either a preliminary hearing or a final hearing, the revocation of his probation did not meet the standards of due process prescribed in *Morrissey*, which we have here held applicable to probation revocations. Accordingly, respondent was entitled to a writ of habeas corpus. On remand, the District Court should allow the State an opportunity to conduct such a hearing. As to whether the State must provide counsel, respondent's admission to having committed another serious crime creates the very sort of situation in which counsel need not ordinarily be provided. But because of respondent's subsequent assertions regarding that admission, we conclude that the failure of the Department to provide respondent with the assistance of counsel should be re-examined in light of this opinion. The general guidelines outlined above should be applied in the first instance by those charged with conducting the revocation hearing.

Affirmed in part, reversed in part, and remanded.

Part V: Juvenile Justice

Breed v. Jones (1975)
421 U.S. 519

In this case, the Supreme Court was asked to determine if a juvenile is first adjudicated delinquent in a juvenile court, is a subsequent trail in an adult criminal court a violation of the Double Jeopardy Clause. The Court said that it was indeed a violation of the Fifth and Fourteenth Amendments. Because of this ruling, many juvenile courts now conduct waiver hearings *to determine if a juvenile should be tried in adult court.*

We granted certiorari to decide whether the prosecution of respondent as an adult, after Juvenile Court proceedings which resulted in a finding that respondent had violated a criminal statute and a subsequent finding that he was unfit for treatment as a juvenile, violated the Fifth and Fourteenth Amendments to the United States Constitution.

On February 9, 1971, a petition was filed in the Superior Court of California, County of Los Angeles, Juvenile Court, alleging that respondent, then 17 years of age, was a person described by Cal. Welf. & Inst'ns Code § 602 (1966), in that, on or about February 8, while armed with a deadly weapon, he had committed acts which, if committed by an adult, would constitute the crime of robbery in violation of Cal. Penal Code § 211 (1970). The following day, a detention hearing was held, at the conclusion of which respondent was ordered detained pending a hearing on the petition.

The jurisdictional or adjudicatory hearing was conducted on March 1, pursuant to Cal. Welf. & Inst'ns Code § 701 (1966). After taking testimony from two prosecution witnesses and respondent, the Juvenile Court found that the allegations in the petition were true and that respondent was a person described by § 602, and it sustained the petition. The proceedings were continued for a dispositional hearing, pending which the court ordered that respondent remain detained.

At a hearing conducted on March 15, the Juvenile Court indicated its intention to find respondent "not... amenable to the care, treatment and training program available through the facilities of the juvenile court" under Cal. Welf. & Inst'ns Code § 707 (Supp. 1967). Respondent's counsel orally moved "to continue the matter on the ground of surprise," contending that respondent "was not informed that it was going to be a fitness hearing." The court continued the matter for one week, at which time, having considered the report of the probation officer assigned to the case and having heard her testimony, it declared respondent "unfit for treatment as a juvenile," and ordered that he be prosecuted as an adult.

Thereafter, respondent filed a petition for a writ of habeas corpus in Juvenile Court, raising the same double jeopardy claim now presented. Upon the denial of that petition, respondent sought habeas corpus relief in the California Court of Appeal, Second Appellate District. Although it initially stayed the criminal prosecution pending against respondent, that court denied the petition. The Supreme Court of California denied respondent's petition for hearing.

After a preliminary hearing respondent was ordered held for trial in Superior Court, where an information was subsequently filed accusing him of having committed robbery, in violation of Cal. Penal Code § 211(1970), while armed with a deadly weapon, on or about February 8, 1971. Respondent entered a plea of not guilty, and he also pleaded that he had "already been placed once in jeopardy and convicted of the offense charged, by the judgment of the Superior Court of the County of Los Angeles, Juvenile Court, rendered... on the 1st day of March, 1971." By stipulation, the case was submitted to the court on the transcript of the preliminary hearing. The court found respondent guilty of robbery in the first degree under Cal. Penal Code § 211a (1970) and ordered that he be committed to the California Youth Authority. No appeal was taken from the judgment of conviction.

On December 10, 1971, respondent, through his mother as *guardian ad litem,* filed the instant petition for a writ of habeas corpus in the United States District Court for the Central District of California. In his petition he alleged that his transfer to adult court pursuant to Cal. Welf. & Inst'ns Code § 707 and subsequent trial there "placed him in double jeopardy." The District Court denied the petition, rejecting respondent's contention that jeopardy attached at his adjudicatory hearing. It concluded that the "distinctions between the preliminary procedures and hearings provided by California law for juveniles and a criminal trial are many and apparent and the effort of respondent to relate them is unconvincing," and that "even assuming jeopardy attached during the preliminary juvenile proceedings... it is clear that no new jeopardy arose by the juvenile proceeding sending the case to the criminal court."

The Court of Appeals reversed, concluding that applying double jeopardy protection to juvenile proceedings would not "impede the juvenile courts in carrying out their basic goal of rehabilitating the erring youth," and that the contrary result might "do irreparable harm to or destroy their confidence in our judicial system." The court therefore held that the Double Jeopardy Clause "is fully applicable to juvenile court proceedings."

Turning to the question whether there had been a constitutional violation in this case, the Court of Appeals pointed to the power of the Juvenile Court to "impose severe restrictions upon the juvenile's liberty" in support of its conclusion that jeopardy attached in respondent's adjudicatory hearing. It rejected petitioner's contention that no new jeopardy attached when respondent was referred to Superior Court and subsequently tried and convicted, finding "continuing jeopardy" principles advanced by petitioner inapplicable. Finally, the Court of Appeals observed that acceptance of petitioner's position would "allow the prosecution to review in advance the accused's defense and, as here, hear him testify about the crime charged," a procedure it found offensive to "our concepts of basic, even-handed fairness." The court therefore held that once jeopardy attached at the adjudicatory hearing, a minor could not be retried as an adult or a juvenile "absent some exception to the double jeopardy prohibition," and that there "was none here."

We granted certiorari because of a conflict between Courts of Appeals and the highest courts of a number of States on the issue presented in this case and similar issues and because of the importance of final resolution of the issue to the administration of the juvenile-court system.

I.

The parties agree that, following his transfer from Juvenile Court, and as a defendant to a felony information, respondent was entitled to the full protection of the Double Jeopardy Clause of the Fifth Amendment, as applied to the States through the Fourteenth Amendment. In addition, they agree that respondent was put in jeopardy by the proceedings on that information, which resulted in an adjudication that he was guilty of robbery in the first degree and in a sentence of commitment. Finally, there is no dispute that the petition filed in Juvenile Court and the information filed in Superior Court related to the "same offence" within the meaning of the constitutional prohibition. The point of disagreement between the parties, and the question for our decision, is whether, by reason of the proceedings in Juvenile Court, respondent was "twice put in jeopardy."

II.

Jeopardy denotes risk. In the constitutional sense, jeopardy describes the risk that is traditionally associated with a criminal prosecution. Although the constitutional language, "jeopardy of life or limb," suggests proceedings in which only the most serious penalties can be imposed, the Clause has long been construed to mean something far broader than its literal language. At the same time, however, we have held that the risk to which the Clause refers is not present in proceedings that are not "essentially criminal."

Although the juvenile court system had its genesis in the desire to provide a distinctive procedure and setting to deal with the problems of youth, including those manifested by antisocial conduct, our decisions in recent years have recognized that there is a gap between the originally benign conception of the system and its realities. With the exception of *McKeiver v. Pennsylvania* (1971), the Court's response to that perception has been to make applicable in juvenile proceedings constitutional guarantees associated with traditional criminal prosecutions. In so doing the Court has evinced awareness of the threat which such a process represents to the efforts of the juvenile-court system, functioning in a unique manner, to ameliorate the harshness of criminal justice when applied to youthful offenders. That the system has fallen short of the high expectations of its sponsors in no way detracts from the broad social benefits sought or from those benefits that can survive constitutional scrutiny.

We believe it is simply too late in the day to conclude, as did the District Court in this case, that a juvenile is not put in jeopardy at a proceeding whose object is to determine whether he has committed acts that violate a criminal law and whose potential consequences include both the stigma inherent in such a determination and the deprivation of liberty for many years. For it is clear under our cases that determining the relevance of constitutional policies, like determining the applicability of constitutional rights, in juvenile proceedings, requires that courts eschew "the 'civil' label-of-convenience which has been attached to juvenile proceedings," and that "the juvenile process... be candidly appraised."

As we have observed, the risk to which the term jeopardy refers is that traditionally associated with "actions intended to authorize criminal punishment to vindicate public justice." Because of its purpose and potential consequences, and the nature and resources of the State, such a proceeding imposes heavy pressures and burdens— psychological, physical, and financial—on a person charged. The purpose of the Double Jeopardy Clause is to require that he be subject to the experience only once "for the same offence."

In *In re Gault*, this Court concluded that, for purposes of the right to counsel, a "proceeding where the issue is whether the child will be found to be 'delinquent' and subjected to the loss of his liberty for years is comparable in seriousness to a felony prosecution." The Court stated that the term "delinquent" had "come to involve only slightly less stigma than the term 'criminal' applied to adults," and that, for purposes of the privilege against self-incrimination, "commitment is a deprivation of liberty. It is incarceration against one's will, whether it is called 'criminal' or 'civil.'"

Thus, in terms of potential consequences, there is little to distinguish an adjudicatory hearing such as was held in this case from a traditional criminal prosecution. For that reason, it engenders elements of "anxiety and insecurity" in a juvenile, and imposes a "heavy personal strain." And we can expect that, since our decisions implementing fundamental fairness in the juvenile-court system, hearings have been prolonged, and some of the burdens incident to a juvenile's defense increased, as the system has assimilated the process thereby imposed.

We deal here, not with "the formalities of the criminal adjudicative process," but with an analysis of an aspect of the juvenile-court system in terms of the kind of risk to which jeopardy refers. Under our decisions we can find no persuasive distinction in that regard between the proceeding conducted in this case pursuant to Cal. Welf. & Inst'ns Code § 701 and a criminal prosecution, each of which is designed "to vindicate the very vital interest in enforcement of criminal laws." We therefore conclude that respondent was put in jeopardy at the adjudicatory hearing. Jeopardy attached when respondent was "put to trial before the trier of the facts," that is, when the Juvenile Court, as the trier of the facts, began to hear evidence.

Petitioner argues that, even assuming jeopardy attached at respondent's adjudicatory hearing, the procedure by which he was transferred from Juvenile Court and tried on a felony information in Superior Court did not violate the Double Jeopardy Clause. The argument is supported by two distinct, but in this case overlapping, lines of analysis. First, petitioner reasons that the procedure violated none of the policies of the Double Jeopardy Clause or that, alternatively, it should be upheld by analogy to those cases which permit retrial of an accused who has obtained reversal of a conviction on appeal. Second, pointing to this Court's concern for "the juvenile court's assumed ability to function in a unique manner," petitioner urges that, should we conclude traditional principles "would otherwise bar a transfer to adult court after a delinquency adjudication," we should avoid that result here because it "would diminish the flexibility and informality of juvenile court proceedings without conferring any additional due process benefits upon juveniles charged with delinquent acts."

A.

We cannot agree with petitioner that the trial of respondent in Superior Court on an information charging the same offense as that for which he had been tried in Juvenile Court violated none of the policies of the Double Jeopardy Clause. For, even accepting petitioner's premise that respondent "never faced the risk of more than one punishment," we have pointed out that "the Double Jeopardy Clause... is written in terms of potential or risk of trial and conviction, not punishment." And we have recently noted: "The policy of avoiding multiple trials has been regarded as so important that exceptions to the principle have been only grudgingly allowed. Initially, a new trial was thought to be unavailable after appeal, whether requested by the prosecution or the defendant.... It was not until 1896 that it was made clear that a defendant could seek a new trial after conviction, even though the Government enjoyed no similar right.... Following the same policy, the Court has granted the Government the right to retry a defendant after a mistrial only where 'there is a manifest necessity for the act, or the ends of public justice would otherwise be defeated.'"

Respondent was subjected to the burden of two trials for the same offense; he was twice put to the task of marshaling his resources against those of the State, twice subjected to the "heavy personal strain" which such an experience represents. We turn, therefore, to inquire whether either traditional principles or "the juvenile court's assumed ability to function in a unique manner," supports an exception to the "constitutional policy of finality" to which respondent would otherwise be entitled.

B.

In denying respondent's petitions for writs of habeas corpus, the California Court of Appeal first, and the United States District Court later, concluded that no new jeopardy arose as a result of his transfer from Juvenile Court and trial in Superior Court. In the view of those courts, the jeopardy that attaches at an adjudicatory hearing continues until there is a final disposition of the case under the adult charge.

The phrase "continuing jeopardy" describes both a concept and a conclusion. As originally articulated by Mr. Justice Holmes in his dissent in *Kepner v. United States* (1904), the concept has proved an interesting model for comparison with the system of constitutional protection which the Court has in fact derived from the rather ambiguous language and history of the Double Jeopardy Clause. Holmes' view has "never been adopted by a majority of this Court."

The conclusion, "continuing jeopardy," as distinguished from the concept, has occasionally been used to explain why an accused who has secured the reversal of a conviction on appeal may be retried for the same offense. Probably a more satisfactory explanation lies in analysis of the respective interests involved. Similarly, the fact that the proceedings against respondent had not "run their full course," within the contemplation of the California Welfare and Institutions Code, at the time of transfer, does not satisfactorily explain why respondent should be deprived of the constitutional protection against a second trial. If there is to be an exception to that protection in the context of the juvenile-court system, it must be justified by interests of society, reflected in that unique institution, or of juveniles themselves, of sufficient substance to render tolerable the costs and burdens, noted earlier, which the exception will entail in individual cases.

C.

The possibility of transfer from juvenile court to a court of general criminal jurisdiction is a matter of great significance to the juvenile. At the same time, there appears to be widely shared agreement that not all juveniles can benefit from the special features and programs of the juvenile-court system and that a procedure for transfer to an adult court should be available. This general agreement is reflected in the fact that an overwhelming majority of jurisdictions permits transfer in certain circumstances. As might be expected, the statutory provisions differ in numerous details. Whatever their differences, however, such transfer provisions represent an attempt to impart to the juvenile-court system the flexibility needed to deal with youthful offenders who cannot benefit from the specialized guidance and treatment contemplated by the system.

We do not agree with petitioner that giving respondent the constitutional protection against multiple trials in this context will diminish flexibility and informality to the extent that those qualities relate uniquely to the goals of the juvenile-court system. We agree that such a holding will require, in most cases, that the transfer decision be made prior to an adjudicatory hearing. To the extent that evidence concerning the alleged offense is considered relevant, it may be that, in those cases where transfer is considered and rejected, some added burden will be imposed on the juvenile courts by reason of duplicative proceedings. Finally, the nature of the evidence considered at a transfer hearing may in some States require that, if transfer is rejected, a different judge preside at the adjudicatory hearing.

We recognize that juvenile courts, perhaps even more than most courts, suffer from the problems created by spiraling caseloads unaccompanied by enlarged resources and manpower. And courts should be reluctant to impose on the juvenile-court system any additional requirements which could so strain its resources as to endanger its unique functions. However, the burdens that petitioner envisions appear to us neither qualitatively nor quantitatively sufficient to justify a departure in this context from the fundamental prohibition against double jeopardy.

 A requirement that transfer hearings be held prior to adjudicatory hearings affects not at all the nature of the latter proceedings. More significantly, such a requirement need not affect the quality of decisionmaking at transfer hearings themselves. In *Kent v. United States*, the Court held that hearings under the statute there involved "must measure up to the essentials of due process and fair treatment." However, the Court has never attempted to prescribe criteria for, or the nature and quantum of evidence that must support, a decision to transfer a juvenile for trial in adult court. We require only that, whatever the relevant criteria, and whatever the evidence demanded, a State determine whether it wants to treat a juvenile within the juvenile-court system before entering upon a proceeding that may result in an adjudication that he has violated a criminal law and in a substantial deprivation of liberty, rather than subject him to the expense, delay, strain, and embarrassment of two such proceedings.

Moreover, we are not persuaded that the burdens petitioner envisions would pose a significant problem for the administration of the juvenile-court system. The large number of jurisdictions that presently require that the transfer decision be made prior to an adjudicatory hearing, and the absence of any indication that the juvenile courts in those jurisdictions have not been able to perform their task within that framework, suggest the contrary. The likelihood that in many cases the lack of need or basis for a transfer hearing can be recognized promptly reduces the number of cases in which a commitment of resources is necessary. In addition, we have no reason to believe that the resources available to those who recommend transfer or participate in the process leading to transfer decisions are inadequate to enable them to gather the information relevant to informed decision prior to an adjudicatory hearing.

To the extent that transfer hearings held prior to adjudication result in some duplication of evidence if transfer is rejected, the burden on juvenile courts will tend to be offset somewhat by the cases in which, because of transfer, no further proceedings in juvenile court are required. Moreover, when transfer has previously been rejected, juveniles may well be more likely to admit the commission of the offense charged, thereby obviating the need for adjudicatory hearings, than if transfer remains a possibility. Finally, we note that those States which presently require a different judge to preside at an adjudicatory hearing if transfer is rejected also permit waiver of that requirement. Where the requirement is not waived, it is difficult to see a substantial strain on judicial resources.

Quite apart from our conclusions with respect to the burdens on the juvenile-court system envisioned by petitioner, we are persuaded that transfer hearings prior to adjudication will aid the objectives of that system. What concerns us here is the dilemma that the possibility of transfer after an adjudicatory hearing presents for a juvenile, a dilemma to which the Court of Appeals alluded. Because of that possibility, a juvenile, thought to be the beneficiary of special consideration, may in fact suffer substantial disadvantages. If he appears uncooperative, he runs the risk of an adverse adjudication, as well as of an unfavorable dispositional recommendation. If, on the other hand, he is cooperative, he runs the risk of prejudicing his chances in adult court if transfer is ordered. We regard a procedure that results in such a dilemma as at odds with the goal that, to the extent fundamental fairness permits, adjudicatory hearings be informal and nonadversary. Knowledge of the risk of transfer after an adjudicatory hearing can only undermine the potential for informality and cooperation which was intended to be the hallmark of the juvenile-court system. Rather than concerning themselves with the matter at hand, establishing innocence or seeking a disposition best suited to individual correctional needs, the juvenile and his attorney are pressed into a posture of adversary wariness that is conducive to neither.

IV.

We hold that the prosecution of respondent in Superior Court, after an adjudicatory proceeding in Juvenile Court, violated the Double Jeopardy Clause of the Fifth Amendment, as applied to the States through the Fourteenth Amendment. The mandate of the Court of Appeals, which was stayed by that court pending our decision, directs the District Court "to issue a writ of habeas corpus directing the state court, within 60 days, to vacate the adult conviction of Jones and either set him free or remand him to the juvenile court for disposition." Since respondent is no longer subject to the jurisdiction of the California Juvenile Court, we vacate the judgment and remand the case to the Court of Appeals for such further proceedings consistent with this opinion as may be appropriate in the circumstances.

So ordered.

In Re Gault (1967)
387 U.S. 1

In this case, the Supreme Court was called upon to define the procedural protections that a juvenile is entitled to in hearings where incarceration is possible. The resulting list has had an enormous impact on the administration of the Juvenile Justice System since this landmark decision was handed down.

This is an appeal under 28 U. S. C. § 1257 (2) from a judgment of the Supreme Court of Arizona affirming the dismissal of a petition for a writ of habeas corpus. The petition sought the release of Gerald Francis Gault, appellants' 15-year-old son, who had been committed as a juvenile delinquent to the State Industrial School by the Juvenile Court of Gila County, Arizona. The Supreme Court of Arizona affirmed dismissal of the writ against various arguments which included an attack upon the constitutionality of the Arizona Juvenile Code because of its alleged denial of procedural due process rights to juveniles charged with being "delinquents." The court agreed that the constitutional guarantee of due process of law is applicable in such proceedings. It held that Arizona's Juvenile Code is to be read as "impliedly" implementing the "due process concept." It then proceeded to identify and describe "the particular elements which constitute due process in a juvenile hearing." It concluded that the proceedings ending in commitment of Gerald Gault did not offend those requirements. We do not agree, and we reverse. We begin with a statement of the facts.

I.

On Monday, June 8, 1964, at about 10 a. m., Gerald Francis Gault and a friend, Ronald Lewis, were taken into custody by the Sheriff of Gila County. Gerald was then still subject to a six months' probation order which had been entered on February 25, 1964, as a result of his having been in the company of another boy who had stolen a wallet from a lady's purse. The police action on June 8 was taken as the result of a verbal complaint by a neighbor of the boys, Mrs. Cook, about a telephone call made to her in which the caller or callers made lewd or indecent remarks. It will suffice for purposes of this opinion to say that the remarks or questions put to her were of the irritatingly offensive, adolescent, sex variety.

At the time Gerald was picked up, his mother and father were both at work. No notice that Gerald was being taken into custody was left at the home. No other steps were taken to advise them that their son had, in effect, been arrested. Gerald was taken to the Children's Detention Home. When his mother arrived home at about 6 o'clock, Gerald was not there. Gerald's older brother was sent to look for him at the trailer home of the Lewis family. He apparently learned then that Gerald was in custody. He so informed his mother. The two of them went to the Detention Home. The deputy probation officer, Flagg, who was also superintendent of the Detention Home, told Mrs. Gault "why Jerry was there" and said that a hearing would be held in Juvenile Court at 3 o'clock the following day, June 9.

Officer Flagg filed a petition with the court on the hearing day, June 9, 1964. It was not served on the Gaults. Indeed, none of them saw this petition until the habeas corpus hearing on August 17, 1964. The petition was entirely formal. It made no reference to any factual basis for the judicial action which it initiated. It recited only that "said minor is under the age of eighteen years, and is in need of the protection of this Honorable Court; and that said minor is a delinquent minor." It prayed for a hearing and an order regarding "the care and custody of said minor." Officer Flagg executed a formal affidavit in support of the petition.

On June 9, Gerald, his mother, his older brother, and Probation Officers Flagg and Henderson appeared before the Juvenile Judge in chambers. Gerald's father was not there. He was at work out of the city. Mrs. Cook, the complainant, was not there. No one was sworn at this hearing. No transcript or recording was made. No memorandum or record of the substance of the proceedings was prepared. Our information about the proceedings and the subsequent hearing on June 15, derives entirely from the testimony of the Juvenile Court Judge, Mr. and Mrs. Gault and Officer Flagg at the habeas corpus proceeding conducted two months later. From this, it appears that at the June 9 hearing Gerald was questioned by the judge about the telephone call. There was conflict as to what he said. His mother recalled that Gerald said he only dialed Mrs. Cook's number and handed the telephone to his friend, Ronald. Officer Flagg recalled that Gerald had admitted making the lewd remarks. Judge McGhee testified that Gerald "admitted making one of these lewd statements." At the conclusion of the hearing, the judge said he would "think about it." Gerald was taken back to the Detention Home. He was not sent to his own home with his parents. On June 11 or 12, after having been detained since June 8, Gerald was released and driven home. There is no explanation in the record as to why he was kept in the Detention Home or why he was released. At 5 p. m. on the day of Gerald's release, Mrs. Gault received a note signed by Officer Flagg. It was on plain paper, not letterhead. Its entire text was as follows:

"Mrs. Gault:

"Judge McGHEE has set Monday June 15, 1964 at 11:00 A. M. as the date and time for further Hearings on Gerald's delinquency."

At the appointed time on Monday, June 15, Gerald, his father and mother, Ronald Lewis and his father, and Officers Flagg and Henderson were present before Judge McGhee. Witnesses at the habeas corpus proceeding differed in their recollections of Gerald's testimony at the June 15 hearing. Mr. and Mrs. Gault recalled that Gerald again testified that he had only dialed the number and that the other boy had made the remarks. Officer Flagg agreed that at this hearing Gerald did not admit making the lewd remarks. But Judge McGhee recalled that "there was some admission again of some of the lewd statements. He—he didn't admit any of the more serious lewd statements." Again, the complainant, Mrs. Cook, was not present. Mrs. Gault asked that Mrs. Cook be present "so she could see which boy that done the talking, the dirty talking over the phone." The Juvenile Judge said "she didn't have to be present at that hearing." The judge did not speak to Mrs. Cook or communicate with her at any time. Probation Officer Flagg had talked to her once—over the telephone on June 9.

At this June 15 hearing a "referral report" made by the probation officers was filed with the court, although not disclosed to Gerald or his parents. This listed the charge as "Lewd Phone Calls." At the conclusion of the hearing, the judge committed Gerald as a juvenile delinquent to the State Industrial School "for the period of his minority that is, until 21, unless sooner discharged by due process of law." An order to that effect was entered. It recites that "after a full hearing and due deliberation the Court finds that said minor is a delinquent child, and that said minor is of the age of 15 years."

No appeal is permitted by Arizona law in juvenile cases. On August 3, 1964, a petition for a writ of habeas corpus was filed with the Supreme Court of Arizona and referred by it to the Superior Court for hearing.

At the habeas corpus hearing on August 17, Judge McGhee was vigorously cross-examined as to the basis for his actions. He testified that he had taken into account the fact that Gerald was on probation. He was asked "under what section of . . . the code you found the boy delinquent?"

His answer is set forth in the margin. In substance, he concluded that Gerald came within ARS § 8-201-6 (a), which specifies that a "delinquent child" includes one "who has violated a law of the state or an ordinance or regulation of a political subdivision thereof." The law which Gerald was found to have violated is ARS § 13-377. This section of the Arizona Criminal Code provides that a person who "in the presence or hearing of any woman or child . . . uses vulgar, abusive or obscene language, is guilty of a misdemeanor. . . ." The penalty specified in the Criminal Code, which would apply to an adult, is $ 5 to $ 50, or imprisonment for not more than two months. The judge also testified that he acted under ARS § 8-201-6 (d) which includes in the definition of a "delinquent child" one who, as the judge phrased it, is "habitually involved in immoral matters."

Asked about the basis for his conclusion that Gerald was "habitually involved in immoral matters," the judge testified, somewhat vaguely, that two years earlier, on July 2, 1962, a "referral" was made concerning Gerald, "where the boy had stolen a baseball glove from another boy and lied to the Police Department about it." The judge said there was "no hearing," and "no accusation" relating to this incident, "because of lack of material foundation." But it seems to have remained in his mind as a relevant factor. The judge also testified that Gerald had admitted making other nuisance phone calls in the past which, as the judge recalled the boy's testimony, were "silly calls, or funny calls, or something like that."

The Superior Court dismissed the writ, and appellants sought review in the Arizona Supreme Court. That court stated that it considered appellants' assignments of error as urging (1) that the Juvenile Code, ARS § 8-201 to § 8-239, is unconstitutional because it does not require that parents and children be apprised of the specific charges, does not require proper notice of a hearing, and does not provide for an appeal; and (2) that the proceedings and order relating to Gerald constituted a denial of due process of law because of the absence of adequate notice of the charge and the hearing; failure to notify appellants of certain constitutional rights including the rights to counsel and to confrontation, and the privilege against self-incrimination; the use of unsworn hearsay testimony; and the failure to make a record of the proceedings. Appellants further asserted that it was error for the Juvenile Court to remove Gerald from the custody of his parents without a showing and finding of their unsuitability, and alleged a miscellany of other errors under state law.

The Supreme Court handed down an elaborate and wide-ranging opinion affirming dismissal of the writ and stating the court's conclusions as to the issues raised by appellants and other aspects of the juvenile process. In their jurisdictional statement and brief in this Court, appellants do not urge upon us all of the points passed upon by the Supreme Court of Arizona. They urge that we hold the Juvenile Code of Arizona invalid on its face or as applied in this case because, contrary to the Due Process Clause of the Fourteenth Amendment, the juvenile is taken from the custody of his parents and committed to a state institution pursuant to proceedings in which the Juvenile Court has virtually unlimited discretion, and in which the following basic rights are denied:

1. Notice of the charges;
2. Right to counsel;
3. Right to confrontation and cross-examination;
4. Privilege against self-incrimination;
5. Right to a transcript of the proceedings; and
6. Right to appellate review.

We shall not consider other issues which were passed upon by the Supreme Court of Arizona. We emphasize that we indicate no opinion as to whether the decision of that court with respect to such other issues does or does not conflict with requirements of the Federal Constitution.

II.

The Supreme Court of Arizona held that due process of law is requisite to the constitutional validity of proceedings in which a court reaches the conclusion that a juvenile has been at fault, has engaged in conduct prohibited by law, or has otherwise misbehaved with the consequence that he is committed to an institution in which his freedom is curtailed. This conclusion is in accord with the decisions of a number of courts under both federal and state constitutions.

This court has not heretofore decided the precise question. In *Kent v. United States* (1966), we considered the requirements for a valid waiver of the "exclusive" jurisdiction of the Juvenile Court of the District of Columbia so that a juvenile could be tried in the adult criminal court of the District. Although our decision turned upon the language of the statute, we emphasized the necessity that "the basic requirements of due process and fairness" be satisfied in such proceedings. *Haley v. Ohio* (1948) involved the admissibility, in a state criminal court of general jurisdiction, of a confession by a 15-year-old boy. The Court held that the Fourteenth Amendment applied to prohibit the use of the coerced confession. MR. JUSTICE DOUGLAS said, "Neither man nor child can be allowed to stand condemned by methods which flout constitutional requirements of due process of law." To the same effect is *Gallegos v. Colorado* (1962). Accordingly, while these cases relate only to restricted aspects of the subject, they unmistakably indicate that, whatever may be their precise impact, neither the Fourteenth Amendment nor the Bill of Rights is for adults alone.

We do not in this opinion consider the impact of these constitutional provisions upon the totality of the relationship of the juvenile and the state. We do not even consider the entire process relating to juvenile "delinquents." For example, we are not here concerned with the procedures or constitutional rights applicable to the pre-judicial stages of the juvenile process, nor do we direct our attention to the post-adjudicative or dispositional process. We consider only the problems presented to us by this case. These relate to the proceedings by which a determination is made as to whether a juvenile is a "delinquent" as a result of alleged misconduct on his part, with the consequence that he may be committed to a state institution. As to these proceedings, there appears to be little current dissent from the proposition that the Due Process Clause has a role to play. The problem is to ascertain the precise impact of the due process requirement upon such proceedings.

From the inception of the juvenile court system, wide differences have been tolerated—indeed insisted upon— between the procedural rights accorded to adults and those of juveniles. In practically all jurisdictions, there are rights granted to adults which are withheld from juveniles. In addition to the specific problems involved in the present case, for example, it has been held that the juvenile is not entitled to bail, to indictment by grand jury, to a public trial or to trial by jury. It is frequent practice that rules governing the arrest and interrogation of adults by the police are not observed in the case of juveniles.

The history and theory underlying this development are well-known, but a recapitulation is necessary for purposes of this opinion. The Juvenile Court movement began in this country at the end of the last century. From the juvenile court statute adopted in Illinois in 1899, the system has spread to every State in the Union, the District of Columbia, and Puerto Rico. The constitutionality of Juvenile Court laws has been sustained in over 40 jurisdictions against a variety of attacks.

The early reformers were appalled by adult procedures and penalties, and by the fact that children could be given long prison sentences and mixed in jails with hardened criminals. They were profoundly convinced that society's duty to the child could not be confined by the concept of justice alone. They believed that society's role was not to ascertain whether the child was "guilty" or "innocent," but "What is he, how has he become what he is, and what had best be done in his interest and in the interest of the state to save him from a downward career." The child— essentially good, as they saw it—was to be made "to feel that he is the object of the state's care and solicitude," not that he was under arrest or on trial. The rules of criminal procedure were therefore altogether inapplicable. The apparent rigidities, technicalities, and harshness which they observed in both substantive and procedural criminal law were therefore to be discarded. The idea of crime and punishment was to be abandoned. The child was to be "treated" and "rehabilitated" and the procedures, from apprehension through institutionalization, were to be "clinical" rather than punitive.

These results were to be achieved, without coming to conceptual and constitutional grief, by insisting that the proceedings were not adversary, but that the state was proceeding as *parens patriae*. The Latin phrase proved to be a great help to those who sought to rationalize the exclusion of juveniles from the constitutional scheme; but its meaning is murky and its historic credentials are of dubious relevance. The phrase was taken from chancery practice, where, however, it was used to describe the power of the state to act *in loco parentis* for the purpose of protecting the property interests and the person of the child. But there is no trace of the doctrine in the history of criminal jurisprudence. At common law, children under seven were considered incapable of possessing criminal intent. Beyond that age, they were subjected to arrest, trial, and in theory to punishment like adult offenders. In these old days, the state was not deemed to have authority to accord them fewer procedural rights than adults.

The right of the state, as *parens patriae*, to deny to the child procedural rights available to his elders was elaborated by the assertion that a child, unlike an adult, has a right "not to liberty but to custody." He can be made to attorn to his parents, to go to school, etc. If his parents default in effectively performing their custodial functions—that is, if the child is "delinquent"—the state may intervene. In doing so, it does not deprive the child of any rights, because he has none. It merely provides the "custody" to which the child is entitled. On this basis, proceedings involving juveniles were described as "civil" not "criminal" and therefore not subject to the requirements which restrict the state when it seeks to deprive a person of his liberty.

Accordingly, the highest motives and most enlightened impulses led to a peculiar system for juveniles, unknown to our law in any comparable context. The constitutional and theoretical basis for this peculiar system is—to say the least—debatable. And in practice, as we remarked in the *Kent* case, the results have not been entirely satisfactory. Juvenile Court history has again demonstrated that unbridled discretion, however benevolently motivated, is frequently a poor substitute for principle and procedure. In 1937, Dean Pound wrote: "The powers of the Star Chamber were a trifle in comparison with those of our juvenile courts . . . ." The absence of substantive standards has not necessarily meant that children receive careful, compassionate, individualized treatment. The absence of procedural rules based upon constitutional principle has not always produced fair, efficient, and effective procedures. Departures from established principles of due process have frequently resulted not in enlightened procedure, but in arbitrariness. The Chairman of the Pennsylvania Council of Juvenile Court Judges has recently observed: "Unfortunately, loose procedures, high-handed methods and crowded court calendars, either singly or in combination, all too often, have resulted in depriving some juveniles of fundamental rights that have resulted in a denial of due process."

Failure to observe the fundamental requirements of due process has resulted in instances, which might have been avoided, of unfairness to individuals and inadequate or inaccurate findings of fact and unfortunate prescriptions of remedy. Due process of law is the primary and indispensable foundation of individual freedom. It is the basic and essential term in the social compact that defines the rights of the individual and delimits the powers which the state may exercise. As Mr. Justice Frankfurter has said: "The history of American freedom is, in no small measure, the history of procedure." But in addition, the procedural rules which have been fashioned from the generality of due process are our best instruments for the distillation and evaluation of essential facts from the conflicting welter of data that life and our adversary methods present. It is these instruments of due process which enhance the possibility that truth will emerge from the confrontation of opposing versions and conflicting data. "Procedure is to law what 'scientific method' is to science."

It is claimed that juveniles obtain benefits from the special procedures applicable to them which more than offset the disadvantages of denial of the substance of normal due process. As we shall discuss, the observance of due process standards, intelligently and not ruthlessly administered, will not compel the States to abandon or displace any of the substantive benefits of the juvenile process. But it is important, we think, that the claimed benefits of the juvenile process should be candidly appraised. Neither sentiment nor folklore should cause us to shut our eyes, for example, to such startling findings as that reported in an exceptionally reliable study of repeaters or recidivism conducted by the Stanford Research Institute for the President's Commission on Crime in the District of Columbia. This Commission's Report states:

"In fiscal 1966 approximately 66 percent of the 16- and 17-year-old juveniles referred to the court by the Youth Aid Division had been before the court previously. In 1965, 56 percent of those in the Receiving Home were repeaters. The SRI study revealed that 61 percent of the sample Juvenile Court referrals in 1965 had been previously referred at least once and that 42 percent had been referred at least twice before."

Certainly, these figures and the high crime rates among juveniles to which we have referred, could not lead us to conclude that the absence of constitutional protections reduces crime, or that the juvenile system, functioning free of constitutional inhibitions as it has largely done, is effective to reduce crime or rehabilitate offenders. We do not mean by this to denigrate the juvenile court process or to suggest that there are not aspects of the juvenile system relating to offenders which are valuable. But the features of the juvenile system which its proponents have asserted are of unique benefit will not be impaired by constitutional domestication. For example, the commendable principles relating to the processing and treatment of juveniles separately from adults are in no way involved or affected by the procedural issues under discussion. Further, we are told that one of the important benefits of the special juvenile court procedures is that they avoid classifying the juvenile as a "criminal." The juvenile offender is now classed as a "delinquent." There is, of course, no reason why this should not continue. It is disconcerting, however, that this term has come to involve only slightly less stigma than the term "criminal" applied to adults. It is also emphasized that in practically all jurisdictions, statutes provide that an adjudication of the child as a delinquent shall not operate as a civil disability or disqualify him for civil service appointment. There is no reason why the application of due process requirements should interfere with such provisions.

Beyond this, it is frequently said that juveniles are protected by the process from disclosure of their deviational behavior. As the Supreme Court of Arizona phrased it in the present case, the summary procedures of Juvenile Courts are sometimes defended by a statement that it is the law's policy "to hide youthful errors from the full gaze of the public and bury them in the graveyard of the forgotten past." This claim of secrecy, however, is more rhetoric than reality. Disclosure of court records is discretionary with the judge in most jurisdictions. Statutory restrictions almost invariably apply only to the court records, and even as to those the evidence is that many courts routinely furnish information to the FBI and the military, and on request to government agencies and even to private employers. Of more importance are police records. In most States, the police keep a complete file of juvenile "police contacts" and have complete discretion as to disclosure of juvenile records. Police departments receive requests for information from the FBI and other law-enforcement agencies, the Armed Forces, and social service agencies, and most of them generally comply. Private employers word their application forms to produce information concerning juvenile arrests and court proceedings, and in some jurisdictions information concerning juvenile police contacts is furnished private employers as well as government agencies.

In any event, there is no reason why, consistently with due process, a State cannot continue, if it deems it appropriate, to provide and to improve provision for the confidentiality of records of police contacts and court action relating to juveniles. It is interesting to note, however, that the Arizona Supreme Court used the confidentiality argument as a justification for the type of notice which is here attacked as inadequate for due process purposes. The parents were given merely general notice that their child was charged with "delinquency." No facts were specified. The Arizona court held, however, as we shall discuss, that in addition to this general "notice," the child and his parents must be advised "of the facts involved in the case" no later than the initial hearing by the judge. Obviously, this does not "bury" the word about the child's transgressions. It merely defers the time of disclosure to a point when it is of limited use to the child or his parents in preparing his defense or explanation.

Further, it is urged that the juvenile benefits from informal proceedings in the court. The early conception of the Juvenile Court proceeding was one in which a fatherly judge touched the heart and conscience of the erring youth by talking over his problems, by paternal advice and admonition, and in which, in extreme situations, benevolent and wise institutions of the State provided guidance and help "to save him from a downward career." Then, as now, goodwill and compassion were admirably prevalent. But recent studies have, with surprising unanimity, entered sharp dissent as to the validity of this gentle conception. They suggest that the appearance as well as the actuality of fairness, impartiality and orderliness—in short, the essentials of due process—may be a more impressive and more therapeutic attitude so far as the juvenile is concerned. For example, in a recent study, the sociologists Wheeler and Cottrell observe that when the procedural laxness of the "parens patriae" attitude is followed by stern disciplining, the contrast may have an adverse effect upon the child, who feels that he has been deceived or enticed.

They conclude as follows: "Unless appropriate due process of law is followed, even the juvenile who has violated the law may not feel that he is being fairly treated and may therefore resist the rehabilitative efforts of court personnel." Of course, it is not suggested that juvenile court judges should fail appropriately to take account, in their demeanor and conduct, of the emotional and psychological attitude of the juveniles with whom they are confronted. While due process requirements will, in some instances, introduce a degree of order and regularity to Juvenile Court proceedings to determine delinquency, and in contested cases will introduce some elements of the adversary system, nothing will require that the conception of the kindly juvenile judge be replaced by its opposite, nor do we here rule upon the question whether ordinary due process requirements must be observed with respect to hearings to determine the disposition of the delinquent child.

Ultimately, however, we confront the reality of that portion of the Juvenile Court process with which we deal in this case. A boy is charged with misconduct. The boy is committed to an institution where he may be restrained of liberty for years. It is of no constitutional consequence—and of limited practical meaning—that the institution to which he is committed is called an Industrial School. The fact of the matter is that, however euphemistic the title, a "receiving home" or an "industrial school" for juveniles is an institution of confinement in which the child is incarcerated for a greater or lesser time. His world becomes "a building with whitewashed walls, regimented routine and institutional hours . . . ." Instead of mother and father and sisters and brothers and friends and classmates, his world is peopled by guards, custodians, state employees, and "delinquents" confined with him for anything from waywardness to rape and homicide.

In view of this, it would be extraordinary if our Constitution did not require the procedural regularity and the exercise of care implied in the phrase "due process." Under our Constitution, the condition of being a boy does not justify a kangaroo court. The traditional ideas of Juvenile Court procedure, indeed, contemplated that time would be available and care would be used to establish precisely what the juvenile did and why he did it—was it a prank of adolescence or a brutal act threatening serious consequences to himself or society unless corrected? Under traditional notions, one would assume that in a case like that of Gerald Gault, where the juvenile appears to have a home, a working mother and father, and an older brother, the Juvenile Judge would have made a careful inquiry and judgment as to the possibility that the boy could be disciplined and dealt with at home, despite his previous transgressions. Indeed, so far as appears in the record before us, except for some conversation with Gerald about his school work and his "wanting to go to . . . Grand Canyon with his father," the points to which the judge directed his attention were little different from those that would be involved in determining any charge of violation of a penal statute. The essential difference between Gerald's case and a normal criminal case is that safeguards available to adults were discarded in Gerald's case. The summary procedure as well as the long commitment was possible because Gerald was 15 years of age instead of over 18.

If Gerald had been over 18, he would not have been subject to Juvenile Court proceedings. For the particular offense immediately involved, the maximum punishment would have been a fine of $ 5 to $ 50, or imprisonment in jail for not more than two months. Instead, he was committed to custody for a maximum of six years. If he had been over 18 and had committed an offense to which such a sentence might apply, he would have been entitled to substantial rights under the Constitution of the United States as well as under Arizona's laws and constitution. The United States Constitution would guarantee him rights and protections with respect to arrest, search and seizure, and pretrial interrogation. It would assure him of specific notice of the charges and adequate time to decide his course of action and to prepare his defense. He would be entitled to clear advice that he could be represented by counsel, and, at least if a felony were involved, the State would be required to provide counsel if his parents were unable to afford it. If the court acted on the basis of his confession, careful procedures would be required to assure its voluntariness. If the case went to trial, confrontation and opportunity for cross-examination would be guaranteed. So wide a gulf between the State's treatment of the adult and of the child requires a bridge sturdier than mere verbiage, and reasons more persuasive than cliché can provide. As Wheeler and Cottrell have put it, "The rhetoric of the juvenile court movement has developed without any necessarily close correspondence to the realities of court and institutional routines."

In *Kent v. United States*, we stated that the Juvenile Court Judge's exercise of the power of the state as *parens patriae* was not unlimited. We said that "the admonition to function in a 'parental' relationship is not an invitation to procedural arbitrariness." With respect to the waiver by the Juvenile Court to the adult court of jurisdiction over an offense committed by a youth, we said that "there is no place in our system of law for reaching a result of such tremendous consequences without ceremony—without hearing, without effective assistance of counsel, without a statement of reasons." We announced with respect to such waiver proceedings that while "We do not mean . . . to indicate that the hearing to be held must conform with all of the requirements of a criminal trial or even of the usual administrative hearing; but we do hold that the hearing must measure up to the essentials of due process and fair treatment." We reiterate this view, here in connection with a juvenile court adjudication of "delinquency," as a requirement which is part of the Due Process Clause of the Fourteenth Amendment of our Constitution.

We now turn to the specific issues which are presented to us in the present case.

III.

NOTICE OF CHARGES.

Appellants allege that the Arizona Juvenile Code is unconstitutional or alternatively that the proceedings before the Juvenile Court were constitutionally defective because of failure to provide adequate notice of the hearings. No notice was given to Gerald's parents when he was taken into custody on Monday, June 8. On that night, when Mrs. Gault went to the Detention Home, she was orally informed that there would be a hearing the next afternoon and was told the reason why Gerald was in custody. The only written notice Gerald's parents received at any time was a note on plain paper from Officer Flagg delivered on Thursday or Friday, June 11 or 12, to the effect that the judge had set Monday, June 15, "for further Hearings on Gerald's delinquency."

A "petition" was filed with the court on June 9 by Officer Flagg, reciting only that he was informed and believed that "said minor is a delinquent minor and that it is necessary that some order be made by the Honorable Court for said minor's welfare." The applicable Arizona statute provides for a petition to be filed in Juvenile Court, alleging in general terms that the child is "neglected, dependent, or delinquent." The statute explicitly states that such a general allegation is sufficient, "without alleging the facts." There is no requirement that the petition be served and it was not served upon, given to, or shown to Gerald or his parents.

The Supreme Court of Arizona rejected appellants' claim that due process was denied because of inadequate notice. It stated that "Mrs. Gault knew the exact nature of the charge against Gerald from the day he was taken to the detention home." The court also pointed out that the Gaults appeared at the two hearings "without objection." The court held that because "the policy of the juvenile law is to hide youthful errors from the full gaze of the public and bury them in the graveyard of the forgotten past," advance notice of the specific charges or basis for taking the juvenile into custody and for the hearing is not necessary. It held that the appropriate rule is that "the infant and his parent or guardian will receive a petition only reciting a conclusion of delinquency. But no later than the initial hearing by the judge, they must be advised of the facts involved in the case. If the charges are denied, they must be given a reasonable period of time to prepare."

We cannot agree with the court's conclusion that adequate notice was given in this case. Notice, to comply with due process requirements, must be given sufficiently in advance of scheduled court proceedings so that reasonable opportunity to prepare will be afforded, and it must "set forth the alleged misconduct with particularity." It is obvious, as we have discussed above, that no purpose of shielding the child from the public stigma of knowledge of his having been taken into custody and scheduled for hearing is served by the procedure approved by the court below. The "initial hearing" in the present case was a hearing on the merits. Notice at that time is not timely; and even if there were a conceivable purpose served by the deferral proposed by the court below, it would have to yield to the requirements that the child and his parents or guardian be notified, in writing, of the specific charge or factual allegations to be considered at the hearing, and that such written notice be given at the earliest practicable time, and in any event sufficiently in advance of the hearing to permit preparation. Due process of law requires notice of the sort we have described—that is, notice which would be deemed constitutionally adequate in a civil or criminal proceeding. It does not allow a hearing to be held in which a youth's freedom and his parents' right to his custody are at stake without giving them timely notice, in advance of the hearing, of the specific issues that they must meet. Nor, in the circumstances of this case, can it reasonably be said that the requirement of notice was waived.

IV.

RIGHT TO COUNSEL.

Appellants charge that the Juvenile Court proceedings were fatally defective because the court did not advise Gerald or his parents of their right to counsel, and proceeded with the hearing, the adjudication of delinquency and the order of commitment in the absence of counsel for the child and his parents or an express waiver of the right thereto. The Supreme Court of Arizona pointed out that "there is disagreement among the various jurisdictions as to whether the court must advise the infant that he has a right to counsel." It noted its own decision in *Arizona State Dept. of Public Welfare v. Barlow* (1956), to the effect "that the parents of an infant in a juvenile proceeding cannot be denied representation by counsel of their choosing." It referred to a provision of the Juvenile Code which it characterized as requiring "that the probation officer shall look after the interests of neglected, delinquent and dependent children," including representing their interests in court. The court argued that "The parent and the probation officer may be relied upon to protect the infant's interests."

Accordingly, it rejected the proposition that "due process requires that an infant have a right to counsel." It said that juvenile courts have the discretion, but not the duty, to allow such representation; it referred specifically to the situation in which the Juvenile Court discerns conflict between the child and his parents as an instance in which this discretion might be exercised. We do not agree. Probation officers, in the Arizona scheme, are also arresting officers. They initiate proceedings and file petitions which they verify, as here, alleging the delinquency of the child; and they testify, as here, against the child. And here the probation officer was also superintendent of the Detention Home. The probation officer cannot act as counsel for the child. His role in the adjudicatory hearing, by statute and in fact, is as arresting officer and witness against the child. Nor can the judge represent the child. There is no material difference in this respect between adult and juvenile proceedings of the sort here involved.

In adult proceedings, this contention has been foreclosed by decisions of this Court. A proceeding where the issue is whether the child will be found to be "delinquent" and subjected to the loss of his liberty for years is comparable in seriousness to a felony prosecution. The juvenile needs the assistance of counsel to cope with problems of law, to make skilled inquiry into the facts, to insist upon regularity of the proceedings, and to ascertain whether he has a defense and to prepare and submit it. The child "requires the guiding hand of counsel at every step in the proceedings against him." Just as in *Kent v. United States*, we indicated our agreement with the United States Court of Appeals for the District of Columbia Circuit that the assistance of counsel is essential for purposes of waiver proceedings, so we hold now that it is equally essential for the determination of delinquency, carrying with it the awesome prospect of incarceration in a state institution until the juvenile reaches the age of 21.

During the last decade, court decisions, experts, and legislatures have demonstrated increasing recognition of this view. In at least one-third of the States, statutes now provide for the right of representation by retained counsel in juvenile delinquency proceedings, notice of the right, or assignment of counsel, or a combination of these. In other States, court rules have similar provisions.

The President's Crime Commission has recently recommended that in order to assure "procedural justice for the child," it is necessary that "Counsel . . . be appointed as a matter of course wherever coercive action is a possibility, without requiring any affirmative choice by child or parent." As stated by the authoritative "Standards for Juvenile and Family Courts," published by the Children's Bureau of the United States Department of Health, Education, and Welfare:

"As a component part of a fair hearing required by due process guaranteed under the 14th amendment, notice of the right to counsel should be required at all hearings and counsel provided upon request when the family is financially unable to employ counsel."

This statement was "reviewed" by the National Council of Juvenile Court Judges at its 1965 Convention and they "found no fault" with it.

The New York Family Court Act contains the following statement:

"This act declares that minors have a right to the assistance of counsel of their own choosing or of law guardians in neglect proceedings under article three and in proceedings to determine juvenile delinquency and whether a person is in need of supervision under article seven. This declaration is based on a finding that counsel is often indispensable to a practical realization of due process of law and may be helpful in making reasoned determinations of fact and proper orders of disposition."

The Act provides that "At the commencement of any hearing" under the delinquency article of the statute, the juvenile and his parent shall be advised of the juvenile's "right to be represented by counsel chosen by him or his parent . . . or by a law guardian assigned by the court . . . ."

The California Act (1961) also requires appointment of counsel.

We conclude that the Due Process Clause of the Fourteenth Amendment requires that in respect of proceedings to determine delinquency which may result in commitment to an institution in which the juvenile's freedom is curtailed, the child and his parents must be notified of the child's right to be represented by counsel retained by them, or if they are unable to afford counsel, that counsel will be appointed to represent the child.

At the habeas corpus proceeding, Mrs. Gault testified that she knew that she could have appeared with counsel at the juvenile hearing. This knowledge is not a waiver of the right to counsel which she and her juvenile son had, as we have defined it. They had a right expressly to be advised that they might retain counsel and to be confronted with the need for specific consideration of whether they did or did not choose to waive the right. If they were unable to afford to employ counsel, they were entitled in view of the seriousness of the charge and the potential commitment, to appointed counsel, unless they chose waiver. Mrs. Gault's knowledge that she could employ counsel was not an "intentional relinquishment or abandonment" of a fully known right.

V.

CONFRONTATION, SELF-INCRIMINATION, CROSS-EXAMINATION.

Appellants urge that the writ of habeas corpus should have been granted because of the denial of the rights of confrontation and cross-examination in the Juvenile Court hearings, and because the privilege against self-incrimination was not observed. The Juvenile Court Judge testified at the habeas corpus hearing that he had proceeded on the basis of Gerald's admissions at the two hearings. Appellants attack this on the ground that the admissions were obtained in disregard of the privilege against self-incrimination. If the confession is disregarded, appellants argue that the delinquency conclusion, since it was fundamentally based on a finding that Gerald had made lewd remarks during the phone call to Mrs. Cook, is fatally defective for failure to accord the rights of confrontation and cross-examination which the Due Process Clause of the Fourteenth Amendment of the Federal Constitution guarantees in state proceedings generally.

Our first question, then, is whether Gerald's admission was improperly obtained and relied on as the basis of decision, in conflict with the Federal Constitution. For this purpose, it is necessary briefly to recall the relevant facts.

Mrs. Cook, the complainant, and the recipient of the alleged telephone call, was not called as a witness. Gerald's mother asked the Juvenile Court Judge why Mrs. Cook was not present and the judge replied that "she didn't have to be present." So far as appears, Mrs. Cook was spoken to only once, by Officer Flagg, and this was by telephone. The judge did not speak with her on any occasion. Gerald had been questioned by the probation officer after having been taken into custody. The exact circumstances of this questioning do not appear but any admissions Gerald may have made at this time do not appear in the record. Gerald was also questioned by the Juvenile Court Judge at each of the two hearings. The judge testified in the habeas corpus proceeding that Gerald admitted making "some of the lewd statements . . . but not any of the more serious lewd statements." There was conflict and uncertainty among the witnesses at the habeas corpus proceeding—the Juvenile Court Judge, Mr. and Mrs. Gault, and the probation officer— as to what Gerald did or did not admit.

We shall assume that Gerald made admissions of the sort described by the Juvenile Court Judge, as quoted above. Neither Gerald nor his parents were advised that he did not have to testify or make a statement, or that an incriminating statement might result in his commitment as a "delinquent."

The Arizona Supreme Court rejected appellants' contention that Gerald had a right to be advised that he need not incriminate himself. It said: "We think the necessary flexibility for individualized treatment will be enhanced by a rule which does not require the judge to advise the infant of a privilege against self-incrimination."

In reviewing this conclusion of Arizona's Supreme Court, we emphasize again that we are here concerned only with a proceeding to determine whether a minor is a "delinquent" and which may result in commitment to a state institution. Specifically, the question is whether, in such a proceeding, an admission by the juvenile may be used against him in the absence of clear and unequivocal evidence that the admission was made with knowledge that he was not obliged to speak and would not be penalized for remaining silent. In light of *Miranda v. Arizona* (1966), we must also consider whether, if the privilege against self-incrimination is available, it can effectively be waived unless counsel is present or the right to counsel has been waived.

It has long been recognized that the eliciting and use of confessions or admissions require careful scrutiny. Dean Wigmore states:

"The ground of distrust of confessions made in certain situations is, in a rough and indefinite way, judicial experience. There has been no careful collection of statistics of untrue confessions, nor has any great number of instances been even loosely reported . . . . but enough have been verified to fortify the conclusion, based on ordinary observation of human conduct, that under certain stresses a person, especially one of defective mentality or peculiar temperament, may falsely acknowledge guilt. This possibility arises wherever the innocent person is placed in such a situation that the untrue acknowledgment of guilt is at the time the more promising of two alternatives between which he is obliged to choose; that is, he chooses any risk that may be in falsely acknowledging guilt, in preference to some worse alternative associated with silence.

. . . .

"The principle, then, upon which a confession may be excluded is that it is, under certain conditions, testimonially untrustworthy . . . . The essential feature is that the principle of exclusion is a testimonial one, analogous to the other principles which exclude narrations as untrustworthy . . . ."

This Court has emphasized that admissions and confessions of juveniles require special caution. In *Haley v. Ohio*, where this Court reversed the conviction of a 15-year-old boy for murder, MR. JUSTICE DOUGLAS said:

"What transpired would make us pause for careful inquiry if a mature man were involved. And when, as here, a mere child— an easy victim of the law—is before us, special care in scrutinizing the record must be used. Age 15 is a tender and difficult age for a boy of any race. He cannot be judged by the more exacting standards of maturity. That which would leave a man cold and unimpressed can overawe and overwhelm a lad in his early teens. This is the period of great instability which the crisis of adolescence produces. A 15-year-old lad, questioned through the dead of night by relays of police, is a ready victim of the inquisition. Mature men possibly might stand the ordeal from midnight to 5 a. m. But we cannot believe that a lad of tender years is a match for the police in such a contest. He needs counsel and support if he is not to become the victim first of fear, then of panic. He needs someone on whom to lean lest the overpowering presence of the law, as he knows it, crush him. No friend stood at the side of this 15-year-old boy as the police, working in relays, questioned him hour after hour, from midnight until dawn. No lawyer stood guard to make sure that the police went so far and no farther, to see to it that they stopped short of the point where he became the victim of coercion. No counsel or friend was called during the critical hours of questioning."

In *Haley*, as we have discussed, the boy was convicted in an adult court, and not a juvenile court. In notable decisions, the New York Court of Appeals and the Supreme Court of New Jersey have recently considered decisions of Juvenile Courts in which boys have been adjudged "delinquent" on the basis of confessions obtained in circumstances comparable to those in *Haley*. In both instances, the State contended before its highest tribunal that constitutional requirements governing inculpatory statements applicable in adult courts do not apply to juvenile proceedings. In each case, the State's contention was rejected, and the juvenile court's determination of delinquency was set aside on the grounds of inadmissibility of the confession.

The privilege against self-incrimination is, of course, related to the question of the safeguards necessary to assure that admissions or confessions are reasonably trustworthy, that they are not the mere fruits of fear or coercion, but are reliable expressions of the truth. The roots of the privilege are, however, far deeper. They tap the basic stream of religious and political principle because the privilege reflects the limits of the individual's attornment to the state and—in a philosophical sense—insists upon the equality of the individual and the state. In other words, the privilege has a broader and deeper thrust than the rule which prevents the use of confessions which are the product of coercion because coercion is thought to carry with it the danger of unreliability. One of its purposes is to prevent the state, whether by force or by psychological domination, from overcoming the mind and will of the person under investigation and depriving him of the freedom to decide whether to assist the state in securing his conviction.

It would indeed be surprising if the privilege against self-incrimination were available to hardened criminals but not to children. The language of the Fifth Amendment, applicable to the States by operation of the Fourteenth Amendment, is unequivocal and without exception. And the scope of the privilege is comprehensive. As MR. JUSTICE WHITE, concurring, stated in *Murphy v. Waterfront Commission* (1964):

"The privilege can be claimed in any proceeding, be it criminal or civil, administrative or judicial, investigatory or adjudicatory . . . it protects any disclosures which the witness may reasonably apprehend could be used in a criminal prosecution or which could lead to other evidence that might be so used."

With respect to juveniles, both common observation and expert opinion emphasize that the "distrust of confessions made in certain situations" ... is imperative in the case of children from an early age through adolescence. In New York, for example, the recently enacted Family Court Act provides that the juvenile and his parents must be advised at the start of the hearing of his right to remain silent. The New York statute also provides that the police must attempt to communicate with the juvenile's parents before questioning him, and that absent "special circumstances" a confession may not be obtained from a child prior to notifying his parents or relatives and releasing the child either to them or to the Family Court.

. . . .

The authoritative "Standards for Juvenile and Family Courts" concludes that, "Whether or not transfer to the criminal court is a possibility, certain procedures should always be followed. Before being interviewed by the police, the child and his parents should be informed of his right to have legal counsel present and to refuse to answer questions or be fingerprinted if he should so decide."

Against the application to juveniles of the right to silence, it is argued that juvenile proceedings are "civil" and not "criminal," and therefore the privilege should not apply. It is true that the statement of the privilege in the Fifth Amendment, which is applicable to the States by reason of the Fourteenth Amendment, is that no person "shall be compelled in any criminal case to be a witness against himself." However, it is also clear that the availability of the privilege does not turn upon the type of proceeding in which its protection is invoked, but upon the nature of the statement or admission and the exposure which it invites. The privilege may, for example, be claimed in a civil or administrative proceeding, if the statement is or may be inculpatory.

It would be entirely unrealistic to carve out of the Fifth Amendment all statements by juveniles on the ground that these cannot lead to "criminal" involvement. In the first place, juvenile proceedings to determine "delinquency," which may lead to commitment to a state institution, must be regarded as "criminal" for purposes of the privilege against self-incrimination. To hold otherwise would be to disregard substance because of the feeble enticement of the "civil" label-of-convenience, which has been attached to juvenile proceedings. Indeed, in over half of the States, there is not even assurance that the juvenile will be kept in separate institutions, apart from adult "criminals." In those States, juveniles may be placed in or transferred to adult penal institutions after having been found "delinquent" by a juvenile court. For this purpose, at least, commitment is a deprivation of liberty. It is incarceration against one's will, whether it is called "criminal" or "civil." And our Constitution guarantees that no person shall be "compelled" to be a witness against himself when he is threatened with deprivation of his liberty—a command which this Court has broadly applied and generously implemented in accordance with the teaching of the history of the privilege and its great office in mankind's battle for freedom.

In addition, apart from the equivalence for this purpose of exposure to commitment as a juvenile delinquent and exposure to imprisonment as an adult offender, the fact of the matter is that there is little or no assurance in Arizona, as in most if not all of the States, that a juvenile apprehended and interrogated by the police or even by the Juvenile Court itself will remain outside of the reach of adult courts as a consequence of the offense for which he has been taken into custody. In Arizona, as in other States, provision is made for Juvenile Courts to relinquish or waive jurisdiction to the ordinary criminal courts. In the present case, when Gerald Gault was interrogated concerning violation of a section of the Arizona Criminal Code, it could not be certain that the Juvenile Court Judge would decide to "suspend" criminal prosecution in court for adults by proceeding to an adjudication in Juvenile Court.

It is also urged, as the Supreme Court of Arizona here asserted, that the juvenile and presumably his parents should not be advised of the juvenile's right to silence because confession is good for the child as the commencement of the assumed therapy of the juvenile court process, and he should be encouraged to assume an attitude of trust and confidence toward the officials of the juvenile process. This proposition has been subjected to widespread challenge on the basis of current reappraisals of the rhetoric and realities of the handling of juvenile offenders.

In fact, evidence is accumulating that confessions by juveniles do not aid in "individualized treatment," as the court below put it, and that compelling the child to answer questions, without warning or advice as to his right to remain silent, does not serve this or any other good purpose. In light of the observations of Wheeler and Cottrell, and others, it seems probable that where children are induced to confess by "paternal" urgings on the part of officials and the confession is then followed by disciplinary action, the child's reaction is likely to be hostile and adverse—the child may well feel that he has been led or tricked into confession and that despite his confession, he is being punished.

Further, authoritative opinion has cast formidable doubt upon the reliability and trustworthiness of "confessions" by children. This Court's observations in *Haley v. Ohio* are set forth above. The recent decision of the New York Court of Appeals referred to above, In the *Matters of Gregory W. and Gerald S.*, deals with a dramatic and, it is to be hoped, extreme example. Two 12-year-old Negro boys were taken into custody for the brutal assault and rape of two aged domestics, one of whom died as the result of the attack. One of the boys was schizophrenic and had been locked in the security ward of a mental institution at the time of the attacks. By a process that may best be described as bizarre, his confession was obtained by the police. A psychiatrist testified that the boy would admit "whatever he thought was expected so that he could get out of the immediate situation." The other 12-year-old also "confessed." Both confessions were in specific detail, albeit they contained various inconsistencies. The Court of Appeals, in an opinion by Keating, J., concluded that the confessions were products of the will of the police instead of the boys. The confessions were therefore held involuntary and the order of the Appellate Division affirming the order of the Family Court adjudging the defendants to be juvenile delinquents was reversed.

A similar and equally instructive case has recently been decided by the Supreme Court of New Jersey. The body of a 10-year-old girl was found. She had been strangled. Neighborhood boys who knew the girl were questioned. The two appellants, aged 13 and 15, confessed to the police, with vivid detail and some inconsistencies. At the Juvenile Court hearing, both denied any complicity in the killing. They testified that their confessions were the product of fear and fatigue due to extensive police grilling. The Juvenile Court Judge found that the confessions were voluntary and admissible. On appeal, in an extensive opinion by Proctor, J., the Supreme Court of New Jersey reversed. It rejected the State's argument that the constitutional safeguard of voluntariness governing the use of confessions does not apply in proceedings before the Juvenile Court. It pointed out that under New Jersey court rules, juveniles under the age of 16 accused of committing a homicide are tried in a proceeding which "has all of the appurtenances of a criminal trial," including participation by the county prosecutor, and requirements that the juvenile be provided with counsel, that a stenographic record be made, etc. It also pointed out that under New Jersey law, the confinement of the boys after reaching age 21 could be extended until they had served the maximum sentence which could have been imposed on an adult for such a homicide, here found to be second-degree murder carrying up to 30 years' imprisonment. The court concluded that the confessions were involuntary, stressing that the boys, contrary to statute, were placed in the police station and there interrogated; that the parents of both boys were not allowed to see them while they were being interrogated; that inconsistencies appeared among the various statements of the boys and with the objective evidence of the crime; and that there were protracted periods of questioning. The court noted the State's contention that both boys were advised of their constitutional rights before they made their statements, but it held that this should not be given "significant weight in our determination of voluntariness." Accordingly, the judgment of the Juvenile Court was reversed.

In a recent case before the Juvenile Court of the District of Columbia, Judge Ketcham rejected the proffer of evidence as to oral statements made at police headquarters by four juveniles who had been taken into custody for alleged involvement in an assault and attempted robbery. The court explicitly stated that it did not rest its decision on a showing that the statements were involuntary, but because they were untrustworthy. Judge Ketcham said:

"Simply stated, the Court's decision in this case rests upon the considered opinion—after nearly four busy years on the Juvenile Court bench during which the testimony of thousands of such juveniles has been heard—that the statements of adolescents under 18 years of age who are arrested and charged with violations of law are frequently untrustworthy and often distort the truth."

We conclude that the constitutional privilege against self-incrimination is applicable in the case of juveniles as it is with respect to adults. We appreciate that special problems may arise with respect to waiver of the privilege by or on behalf of children, and that there may well be some differences in technique—but not in principle—depending upon the age of the child and the presence and competence of parents. The participation of counsel will, of course, assist the police, Juvenile Courts and appellate tribunals in administering the privilege. If counsel was not present for some permissible reason when an admission was obtained, the greatest care must be taken to assure that the admission was voluntary, in the sense not only that it was not coerced or suggested, but also that it was not the product of ignorance of rights or of adolescent fantasy, fright or despair.

The "confession" of Gerald Gault was first obtained by Officer Flagg, out of the presence of Gerald's parents, without counsel and without advising him of his right to silence, as far as appears. The judgment of the Juvenile Court was stated by the judge to be based on Gerald's admissions in court. Neither "admission" was reduced to writing, and, to say the least, the process by which the "admissions" were obtained and received must be characterized as lacking the certainty and order which are required of proceedings of such formidable consequences. Apart from the "admissions," there was nothing upon which a judgment or finding might be based. There was no sworn testimony. Mrs. Cook, the complainant, was not present. The Arizona Supreme Court held that "sworn testimony must be required of all witnesses including police officers, probation officers and others who are part of or officially related to the juvenile court structure." We hold that this is not enough. No reason is suggested or appears for a different rule in respect of sworn testimony in juvenile courts than in adult tribunals. Absent a valid confession adequate to support the determination of the Juvenile Court, confrontation and sworn testimony by witnesses available for cross-examination were essential for a finding of "delinquency" and an order committing Gerald to a state institution for a maximum of six years.

The recommendations in the Children's Bureau's "Standards for Juvenile and Family Courts" are in general accord with our conclusions. They state that testimony should be under oath and that only competent, material and relevant evidence under rules applicable to civil cases should be admitted in evidence.

As we said in *Kent v. United States* (1966), with respect to waiver proceedings, "there is no place in our system of law for reaching a result of such tremendous consequences without ceremony . . . ." We now hold that, absent a valid confession, a determination of delinquency and an order of commitment to a state institution cannot be sustained in the absence of sworn testimony subjected to the opportunity for cross-examination in accordance with our law and constitutional requirements.

VI.

APPELLATE REVIEW AND TRANSCRIPT OF PROCEEDINGS.

Appellants urge that the Arizona statute is unconstitutional under the Due Process Clause because, as construed by its Supreme Court, "there is no right of appeal from a juvenile court order . . . ." The court held that there is no right to a transcript because there is no right to appeal and because the proceedings are confidential and any record must be destroyed after a prescribed period of time. Whether a transcript or other recording is made, it held, is a matter for the discretion of the juvenile court.

This Court has not held that a State is required by the Federal Constitution "to provide appellate courts or a right to appellate review at all." In view of the fact that we must reverse the Supreme Court of Arizona's affirmance of the dismissal of the writ of habeas corpus for other reasons, we need not rule on this question in the present case or upon the failure to provide a transcript or recording of the hearings—or, indeed, the failure of the Juvenile Judge to state the grounds for his conclusion. In the context of a decision of the juvenile court waiving jurisdiction to the adult court, which by local law, was permissible: ". . . it is incumbent upon the Juvenile Court to accompany its waiver order with a statement of the reasons or considerations therefor." As the present case illustrates, the consequences of failure to provide an appeal, to record the proceedings, or to make findings or state the grounds for the juvenile court's conclusion may be to throw a burden upon the machinery for habeas corpus, to saddle the reviewing process with the burden of attempting to reconstruct a record, and to impose upon the Juvenile Judge the unseemly duty of testifying under cross-examination as to the events that transpired in the hearings before him.

For the reasons stated, the judgment of the Supreme Court of Arizona is reversed and the cause remanded for further proceedings not inconsistent with this opinion.

It is so ordered.

In Re Winship (1970)
397 U.S. 358

In an adult criminal trial, the state must prove every element of the criminal offense beyond a reasonable doubt. Juvenile courts, up until this case was handed down, used the preponderance of the evidence standard that is used by civil courts.

Constitutional questions decided by this Court concerning the juvenile process have centered on the adjudicatory stage at "which a determination is made as to whether a juvenile is a 'delinquent' as a result of alleged misconduct on his part, with the consequence that he may be committed to a state institution." *Gault* decided that, although the Fourteenth Amendment does not require that the hearing at this stage conform with all the requirements of a criminal trial or even of the usual administrative proceeding, the Due Process Clause does require application during the adjudicatory hearing of "'the essentials of due process and fair treatment.'" This case presents the single, narrow question whether proof beyond a reasonable doubt is among the "essentials of due process and fair treatment" required during the adjudicatory stage when a juvenile is charged with an act which would constitute a crime if committed by an adult.

Section 712 of the New York Family Court Act defines a juvenile delinquent as "a person over seven and less than sixteen years of age who does any act which, if done by an adult, would constitute a crime." During a 1967 adjudicatory hearing, conducted pursuant to § 742 of the Act, a judge in New York Family Court found that appellant, then a 12-year-old boy, had entered a locker and stolen $ 112 from a woman's pocketbook. The petition which charged appellant with delinquency alleged that his act, "if done by an adult, would constitute the crime or crimes of Larceny." The judge acknowledged that the proof might not establish guilt beyond a reasonable doubt, but rejected appellant's contention that such proof was required by the Fourteenth Amendment. The judge relied instead on § 744 (b) of the New York Family Court Act which provides that "any determination at the conclusion of an adjudicatory hearing that a juvenile did an act or acts must be based on a preponderance of the evidence." During a subsequent dispositional hearing, appellant was ordered placed in a training school for an initial period of 18 months, subject to annual extensions of his commitment until his 18th birthday—six years in appellant's case. The Appellate Division of the New York Supreme Court, First Judicial Department, affirmed without opinion. The New York Court of Appeals then affirmed by a four-to-three vote, expressly sustaining the constitutionality of § 744. We noted probable jurisdiction. We reverse.

I.

The requirement that guilt of a criminal charge be established by proof beyond a reasonable doubt dates at least from our early years as a Nation. The "demand for a higher degree of persuasion in criminal cases was recurrently expressed from ancient times, though its crystallization into the formula 'beyond a reasonable doubt' seems to have occurred as late as 1798. It is now accepted in common law jurisdictions as the measure of persuasion by which the prosecution must convince the trier of all the essential elements of guilt." Although virtually unanimous adherence to the reasonable-doubt standard in common-law jurisdictions may not conclusively establish it as a requirement of due process, such adherence does "reflect a profound judgment about the way in which law should be enforced and justice administered."

Expressions in many opinions of this Court indicate that it has long been assumed that proof of a criminal charge beyond a reasonable doubt is constitutionally required. Mr. Justice Frankfurter stated that "it is the duty of the Government to establish . . . guilt beyond a reasonable doubt. This notion—basic in our law and rightly one of the boasts of a free society—is a requirement and a safeguard of due process of law in the historic, procedural content of 'due process.'" In a similar vein, the Court said in *Brinegar v. United States* that "guilt in a criminal case must be proved beyond a reasonable doubt and by evidence confined to that which long experience in the common-law tradition, to some extent embodied in the Constitution, has crystallized into rules of evidence consistent with that standard. These rules are historically grounded rights of our system, developed to safeguard men from dubious and unjust convictions, with resulting forfeitures of life, liberty, and property." *Davis v. United States* stated that the requirement is implicit in "constitutions . . . which recognize the fundamental principles that are deemed essential for the protection of life and liberty." In *Davis*, a murder conviction was reversed because the trial judge instructed the jury that it was their duty to convict when the evidence was equally balanced regarding the sanity of the accused. This Court said: "On the contrary, he is entitled to an acquittal of the specific crime charged if upon all the evidence there is reasonable doubt whether he was capable in law of committing crime. . . . No man should be deprived of his life under the forms of law unless the jurors who try him are able, upon their consciences, to say that the evidence before them . . . is sufficient to show beyond a reasonable doubt the existence of every fact necessary to constitute the crime charged."

The reasonable-doubt standard plays a vital role in the American scheme of criminal procedure. It is a prime instrument for reducing the risk of convictions resting on factual error. The standard provides concrete substance for the presumption of innocence—that bedrock "axiomatic and elementary" principle whose "enforcement lies at the foundation of the administration of our criminal law." As the dissenters in the New York Court of Appeals observed, and we agree, "a person accused of a crime . . . would be at a severe disadvantage, a disadvantage amounting to a lack of fundamental fairness, if he could be adjudged guilty and imprisoned for years on the strength of the same evidence as would suffice in a civil case."

The requirement of proof beyond a reasonable doubt has this vital role in our criminal procedure for cogent reasons. The accused during a criminal prosecution has at stake interests of immense importance, both because of the possibility that he may lose his liberty upon conviction and because of the certainty that he would be stigmatized by the conviction. Accordingly, a society that values the good name and freedom of every individual should not condemn a man for commission of a crime when there is reasonable doubt about his guilt. As we said in *Speiser v. Randall*: "There is always in litigation a margin of error, representing error in factfinding, which both parties must take into account. Where one party has at stake an interest of transcending value—as a criminal defendant his liberty—this margin of error is reduced as to him by the process of placing on the other party the burden of . . . persuading the factfinder at the conclusion of the trial of his guilt beyond a reasonable doubt. Due process commands that no man shall lose his liberty unless the Government has borne the burden of . . . convincing the factfinder of his guilt." To this end, the reasonable-doubt standard is indispensable, for it "impresses on the trier of fact the necessity of reaching a subjective state of certitude of the facts in issue."

Moreover, use of the reasonable-doubt standard is indispensable to command the respect and confidence of the community in applications of the criminal law. It is critical that the moral force of the criminal law not be diluted by a standard of proof that leaves people in doubt whether innocent men are being condemned. It is also important in our free society that every individual going about his ordinary affairs have confidence that his government cannot adjudge him guilty of a criminal offense without convincing a proper factfinder of his guilt with utmost certainty.

Lest there remain any doubt about the constitutional stature of the reasonable-doubt standard, we explicitly hold that the Due Process Clause protects the accused against conviction except upon proof beyond a reasonable doubt of every fact necessary to constitute the crime with which he is charged.

II.

We turn to the question whether juveniles, like adults, are constitutionally entitled to proof beyond a reasonable doubt when they are charged with violation of a criminal law. The same considerations that demand extreme caution in factfinding to protect the innocent adult apply as well to the innocent child. We do not find convincing the contrary arguments of the New York Court of Appeals. *Gault* rendered untenable much of the reasoning relied upon by that court to sustain the constitutionality of § 744 (b). The Court of Appeals indicated that a delinquency adjudication "is not a 'conviction' (§ 781); that it affects no right or privilege, including the right to hold public office or to obtain a license (§ 782); and a cloak of protective confidentiality is thrown around all the proceedings. The court said further: "The delinquency status is not made a crime; and the proceedings are not criminal. There is, hence, no deprivation of due process in the statutory provision challenged by appellant . . . ." In effect the Court of Appeals distinguished the proceedings in question here from a criminal prosecution by use of what *Gault* called the "'civil' label-of-convenience which has been attached to juvenile proceedings." But *Gault* expressly rejected that distinction as a reason for holding the Due Process Clause inapplicable to a juvenile proceeding. The Court of Appeals also attempted to justify the preponderance standard on the related ground that juvenile proceedings are designed "not to punish, but to save the child." Again, however, *Gault* expressly rejected this justification. We made clear in that decision that civil labels and good intentions do not themselves obviate the need for criminal due process safeguards in juvenile courts, for "a proceeding where the issue is whether the child will be found to be 'delinquent' and subjected to the loss of his liberty for years is comparable in seriousness to a felony prosecution."

Nor do we perceive any merit in the argument that to afford juveniles the protection of proof beyond a reasonable doubt would risk destruction of beneficial aspects of the juvenile process. Use of the reasonable-doubt standard during the adjudicatory hearing will not disturb New York's policies that a finding that a child has violated a criminal law does not constitute a criminal conviction, that such a finding does not deprive the child of his civil rights, and that juvenile proceedings are confidential. Nor will there be any effect on the informality, flexibility, or speed of the hearing at which the factfinding takes place. And the opportunity during the post-adjudicatory or dispositional hearing for a wide-ranging review of the child's social history and for his individualized treatment will remain unimpaired. Similarly, there will be no effect on the procedures distinctive to juvenile proceedings that are employed prior to the adjudicatory hearing.

The Court of Appeals observed that "a child's best interest is not necessarily, or even probably, promoted if he wins in the particular inquiry which may bring him to the juvenile court." It is true, of course, that the juvenile may be engaging in a general course of conduct inimical to his welfare that calls for judicial intervention. But that intervention cannot take the form of subjecting the child to the stigma of a finding that he violated a criminal law and to the possibility of institutional confinement on proof insufficient to convict him were he an adult.

We conclude, as we concluded regarding the essential due process safeguards applied in *Gault*, that the observance of the standard of proof beyond a reasonable doubt "will not compel the States to abandon or displace any of the substantive benefits of the juvenile process."

Finally, we reject the Court of Appeals' suggestion that there is, in any event, only a "tenuous difference" between the reasonable-doubt and preponderance standards. The suggestion is singularly unpersuasive. In this very case, the trial judge's ability to distinguish between the two standards enabled him to make a finding of guilt that he conceded he might not have made under the standard of proof beyond a reasonable doubt. Indeed, the trial judge's action evidences the accuracy of the observation of commentators that "the preponderance test is susceptible to the misinterpretation that it calls on the trier of fact merely to perform an abstract weighing of the evidence in order to determine which side has produced the greater quantum, without regard to its effect in convincing his mind of the truth of the proposition asserted."

III.

In sum, the constitutional safeguard of proof beyond a reasonable doubt is as much required during the adjudicatory stage of a delinquency proceeding as are those constitutional safeguards applied in Gault—notice of charges, right to counsel, the rights of confrontation and examination, and the privilege against self-incrimination. We therefore hold, in agreement with Chief Judge Fuld in dissent in the Court of Appeals, "that, where a 12-year-old child is charged with an act of stealing which renders him liable to confinement for as long as six years, then, as a matter of due process . . . the case against him must be proved beyond a reasonable doubt."

Reversed.

McKeiver v. Pennsylvania (1971)
403 U.S. 528

These cases present the narrow but precise issue whether the Due Process Clause of the Fourteenth Amendment assures the right to trial by jury in the adjudicative phase of a state juvenile court delinquency proceeding.

I.

The issue arises understandably, for the Court in a series of cases already has emphasized due process factors protective of the juvenile:

1. *Haley v. Ohio* (1948), concerned the admissibility of a confession taken from a 15-year-old boy on trial for first-degree murder. It was held that, upon the facts there developed, the Due Process Clause barred the use of the confession. MR. JUSTICE DOUGLAS, in an opinion in which three other Justices joined, said, "Neither man nor child can be allowed to stand condemned by methods which flout constitutional requirements of due process of law."

2. *Gallegos v. Colorado* (1962), where a 14-year-old was on trial, is to the same effect.

3. *Kent v. United States* (1966), concerned a 16-year-old charged with housebreaking, robbery, and rape in the District of Columbia. The issue was the propriety of the juvenile court's waiver of jurisdiction "after full investigation," as permitted by the applicable statute. It was emphasized that the latitude the court possessed within which to determine whether it should retain or waive jurisdiction "assumes procedural regularity sufficient in the particular circumstances to satisfy the basic requirements of due process and fairness, as well as compliance with the statutory requirement of a 'full investigation.'"

4. *In re Gault* (1967), concerned a 15-year-old, already on probation, committed in Arizona as a delinquent after being apprehended upon a complaint of lewd remarks by telephone. Mr. Justice Fortas, in writing for the Court, reviewed the cases just cited and observed,

"Accordingly, while these cases relate only to restricted aspects of the subject, they unmistakably indicate that, whatever may be their precise impact, neither the Fourteenth Amendment nor the Bill of Rights is for adults alone."

The Court focused on "the proceedings by which a determination is made as to whether a juvenile is a 'delinquent' as a result of alleged misconduct on his part, with the consequence that he may be committed to a state institution" and, as to this, said that "there appears to be little current dissent from the proposition that the Due Process Clause has a role to play." *Kent* was adhered to: "We reiterate this view, here in connection with a juvenile court adjudication of 'delinquency,' as a requirement which is part of the Due Process Clause of the Fourteenth Amendment of our Constitution." Due process, in that proceeding, was held to embrace adequate written notice; advice as to the right to counsel, retained or appointed; confrontation; and cross-examination. The privilege against self-incrimination was also held available to the juvenile. The Court refrained from deciding whether a State must provide appellate review in juvenile cases or a transcript or recording of the hearings.

5. *DeBacker v. Brainard* (1969) presented, by state habeas corpus, a challenge to a Nebraska statute providing that juvenile court hearings "shall be conducted by the judge without a jury in an informal manner." However, because that appellant's hearing had antedated the decisions in *Duncan v. Louisiana* (1968), and *Bloom v. Illinois* (1968), and because *Duncan* and *Bloom* had been given only prospective application by *DeStefano v. Woods* (1968), DeBacker's case was deemed an inappropriate one for resolution of the jury trial issue. His appeal was therefore dismissed. MR. JUSTICE BLACK and MR. JUSTICE DOUGLAS, in separate dissents, took the position that a juvenile is entitled to a jury trial at the adjudicative stage. MR. JUSTICE BLACK described this as "a right which is surely one of the fundamental aspects of criminal justice in the English-speaking world," and MR. JUSTICE DOUGLAS described it as a right required by the Sixth and Fourteenth Amendments "where the delinquency charged is an offense that, if the person were an adult, would be a crime triable by jury."

6. *In re Winship* (1970), concerned a 12-year-old charged with delinquency for having taken money from a woman's purse. The Court held that "the Due Process Clause protects the accused against conviction except upon proof beyond a reasonable doubt of every fact necessary to constitute the crime with which he is charged," at and then went on to hold that this standard was applicable, too, "during the adjudicatory stage of a delinquency proceeding."

From these six cases—*Haley, Gallegos, Kent, Gault, DeBacker,* and *Winship*—it is apparent that:

1. Some of the constitutional requirements attendant upon the state criminal trial have equal application to that part of the state juvenile proceeding that is adjudicative in nature. Among these are the rights to appropriate notice, to counsel, to confrontation and to cross-examination, and the privilege against self-incrimination. Included, also, is the standard of proof beyond a reasonable doubt.

2. The Court, however, has not yet said that all rights constitutionally assured to an adult accused of crime also are to be enforced or made available to the juvenile in his delinquency proceeding. Indeed, the Court specifically has refrained from going that far:

"We do not mean by this to indicate that the hearing to be held must conform with all of the requirements of a criminal trial or even of the usual administrative hearing; but we do hold that the hearing must measure up to the essentials of due process and fair treatment."

3. The Court, although recognizing the high hopes and aspirations of Judge Julian Mack, the leaders of the Jane Addams School and the other supporters of the juvenile court concept, has also noted the disappointments of the system's performance and experience and the resulting widespread disaffection. There have been, at one and the same time, both an appreciation for the juvenile court judge who is devoted, sympathetic, and conscientious, and a disturbed concern about the judge who is untrained and less than fully imbued with an understanding approach to the complex problems of childhood and adolescence. There has been praise for the system and its purposes, and there has been alarm over its defects.

4. The Court has insisted that these successive decisions do not spell the doom of the juvenile court system or even deprive it of its "informality, flexibility, or speed." On the other hand, a concern precisely to the opposite effect was expressed by two dissenters in *Winship*.

II.

With this substantial background already developed, we turn to the facts of the present cases:

Joseph McKeiver, then age 16, in May 1968 was charged with robbery, larceny, and receiving stolen goods (felonies under Pennsylvania law as acts of juvenile delinquency. At the time of the adjudication hearing he was represented by counsel. His request for a jury trial was denied and his case was heard by Judge Theodore S. Gutowicz of the Court of Common Pleas, Family Division, Juvenile Branch, of Philadelphia County, Pennsylvania. McKeiver was adjudged a delinquent upon findings that he had violated a law of the Commonwealth. He was placed on probation. On appeal, the Superior Court affirmed without opinion.

Edward Terry, then age 15, in January 1969 was charged with assault and battery on a police officer and conspiracy as acts of juvenile delinquency. His counsel's request for a jury trial was denied and his case was heard by Judge Joseph C. Bruno of the same Juvenile Branch of the Court of Common Pleas of Philadelphia County. Terry was adjudged a delinquent on the charges. This followed an adjudication and commitment in the preceding week for an assault on a teacher. He was committed, as he had been on the earlier charge, to the Youth Development Center at Cornwells Heights. On appeal, the Superior Court affirmed without opinion.

The Supreme Court of Pennsylvania granted leave to appeal in both cases and consolidated them. The single question considered, as phrased by the court, was "whether there is a constitutional right to a jury trial in juvenile court." The answer, one justice dissenting, was in the negative. We noted probable jurisdiction.

The details of the McKeiver and Terry offenses are set forth in Justice Roberts' opinion for the Pennsylvania court... McKeiver's offense was his participating with 20 or 30 youths who pursued three young teenagers and took 25 cents from them; that McKeiver never before had been arrested and had a record of gainful employment; that the testimony of two of the victims was described by the court as somewhat inconsistent and as "weak"; and that Terry's offense consisted of hitting a police officer with his fists and with a stick when the officer broke up a boys' fight Terry and others were watching.

Barbara Burrus and approximately 45 other black children, ranging in age from 11 to 15 years, 3 were the subjects of juvenile court summonses issued in Hyde County, North Carolina, in January 1969.
The charges arose out of a series of demonstrations in the county in late 1968 by black adults and children protesting school assignments and a school consolidation plan. Petitions were filed by North Carolina state highway patrolmen. Except for one

relating to James Lambert Howard, the petitions charged the respective juveniles with willfully impeding traffic. The charge against Howard was that he willfully made riotous noise and was disorderly in the O. A. Peay School in Swan Quarter; interrupted and disturbed the school during its regular sessions; and defaced school furniture. The acts so charged are misdemeanors under North Carolina law.

The several cases were consolidated into groups for hearing before District Judge Hallett S. Ward, sitting as a juvenile court. The same lawyer appeared for all the juveniles. Over counsel's objection, made in all except two of the cases, the general public was excluded. A request for a jury trial in each case was denied.

The evidence as to the juveniles other than Howard consisted solely of testimony of highway patrolmen. No juvenile took the stand or offered any witness. The testimony was to the effect that on various occasions the juveniles and adults were observed walking along Highway 64 singing, shouting, clapping, and playing basketball. As a result, there was interference with traffic. The marchers were asked to leave the paved portion of the highway and they were warned that they were committing a statutory offense. They either refused or left the roadway and immediately returned. The juveniles and participating adults were taken into custody. Juvenile petitions were then filed with respect to those under the age of 16.

The evidence as to Howard was that on the morning of December 5, he was in the office of the principal of the O. A. Peay School with 15 other persons while school was in session and was moving furniture around; that the office was in disarray; that as a result the school closed before noon; and that neither he nor any of the others was a student at the school or authorized to enter the principal's office.

In each case the court found that the juvenile had committed "an act for which an adult may be punished by law." A custody order was entered declaring the juvenile a delinquent "in need of more suitable guardianship" and committing him to the custody of the County Department of Public Welfare for placement in a suitable institution "until such time as the Board of Juvenile Correction or the Superintendent of said institution may determine, not inconsistent with the laws of this State." The court, however, suspended these commitments and placed each juvenile on probation for either one or two years conditioned upon his violating none of the State's laws, upon his reporting monthly to the County Department of Welfare, upon his being home by 11 p. m. each evening, and upon his attending a school approved by the Welfare Director. None of the juveniles has been confined on these charges.

On appeal, the cases were consolidated into two groups. The North Carolina Court of Appeals affirmed. In its turn the Supreme Court of North Carolina deleted that portion of the order in each case relating to commitment, but otherwise affirmed. Two justices dissented without opinion. We granted certiorari.

III.

It is instructive to review, as an illustration, the substance of Justice Roberts' opinion for the Pennsylvania court. He observes that "for over sixty-five years the Supreme Court gave no consideration at all to the constitutional problems involved in the juvenile court area"; that *Gault* "is somewhat of a paradox, being both broad and narrow at the same time"; that it "is broad in that it evidences a fundamental and far-reaching disillusionment with the anticipated benefits of the juvenile court system"; that it is narrow because the court enumerated four due process rights which it held applicable in juvenile proceedings, but declined to rule on two other claimed rights that as a consequence the Pennsylvania court was "confronted with a sweeping rationale and a carefully tailored holding," that the procedural safeguards "*Gault* specifically made applicable to juvenile courts have already caused a significant 'constitutional domestication' of juvenile court proceedings," that those safeguards and other rights, including the reasonable-doubt standard established by *Winship*, "insure that the juvenile court will operate in an atmosphere which is orderly enough to impress the juvenile with the gravity of the situation and the impartiality of the tribunal and at the same time informal enough to permit the benefits of the juvenile system to operate" that the "proper inquiry, then, is whether the right to a trial by jury is 'fundamental' within the meaning of *Duncan*, in the context of a juvenile court which operates with all of the above constitutional safeguards," and that his court's inquiry turned "upon whether there are elements in the juvenile process which render the right to a trial by jury less essential to the protection of an accused's rights in the juvenile system than in the normal criminal process."

Justice Roberts then concluded that such factors do inhere in the Pennsylvania juvenile system: (1) Although realizing that "faith in the quality of the juvenile bench is not an entirely satisfactory substitute for due process," the judges in the juvenile courts "do take a different view of their role than that taken by their counterparts in the criminal courts." (2) While one regrets its inadequacies, "the juvenile system has available and utilizes much more fully various diagnostic and rehabilitative services" that are "far superior to those available in the regular criminal process." (3) Although conceding that the post-adjudication process "has in many respects fallen far short of its goals, and its reality is far harsher than its theory," the end result of a declaration of delinquency "is significantly different from and less onerous than a finding of criminal guilt" and "we are not yet convinced that the current practices do not contain the seeds from which a truly appropriate system can be brought forth." (4) Finally, "of all the possible due process rights which could be applied in the juvenile courts, the right to trial by jury is the one which would most likely be disruptive of the unique nature of the juvenile process." It is the jury trial that "would probably require substantial alteration of the traditional practices." The other procedural rights held applicable to the juvenile process "will give the juveniles sufficient protection" and the addition of the trial by jury "might well destroy the traditional character of juvenile proceedings."

The court concluded that it was confident "that a properly structured and fairly administered juvenile court system can serve our present societal needs without infringing on individual freedoms."

IV.

The right to an impartial jury "in all criminal prosecutions" under federal law is guaranteed by the Sixth Amendment. Through the Fourteenth Amendment that requirement has now been imposed upon the States "in all criminal cases which—were they to be tried in a federal court—would come within the Sixth Amendment's guarantee." This is because the Court has said it believes "that trial by jury in criminal cases is fundamental to the American scheme of justice."

This, of course, does not automatically provide the answer to the present jury trial issue, if for no other reason than that the juvenile court proceeding has not yet been held to be a "criminal prosecution," within the meaning and reach of the Sixth Amendment, and also has not yet been regarded as devoid of criminal aspects merely because it usually has been given the civil label.

Little, indeed, is to be gained by any attempt simplistically to call the juvenile court proceeding either "civil" or "criminal." The Court carefully has avoided this wooden approach. Before *Gault* was decided in 1967, the Fifth Amendment's guarantee against self-incrimination had been imposed upon the state criminal trial. So, too, had the Sixth Amendment's rights of confrontation and cross-examination. Yet the Court did not automatically and peremptorily apply those rights to the juvenile proceeding. A reading of *Gault* reveals the opposite. And the same separate approach to the standard-of-proof issue is evident from the carefully separated application of the standard, first to the criminal trial, and then to the juvenile proceeding, displayed in *Winship*.

Thus, accepting "the proposition that the Due Process Clause has a role to play." Our task here with respect to trial by jury, as it was in *Gault* with respect to other claimed rights, "is to ascertain the precise impact of the due process requirement."

V.

The Pennsylvania juveniles' basic argument is that they were tried in proceedings "substantially similar to a criminal trial." They say that a delinquency proceeding in their State is initiated by a petition charging a penal code violation in the conclusory language of an indictment; that a juvenile detained prior to trial is held in a building substantially similar to an adult prison; that in Philadelphia juveniles over 16 are, in fact, held in the cells of a prison; that counsel and the prosecution engage in plea bargaining; that motions to suppress are routinely heard and decided; that the usual rules of evidence are applied; that the customary common-law defenses are available; that the press is generally admitted in the Philadelphia juvenile courtrooms; that members of the public enter the room; that arrest and prior record may be reported by the press (from police sources, however, rather than from the juvenile court records); that, once adjudged delinquent, a juvenile may be confined until his majority in what amounts to a prison, describing the state correctional institution at Camp Hill as a "maximum security prison for adjudged delinquents and youthful criminal offenders"); and that the stigma attached upon delinquency adjudication approximates that resulting from conviction in an adult criminal proceeding.

The North Carolina juveniles particularly urge that the requirement of a jury trial would not operate to deny the supposed benefits of the juvenile court system; that the system's primary benefits are its discretionary intake procedure permitting disposition short of adjudication, and its flexible sentencing permitting emphasis on rehabilitation; that realization of these benefits does not depend upon dispensing with the jury; that adjudication of factual issues on the one hand and disposition of the case on the other are very different matters with very different purposes; that the purpose of the former is indistinguishable from that of the criminal trial; that the jury trial provides an independent protective factor; that experience has shown that jury trials in juvenile courts are manageable; that no reason exists why protection traditionally accorded in criminal proceedings should be denied young people subject to involuntary incarceration for lengthy periods; and that the juvenile courts deserve healthy public scrutiny.

VI.

All the litigants here agree that the applicable due process standard in juvenile proceedings, as developed by *Gault* and *Winship*, is fundamental fairness. As that standard was applied in those two cases, we have an emphasis on factfinding procedures. The requirements of notice, counsel, confrontation, cross-examination, and standard of proof naturally flowed from this emphasis. But one cannot say that in our legal system the jury is a necessary component of accurate factfinding. There is much to be said for it, to be sure, but we have been content to pursue other ways for determining facts. Juries are not required, and have not been, for example, in equity cases, in workmen's compensation, in probate, or in deportation cases. Neither have they been generally used in military trials. In *Duncan* the Court stated, "We would not assert, however, that every criminal trial—or any particular trial—held before a judge alone is unfair or that a defendant may never be as fairly treated by a judge as he would be by a jury." In *DeStefano*, for this reason and others, the Court refrained from retrospective application of *Duncan*, an action it surely would have not taken had it felt that the integrity of the result was seriously at issue. And in *Williams v. Florida* (1970), the Court saw no particular magic in a 12-man jury for a criminal case, thus revealing that even jury concepts themselves are not inflexible.

We must recognize, as the Court has recognized before, that the fond and idealistic hopes of the juvenile court proponents and early reformers of three generations ago have not been realized. The devastating commentary upon the system's failures as a whole, contained in the President's Commission on Law Enforcement and Administration of Justice, *Task Force Report: Juvenile Delinquency and Youth Crime* (1967), reveals the depth of disappointment in what has been accomplished. Too often the juvenile court judge falls far short of that stalwart, protective, and communicating figure the system envisaged. The community's unwillingness to provide people and facilities and to be concerned, the insufficiency of time devoted, the scarcity of professional help, the inadequacy of dispositional alternatives, and our general lack of knowledge all contribute to dissatisfaction with the experiment.

The Task Force Report, however, also said, "To say that juvenile courts have failed to achieve their goals is to say no more than what is true of criminal courts in the United States. But failure is most striking when hopes are highest."

Despite all these disappointments, all these failures, and all these shortcomings, we conclude that trial by jury in the juvenile court's adjudicative stage is not a constitutional requirement. We so conclude for a number of reasons:

1. The Court has refrained, in the cases heretofore decided, from taking the easy way with a flat holding that all rights constitutionally assured for the adult accused are to be imposed upon the state juvenile proceeding. What was done in *Gault* and in *Winship* is aptly described in *Commonwealth v. Johnson*: "It is clear to us that the Supreme Court has properly attempted to strike a judicious balance by injecting procedural orderliness into the juvenile court system. It is seeking to reverse the trend whereby 'the child receives the worst of both worlds . . . .'"

2. There is a possibility, at least, that the jury trial, if required as a matter of constitutional precept, will remake the juvenile proceeding into a fully adversary process and will put an effective end to what has been the idealistic prospect of an intimate, informal protective proceeding.

3. The Task Force Report, although concededly pre-*Gault*, is notable for its not making any recommendation that the jury trial be imposed upon the juvenile court system. This is so despite its vivid description of the system's deficiencies and disappointments. Had the Commission deemed this vital to the integrity of the juvenile process, or to the handling of juveniles, surely a recommendation or suggestion to this effect would have appeared. The intimations, instead, are quite the other way. Further, it expressly recommends against abandonment of the system and against the return of the juvenile to the criminal courts.

4. The Court specifically has recognized by dictum that a jury is not a necessary part even of every criminal process that is fair and equitable.

5. The imposition of the jury trial on the juvenile court system would not strengthen greatly, if at all, the factfinding function, and would, contrarily, provide an attrition of the juvenile court's assumed ability to function in a unique manner. It would not remedy the defects of the system. Meager as has been the hoped-for advance in the juvenile field, the alternative would be regressive, would lose what has been gained, and would tend once again to place the juvenile squarely in the routine of the criminal process.

6. The juvenile concept held high promise. We are reluctant to say that, despite disappointments of grave dimensions, it still does not hold promise, and we are particularly reluctant to say, as do the Pennsylvania appellants here, that the system cannot accomplish its rehabilitative goals. So much depends on the availability of resources, on the interest and commitment of the public, on willingness to learn, and on understanding as to cause and effect and cure. In this field, as in so many others, one perhaps learns best by doing. We are reluctant to disallow the States to experiment further and to seek in new and different ways the elusive answers to the problems of the young, and we feel that we would be impeding that experimentation by imposing the jury trial. The States, indeed, must go forward. If, in its wisdom, any State feels the jury trial is desirable in all cases, or in certain kinds, there appears to be no impediment to its installing a system embracing that feature. That, however, is the State's privilege and not its obligation.

7. Of course there have been abuses. The Task Force Report has noted them. We refrain from saying at this point that those abuses are of constitutional dimension. They relate to the lack of resources and of dedication rather than to inherent unfairness.

8. There is, of course, nothing to prevent a juvenile court judge, in a particular case where he feels the need, or when the need is demonstrated, from using an advisory jury.

9. "The fact that a practice is followed by a large number of states is not conclusive in a decision as to whether that practice accords with due process, but it is plainly worth considering in determining whether the practice 'offends some principle of justice so rooted in the traditions and conscience of our people as to be ranked as fundamental.' It therefore is of more than passing interest that at least 29 States and the District of Columbia by statute deny the juvenile a right to a jury trial in cases such as these. The same result is achieved in other States by judicial decision. 8 In 10 States statutes provide for a jury trial under certain circumstances.

10. Since *Gault* and since *Duncan* the great majority of States, in addition to Pennsylvania and North Carolina, that have faced the issue have concluded that the considerations that led to the result in those two cases do not compel trial by jury in the juvenile court.

11. Stopping short of proposing the jury trial for juvenile proceedings are the Uniform Juvenile Court Act, § 24 (a), approved in July 1968 by the National Conference of Commissioners on Uniform State Laws; the Standard Juvenile Court Act, Art. V, § 19, proposed by the National Council on Crime and Delinquency; and the Legislative Guide for Drafting Family and Juvenile Court Acts § 29 (a).

12. If the jury trial were to be injected into the juvenile court system as a matter of right, it would bring with it into that system the traditional delay, the formality, and the clamor of the adversary system and, possibly, the public trial. It is of interest that these very factors were stressed by the District Committee of the Senate when, through Senator Tydings, it recommended, and Congress then approved, as a provision in the District of Columbia Crime Bill, the abolition of the jury trial in the juvenile court.

13. Finally, the arguments advanced by the juveniles here are, of course, the identical arguments that underlie the demand for the jury trial for criminal proceedings. The arguments necessarily equate the juvenile proceeding—or at least the adjudicative phase of it—with the criminal trial. Whether they should be so equated is our issue. Concern about the inapplicability of exclusionary and other rules of evidence, about the juvenile court judge's possible awareness of the juvenile's prior record and of the contents of the social file; about repeated appearances of the same familiar witnesses in the persons of juvenile and probation officers and social workers—all to the effect that this will create the likelihood of pre-judgment—chooses to ignore, it seems to us, every aspect of fairness, of concern, of sympathy, and of paternal attention that the juvenile court system contemplates.

If the formalities of the criminal adjudicative process are to be superimposed upon the juvenile court system, there is little need for its separate existence. Perhaps that ultimate disillusionment will come one day, but for the moment we are disinclined to give impetus to it.

Affirmed.

Schall v. Martin (1984)
467 U.S. 253

In this case, the Supreme Court was asked to evaluate the constitutionality of a New York statute that provided for the preventive detention of juveniles accused of crimes.

Section 320.5(3)(b) of the New York Family Court Act authorizes pretrial detention of an accused juvenile delinquent based on a finding that there is a "serious risk" that the child "may before the return date commit an act which if committed by an adult would constitute a crime." Appellees brought suit on behalf of a class of all juveniles detained pursuant to that provision. The District Court struck down § 320.5(3)(b) as permitting detention without due process of law and ordered the immediate release of all class members. The Court of Appeals for the Second Circuit affirmed, holding the provision "unconstitutional as to all juveniles" because the statute is administered in such a way that "the detention period serves as punishment imposed without proof of guilt established according to the requisite constitutional standard." We noted probable jurisdiction, and now reverse. We conclude that preventive detention under the FCA serves a legitimate state objective, and that the procedural protections afforded pretrial detainees by the New York statute satisfy the requirements of the Due Process Clause of the Fourteenth Amendment to the United States Constitution.

I.

Appellee Gregory Martin was arrested on December 13, 1977, and charged with first-degree robbery, second-degree assault, and criminal possession of a weapon based on an incident in which he, with two others, allegedly hit a youth on the head with a loaded gun, and stole his jacket and sneakers. Martin had possession of the gun when he was arrested. He was 14 years old at the time and, therefore, came within the jurisdiction of New York's Family Court. The incident occurred at 11:30 at night, and Martin lied to the police about where and with whom he lived. He was consequently detained overnight.

A petition of delinquency was filed, and Martin made his "initial appearance" in Family Court on December 14th, accompanied by his grandmother. The Family Court Judge, citing the possession of the loaded weapon, the false address given to the police, and the lateness of the hour, as evidencing a lack of supervision, ordered Martin detained under § 320.5(3)(b). A probable-cause hearing was held five days later, on December 19th, and probable cause was found to exist for all the crimes charged. At the factfinding hearing held December 27-29, Martin was found guilty on the robbery and criminal possession charges. He was adjudicated a delinquent and placed on two years' probation. He had been detained pursuant to § 320.5(3)(b), between the initial appearance and the completion of the factfinding hearing, for a total of 15 days.

Appellees Luis Rosario and Kenneth Morgan, both age 14, were also ordered detained pending their factfinding hearings. Rosario was charged with attempted first-degree robbery and second-degree assault for an incident in which he, with four others, allegedly tried to rob two men, putting a gun to the head of one of them and beating both about the head with sticks. At the time of his initial appearance, on March 15, 1978, Rosario had another delinquency petition pending for knifing a student, and two prior petitions had been adjusted. Probable cause was found on March 21. On April 11, Rosario was released to his father, and the case was terminated without adjustment on September 25, 1978.

Kenneth Morgan was charged with attempted robbery and attempted grand larceny for an incident in which he and another boy allegedly tried to steal money from a 14-year-old girl and her brother by threatening to blow their heads off and grabbing them to search their pockets. Morgan, like Rosario, was on release status on another petition (for robbery and criminal possession of stolen property) at the time of his initial appearance on March 27, 1978. He had been arrested four previous times, and his mother refused to come to court because he had been in trouble so often she did not want him home. A probable-cause hearing was set for March 30, but was continued until April 4, when it was combined with a factfinding hearing. Morgan was found guilty of harassment and petit larceny and was ordered placed with the Department of Social Services for 18 months. He was detained a total of eight days between his initial appearance and the factfinding hearing.

On December 21, 1977, while still in preventive detention pending his factfinding hearing, Gregory Martin instituted a habeas corpus class action on behalf of "those persons who are, or during the pendency of this action will be, preventively detained pursuant to" § 320.5(3)(b) of the FCA. Rosario and Morgan were subsequently added as additional named plaintiffs. These three class representatives sought a declaratory judgment that § 320.5(3)(b) violates the Due Process and Equal Protection Clauses of the Fourteenth Amendment.

In an unpublished opinion, the District Court certified the class. The court also held that appellees were not required to exhaust their state remedies before resorting to federal habeas because the highest state court had already rejected an identical challenge to the juvenile preventive detention statute. Exhaustion of state remedies, therefore, would be "an exercise in futility."

At trial, appellees offered in evidence the case histories of 34 members of the class, including the three named petitioners. Both parties presented some general statistics on the relation between pretrial detention and ultimate disposition. In addition, there was testimony concerning juvenile proceedings from a number of witnesses, including a legal aid attorney specializing in juvenile cases, a probation supervisor, a child psychologist, and a Family Court Judge. On the basis of this evidence, the District Court rejected the equal protection challenge as "insubstantial," but agreed with appellees that pretrial detention under the FCA violates due process. The court ordered that "all class members in custody pursuant to Family Court Act shall be released forthwith."

The Court of Appeals affirmed. After reviewing the trial record, the court opined that "the vast majority of juveniles detained under § 320.5(3)(b) either have their petitions dismissed before an adjudication of delinquency or are released after adjudication." The court concluded from that fact that § 320.5(3)(b) "is utilized principally, not for preventive purposes, but to impose punishment for unadjudicated criminal acts." The early release of so many of those detained contradicts any asserted need for pretrial confinement to protect the community. The court therefore concluded that § 320.5(3)(b) must be declared unconstitutional as to all juveniles. Individual litigation would be a practical impossibility because the periods of detention are so short that the litigation is mooted before the merits are determined.

II.

There is no doubt that the Due Process Clause is applicable in juvenile proceedings. "The problem," we have stressed, "is to ascertain the precise impact of the due process requirement upon such proceedings." We have held that certain basic constitutional protections enjoyed by adults accused of crimes also apply to juveniles. ...But the Constitution does not mandate elimination of all differences in the treatment of juveniles. The State has "a *parens patriae* interest in preserving and promoting the welfare of the child," which makes a juvenile proceeding fundamentally different from an adult criminal trial. We have tried, therefore, to strike a balance—to respect the "informality" and "flexibility" that characterize juvenile proceedings, and yet to ensure that such proceedings comport with the "fundamental fairness" demanded by the Due Process Clause.

The statutory provision at issue in these cases, § 320.5(3)(b), permits a brief pretrial detention based on a finding of a "serious risk" that an arrested juvenile may commit a crime before his return date. The question before us is whether preventive detention of juveniles pursuant to § 320.5(3)(b) is compatible with the "fundamental fairness" required by due process. Two separate inquiries are necessary to answer this question. First, does preventive detention under the New York statute serve a legitimate state objective? And, second, are the procedural safeguards contained in the FCA adequate to authorize the pretrial detention of at least some juveniles charged with crimes?

A.

Preventive detention under the FCA is purportedly designed to protect the child and society from the potential consequences of his criminal acts. When making any detention decision, the Family Court judge is specifically directed to consider the needs and best interests of the juvenile as well as the need for the protection of the community. In *Bell v. Wolfish*, we left open the question whether any governmental objective other than ensuring a detainee's presence at trial may constitutionally justify pretrial detention. As an initial matter, therefore, we must decide whether, in the context of the juvenile system, the combined interest in protecting both the community and the juvenile himself from the consequences of future criminal conduct is sufficient to justify such detention.

The "legitimate and compelling state interest" in protecting the community from crime cannot be doubted. We have stressed before that crime prevention is "a weighty social objective," and this interest persists undiluted in the juvenile context. The harm suffered by the victim of a crime is not dependent upon the age of the perpetrator. And the harm to society generally may even be greater in this context given the high rate of recidivism among juveniles.

The juvenile's countervailing interest in freedom from institutional restraints, even for the brief time involved here, is undoubtedly substantial as well. But that interest must be qualified by the recognition that juveniles, unlike adults, are always in some form of custody. Children, by definition, are not assumed to have the capacity to take care of themselves. They are assumed to be subject to the control of their parents, and if parental control falters, the State must play its part as *parens patriae*.

In this respect, the juvenile's liberty interest may, in appropriate circumstances, be subordinated to the State's "*parens patriae* interest in preserving and promoting the welfare of the child."

The New York Court of Appeals, in upholding the statute at issue here, stressed at some length "the desirability of protecting the juvenile from his own folly." Society has a legitimate interest in protecting a juvenile from the consequences of his criminal activity—both from potential physical injury which may be suffered when a victim fights back or a policeman attempts to make an arrest and from the downward spiral of criminal activity into which peer pressure may lead the child.

The substantiality and legitimacy of the state interests underlying this statute are confirmed by the widespread use and judicial acceptance of preventive detention for juveniles. Every State, as well as the United States in the District of Columbia, permits preventive detention of juveniles accused of crime. A number of model juvenile justice Acts also contain provisions permitting preventive detention. And the courts of eight States, including the New York Court of Appeals, have upheld their statutes with specific reference to protecting the juvenile and the community from harmful pretrial conduct, including pretrial crime.

"The fact that a practice is followed by a large number of states is not conclusive in a decision as to whether that practice accords with due process, but it is plainly worth considering in determining whether the practice 'offends some principle of justice so rooted in the traditions and conscience of our people as to be ranked as fundamental.' In light of the uniform legislative judgment that pretrial detention of juveniles properly promotes the interests both of society and the juvenile, we conclude that the practice serves a legitimate regulatory purpose compatible with the "fundamental fairness" demanded by the Due Process Clause in juvenile proceedings.

Of course, the mere invocation of a legitimate purpose will not justify particular restrictions and conditions of confinement amounting to punishment. It is axiomatic that "due process requires that a pretrial detainee not be punished." Even given, therefore, that pretrial detention may serve legitimate regulatory purposes, it is still necessary to determine whether the terms and conditions of confinement under § 320.5(3)(b) are in fact compatible with those purposes. "A court must decide whether the disability is imposed for the purpose of punishment or whether it is but an incident of some other legitimate governmental purpose." Absent a showing of an express intent to punish on the part of the State, that determination generally will turn on "whether an alternative purpose to which the restriction may rationally be connected is assignable for it, and whether it appears excessive in relation to the alternative purpose assigned to it."

There is no indication in the statute itself that preventive detention is used or intended as a punishment. First of all, the detention is strictly limited in time. If a juvenile is detained at his initial appearance and has denied the charges against him, he is entitled to a probable-cause hearing to be held not more than three days after the conclusion of the initial appearance or four days after the filing of the petition, whichever is sooner. If the Family Court judge finds probable cause, he must also determine whether continued detention is necessary pursuant to § 320.5(3)(b).

Detained juveniles are also entitled to an expedited factfinding hearing. If the juvenile is charged with one of a limited number of designated felonies, the factfinding hearing must be scheduled to commence not more than 14 days after the conclusion of the initial appearance. If the juvenile is charged with a lesser offense, then the factfinding hearing must be held not more than three days after the initial appearance. In the latter case, since the times for the probable-cause hearing and the factfinding hearing coincide, the two hearings are merged.

Thus, the maximum possible detention under § 320.5(3)(b) of a youth accused of a serious crime, assuming a 3-day extension of the factfinding hearing for good cause shown, is 17 days. The maximum detention for less serious crimes, again assuming a 3-day extension for good cause shown, is six days. These time frames seem suited to the limited purpose of providing the youth with a controlled environment and separating him from improper influences pending the speedy disposition of his case.

The conditions of confinement also appear to reflect the regulatory purposes relied upon by the State. When a juvenile is remanded after his initial appearance, he cannot, absent exceptional circumstances, be sent to a prison or lockup where he would be exposed to adult criminals. Instead, the child is screened by an "assessment unit" of the Department of Juvenile Justice. The assessment unit places the child in either nonsecure or secure detention. Nonsecure detention involves an open facility in the community, a sort of "halfway house," without locks, bars, or security officers where the child receives schooling and counseling and has access to recreational facilities.

Secure detention is more restrictive, but it is still consistent with the regulatory and *parens patriae* objectives relied upon by the State. Children are assigned to separate dorms based on age, size, and behavior. They wear street clothes provided by the institution and partake in educational and recreational programs and counseling sessions run by trained social workers. Misbehavior is punished by confinement to one's room. We cannot conclude from this record that the controlled environment briefly imposed by the State on juveniles in secure pretrial detention "is imposed for the purpose of punishment" rather than as "an incident of some other legitimate governmental purpose."

The Court of Appeals, of course, did conclude that the underlying purpose of § 320.5(3)(b) is punitive rather than regulatory. But the court did not dispute that preventive detention might serve legitimate regulatory purposes or that the terms and conditions of pretrial confinement in New York are compatible with those purposes. Rather, the court invalidated a significant aspect of New York's juvenile justice system based solely on some case histories and a statistical study which appeared to show that "the vast majority of juveniles detained under § 320.5(3)(b) either have their petitions dismissed before an adjudication of delinquency or are released after adjudication." The court assumed that dismissal of a petition or failure to confine a juvenile at the dispositional hearing belied the need to detain him prior to factfinding and that, therefore, the pretrial detention constituted punishment. Since punishment imposed without a prior adjudication of guilt is per se illegitimate, the Court of Appeals concluded that no juveniles could be held pursuant to § 320.5(3)(b).

There are some obvious flaws in the statistics and case histories relied upon by the lower court. But even assuming it to be the case that "by far the greater number of juveniles incarcerated under § 320.5(3)(b) will never be confined as a consequence of a disposition imposed after an adjudication of delinquency," we find that to be an insufficient ground for upsetting the widely shared legislative judgment that preventive detention serves an important and legitimate function in the juvenile justice system. We are unpersuaded by the Court of Appeals' rather cavalier equation of detentions that do not lead to continued confinement after an adjudication of guilt and "wrongful" or "punitive" pretrial detentions.

Pretrial detention need not be considered punitive merely because a juvenile is subsequently discharged subject to conditions or put on probation. In fact, such actions reinforce the original finding that close supervision of the juvenile is required. Lenient but supervised disposition is in keeping with the Act's purpose to promote the welfare and development of the child. As the New York Court of Appeals noted:

"It should surprise no one that caution and concern for both the juvenile and society may indicate the more conservative decision to detain at the very outset, whereas the later development of very much more relevant information may prove that while a finding of delinquency was warranted, placement may not be indicated."

Even when a case is terminated prior to factfinding, it does not follow that the decision to detain the juvenile pursuant to § 320.5(3)(b) amounted to a due process violation. A delinquency petition may be dismissed for any number of reasons collateral to its merits, such as the failure of a witness to testify. The Family Court judge cannot be expected to anticipate such developments at the initial hearing. He makes his decision based on the information available to him at that time, and the propriety of the decision must be judged in that light. Consequently, the final disposition of a case is "largely irrelevant" to the legality of a pretrial detention.

It may be, of course, that in some circumstances detention of a juvenile would not pass constitutional muster. But the validity of those detentions must be determined on a case-by-case basis. Section 320.5(3)(b) is not invalid "on its face" by reason of the ambiguous statistics and case histories relied upon by the court below. We find no justification for the conclusion that, contrary to the express language of the statute and the judgment of the highest state court, § 320.5(3)(b) is a punitive rather than a regulatory measure. Preventive detention under the FCA serves the legitimate state objective, held in common with every State in the country, of protecting both the juvenile and society from the hazards of pretrial crime.

B.

Given the legitimacy of the State's interest in preventive detention, and the nonpunitive nature of that detention, the remaining question is whether the procedures afforded juveniles detained prior to factfinding provide sufficient protection against erroneous and unnecessary deprivations of liberty. In *Gerstein v. Pugh*, we held that a judicial determination of probable cause is a prerequisite to any extended restraint on the liberty of an adult accused of crime. We did not, however, mandate a specific timetable. Nor did we require the "full panoply of adversary safeguards—counsel, confrontation, cross-examination, and compulsory process for witnesses." Instead, we recognized "the desirability of flexibility and experimentation by the States." *Gerstein* arose under the Fourth Amendment, but the same concern with "flexibility" and "informality," while yet ensuring adequate predetention procedures, is present in this context.

In many respects, the FCA provides far more predetention protection for juveniles than we found to be constitutionally required for a probable-cause determination for adults in *Gerstein*. The initial appearance is informal, but the accused juvenile is given full notice of the charges against him and a complete stenographic record is kept of the hearing. The juvenile appears accompanied by his parent or guardian. He is first informed of his rights, including the right to remain silent and the right to be represented by counsel chosen by him or by a law guardian assigned by the court. The initial appearance may be adjourned for no longer than 72 hours or until the next court day, whichever is sooner, to enable an appointed law guardian or other counsel to appear before the court. When his counsel is present, the juvenile is informed of the charges against him and furnished with a copy of the delinquency petition. A representative from the presentment agency appears in support of the petition.

The nonhearsay allegations in the delinquency petition and supporting depositions must establish probable cause to believe the juvenile committed the offense. Although the Family Court judge is not required to make a finding of probable cause at the initial appearance, the youth may challenge the sufficiency of the petition on that ground. Thus, the juvenile may oppose any recommended detention by arguing that there is not probable cause to believe he committed the offense or offenses with which he is charged. If the petition is not dismissed, the juvenile is given an opportunity to admit or deny the charges.

At the conclusion of the initial appearance, the presentment agency makes a recommendation regarding detention. A probation officer reports on the juvenile's record, including other prior and current Family Court and probation contacts, as well as relevant information concerning home life, school attendance, and any special medical or developmental problems. He concludes by offering his agency's recommendation on detention. Opposing counsel, the juvenile's parents, and the juvenile himself may all speak on his behalf and challenge any information or recommendation. If the judge does decide to detain the juvenile under § 320.5(3)(b), he must state on the record the facts and reasons for the detention.

As noted, a detained juvenile is entitled to a formal, adversarial probable-cause hearing within three days of his initial appearance, with one 3-day extension possible for good cause shown. The burden at this hearing is on the presentment agency to call witnesses and offer evidence in support of the charges. Testimony is under oath and subject to cross-examination. The accused juvenile may call witnesses and offer evidence in his own behalf. If the court finds probable cause, the court must again decide whether continued detention is necessary under § 320.5(3)(b). Again, the facts and reasons for the detention must be stated on the record.

In sum, notice, a hearing, and a statement of facts and reasons are given prior to any detention under § 320.5(3)(b). A formal probable-cause hearing is then held within a short while thereafter, if the factfinding hearing is not itself scheduled within three days. These flexible procedures have been found constitutionally adequate under the Fourth Amendment. Appellees have failed to note any additional procedures that would significantly improve the accuracy of the determination without unduly impinging on the achievement of legitimate state purposes.

Appellees argue, however, that the risk of erroneous and unnecessary detentions is too high despite these procedures because the standard for detention is fatally vague. Detention under § 320.5(3)(b) is based on a finding that there is a "serious risk" that the juvenile, if released, would commit a crime prior to his next court appearance. We have already seen that detention of juveniles on that ground serves legitimate regulatory purposes. But appellees claim, and the District Court agreed, that it is virtually impossible to predict future criminal conduct with any degree of accuracy. Moreover, they say, the statutory standard fails to channel the discretion of the Family Court judge by specifying the factors on which he should rely in making that prediction. The procedural protections noted above are thus, in their view, unavailing because the ultimate decision is intrinsically arbitrary and uncontrolled.

Our cases indicate, however, that from a legal point of view there is nothing inherently unattainable about a prediction of future criminal conduct. Such a judgment forms an important element in many decisions, and we have specifically rejected the contention, based on the same sort of sociological data relied upon by appellees and the District Court, "that it is impossible to predict future behavior and that the question is so vague as to be meaningless."

We have also recognized that a prediction of future criminal conduct is "an experienced prediction based on a host of variables" which cannot be readily codified. Judge Quinones of the Family Court testified at trial that he and his colleagues make a determination under § 320.5(3)(b) based on numerous factors including the nature and seriousness of the charges; whether the charges are likely to be proved at trial; the juvenile's prior record; the adequacy and effectiveness of his home supervision; his school situation, if known; the time of day of the alleged crime as evidence of its seriousness and a possible lack of parental control; and any special circumstances that might be brought to his attention by the probation officer, the child's attorney, or any parents, relatives, or other responsible persons accompanying the child. The decision is based on as much information as can reasonably be obtained at the initial appearance.

Given the right to a hearing, to counsel, and to a statement of reasons, there is no reason that the specific factors upon which the Family Court judge might rely must be specified in the statute. As the New York Court of Appeals concluded, "To a very real extent Family Court must exercise a substitute parental control for which there can be no particularized criteria." There is also no reason, we should add, for a federal court to assume that a state court judge will not strive to apply state law as conscientiously as possible.

It is worth adding that the Court of Appeals for the Second Circuit was mistaken in its conclusion that "individual litigation . . . is a practical impossibility because the periods of detention are so short that the litigation is mooted before the merits are determined." In fact, one of the juveniles in the very case histories upon which the court relied was released from pretrial detention on a writ of habeas corpus issued by the State Supreme Court. New York courts also have adopted a liberal view of the doctrine of "capable of repetition, yet evading review" precisely in order to ensure that pretrial detention orders are not unreviewable. In *People ex rel. Wayburn v. Schupf,* the court declined to dismiss an appeal from the grant of a writ of habeas corpus despite the technical mootness of the case.

"Because the situation is likely to recur . . . and the substantial issue may otherwise never be reached (in view of the predictably recurring happenstance that, however expeditiously an appeal might be prosecuted, fact-finding and dispositional hearings normally will have been held and a disposition made before the appeal could reach us), . . . we decline to dismiss the appeal on the ground of mootness."

The required statement of facts and reasons justifying the detention and the stenographic record of the initial appearance will provide a basis for the review of individual cases. Pretrial detention orders in New York may be reviewed by writ of habeas corpus brought in State Supreme Court. And the judgment of that court is appealable as of right and may be taken directly to the Court of Appeals if a constitutional question is presented. Permissive appeal from a Family Court order may also be had to the Appellate Division. Or a motion for reconsideration may be directed to the Family Court judge. These post-detention procedures provide a sufficient mechanism for correcting on a case-by-case basis any erroneous detentions ordered under § 320.5(3). Such procedures may well flesh out the standards specified in the statute.

III.

The dissent would apparently have us strike down New York's preventive detention statute on two grounds: first, because the preventive detention of juveniles constitutes poor public policy, with the balance of harms outweighing any positive benefits either to society or to the juveniles themselves, and, second, because the statute could have been better drafted to improve the quality of the decisionmaking process. But it is worth recalling that we are neither a legislature charged with formulating public policy nor an American Bar Association committee charged with drafting a model statute. The question before us today is solely whether the preventive detention system chosen by the State of New York and applied by the New York Family Court comports with constitutional standards. Given the regulatory purpose for the detention and the procedural protections that precede its imposition, we conclude that § 320.5(3)(b) of the New York FCA is not invalid under the Due Process Clause of the Fourteenth Amendment.

The judgment of the Court of Appeals is Reversed.

CPSIA information can be obtained
at www.ICGtesting.com
Printed in the USA
BVHW070302270819
556725BV00008B/66/P